Multimedia and Print Resources for Students

The Crosson/Needles *Managerial Accounting* program keeps you engaged and on track for success in your accounting class. Following is a comprehensive list and description of all the multimedia and print resources available to you and where you can find each resource.

Resource	Description	Where to Find
Online Study Center	Contains resources (see below) to help you succeed in your accounting course. Organized by chapter; look for these sections: Prepare for Class, Improve Your Grade, General Resources, and ACE the Test.	http://college.hmco.com/accounting/needles/man_acc/8e/student_home.html
Your Guide to an "A"	Premium web resources that focus on helping you improve your grade. Content is available through a passkey.	Online Study Center; passkeys provided with new books. To purchase a passkey click on the Bookstore link at the Online Study Center or visit **college.hmco.com/info/needles.**
Smarthinking	This online tutoring center provides real-time access to experienced e-tutors.	Online Study Center; to purchase Smarthinking click on the Bookstore link at the Online Study Center or visit **college.hmco.com/info/needles.**
Electronic Working Papers	These Excel files contain templates for all end-of-chapter assignments with an easy-to-use interface.	Purchase at your bookstore or click on the Bookstore link at the Online Study Center or visit **college.hmco.com/info/needles.**
Working Papers (print)	Provide accounting forms for solving all end-of-chapter assignments.	Purchase at your bookstore or click on the Bookstore link at the Online Study Center or visit **college.hmco.com/info/needles.**
HMAccounting Tutor	Reinforce your understanding of accounting concepts and procedures with animated demonstration problems and tutorials that match your text's Learning Objectives.	Online Study Center: Improve Your Grade (part of Your Guide to an "A")
ACE Tests	How well do you know the chapter? Find out with these interactive practice tests.	Online Study Center: ACE the Test
ACE+ Tests	More interactive practice tests!	Online Study Center: ACE the Test (part of Your Guide to an "A")
Audio Chapter Reviews and Quizzes	Study on the go! Review the chapter with an audio summary of key concepts and terms; test your understanding with an audio quiz.	Online Study Center: Improve Your Grade (part of Your Guide to an "A")
Demonstration Videos	Review concepts with video and animation, explained by the text authors.	Online Study Center: Improve Your Grade (part of Your Guide to an "A")
Study Guide	The online Study Guide provides a thorough review of each learning objective, a detailed outline, true/false and multiple-choice questions, and exercises. Answers are included.	Online Study Center: Improve Your Grade (part of Your Guide to an "A")
Answers to Stop, Review, and Apply Questions	Here are all the answers to the Stop, Review, and Apply questions and exercises in your textbook.	Online Study Center: Improve Your Grade
Crossword Puzzles	Crossword puzzles can be used to practice glossary terms and to study for exams.	Online Study Center: Improve Your Grade (part of Your Guide to an "A")
Flashcards	Review important definitions with interactive flashcards.	Online Study Center: Improve Your Grade (part of Your Guide to an "A")
To the Student	Learn how to study accounting successfully, improve your grade, and make the most out of your course.	Online Study Center: General Resources
Learning Objectives	Preview the Learning Objectives to get a head start on the chapter. Text content and end-of-chapter assignments are correlated to Learning Objectives.	Online Study Center: home page; textbook
Glossary	Use the electronic glossary to look up important terms and definitions.	Online Study Center: General Resources (complete glossary) and Improve Your Grade (glossary by chapter)
Chapter Outlines	Download chapter outlines to organize notes.	Online Study Center: Prepare for Class
Chapter Review	A one-stop shop for important points and concepts covered throughout the chapter.	Online Study Center: Improve Your Grade
Company Links	Here are hot links to companies featured in your text.	Online Study Center: Improve Your Grade

Managerial
Accounting

Eighth Edition

Susan V. Crosson, M.S. Accounting, C.P.A.
Santa Fe Community College, Florida

Belverd E. Needles, Jr., Ph.D., C.P.A., C.M.A.
DePaul University

Houghton Mifflin Company   Boston   New York

To my family—Bruce, Brent, and Courtney Crosson—and
in loving memory of my parents, Helen and Bryce Van Valkenburgh
To Professor Reginald R. Rushing, Texas Tech University (Deceased)
To Professor Joseph Goodman, Chicago State University

Executive Publisher: George Hoffman
Senior Sponsoring Editor: Ann West
Senior Marketing Manager: Mike Schenk
Marketing Coordinator: Erin Lane
Senior Development Editor: Chere Bemelmans
Editorial Assistant: Diane Akerman
Project Editor: Margaret M. Kearney
Art and Design Manager: Gary Crespo
Cover Design Manager: Anne S. Katzeff
Senior Photo Editor: Jennifer Meyer Dare
Composition Buyer: Chuck Dutton

Cover photo © Oliver Benn/Stone/Getty Images

COMPANY LOGO CREDITS: p. 54, Courtesy of Southwest Airlines; p. 112, Reprinted with permission of Cold Stone Creamery; p. 198, Photo courtesy of La-Z-Boy Inc.; p. 292, Reprinted with permission of Johnson & Johnson; p. 348, Reprinted with permission of Vail Resorts; p. 488, The Palm logo is a registered trademark owned by or licensed to Palm, Inc. (*Continued on p. xxviii*)

PHOTO CREDITS: p. 3, Getty Images; p. 10, © Richard T. Nowitz/Corbis; p. 17, © Leif Skoogfors/Corbis; p. 53, Getty Images; p. 54, © Southwest Airlines; p. 59, © Southwest Airlines; p. 111, Lon C. Diehl/PhotoEdit; p. 115, © Ed Bock/Corbis; p. 126, © Royalty-Free/Corbis; p. 155, Getty Images; p. 156, ©Louis Psihoyos/Corbis; p. 160, © Charles O'Rear/Corbis; p. 197, AP Images; p.202, dpa/Landov; p. 213, © Chuck Savage/Corbis (*Continued on page xxviii*)

Printed in the U.S.A.

Library of Congress Control Number: 2006936637

Instructor's examination copy
  ISBN-10: 0-618-83351-X
  ISBN-13: 978-0-618-83351-1
For orders, use student text ISBNs
  ISBN-10: 0-618-77718-0
  ISBN-13: 978-0-618-77718-1

1 2 3 4 5 6 7 8 9-VH-11 10 09 08 07

Brief Contents

Contents

Preface

This revision of *Managerial Accounting* is the most significant in the book's long history. The substantial changes we have made meet the needs of today's students, who not only face a business world increasingly complicated by ethical issues, globalization, and technology, but who also have more demands on their time. To help them meet these challenges, we place a heavy emphasis on developing their decision-making and critical-thinking skills and on providing information that is easy to understand and process.

Our primary focus is on showing students how successful managers use the tools and techniques of managerial accounting to make decisions about both day-to-day operations and long-term tactics and strategy. Our hope is not to make expert accountants of students, but to enable them to become knowledgeable, informed managers who use their organization's resources ethically and wisely and who, in doing so, protect and promote stakeholders' interests.

We invite you to read the User's Guide that follows this preface to get a sense of how this book and its many learning aids were designed to support a variety of learning styles and help students become effective managers skilled in using accounting information. Here, we elaborate on exactly what we set out to achieve in this eighth edition.

Streamlined Coverage and Redesign of Text

To make the text more readable, visually appealing, and pedagogically useful, we broke it into "user-friendly" portions with bulleted and numbered lists and added new Focus on Business boxes, line art, photographs, and end-of-section review material.

▶ New line art clarifies concepts and appeals to students who are visual learners.

▶ Photographs, with captions that underscore concepts in the text, increase visual interest.

▶ For learners who favor a hands-on approach, a new feature called "Stop• Review•Apply" presents review questions related to specific learning objectives. Many of these sections also include short exercises and their solutions. The Online Study Center (student website) provides the answers to the review questions, as well as many other resources for all types of learners.

We also reduced excessive detail, shortened headings, and simplified explanations. Last but not least, we made the text more accessible to students by using well-known companies to illustrate the concepts and techniques of managerial accounting.

Emphasis on Accounting Information and Successful Decision Making

Throughout the text, we increased our emphasis on how managers use accounting information to make operating, tactical, and strategic decisions, thus providing a uniform framework for developing decision-making skills.

▶ Each chapter opening includes a Decision Point that shows how managers of a well-known company—one that most students will immediately recognize—use accounting information to make decisions. The Decision Point poses questions that challenge students to think about the relationship between this information and the decisions management makes.

▷ The company discussed in the Decision Point is highlighted in the chapter and is revisited in "A Look Back At," a new feature that shows how the questions introduced in the Decision Point can now be answered.

Applying Accounting Concepts to Real Businesses

Today, management's use of accounting information goes far beyond computing the cost of products and services. In *Managerial Accounting*, we explore the full range of innovative systems that managers in our value-centered economy use to make critical decisions about product quality, customer service, and long-term relationships.

▷ Rather than focusing on the technical details of cost accounting, we emphasize the management process critical to operating a successful business. A piece of line art that appears in the first section of each chapter highlights managerial activities important at each stage of the management process.

▷ We emphasize the approaches learned from the most progressive companies, such as how to manage supply chains, analyze value chains, operate in a just-in-time environment, utilize activity-based management, apply the theory of constraints, and improve quality.

▷ We discuss the latest in management models and technology and emphasize that performance measurement and evaluation are essential to a manager's success in today's competitive environment.

▷ Service businesses, in which many students will ultimately work, receive expanded emphasis in the text discussion and the chapter assignments.

Ethical Financial Reporting

We believe students need to know more about what constitutes ethical financial reporting and good corporate governance. We revised the text to address this need.

▷ The previews at the start of many chapters point out ethical and governance issues related to the topics discussed in the chapter.

▷ In the end-of-chapter material, we continue to provide short cases based on realistic situations that require students to address an ethical dilemma directly related to the chapter content.

Reorganized Assignment Material

This text has always provided a rich assortment of assignments that address professors' needs. While keeping the range and depth of assignments from previous editions, we have simplified their organization for easier use.

▷ The end-of-chapter assignments are organized into two main sections: Building Your Basic Knowledge and Skills—which consists of Short Exercises, Exercises, Problems, and Alternate Problems—and Enhancing Your Knowledge, Skills, and Critical Thinking—which consists of cases.

▶ Many of the problems have a requirement labeled "Manager Insight." These requirements challenge students to think about the numbers and how they're used in business decision making.

▶ Cases are grouped by skill: Conceptual Understanding; Interpreting Management Reports; Decision Analysis Using Excel; Ethical Dilemma; Internet; Group Activity; and Business Communication.

New Instructional Technologies for Today's Business Environment

New technologies are today a driving force behind business growth and accounting education. For this eighth edition of *Managerial Accounting*, we developed an integrated text and technology program to help instructors take advantage of the opportunities created by new instructional technologies. Whether an instructor wants to incorporate new instructional strategies, develop students' core skills and competencies, or integrate technology into the classroom, this edition provides a total solution. (See the inside back cover of the book for a complete listing of supplements.)

Course Management

We know that homework and practice are integral parts of accounting courses and that grading homework and tests can be a challenge. The **Eduspace**® online learning tool pairs the widely recognized resources of Blackboard with quality, text-specific content from Houghton Mifflin. Auto-graded homework for end-of-chapter short exercises, exercises, and problems; algorithmic practice exercises; SMARTHINKING online tutoring; multimedia ebook with links to tutorials; demonstration videos; and other text-supporting content come ready to use. Premium Blackboard course cartridges and WebCT ePacks are also available.

HMTesting

HMTesting—now powered by D*iploma*®—contains the computerized version of the Test Bank. HMTesting provides instructors with the tools they need to create, customize, and deliver multiple types of tests. Instructors can select, edit, and add questions—some with algorithms—or generate randomly selected questions to produce a test master for easy duplication. All test questions are now tagged with AACSB learning outcomes, learning objectives, and key concepts. Online Testing and Gradebook functions allow instructors to administer tests via their local area network or the Internet, set up classes, record grades from tests or assignments, analyze grades, and compile class and individual statistics. HMTesting can be used on both PCs and Apple computers.

The Test Bank is also available in print. The printed Test Bank provides the same questions found in **HMTesting**—more than 2,000 true-false, multiple choice, short essay, and critical-thinking questions, as well as exercises and problems, all of which test students' ability to recall, comprehend, apply, and analyze information. Two achievement tests are provided for each chapter.

Instructor and Student Websites

The Online Teaching and Online Study Centers provide professors and students with text-specific resources that reinforce key concepts in the *Managerial Accounting* teaching and learning system. Both websites can be accessed at college.hmco.com/info/needles.

For instructors, the Online Teaching Center includes password-protected course materials, such as completely revised PowerPoint slides with video and original content; Classroom Response System content; sample syllabi; the *Accounting Instructor's Report*, which explores a wide range of contemporary teaching issues; and Electronic Solutions, which are fully functioning Excel spreadsheets for all exercises, problems, and cases in the text.

For students, the Online Study Center provides access to supplementary materials, such as ACE practice tests, answers to Stop, Review, and Apply questions, weblinks to companies discussed in the text, chapter outlines and summaries, glossaries (chapter-based and complete), and much more. In addition, all new texts are packaged with a passkey providing access to "Your Guide to an 'A'" resources. This material includes additional (ACE+) self-test quizzes, Flashcards, crossword puzzles, the complete *Study Guide*, Demonstration Videos, HMAccounting Tutor, and audio chapter reviews (MP3/ iPod-based chapter summaries and quizzes). See the endpapers of the text for a complete listing of all the student supplements available.

The Bottom Line

Although we have done more in this revision than in any previous one to make accounting concepts accessible to students, there is one thing we have not changed: we still teach students how to use the accounting information and systems that provide the data needed to make business decisions and that tell a company's story. For management, both financial information and nonfinancial information are a means of guiding a company's progress and profitability. Our goal is to improve students' understanding of the "story" revealed in a company's financial and nonfinancial data, and never has that goal been as critical as in current times, with business events underscoring this fact: accounting really matters.

To follow the "story," students have to learn how to think. *Managerial Accounting* teaches students to think about what they are reading, how they might make management decisions, and what roles they might play as future users of accounting information. Students also have to learn how to analyze and interpret data—where did the numbers come from? What is the meaning behind the numbers? What do the numbers say about a company's financial health? Today, business students need to learn more than how to make decisions about day-to-day operations; they also must learn how to analyze data from tactical and strategic perspectives to plan their organization's future. *Managerial Accounting*, Eighth Edition, focuses on teaching students to do just that.

Acknowledgments

A successful textbook is a collaborative effort. We are grateful to the many professors, other professional colleagues, and students who have taught and studied from our book, and we thank all of them for their constructive comments. In the space available, we cannot possibly mention everyone who has been helpful, but we do want to recognize those who made special contributions to our efforts in preparing the eighth edition of *Managerial Accounting*.

We wish to express our deep appreciation to colleagues at Santa Fe Community College and DePaul University, who have been extremely supportive and encouraging.

We thank Eric Blazer (Millersville University) for the study guide, and Judy R. Colwell (Northern Oklahoma College) for the test bank. We thank Edward H. Julius (California Lutheran University) for his contributions to the study guide and Eduspace course. We also thank Jeri Condit for creating the PowerPoint slides; Linda Burkell for HMAccounting Tutor and Demonstration Videos; and

Cathy Larson for her accuracy review of the text and solutions. Sarah Evans deserves special recognition for her thoroughness and clarity in editing portions of the text and laying out the eighth edition.

Also very important to the quality of this book is the supportive collaboration of our senior sponsoring editor, Ann West; senior development editor, Chere Bemelmans; editorial assistant, Diane Akerman; and project editor, Margaret Kearney—to whom we give special thanks.

Others who have had a major impact on this book through their reviews, suggestions, and participation in surveys, interviews, and focus groups are listed below. We cannot begin to say how grateful we are for the feedback from the many professors who have generously shared their responses and teaching experiences with us.

Daneen Adams, *Santa Fe Community College*
Sheryl Alley, *Ball State University*
Felix Amenkhienan, *Radford University*
Gregory D. Barnes, *Clarion University*
Mohamed E. Bayou, *The University of Michigan—Dearborn*
Charles M. Betts, *Delaware Technical and Community College*
Michael C. Blue, *Bloomsburg University*
Gary R. Bower, *Community College of Rhode Island*
Charles Bunn, *Wake Technical College*
Lee Cannell, *El Paso Community College*
Judy Colwell, *Northern Oklahoma University*
Constance Cooper, *University of Cincinnati*
John D. Cunha, *University of California—Berkeley*
Mark W. Dawson, *Duquesne University*
Patricia A. Doherty, *Boston University*
Lizabeth England, *American Language Academy*
David Fetyko, *Kent State University*
Sue Garr, *Wayne State University*
Roxanne Gooch, *Cameron University*
Christine Uber Grosse, *The American Graduate School of International Management*
Dennis A. Gutting, *Orange County Community College*
John Hancock, *University of California—Davis Graduate School of Management*
Yvonne Hatami, *Borough of Manhattan Community College*
Lyle Hicks, *Danville Area Community College*
Harry Hooper, *Santa Fe Community College*
Marianne James, *California State University, Los Angeles*
Edward H. Julius, *California Lutheran University*
Howard A. Kanter, *DePaul University*
Debbie Luna, *El Paso Community College*
Kevin McClure, *ESL Language Center*
George McGowan
Josie Mathias, *Mercer County Community College*
Gail A. Mestas
Jenine Moscove
Beth Brooks Patel, *University of California—Berkeley*
Ronald Picker, *St. Mary of the Wood College*
LaVonda Ramey, *Schoolcraft College*
Alan Ransom, *Cypress College*
Roberta Rettner, *American Ways*
Gayle Richardson, *Bakersfield College*
Larry Roman, *Cuyahoga Community College East*
James B. Rosa, *Queensborough Community College*
Donald Shannon, *DePaul University*
S. Murray Simons, *Northeastern University*
Marion Taube, *University of Pittsburgh*
Kathleen Villani, *Queensborough Community College*

Vicki Vorell, Cuyahoga Community College West
John Weber, DeVry Institute
Kay Westerfield, University of Oregon
Andy Williams, Edmunds Community College

Finally, we want to thank the facilitators for the last five years of COAE (Conference on Accounting Education):

2006 COAE Facilitators
Salvador Aceves, *University of San Francisco*
Rita Grant, *Grand Valley State University*
Emmanuel Onifade, *Morehouse College*
Janet Papiernik, *Indiana University—Purdue University*
Andy Williams, *Edmonds Community College*

2005 COAE Facilitators
Peter Aghimien, *Indiana University, South Bend*
Charles Bunn, *Wake Technical College*
James Dougher, *DeVry University*
Frank Lordi, *Widener University*
Elizabeth Murphy, *DePaul University*
Karen Novey, *Robert Morris College*
Wendy Tietz, *Kent State University*

2004 COAE Facilitators
Star Brown, *Western Piedmont Community College*
Rosie Bukics, *Lafayette College*
Stanley Chu, *Borough of Manhattan Community College*
Michael Cottrill, *Northeastern University*
Mark Mitschow, *SUNY—Genesee*
Elizabeth Murphy, *DePaul University*

2003 COAE Facilitators
Charlene Abendroth, *California State University*
Daneen Adams, *Santa Fe Community College*
Richard Fern, *Eastern Kentucky University*
Terry Grant, *Mississippi College*
Yvonne Hatami, *Borough of Manhattan Community College*
Rodger Holland, *Columbus State University*

2002 COAE Facilitators
Sharon Bell, *University of North Carolina—Pembroke*
Mark Henry, *Victoria College*
Harry Hooper, *Santa Fe Community College*
Richard Irvine, *Pensacola Junior College*
Nancy Kelly, *Middlesex Community College*
Paul Mihalek, *University of Hartford*
Paul Weitzel, *Eastern Shore Community College*

2001 COAE Facilitators
Salvador Aceves, *University of San Francisco*
Betty Habershon, *Prince George's Community College*
Jim Mazza, *Heald College*
Roselyn Morris, *Southwest Texas State University*
Ginger Parker, *Creighton University*
David Rogers, *Mesa State College*
Jeanne Yamamura, *University of Nevada—Reno*

—S.C. and B.N.

User's Guide to *Managerial Accounting*

We have designed *Managerial Accounting* with you—the student—in mind. Becoming familiar with this textbook will help you succeed in this course: you will study more effectively and improve your grades on tests and assignments. The following User's Guide will introduce you to your *Managerial Accounting* textbook.

Preview the Chapter

Use these features to preview the chapter. First, become familiar with the **Learning Objectives** (they appear throughout the chapter). Review the Decision Point; this feature tells you how a leading business uses accounting information.

1 Each **Chapter Preview** focuses on management issues; many also present ethical issues. As you read this section, consider the following: Why are the concepts in this chapter important to managers? What are the ethical issues?

2 The **Learning Objectives (LOs)** help guide you toward mastery of the material. These brief statements summarize what you should know after reading the chapter. You will see many references to **LOs** throughout each chapter.

CHAPTER

1

The Changing Business Environment: A Manager's Perspective

1 Management is expected to ensure that the organization uses its resources wisely, operates profitably, pays its debts, and abides by laws and regulations. To fulfill these expectations, managers establish the goals, objectives, and strategic plans that guide and control the organization's operating, investing, and financing activities. In this chapter, we describe the approaches that managers have developed to meet the challenges of today's changing business environment and the role that management accounting plays in meeting those challenges in an ethical manner.

LEARNING OBJECTIVES

2
LO1 Distinguish management accounting from financial accounting and explain how management accounting supports the management process.

LO2 Describe the value chain and its usefulness in analyzing a business.

LO3 Identify the management tools used for continuous improvement.

LO4 Explain the balanced scorecard and its relationship to performance measures.

LO5 Prepare an analysis of nonfinancial data.

LO6 Identify the standards of ethical conduct for management accountants.

2

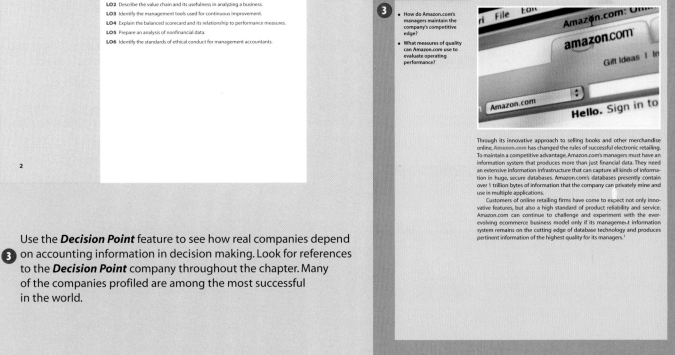

DECISION POINT
A MANAGER'S FOCUS AMAZON.COM

3
- How do Amazon.com's managers maintain the company's competitive edge?
- What measures of quality can Amazon.com use to evaluate operating performance?

Through its innovative approach to selling books and other merchandise online, Amazon.com has changed the rules of successful electronic retailing. To maintain a competitive advantage, Amazon.com's managers must have an information system that produces more than just financial data. They need an extensive information infrastructure that can capture all kinds of information in huge, secure databases. Amazon.com's databases presently contain over 1 trillion bytes of information that the company can privately mine and use in multiple applications.

Customers of online retailing firms have come to expect not only innovative features, but also a high standard of product reliability and service. Amazon.com can continue to challenge and experiment with the ever-evolving ecommerce business model only if its management information system remains on the cutting edge of database technology and produces pertinent information of the highest quality for its managers.[1]

3 Use the **Decision Point** feature to see how real companies depend on accounting information in decision making. Look for references to the **Decision Point** company throughout the chapter. Many of the companies profiled are among the most successful in the world.

Reinforce What You Read

As you read each chapter, use the features described below to reinforce the concepts. Look for the LO before each main section, and note boldface words: they are terms and definitions you should know. Use the *Stop, Review, and Apply* questions at the end of each main section to assess your understanding of the material.

4 *Learning Objectives* introduce the key points of each section and are integrated throughout the text.

5 **Boldface** terms call out important concepts and their definitions. These words also appear in a glossary at the end of the chapter.

6 *Study Notes* highlight important information and provide useful tips on ways to avoid common mistakes.

7 **Photographs** with detailed captions reinforce concepts in the textbook and show how accounting is used in the business world.

8 *Stop, Review, and Apply* features at the end of every section help you review important concepts in the section. These questions can also be used for discussion in class.

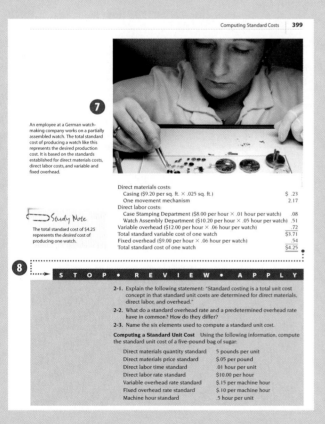

Reinforce Concepts Visually

These features visually reinforce the concepts in your textbook. Line art helps explain concepts, exhibits show financial statements and other information, and tables include material to support topics covered in the chapter.

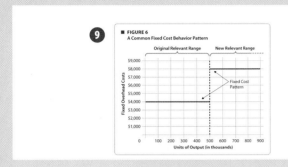

9 An abundance of **line art** illustrates the relationships between concepts and processes.

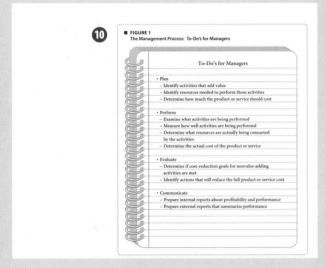

10 Each chapter includes a graphic that highlights managerial activities important at each stage of the management process.

Exhibit 2 presents a customer-related income statement for DAI. A similar format can be used to create an income statement for any cost object. Service organizations typically group clients according to significant characteristics, such as the length of time required to perform the service or the frequency of the service. In our example, Fran Teerlink can use the ABC information to review the profitability of each customer or customer group. He can also use it to compare selling and administrative costs across customer groups and as a basis for making changes in selling and administrative activities that will increase his company's profitability.

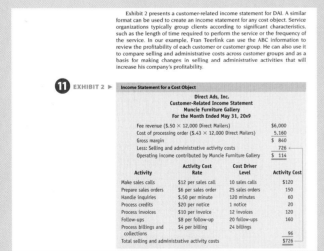

11 **Exhibits** throughout the text show financial information.

12 **Tables** present factual information referred to in the text.

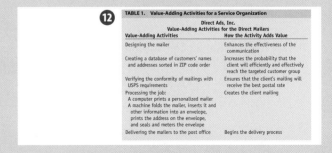

Learn Why Accounting Is Relevant

These features demonstrate how and why accounting is relevant. *Focus on Business Practice* boxes introduce you to real companies and real issues. Well-known public companies are used throughout to relate concepts to the real world.

13 *Focus on Business Practice* boxes highlight the relevance of accounting to business today.

14 The textbook refers to over 200 public, private, and not-for-profit companies. The **Needles Online Study Center** website (**http://college.hmco.com/info/needles**) provides a direct link to the websites of these companies. The book also has a company name index.

15 The approaches learned from the most progressive companies, including ways to improve quality, are emphasized throughout.

(Right-hand sample pages)

13

FOCUS ON BUSINESS PRACTICE
Just-in-Time Who's Who

- Eli Whitney perfected the concept of interchangeable parts in 1799, when he produced 10,000 muskets for the U.S. Army for the low price of $13.40 per musket.
- In the late 1890s, Frederick W. Taylor used his ideas of scientific management to standardize work through time studies.
- In the early twentieth century, Frank and Lillian Galbraith (parents of the authors of *Cheaper by the Dozen*) focused on eliminating waste by studying worker motivation and using motion studies and process charting.
- Starting in 1910, Henry Ford and Charles E. Sorensen arranged all the elements of manufacturing into a continuous system called the *production line*.
- After World War II, Taichii Ohno and Shigeo Shingo recognized the importance of inventory management, and they perfected the Toyota production system, also known as the *just-in-time system (JIT)*.[5]

◆ Goods should be produced only when needed.

◆ Workers must be multiskilled and must participate in improving efficiency and product quality.

Application of these concepts creates a JIT operating environment. Here, we describe the elements used in a JIT operating environment to enhance productivity, eliminate waste, reduce costs, and improve product quality.

Minimum Inventory Levels

Maintaining minimum inventory levels is fundamental to the JIT operating philosophy. In the traditional manufacturing environment, parts, materials, and supplies are purchased far in advance and stored until the production department needs them. In contrast, in a JIT environment, materials and parts are

A basic rule in a JIT operating environment is to keep inventory at a minimum. Doing so has many advantages, including reducing the amount of storage space needed, the amount of materials handling, and the amount of capital tied up in inventory. Maintaining minimum inventory levels does, however, increase the risk of stock depletions, so employees must keep a careful eye on inventory. The employee shown here is checking inventory in an electronics warehouse.

(Left-hand sample page)

Recognition of Quality

LO5 Recognize the awards and organizations that promote quality.

Many awards and organizations have been established to recognize and promote the importance of quality. Two of the most prestigious awards are the Deming prizes and the Malcolm Baldrige Quality Award. In addition, the International Organization for Standardization works to promote quality standards worldwide.

In 1951, the Japanese Union of Scientists and Engineers established the Deming Application Prize to honor individuals or groups who have contributed to the development and dissemination of total quality control. Consideration for the prize was originally limited to Japanese companies, but interest in it was so great that the rules were revised to allow the participation of companies outside Japan. Today, the organization awards several **Deming prizes** to companies and individuals that achieve distinctive results by carrying out total quality control. Recent winners of Deming prizes include the following:

14

Hosei Brake Industry Co., Limited (Japan)

Krishna Maruti Limited, Seat Division (India)

Rane Engine Valves Limited (India)

Rane TRW Steering Systems Limited, Steering Gear Division (India)

GC Corporation (Japan)

Thai Acrylic Fibre Co., Limited (Thailand).[5]

In 1987, the U.S. Congress created the **Malcolm Baldrige Quality Award** to recognize U.S. organizations for their achievements in quality and business performance and to raise awareness of the importance of quality and performance excellence. Organizations are evaluated on the basis of the Baldrige performance excellence criteria, a set of standards that is divided into seven categories: leadership, strategic planning, customer and market focus, information and analysis, human resource focus, process management, and business results. Thousands of organizations throughout the world accept the Baldrige criteria as the standards for performance excellence and use them for training and self-assessment, whether they plan to compete for the award or not. Award winners are showcased annually on the Internet (www.quality.nist.gov) and are encouraged to share their best practices with others. The following were among the winners of the Baldrige Award in 2005:

Sunny Fresh Foods, Inc., Monticello, Minn. (manufacturing)

DynMcDermott Petroleum Operations, New Orleans, La. (service)

Park Place Lexus, Plano, Tex. (small business)

Richland College, Dallas, Tex. (education)

Jenks Public Schools, Jenks, Okla. (education)

Bronson Methodist Hospital, Kalamazoo, Mich. (health care)

Customer Satisfaction The sale and shipment of a product does not mark the end of performance measurement. Customer follow-up helps in evaluating total customer satisfaction. Measures used to determine the degree of customer satisfaction include (1) the number and types of customer complaints, (2) the number and causes of warranty claims, and (3) the percentage of shipments returned by customers (or the percentage of shipments accepted by customers). Several companies have developed their own customer satisfaction indexes from these measures so that they can compare different product lines over different time periods.

Table 2 lists specific examples of the many nonfinancial measures used to monitor quality. These measures help a company continuously produce higher-quality products, improve production processes, and reduce throughput time and costs.

15 ### Measuring Service Quality

The quality of services rendered can be measured and analyzed. Many of the costs of conformance and nonconformance for a product apply to the development and delivery of a service. Flaws in service design lead to poor-quality services. Timely service delivery is as important as timely product shipments. Customer satisfaction in a service business can be measured by services accepted or rejected, the number of complaints, and the number of returning customers. Poor service development leads to internal and external failure costs.

Many of the costs-of-quality categories and several of the nonfinancial measures of quality can be applied directly to services and can be adopted by any type of service company. For example, the service departments of **Mercedes-Benz** dealers ask customers to complete a short three-question form when they pay their bills, **Chubb Insurance Company** sends a brief questionnaire to customers after every claim, and **PBS** provides phone, fax, and email addresses where viewers can record their comments about the system's programming.

Summarize and Review

The end-of-chapter features provide summary, review, and assignments for practice. ***A Look Back At*** relates the chapter's concepts to the company you read about in the ***Decision Point*** at the beginning of the chapter. Review sections include a ***Review of Learning Objectives*** and a ***Review of Concepts and Terminology***.

16 ***A Look Back At*** shows how the concepts learned in the chapter can be used to evaluate a company's performance.

17 The ***Chapter Review*** restates each learning objective and its main ideas.

17 CHAPTER REVIEW

REVIEW of Learning Objectives

LO1 Describe a management information system, and explain how it enhances management decision making.

In a management information system (MIS), the primary focus is on the management of activities, not on costs. By focusing on activities, an MIS provides managers with improved knowledge of the processes for which they are responsible. The MIS pinpoints resource usage for each activity and fosters managerial decisions that lead to continuous improvement throughout the organization.

As managers plan, they use the MIS database to obtain relevant and reliable information for formulating strategic plans, making forecasts, and preparing budgets. When managers perform their duties, they use the financial and nonfinancial information in the MIS database to implement decisions about personnel, resources, and activities that will minimize waste and improve the quality of their organization's products or services. When they evaluate performance, managers identify and track financial and nonfinancial performance measures to evaluate all major business functions. By enabling the timely comparison of actual to expected performance, the MIS allows managers to reward performance promptly, take speedy corrective actions, and analyze and revise performance measurement plans. And when they communicate, managers are able to generate customized reports that evaluate performance and provide useful real-time information for decision making.

LO2 Define *total quality management (TQM),* and identify financial and nonfinancial measures of quality.

Total quality management is an organizational environment in which all business functions work together to build quality into a firm's products or services. The costs of quality are measures of the costs that are specifically related to the achievement or nonachievement of product or service quality. The costs of quality have two components. One is the cost of conforming to a customer's product or service standards by preventing defects and failures and by appraising quality and performance. The other is the cost of nonconformance—the costs incurred when defects are discovered before a product is shipped and the costs incurred after a defective product or faulty service is delivered to the customer.

The objective of TQM is to reduce or eliminate the costs of nonconformance, the internal and external failure costs that are associated with customer dissatisfaction. To this end, managers can justify high initial costs of conformance if they minimize the total costs of quality over the product's or service's life cycle.

LO3 Use measures of quality to evaluate operating performance.

Nonfinancial measures of quality are related to product design, vendor performance, production performance, delivery cycle time, and customer satisfaction. Those measures, together with the costs of quality, help a firm meet its goal of continuously improving product or service quality and the production process.

LO4 Discuss the evolving concept of quality.

A manager's concept of quality must continuously evolve to fulfill customers' needs and expectations and to meet the demands of the changing business environment. Quality has many dimensions that extend beyond the mere creation and delivery of a product or service. Managers must satisfy customers today and create innovative products and services for tomorrow. The evolving concept of quality means more than having zero defects in a product or service; it means doing everything possible to have zero defections of customers.

Study Note

Some ISO standards vary between countries. For example, the standard size of computer paper in the United States is different from the standard size in European countries.

The International Organization for Standardization (ISO) is a worldwide federation of national standards bodies from over 130 countries. It promotes standardization with a view to facilitating the international exchange of goods and services. For example, by developing a standard format for credit cards, standard film speed codes, and standard graphical symbols for use on equipment and diagrams, the ISO has saved time and money for both individuals and businesses worldwide.

To standardize quality management and quality assurance, the ISO has developed **ISO 9000**, a set of guidelines for businesses that covers the design, development, production, final inspection and testing, installation, and servicing of products, processes, and services. Because many organizations do business only with ISO-certified companies, these guidelines have been adopted worldwide. To become ISO certified, an organization must pass a rigorous third-party audit of its manufacturing and service processes. As a result, certified companies have detailed documentation of their operations. The ISO 14000 series provides a similar framework for environmental management.[6]

STOP • REVIEW • APPLY

5-1. Identify two awards for quality, and explain the purpose of each.

5-2. Why is ISO certification advantageous for a company?

16 A LOOK BACK AT

AMAZON.COM

This chapter's Decision Point posed the following questions:

- **How do Amazon.com's managers maintain the company's competitive edge?**
- **What measures of quality can Amazon.com use to evaluate operating performance?**

Doing business over the Internet has added a rich dimension to quality. At Amazon.com, the quality of a customer's experience is enhanced by the company's management information system. By maintaining customer profiles based on previous visits and purchases, Amazon.com can greet customers as they return to the site with a web page customized to their preferences. And by integrating its supply-chain software with its warehousing and data-mining applications, Amazon.com can ensure timely and efficient deliveries to its warehouses and its customers.

Amazon.com's managers also use their information system's highly developed infrastructure to meet the changing expectations of their diverse customer base. In assessing customer satisfaction and the responsiveness of the company's supply chain and value chain, these managers use both nonfinancial and financial measures. To maintain a competitive edge, they will continue to need detailed, real-time information, both financial and nonfinancial, about every aspect of the company's operations and the highly competitive environment of ecommerce.

LO5 Recognize the awards and organizations that promote quality.

The importance of quality has been acknowledged worldwide through the granting of numerous awards, certificates, and prizes for quality. Two of the most prestigious awards are the Deming prizes and the Malcolm Baldrige Quality Award. In addition, the International Organization for Standardization promotes quality management through the ISO 9000 standards.

18 REVIEW of Concepts and Terminology

The following concepts and terms were introduced in this chapter:

Appraisal costs: The costs of activities that measure, evaluate, or audit products, processes, or services to ensure their conformance to quality standards and performance requirements; a cost of conformance. **(LO2)**

Benchmarking: The measurement of the gap between the quality of a company's process and the quality of a parallel process at the best-in-class company. **(LO4)**

Computer-aided design (CAD): A computer-based engineering system with a built-in program to detect product design flaws. **(LO2)**

Computer-integrated manufacturing (CIM) systems: Systems in which manufacturing and its support operations are coordinated by computer. **(LO2)**

Costs of conformance: The costs incurred in producing a quality product or service. **(LO2)**

Costs of nonconformance: The costs incurred to correct defects in a product or service. **(LO2)**

Costs of quality: The costs that are specifically associated with the achievement or nonachievement of product or service quality. **(LO2)**

Delivery cycle time: The time between the acceptance of an order and the final delivery of the product or service. **(LO2)**

Delivery time: The time between the completion of a product and its receipt by the customer. **(LO2)**

Deming prizes: Prizes awarded by the Japanese Union of Scientists and Engineers to companies that achieve distinctive results by carrying out total quality control. **(LO5)**

Enterprise resource planning (ERP) system: An integrated information system that manages all major business functions of an organization through an easy-to-access, centralized data warehouse. **(LO1)**

External failure costs: The costs incurred after the delivery of a defective product or service; a cost of nonconformance. **(LO2)**

Internal failure costs: The costs incurred when defects are discovered before a product or service is delivered to a customer; a cost of nonconformance. **(LO2)**

ISO 9000: A set of quality management guidelines established by the International Organization for Standardization. **(LO5)**

Kaizen: The gradual and ongoing improvement of quality and cost reduction in a business. **(LO4)**

Malcolm Baldrige Quality Award: An award established by the U.S. Congress to recognize U.S. organizations for their achievements in quality and business performance and to raise awareness about the importance of quality and performance excellence. **(LO5)**

Management information system (MIS): A management reporting system that identifies, monitors, and maintains continuous, detailed analyses of a company's activities and provides managers with timely measures of operating results. **(LO1)**

Prevention costs: The costs associated with the prevention of defects and failures in products and services; a cost of conformance. **(LO2)**

Process mapping: A method of using a flow diagram to indicate process inputs, outputs, constraints, and flows to help managers identify unnecessary efforts and inefficiencies in a business process. **(LO4)**

Production cycle time: The time it takes to make a product. **(LO2)**

Purchase-order lead time: The time it takes a company to process an order and organize so that production can begin. **(LO2)**

Quality: The result of an operating environment in which a product or service meets or conforms to a customer's specifications the first time it is produced or delivered. **(LO2)**

18 Each chapter includes a glossary of the key concepts and terms defined in the chapter. The ***LO*** next to each term indicates the section in which it is discussed.

Want more study aids and review exercises? The ***Study Guide*** for this book provides a thorough review of each learning objective, a detailed outline, true/false and multiple-choice questions, and exercises. Answers are included. Access the Study Guide with "Your Guide to an A" passkey.

Review and Practice

Continue your review of the chapter with the *Review Problem*, which reflects computations or analyses covered in the chapter. For practice at different levels of difficulty, *Chapter Assignments*—from *Short Exercises* to *Cases*—let you develop skills learned in the chapter. All assignments are identified by *Learning Objective* so you can easily review the concepts presented in the text.

19 Not sure if you understand the techniques and calculations? Want to find out if you're ready for a test? The *Review Problem* models main computations or analyses presented in the chapter and end-of-chapter assignments. The answer, often shown in Excel, is provided for immediate feedback.

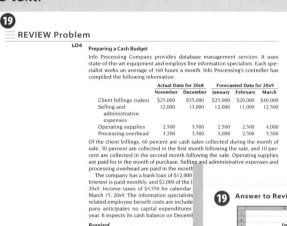

20 **Short Exercises** provide additional practice. Learning Objectives appear in the margin next to all assignments so you can refer to the text for help.

21 Single-topic **exercises** stress the application of the chapter's concepts.

Develop Important Skills

Use these end-of-chapter features to develop important skills. Five problems and three alternate problems per chapter allow extensive application of chapter topics, often covering more than one *Learning Objective*. *Cases* provide opportunities for group assignments, Internet research, analysis with Excel, and critical thinking.

㉒ Most problems include at least one *Manager Insight* question. These questions challenge you to think about how financial information is used for business decision making.

㉓ *Cases* at the end of each chapter have been organized to highlight important skills, such as conceptual understanding, interpretation of financial statements or management reports, Excel analysis, decision making, Internet research, and business communication.

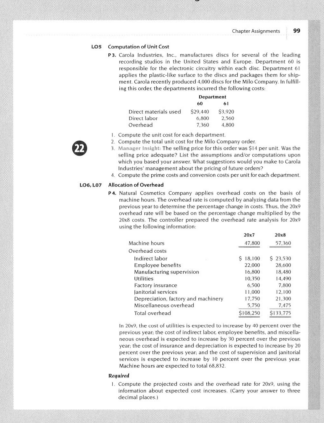

LO5 Computation of Unit Cost

P 3. Carola Industries, Inc., manufactures discs for several of the leading recording studios in the United States and Europe. Department 60 is responsible for the electronic circuitry within each disc. Department 61 applies the plastic-like surface to the discs and packages them for shipment. Carola recently produced 4,000 discs for the Milo Company. In fulfilling this order, the departments incurred the following costs:

	Department	
	60	**61**
Direct materials used	$29,440	$3,920
Direct labor	6,800	2,560
Overhead	7,360	4,800

1. Compute the unit cost for each department.
2. Compute the total unit cost for the Milo Company order.
3. **Manager Insight:** The selling price for this order was $14 per unit. Was the selling price adequate? List the assumptions and/or computations upon which you based your answer. What suggestions would you make to Carola Industries' management about the pricing of future orders?
4. Compute the prime costs and conversion costs per unit for each department.

LO6, LO7 Allocation of Overhead

P 4. Natural Cosmetics Company applies overhead costs on the basis of machine hours. The overhead rate is computed by analyzing data from the previous year to determine the percentage change in costs. Thus, the 20x9 overhead rate will be based on the percentage change multiplied by the 20x8 costs. The controller prepared the overhead rate analysis for 20x9 using the following information:

	20x7	20x8
Machine hours	47,800	57,360
Overhead costs		
Indirect labor	$ 18,100	$ 23,530
Employee benefits	22,000	28,600
Manufacturing supervision	16,800	18,480
Utilities	10,350	14,490
Factory insurance	6,500	7,800
Janitorial services	11,000	12,100
Depreciation, factory and machinery	17,750	21,300
Miscellaneous overhead	5,750	7,475
Total overhead	$108,250	$133,775

In 20x9, the cost of utilities is expected to increase by 40 percent over the previous year; the cost of indirect labor, employee benefits, and miscellaneous overhead is expected to increase by 30 percent over the previous year; the cost of insurance and depreciation is expected to increase by 20 percent over the previous year; and the cost of supervision and janitorial services is expected to increase by 10 percent over the previous year. Machine hours are expected to total 68,832.

Required

1. Compute the projected costs and the overhead rate for 20x9, using the information about expected cost increases. (Carry your answer to three decimal places.)

≡ **ENHANCING Your Knowledge, Skills, and Critical Thinking**

㉓ **Conceptual Understanding Cases**

LO1, LO2 Comparison of Costs in Different Types of Businesses

C 1. H & R Block is a service company that prepares tax returns; Borders is a retail company that sells books and CDs; Indian Motorcycle Corporation is a manufacturing company that makes motorcycles. Show that you understand how these companies differ by giving for each one an example of a direct and an indirect cost, a variable and a fixed cost, a value-adding and a nonvalue-adding cost, and a product and a period cost. Discuss the use of cost classification in these three types of organizations.

LO6, LO7, LO8 Comparison of Approaches to Developing Overhead Rates

C 2. Both Matos Company and Stubee Corporation use predetermined overhead rates for product costing, inventory valuation, and sales quotations. The two businesses are about the same size, and they compete in the corrugated box industry. Because the overhead rate is an estimated measure, Matos Company's management believes that the controller's department should spend little effort in developing it. The company computes the rate annually based on an analysis of the previous year's costs. No one monitors its accuracy during the year. Stubee Corporation takes a different approach. One person in the

---

Interpreting Management Reports

LO3, LO4 ABC and Selling and Administrative Expenses

C 4. Sandy Star, the owner of Star Bakery, wants to know the profitability of each of her bakery's customer groups. She is especially interested in the State Institutions customer group, which is one of the company's largest customer groups. Currently, the bakery is selling doughnuts and snack foods to ten state institutions in three states. The controller has prepared the following income statement for the State Institutions customer group:

Star Bakery
Income Statement for State Institutions Customer Group
For the Year Ended December 31, 20x8

Sales ($5 per case × 50,000 cases)	$250,000
Cost of goods sold ($3.50 per case × 50,000 cases)	175,000
Gross margin	$ 75,000
Less: Selling and administrative activity costs	94,750
Operating income (loss) contributed by State Institutions customer group	($19,750)

Activity	Activity Cost Rate	Actual Cost Driver Level	Activity Cost
Make sales calls	$60 per sales call	60 sales calls	$ 3,600
Prepare sales orders	$10 per sales order	900 sales orders	9,000
Handle inquiries	$5 per minute	1,000 minutes	5,000
Ship products	$1 per case sold	50,000 cases	50,000
Process invoices	$20 per invoice	950 invoices	19,000
Process credits	$20 per notice	40 notices	800
Process billings and collections	$7 per billing	1,050 billings	7,350
Total selling and administrative activity costs			94,750

Decision Analysis Using Excel

LO3, LO4 ABC in Planning and Control

C 5. Refer to the income statement in **C 4** for the State Institutions customer group for the year ended December 31, 20x8. Sandy Star, the owner of Star Bakery, is in the process of budgeting income for 20x9. She has asked the controller to prepare a budgeted income statement for the State Institutions customer group. She estimates that the selling price per case, the number of cases sold, the cost of goods sold per case, and the activity costs for making sales calls, preparing sales orders, and handling inquiries will remain the same for 20x9. She has contracted with a new freight company to ship the 50,000 cases at $.60 per case sold. She has also analyzed the procedures for invoicing, processing credits, billing, and collecting and has decided that it would be less expensive for a customer service agency to do the work. The agency will charge the bakery 1.5 percent of the total sales revenue.

1. Prepare a budgeted income statement for the State Institutions customer group for the year ended December 31, 20x9.
2. Refer to the information in **C 4**. Assuming that the planned activity cost rate and planned annual cost driver level for each selling and administrative activity remain the same in 20x9, calculate the planned activity cost for each activity.
3. Calculate the differences between the planned activity costs (determined in requirement 2) and the State Institutions customer group's budgeted activity costs for 20x9 (determined in 1).
4. Evaluate the results of changing freight companies and outsourcing the customer service activities.

Student Resources and Study Aids

Managerial Accounting offers a variety of print and multimedia tools to complement the way you learn. From study guides to downloadable MP3 audio review files, the Needles *Managerial Accounting* program keeps you engaged and on track for success. The following student resources may come packaged with your new copy of *Managerial Accounting*, or can be purchased separately at your local college bookstore or directly from Houghton Mifflin's virtual bookstore at **http://college.hmco.com/students**.

The **Online Study Center** contains a variety of resources, including ACE practice tests, chapter outlines and reviews, links to companies mentioned in the text, glossaries, and additional appendixes. Content to help you improve your grade is available with the **"Your Guide to an A"** passkey and includes Flashcards, Crossword Puzzles, MP3 audio summaries and quizzes, Demonstration Videos, and the complete Study Guide.

The *Managerial Accounting* **Electronic Working Papers CD** (0-618-77752-0) is an alternative to printed working papers. These Excel-based files contain templates that allow you to work the exercises, problems, and cases in the text; a new interface makes it easy to navigate among assignments. With the Electronic Working Papers CD, you master both accounting concepts and the basic skills required for spreadsheet applications.

Also available are print **Working Papers** (0-618-91002-6), which provide the appropriate accounting forms for solving the exercises, problems, and cases from the text.

The **SMARTHINKING**™ online tutoring center provides real-time access to experienced "e-structors" (online tutors). In addition to live, one-on-one interaction, you can submit questions, assignments, and spreadsheets and receive personalized feedback—usually within 24 hours.

The *Managerial Accounting* **Study Guide** is designed to help you improve your performance in the course. This resource consists of five parts: "Reviewing the Chapter," "Self-Test," "Testing Students' Knowledge," "Applying Your Knowledge," and "Answers." The Study Guide is available with the "Your Guide to an A" passkey.

To help you become familiar with computerized accounting systems used in practice, the **Peachtree Accounting CD** (0-618-62683-2) features the educational version of this leading software program. The experience you gain from working with actual software makes you more desirable as a potential employee.

Check Figures

Chapter 1
P 1. No check figure
P 2. Projected Cost per Unit: $22.25
P 3. No check figure
P 4. 2. Molding, Week 4, Second shift: −23.53%
P 5. Total traffic flow goal, 24,182
P 6. No check figure
P 7. 2. Decrease in number of rejects: 202
P 8. Average output, week eight: 92,899

Chapter 2
P 1. Cost of goods manufactured: $10,163,200
P 2. 2a. Gross Margin: $191,800; 2d. Cost of Goods Manufactured: $312,100
P 3. 2. Total unit cost: $13.72
P 4. 2. Overhead applied to Job 2214: $29,717
P 5. Total costs assigned to the Grater order, activity-based costing method: $69,280.40
P 6. Predetermined overhead rate for 20x9: $5.014 per machine hour
P 7. Total costs assigned to the Kent order, activity-based costing method: $41,805.60
P 8. 1c. Rigger II: $11,665; BioScout: $14,940

Chapter 3
P 1. b. $66,500; i. $57,800
P 2. Manufacturing overhead applied, January 15: $108,000
P 3. 2. $185,073
P 4. 1. Audit revenue, Rainy Day Bakeries: $37,163
P 5. Contract revenue, Job Order No. P-12: $28,990
P 6. Manufacturing overhead applied, September 15: $75,480
P 7. 3. $89,647
P 8. No check figure

Chapter 4
P 1. 1. Cost per equivalent unit: $6.05; ending inventory: $7,225
P 2. 1. Cost per equivalent unit: $2.00; ending inventory: $5,372
P 3. 1. Cost per equivalent unit: $7.00; ending inventory: $37,200
P 4. 1. Cost per equivalent unit: $3.78; ending inventory: $9,455
P 5. 1. Cost per equivalent unit: $4.70; ending inventory: $39,180
P 6. 1. Cost per equivalent unit: $0.59; ending inventory: $1,494
P 7. 1. Cost per equivalent unit: $1.25; ending inventory: $6,572
P 8. 1. Cost per equivalent unit: $213.40; ending inventory: $220,475

Chapter 5
P 1. No check figure
P 2. 1. Product unit cost: $270.00; 4. Product unit cost: $280.47
P 3. 1a. Total materials handling cost rate: 30% per dollar of direct materials
P 4. 3. Total direct cost, toy car work cell: $17,000
P 5. 3. Cost of goods sold: $564,400
P 6. 1. Product unit cost: $878.25
P 7. 3. Product unit cost: $10.43
P 8. 3. Cost of goods sold: $391,520

Chapter 6
P 1. 4. Cost per Job: $81.56
P 2. 1. 7,500 Billable Hours
P 3. 1.a. 3,500 Units
P 4. 2. 190,000 Units
P 5. 3. $805.23 per Job (rounded)
P 6. 1. 740 Systems
P 7. 1.a. 7,900 Units
P 8. 2. 418 Loans

Chapter 7
P 1. 1. Total manufacturing costs budgeted, November: $1,157,000
P 2. 8. Income from operations: $3,086
P 3. 1. Ending cash balance, February: $6,000
P 4. Ending cash balance, February: $17,660
P 5. 1. Projected net income: $101,812
P 6. 7. Manufactured cost per unit: $0.34
P 7. 1. Ending cash balance, February: $19,555
P 8. 1. Net income: $52,404

Chapter 8
P 1. 1. Flexible Budget, Total Cost: $7,248,000
P 2. 2. Operating Income: $194,782
P 3. 1. Flexible Budget, Contribution margin: $88,200
P 4. 3. Economic value added for 20x8: $21,850
P 5. 1. Residual income: ($2,500)
P 6. 2. Operating Income: $418,555
P 7. 3a. Actual Return on Investment: 6.30%
P 8. 3. Economic value added: $126,000

Chapter 9
P 1. Total standard unit cost of front entrance: $8,510
P 2. 2. Flexible budget formula: Total Budgeted Costs = ($.35 x Units Produced) + $10,500
P 3. 1. Direct materials price variance—Metal: $832 (F); 2. Direct labor rate variance—Molding: $510 (F)
P 4. 1.b. Direct materials quantity variance: $3,720 (U); 1.h. Fixed overhead volume variance: $320 (F)
P 5. a. Actual variable overhead: $42,500

P 6. 1. Total standard direct materials cost per unit: $167.52

P 7. 1. Direct materials price variance—Liquid Plastic: $386 (F); 2. Direct labor rate variance—Trimming/Packing: $56 (U)

P 8. 1.a. Direct materials price variance—Chemicals: $12,200 (F); 1.e. Variable overhead spending variance: $100 (U)

Chapter 10

P 1. 1. Cost to make: $1,200,000

P 2. 1. Contribution margin: $6,420

P 3. 1. Operating loss if Baseball line is dropped: ($50,000)

P 4. 2. Contribution margin per machine hour for AZ1: $2.40

P 5. 1. Contribution margin per hour for phone calls: $130

P 6 3. Operating income from further processing, bagel sandwiches with cheese: $.50

P 7. 1. Segment margin for Book X: $223,560

P 8. 2. $68.20

Chapter 11

P 1. 2. Gross Margin-Based Price: $23.04

P 2. 2. Tone Book, Gross Margin-Based Price: $23.39

P 3. Total billing: $14,812.71

P 4. 1. Speed-Calc 4: $78.40; 2. Speed-Calc 5: $88.00

P 5. 1. $19.20

P 6. 2. Gross Margin-Based Price: $27.68

P 7. 1. Product Y14: $520.00; 2. Product Z33, Projected total unit cost: $623.40

P 8. 1. Cost-plus transfer price: $34.08

Chapter 12

P 1. 1. 10.15%

P 2. 1. $99,672

P 3. Positive net present value: $35,540

P 4. 1. HZT Machine: 13.4%; 2. XJS Machine: 5.5 years

P 5. Negative net present value: ($26,895)

P 6. 1. $92,536.50

P 7. 2. Negative net present value: ($7,080)

P 8. 1. ETZ Machine: ($32,379); 2. ETZ Machine: 20.7%; 3. ETZ Machine: 5.4 years

Chapter 13

P 1. 1. Carbondale Company, total costs of conformance: $533,600; 2. Carbondale Company, total costs of nonconformance: 10.30% of Sales

P 2. 1. Delivery cycle time, weekly average: 73.43 hours

P 3. 1. Aspen, total costs of quality as a percentage of sales: 7.28%; 2. Frisco, ratio of costs of conformance to costs of quality: 28.10%

P 4. 1. Partnership Portal, total costs of conformance as a percentage of sales: .58%; 2. Small Business Portal, ratio of costs of nonconformance to costs of quality: 45.03%

P 5. 1. Springs Division is first; Glenwood Division is last

P 6. 1. East Division, total costs of conformance: $348,500; 2. East Division, total costs of nonconformance: 9.5% of sales

P 7. Delivery cycle time, weekly average: 58.04 hours

Chapter 14

P 1. Revenue centers: Housing, Food Service, Bookstore, Foundation

P 2. 1. NuBones total revenue center costs after allocation: $82,292

P 3. 2. Trade Publishing total revenue center costs after allocation: $237,452

P 4. 1. General Dentistry total revenue center costs after allocation: $10,197

P 5. 3. Solo Adventures total revenue center costs after allocation: $165,000

P 6. 2. Commercial Planes total revenue center costs after allocation: $324,509

P 7. 2. Insurance total revenue center costs after allocation: $5,180

P 8. 4. Net income: $100

Chapter 15

P 1. No check figure

P 2. Increase: a, b, e, f, l, m

P 3. 1.c. Receivable turnover, 20x8: 14.1 times; 20x7: 14.4 times; 1.e. Inventory turnover, 20x8: 3.6 times; 20x7: 3.5 times

P 4. 1.b. Quick ratio, Lewis: 1.5 times; Ramsey: 1.2 times; 2.d. Return on equity, Lewis: 8.8%; Ramsey: 4.9%

P 5. Increase: d, h, i

P 6. 1.a. Current ratio, 20x8: 1.5 times; 20x7: 1.5 times; 2.c. Return on assets, 20x8: 5.0%; 20x7: 10.7%

About the Authors

Central to the success of any accounting text is the expertise of its author team. This team brings to the text a wealth of classroom teaching experience, relevant business insight, and pedagogical expertise, as well as first-hand knowledge of today's students.

Susan V. Crosson, M.S., C.P.A.
Santa Fe Community College, Florida

With more than 25 years of teaching experience at the college and university level, Susan Crosson is recognized for her pedagogical expertise in teaching managerial accounting. She has a reputation for being able to engage university students in very large course sections and for encouraging community college students to master accounting. She believes in integrating technology into accounting education and actively uses the Internet to teach online, on-campus, and blended courses. Professor Crosson continues to promote the improvement of accounting education by serving the American Accounting Association and the Florida Institute of CPAs on a variety of committees, task forces, and sections. She is a past recipient of an IMA Faculty Development Grant to blend technology into the classroom, the Florida Association of Community Colleges Professor of the Year Award for Instructional Excellence, and the University of Oklahoma's Halliburton Education Award for Excellence.

Belverd E. Needles. Jr., Ph.D., C.P.A., C.M.A.
DePaul University

During his more than 30 years of teaching beginning accounting students, Belverd Needles has been an acknowledged innovator in accounting education. He has won teaching and education awards from DePaul University, the American Accounting Association, the Illinois CPA Society, the American Institute of CPAs, and the national honorary society, Beta Alpha Psi. The Conference on Accounting Education, started by Dr. Needles and sponsored by Houghton Mifflin, has been in existence for over 20 years and has helped more than 2,000 accounting instructors improve their teaching. Dr. Needles is editor of the *Accounting Instructors' Report*, a newsletter that thousands of accounting teachers rely on for new ideas in accounting education.

COMPANY LOGO CREDITS (*Continued*):

p. 536, Courtesy of Air Products; p. 576, Amazon, Amazon.com, the Amazon.com logo, and 1-Click are registered trademarks of Amazon.com Inc. or its affiliates; p. 618, Logo is a registered trademark licensed to Publix Super Markets, Inc., and reprinted with permission.

PHOTO CREDITS (*Continued*):

p. 245, Daniel Acker/Bloomberg News/Landov; p. 254, Getty Images; p. 258, AP Images; p. 291, Tony Freeman/PhotoEdit; p. 293, Bloomberg News/Landov; p. 311, Time Life Pictures/Getty Images; p. 347, AFP/Getty images; p. 355, © Jim Richardson/Corbis; p. 356, © Alan Klehr; p. 393, Daniel Acker/Bloomberg News/:amdpv; p. 399, REUTERS/Arnd Wiegmann/Landov; p. 405, AP Images; p. 443, AP Images; p. 450, © Sherwin Crasto/Reuters/Corbis; p. 461, © Greg Smith/Corbis; p. 487, AFP/Getty Images; p. 500, Tom Prettyman/PhotoEdit; p. 504, AP Images; p. 535, Photo Courtesy of Air Products; p. 539, AP Images; p. 551, AP Images; p. 575, Richard Levine/Alamy; p. 581, SPL/Photo Researchers; p. 592, Getty Images; p. 617, Robert W. Ginn/PhotoEdit; p. 624, Keith Brofsky/Photodisc Green/Getty Images; p. 630, Walt Disney Pictures/The Kobal Collection/Marks, Elliot; p. 657, AP Images; p. 676, © Syracuse Newspapers/Gary Walts/The Image Works.

Managerial
Accounting

The Changing Business Environment: A Manager's Perspective

Management is expected to ensure that the organization uses its resources wisely, operates profitably, pays its debts, and abides by laws and regulations. To fulfill these expectations, managers establish the goals, objectives, and strategic plans that guide and control the organization's operating, investing, and financing activities. In this chapter, we describe the approaches that managers have developed to meet the challenges of today's changing business environment and the role that management accounting plays in meeting those challenges in an ethical manner.

LEARNING OBJECTIVES

LO1 Distinguish management accounting from financial accounting and explain how management accounting supports the management process.

LO2 Describe the value chain and its usefulness in analyzing a business.

LO3 Identify the management tools used for continuous improvement.

LO4 Explain the balanced scorecard and its relationship to performance measures.

LO5 Prepare an analysis of nonfinancial data.

LO6 Identify the standards of ethical conduct for management accountants.

WAL-MART STORES, INC.

- What is Wal-Mart's strategic plan?

- What management accounting tools does Wal-Mart use to stay ahead of its competitors?

- What role does management accounting play in Wal-Mart's endeavors?

If organizations are to prosper, they must identify the factors that are critical to their success. Key success factors include satisfying customer needs, developing efficient operating processes, fostering career paths for employees, and being an innovative leader in marketing products and services. **Wal-Mart** had all these factors in mind when it entered the grocery business in 1988 (it is now the largest grocer in the United States) and when it began marketing toys (it now has 28 percent of that market). What drives Wal-Mart's success? Wal-Mart's CEO, Lee Scott, sums up his company's strategy this way:"What we look at is, when you end the year, did you produce the record results you wanted and are you positioned to do that again next year?"[1]

The Role of Management Accounting

LO 1   Distinguish management accounting from financial accounting and explain how management accounting supports the management process.

To plan and control an organization's operations, to measure its performance, and to make decisions about pricing products or services and many other matters, managers need accurate and timely accounting information. To do their jobs efficiently, employees who handle daily operations, such as managing the flow of materials into a production system, also rely on accurate and timely accounting information. The role of management accounting is to provide an information system that enables persons throughout an organization to make informed decisions, to be more effective at their jobs, and to improve the organization's performance.

The need for management accounting information exists regardless of the type of organization—manufacturing, retail, service, or governmental—or its size. Although multidivisional corporations need more information and more complex accounting systems than small ones, even small businesses need certain types of management accounting information to ensure efficient operating conditions. The precise type of information needed depends on an organization's goals and the nature of its operations.

In 1982, the Institute of Management Accountants (IMA) defined **management accounting** as

> the process of identification, measurement, accumulation, analysis, preparation, interpretation, and communication of financial information used by management to plan, evaluate, and control within the organization and to assure appropriate use of and accountability for its resources.[2]

Since this definition was written, the importance of nonfinancial information has increased significantly. Today, management accounting information includes such nonfinancial data as the time needed to complete one cycle of the production process or to rework production errors, as well as nonfinancial data pertaining to customer satisfaction.

Management Accounting and Financial Accounting: A Comparison

Both management accounting and financial accounting assist decision makers by identifying, measuring, and processing relevant information and communicating this information through reports. Both provide managers with key measures of a company's performance and with cost information for valuing inventories on the balance sheet. Despite the overlap in their functions, management accounting and financial accounting differ in a number of ways. Table 1 summarizes these differences.

Management accounting provides managers and employees with the information they need to make informed decisions, to perform their jobs effectively, and to achieve their organization's goals. Thus, the primary users of management accounting information are people inside the organization. Financial accounting takes the actual results of management decisions about operating, investing, and financing activities and prepares financial statements for parties outside the organization—owners or stockholders, lenders, customers, and governmental agencies. Although these reports are prepared

Study Note

Management accounting is *not* a subordinate activity to financial accounting. Rather, it is a process that includes financial accounting, tax accounting, information analysis, and other accounting activities.

TABLE 1. Comparison of Management and Financial Accounting		
Areas of Comparison	**Management Accounting**	**Financial Accounting**
Primary users	Managers, employees, supply chain partners	Owners or stockholders, lenders, customers, governmental agencies
Report format	Flexible, driven by user's needs	Based on generally accepted accounting principles
Purpose of reports	Provide information for planning, control, performance measurement, and decision making	Report on past performance
Nature of information	Objective and verifiable for decision making; more subjective for planning (relies on estimates)	Objective and verifiable
Units of measure	Monetary at historical or current market or projected values; physical measures of time or number of objects	Monetary at historical and current market values
Frequency of reports	Prepared as needed; may or may not be on a periodic basis	Prepared on a periodic basis

primarily for external use, managers also rely on them in evaluating an organization's performance.

Because management accounting reports are for internal use, their format can be flexible, driven by the user's needs. They may report either historical or future-oriented information without any formal guidelines or restrictions. In contrast, financial accounting reports, which focus on past performance, must follow standards and procedures specified by generally accepted accounting principles.

The information in management accounting reports may be objective and verifiable, expressed in monetary terms or in physical measures of time or objects; if needed for planning purposes, the information may be based on estimates, and in such cases, it will be more subjective. In contrast, the statements that financial accounting provides must be based on objective and verifiable information, which is generally historical in nature and measured in monetary terms. Management accounting reports are prepared as often as needed—annually, quarterly, monthly, or even daily. Financial statements, on the other hand, are prepared and distributed periodically, usually on a quarterly and annual basis.

Management Accounting and the Management Process

As we noted at the beginning of the chapter, management is expected to ensure that the organization uses its resources wisely, operates profitably, pays its debts, and abides by laws and regulations. To fulfill these expectations, managers establish the goals, objectives, and strategic plans that guide and control the organization's operating, investing, and financing activities.

 Study Note

Financial accounting must adhere to the conventions of consistency and comparability to ensure the usefulness of information to parties outside the firm. Management accounting, on the other hand, can use innovative analyses and presentation techniques to enhance the usefulness of information to people within the firm.

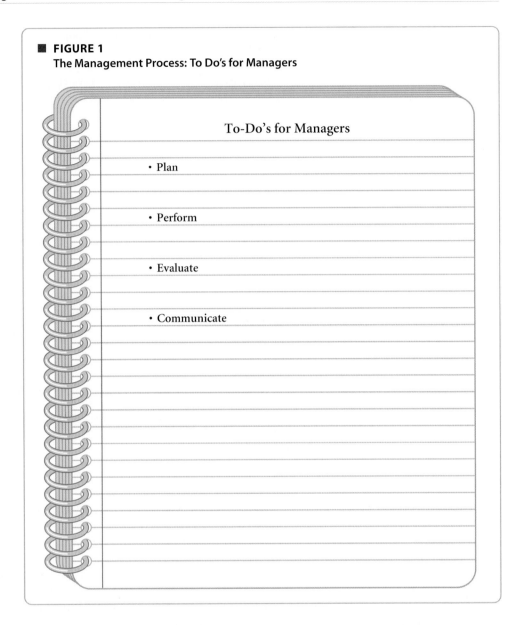

■ **FIGURE 1**
The Management Process: To Do's for Managers

To-Do's for Managers

• Plan

• Perform

• Evaluate

• Communicate

Although management actions differ from organization to organization, they generally follow a four-stage management process. As illustrated in Figure 1, the four stages of this process are planning, performing, evaluating, and communicating. Management accounting supports each stage of the process.

Planning Figure 2 shows the overall framework in which planning takes place. The overriding goal of a business is to increase the value of the stakeholders' interest in the business. It specifies the business's end point, or ideal state. For example, **Wal-Mart's** end point is "to become the worldwide leader in retailing."

A company's **mission statement** describes the fundamental way in which the company will achieve its goal of increasing stakeholders' value. It also expresses the company's identity and unique character; for instance, in its mission statement, Wal-Mart says that it wants "to give ordinary folk the chance to buy the same things as rich people." The mission statement is essential to the planning process, which must consider how to add value through strategic objectives, tactical objectives, and operating objectives.

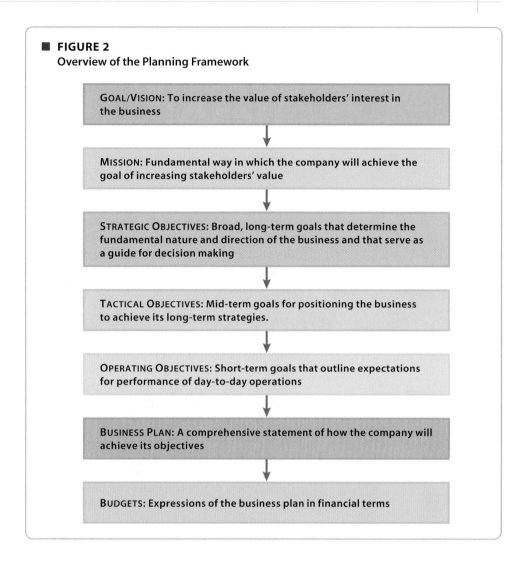

■ **FIGURE 2**
Overview of the Planning Framework

> GOAL/VISION: To increase the value of stakeholders' interest in the business

> MISSION: Fundamental way in which the company will achieve the goal of increasing stakeholders' value

> STRATEGIC OBJECTIVES: Broad, long-term goals that determine the fundamental nature and direction of the business and that serve as a guide for decision making

> TACTICAL OBJECTIVES: Mid-term goals for positioning the business to achieve its long-term strategies.

> OPERATING OBJECTIVES: Short-term goals that outline expectations for performance of day-to-day operations

> BUSINESS PLAN: A comprehensive statement of how the company will achieve its objectives

> BUDGETS: Expressions of the business plan in financial terms

▸ **Strategic objectives** are broad, long-term goals that determine the fundamental nature and direction of a business and that serve as a guide for decision making. Strategic objectives involve such basic issues as what a company's main products or services will be, who its primary customers will be, and where it will operate. They stake out the strategic position that a company will occupy in the market—whether it will be a cost leader, quality leader, or niche satisfier. For example, Wal-Mart's strategic objective in entering the grocery and toy markets in the late 1980s was to become the low-cost leader in those markets. In 2006, Wal-Mart was considering entering the banking field—a strategy that its management believed would give customers a better deal.[3]

▸ **Tactical objectives** are mid-term goals that position an organization to achieve its long-term strategies. These objectives, which usually cover a three- to five-year period, lay the groundwork for attaining the company's strategic objectives. For example, to implement its banking strategy, Wal-Mart applied for federal deposit insurance, a requirement for any bank.

▸ **Operating objectives** are short-term goals that outline expectations for the performance of day-to-day operations. Operating objectives link to performance targets and specify how success will be measured. Wal-Mart's operating objectives focus on increasing sales, earnings per share, and real profit dollars everyday—as evidenced by the daily posting of the company's stock price in every store.

To develop strategic, tactical, and operating objectives, managers must formulate a business plan. A **business plan** is a comprehensive statement of how a company will achieve its objectives. It is usually expressed in financial terms in the form of budgets, and it often includes performance goals for individuals, teams, products, or services. Management accounting supports the planning process by providing the information that managers need to develop strategic, tactical, and operating objectives and the comprehensive business plan.

To illustrate the role of management accounting in the planning process, let's suppose that Anna Wang is about to open her own retail grocery store called Good Foods Store. Wang's goal is to obtain an income from the business and to increase the value of her investment in it. After reading about how traditional grocers are being squeezed out by low-cost competitors like Wal-Mart and quality-focused stores like **Whole Foods Market**, Wang has decided that her business's mission is to attract upscale customers and retain them by selling high-quality foods and providing excellent service in a pleasant atmosphere.

Wang's strategic objectives call for buying high-quality fresh foods from local growers and international distributors and reselling these items to consumers. Her tactical objectives include implementing a stable supply chain of high-quality suppliers and a database to track customers' preferences. Her operating objectives call for courteous and efficient customer service. To measure performance in this area, she decides to keep a record of the number and type of complaints about poor customer service.

Before Wang can open her store, she needs to apply to a local bank for a start-up loan. To do so, she must have a business plan that provides a full description of the business, including a complete operating budget for the first two years of operations. The budget must include a forecasted income statement, a forecasted statement of cash flows, and a forecasted balance sheet for both years.

Because Wang does not have a financial background, she consults a local accounting firm for help in developing her business plan. To provide relevant input for the plan, she has to determine the types of products she wants to sell; the volume of sales she anticipates; the selling price for each product; the monthly costs of leasing or purchasing facilities, employing personnel, and maintaining the facilities; and the number of display counters, storage units, and cash registers that she will need.

FOCUS ON BUSINESS PRACTICE
What's Going On in the Grocery Business?

Over the last five years, sales at large supermarket chains, such as **Kroger**, **Safeway**, and **Albertson's**, have been flat and profits weak because both ends of their customer market are being squeezed. Large-scale retailers like **Wal-Mart** and **Costco** are attracting cost-conscious grocery shoppers, and upscale grocery customers are being lured to specialty grocers like **Trader Joe's** and **Whole Foods Market**. Albertson's strategy to combat its flat sales and profits was to sell itself to other retailers, like **Supervalu** and **CVS**, to form larger businesses. Other grocery chains are using the planning framework to reconsider their company's mission and strategic options. Some are adding new products and services, such as walk-in medical clinics; others are closing stores and downsizing; still others are entering new geographic markets.[4]

Performing Planning alone does not guarantee satisfactory operating results. Management must implement the business plan in ways that make optimal use of available resources. Smooth operations require one or more of the following:

- Hiring and training personnel
- Matching human and technical resources to the work that must be done
- Purchasing or leasing facilities
- Maintaining an inventory of products for sale
- Identifying operating activities, or tasks, that minimize waste and improve the quality of products or services

Managers execute the business plan by overseeing the company's daily operations. In small companies like Anna Wang's, managers generally have frequent direct contact with their employees. They supervise them and interact with them to help them learn a task or improve their performance. In larger, more complex organizations, there is usually less direct contact between managers and employees. Instead of directly observing employees, managers in large companies like Wal-Mart monitor their employees' performance by measuring the time taken to complete an activity (such as how long it takes to process customer sales) or the frequency of an activity (such as the number of customers served per hour).

To illustrate how management accounting provides information to support the performance of managers, let's assume that Good Foods Store is now open for business. The budget prepared for the store's first two years of operation provides the link between the business plan and the execution of the plan. Items that relate to the business plan appear in the budget and become authorizations for expenditures. They include such matters as spending on store fixtures, hiring employees, developing advertising campaigns, and pricing items for special sales.

Critical to managing any retail business is the supply chain. As Figure 3 shows, the **supply chain** (also called the *supply network*) is the path that leads from the suppliers of the materials from which a product is made to the final consumer. In the supply chain for grocery stores, produce and other items flow from growers and suppliers to manufacturers or distributors to retailers to consumers. Wang must coordinate deliveries from local growers and international distributors so that she meets the demands of her customers without having too much inventory on hand, which would tie up cash, or being out of stock

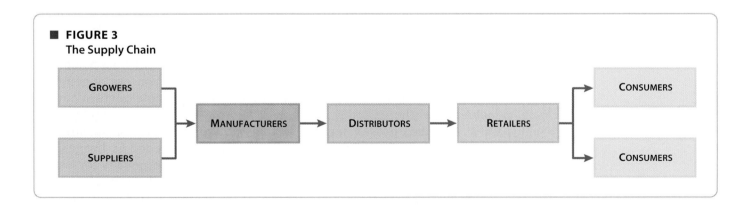

■ **FIGURE 3**
The Supply Chain

The supply chain is the path that leads from suppliers to the final consumer. In the supply chain for grocery stores, produce flows from growers and suppliers to manufacturers or distributors to retailers to consumers. The supply chain for this farmer's market is much shorter: grower to consumer.

when a customer asks for a certain product. Management accounting information about deliveries and sales will help her manage the supply chain.

Evaluating When managers evaluate operating results, they compare the organization's actual performance with the performance levels they established in the planning stage. They earmark any significant variations for further analysis so that they can correct the problems. If the problems are the result of a change in the organization's operating environment, the managers may revise the original objectives. Ideally, the adjustments made in the evaluation stage will improve the company's performance.

To evaluate how well Good Foods Store is doing, Anna Wang will compare the amounts estimated in the budget with actual results. If any differences appear, she will analyze why they have occurred. The reasons for these differences may lead Wang to change parts of her original business plan. In addition to reviewing employees' performance with regard to financial goals, such as avoiding waste, Wang will want to review how well her employees served customers. As noted earlier, she decided to monitor service quality by keeping a record of the number and type of complaints about poor customer service. Her review of this record may help her develop new and better strategies.

Communicating Whether accounting reports are prepared for internal or external use, they must provide accurate information and clearly communicate this information to the reader. Internal reports that provide inaccurate information or present information in such a way that it is unclear to the employee or the manager can have a negative effect on a company's operations and ultimately on its profitability. Full disclosure and transparency in financial statements issued to external parties is a basic concept of generally accepted accounting principles, and violation of this principle can result in stiff penalties. After the reporting violations by **Enron**, **WorldCom**, and other companies, Congress passed legislation that requires the top management of companies that file financial statements with the Securities and Exchange Commission to certify that these statements are accurate. The penalty for issuing false public reports can be loss of compensation, fines, and jail time.

The key to producing a management accounting report that communicates accurate and useful information whose meaning is transparent to the reader is to apply the four *w*'s: why, who, what, and when.

▶ W*hy*? Know the purpose of the report. Focus on it as you write.

▶ W*ho*? Identify the audience for your report. Communicate at a level that matches your readers' understanding of the issue and their familiarity with accounting information. A detailed, informal report may be appropriate for your manager, but a more concise summary may be necessary for other audiences, such as the president or board of directors of your organization.

▶ W*hat*? What information is needed, and what method of presentation is best? Select relevant information from reliable sources. You may draw information from pertinent documents or from interviews with knowledgeable managers and employees. The information should be not only relevant, but also easy to read and understand. You may need to include visual aids, such as bar charts or graphs, to present the information clearly.

▶ W*hen*? Know the due date for the report. Strive to prepare an accurate report on a timely basis. If the report is urgently needed, you may have to sacrifice some accuracy in the interest of timeliness.

The four *w*'s are also applicable to financial accounting reports. Assume that Anna Wang has hired Sal Chavez to be her company's accountant. In the financial statements that he prepares, the purpose—or *why*—is to report on the financial health of Good Foods Store. In this case, Wang, her bank and other creditors, and potential investors are the *who*. The *what* consists of disclosures about assets, liabilities, product costs, and sales. The required reporting deadline for the accounting period answers the question of *when*.

Wang will also want periodic internal reports on various aspects of her store's operations. For example, a monthly report may summarize the costs of ordering products from international distributors and the related shipping charges. If the costs in the monthly reports appear to be too high, she may ask Sal Chavez to conduct a special study. The results of such a study might result in a memorandum report like the one shown in Exhibit 1.

EXHIBIT 1 ▶

A Management Accounting Report
Memorandum

When:	Today's Date
Who:	To: A. Wang, Good Foods Store
	From: Sal Chavez, Accountant
Why:	Re: International Distributors Ordering and Shipping Costs—Analysis and Recommendations
What:	As you requested, I have analyzed the ordering and shipping costs incurred when buying from international distributors. I found that during the past year, these costs were 9 percent of sales, or $36,000.
	On average, we are placing about two orders per week, or eight orders per month. Placing each order requires about two and one-half hours of an employee's time. Further, the international distributors charge a service fee for each order, and shippers charge high rates for orders as small as ours.
	My recommendations are (1) to reduce orders to four per month (the products' freshness will not be affected if we order at least once a week) and (2) to begin placing orders through the international distributors' websites (our international distributors do not charge a service fee for online orders). If we follow these recommendations, I project that the costs of receiving products will be reduced to 4 percent of sales, or $16,000, annually—a savings of $20,000.

In summary, management accounting can provide a constant stream of relevant information. Compare Wang's activities and information needs with the steps of the management process shown in Figure 1. She started with a business plan, implemented the plan, and evaluated the results. Accounting information helped her develop her business plan, communicate that plan to her bank and employees, evaluate the performance of her employees, and report the results of operations. As you can see, accounting plays a critical role in managing the operations of any organization.

STOP • REVIEW • APPLY

1-1. What is management accounting, and how is it similar to financial accounting?

1-2. What is the supply chain?

1-3. What are the four *w*'s of report preparation? Explain the importance of each.

1-4. A financial report often contains estimates and projections. How does the writer of such a report make sure that the reader understands the uncertainties involved?

Suggested answers to all Stop, Review, and Apply questions are available at http://college.hmco.com/accounting/needles/man_acc/8e/student_home.html.

Value Chain Analysis

LO2 Describe the value chain and its usefulness in analyzing a business.

Each step in the manufacture of a product or the delivery of a service can be thought of as a link in a chain that adds value to the product or service. This concept of how a business fulfills its mission and objectives is known as the **value chain**. As shown in Figure 4, the steps that add value to a product or service—which range from research and development to customer service— are known as **primary processes**. The value chain also includes **support services**, such as legal services and management accounting. These services facilitate the primary processes but do not add value to the final product or service. Their roles are critical, however, to making the primary processes as efficient and effective as possible.

Primary Processes and Support Services

Let's assume that Good Foods Store has had some success, and Anna Wang now wants to determine the feasibility of making and selling her own brand of candy. The primary processes that will add value to the new candy are as follows:

Research and development: developing new and better products or services. Wang plans to add value by developing a candy that has less sugar content than similar confections.

Design: creating improved and distinctive shapes, labels, or packages for products. For example, a package that is attractive and that describes the desirable features of Wang's new candy will add value to the product.

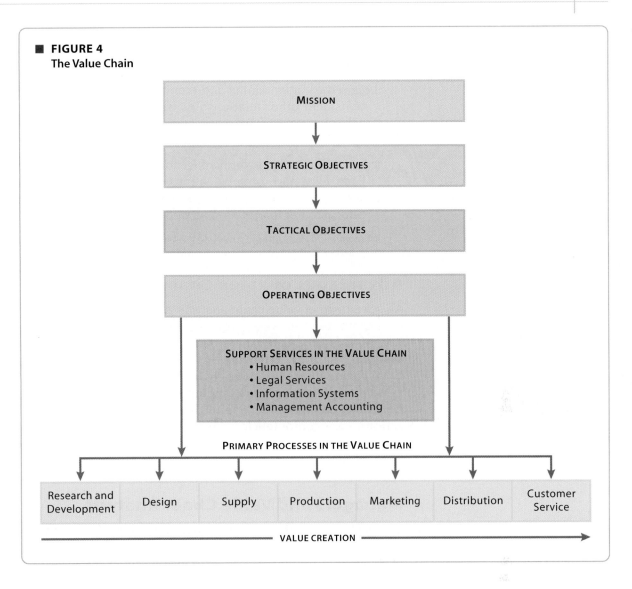

■ **FIGURE 4**
The Value Chain

Supply: purchasing materials for products or services. Wang will want to purchase high-quality sugar, chocolate, and other ingredients for the candy, as well as high-quality packaging.

Production: manufacturing the product or service. To add value to the new candy, Wang will want to implement efficient manufacturing and packaging processes.

Marketing: communicating information about the products or services and selling them. Attractive advertisements will facilitate sale of the new candy to customers.

Distribution: delivering the product or service to the customer. Courteous and efficient service for in-store customers will add value to the product. Wang may also want to accommodate Internet customers by providing shipping.

Customer service: following up with service after sales or providing warranty service. For example, Wang may offer free replacement of any candy that does not satisfy the customer. She could also use questionnaires to measure customer satisfaction.

The services that support the primary processes are as follows:

Human resources: hiring and training employees to carry out all the functions of the business. Wang will need to hire and train personnel to make the new candy.

Legal services: maintaining and monitoring all contracts, agreements, obligations, and other relationships with outside parties. For example, Wang will want legal advice when applying for a trademark for the new candy's name and when signing contracts with suppliers.

Information systems: establishing and maintaining technological means of controlling and communicating within the organization. Wang will want a computerized accounting system that keeps not only financial records, but customer information as well.

Management accounting: provides essential information in any business.

Advantages of Value Chain Analysis

Study Note

A company cannot succeed by trying to do everything at the highest level. It has to focus on its core competencies to give customers the best value.

An advantage of value chain analysis is that it allows a company to focus on its core competencies. A **core competency** is the thing that a company does best. It is what gives a company an advantage over its competitors. For example, **Wal-Mart** is known for having the lowest prices; that is its core competency.

A common result of value chain analysis is outsourcing, which can also be of benefit to a business. **Outsourcing** is the engagement of other companies to perform a process or service in the value chain that is not among an organization's core competencies. For instance, Wal-Mart outsources its inventory management to its vendors, who monitor and stock Wal-Mart's stores and warehouses.

Managers and Value Chain Analysis

In today's competitive business environment, analysis of the value chain is critical to most companies' survival. Managers at Wal-Mart and other organizations must provide the highest value to customers at the lowest cost, and low cost often equates with the speed at which the primary processes of the value chain are executed. Time to market is very important.

Managers must also make the services that support the primary processes as efficient as possible. These services are essential and cannot be eliminated, but because they do not add value to the final product, they must be implemented as economically as possible. Businesses have been making progress in this area. For example, over the past ten years, the cost of the accounting function in many companies as a percentage of total revenue has declined from 6 percent to 2 percent. Technology has played a big role in making this economy possible.

As a support service, management accounting must be efficient and provide value to managers by developing information that is useful for decision making. For example, to determine whether manufacturing and selling her own brand of candy will be profitable, Anna Wang will need accurate information about the cost of the candy. She knows that if her candy is to be competitive, she cannot sell it for more than $10 per pound. Further, she has an idea of how much candy she can sell in the first year. Based on this information, her accountant, Sal Chavez, analyzes the value chain and projects the initial costs per pound shown in Exhibit 2. The total cost of $8 per pound worries Wang because with a selling price of $10, it leaves only $2, or 20 percent of revenue, to cover all the support services and provide a profit. Wang believes that if the enterprise is to be successful, this percentage, called the *margin*, must be at

EXHIBIT 2 ▶ **Value Chain Analysis**

Good Foods Store
Projected Costs of New Candy
June 1, 20x9

Primary Process	Initial Costs per Pound	Revised Costs per Pound
Research and development	$ .25	$ .25
Design	.10	.10
Supply	1.10	.60
Production	4.50	3.50
Marketing	.50	.50
Distribution	.90	.90
Customer service	.65	.65
Total cost	$8.00	$6.50

least 35 percent. Since the selling price is constrained by the competition, she must find a way to reduce costs.

Chavez tells her that the company could achieve a lower total cost per pound by selling a higher volume of candy, but that is not realistic for the new product. He also points out that the largest projected costs in the store's value chain are for supply and production. Because Wang plans to order ingredients from a number of suppliers, her orders would not be large enough to qualify for quantity discounts and savings on shipping. Using a single supplier could reduce the supply cost by $.50 per unit. Another way of reducing the cost of production would be to outsource this process to a candy manufacturer, whose high volume of products would allow it to produce the candy at a much lower cost than could be done at Good Foods Store. Outsourcing would reduce the production cost to $3.50 per unit. Thus, the total unit cost would be reduced to $6.50, as shown in Exhibit 2. This per unit cost would enable the company to sell the candy at a competitive $10 per pound and make the targeted margin of 35 percent ($3.50 ÷ $10).

This value chain analysis illustrates two important points. First, Good Food Store's mission is as a retailer. The company has no experience in making candy. Manufacturing candy would require a change in the company's mission and major changes in the way it does business. Second, outsourcing portions of the value chain that are not part of a business's core competency is often the best business policy. Since Good Foods Store does not have a core competency in manufacturing candy, it would not be competitive in this field. Anna Wang would be better off having an experienced candy manufacturer produce the candy according to her specifications and then selling the candy under her store's label. As Wang's business grows, increased volume may allow her to reconsider undertaking the manufacture of candy.

S T O P • R E V I E W • A P P L Y

2-1. What is the value chain?

2-2. What are primary processes and support services? How do primary processes and support services differ?

2-3. Is it better for a company to have a primary process or a support service as a core competency?

The Total Cost per Unit of Primary Processes and Support Services   The following unit costs were determined by dividing the total costs of each component by the number of products produced. From these unit costs, determine the total cost per unit of primary processes and the total cost per unit of support services.

Research and development	$ 1.25
Human resources	1.35
Design	.15
Supply	1.10
Legal services	.40
Production	4.00
Marketing	.80
Distribution	.90
Customer service	.65
Information systems	.75
Management accounting	.10
Total cost per unit	$11.45

SOLUTION

Primary processes:

Research and development	$1.25
Design	.15
Supply	1.10
Production	4.00
Marketing	.80
Distribution	.90
Customer service	.65
Total cost per unit	$8.85

Support services:

Human resources	$1.35
Legal services	.40
Information systems	.75
Management accounting	.10
Total cost per unit	$2.60

Continuous Improvement

Today, managers in all parts of the world have ready access to international markets and to current information for informed decision making. As a result, global competition has increased significantly. One of the most valuable lessons gained from this increase in competition is that management cannot afford to become complacent. The concept of **continuous improvement** evolved to avoid such complacency. Organizations that adhere to continuous

FOCUS ON BUSINESS PRACTICE

Becoming a Leader: What Qualities, Skills, and Education Do CEOs Possess?

According to the consulting firm Leadership Worth Following, top business leaders have vision, good judgment, and excellent communication skills and are futurists who persevere and adapt. A profile of leading CEOs reveals the following:

- The average age is 52 for men and 47 for women.

- About 97 percent have an undergraduate degree, and 38 percent have an MBA.

- About 33 percent have international experience.

- Women occupy many leadership positions in health care, consumer products, and financial services, but very few women are leaders in the manufacturing, chemical, entertainment, and wholesale businesses.

- On average, women CEOs receive about 30 percent less in pay, bonuses, and options than male CEOs.[5]

improvement are never satisfied with what is; they constantly seek improved quality and lower cost through better methods, products, services, processes, or resources. In response to this concept, several important management tools have emerged. These tools help companies remain competitive by focusing on continuous improvement of business methods.

Management Tools for Continuous Improvement

Among the management tools that companies use are the just-in-time operating philosophy, total quality management, activity-based management, and the theory of constraints.

Just-in-Time Operating Philosophy
The **just-in-time (JIT) operating philosophy** requires that all resources—materials, personnel, and facilities—be acquired and used only when they are needed. Its objectives are to improve productivity and eliminate waste. In a JIT environment, production processes are consolidated, and workers are trained to be multiskilled so that they can operate several different machines. Materials and supplies are scheduled for delivery just at the time they are needed in the production process, which significantly reduces inventories of materials. Goods are produced continuously, so work in process inventories are very small. Production is usually started only when an order is received, and the ordered goods are shipped when completed, which reduces the inventories of finished goods.

Adopting the JIT operating philosophy reduces production time and costs, investment in materials inventory, and materials waste, and it results in higher-quality goods. Funds that are no longer invested in inventory can be redirected according to the goals of the company's business plan. Management accounting responds to a JIT operating environment by providing an information system that is sensitive to changes in production processes. JIT methods help retailers like **Wal-Mart** and manufacturers like **Harley-Davidson** assign more accurate costs to their products and identify the costs of waste and inefficient operation. Wal-Mart, for example, requires vendors to restock inventory

The JIT operating philosophy requires that all resources be acquired and used only when needed. After implementing JIT and other reforms in 1981, Harley-Davidson's breakeven point dropped from 53,000 bikes to 35,000 bikes. For JIT to work, Harley-Davidson must trust suppliers to deliver the materials it needs at 100 percent quality.

often and pays them only when the goods sell. This minimizes the funds invested in inventory and allows the retailer to focus on offering high-demand merchandise at attractive prices.

Total Quality Management

Total quality management (TQM) requires that all parts of a business work together to build quality into the business's product or service. Improved quality of both the product or service and the work environment is TQM's goal. Workers act as team members and are empowered to make operating decisions that improve quality in both areas.

TQM has many of the same characteristics as the JIT operating philosophy. It focuses on improving product or service quality by identifying and reducing or eliminating the causes of waste. The emphasis is on examining current operations to spot possible causes of poor quality and on using resources efficiently and effectively to improve quality and reduce the time needed to complete a task or provide a service. Like JIT, TQM results in reduced waste of materials, higher-quality goods, and lower production costs in manufacturing environments, such as those of Wal-Mart's vendors, and helps Wal-Mart realize time savings and provide higher-quality services.

To determine the impact of poor quality on profits, TQM managers use accounting information about the costs of quality. The **costs of quality** include both the costs of achieving quality (such as training costs and inspection costs) and the costs of poor quality (such as the costs of rework and of handling customer complaints). Managers use information about the costs of quality to relate their organization's business plan to its daily operating activities, to stimulate improvement by sharing this information with all employees, to identify opportunities for reducing costs and customer dissatisfaction, and to determine the costs of quality relative to net income. For retailers like Wal-Mart and Good Foods Store, TQM results in a quality customer experience before, during, and after the sale.

Activity-Based Management

Activity-based management (ABM) is an approach to managing an organization that identifies all major operating activities or tasks, determines the resources consumed by each of those activities and the cause of the resource usage, and categorizes the activities as either adding value to a product or service or not adding value. ABM includes a management accounting practice called activity-based costing. **Activity-based costing (ABC)** identifies all of an organization's major operating activities (both production and nonproduction), traces costs to those activities or cost pools, and then assigns costs to the products or services that use the resources supplied by those activities.

Activities that add value to a product or service, as perceived by the customer, are known as **value-adding activities**. All other activities are called **nonvalue-adding activities**; they add cost to a product or service but do not increase its market value. ABM eliminates nonvalue-adding activities that do not support the organization; those that do support the organization are focal points for cost reduction. ABM results in reduced costs, reduced waste of resources, increased efficiency, and increased customer satisfaction. In addition, ABC produces more accurate costs than traditional cost allocation methods, which leads to improved decision making.

Theory of Constraints

According to the **theory of constraints (TOC)**, limiting factors, or bottlenecks, occur during the production of any product or service, but once managers identify such a constraint, they can focus their attention and resources on it and achieve significant improvements. TOC thus

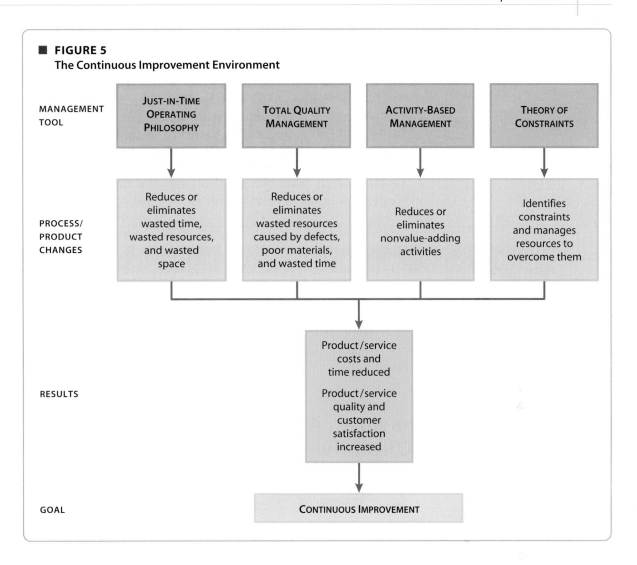

■ FIGURE 5
The Continuous Improvement Environment

MANAGEMENT TOOL	JUST-IN-TIME OPERATING PHILOSOPHY	TOTAL QUALITY MANAGEMENT	ACTIVITY-BASED MANAGEMENT	THEORY OF CONSTRAINTS
PROCESS/ PRODUCT CHANGES	Reduces or eliminates wasted time, wasted resources, and wasted space	Reduces or eliminates wasted resources caused by defects, poor materials, and wasted time	Reduces or eliminates nonvalue-adding activities	Identifies constraints and manages resources to overcome them
RESULTS		Product/service costs and time reduced / Product/service quality and customer satisfaction increased		
GOAL		CONTINUOUS IMPROVEMENT		

helps managers set priorities for how they spend their time and resources. In identifying constraints, managers rely on the information that management accounting provides.

To illustrate TOC, suppose Anna Wang wants to increase sales of store-roasted coffees. After reviewing management accounting reports, she concludes that the limited production capacity of her equipment—a roaster that can roast only 100 pounds of coffee beans per hour—limits the sales of the store's coffee. To overcome this constraint, she can rent or purchase a second roaster. The increase in production will enable her to increase coffee sales.

TOC complements JIT, TQM, and ABM by focusing resources on efforts that will yield the most effective improvements.

Achieving Continuous Improvement

JIT, TQM, ABM, and TOC all make a contribution to continuous improvement, as shown in Figure 5. In the just-in-time operating environment, management wages war on wasted time, wasted resources, and wasted space. All employees are encouraged to look for ways of improving processes and saving time. Total quality management focuses on improving the quality of the product or service and the work environment. It pursues continuous improvement by reducing the number of defective products and the time needed to complete a task or provide a service. Activity-based management seeks continuous improvement by emphasizing the ongoing reduction or elimination of nonvalue-adding activities. The theory of constraints helps managers focus resources on efforts that will produce the most effective improvements.

Each of these management tools can be used individually, or parts of them can be combined to create a new operating environment. They are applicable in service businesses, such as banking, as well as in manufacturing and retail businesses. By focusing attention on continuous improvement and fine-tuning of operations, they contribute to the same results in any organization: a reduction in product or service costs and delivery time, an improvement in the quality of the product or service, and an increase in customer satisfaction.

S T O P • R E V I E W • A P P L Y

3-1. How does a company know whether the quality of its products or services is improving?

3-2. What is the goal of all the management approaches described in this chapter?

Performance Measures: A Key to Achieving Organizational Objectives

LO4   Explain the balanced scorecard and its relationship to performance measures.

Performance measures are quantitative tools that gauge an organization's performance in relation to a specific goal or an expected outcome. Performance measures may be financial or nonfinancial. Financial performance measures include return on investment, net income as a percentage of sales, and the costs of poor quality as a percentage of sales. Such measures use monetary information to gauge the performance of a profit-generating organization or its segments—its divisions, departments, product lines, sales territories, or operating activities.

Nonfinancial performance measures include the number of times an activity occurs or the time taken to perform a task. Examples are number of customer complaints, number of orders shipped the same day, and the time taken to fill an order. Such performance measures are useful in reducing or eliminating waste and inefficiencies in operating activities.

Using Performance Measures in the Management Process

Managers use performance measures in all stages of the management process. In the planning stage, they establish performance measures that will support the organization's mission and the objectives of its business plan, such as reducing costs and increasing quality, efficiency, timeliness, and customer satisfaction. As you will recall from earlier in the chapter, Anna Wang selected the number of customer complaints as a performance measure to monitor the quality of service at Good Foods Store.

As managers perform their duties, they use the performance measures they established in the planning stage to guide and motivate employees and to assign costs to products, departments, and operating activities. Anna Wang will record the number of customer complaints during the year. She can group the information by type of complaint or by the employee involved in the service.

When evaluating performance, managers use the information that performance measures have provided to analyze significant differences between actual and planned performance and to identify ways of improving performance. By comparing the actual and planned number of customer complaints, Wang can identify problem areas and develop solutions.

When communicating with stakeholders, managers use information derived from performance measurement to report results and develop new budgets. If Wang needed formal reports, she could prepare performance evaluations based on this information.

The Balanced Scorecard

If an organization is to achieve its mission and objectives, it must identify the areas in which it needs to excel and establish measures of performance in these critical areas. As we have indicated, effective performance measurement requires an approach that uses both financial and nonfinancial measures that are tied to a company's mission and objectives. One such approach that has gained wide acceptance is the balanced scorecard.

The **balanced scorecard** is a framework that links the perspectives of an organization's four stakeholder groups to the organization's mission, objectives, resources, and performance measures. The four stakeholder groups are as follows:

Study Note

The balanced scorecard focuses all perspectives of a business on accomplishing the business's mission.

▶ Stakeholders with a financial perspective (owners, investors, and creditors) value improvements in financial measures, such as net income and return on investment.

▶ Stakeholders with a learning and growth perspective (employees) value high wages, job satisfaction, and opportunities to fulfill their potential.

▶ Stakeholders who focus on the business's internal processes value the safe and cost-effective production of high-quality products.

▶ Stakeholders with a customer perspective value high-quality products that are low in cost.

Although their perspectives differ, these stakeholder groups may be interested in the same measurable performance goals. For example, holders of

FOCUS ON BUSINESS PRACTICE

How Does the Balanced Scorecard Measure Success at Futura Industries?

Futura Industries is not a famous company, but it is one of the best. Based in Utah, it is rated as that state's top privately owned employer and serves a high-end niche in such diverse markets as floor coverings, electronics, transportation, and shower doors. In achieving its success, Futura uses the balanced scorecard. Futura has developed the following performance measures:

● Employee turnover is a measure of learning and growth.

● Percentage of sales from new products and total production cost per standard hour are measures of the company's internal processes.

● Number of customers' complaints and percentage of materials returned are the measures of customer satisfaction.

● Income and gross margin are among the measures of financial performance.[6]

■ **FIGURE 6**
The Balanced Scorecard for Good Foods Store

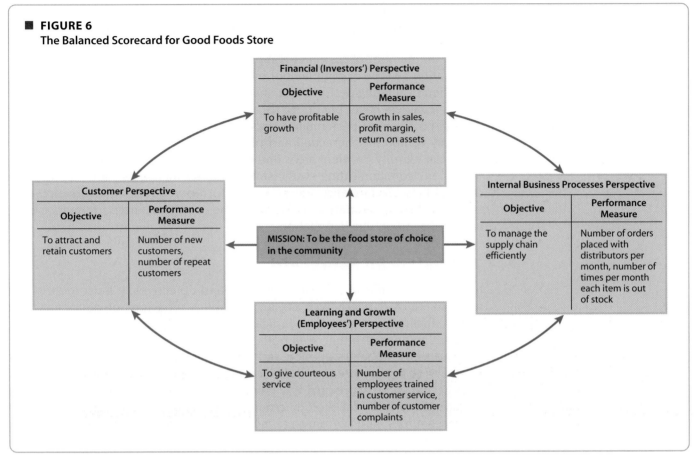

Source: Adapted from Robert S. Kaplan and David P. Norton, "The Balanced Scorecard: Measures That Drive Performance,"
Harvard Business Review, July-August 2005.

Study Note

The balanced scorecard provides a way of linking the management of employees, internal business processes, and customer needs to external financial results. In other words, if managers can foster excellent performance for three of the stakeholder groups, good financial results will occur for the investor stakeholder group.

both the customer and internal business processes perspectives are interested in performance that results in high-quality products.

Figure 6 applies the balanced scorecard to Good Foods Store. The company's mission is to be the food store of choice in the community. This mission is at the center of the company's balanced scorecard. Surrounding it are the four interrelated perspectives.

At the base of the scorecard is the learning and growth perspective. Here, part of the objective, or performance goal, is to provide courteous service. Because training employees in customer service should result in courteous service, performance related to this objective can be measured in terms of how many employees have received training. The number of customer complaints is another measure of courteous service.

From the perspective of internal business processes, the objective is to help achieve the company's mission by managing the supply chain efficiently, which should contribute to customer satisfaction. Efficiency in the ordering process can be measured by recording the number of orders placed with distributors each month and the number of times per month that customers ask for items that are not in stock.

If the objectives of the learning and growth and internal business processes perspectives are met, this should result in attracting customers and retaining them, which is the objective of the customer perspective. Performance related to this objective is measured by tracking the number of new customers and the number of repeat customers. Satisfied customers should help achieve the objective of the financial perspective, which is profitable growth. Profitable growth is measured by growth in sales, profit margin, and return on assets.

Benchmarking

The balanced scorecard enables a company to determine whether it is making continuous improvement in its operations. But to ensure its success, a company must also compare its performance with that of similar companies in the same industry. **Benchmarking** is a technique for determining a company's competitive advantage by comparing its performance with that of its closest competitors. **Benchmarks** are measures of the best practices in an industry. To obtain information about benchmarks in the retail grocery industry, Anna Wang might join a trade association for small retail shops or food stores. Information about these benchmarks would be useful to her in setting targets for the performance measures in Good Foods Store's balanced scorecard.

S T O P • R E V I E W • A P P L Y

4-1. In what sense is the balanced scorecard "balanced"?

4-2. What are performance measures? Give examples of both financial and nonfinancial performance measures.

4-3. How does the balanced scorecard help managers evaluate performance?

Analysis of Nonfinancial Data in a Retail Organization

LO5 Prepare an analysis of nonfinancial data.

As we have noted throughout this chapter, managers use many kinds of nonfinancial measures to determine whether performance targets for internal business processes and customer satisfaction are being met. The following example illustrates how Good Foods Store can use nonfinancial data to analyze changes in performance at its checkout registers.

Lucy Bass supervises checkout procedures at Good Foods Store. The store has three registers to record customer sales. In the past, each register served an average of 30 customers per hour. However, on November 1, 20x9, Bass implemented a new scanning procedure that has reduced the number of customers served per hour.

Data on the number of customers served for the three-month period ended December 31, 20x9, are shown in Part A of Exhibit 3. Each register operated an average of 170 hours per month. Register 1 is always the busiest. Registers 2 and 3 receive progressively less business. Bass is preparing a report for Anna Wang on the effects of the new procedure.

Part B of Exhibit 3 shows Bass's analysis of the number of customers served at each register over the three months. She computed the number of customers served per hour by dividing the number of customers served by the register's monthly average operating hours (170). By averaging the customer service rates for the three registers, she got 28.43 customers per hour per register for November and 28.83 customers for December. As you can see, the service rate decreased in November. But December's average is higher than November's, which means that the register clerks, as a group, are becoming more accustomed to the new procedure. Part C of Exhibit 3 is a graphic comparison of the number of customers served per hour.

EXHIBIT 3 ▶

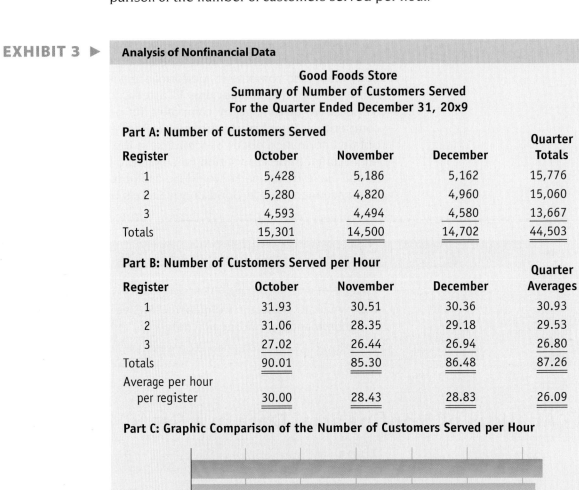

Analysis of Nonfinancial Data

Good Foods Store
Summary of Number of Customers Served
For the Quarter Ended December 31, 20x9

Part A: Number of Customers Served

Register	October	November	December	Quarter Totals
1	5,428	5,186	5,162	15,776
2	5,280	4,820	4,960	15,060
3	4,593	4,494	4,580	13,667
Totals	15,301	14,500	14,702	44,503

Part B: Number of Customers Served per Hour

Register	October	November	December	Quarter Averages
1	31.93	30.51	30.36	30.93
2	31.06	28.35	29.18	29.53
3	27.02	26.44	26.94	26.80
Totals	90.01	85.30	86.48	87.26
Average per hour per register	30.00	28.43	28.83	26.09

Part C: Graphic Comparison of the Number of Customers Served per Hour

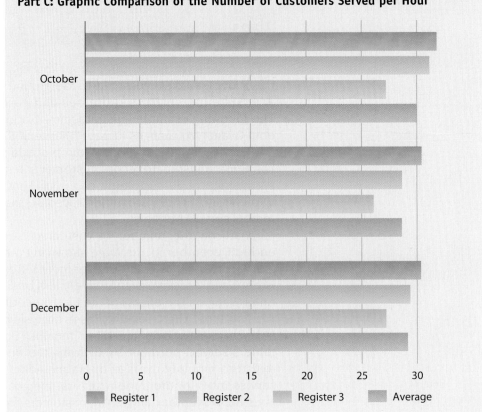

Register 1   Register 2   Register 3   Average

S T O P • R E V I E W • A P P L Y

5-1. Which is more important in managing a company: financial data or non-financial data?

5-2. Postal Services Inc. is having a problem with its three fully automated postal processing machines. The time for each operation has been increasing at an erratic rate. Management has asked that the time intervals be analyzed to see if the cause of the problem can be determined. The number of letters processed (in thousands) per shift during the previous week is as follows:

	Machine Number	Monday	Tuesday	Wednesday	Thursday	Friday
First shift:						
K	1	640	630	620	610	600
A	2	730	730	730	720	730
G	3	740	720	710	690	680
Second shift:						
D	1	420	410	410	400	398
B	2	650	650	660	660	670
F	3	520	520	510	504	502

From this information, assess the operations of the three machines.

Standards of Ethical Conduct

LO6   Identify the standards of ethical conduct for management accountants.

Managers are responsible to external parties (e.g., owners, creditors, governmental agencies, and the local community) for the proper use of organizational resources and the financial reporting of their actions. Conflicts may arise that require managers to balance the interests of all external parties, and management accountants have a responsibility to help them balance those interests. For example, the community wants a safe living environment, while owners seek to maximize profits. If management decides to

FOCUS ON BUSINESS PRACTICE
What Is Management's Responsibility for the Financial Statements?

Top-level managers have not only an ethical responsibility to ensure that the financial statements issued by their companies adhere to the principles of full disclosure and transparency; today, they have a legal responsibility as well. The Securities and Exchange Commission (SEC) requires the chief executive officers and chief financial officers of companies filing reports with the SEC to certify that those reports contain no untrue statements and include all facts needed to ensure that the reports are not misleading. In addition, the SEC requires managers to ensure that the information in reports filed with the SEC "is recorded, processed, summarized and reported on a timely basis."[7]

▼ **EXHIBIT 4**

Statement of Ethical Professional Practice

Members of IMA shall behave ethically. A commitment to ethical professional practice includes: overarching principles that express our values, and standards that guide our conduct.

PRINCIPLES

IMA's overarching ethical principles include: Honesty, Fairness, Objectivity, and Responsibility. Members shall act in accordance with these principles and shall encourage others within their organizations to adhere to them.

STANDARDS

A member's failure to comply with the following standards may result in disciplinary action.

I. COMPETENCE

Each member has a responsibility to:
1. Maintain an appropriate level of professional expertise by continually developing knowledge and skills.
2. Perform professional duties in accordance with relevant laws, regulations, and technical standards.
3. Provide decision support information and recommendations that are accurate, clear, concise, and timely.
4. Recognize and communicate professional limitations or other constraints that would preclude responsible judgment or successful performance of an activity.

II. CONFIDENTIALITY

Each member has a responsibility to:
1. Keep information confidential except when disclosure is authorized or legally required.
2. Inform all relevant parties regarding appropriate use of confidential information. Monitor subordinates' activities to ensure compliance.
3. Refrain from using confidential information for unethical or illegal advantage.

III. INTEGRITY

Each member has a responsibility to:
1. Mitigate actual conflicts of interest. Regularly communicate with business associates to avoid apparent conflicts of interest. Advise all parties of any potential conflicts.
2. Refrain from engaging in any conduct that would prejudice carrying out duties ethically.
3. Abstain from engaging in or supporting any activity that might discredit the profession.

IV. CREDIBILITY

Each member has a responsibility to:
1. Communicate information fairly and objectively.
2. Disclose all relevant information that could reasonably be expected to influence an intended user's understanding of the reports, analyses, or recommendations.
3. Disclose delays or deficiencies in information, timeliness, processing, or internal controls in conformance with organization policy and/or applicable law.

RESOLUTION OF ETHICAL CONFLICT

In applying the Standards of Ethical Professional Practice, you may encounter problems identifying unethical behavior or resolving an ethical conflict. When faced with ethical issues, you should follow your organization's established policies on the resolution of such conflict. If these policies do not resolve the ethical conflict, you should consider the following courses of action:

Discuss the issue with your immediate supervisor except when it appears that the supervisor is involved. In that case, present the issue to the next level. If you cannot achieve a satisfactory resolution, submit the issue to the next management level. If your immediate superior is the chief executive officer or equivalent, the acceptable reviewing authority may be a group such as the audit committee, executive committee, board of directors, board of trustees, or owners. Contact with levels above the immediate superior should be initiated only with your superior's knowledge, assuming he or she is not involved. Communication of such problems to authorities or individuals not employed or engaged by the organization is not considered appropriate, unless you believe there is a clear violation of the law.

Clarify relevant ethical issues by initiating a confidential discussion with an IMA Ethics Counselor or other impartial advisor to obtain a better understanding of possible courses of action.

Consult your own attorney as to legal obligations and rights concerning the ethical conflict.

Source: IMA Statement of Ethical Professional Practice, Institute of Management Accountants, www.imanet.org. Reprinted by permission.

purchase an expensive device to extract pollutants from the production process, it will protect the community, but profits will decline. The benefit will be greater for the community than for the owners. On the other hand, management could achieve higher profits for the owners by purchasing a less expensive, less effective antipollution device that would not protect the community as well. Such conflicts between external parties can create ethical dilemmas for management and for accountants.

To be viewed credibly by the various parties who rely on the information they provide, management accountants must adhere to the highest standards of performance. To provide guidance, the Institute of Management Accountants has issued standards of ethical conduct for practitioners of management accounting and financial management. Those standards, presented in Exhibit 4, emphasize that management accountants have responsibilities in the areas of competence, confidentiality, integrity, and credibility.

STOP • REVIEW • APPLY

6-1. If you encounter financial irregularities in your company, what should your first step be? What is your last recourse?

6-2. Why is it so important for management accountants to maintain their integrity?

A LOOK BACK AT

WAL-MART STORES, INC.

The Decision Point at the beginning of this chapter focused on **Wal-Mart,** a company whose mission is to give ordinary folk the chance to buy the same things as rich people around the world. It posed these questions:

- **What is Wal-Mart's strategic plan?**
- **What management accounting tools does Wal-Mart use to stay ahead of its competitors?**
- **What role does management accounting play in Wal-Mart's endeavors?**

Wal-Mart's strategic plan focuses on achieving the company's objective of being the low-cost leader in the markets that it enters. This strategy drives the way Wal-Mart' managers address stakeholder perspectives, as well as how they formulate tactical and operating plans. To stay agile, flexible, and ahead of its competitors, Wal-Mart uses management tools like supply and value chains to standardize requirements and procedures and keep the costs of doing business low. These cost containment measures demonstrate Wal-Mart's resolve to remain an industry leader. But what role does management accounting play in this endeavor?

Management accounting provides the information necessary for effective decision making. Wal-Mart's managers use management accounting information in making decisions about everything from entering new markets like banking and religious books, to selecting vendors and products, to developing and implementing new supply chain processes, to pricing, marketing, and distributing goods.

Management accounting also provides Wal-Mart's managers with objective data that they can use to measure the company's performance in terms of its key success factor—cost. Among the management accounting tools used are budgets, which set daily operating goals for stores and provide targets for evaluating a store's performance. As Wal-Mart strives to improve its sales, earnings per share, and profitability by maintaining its record of successes, it will continue to rely on the information that management accounting provides.

CHAPTER REVIEW

REVIEW of Learning Objectives

LO1 Distinguish management accounting from financial accounting and explain how management accounting supports the management process.

Management accounting is the process of identifying, measuring, accumulating, analyzing, preparing, interpreting, and communicating information that management uses to plan, evaluate, and control an organization and to ensure that its resources are used and accounted for appropriately. Management accounting reports provide information for planning, control, performance measurement, and decision making to managers and employees when they need such information. These reports have a flexible format; they can present either historical or future-oriented information expressed in dollar amounts or physical measures. In contrast, financial accounting reports provide information about an organization's past performance to owners, lenders, customers, and governmental agencies on a periodic basis. Financial accounting reports follow strict guidelines defined by generally accepted accounting principles.

Management accounting supports each stage of the management process. When managers plan, they use management accounting information to establish strategic, tactical, and operating objectives that reflect their company's mission and to formulate a comprehensive business plan for achieving those objectives. The plan is usually expressed in financial terms in the form of budgets. When managers implement the plan, they use the information provided in the budgets. In evaluating performance, managers compare actual performance with planned performance and take steps to correct any problems. Reports reflect the results of planning, executing, and evaluating operations and may be prepared for external or internal use.

LO2 Describe the value chain and its usefulness in analyzing a business.

The value chain conceives of each step in the production of a product or the delivery of a service as a link in a chain that adds value to the product or service. These value-adding steps—research and development, design, supply, production, marketing, distribution, and customer service—are known as primary processes. The value chain also includes support services—human resources, legal services, information services, and management accounting. Support services facilitate the primary processes but do not add value to the final product. Value chain analysis enables a company to focus on its core competencies. Parts of the value chain that are not core competencies are frequently outsourced.

LO3 Identify the management tools used for continuous improvement.

Management tools for continuous improvement include the just-in-time (JIT) operating philosophy, total quality management (TQM), activity-based management (ABM), and the theory of constraints (TOC). These tools are designed to help businesses meet the demands of global competition by reducing resource waste and costs and by improving product or service quality, thereby increasing customer satisfaction.

Management accounting responds to a just-in-time operating environment by providing an information system that is sensitive to changes in production processes. In a total quality management environment, management accounting provides information about the costs of quality. Activity-based management's assignment of overhead costs to products or services relies on the accounting practice known as activity-based costing (ABC). In businesses that use the theory of constraints, management accounting identifies process or product constraints.

LO4 Explain the balanced scorecard and its relationship to performance measures.

The balanced scorecard links the perspectives of an organization's stakeholder groups—financial (investors and owners), learning and growth (employees), internal business processes, and customers—to the organization's mission, objectives, resources, and performance measures. Performance measures are used to assess whether the objectives of each of the four perspectives are being met. Benchmarking is a technique for determining a company's competitive advantage by comparing its performance with that of its industry peers.

LO5 Prepare an analysis of nonfinancial data.

Using management tools like TQM and ABM and comprehensive frameworks like the balanced scorecard requires analysis of both financial and nonfinancial data. In analyzing nonfinancial data, it is important to compare performance measures with the objectives that are to be achieved.

LO6 Identify the standards of ethical conduct for management accountants.

Standards of ethical conduct for management accountants emphasize practitioners' responsibilities in the areas of competence, confidentiality, integrity, and credibility. These standards of conduct help management accountants recognize and avoid situations that could compromise their ability to supply management with accurate and relevant information.

REVIEW of Concepts and Terminology

The following concepts and terms were introduced in this chapter:

Activity-based costing (ABC): A management accounting practice that identifies all of an organization's major operating activities (both production and nonproduction), traces costs to those activities, and then assigns costs to the products or services that use the resources and services supplied by the activities. **(LO3)**

Activity-based management (ABM): An approach to managing an organization that identifies all major operating activities, determines the resources consumed by each of those activities and the cause of the resource usage, categorizes the activities as either adding value to a product or service or not adding value, and seeks to eliminate or reduce nonvalue-adding activities. **(LO3)**

Balanced scorecard: A framework that links the perspectives of an organization's stakeholder groups to the organization's mission, objectives, resources, and performance measures. **(LO4)**

Benchmarking: A technique for determining a company's competitive advantage by comparing its performance with that of its best competitors. **(LO4)**

Benchmarks: Measures of the best practices in an industry. **(LO4)**

Business plan: A comprehensive statement of how a company will achieve its objectives. **(LO1)**

Continuous improvement: The management concept that one should never be satisfied with what is, but should instead constantly seek improved efficiency and lower cost through better methods, products, services, processes, or resources. **(LO3)**

Core competency: The thing a company does best and that gives it an advantage over its competitors. **(LO2)**

Costs of quality: Both the costs of achieving quality and the costs of poor quality in the manufacture of a product or the delivery of a service. **(LO3)**

Just-in-time (JIT) operating philosophy: A management tool aimed at improving productivity and eliminating waste by requiring that all resources—materials, personnel, and facilities—be acquired and used only as needed. **(LO3)**

Management accounting: The process of identifying, measuring, accumulating, analyzing, preparing, interpreting, and communicating information that management uses to plan, evaluate, and control an organization and to ensure that its resources are used and accounted for appropriately. **(LO1)**

Mission statement: A description of the fundamental way in which a business will achieve its goal of increasing the value of the owners' interest in the business. **(LO1)**

Nonvalue-adding activities: Activities that add cost to a product or service but do not increase its market value. **(LO3)**

Operating objectives: Short-term goals that outline expectations for the performance of day-to-day operations. **(LO1)**

Outsourcing: The engagement of other companies to perform a process or service in the value chain that is not among an organization's core competencies. **(LO2)**

Performance measures: Quantitative tools that gauge an organization's performance in relation to a specific goal or expected outcome. **(LO4)**

Primary processes: Components of the value chain that add value to a product or service. **(LO2)**

Strategic objectives: Broad, long-term goals that determine the fundamental nature and direction of a business and that serve as a guide for decision making. **(LO1)**

Supply chain: The path that leads from the suppliers of the materials from which a product is made to the final consumer. Also called the *supply network.* **(LO1)**

Support services: Components of the value chain that facilitate the primary processes but do not add value to a product or service. **(LO2)**

Tactical objectives: Interim goals that position a business to achieve its long-term strategies. **(LO1)**

Theory of constraints (TOC): A management theory that contends that limiting factors, or bottlenecks, occur during the production of any product or service, but that once managers identify such a constraint, they can focus their attention and resources on it and achieve significant improvements. **(LO3)**

Total quality management (TQM): A management tool that requires that all parts of a business work together to build quality into the business's product or service. **(LO3)**

Value-adding activities: Activities that add value to a product or service as perceived by the customer. **(LO3)**

Value chain: A way of defining a business as a set of primary processes and support services that link together to add value to a business's products or services, thus fulfilling the business's mission and objectives. **(LO2)**

≡ REVIEW Problem

LO5   Analysis of Nonfinancial Data

Good Foods Store employs chefs who specialize in gourmet baked goods and bistro foods. Anna Wang prepared the following table estimating the number of hours that the chefs would work during June:

	A	B	C	D	E	F
1	**Estimated Hours to Be Worked**					
2		Week 1	Week 2	Week 3	Week 4	Totals
3	Baked goods	80	80	80	80	320
4	Bistro goods	120	120	120	120	480
5						

On July 2, Anna Wang assembled the following data on the actual number of hours worked:

	A	B	C	D	E	F
1	**Actual Hours Worked**					
2		Week 1	Week 2	Week 3	Week 4	Totals
3	Baked goods	96	108	116	116	436
4	Bistro goods	104	108	116	108	436
5						

Anna Wang is concerned about the excess hours worked during June.

Required

1. For each group of chefs (Baked goods and Bistro goods), prepare an analysis that shows the estimated hours, the actual hours worked, and the number of hours under or over the estimates for each week and in total.

2. Using the same information, prepare a line graph for a each group of chefs. Place the weeks on the *x* axis and the number of hours on the *y* axis.
3. Using the information from 1 and 2, identify the group of chefs who worked more hours than Anna Wang had planned and offer several reasons for the additional hours.

Answer to Review Problem

1.

Baked Goods Chefs

	A	B	C	D
	Week	Estimated Hours	Actual Hours	Hours Under or (Over) Estimate
1	80	96	(16)
2	80	108	(28)
3	80	116	(36)
4	80	116	(36)
Total	320	436	(116)

Bistro Goods Chefs

	A	B	C	D
	Week	Estimated Hours	Actual Hours	Hours Under or (Over) Estimate
1	120	104	16
2	120	108	12
3	120	116	4
4	120	108	12
Total	480	436	44

2.

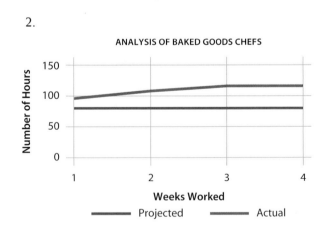

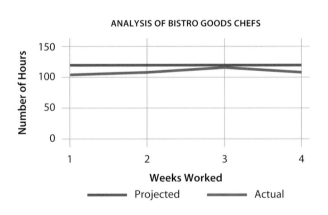

3. The baked goods chefs worked more hours than Wang had planned. The following are possible reasons for the additional hours:
   a. The quality of the materials may have been poor, which would have required extra work by the chefs.
   b. One of the chefs may have been recently hired and inexperienced. He would therefore have worked more slowly than anticipated, and the other chefs may have taken extra time to train him.

c. The equipment may have broken, in which case the chefs would have had to wait until it was repaired.

d. Wang may have underestimated the time required for baked goods.

CHAPTER ASSIGNMENTS

BUILDING Your Basic Knowledge and Skills

Short Exercises

LO1 **Management Accounting Versus Financial Accounting**

SE 1. Management accounting differs from financial accounting in a number of ways. Indicate whether each of the following characteristics relates to management accounting (MA) or financial accounting (FA):

1. Focuses on various segments of the business entity
2. Demands objectivity
3. Relies on the criterion of usefulness rather than formal guidelines in reporting information
4. Measures units in historical dollars
5. Reports information on a regular basis
6. Uses only monetary measures for reports
7. Adheres to generally accepted accounting principles
8. Prepares reports whenever needed

LO1 **Strategic Positioning**

SE 2. Organizations stake out different strategic positions to add value and achieve success. Some strive to be low-cost leaders like **Wal-Mart**, while others become the high-end quality leaders like **Whole Foods Market**. Identify which of the following organizations are low-cost leaders (C) and which are quality leaders (Q):

1. Nordstrom's
2. Harvard University
3. Local community college
4. Lexus
5. Kia
6. Rent-a-Wreck
7. Hertz Rental Cars
8. Coca-Cola
9. Store-brand soda

LO1 **The Management Process**

SE 3. Indicate whether each of the following management activities in a department store is part of planning (PL), performing (PE), evaluating (E), or communicating (C):

1. Completing a balance sheet and income statement at the end of the year
2. Training a clerk to complete a cash sale
3. Meeting with department managers to develop performance measures for sales personnel
4. Renting a local warehouse to store excess inventory of clothing
5. Evaluating the performance of the shoe department by examining the significant differences between its actual and planned expenses for the month
6. Preparing an annual budget of anticipated sales for each department and the entire store

LO1 **Report Preparation**

SE 4. Melissa Mertz, president of Mertz Industries, asked controller Rick Caputo to prepare a report on the use of electricity by each of the organization's five divisions. Increases in electricity costs in the divisions ranged from 20 to 35 percent over the past year. What questions should Rick ask before he begins his analysis?

LO1, LO2 **The Supply Chain and the Value Chain**

SE 5. Indicate whether each of the following is part of the supply chain (SC), a primary process (PP) in the value chain, or a support service (SS) in the value chain:

1. Human resources
2. Research and development
3. Supplier
4. Management accounting
5. Customer service
6. Retailer

LO2 **The Value Chain**

SE 6. The following unit costs were determined by dividing the total costs of each component by the number of products produced. From these unit costs, determine the total cost per unit of primary processes and the total cost per unit of support services.

Research and development	$ 1.40
Human resources	1.45
Design	0.15
Supply	1.10
Legal services	0.50
Production	4.00
Marketing	0.80
Distribution	0.90
Customer service	0.65
Information systems	0.85
Management accounting	0.20
Total cost per unit	$12.00

LO3 **JIT and Continuous Improvement**

SE 7. The just-in-time operating environment focuses on reducing or eliminating the waste of resources. Resources include physical assets such as machinery and buildings, labor time, and materials and parts used in the production process. Choose one of those resources and describe how it could be wasted. How can an organization prevent the waste of that resource? How can the concept of continuous improvement be implemented to reduce the waste of that resource?

LO4 **The Balanced Scorecard: Stakeholder Values**

SE 8. In the balanced scorecard approach, stakeholder groups with different perspectives value different performance goals. Sometimes, however, they may be interested in the same goal. Indicate which stakeholder groups—financial (F), learning and growth (L), internal business processes (P), and customers (C)—value the following performance goals:

1. High wages
2. Safe products
3. Low-priced products
4. Improved return on investment

5. Job security
6. Cost-effective production processes

LO5 **Analysis of Nonfinancial Data**

SE 9. Precision Technologies has been having a problem with the computerized welding operation in its extractor assembly line. The extractors are used to separate metal shavings into piles of individual metals for recycling and scrap sales. The time for each welding operation has been increasing at an erratic rate. Management has asked that the time intervals be analyzed to see if the cause of the problem can be determined. The number of parts welded per shift during the previous week is as follows:

	Machine Number	Monday	Tuesday	Wednesday	Thursday	Friday
First shift:						
Kovacs	1	642	636	625	617	602
Abington	2	732	736	735	729	738
Geisler	3	745	726	717	694	686
Second shift:						
Deragon	1	426	416	410	404	398
Berwager	2	654	656	661	664	670
Grass	3	526	524	510	504	502

What can you deduce from this information that may help management solve the welding operation problem?

LO6 **Ethical Conduct**

SE 10. Tyler Jones, a management accountant for Pegstone Cosmetics Company, has lunch every day with his friend Joe Blaik, who is a management accountant for Shepherd Cosmetics, Inc., a competitor of Pegstone Cosmetics. Last week, Jones couldn't decide how to treat some information in a report he was preparing, so he discussed it with Blaik. Is Jones adhering to the ethical standards of management accountants? Defend your answer.

Exercises

LO1 **Management Accounting Versus Financial Accounting**

E 1. Explain this statement: "It is impossible to distinguish the point at which financial accounting ends and management accounting begins."

LO1 **The Management Process**

E 2. Indicate whether each of the following management activities in a community hospital is part of planning (PL), performing (PE), evaluating (E), or communicating (C):

1. Leasing five ambulances for the current year
2. Comparing the actual number with the planned number of patient days in the hospital for the year
3. Developing a strategic plan for a new pediatric wing
4. Preparing a report showing the past performance of the emergency room
5. Developing standards, or expectations, for performance in the hospital admittance area for next year
6. Preparing the hospital's balance sheet and income statement and distributing them to the board of directors
7. Maintaining an inventory of bed linens and bath towels

8. Formulating a corporate policy for the treatment and final disposition of hazardous waste materials
9. Preparing a report on the types and amounts of hazardous waste materials removed from the hospital in the last three months
10. Recording the time taken to deliver food trays to patients

LO1   Report Preparation

E 3. Jeff Johnson is the sales manager for Sunny Days Greeting Cards, Inc. At the beginning of the year, the organization introduced a new line of humorous birthday cards to the U.S. market. Management held a strategic planning meeting on August 31 to discuss next year's operating activities. One item on the agenda was to review the success of the new line of cards and decide if there was a need to change the selling price or to stimulate sales volume in the five sales territories. Johnson was asked to prepare a report addressing those issues and to present it at the meeting. His report was to include the profits generated in each sales territory by the new card line only.

On August 31, Johnson arrived at the meeting late and immediately distributed his report to the strategic planning team. The report consisted of comments made by seven of Johnson's leading sales representatives. The comments were broad in scope and touched only lightly on the success of the new card line. Johnson was pleased that he had met the deadline for distributing the report, but the other team members were disappointed in the information he provided.

Using the four w's for report presentation, comment on Johnson's effectiveness in preparing his report.

LO1   The Planning Framework

E 4. Edward Ortez has just opened a company that imports fine ceramic gifts from Mexico and sells them over the Internet. In planning his business, Ortez did the following:

1. Listed his expected expenses and revenues for the first six months of operations
2. Decided that he wanted the company to provide him with income for a good lifestyle and funds for retirement
3. Determined that he would keep his expenses low and generate enough revenues during the first two months of operations so that he would have a positive cash flow by the third month
4. Decided to focus his business on providing customers with the finest Mexican ceramics at a favorable price
5. Developed a complete list of goals, objectives, procedures, and policies relating to how he would find, buy, store, sell, and ship goods and collect payment
6. Decided not to have a retail operation but to rely solely on the Internet to market the products
7. Decided to expand his website to include ceramics from other Central American countries over the next five years

Match each of Ortez's actions to the components of the planning framework: goal, mission, strategic objectives, tactical objectives, operating objectives, business plan, and budget.

LO1   The Supply Chain

E 5. In recent years, **United Parcel Service (UPS)** has been positioning itself as a solver of supply chain issues. Visit its website and read one of the case studies related to its supply chain solutions. Explain how UPS helped improve the supply chain of the business featured in the case.

LO2 **The Value Chain**

E 6. As mentioned in **E4**, Edward Ortez recently opened his own company. He has been thinking of ways to improve the business. Here is a list of the actions that he will be undertaking:

1. Engaging an accountant to help analyze progress in meeting the objectives of the company
2. Hiring a company to handle payroll records and employee benefits
3. Developing a logo for labeling and packaging the ceramics
4. Making gift packages by placing gourmet food products in ceramic pots and wrapping them in plastic
5. Engaging an attorney to write contracts
6. Traveling to Mexico himself to arrange for the purchase of products and their shipment back to the company
7. Arranging new ways of taking orders over the Internet and shipping the products
8. Keeping track of the characteristics of customers and the number and types of products they buy
9. Following up with customers to see if they received the products and if they are happy with them
10. Arranging for an outside firm to keep the accounting records
11. Distributing brochures that display the ceramics and refer to the website

Classify each of Ortez's actions as one of the value chain's primary processes—research and development, design, supply, production, marketing, distribution, or customer service—or as a support service—human resources, legal services, information systems, or management accounting. Of the 11 actions, which are the most likely candidates for outsourcing? Why?

LO3 **Management Tools**

E 7. Recently, you were dining with four chief financial officers (CFOs) who were attending a seminar on management tools and approaches to improving operations. During dinner, the CFOs shared information about their organizations' current operating environments. Excerpts from the dinner conversation appear below. Indicate whether each excerpt describes activity-based management (ABM), the just-in-time (JIT) operating philosophy, total quality management (TQM), or the theory of constraints (TOC).

CFO 1: We think quality can be achieved through carefully designed production processes. We focus on minimizing the time needed to move, store, queue, and inspect our materials and products. We've reduced inventories by purchasing and using materials only when they're needed.

CFO 2: Your approach is good. But we're more concerned with our total operating environment, so we have a strategy that asks all employees to contribute to the quality of both our products and our work environment. We focus on eliminating poor product quality by reducing waste and inefficiencies in our current operating methods.

CFO 3: Our organization has adopted a strategy for producing high-quality products that incorporates many of your approaches. We also want to manage our resources effectively, and we do it by monitoring operating activities. We analyze all activities to eliminate or reduce the ones that don't add value to products.

CFO 4: All of your approaches are good, but how do you set priorities for your management efforts? We find that we achieve the greatest improvements by focusing our time and resources on the bottlenecks in our production processes.

LO3 TQM and Value

E 8. De Silva Dry Cleaners recently adopted total quality management. Jorge De Silva, the owner, has hired you as a consultant. Classify each of the following activities as either value-adding (V) or nonvalue-adding (NV):

1. Providing same-day service
2. Closing the store on weekends
3. Providing free delivery service
4. Having a seamstress on site
5. Making customers pay for parking

LO4 The Balanced Scorecard

E 9. Connie's Takeout caters to young professionals who want a good meal at home but do not have time to prepare it. Connie's has developed the following business objectives:

1. To provide fast, courteous service
2. To manage the inventory of food carefully
3. To have repeat customers
4. To be profitable and grow

Connie's has also developed the following performance measures:

5. Growth in revenues per quarter and net income
6. Average unsold food at the end of the business day as a percentage of the total food purchased that day
7. Average customer time at the counter before being waited on
8. Percentage of customers who have shopped in the store before

Match each of these objectives and performance measures with the four perspectives of the balanced scorecard: financial perspective, learning and growth perspective, internal business processes perspective, and customer perspective.

LO5 Nonfinancial Data Analysis

E 10. Bluegrass Landscaping specializes in lawn installations requiring California bluegrass sod. The sod comes in 1-yard squares. To evaluate performance in laying sod, Bluegrass Landscaping uses the guideline of 500 square yards per person per hour. The company collected the following data about its operations during the first week of March:

Employee	Hours Worked	Square Yards of Sod Planted
S. Elway	38	18,240
R. Mahoney	45	22,500
N. Fenton	40	19,800
O. Pfister	42	17,640
B. Onski	44	22,880
J. Mantero	45	21,500

Evaluate the performance of the six employees.

LO5 **Nonfinancial Data Analysis**

E 11. Mother's Cookie Company recently adopted total quality management. According to a quality performance measure set by Elián Gomez, the vice president in charge of production, no more than ten cookies should be rejected per day. Data gathered for a recent week showed that the actual number of rejected cookies per day was as follows.

Day	Actual Number of Rejected Cookies
Monday	5
Tuesday	6
Wednesday	7
Thursday	4
Friday	8
Total	30

Analyze the activity for the week by preparing a table showing each day's maximum number of rejected cookies allowed, actual number of rejected cookies, and variance from the maximum number allowed. Compute the daily average for each column. Based on the information in your table, how successful was Gomez in increasing the quality of the company's cookies?

LO5 **Nonfinancial Data Analysis**

E 12. Sara Fowler, who is in charge of information technology at Cergo Corporation, must decide whether to purchase additional memory for her department's three computers or to buy additional new computers to increase her department's productivity. Six weeks ago, Fowler installed additional memory on Computer CM. She is impressed with the processing improvement, but she has yet to decide between the two courses of action. Information on the number of bytes processed per nanosecond by each computer for the past ten weeks is as follows:

Computer	One	Two	Three	Four	Five	Six	Seven	Eight	Nine	Ten
									Week	
CM	51	52	53	50	80	82	84	87	88	89
CN	52	51	52	52	54	54	53	54	54	54
CP	50	49	50	48	50	52	51	50	52	50

Fowler has asked you to analyze the two courses of action based on the assumption that two memory upgrades can be purchased for the price of one new computer. Your analysis is to include the computation of the average weekly output per nanosecond for Computers CN and CP, a comparison of that average with the output of Computer CM, and the computation of the weekly difference between the average output and the output of Computer CM. What course of action do you recommend?

LO6 **Ethical Conduct**

E 13. Katrina Kim went to work for Billings Industries five years ago. She was recently promoted to cost accounting manager and now has a new boss, Vic Howard, the corporate controller. Last week, Kim and Howard went to a two-day professional development program on accounting changes in the manufacturing environment. During the first hour of the first day's program, Howard disappeared, and Kim didn't see him again until the cocktail hour. The same thing happened on the second day. During the trip home, Kim asked Howard if he had enjoyed the conference. He replied:

> Katrina, the golf course was excellent. You play golf. Why don't you join me during the next conference? I haven't sat in on one of those sessions in ten years. This is my R&R time. Those sessions are for the new people. My experience is enough to keep me current. Plus, I have excellent people to help me as we adjust our accounting system to the changes being implemented on the production floor.

Does Katrina Kim have an ethical dilemma? If so, what is it? What are her options? How would you solve her problem? Be prepared to defend your answer.

LO6 **Ethical Responsibility**

E 14. Rank in order of importance the management accountant's four areas of responsibility: competence, confidentiality, integrity, and credibility. Explain the reasons for your ranking.

LO6 **Corporate Ethics**

E 15. To answer the following questions, conduct a search of several companies' websites: (1) Does the company have an ethics statement? (2) Does it express a commitment to environmental or social issues? (3) In your opinion, is the company ethically responsible? Select one of the companies you researched and write a brief description of your findings.

Problems

LO1 **Report Preparation**

P 1. Classic Industries, Inc., is deciding whether to expand its line of women's clothing called Pants by Olene. Sales in units of this product were 22,500, 28,900, and 36,200 in 20x7, 20x8, and 20x9, respectively. The product has been very profitable, averaging 35 percent profit (above cost) over the three-year period. The company has ten sales representatives covering seven states in the Northeast. Production capacity at present is about 40,000 pants per year. There is adequate plant space for additional equipment, and the labor needed can be easily hired and trained.

The organization's management is made up of four vice presidents: the vice president of marketing, the vice president of production, the vice president of finance, and the vice president of management information systems. Each vice president is directly responsible to the president, Teresa Jefferson.

Required

1. What types of information will Jefferson need before she can decide whether to expand the Pants by Olene line?
2. Assume that one report needed to support Jefferson's decision is an analysis of sales, broken down by sales representative, over the past three years. How would each of the four *w*'s pertain to this report?
3. Design a format for the report described in **2**.

LO2 **The Value Chain**

P 2. Zeigler Electronics is a manufacturer of cell phones, a highly competitive business. Zeigler's phones carry a price of $99, but competition forces the company to offer significant discounts and rebates. As a result, the average price of Zeigler's cell phones has dropped to around $50, and the company is losing money. Management is applying value chain analysis to the company's operations in an effort to reduce costs and improve product quality. A study by the company's management accountant has determined the following per unit costs for primary processes:

Primary Process	Cost per Unit
Research and development	$ 2.50
Design	3.50
Supply	4.50
Production	6.70
Marketing	8.00
Distribution	1.90
Customer service	.50
Total cost	$27.60

To generate a gross margin large enough for the company to cover its overhead costs and earn a profit, Zeigler must lower its total cost per unit for primary processes to no more than $20. After analyzing operations, management reached the following conclusions about primary processes:

- Research and development and design are critical functions because the market and competition require constant development of new features with "cool" designs at lower cost. Nevertheless, management feels that the cost per unit of these processes must be reduced by 10 percent.
- Six different suppliers currently provide the components for the cell phones. Ordering these components from just two suppliers and negotiating lower prices could result in a savings of 15 percent.
- The cell phones are currently manufactured in Mexico. By shifting production to China, the unit cost of production can be lowered by 20 percent.
- Most cell phones are sold through wireless communication companies that are trying to attract new customers with low-priced cell phones. Management believes that these companies should bear more of the marketing costs and that it is feasible to renegotiate its marketing arrangements with them so that they will bear 35 percent of the current marketing costs.
- Distribution costs are already very low, but management will set a target of reducing the cost per unit by 10 percent.
- Customer service is a weakness of the company and has resulted in lost sales. Management therefore proposes increasing the cost per unit of customer service by 50 percent.

Required

1. Prepare a table showing the current cost per unit of primary processes and the projected cost per unit based on management's proposals for cost reduction.
2. **Manager Insight:** Will management's proposals for cost reduction achieve the targeted total cost per unit? What further steps should management take to reduce costs? Which steps that management is proposing do you believe will be the most difficult to accomplish?
3. **Manager Insight:** What are the company's support services? What role should these services play in the value chain analysis?

LO4 The Balanced Scorecard and Benchmarking

P 3. Bychowski Associates is an independent insurance agency that sells business, automobile, home, and life insurance. Myra Bychowski, senior partner of the agency, recently attended a workshop at the local university in which the balanced scorecard was presented as a way of focusing all of a company's functions on its mission. After the workshop, she met with her managers in a weekend brainstorming session. The group determined that Bychowski Associates' mission was to provide high-quality, innovative risk-protection services to individuals and businesses. To ensure that the agency would fulfill this mission, the group established the following objectives:

- To provide a sufficient return on investment by increasing sales and maintaining the liquidity needed to support operations
- To add value to the agency's services by training employees to be knowledgeable and competent
- To retain customers and attract new customers
- To operate an efficient and cost-effective office support system for customer agents

To determine the agency's progress in meeting these objectives, the group established the following performance measures:

- Number of new ideas for customer insurance
- Percentage of customers who rate services as excellent
- Average time for processing insurance applications
- Number of dollars spent on training
- Growth in revenues for each type of insurance
- Average time for processing claims
- Percentage of employees who complete 40 hours of training during the year
- Percentage of new customer leads that result in sales
- Cash flow
- Number of customer complaints
- Return on assets
- Percentage of customers who renew policies
- Percentage of revenue devoted to office support system (information systems, accounting, orders, and claims processing)

Required

1. Prepare a balanced scorecard for Bychowski Associates by stating the agency's mission and matching its four objectives to the four stakeholder perspectives: the financial, learning and growth, internal business processes, and customer perspectives. Indicate which of the agency's performance measures would be appropriate for each objective.

2. **Manager Insight:** Bychowski Associates is a member of an association of independent insurance agents that provides industry statistics about many aspects of operating an insurance agency. What is benchmarking, and in what ways would the industry statistics assist Bychowski Associates in further developing its balanced scorecard?

LO5 **Nonfinancial Data Analysis**

P 4. Action Skateboards, Inc., manufactures state-of-the-art skateboards and related equipment. The production process involves the following departments and tasks: the Molding Department, where the board's base is molded; the Sanding Department, where the base is sanded after being taken out of the mold; the Fiber-Ap Department, where a fiberglass coating is applied; and the Assembling Department, where the wheels are attached and the board is inspected. After the board is molded, all processes are performed by hand.

Linda Raymond, the manager of the firm's California branch, is concerned about the number of hours her employees are working.

The California plant has a two-shift labor force. The actual hours worked for the past four weeks are as follows:

Actual Hours Worked—First Shift

Department	Week 1	Week 2	Week 3	Week 4	Totals
Molding	420	432	476	494	1,822
Sanding	60	81	70	91	302
Fiber-Ap	504	540	588	572	2,204
Assembling	768	891	952	832	3,443

Actual Hours Worked—Second Shift

Department	Week 1	Week 2	Week 3	Week 4	Totals
Molding	360	357	437	462	1,616
Sanding	60	84	69	99	312
Fiber-Ap	440	462	529	506	1,937
Assembling	670	714	782	726	2,892

Expected labor hours per product for each operation are Molding, 3.4 hours; Sanding, 0.5 hour; Fiber-Ap, 4.0 hours; and Assembling, 6.5 hours. Actual units completed are as follows:

Week	First Shift	Second Shift
1	120	100
2	135	105
3	140	115
4	130	110

Required

1. Prepare an analysis of each week to determine the average actual labor hours worked per board for each phase of the production process and for each shift. Carry your solution to two decimal places.
2. Using the information from 1 and the expected labor hours per board for each department, prepare an analysis showing the differences in each phase for each shift. Identify possible reasons for the differences.

LO5 **Nonfinancial Data Analysis**

P 5. The flow of passenger traffic is an important factor in an airport's success, and over the past year, heightened security measures at Winnebago County Airport in Rockford, Illinois, have slowed passenger flow significantly. The airport uses eight metal detectors to screen passengers for weapons. The facility is open from 6:00 A.M. to 10:00 P.M. daily, and the present machinery allows a maximum of 45,000 passengers to be checked each day.

The security team has selected four of the metal detectors for special analysis to determine if additional equipment is needed or if funding an additional homeland security officer could solve the problem. The additional homeland security officer would be responsible for guiding people to different machines and instructing them on the detection process. Because this solution would be less expensive than acquiring new machines, the team decides to fund a position for this function on a trial basis. The team hopes that this procedure will speed up the flow of passenger traffic by at least 10 percent. Manufacturers of the machinery have stated that each machine can handle an average of 400 passengers per hour. Data on passenger traffic through the four machines for the past 10 days are as follows:

Passengers Checked by Metal Detectors

Date	Machine 1	Machine 2	Machine 3	Machine 4	Totals
March 6	5,620	5,490	5,436	5,268	21,814
March 7	5,524	5,534	5,442	5,290	21,790
March 8	5,490	5,548	5,489	5,348	21,875
March 9	5,436	5,592	5,536	5,410	21,974
March 10	5,404	5,631	5,568	5,456	22,059
March 11	5,386	5,667	5,594	5,496	22,143
March 12	5,364	5,690	5,638	5,542	22,234
March 13	5,678	6,248	6,180	6,090	24,196
March 14	5,720	6,272	6,232	6,212	24,436
March 15	5,736	6,324	6,372	6,278	24,710

In the past, passenger flow has favored Machine 1 because of its location. Overflow traffic goes to Machine 2, Machine 3, and Machine 4, in that order. The new homeland security officer, Lynn Hedlund, began her duties on March 13. If her work results in at least a 10 percent increase in the number of passengers handled, the security team plans to fund another homeland security officer for the other four machines rather than purchasing additional metal detectors.

Required

1. Calculate the average daily traffic flow for the period March 6–12 and then calculate management's traffic flow goal.
2. Manager Insight: Calculate the average traffic flow for the period March 13–15. Did the additional homeland security officer's work result in the minimum increase in flow set by the security team, or should airport officials purchase additional metal detectors?
3. Manager Insight: Is there anything unusual in the analysis of passenger traffic flow that the security team should look into? Explain your answer.

Alternate Problems

LO1   **Report Preparation**

P 6. Sam Ratha recently purchased Yard & More, Inc., a wholesale distributor of equipment and supplies for lawn and garden care. The organization, which is headquartered in Baltimore, has four distribution centers that service 14 eastern states. The centers are located in Boston, Massachusetts; Rye, New York; Reston, Virginia; and Lawrenceville, New Jersey. The company's profits for 20x7, 20x8, and 20x9 were $225,400, $337,980, and $467,200, respectively.

Shortly after purchasing the organization, Ratha appointed people to the following positions: vice president, marketing; vice president, distribution; corporate controller; and vice president, research and development. Ratha has called a meeting of his management group. He wants to create a deluxe retail lawn and garden center that would include a large, fully landscaped plant and tree nursery. The purposes of the retail center would be (1) to test equipment and supplies before selecting them for sales and distribution and (2) to showcase the effects of using the company's products. The retail center must also make a profit on sales.

Required

1. What types of information will Ratha need before deciding whether to create the retail lawn and garden center?
2. To support his decision, Ratha will need a report from the vice president of research and development analyzing all possible plants and trees that could be planted and their ability to grow in the places where the new retail center might be located. How would each of the four *w*'s pertain to this report?
3. Design a format for the report in **2**.

LO5 **Nonfinancial Data Analysis**

P 7. Holiday Candy Company, which recently developed a strategic plan based on total quality management, wants its candy canes to have the highest quality of color, texture, shape, and taste possible. To ensure that quality standards are met, management has chosen many quality performance measures, including the number of rejected candy canes. Working with Luisa Ortes, the production supervisor, management has decided that no more than 50 candy canes should be rejected each day.

Using data on rejections in Week 1, Luisa Ortes prepared the following summary and graph:

Week 1	Maximum Number of Rejected Candy Canes Allowed	Actual Number of Rejected Candy Canes	Variance Under (Over) Allowed Maximum
Monday	50	60	(10)
Tuesday	50	63	(13)
Wednesday	50	58	(8)
Thursday	50	59	(9)
Friday	50	62	(12)
Total for the week	250	302	(52)
Daily average	50	60.4	

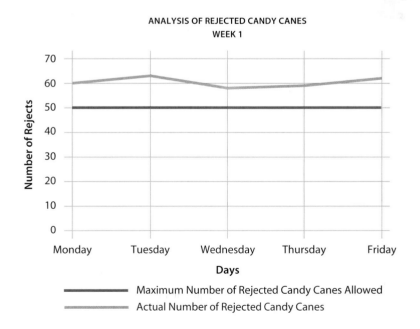

ANALYSIS OF REJECTED CANDY CANES
WEEK 1

— Maximum Number of Rejected Candy Canes Allowed
— Actual Number of Rejected Candy Canes

Because the variance was 20.8 percent (52 ÷ 250), Ortes decided to analyze the data further. She found that the rejected candy canes contained too little sugar (ingredients), were not circular (shaping), or were under-cooked (cooking time). The number of rejects in each category appears below.

Week 1	Reasons for Rejects
Ingredients	40
Shaping	195
Cooking time	67
Total	302

The following week, Ortes reviewed the recipe with the cooks. She trained them to measure ingredients more precisely, to shape the candy more carefully, and to time the cooking process more accurately. Then, in Week 3, she gathered the following information on the actual number of rejected candy canes and reasons for the rejects:

Week 3	Actual Number of Rejects	Week 3	Reasons for Rejects
Monday	20	Ingredients	7
Tuesday	21	Shaping	63
Wednesday	22	Cooking time	30
Thursday	19	Total	100
Friday	18		
Total	100		

Required

1. Analyze the activity in Week 3 by preparing a table showing each day's maximum number of rejected candy canes allowed, actual number of rejected candy canes, and variance under (over) the maximum number allowed. In addition, prepare a graph comparing the maximum and actual numbers for each day of Week 3.
2. Analyze how the reasons for rejecting candy canes changed from Week 1 to Week 3 by preparing a table showing the number of times each reason occurred each week. In addition, prepare a graph comparing the reasons for rejects each week.
3. Manager Insight: How successful was Ortes in increasing the quality of Holiday's candy canes? What recommendations, if any, would you make about monitoring candy cane production in the future?

LO5 **Nonfinancial Data Analysis**

P 8. Texas State Bank was founded in 1869. It has had a record of slow, steady growth since its inception. Management has always kept the processing of information as current as technology allows. Leslie Oistins, manager of the Brazas branch, is upgrading the check-sorting equipment in her office. There are ten check-sorting machines in operation. Information on the number of checks sorted by machine during the past eight weeks is at the top of the following page.

The Brazas branch has increased its checking business significantly over the past two years. Oistins must decide whether to purchase additional check-sorting machines or attachments for the existing machines to increase productivity. Five weeks ago the Colonnade Company convinced her to experiment with one such attachment, and it was placed on Machine BD. Oistins is impressed with the attachment but has yet to

				Week				
Machine	One	Two	Three	Four	Five	Six	Seven	Eight
AA	89,260	89,439	89,394	90,288	90,739	90,658	90,676	90,630
AB	91,420	91,237	91,602	91,969	91,950	92,502	92,446	92,816
AC	94,830	95,020	94,972	95,922	96,401	96,315	96,334	96,286
AD	91,970	91,786	92,153	92,522	92,503	93,058	93,002	93,375
AE	87,270	87,445	87,401	88,275	88,716	88,636	88,654	88,610
BA	92,450	92,265	92,634	93,005	92,986	93,544	93,488	93,862
BB	91,910	92,094	92,048	92,968	93,433	93,349	93,368	93,321
BC	90,040	89,860	90,219	90,580	90,562	91,105	91,051	91,415
BD	87,110	87,190	87,210	130,815	132,320	133,560	134,290	135,770
BE	94,330	94,519	94,471	95,416	95,893	95,807	95,826	95,778

decide between the two courses of action. Labor costs are not a factor in her decision.

Required

1. Compute the average weekly output of all machines except BD.
2. Compare the weekly output of Machine BD with the average weekly output of the nine machines without the attachment. Compute the weekly difference in the number of checks and the percentage change (difference divided by the average weekly output of the nine machines).
3. Manager Insight: Assume that Colonnade's attachment costs about the same as a new check-sorting machine. Which alternative would you recommend that Oistins choose?
4. Manager Insight: Would you change your recommendation if two attachments could be purchased for the price of one check-sorting machine? Does this decision require more data?
5. Manager Insight: If three attachments could be purchased for the price of one check-sorting machine, what action would you recommend?

ENHANCING Your Knowledge, Skills, and Critical Thinking

Conceptual Understanding Cases

LO2 The Value Chain and Core Competency

C 1. Medical Products Company (MPC) is known for developing innovative and high-quality products for use in hospitals and medical and dental offices. Its latest product is a nonporous, tough, and very thin disposable glove that will not leak or split and molds tightly to the hand, making it ideal for use in medical and dental procedures. MPC buys the material it uses in making the gloves from another company, which manufactures it according to MPC's exact specifications and quality standards. MPC makes two models of the glove—one white and one transparent—in its own plant and sells them through independent agents who represent various manufacturers. When an agent informs MPC of a sale, MPC ships the order directly to the buyer. MPC advertises the gloves in professional journals and gives free samples to physicians and dentists. It provides a product warranty and periodically surveys users about the product's quality.

Briefly explain how MPC accomplishes each of the primary processes in the value chain. What is a core competency? Which one of the primary processes would you say is MPC's core competency? Explain your choice.

LO4 **Performance Measures and the Balanced Scorecard**

C 2. In 2005, **General Motors Corporation (GM)** sold 9.2 million vehicles worldwide, the second-largest volume in the company's history. The good news was that sales increased in three of GM's four business regions, and all-time sales records were set for the Asia Pacific, Latin America, and Africa and Middle East regions. The bad news was that unit sales were down 3.1 percent in North America. As a result, GM's share of the global automotive market was 14.2 percent in 2005, down from 14.4 percent in 2004. The company is therefore revamping the way it does business. For example, it is investing $545 million in five core Michigan plants, pursuing hybrid technologies and alternative fuels, and seeking sensible labor contracts with its unions. Before answering the following questions, do a quick Internet search to determine what else GM is doing to revitalize itself.

1. What financial and other performance measures mentioned in the chapter would have prompted GM to revitalize itself?
2. The balanced scorecard uses performance measures that are linked to the perspectives of all stakeholder groups. Who are GM's stakeholders, and what performance measures do they value?
3. In your opinion, what options does GM have for revitalization?

Interpreting Management Reports

LO1 **Management Information**

C 3. Obtain a copy of a recent annual report of a publicly held organization in which you have a particular interest. (Copies of annual reports are available at your campus library, at a local public library, on the Internet, or by direct request to an organization.) Assume that you have just been appointed to a middle-management position in a division of the organization you have chosen. You are interested in obtaining information that will help you better manage the activities of your division, and you have decided to study the contents of the annual report in an attempt to learn as much as possible.

You particularly want to know about the following: (1) size of inventory maintained; (2) ability to earn income; (3) reliance on debt financing; (4) types, volume, and prices of products or services sold; (5) type of production process used; (6) management's long-range strategies; (7) success (profitability) of the division's various product lines; (8) efficiency of operations; and (9) operating details of your division.

1. Write a brief description of the organization and its products or services and activities.
2. Based on a review of the financial statements and the accompanying disclosure notes, prepare a written summary of information pertaining to items 1 through 9 above.
3. Can you find any of the information in which you are interested in other sections of the annual report? If so, which information, and in which sections of the report is it?
4. The annual report also includes other types of information that you may find helpful in your new position. In outline form, summarize this additional information.

LO1 **Management Information Needs**

C 4. In **C 3**, you examined your new employer's annual report and found some useful information. However, you are interested in knowing whether your division's products or services are competitive, and you were unable to find the necessary information in the annual report.

1. What kinds of information about your competition do you want to find?
2. Why is this information relevant? (Link your response to a particular decision about your organization's products or services. For example, you might seek information to help you determine a new selling price.)
3. From what sources could you obtain the information you need?
4. When would you want to obtain this information?
5. Create a report that will communicate your findings to your superior.

Decision Analysis Using Excel

Nonfinancial Data Analysis

LO5

C 5. Aviation Products Company is a subcontractor that specializes in producing housings for landing gears on jet airplanes. Its production process begins with Machine 1, which bends metal into cylinder-shaped housings and trims off the rough edges. Machine 2 welds the seam of the cylinder and pushes the entire piece into a large die to mold the housing into its final shape.

Joe Mee, the production supervisor, believes that the current process creates too much scrap (i.e., wasted metal). To verify this, James Kincaid, the company's accountant, began comparing the amounts of scrap generated in the last four weeks with the amounts of scrap the company anticipated for that period. Kincaid could not complete his analysis; his incomplete report appears below. Mee asks you to complete the report and submit a recommendation to him.

Aviation Products Company
Comparison of Actual Scrap and Expected Scrap
Four-Week Period

	Scrap in Pounds		Difference Under (Over)	
	Actual	Expected	Pounds	Percentage
Machine 1				
Week 1	36,720	36,720		
Week 2	54,288	36,288		
Week 3	71,856	35,856		
Week 4	82,440	35,640		
Machine 2				
Week 1	43,200	18,180		
Week 2	39,600	18,054		
Week 3	7,200	18,162		
Week 4	18,000	18,108		

1. Present the information in two ways:
   a. Prepare a table that shows the difference between the actual and expected scrap in pounds per machine per week. Calculate the difference in pounds and as a percentage (divide the difference in pounds by the expected pounds of scrap for each week). If the actual poundage of scrap is less than the expected poundage, record the difference as a negative. (This means there is less scrap than expected.)
   b. Prepare a line graph for each machine showing the weeks on the x axis and the pounds of scrap on the y axis.

2. Examine the differences for the four weeks for each machine, and determine which machine operation is creating excessive scrap.
3. What could be causing this problem?
4. What could Mee do to encourage early identification of the specific cause of such problems?

LO5 **Nonfinancial Data Analysis**

C 6. Refer to assignment **P 4** in this chapter. Linda Raymond needs to analyze the work performed by each shift in each department during Weeks 1 through 4.

1. For each department, calculate the average labor hours worked per board for each shift during Weeks 1 through 4. Carry your solution to two decimal places. (Note: Hours worked per board = hours worked each week ÷ boards produced each week.)
2. Using Excel's ChartWizard and the information from **1**, prepare a line graph for each department that compares the hours per board worked by the first and second shifts and the estimate for that department during Weeks 1 through 4. The following is the suggested format to use for the information table needed to complete the line graph for the Molding Department:

Molding Department

	Week 1	Week 2	Week 3	Week 4
First shift	3.50	3.20	3.40	3.80
Second shift	3.60	3.40	3.80	4.20
Estimated	3.40	3.40	3.40	3.40

3. Examine the four graphs that you prepared in **2**. Which shift is more efficient in all four departments? List some reasons for the differences between the shifts.

Ethical Dilemma Case

LO6 **Professional Ethics**

C 7. Mark Taylor is the controller for Krohm Corporation. He has been with the company for 17 years and is being considered for the job of chief financial officer. His boss, who is the current chief financial officer and former company controller, will be Krohm Corporation's new president. Taylor has just discussed the year-end closing with his boss, who made the following statement during their conversation:

> Mark, why are you being so inflexible? I'm only asking you to postpone the $2,500,000 write-off of obsolete inventory for ten days so that it won't appear on this year's financial statements. Ten days! Do it. Your promotion is coming up, you know. Make sure you keep all the possible outcomes in mind as you complete your year-end work. Oh, and keep this conversation confidential—just between you and me. Okay?

Identify the ethical issue or issues involved, and state the appropriate solution to the problem. Be prepared to defend your answer.

Internet Case

LO4 **Comparison of Performance Measures**

C 8. Honda Motor Company makes a green car called the Insight. Toyota Motor Company also makes a green car, which it calls the Prius. Search the websites of both these companies for data concerning the success of their green cars. (**Hint:** Review annual reports and press releases, or use the company's search engine.)

1. List the financial and nonfinancial performance measures that Toyota uses. List the measures used by Honda.
2. Use the data you found to prepare a brief comparison of the two cars. Do the two companies use comparable performance measures? If so, use these measures to evaluate the performance of the Prius and the Insight. If the measures are not comparable, how do they differ?

Group Activity Case

LO5 **Management Information Needs**

C 9. McDonald's is a leading competitor in the fast-food restaurant business. One component of McDonald's marketing strategy is to increase sales by expanding its foreign markets. At present, more than 40 percent of McDonald's restaurants are located outside the United States. In making decisions about opening restaurants in foreign markets, the company uses quantitative and qualitative financial and nonfinancial information. The following types of information would be important to such a decision: the cost of a new building (quantitative financial information), the estimated number of hamburgers to be sold in the first year (quantitative nonfinancial information), and site desirability (qualitative information).

You are a member of a management team that must decide whether to open a new restaurant in England. Identify at least two examples each of the (a) quantitative financial, (b) quantitative nonfinancial, and (c) qualitative information that you will need before you can make a decision.

Your instructor will divide the class into groups to discuss this case. Summarize your group's discussion and select someone from the group to present the group's findings to the rest of the class.

Business Communication Case

LO1 **Report Preparation**

C 10. The registrar's office of Polk Community College is responsible for maintaining a record of each student's grades and credits for use by students, instructors, and administrators.

1. Assume that you are a manager in the registrar's office and that you recently joined a team of managers to review the grade-reporting process. Explain how you would prepare a report of grades for students' use and the same report for instructors' use by answering the following questions:
   a. Who will read the grade report?
   b. Why is the grade report necessary?
   c. What information should the grade report contain?
   d. When is the grade report due?
2. Why does the information in a grade report for students' use and in a grade report for instructors' use differ?
3. Visit the registrar's office of your school in person or through your school's website. Obtain a copy of your grade report and a copy of the form that the registrar's office uses to report grades to instructors. Compare the information that these reports supply with the information you listed in 1. Explain any differences.
4. What can the registrar's office do to make sure that its grade reports are effective in communicating all necessary information to readers?

Cost Concepts and Cost Allocation

One of a company's primary goals is to be profitable. Because a company's owners expect to earn profits, managers have a responsibility to use the company's resources ethically and wisely so that they generate revenues that exceed the costs of the company's operating, investing, and financing activities. In this chapter, we describe how managers use information about costs, classify costs, compile product unit costs, and allocate overhead costs using the traditional method and the activity-based approach.

LEARNING OBJECTIVES

LO1 Describe how managers use information about costs.

LO2 Explain how managers classify costs and how they use these cost classifications.

LO3 Compare how service, retail, and manufacturing organizations report costs on their financial statements and how they account for inventories.

LO4 Describe the flow of costs through a manufacturer's inventory accounts.

LO5 Define *product unit cost* and compute the unit cost of a product or service.

LO6 Define *cost allocation* and explain how cost objects, cost pools, and cost drivers are used to assign overhead costs.

LO7 Using the traditional method of allocating overhead costs, calculate product or service unit cost.

LO8 Using activity-based costing to assign overhead costs, calculate product or service unit cost.

SOUTHWEST AIRLINES

- How do managers at Southwest Airlines determine the cost of selling tickets or of operating a flight?

- How do they use cost information?

With more than 3,000 flights a day, an average trip length of 793 miles, an average of 69.5 percent of its flights full, and an average one-way fare of $92.63, **Southwest Airlines** is the nation's leading high-frequency, short-haul, low-fare carrier. It is also the only large domestic airline to have remained profitable for more than 31 years. For nine years running, *Fortune* magazine has recognized Southwest as the most admired airline in the world, and for the past five years, *Business Ethics* magazine has included Southwest in its "100 Best Corporate Citizens" list.

To have achieved such a status and to maintain it, managers at Southwest must know the costs that the airline is incurring, including the cost of selling tickets and the cost of operating a flight. Online ticket sales generate approximately 65 percent of Southwest's passenger revenues, so classifying and analyzing the costs of these sales is very important to the company's profitability.[1]

Cost Information

One of a company's primary goals is to be profitable. Because a company's owners expect to earn profits, managers have a responsibility to use the company's resources wisely and to generate revenues that will exceed the costs of the company's operating, investing, and financing activities. In this chapter, we focus on costs related to the operating activities of manufacturing, retail, and service organizations. We begin by looking at how managers in these different organizations use information about costs.

Managers' Use of Cost Information

Managers use information about operating costs to plan, perform, evaluate, and communicate the results of operating activities. Figure 1 provides an overview of how managers use operating costs.

Planning When they plan, managers in service organizations, such as **Southwest Airlines**, **Federal Express** and **USAA**, use the estimated costs of rendering services to develop budgets, estimate revenues, and manage the organization's work force. In retail companies, such as **Wal-Mart** and **Target**, managers work with estimates of the cost of merchandise purchases to develop budgets for purchases and net income, as well as to determine the selling prices or sales units required to cover all costs. Managers of manufacturing companies, such as **Apple**, **Motorola**, and **Honda**, use estimates of product costs to develop budgets for production, materials, labor, and overhead, as well as to determine the selling price or sales level required to cover all costs.

Performing Managers in service organizations find the estimated cost of services helpful in monitoring profitability and making decisions about such matters as bidding on future business, lowering or negotiating their fees, or dropping one of their services.

Colleen Barrett, president of Southwest Airlines, is shown here with some of the company's pilots. She believes that a stable work environment encourages learning and personal growth and helps fulfill Southwest's mission of providing the highest quality of customer service. Like managers in other service organizations, Barrett and her management team use cost information to plan work force levels, estimate the cost of labor, and evaluate performance.

■ **FIGURE 1**
The Management Process: To-Do's for Managers

To-Do's for Managers

- Plan
  - Estimate operating costs
  - Estimate sales volume
  - Set prices
  - Prepare budgets

- Perform
  - Monitor profitability of products and services
  - Make decisions concerning products and services
  - Compute the unit cost of a product or service

- Evaluate
  - Compute variances between estimated and actual costs
  - Analyze variances, address causes, and revise future plans

- Communicate
  - Prepare internal reports for management
  - Prepare external reports for stakeholders

In retail organizations, such as Good Foods Store, which we used as an example in the last chapter, managers work with the estimated cost of merchandise purchases to predict gross margin, operating income, and value of merchandise sold. They also use this information to make decisions about matters like reducing selling prices for clearance sales, lowering selling prices for bulk sales, or dropping a product line.

Managers of manufacturing companies use estimated product costs to predict the gross margin and operating income on sales and to make decisions about such matters as dropping a product line, outsourcing the manufacture of a part to another company, bidding on a special order, or negotiating a selling price. In this chapter, we will use The Choice Candy Company, a hypothetical manufacturer of gourmet chocolate candy bars, to illustrate how managers of manufacturing companies use cost information.

Evaluating When managers evaluate performance, they want to know about significant differences between the estimated costs and actual costs of their products, merchandise purchases, or services. The identification of variances between estimated and actual costs helps them determine the causes of cost overruns, which may enable them to make decisions that will avoid such problems in the future.

Communicating When managers look at external reports, they expect income statements that communicate the actual costs of operating activities and balance sheets that show the value of inventory. They also expect internal performance reports that summarize their plans, their performance outcomes, and their evaluation of performance, such as the variance analyses done in the evaluating stage of the management process.

Cost Information and Organizations

Although all organizations use cost information to determine profits and selling prices and to value inventories, different types of organizations have different types of costs.

▶ Service organizations like **Southwest Airlines** need information about the costs of providing services, which include the costs of labor and related overhead.

▶ Retail organizations like **Wal-Mart** and Good Foods Store need information about the costs of purchasing products for resale. These costs include adjustments for freight-in costs, purchase returns and allowances, and purchase discounts.

▶ Manufacturing organizations like **Coca-Cola** and the Choice Candy Company need information about the costs of manufacturing products. Product costs include the costs of direct materials, direct labor, and overhead.

Among the other costs that organizations incur are the costs of marketing, distributing, installing, and repairing a product or the costs of marketing and supporting the delivery of services. Ultimately, a company is profitable only when its revenues from sales or services rendered exceed all its costs.

S T O P • R E V I E W • A P P L Y

1-1. How do managers use information about costs?

1-2. Do managers in all organizations need the same type of cost information?

Suggested answers to all Stop, Review, and Apply questions are available at http://college.hmco.com/accounting/needles/man_acc/8e/student_home.html.

Cost Classifications and Their Uses

LO2 Explain how managers classify costs and how they use these cost classifications.

A single cost can be classified and used in several ways, depending on the purpose of the analysis. Figure 2 provides an overview of commonly used cost classifications. These classifications enable managers to do the following:

1. Control costs by determining which are traceable to a particular cost object, such as a service or product

■ **FIGURE 2**
Overview of Cost Classifications

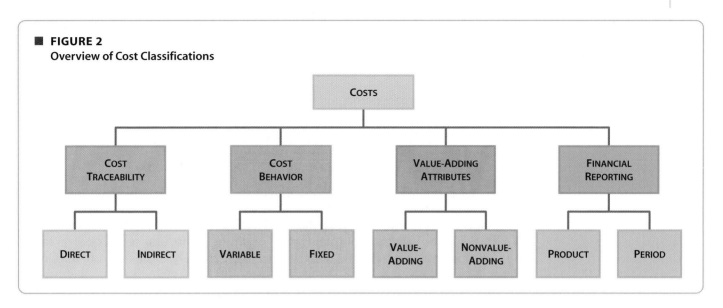

2. Calculate the number of units that must be sold to achieve a certain level of profit (cost behavior)

3. Identify the costs of activities that do and do not add value to a product or service

4. Classify costs for the preparation of financial statements

Cost classifications are important in all types of organizations. They help managers select and use relevant information to improve the efficiency of operations, provide quality products or services, and satisfy customer needs.

Cost Traceability

Managers trace costs to cost objects, such as products or services, sales territories, departments, or operating activities, to develop a fairly accurate measurement of costs. They use both direct and indirect measures of costs to support pricing decisions or decisions to reallocate resources to other cost objects. **Direct costs** are costs that can be conveniently and economically traced to a cost object. For example, the wages of a **Southwest Airlines** flight crew can be conveniently traced to a flight because the time worked and the hourly wages are shown on time cards and payroll records. Similarly, jet fuel (1.2 billion gallons consumed in 2004) costs for a flight can be easily traced.

In some cases, even though a material becomes part of a finished product or service, the expense of tracing its cost is too great. Some examples include the nails used in furniture, the salt used in candy, and the rivets used in airplanes. Such costs are considered indirect costs of the product or service. **Indirect costs** are costs that cannot be conveniently and economically traced to a cost object. For the sake of accuracy, however, indirect costs must be included in the cost of a product or service. Because they are difficult to trace, management uses a formula to assign them. For example, Southwest Airlines' insurance costs cannot be conveniently traced to individual flights; management solves the problem by assigning a portion of the insurance costs to each flight flown.

The following examples illustrate cost objects and their direct and indirect costs in service, retail, and manufacturing organizations:

▶ In a service organization, such as an accounting firm, costs can be traced to a specific service, such as preparation of tax returns. Direct costs for such a service include the costs of government reporting forms, computer usage, and the accountant's labor. Indirect costs include the costs of supplies, office rental, utilities, secretarial labor, telephone usage, and depreciation of office furniture.

▶ In a retail organization, such as Good Foods Store, costs can be traced to a department. For example, the direct costs of the produce department include the costs of fruits and vegetables and the wages of employees working in that department. Indirect costs include the costs of utilities to cool the produce displays and the storage and handling of the produce.

▶ In a manufacturing organization, such as The Choice Candy Company, costs can be traced to the product. Direct costs include the costs of the materials and labor needed to make the candy. Indirect costs include the costs of utilities, depreciation of plant and equipment, insurance, property taxes, inspection, supervision, maintenance of machinery, storage, and handling.

Cost Behavior

Managers are also interested in the way costs respond to changes in volume or activity. By analyzing those patterns of behavior, they gain information about how changes in selling prices or operating costs affect the company's net income, and they can then make adjustments so that the company obtains a certain level of profit.

Costs can be separated into variable costs and fixed costs. A **variable cost** is a cost that changes in direct proportion to a change in productive output (or some other measure of volume). A **fixed cost** is a cost that remains constant within a defined range of activity or time period.

All types of organizations have variable and fixed costs. The following are a few examples:

▶ Because the number of passengers drives the consumption of food and beverages on a flight, the cost of peanuts and beverages is a variable cost for Southwest Airlines. Fixed costs include the depreciation on the plane and the salaries and benefits of the flight and ground crews.

▶ The variable costs of Good Foods Store include the cost of groceries sold and any sales commissions. Fixed costs include the costs of building and lot rental, depreciation on store equipment, and the manager's salary.

▶ The variable costs of The Choice Candy Company include the costs of direct materials (e.g., sugar, cocoa), direct labor, indirect materials (e.g., salt), and indirect labor (e.g., inspection and maintenance labor). Fixed costs include the costs of supervisors' salaries and depreciation on buildings.

As a grocery store sells more products or as a candy manufacturer increases its output of products, its variable costs will increase proportionately. But its

FOCUS ON BUSINESS PRACTICE

How Does an Airline Manage Its Fixed Costs?

One of **Southwest Airlines'** nonfinancial performance measures is a 20-minute turnaround time on the ground. This standard helps Southwest efficiently manage the many fixed costs of running an airline. If additional security measures or other circumstances forced Southwest to add even 10 minutes to its ground turnaround time, it would result in higher fixed costs because the company would need additional planes to keep to its daily flight schedule. For an airline to be profitable, it needs to maximize its fleet's time in the air and minimize its time on the ground.[2]

A fixed cost is a cost that remains constant within a defined range of activity or time period. For Southwest Airlines, fixed costs include the salaries and benefits of ground crews. By keeping turnaround time on the ground to 20 minutes, Southwest minimizes the number of planes it needs to keep to daily schedules, thus avoiding some higher fixed costs.

fixed costs will remain the same for a specified period. Its rent, for example, will not change over the term of the lease, and its property taxes will remain the same until the next assessment.

Value-Adding Versus Nonvalue-Adding Costs

A **value-adding cost** is the cost of an activity that increases the market value of a product or service. A **nonvalue-adding cost** is the cost of an activity that adds cost to a product or service but does not increase its market value. Costs incurred to improve the quality of a product are value-adding costs if the customer is willing to pay more for the higher-quality product; otherwise, they are nonvalue-adding costs because they do not increase the product's market value.

Managers examine the value-adding attributes of their company's operating activities and, wherever possible, reduce or eliminate activities that do not directly add value to the company's products or services. For example, the costs of administrative activities, such as accounting and human resource management, are nonvalue-adding costs; they are necessary for the operation of the business, but they do not add value to the products or services produced, so they are monitored closely. Information about value-adding and nonvalue-adding costs influences the design of future products or services.

Cost Classifications for Financial Reporting

For purposes of preparing financial statements, managers classify costs as product costs or period costs. **Product costs**, or *inventoriable* costs, are costs assigned to inventory; they include direct materials, direct labor, and overhead. Product costs appear on the income statement as cost of goods sold and on the balance sheet as inventory. **Period costs**, or *noninventoriable* costs, are costs of resources used during the accounting period that are not assigned to products. They appear as operating expenses on the income statement. For example, among the period costs listed on the income statement are selling, administrative, and general expenses.

Study Note

Product costs and period costs can be explained by using the matching rule. Product costs must be charged to the period in which the product generates revenue, and period costs are charged against the revenue of the current period.

TABLE 1. Examples of Cost Classifications for a Candy Manufacturer

Cost Examples	Traceability to Product	Cost Behavior	Value Attribute	Financial Reporting
Sugar for candy	Direct	Variable	Value-adding	Product (direct materials)
Labor for mixing	Direct	Variable	Value-adding	Product (direct labor)
Labor for supervision	Indirect	Fixed	Nonvalue-adding	Product (overhead)
Depreciation on mixing machine	Indirect	Fixed	Value-adding	Product (overhead)
Sales commission	—*	Variable	Value-adding†	Period
Accountant's salary	—*	Fixed	Nonvalue-adding	Period

*Sales commissions and accountants' salaries cannot be directly or indirectly traced to a cost object; they are not product costs.

†Sales commissions can be value-adding because customers' perceptions of the salesperson and the selling experience can strongly affect their perceptions of the product's market value.

Table 1 shows how some costs of a candy manufacturer can be classified in terms of traceability, behavior, value attribute, and financial reporting.

S T O P • R E V I E W • A P P L Y

2-1. Why do managers use different classifications of costs?

2-2. Are the costs of a product always traceable as direct or indirect costs?

2-3. What is the difference between a value-adding cost and a nonvalue-adding cost?

2-4. What are product costs and period costs?

Financial Statements and the Reporting of Costs

LO3 Compare how service, retail, and manufacturing organizations report costs on their financial statements and how they account for inventories.

Managers prepare financial statements at least once a year to communicate the results of their management activities for the period. The key to preparing an income statement or a balance sheet in any kind of organization is to determine its cost of goods or services sold and the value of its inventories, if any.

Cost Reporting and Accounting for Inventories

Because the operations of service and retail organizations differ from those of manufacturers, the accounts presented in their financial statements differ as well. For example, because service organizations like **Southwest Airlines** and **United Parcel Service (UPS)** sell services and not products, they maintain no inventories for sale or resale. As a result, unlike manufacturing and retail organizations, they have no inventory accounts on their balance sheets. When preparing income statements, they calculate the cost of sales rather than the cost of goods sold, using the following equation:

$$\text{Cost of Sales} = \text{Net Cost of Services Sold}$$

For instance, suppose that Good Foods Store, the retail shop that we used as an example in the last chapter, employs UPS to deliver its products. The cost of sales for UPS would include the wages and salaries of personnel plus the expense of the trucks, planes, supplies, and anything else that UPS uses to deliver packages for Good Foods Store.

Retail organizations, such as **Wal-Mart** and Good Foods Store, which purchase products ready for resale, maintain just one inventory account on the balance sheet. Called the Merchandise Inventory account, it reflects the costs of goods held for resale. Retail organizations include the cost of purchases in the calculation of cost of goods sold, as follows:

$$\text{Cost of Goods Sold} = \begin{array}{c}\text{Beginning}\\\text{Merchandise}\\\text{Inventory}\end{array} + \begin{array}{c}\text{Net Cost of}\\\text{Purchases}\end{array} - \begin{array}{c}\text{Ending}\\\text{Merchandise}\\\text{Inventory}\end{array}$$

Suppose that Good Foods Store had a balance of $3,000 in its Merchandise Inventory account on December 31, 20x8. During the next year, its purchases of food products totaled $23,000 (adjusted for purchase discounts, returns and allowances, and freight-in). On December 31, 20x9, its Merchandise Inventory balance was $4,500. The cost of goods sold for 20x9 is thus $21,500:

$$\text{Cost of Goods Sold} = \$3,000 + \$23,000 - \$4,500 = \$21,500$$

Manufacturing organizations like The Choice Candy Company, which make products for sale, maintain three inventory accounts on the balance sheet: the Materials Inventory, Work in Process Inventory, and Finished Goods Inventory accounts. The Materials Inventory account shows the cost of materials that have been purchased but not used in the production process. During the production process, the costs of manufacturing the product are accumulated in the Work in Process Inventory account; the balance of this account represents the costs of the unfinished product. Once the product is complete and ready for sale, its cost is transferred to the Finished Goods Inventory account; the balance in this account is the cost of the unsold completed product. When the product is sold, the manufacturing organization uses the following equation to calculate the cost of goods sold:

$$\text{Cost of Goods Sold} = \begin{array}{c}\text{Beginning}\\\text{Finished Goods}\\\text{Inventory}\end{array} + \begin{array}{c}\text{Cost of}\\\text{Goods}\\\text{Manufactured}\end{array} - \begin{array}{c}\text{Ending}\\\text{Finished Goods}\\\text{Inventory}\end{array}$$

For example, suppose that The Choice Candy Company had a balance of $52,000 in its Finished Goods Inventory account on December 31, 20x8. During the next year, the cost of the products that the company manufactured totaled $144,000. On December 31, 20x9, its Finished Goods Inventory balance was $78,000. The cost of goods sold for 20x9 is thus $118,000:

$$\text{Cost of Goods Sold} = \$52,000 + \$144,000 - \$78,000 = \$118,000$$

Remember that all organizations—service, retail, and manufacturing—use the following income statement format:

$$\text{Sales} - \begin{array}{c}\text{Cost of Sales}\\\text{or}\\\text{Cost of Goods Sold}\end{array} = \begin{array}{c}\text{Gross}\\\text{Margin}\end{array} - \begin{array}{c}\text{Operating}\\\text{Expenses}\end{array} = \text{Operating Income}$$

FIGURE 3
Financial Statements of Service, Retail, and Manufacturing Organizations

	Service Company	Retail Company	Manufacturing Company
Income Statement	Sales – Cost of sales Gross margin – Operating expenses Operating income	Sales – Cost of goods sold* Gross margin – Operating expenses Operating income *Cost of goods sold: Beginning merchandise inventory + Net cost of purchases Cost of goods available for sale – Ending merchandise inventory Cost of goods sold	Sales – Cost of goods sold† Gross margin – Operating expenses Operating income † Cost of goods sold: Beginning finished goods inventory + Cost of goods manufactured Cost of goods available for sale – Ending finished goods inventory Cost of goods sold
Balance Sheet (current assets section)	No inventory accounts	One inventory account: Merchandise Inventory (finished product ready for sale)	Three inventory accounts: Materials Inventory (unused materials) Work in Process Inventory (unfinished product) Finished Goods Inventory (finished product ready for sale)
Example with numbers		Income Statement: Beg. merchandise inventory $ 3,000 + Net cost of purchases 23,000 Cost of goods available for sale $26,000 – End. merchandise inventory 4,500 Cost of goods sold $21,500 Balance Sheet: Merchandise inventory, ending $ 4,500	Income Statement: Beg. finished goods inventory $ 52,000 + Cost of goods manufactured 144,000 Cost of goods available for sale $196,000 – End. finished goods inventory 78,000 Cost of goods sold $118,000 Balance Sheet: Finished goods inventory, ending $ 78,000

Figure 3 compares the financial statements of service, retail, and manufacturing organizations. Note in particular the differences in inventory accounts and cost of goods sold. As pointed out earlier, product costs, or inventoriable costs, appear as inventory on the balance sheet and as cost of goods sold on the income statement. Period costs, also called *noninventoriable costs* or *selling, administrative, and general expenses,* are reflected in the operating expenses on the income statement.

Statement of Cost of Goods Manufactured

The key to preparing an income statement for a manufacturing organization is computing its cost of goods sold, which means that you must first determine the cost of goods manufactured. This dollar amount is calculated on the **statement of cost of goods manufactured**, a special report based on an analysis of the Work in Process Inventory account. At the end of an accounting period, the flow of all manufacturing costs incurred during the period is sum-

EXHIBIT 1 ▶ **Statement of Cost of Goods Manufactured and Partial Income Statement for a Manufacturing Organization**

The Choice Candy Company
Statement of Cost of Goods Manufactured
For the Year Ended December 31, 20x9

Direct materials used		
Materials inventory, December 31, 20x8	$100,000	
Direct materials purchased	200,000	
Cost of direct materials available for use	$300,000	
Less materials inventory, December 31, 20x9	50,000	
Step 1: Cost of direct materials used		$250,000
Direct labor		120,000
Overhead		60,000
Step 2: Total manufacturing costs		$430,000
Add work in process inventory, December 31, 20x8		20,000
Total cost of work in process during the year		$450,000
Less work in process inventory, December 31, 20x9		150,000
Step 3: Cost of goods manufactured		$300,000

The Choice Candy Company
Income Statement
For the Year Ended December 31, 20x9

Sales		$500,000
Cost of goods sold		
Finished goods inventory, December 31, 20x8	$ 78,000	
Cost of goods manufactured	300,000	
Cost of finished goods available for sale	$378,000	
Less finished goods inventory, December 31, 20x9	138,000	
Cost of goods sold		240,000
Gross margin		$260,000
Selling and administrative expenses		160,000
Operating income		$100,000

marized in this statement. Exhibit 1 shows The Choice Candy Company's statement of cost of goods manufactured for the year ended December 31, 20x9. It is helpful to think of the statement of cost of goods manufactured as being developed in three steps, as described below.

Step 1 *Compute the cost of direct materials used during the accounting period.* To do this, add the beginning balance in the Materials Inventory account to the direct materials purchased ($100,000 + $200,000). The subtotal ($300,000) represents the cost of direct materials available for use during the accounting period. Next, subtract the ending balance of the Materials Inventory account from the cost of direct materials available for use. The difference is the cost of direct materials used during the period ($300,000 − $50,000 = $250,000).

Step 2 *Calculate total manufacturing costs for the period.* As shown in Exhibit 1, the costs of direct materials used ($250,000) and direct labor ($120,000) are added to total overhead costs incurred during the period ($60,000) to arrive at total manufacturing costs ($430,000).

Study Note

An alternative to the cost of goods manufactured calculation uses the cost flow concept that is discussed in LO 4.

Study Note

It is important not to confuse the cost of goods manufactured with the cost of goods sold.

Step 3 *Determine total cost of goods manufactured for the period.* To do so, add the beginning balance in the Work in Process Inventory account to total manufacturing costs to arrive at the total cost of work in process during the period. From this amount, subtract the ending balance in the Work in Process Inventory account to arrive at the cost of goods manufactured ($450,000 − $150,000 = $300,000).

Do not confuse total manufacturing costs with the cost of goods manufactured. To understand the difference between these two amounts, look again at the computations in Exhibit 1. Total manufacturing costs of $430,000 incurred during the period are added to the $20,000 beginning balance in the Work in Process Inventory account to arrive at the total cost of work in process for the period ($430,000 + $20,000 = $450,000). The costs of products still in process at the end of the period ($150,000) are then subtracted from the total cost of work in process during the year. The remainder, $300,000, is the cost of goods manufactured (completed) during the current year. Note that the costs attached to the ending balance of Work in Process Inventory come from the current period's total manufacturing costs; they will not become part of the cost of goods manufactured until the next period, when the products are completed.

Cost of Goods Sold and a Manufacturer's Income Statement

Exhibit 1 shows the relationship between The Choice Candy Company's income statement and its statement of cost of goods manufactured. The total amount of the cost of goods manufactured during the period is carried over to the income statement, where it is used to compute the cost of goods sold. The beginning balance of the Finished Goods Inventory account is added to the cost of goods manufactured to arrive at the total cost of finished goods available for sale during the period ($78,000 + $300,000 = $378,000). The cost of goods sold is then computed by subtracting the ending balance in Finished Goods Inventory (the cost of goods completed but not sold) from the total cost of finished goods available for sale ($378,000 − $138,000 = $240,000). The cost of goods sold is considered an expense in the period in which the goods are sold.

S T O P • R E V I E W • A P P L Y

3-1. How do service, retail, and manufacturing organizations differ, and how do these differences affect accounting for inventories?

3-2. What inventory accounts accumulate the cost information used in the statement of cost of goods manufactured?

3-3. How is the cost of goods manufactured used in computing the cost of goods sold?

Income Statement for a Manufacturing Organization Incomplete inventory and income statement data for Sample Manufacturing Corporation follow. Determine the missing amounts.

	Beginning Finished Goods Inventory		Cost of Goods Manufactured		Ending Finished Goods Inventory
Cost of Goods Sold					
$2,000	$1,000		$5,000		?

SOLUTION:

Cost of Goods Sold		Beginning Finished Goods Inventory		Cost of Goods Manufactured		Ending Finished Goods Inventory
$2,000	=	$1,000	+	$5,000	−	$4,000

Inventory Accounts in Manufacturing Organizations

LO4 Describe the flow of costs through a manufacturer's inventory accounts.

Transforming materials into finished products ready for sale requires a number of production and production-related activities, including purchasing, receiving, inspecting, storing, and moving materials; converting them into finished products using labor, equipment, and other resources; and moving, storing, and shipping the finished products. A manufacturing organization's accounting system tracks these activities as product costs flowing through the Materials Inventory, Work in Process Inventory, and Finished Goods Inventory accounts. The **Materials Inventory account** shows the balance of the cost of unused materials, the **Work in Process Inventory account** shows the manufacturing costs that have been incurred and assigned to partially completed units of product, and the **Finished Goods Inventory account** shows the costs assigned to all completed products that have not been sold.

Document Flows and Cost Flows Through the Inventory Accounts

In many companies, managers accumulate and report manufacturing costs based on documents pertaining to production and production-related activities. Although paper documents are still used for this purpose, electronic documents have become increasingly common. Looking at how the documents for the three elements of product cost relate to the flow of costs through the three inventory accounts provides insight into when an activity must be recorded in the accounting records. Figure 4 summarizes the relationships among the production activities, the documents for each of the three cost elements, and the inventory accounts affected by the activities.

To illustrate document flow and changes in inventory balances for production activities, we continue with our example of The Choice Candy Company.

Purchase of Materials
The same process is used for purchasing both direct and indirect materials. The purchasing process starts with a *purchase request* for specific quantities of materials needed in the manufacturing process but not currently available in the materials storeroom. A qualified manager approves the request. Based on the information in the purchase request, the

■ **FIGURE 4**
Activities, Documents, and Cost Flows Through the Inventory Accounts of a Manufacturing Organization

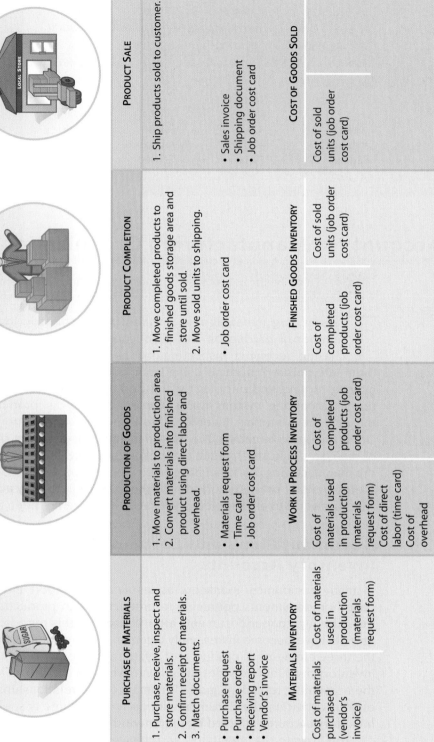

	PURCHASE OF MATERIALS	PRODUCTION OF GOODS	PRODUCT COMPLETION	PRODUCT SALE
ACTIVITIES	1. Purchase, receive, inspect and store materials. 2. Confirm receipt of materials. 3. Match documents.	1. Move materials to production area. 2. Convert materials into finished product using direct labor and overhead.	1. Move completed products to finished goods storage area and store until sold. 2. Move sold units to shipping.	1. Ship products sold to customer.
DOCUMENTS	• Purchase request • Purchase order • Receiving report • Vendor's invoice	• Materials request form • Time card • Job order cost card	• Job order cost card	• Sales invoice • Shipping document • Job order cost card

INVENTORY ACCOUNTS (RELATED DOCUMENTS)

MATERIALS INVENTORY		WORK IN PROCESS INVENTORY		FINISHED GOODS INVENTORY		COST OF GOODS SOLD
Cost of materials purchased (vendor's invoice)	Cost of materials used in production (materials request form)	Cost of materials used in production (materials request form) Cost of direct labor (time card) Cost of overhead	Cost of completed products (job order cost card)	Cost of completed products (job order cost card)	Cost of sold units (job order cost card)	Cost of sold units (job order cost card)

Purchasing Department sends a *purchase order* to a supplier. When the materials arrive, an employee on the receiving dock counts and examines them and prepares a *receiving report*. Later, an accounting clerk matches the information on the receiving report with the descriptions and quantities listed on the purchase order. A materials handler moves the newly arrived materials from the receiving area to the materials storeroom. Soon, The Choice Candy Company receives a *vendor's invoice* from the supplier requesting payment for the purchased materials. The cost of those materials increases the balance of the Materials Inventory account.

Production of Goods When candy bars are scheduled for production, the storeroom clerk receives a *materials request form*. The materials request form is essential for controlling materials. In addition to showing the supervisor's signature of approval, it describes the types and quantities of materials that the storeroom clerk is to send to the production area, and it authorizes the release of those materials from the materials inventory into production. If the appropriate manager has approved the materials request form, the storeroom clerk has the materials handler move the materials to the production floor. The cost of the direct materials transferred will increase the balance of the Work in Process Inventory account and decrease the balance of the Materials Inventory account. The cost of the indirect materials transferred will increase the balance of the Overhead account and decrease the balance of the Materials Inventory account. (We discuss overhead in more detail later in this chapter.)

Each of the production employees who make the candy bars prepares a *time card* to record the number of hours he or she has worked on this and other orders each day. The costs of the direct labor and overhead used to manufacture the candy bars increase the balance of the Work in Process Inventory account. A *job order cost card* can be used to record all costs incurred as the products move through production.

Product Completion and Sale Employees place completed candy bars in cartons and then move the cartons to the finished goods storeroom, where they are kept until they are shipped to customers. The cost of the completed candy bars increases the balance of the Finished Goods Inventory account and decreases the balance of the Work in Process Inventory account.

When candy bars are sold, a clerk prepares a *sales invoice*, and another employee fills the order by removing the candy bars from the storeroom, packaging them, and shipping them to the customer. A *shipping document* shows the quantity of the products that are shipped and gives a description of them. The cost of the candy bars sold increases the Cost of Goods Sold account and decreases the balance of the Finished Goods Inventory account.

The Manufacturing Cost Flow

Manufacturing cost flow is the flow of manufacturing costs (direct materials, direct labor, and overhead) through the Materials Inventory, Work in Process Inventory, and Finished Goods Inventory accounts into the Cost of Goods Sold account. A defined, structured manufacturing cost flow is the foundation for product costing, inventory valuation, and financial reporting. It supplies all the information necessary to prepare the statement of cost of goods manufactured and compute the cost of goods sold, as shown in Exhibit I.

Figure 5 summarizes the manufacturing cost flow as it relates to the inventory accounts and production activity of The Choice Candy Company for the year ended December 31, 20x9. To show the basic flows in this example, we

■ **FIGURE 5**
Manufacturing Cost Flow: An Example Using Actual Costing for The Choice Candy Company

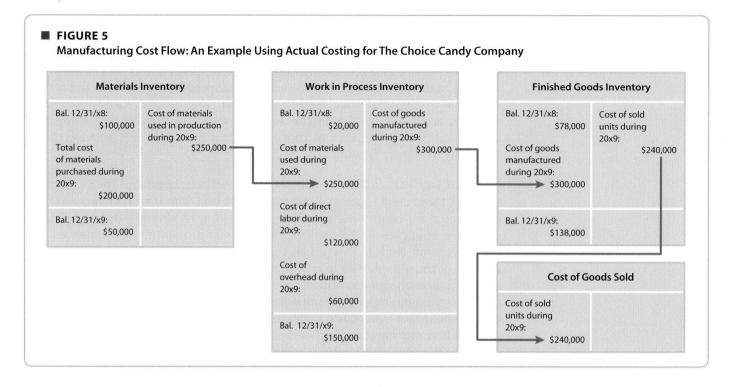

assume that all materials can be traced directly to the candy bars. This means that there are no indirect materials in the Materials Inventory account. We also work with the actual amount of overhead, rather than an estimated amount.

Materials Inventory Because there are no indirect materials in this case, the Materials Inventory account shows the balance of unused direct materials. The cost of direct materials purchased increases the balance of the Materials Inventory account, and the cost of direct materials used by the Production Department decreases it.

Figure 5 shows the flows of material purchased and used through the Materials Inventory T account. Alternatively, the following formula may be used to summarize the activity of The Choice Candy Company's Materials Inventory account during the year:

Materials Inventory, Ending Balance		Materials Inventory, Beginning Balance		Cost of Materials Purchased		Cost of Materials Used
$50,000	=	$100,000	+	$200,000	−	$250,000

Work in Process Inventory The Work in Process Inventory account records the balance of partially completed units of the product. As direct materials and direct labor enter the production process, their costs are added to the Work in Process Inventory account. The cost of overhead for the current period is also added. The total costs of direct materials, direct labor, and overhead incurred and transferred to work in process inventory during an accounting period are called **total manufacturing costs** (also called *current manufacturing costs*). These costs increase the balance of the Work in Process Inventory account.

The cost of all units completed and moved to finished goods inventory during an accounting period is the **cost of goods manufactured**. The cost of goods manufactured for the period decreases the balance of the Work in Process Inventory account.

Figure 5 recaps the inflows of direct materials, direct labor, and overhead into the Work in Process T account and the resulting outflow of completed product costs. The following formulas can also be used to recap the same activity in The Choice Candy Company's Work in Process Inventory account:

Total Manufacturing Costs	=	Cost of Direct Materials Used	+	Direct Labor Costs	+	Overhead Costs
$430,000	=	$250,000	+	$120,000	+	$60,000

Work in Process Inventory, Ending Balance	=	Work in Process Inventory, Beginning Balance	+	Total Manufacturing Costs	−	Cost of Goods Manufactured
$150,000	=	$20,000	+	$430,000	−	$300,000

Finished Goods Inventory The Finished Goods Inventory account holds the balance of costs assigned to all completed products that a manufacturing company has not yet sold. The cost of goods manufactured increases the balance, and the cost of goods sold decreases the balance.

Figure 5 shows the inflow of cost of goods manufactured and the outflow of cost of goods sold to the Finished Goods inventory T account. The following formula may also be used to recap the activity in The Choice Candy Company's Finished Goods Inventory account during the year:

Finished Goods Inventory, Ending Balance	=	Finished Goods Inventory, Beginning Balance	+	Cost of Goods Manufactured	−	Cost of Goods Sold
$138,000	=	$78,000	+	$300,000	−	$240,000

Study Note

Materials Inventory and Work in Process Inventory support the production process, while Finished Goods Inventory supports the sales and distribution functions.

S T O P • R E V I E W • A P P L Y

4-1. Identify and describe the inventory accounts of a manufacturing company.

4-2. What does the term *manufacturing cost flow* mean?

4-3. How do total manufacturing costs differ from the cost of goods manufactured?

Cost Flows in a Manufacturing Organization Given the following information, compute the ending balances of the Materials Inventory, Work in Process Inventory, and Finished Goods Inventory accounts:

Materials Inventory, beginning balance	$ 230
Work in Process Inventory, beginning balance	250
Finished Goods Inventory, beginning balance	380
Direct materials purchased	850
Direct materials placed into production	740
Direct labor costs	970
Overhead costs	350
Cost of goods completed	1,230
Cost of goods sold	935

SOLUTION

Materials Inventory, ending balance:

Materials Inventory, beginning balance	$ 230
Direct materials purchased	850
Direct materials placed into production	(740) ←
Materials Inventory, ending balance	$ 340

Work in Process Inventory, ending balance:

Work in Process Inventory, beginning balance	$ 250
Direct materials placed into production	740 ←
Direct labor costs	970
Overhead costs	350
Cost of goods completed	(1,230) ←
Work in Process Inventory, ending balance	$1,080

Finished Goods Inventory, ending balance:

Finished Goods Inventory, beginning balance	$ 380
Cost of goods completed	1,230 ←
Cost of goods sold	(935)
Finished Goods Inventory, ending balance	$ 675

Elements of Product Costs

LO5   Define *product unit cost* and compute the unit cost of a product or service.

As noted above, product costs include all costs related to the manufacturing process. The three elements of product cost are direct materials costs, direct labor costs, and overhead costs, which are indirect costs.

Direct materials costs are the costs of materials used in making a product that can be conveniently and economically traced to specific units of the product. Some examples of direct materials are the iron ore used in making steel, the sheet metal used in making automobiles, and the sugar used in making candy. Direct materials may also include parts that a company purchases from another manufacturer.

Direct labor costs are the costs of the labor needed to make a product that can be conveniently and economically traced to specific units of the product. For example, the wages of production-line workers are direct labor costs.

Overhead costs (also called *service overhead, factory overhead, factory burden, manufacturing overhead,* or *indirect manufacturing costs*) are production-related costs that cannot be practically or conveniently traced directly to an end product. They include **indirect materials costs**, such as the costs of nails, rivets, lubricants, and small tools, and **indirect labor costs**, such as the costs of labor for machinery and tool maintenance, inspection, engineering design, supervision, and materials handling. Other indirect manufacturing costs include the costs of building maintenance, property taxes, property insurance, depreciation on plant and equipment, rent, and utilities. As indirect costs, overhead costs are allocated to a product's cost using traditional or activity-based costing methods, which we discuss later in the chapter.

To illustrate product costs and the manufacturing process, we'll refer again to The Choice Candy Company. Maggie Evans, the company's founder and

Has Technology Shifted the Elements of Product Costs?

New technology and manufacturing processes have created new patterns of product costs. The three elements of product costs are still direct materials, direct labor, and overhead, but the percentage that each contributes to the total cost of a product has changed. From the 1950s through the 1970s, direct labor was the dominant element, making up over 40 percent of total product cost, while direct materials contributed 35 percent and overhead, around 25 percent. Thus, direct costs, traceable to the product, accounted for 75 percent of total product cost. Improved production technology caused a dramatic shift in the three product cost elements. Machines replaced people, significantly reducing direct labor costs. Today, only 50 percent of the cost of a product is directly traceable to the product; the other 50 percent is overhead, an indirect cost.

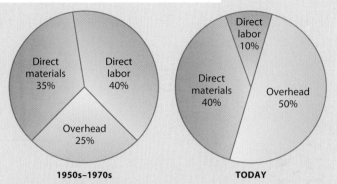

president, has identified the following elements of the product cost of one candy bar:

- *Direct materials costs*: costs of sugar, chocolate, and wrapper

- *Direct labor costs*: costs of labor used in making the candy bar

- *Overhead costs*: indirect materials costs, including the costs of salt and flavorings; indirect labor costs, including the costs of labor to move materials to the production area and to inspect the candy bars during production; other indirect overhead costs, including depreciation on the building and equipment, utilities, property taxes, and insurance

Prime Costs and Conversion Costs

The three elements of manufacturing costs can be grouped into prime costs and conversion costs. **Prime costs** are the primary costs of production; they are the sum of the direct materials costs and direct labor costs. **Conversion costs** are the costs of converting direct materials into a finished product; they are the sum of direct labor costs and overhead costs. These classifications are important for understanding the costing methods discussed in later chapters. Figure 6 summarizes the relationships among the product cost classifications presented so far.

Computing Product Unit Cost

Product unit cost is the cost of manufacturing a single unit of a product. It is made up of the costs of direct materials, direct labor, and overhead. These three cost elements are accumulated as a batch or production run of products is being produced. When the batch or run has been completed, the product unit cost is computed either by dividing the total cost of direct materials, direct labor, and overhead by the total number of units produced, or by determining the cost per unit for each element of the product cost and summing those per-unit costs.

Unit cost information helps managers price products and calculate gross margin and net income. Managers and accountants can calculate product unit

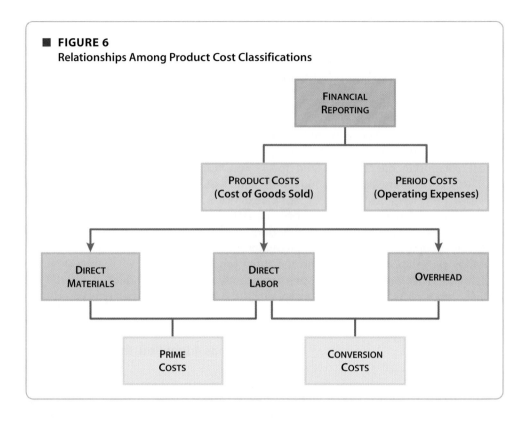

■ **FIGURE 6**
Relationships Among Product Cost Classifications

cost by using the actual costing, the normal costing, or the standard costing method. Table 2 summarizes how these three cost-measurement methods use actual and estimated costs.

Actual Costing Method   The **actual costing** method uses the costs of direct materials, direct labor, and overhead at the end of an accounting period or when actual costs become known to calculate the product unit cost. The actual product unit cost is assigned to the finished goods inventory on the balance sheet and to the cost of goods sold on the income statement. For example, assume that The Choice Candy Company produced 3,000 candy bars on December 28 for Good Foods Store. Sara Kearney, the company's accountant, calculated that the actual costs for the order were direct materials, $540; direct labor, $420; and overhead, $240. The actual product unit cost for the order was $.40, calculated as follows:

Direct materials ($540 ÷ 3,000 candy bars)	$.18
Direct labor ($420 ÷ 3,000 candy bars)	.14
Overhead ($240 ÷ 3,000 candy bars)	.08
Product cost per candy bar ($1,200 ÷ 3,000 candy bars)	$.40

Study Note

Many management decisions require estimates of future costs. Managers often use actual cost as a basis for estimating future cost.

TABLE 2.   Use of Actual and Estimated Costs in Three Cost-Measurement Methods

Product Cost Elements	Actual Costing	Normal Costing	Standard Costing
Direct materials	Actual costs	Actual costs	Estimated costs
Direct labor	Actual costs	Actual costs	Estimated costs
Overhead	Actual costs	Estimated costs	Estimated costs

In this case, the product unit cost was computed after the job was completed and all cost information was known. Sometimes, however, a manufacturer needs to know product unit cost during production, when the actual direct materials costs and direct labor costs are known, but the actual overhead costs are uncertain. In that case, the computation of product unit cost will include an estimate of the overhead, and the normal costing method will be helpful. The use of normal costing is widespread, since many overhead bills, such as utilities, are not received until after products or services are produced and sold.

Normal Costing Method   The **normal costing** method combines the actual direct costs of materials and labor with estimated overhead costs to determine a product unit cost. The normal costing method is simple and allows a smoother, more even assignment of overhead costs to production during an accounting period than is possible with the actual costing method. It also contributes to better pricing decisions and profitability estimates. However, at the end of the accounting period, any difference between the estimated and actual costs must be identified and removed so that the financial statements show only the actual product costs.

Assume that Sara Kearney used normal costing to price the Good Foods Store order for 3,000 candy bars and that overhead was applied to the product's cost using an estimated rate of 60 percent of direct labor costs. In this case, the costs for the order would include the actual direct materials cost of $540, the actual direct labor cost of $420, and an estimated overhead cost of $252 ($420 × 60%). The product unit cost would be $.40:

Direct materials ($540 ÷ 3,000 candy bars)	$.18
Direct labor ($420 ÷ 3,000 candy bars)	.14
Overhead ($252 ÷ 3,000 candy bars)	.08
Product cost per candy bar	
($1,212 ÷ 3,000 candy bars)	$.40

Standard Costing Method   Managers sometimes need product cost information before the accounting period begins so that they can control the cost of operating activities or price a proposed product for a customer. In such situations, product unit costs must be estimated, and the **standard costing** method can be helpful. This method uses estimated or standard costs of direct materials, direct labor, and overhead to calculate the product unit cost.

Assume that The Choice Candy Company is placing a bid to manufacture 2,000 candy bars for a new customer. From standard cost information developed at the beginning of the period, Kearney estimates the following costs: $.20 per unit for direct materials, $.15 per unit for direct labor, and $.09 per unit for overhead (assuming a standard overhead rate of 60 percent of direct labor cost). The standard cost per unit would be $.44:

Direct materials	$.20
Direct labor	.15
Overhead ($.15 × 60%)	.09
Product cost per candy bar	$.44

The $.44 product unit cost is useful in determining the cost of the bid, $880 ($.44 × 2,000 candy bars), estimating the gross margin for the job, and deciding the price to bid for the business. We cover standard costing in more detail in another chapter.

Computing Service Unit Cost

Delivering products, representing people in courts of law, selling insurance policies, and computing people's income taxes are typical of the services performed in many service organizations. Like other services, these are labor-intensive processes supported by indirect materials, indirect labor, and other overhead costs.

Because no products are manufactured in the course of providing services, service organizations have no direct materials costs. As noted, however, they do have both labor and overhead costs, which must be included in the cost of providing a service. The most important cost in a service organization is the direct cost of labor, and the usual standard is applicable; that is, the direct labor cost must be traceable to the service rendered. The indirect costs incurred in performing a service are similar to those incurred in manufacturing a product. They are classified as overhead and, along with direct labor costs, are considered service costs rather than period costs. Just as product costs appear on manufacturers' income statements as cost of goods sold, service costs appear on service organizations' income statements as cost of sales.

To illustrate how to compute service unit cost, assume that Fresh Express, a grocery delivery service in New York City, wants to determine the total cost and unit cost of a typical home grocery delivery. Its policy for the past five years has been to charge a $15 fee per home delivery, but this may now be too low, because operating costs have soared in the past five years. Fresh Express has asked you to compute the actual cost of a home delivery and has given you the following information about its delivery operations:

Study Note

Any material costs in a service organization would be for supplies used in providing services. Because these are indirect materials costs, they are included in overhead.

Direct labor

Monthly salaries:

4 people at $2,500 each	$10,000

Indirect monthly overhead costs:

Supervisor's salary	$ 4,500
Telephone	750
Depreciation	5,000
Delivery supplies	2,460
Customer relations	640
Credit check function	980
Utilities	1,690
Clerical personnel	3,080
Miscellaneous	900
Total overhead costs	$20,000

Home deliveries usually total 1,000 each month. The Delivery Department has other functions in addition to deliveries to homes and offices. After determining how many of the deliveries were home deliveries, you conclude that only 25 percent of the overhead costs of the Delivery Department were applicable to home deliveries. The cost of one home delivery can be computed as:

Direct professional labor cost:	
$10,000 ÷ 1,000	$10.00
Overhead cost:	
$20,000 × 25% ÷ 1,000	5.00
Service cost per home delivery	$15.00

From the service unit cost, you conclude that the present fee of $15.00 just covers the current costs of a home delivery. To allow for a profit margin, the home delivery fee should be raised to $20 or $25. Further analysis using normal or standard costing could also be done for future planning and decisions.

S T O P • R E V I E W • A P P L Y

5-1. What three kinds of costs are included in a product's cost?

5-2. What characteristics identify a cost as part of overhead?

5-3. How do the costing methods used to compute a product's cost per unit affect the three elements of product cost? What is the difference between actual costing and normal costing?

Unit Costs in a Service Business   Fickle Picking Services provides inexpensive, high-quality labor for farmers growing vegetable and fruit crops. In September, Fickle Picking Services paid laborers $4,000 to harvest 500 acres of apples. The company incurred overhead costs of $2,400 for apple-picking services in September. This amount included the costs of transporting the laborers to the orchards; of providing facilities, food, and beverages for the laborers; and of scheduling, billing, and collecting from the farmers. Of this amount, 50 percent was related to picking apples. Compute the cost per acre to pick apples.

SOLUTION

Total cost to pick apples:	$4,000 + (0.50 \times $2,400) = $5,200
Cost per acre to pick apples:	$5,200 \div 500$ acres = $10.40 per acre

Cost Allocation

LO6   Define *cost allocation* and explain how cost objects, cost pools, and cost drivers are used to assign overhead costs.

As noted earlier, the costs of direct materials and direct labor can be easily traced to a product or service, but overhead costs are indirect costs that must be collected and allocated in some manner. **Cost allocation** is the process of assigning a collection of indirect costs to a specific **cost object**, such as a product or service, a department, or an operating activity, using an allocation base known as a **cost driver**. A cost driver might be direct labor hours, direct labor costs, units produced, or another activity base that has a cause-and-effect relationship with the cost. As the cost driver increases in volume, it causes the **cost pool**—the collection of indirect costs assigned to a cost object—to increase in amount.

For example, suppose The Choice Candy Company has a candy machine-maintenance cost pool. The cost pool consists of overhead costs for the supplies and labor needed to maintain the candy machines, the cost object is the candy product, and the cost driver is machine hours. As more machine hours are used, the amount of the cost pool increases, thus increasing the costs assigned to the candy product.

For purposes of product or service costing, cost allocation is defined as the assignment of overhead costs to the product or service (cost object) during an accounting period. It requires (1) the pooling of overhead costs that are affected by a common activity (e.g., machine maintenance) and (2) the selection of a cost driver whose activity level causes a change in the cost pool (e.g., machine hours).

Allocating the Costs of Overhead

Allocating overhead costs to products or services is a four-step process that corresponds to the four stages of the management process:

1. *Planning.* In the first step, managers estimate overhead costs and calculate a rate at which they will assign those costs to products or services.

2. *Performing.* In the second step, this rate is applied to products or services as overhead costs are incurred and recorded during production.

3. *Evaluating.* In the third step, actual overhead costs are recorded as they are incurred, and managers calculate the difference between the estimated (or applied) and actual costs.

4. *Communicating.* In the fourth step, managers report on this difference.

Figure 7 summarizes these four steps in terms of their timing, the procedures involved, and the journal entries they require. It also shows how the cost flows in the various steps affect the accounting records.

Planning the Overhead Rate   Before an accounting period begins, managers determine cost pools and cost drivers and calculate a **predetermined overhead rate** by dividing the cost pool of total estimated overhead costs by the total estimated cost driver level. Grouping all estimated overhead costs into one cost pool and using direct labor hours or machine hours as the cost driver results in a single, plantwide overhead rate. By applying this predetermined rate to all units of production during the period in the same way, managers can better estimate product costs. This step requires no journal entry because no business activity has occurred.

Applying the Overhead Rate   As units of the product or service are produced during the accounting period, the estimated overhead costs are assigned to the product or service using the predetermined overhead rate. The overhead rate for each cost pool is multiplied by that pool's actual cost driver level (e.g., the actual number of direct labor hours used to complete the product). The purpose of this calculation is to assign a consistent overhead cost to each unit produced during the accounting period. A journal entry records the allocation of overhead. For example, the entry to apply overhead to a product is recorded as a debit or increase to the Work in Process Inventory account and a credit or decrease to the Overhead account.

Recording Actual Overhead Costs   The actual overhead costs are recorded as they are incurred during the accounting period. These costs, which include the actual costs of indirect materials, indirect labor, depreciation, property taxes, and other production costs, will be part of the actual product cost. The journal entry made for the actual overhead costs records a debit in the Overhead account and a credit in the asset, contra-asset, or liability accounts affected.

■ **FIGURE 7**
Allocating Overhead Costs: A Four-Step Process

Year 20x8 ├──────────────────────────────┼──────────── Year 20x9 ────────────────────────────────▶
                                      January 1   December 31

	Step 1: Planning the Overhead Rate	Step 2: Applying the Overhead Rate	Step 3: Recording Actual Overhead Costs	Step 4: Reconciling Applied and Actual Overhead Costs
Timing and Procedure	Before the accounting period begins, determine cost pools and cost drivers. Calculate the overhead rate by dividing the cost pool of total estimated overhead costs by the total estimated cost driver level.	During the accounting period, as units are produced, apply overhead costs to products by multiplying the predetermined overhead rate for each cost pool by the actual cost driver level for that pool. Record costs.	Record actual overhead costs as they are incurred during the accounting period.	At the end of the accounting period, calculate and reconcile the difference between applied and actual overhead costs.
Journal Entry	None	Increase Work in Process Inventory account and decrease Overhead account: Dr. Work in Process XX Cr. Overhead XX	Increase Overhead account and decrease asset accounts or increase contra-asset or liability accounts: Dr. Overhead XX Cr. Various Accounts XX	Entry will vary depending on how costs have been applied. If overapplied, increase Overhead and decrease Cost of Goods Sold. If underapplied, increase Cost of Goods Sold and decrease Overhead.

Cost Flow Through the Accounts

Step 2:

Overhead
	Overhead applied using predetermined rate

Work in Process Inventory
Overhead applied using predetermined rate	

Step 3:

Overhead
Actual overhead costs recorded	

Various Asset and Liability Accounts
	Actual costs recorded

Step 4:

Overapplied:
Overhead
Actual overhead costs recorded	Overhead applied using predetermined rate
	Overapplied

Bal. $0

Cost of Goods Sold
Bal.	
	Overapplied

Actual bal.

Underapplied:
Overhead
Actual overhead costs recorded	Overhead applied using predetermined rate
	Underapplied

Bal. $0

Cost of Goods Sold
Bal.	
Underapplied	

Actual bal.

Reconciling the Applied and Actual Overhead Amounts At the end of the accounting period, the difference between the applied and actual overhead costs is calculated and reconciled.

Overapplied Overhead If the overhead costs applied to production during the period are greater than the actual overhead costs, the difference in the amounts represents **overapplied overhead costs**. If this difference is immaterial, the Overhead account is debited or increased and the Cost of Goods Sold or Cost of Sales account is credited or decreased by the difference. If the difference is material for the products produced, adjustments are made to the accounts affected—that is, the Work in Process Inventory, Finished Goods Inventory, and Cost of Goods Sold accounts.

Underapplied Overhead If the overhead costs applied to production during the period are less than the actual overhead costs, the difference represents **underapplied overhead costs**. The Cost of Goods Sold or Cost of Sales account is debited or increased and the Overhead account is credited or decreased by this difference, assuming that the difference is not material.

Actual Cost of Goods Sold or Cost of Sales The adjustment for overapplied or underapplied overhead costs, whether they are immaterial or material, is necessary to reflect the actual overhead costs on the income statement.

The Importance of Good Estimates

A predetermined, or estimated, overhead rate has two main uses. First, it enables managers to make decisions about pricing products or services and controlling costs before some of the actual costs are known. The product or service cost calculated at the end of a period, when all costs are known, is, of course, more accurate. But when the overhead portion of product or service cost is estimated in advance, managers can compare actual and estimated costs throughout the year and more quickly correct any problems that may be causing the under- or overallocation of overhead costs.

Second, an advance estimate allows managers to apply overhead costs to each unit produced in an equitable and timely manner. Actual overhead costs fluctuate from month to month as a result of the timing of the costs and the variability of the amounts. For example, some overhead costs (such as supervisors' salaries and depreciation on equipment) may be expensed monthly. Others (like payroll taxes) may be paid quarterly, and still others (like property taxes and insurance) may be paid annually. In addition, indirect hourly labor costs (such as the costs of machine maintenance and materials handling) fluctuate with changes in output levels.

The successful allocation of overhead costs depends on two factors. One is a careful estimate of the total overhead costs. The other is a good forecast of the cost driver level.

An accurate estimate of total overhead costs is crucial. If the estimate is wrong, the overhead rate will be wrong. This will cause an overstatement or understatement of the product or service unit cost. If an organization relies on information that overstates its unit cost, it may fail to bid on profitable projects because the costs appear too high. If it relies on information that understates its unit cost, the projects that it accepts may not be as profitable as expected. So, to have reliable product or service unit costs, managers must be careful to include all overhead items and to forecast the costs of those items accurately.

The budgeting process usually includes estimating overhead costs. Managers who use production-related resources will provide cost estimates for direct and indirect production activities. For example, the managers for materials handling and inspection at The Choice Candy Company estimate the costs related to their departments' activities, and Sara Kearney, the accountant, includes their cost estimates in developing total overhead costs.

Managers also need to provide accurate estimates of cost driver levels. An understated cost driver level will cause an overstatement of the predetermined overhead rate (the cost is spread over a lesser level), and an overstated cost driver level will cause an understatement of the predetermined overhead rate (the cost is spread over a greater level).

In the following sections, we present two approaches to allocating overhead. We use the first two steps of the four-step overhead allocation process to demonstrate these approaches.

S T O P • R E V I E W • A P P L Y

6-1. Explain the relationship among cost objects, cost pools, and cost drivers. Give an example of each.

6-2. What are the two main uses of a predetermined overhead rate?

6-3. List the four steps involved in allocating overhead costs. Briefly explain each step.

Allocating Overhead: The Traditional Approach

LO7 Using the traditional method of allocating overhead costs, calculate product or service unit cost.

The traditional approach to applying overhead costs to a product or service is to use a single predetermined overhead rate. This approach is especially useful when companies manufacture only one product or a few very similar products that require the same production processes and production-related activities, such as setup, inspection, and materials handling. The total overhead costs constitute one cost pool, and a traditional activity base—such as direct labor hours, direct labor costs, machine hours, or units of production—is the cost driver.

As we continue with our example of The Choice Candy Company, let's assume that the company will be selling two product lines in the coming year—plain candy bars and candy bars with nuts—and that Sara Kearney chooses direct labor hours as the cost driver. Kearney estimates that total overhead costs for the next year will be $20,000 and that total direct labor hours (DLH) worked will be 400,000 hours.

Table 3 summarizes the first two steps in the traditional approach to allocating overhead costs. In the first step, Kearney uses the following formula to compute the rate at which overhead costs will be applied:

$$\text{Predetermined Overhead Rate} = \frac{\$20,000}{400,000 \text{ DLH}} = \$.05 \text{ per DLH}$$

TABLE 3. Allocating Overhead Costs and Calculating Product Unit Cost: Traditional Approach

Step 1. Calculate overhead rate for cost pool:

$$\frac{\text{Estimated Total Overhead Costs}}{\text{Estimated Total Cost Driver Level}} = \frac{\$20,000}{400,000\ (\text{DLH})} = \$.05 \text{ per DLH}$$

Step 2. Apply predetermined overhead rate to products:

	Plain Candy Bars	**Candy Bars with Nuts**
	Predetermined Overhead Rate × Actual Cost Driver Level = Cost Applied to Production	Predetermined Overhead Rate × Actual Cost Driver Level = Cost Applied to Production
Overhead applied: $.05 per DLH	$.05 × 250,000 DLH = $12,500	$.05 × 150,000 DLH = $7,500
Overhead cost per unit: Cost Applied ÷ Number of Units	$12,500 ÷ 100,000 = $.13	$7,500 ÷ 50,000 = $.15

Product unit cost using normal costing:

	Plain Candy Bars	**Candy Bars with Nuts**
Product costs per unit:		
Direct materials	$.18	$.21
Direct labor	.14	.16
Applied overhead	.13	.15
Product unit cost	$.45	$.52

In the second step, Kearney applies the predetermined overhead rate to the products. During the year, The Choice Candy Company actually uses 250,000 direct labor hours to produce 100,000 plain candy bars and 150,000 direct labor hours to produce 50,000 candy bars with nuts. When Kearney applies the predetermined overhead rate during the year, the portion of the overhead cost applied to the plain candy bars totals $12,500 ($.05 × 250,000 DLH), or $.13 per unit ($12,500 ÷ 100,000 units), and the portion applied to the candy bars with nuts totals $7,500 ($.05 × 150,000 DLH), or $.15 per unit ($7,500 ÷ 50,000 units).

Kearney also wanted to calculate the product unit cost for the accounting period using normal costing. She gathered the following data for the two product lines:

	Plain Candy Bars	Candy Bars with Nuts
Actual direct materials cost per unit	$.18	$.21
Actual direct labor cost per unit	.14	.16
Prime cost per unit	$.32	$.37

At the bottom of Table 3 is Kearney's calculation of the normal product unit cost for each product line. The product unit cost of the candy bar with nuts ($.52) is higher than the plain candy bar's cost ($.45) because producing the candy bar with nuts required more expensive materials and more labor time.

Study Note

Don't make the mistake of thinking that because a cost is not traced directly to a product, it is not a product cost. All manufacturing costs, both direct and indirect, are product costs.

7-1. How many overhead cost pools are used in the traditional approach to cost allocation?

7-2. What are three examples of activity bases that are often used in the traditional approach to allocating overhead?

Computation of Overhead Rate Compute the overhead rate per service request for the Sample Service Company if estimated overhead costs are $15,000 and the number of estimated service requests is 5,000.

SOLUTION

$$\frac{\text{Predetermined Overhead}}{\text{Rate per Service Request}} = \frac{\text{Total Estimated Overhead Costs}}{\text{Total Estimated Service Requests}}$$

$$= \frac{\$15,000}{5,000}$$

$$= \$3.00$$

Application of Overhead Rate Calculate the amount of overhead costs applied if the predetermined overhead rate is $3 per direct labor hour and 1,000 direct labor hours were worked.

SOLUTION

Overhead Costs Applied = $3 per Direct Labor Hour

$$\times\ 1,000$$

$$= \$3,000$$

Allocating Overhead: The ABC Approach

LO8 Using activity-based costing to assign overhead costs, calculate product or service unit cost.

Activity-based costing (ABC) is a more accurate method of assigning overhead costs to products or services than the traditional approach. It categorizes all indirect costs by activity, traces the indirect costs to those activities, and assigns activity costs to products or services using a cost driver related to the cause of the cost. A company that uses ABC identifies production-related activities and the events and circumstances that cause, or drive, those activities, such as number of inspections or maintenance hours. As a result, many smaller activity pools are created from the single overhead cost pool used in the traditional method. This means that managers will calculate an overhead rate, or activity cost rate, for each activity pool and then use that rate and a cost driver amount to determine the portion of overhead costs to assign to a product or service produced. Managers must select an appropriate number of activity pools for overhead, and a system must be designed to capture the actual cost driver amounts. Because each activity pool requires a cost driver, the benefit of grouping overhead costs into several smaller pools to obtain more accurate estimates of products or services is offset by the additional costs of measuring many different cost drivers.

ABC will improve the accuracy of product or service cost estimates for organizations that sell many different types of products or services (product diversity) or that use varying, significant amounts of different production-related activities to complete the products or services (process complexity). More careful cost allocation means that managers will have better information for decision making, especially when it comes to making decisions about pricing, outsourcing processes to other organizations, or choosing to keep a product or service item or drop it from the product line.

For other organizations, some products or services are more complicated to manufacture, store, move, package, or ship than others (process complexity). For example, a distributor of dairy products and eggs receives, stores, selects, moves, consolidates, packs, and ships items to various stores like **Wal-Mart** or Good Foods Store or to production facilities like The Choice Candy Company's factory. The distributor's greatest costs are overhead costs, which under the traditional method are assigned based on what it costs to purchase an item for resale. With the traditional method, more expensive items like whipping cream receive a greater allocation of overhead costs than do less expensive items like eggs. However, because some items, like the eggs, are more delicate than others, it may cost the distributor more to move, store, pack, and ship them. If ABC were used, the cost of the more delicate items like the eggs would increase to reflect a fairer allocation of the distributor's overhead costs. Thus, by assigning overhead costs based on the relative use of overhead resources, ABC would provide managers with better information for making decisions, such as pricing, choosing to discontinue selling certain items, or reducing the amount of storage space.

Planning Overhead Rates

As discussed earlier, Sara Kearney, the accountant for The Choice Candy Company, calculated product unit cost by computing one overhead rate for one cost pool and applying that rate to the direct labor hours used to manufacture plain candy bars and candy bars with nuts. As we continue with our example, we find that Maggie Evans, president of The Choice Candy Company, is concerned about the product cost for each type of candy bar. Evans believes that the difference in cost between the plain and nut candy bars should be more than $.07 ($.52 − $.45). She has asked Kearney to review her estimate. Kearney

TABLE 4.   Allocating Overhead Costs and Calculating Product Unit Cost: ABC Approach

Step 1. Calculate activity cost rate for cost pool:

$$\frac{\text{Estimated Total Activity Costs}}{\text{Estimated Total Cost Driver Level}} = \text{Activity Cost Rate for Cost Pool}$$

Activity	Estimated Total Activity Costs	Estimated Total Cost Driver Level	Activity Cost Rate for Cost Pool
Setup	$ 7,000	700 setups	$7,000 ÷ 700 = $10 per setup
Inspection	6,000	500 inspections	$6,000 ÷ 500 = $12 per inspection
Packaging	5,000	2,000 packaging hours	$5,000 ÷ 2,000 = $2.50 per packaging hour
Building	2,000	10,000 machine hours	$2,000 ÷ 10,000 = $.20 per machine hour
	$20,000		

Step 2. Apply predetermined activity cost rates to products:

	Plain Candy Bars	Candy Bars with Nuts
Activity Pool	**Predetermined Overhead Rate × Actual Cost Driver Level = Cost Applied to Production**	**Predetermined Overhead Rate × Actual Cost Driver Level = Cost Applied to Production**
Setup	$10 × 300 = $3,000	$10 × 400 = $ 4,000
Inspection	$12 × 150 = 1,800	$12 × 350 = 4,200
Packaging	$2.50 × 600 = 1,500	$2.50 × 1,400 = 3,500
Building	$.20 × 4,000 = 800	$.20 × 6,000 = 1,200
Total overhead applied	$7,100	$12,900

Applied overhead cost per unit:

Cost Applied ÷ Number of Units	$7,100 ÷ 100,000 = $.07	$12,900 ÷ 50,000 = $.26

Product unit cost using normal costing:

	Plain Candy Bars	Candy Bars with Nuts
Product costs per unit:		
Direct materials	$.18	$.21
Direct labor	.14	.16
Applied overhead	.07	.26
Product unit cost	$.39	$.63

found no errors when she rechecked the calculation of direct materials costs and direct labor costs. However, she believes that the traditional approach to assigning overhead cost could be misleading, so she wants to use activity-based costing to obtain a more accurate estimate of product cost. Table 4 illustrates the use of ABC to assign overhead costs to two product lines.

Kearney analyzed the production-related activities and decided that the estimated $20,000 in overhead cost could be grouped into four activity pools. The first activity, setup, includes estimated total costs of $7,000 for indirect labor and indirect materials used in preparing machines for each batch of products. The second activity, inspection, includes $6,000 for salaries and indirect materials costs, indirect labor, and depreciation on testing equipment. The third activity, packaging, includes estimated total costs of $5,000 for indirect materials, indirect labor, and equipment depreciation. The last activity, building operations, includes estimated total overhead costs of $2,000 for building depreciation, maintenance, janitorial wages, property taxes, insurance, security, and all other costs not related to the first three activities.

After identifying the four activity pools, Kearney selected a cost driver and estimated the cost driver level for each activity pool. The following schedule shows those amounts by product line and in total:

Estimated Cost Driver Level

Cost Driver	Plain	Nut	Total
Number of setups	300	400	700
Number of inspections	150	350	500
Packaging hours	600	1,400	2,000
Machine hours	4,000	6,000	10,000

After identifying activity pools, estimated activity pool amounts, cost drivers, and estimated cost driver levels, Kearney performed Step 1 of the overhead allocation process by calculating the activity cost rate for each activity pool. The activity cost rate is the estimated activity pool amount divided by the estimated cost driver level. Step 1 of Table 4 shows that the activity cost rates are $10 per setup, $12 per inspection, $2.50 per packaging hour, and $.20 per machine hour.

Study Note

Under ABC, activity pools are allocated to cost objects using multiple cost drivers.

Applying the Overhead Rates

In Step 2, Kearney applied overhead to the two product lines using the cost driver level for each cost driver multiplied by the activity cost rate shown in the preceding schedule. Step 2 of Table 4 shows those calculations. For example, Kearney applied $3,000 in setup costs ($10 × 300 setups) to the plain candy bar line and $4,000 ($10 × 400 setups) to the nut candy bar line. After applying the overhead costs from the four activity pools to the product lines, Kearney estimated that total overhead costs of $7,100, or $.07 per bar ($7,100 ÷ 100,000 units), should be applied to the plain candy bar line and that $12,900, or $.26 per bar ($12,900 ÷ 50,000 units), should be applied to the nut candy bar line.

Kearney also wanted to calculate the unit cost for each product line using normal costing. Her calculations appear at the bottom of Table 4. The product unit cost is $.39 for the plain line and $.63 for the nut line.

Kearney presented the following information to Maggie Evans:

	Plain	Nut
Product unit cost: Traditional approach with one overhead cost pool	$.45	$.52
Product unit cost: ABC with four activity pools	.39	.63
Difference: Decrease (increase)	$.06	($.11)

Because ABC assigned more costs to the product line that used more resources, it provided a more accurate estimate of product unit cost. The increased information about the production requirements for the nut candy bar line that went into the ABC calculation of product unit cost also provided valuable insights. Evans found that the candy bars with nuts cost more to manufacture because the different ingredients require more setups and machine hours and because more inspections are needed to test the candy quality. Because the nut candy bar line requires more production and production-related activities, its product unit cost is higher. Based on this analysis, Evans may want to reconsider some of her decisions about the manufacture and sale of these two product lines.

S T O P • R E V I E W • A P P L Y

8-1. How does traditional overhead allocation differ from ABC overhead allocation?

8-2. How many overhead cost pools are used in the ABC approach to cost allocation?

8-3. What allocation measure does ABC use to relate an activity pool to a cost object? Explain your answer.

A LOOK BACK AT

SOUTHWEST AIRLINES

In this chapter's Decision Point, we posed these questions:

- **How do managers at Southwest Airlines determine the cost of selling tickets or of operating a flight?**
- **How do they use cost information?**

To determine the cost of selling tickets online or the cost of operating a flight, managers at Southwest Airlines must conduct complex analyses of many costs. When determining the cost of online ticket sales, Southwest's managers analyze the costs of direct labor and materials, as well as the costs of activities needed to support these sales, such as supervision, equipment maintenance, depreciation, and utilities. When determining the cost of operating a flight, they analyze the costs of the materials (e.g., peanuts, drinks, and jet fuel) and labor used (e.g., flight attendants and pilot), as well as overhead costs, such as aircraft maintenance and depreciation. Southwest's managers also consider any other relevant selling, administrative, or general operating costs that the flight incurs.

Classifying and analyzing costs helps managers make decisions that will sustain Southwest's profitability. All costs must be analyzed in terms of their traceability and behavior and in terms of whether they add value and how they affect the financial statements. Because many costs cannot be directly traced to specific flights, activities, or departments, managers must use a method of allocation to assign them. Possibilities include traditional allocation methods and the activity-based costing method, both of which we introduced in this chapter.

CHAPTER REVIEW

REVIEW of Learning Objectives

LO1 Describe how managers use information about costs.

Managers in manufacturing, retail, and service organizations use information about operating costs and product or service costs to prepare budgets, make pricing and other decisions, calculate variances between estimated and actual costs, and communicate results.

LO2 Explain how managers classify costs and how they use these cost classifications.

A single cost can be classified as a direct or an indirect cost, a variable or a fixed cost, a value-adding or a nonvalue-adding cost, and a product or a period cost. These cost classifications enable managers to control costs by tracing them to cost objects, to calculate the number of units that must be sold to obtain a certain level of profit, to identify the costs of activities that do and do not add value to a product or service, and to prepare financial statements for parties outside the organization.

LO3 Compare how service, retail, and manufacturing organizations report costs on their financial statements and how they account for inventories.

Because the operations of service, retail, and manufacturing organizations differ, their financial statements differ as well. A service organization maintains no inventory accounts on its balance sheet. The cost of sales on its income statement reflects the net cost of the services sold. A retail organization, which purchases products ready for resale, maintains only a Merchandise Inventory account, which is used to record and account for items in inventory. The cost of goods sold is simply the difference between the cost of goods available for sale and the ending merchandise inventory. A manufacturing organization, because it creates a product, maintains three inventory accounts: Materials Inventory, Work in Process Inventory, and Finished Goods Inventory. Manufacturing costs flow through all three inventory accounts. During the accounting period, the cost of completed products is transferred to the Finished Goods Inventory account, and the cost of units that have been manufactured and sold is transferred to the Cost of Goods Sold account.

LO4 Describe the flow of costs through a manufacturer's inventory accounts.

The flow of costs through the inventory accounts begins when costs for direct materials, direct labor, and overhead are incurred. Materials costs flow first into the Materials Inventory account, which is used to record the costs of materials when they are received and again when they are issued for use in a production process. All manufacturing-related costs—direct materials, direct labor, and overhead—are recorded in the Work in Process Inventory account as the production process begins. When products are completed, their costs are transferred from the Work in Process Inventory account to the Finished Goods Inventory account. Costs remain in the Finished Goods Inventory account until the products are sold, at which time they are transferred to the Cost of Goods Sold account.

LO5 Define *product unit cost* and compute the unit cost of a product or service.

Direct materials costs are the costs of materials used in making a product that can be conveniently and economically traced to specific product units. Direct labor costs include all labor costs needed to make a product or service that can be conveniently and economically traced to specific product units. All other production-related costs are classified and accounted for as overhead costs. Such costs cannot be conveniently or economically traced to end products or services, so a cost allocation method is used to assign them to products or services.

When a batch of products has been completed, the product unit cost is computed by dividing the total cost of direct materials, direct labor, and overhead by the total number of units produced. The product unit cost can be calculated using the actual, normal, or standard costing method. Under normal costing, the actual costs of direct materials and direct labor are combined with the estimated cost of overhead to determine the product unit cost. Under standard costing, the estimated costs of direct materials, direct labor, and overhead are used to calculate the product unit cost. The components of product cost may be classified as prime costs or conversion costs. Prime costs are the primary costs of production; they are the sum of direct materials costs and direct labor costs. Conversion costs are the costs of converting direct materials into finished product; they are the sum of direct labor costs and overhead costs.

Because no products are manufactured in the course of providing services, service organizations have no materials costs. They do, however, have both direct labor costs and overhead costs, which are similar to those in manufacturing organizations. To determine the cost of performing a service, professional labor and service-related overhead costs are included in the analysis.

LO6 Define *cost allocation* and explain how cost objects, cost pools, and cost drivers are used to assign overhead costs.

Cost allocation is the process of assigning collected indirect costs to a specific cost object using an allocation base known as a cost driver. The allocation of overhead costs requires the pooling of overhead costs that are affected by a common activity and the selection of a cost driver whose activity level causes a change in the cost pool. A cost pool is the collection of overhead costs assigned to a cost object. A cost driver is an activity base that causes the cost pool to increase in amount as the cost driver increases.

Allocating overhead is a four-step process that involves planning a rate at which overhead costs will be assigned to products or services, assigning overhead costs at this predetermined rate to products or services during production, recording actual overhead costs as they are incurred, and reconciling the difference between the actual and applied overhead costs. The Cost of Goods Sold or Cost of Sales account is corrected for an amount of over- or underapplied overhead costs assigned to the products or services. In manufacturing companies, if the difference is material, adjustments are made to the Work in Process Inventory, Finished Goods Inventory, and Cost of Goods Sold accounts.

LO7 Using the traditional method of allocating overhead costs, calculate product or service unit cost.

The traditional method applies overhead costs to a product or service by estimating one predetermined overhead rate and multiplying that rate by the actual cost driver level. The product or service unit cost is computed either by dividing the total product or service cost (the sum of the total applied overhead cost and the actual costs of direct materials and direct labor) by the total number of units produced or by determining the cost per unit for each element of the product's or service's cost and summing those per-unit costs.

LO8 Using activity-based costing to assign overhead costs, calculate product or service unit cost.

When ABC is used, overhead costs are grouped into a number of cost pools related to specific activities. For each activity pool, cost drivers are identified, and cost driver levels are estimated. Each activity cost rate is calculated by dividing the estimated activity pool amount by the estimated cost driver level. Overhead, which is divided into the activity pools, is applied to the product or service by multiplying the various activity cost rates by their actual cost driver levels. The product or service unit cost is computed by dividing the total product or service cost (the sum of the total applied cost pools and the actual costs of direct materials and direct labor) by the total number of units produced.

REVIEW of Concepts and Terminology

The following concepts and terms were introduced in this chapter:

Activity-based costing (ABC): A method of assigning overhead costs that categorizes all indirect costs by activity, traces the indirect costs to those activities, and assigns activity costs to products using a cost driver related to the cause of the cost. **(LO8)**

Actual costing: A method of cost measurement that uses the actual costs of direct materials, direct labor, and overhead to calculate a product or service unit cost. **(LO5)**

Conversion costs: The costs of converting direct materials into a finished product; the sum of direct labor costs and overhead costs. **(LO5)**

Cost allocation: The process of assigning a collection of indirect costs to a specific cost object using an allocation base known as a cost driver. **(LO6)**

Cost driver: An activity base that causes a cost pool to increase in amount as the cost driver increases in volume. **(LO6)**

Cost object: The destination of an assigned, or allocated, cost. **(LO6)**

Cost of goods manufactured: The cost of all units completed and moved to finished goods storage during an accounting period. **(LO4)**

Cost pool: The collection of overhead costs assigned to a cost object. **(LO6)**

Direct costs: Costs that can be conveniently and economically traced to a cost object. **(LO2)**

Direct labor costs: The costs of the labor needed to make a product or perform a service that can be conveniently and economically traced to specific units of the product or service. **(LO5)**

Direct materials costs: The costs of the materials used in making a product that can be conveniently and economically traced to specific units of the product. **(LO5)**

Finished Goods Inventory account: An inventory account that shows the costs assigned to all completed products that have not been sold. **(LO4)**

Fixed cost: A cost that remains constant within a defined range of activity or time period. **(LO2)**

Indirect costs: Costs that cannot be conveniently or economically traced to a cost object. **(LO2)**

Indirect labor costs: The costs of labor for production-related activities that cannot be conveniently or economically traced to a unit of the product or service. **(LO5)**

Indirect materials costs: The costs of materials that cannot be conveniently and economically traced to a unit of the product or service. **(LO5)**

Manufacturing cost flow: The flow of manufacturing costs (direct materials, direct labor, and overhead) through the Materials Inventory, Work in Process Inventory, and Finished Goods Inventory accounts into the Cost of Goods Sold account. **(LO4)**

Materials Inventory account: An inventory account that shows the balance of the cost of unused materials. **(LO4)**

Nonvalue-adding cost: The cost of an activity that adds cost to a product or service but does not increase its market value. **(LO2)**

Normal costing: A method of cost measurement that combines the actual direct costs of materials and labor with estimated overhead costs to determine a product or service unit cost. **(LO5)**

Overapplied overhead costs: The amount by which overhead costs applied using the predetermined overhead rate exceed the actual overhead costs for the accounting period. **(LO6)**

Overhead costs: Production-related costs that cannot be practically or conveniently traced to an end product or service. Also called *factory overhead, factory burden, manufacturing overhead, service overhead,* or *indirect manufacturing costs.* **(LO5)**

Period costs: The costs of resources used during an accounting period that are not assigned to products or services. Also called *noninventoriable costs* or *selling, administrative, and general expenses.* **(LO2)**

Predetermined overhead rate: The rate calculated before an accounting period begins by dividing the cost pool of total estimated overhead costs by the total estimated cost driver for that pool. **(LO6)**

Prime costs: The primary costs of production; the sum of direct materials costs and direct labor costs. **(LO5)**

Product costs: The costs assigned to inventory, which include the costs of direct materials, direct labor, and overhead. Also called *inventoriable costs.* **(LO2)**

Product unit cost: The cost of manufacturing a single unit of a product, computed either by dividing the total cost of direct materials, direct labor, and overhead by the total number of units produced, or by determining the cost per unit for each element of the product cost and summing those per-unit costs. **(LO5)**

Standard costing: A method of cost measurement that uses the estimated costs of direct materials, direct labor, and overhead to calculate a product unit cost. **(LO5)**

Statement of cost of goods manufactured: A formal statement summarizing the flow of all manufacturing costs incurred during an accounting period. **(LO3)**

Total manufacturing costs: The total costs of direct materials, direct labor, and overhead incurred and transferred to Work in Process Inventory during an accounting period. Also called *current manufacturing costs.* **(LO4)**

Underapplied overhead costs: The amount by which actual overhead costs exceed the overhead costs

applied using the predetermined overhead rate for the accounting period. **(LO6)**

Value-adding cost: The cost of an activity that increases the market value of a product or service. **(LO2)**

Variable cost: A cost that changes in direct proportion to a change in productive output (or some other measure of volume). **(LO2)**

Work in Process Inventory account: An inventory account used to record the manufacturing costs incurred and assigned to partially completed units of product. **(LO4)**

REVIEW Problem

LO3, LO4, LO5　**Calculating Cost of Goods Manufactured: Three Fundamental Steps**

Sample Company requires its controller to prepare not only a year-end balance sheet and income statement, but also a statement of cost of goods manufactured. During the year, the company purchased $361,920 of direct materials. The company's direct labor costs for the year were $99,085 (10,430 hours at $9.50 per hour); its indirect labor costs totaled $126,750 (20,280 hours at $6.25 per hour). Account balances for the year were as follows:

Account	Balance
Plant Supervision	$ 42,500
Factory Insurance	8,100
Utilities, Factory	29,220
Depreciation–Factory Building	46,200
Depreciation–Factory Equipment	62,800
Factory Security	9,460
Factory Repair and Maintenance	14,980
Selling and Administrative Expenses	76,480
Materials Inventory, beginning	26,490
Work in Process Inventory, beginning	101,640
Finished Goods Inventory, beginning	148,290
Materials Inventory, ending	24,910
Work in Process Inventory, ending	100,400
Finished Goods Inventory, ending	141,100

Required

1. Compute the cost of materials used during the year.
2. Given the cost of materials used, compute the total manufacturing costs for the year.
3. Given the total manufacturing costs for the year, compute the cost of goods manufactured during the year.
4. If 13,397 units were manufactured during the year, what was the actual product unit cost? (Round your answer to two decimal places.)

Answer to Review Problem

1. Cost of materials used:

Materials inventory, beginning	$ 26,490
Direct materials purchased	361,920
Cost of materials available for use	$388,410
Less materials inventory, ending	24,910
Cost of materials used	$363,500

2. Total manufacturing costs:

Cost of materials used		$363,500
Direct labor costs		99,085
Overhead costs		
Indirect labor	$126,750	
Plant supervision	42,500	
Factory insurance	8,100	
Utilities, factory	29,220	
Depreciation, factory building	46,200	
Depreciation, factory equipment	62,800	
Factory security	9,460	
Factory repair and maintenance	14,980	
Total overhead costs		340,010
Total manufacturing costs		$802,595

3. Cost of goods manufactured:

Total manufacturing costs	$802,595
Add work in process inventory, beginning	101,640
Total cost of work in process during the year	$904,235
Less work in process inventory, ending	100,400
Cost of goods manufactured	$803,835

4. Actual product unit cost:

$$\frac{\text{Cost of Goods Manufactured}}{\text{Number of Units Manufactured}} = \frac{\$803,835}{13,397} = \$60.00^*$$

*Rounded.

CHAPTER ASSIGNMENTS

BUILDING Your Basic Knowledge and Skills

Short Exercises

LO2 **Cost Classifications**

SE 1. Indicate whether each of the following is a direct cost (D), an indirect cost (ID), or neither (N) and a variable (V) or a fixed (F) cost. Also indicate whether each adds value (VA) or does not add value (NVA) to the product and whether each is a product cost (PD) or a period cost (PER).

1. Production supervisor's salary
2. Sales commission
3. Wages of a production-line worker

LO3   Income Statement for a Manufacturing Organization

SE 2. Using the following information from Hakim Company, prepare an income statement through operating income for the year:

Sales	$900,000
Finished goods inventory, beginning	45,000
Cost of goods manufactured	585,000
Finished goods inventory, ending	60,000
Operating expenses	275,000

LO4   Cost Flow in a Manufacturing Organization

SE 3. Given the following information, compute the ending balances of the Materials Inventory, Work in Process Inventory, and Finished Goods Inventory accounts:

Materials Inventory, beginning balance	$ 23,000
Work in Process Inventory, beginning balance	25,750
Finished Goods Inventory, beginning balance	38,000
Direct materials purchased	85,000
Direct materials placed into production	74,000
Direct labor costs	97,000
Overhead costs	35,000
Cost of goods manufactured	123,000
Cost of goods sold	93,375

LO4   Document Flows in a Manufacturing Organization

SE 4. Identify the document needed to support each of the following activities in a manufacturing organization:

1. Placing an order for direct materials with a supplier
2. Recording direct labor time at the beginning and end of each work shift
3. Receiving direct materials at the shipping dock
4. Recording the costs of a specific job requiring direct materials, direct labor, and overhead
5. Issuing direct materials into production
6. Billing the customer for a completed order
7. Fulfilling a request from the Production Scheduling Department for the purchase of direct materials

LO5   Elements of Manufacturing Costs

SE 5. Daisy Luna, the bookkeeper at Candlelight, Inc., must group the costs of manufacturing candles. Indicate whether each of the following items should be classified as direct materials (DM), direct labor (DL), overhead (O), or none of these (N). Also indicate whether each is a prime cost (PC), a conversion cost (CC), or neither (N).

1. Depreciation of the cost of vats to hold melted wax
2. Cost of wax
3. Rent on the factory where candles are made
4. Cost of George's time to dip the wicks into the wax
5. Cost of coloring for candles
6. Cost of Ray's time to design candles for Halloween
7. Sam's commission to sell candles to Candles Plus

LO5   Computation of Product Unit Cost

SE 6. What is the product unit cost for Job 14, which consists of 300 units and has total manufacturing costs of direct materials, $4,500; direct labor,

$7,500; and overhead, $3,600? What are the prime costs and conversion costs per unit?

LO6 Calculation of Underapplied or Overapplied Overhead

SE 7. At year end, records show that actual overhead costs incurred were $25,870 and the amount of overhead costs applied to production was $27,000. Identify the amount of under- or overapplied overhead, and indicate whether the Cost of Goods Sold account should be increased or decreased to reflect actual overhead costs.

LO6, LO7 Computation of Overhead Rate

SE 8. Compute the overhead rate per service request for the Maintenance Department if estimated overhead costs are $18,290 and the number of estimated service requests is 3,100.

LO6, LO7 Allocation of Overhead to Production

SE 9. Calculate the amount of overhead costs applied to production if the predetermined overhead rate is $4 per direct labor hour and 1,200 direct labor hours were worked.

LO8 Activity-Based Costing and Cost Drivers

SE 10. Mazzola Clothiers Company relies on the information from its activity-based costing system when setting prices for its products. Compute ABC rates from the following estimated data for each of the activity centers:

Estimated Activity	Pool Amount	Cost Driver Level
Cutting/Stitching	$5,220,000	145,000 machine hours
Trimming/Packing	998,400	41,600 operator hours
Designing	1,187,500	62,500 designer hours

Exercises

LO1 The Management Process and Operating Costs

E 1. Indicate whether each of the following activities takes place during the planning (PL), performing (PE), evaluating (E), or communicating (C) stage of the management process:

1. Changing regular price to clearance price
2. Reporting results to appropriate personnel
3. Preparing budgets of operating costs
4. Comparing estimated and actual costs to determine variances

LO2 Cost Classifications

E 2. Indicate whether each of the following costs for a bicycle manufacturer is a product or a period cost, a variable or a fixed cost, a value-adding or a nonvalue-adding cost, and, if it is a product cost, a direct or an indirect cost of the bicycle:

	Cost Classification			
Example	Product or Period	Variable or Fixed	Value-adding or Nonvalue-adding	Direct or Indirect
Bicycle tire	Product	Variable	Value-adding	Direct

1. Depreciation on office computer
2. Labor to assemble bicycle
3. Labor to inspect bicycle
4. Internal auditor's salary
5. Lubricant for wheels

LO3 **Comparison of Income Statement Formats**

E 3. Indicate whether each of these equations applies to a service organization (SER), a retail organization (RET), or a manufacturing organization (MANF):

1. Cost of Goods Sold = Beginning Merchandise Inventory + Net Cost of Purchases − Ending Merchandise Inventory
2. Cost of Sales = Net Cost of Services Sold
3. Cost of Goods Sold = Beginning Finished Goods Inventory + Cost of Goods Manufactured − Ending Finished Goods Inventory

LO3 **Statement of Cost of Goods Manufactured**

E 4. During August, Rao Company's purchases of direct materials totaled $139,000; direct labor for the month was 3,400 hours at $8.75 per hour. Rao also incurred the following overhead costs: utilities, $5,870; supervision, $16,600; indirect materials, $6,750; depreciation, $6,200; insurance, $1,830; and miscellaneous, $1,100.

Beginning inventory accounts were as follows: Materials Inventory, $48,600; Work in Process Inventory, $54,250; and Finished Goods Inventory, $38,500. Ending inventory accounts were as follows: Materials Inventory, $50,100; Work in Process Inventory, $48,400; and Finished Goods Inventory, $37,450.

From the information given, prepare a statement of cost of goods manufactured.

LO3 **Statement of Cost of Goods Manufactured and Cost of Goods Sold**

E 5. Treetec Corp. makes irrigation sprinkler systems for tree nurseries. Rama Shih, Treetec's new controller, can find only the following partial information for the past year:

	Oak Division	Loblolly Division	Maple Division	Spruce Division
Direct materials used	$3	$ 7	$ g	$ 8
Total manufacturing costs	6	d	h	14
Overhead	1	3	2	j
Direct labor	a	6	4	4
Ending work in process inventory	b	3	2	5
Cost of goods manufactured	7	20	12	l
Beginning work in process inventory	2	e	3	k
Ending finished goods inventory	2	6	i	9
Beginning finished goods inventory	3	f	5	7
Cost of goods sold	c	18	13	9

Using the information given, compute the unknown values. List the accounts in the proper order, and show subtotals and totals as appropriate.

LO3 **Characteristics of Organizations**

E 6. Indicate whether each of the following is typical of a service organization (SER), a retail organization (RET), or a manufacturing organization (MANF):

1. Maintains only one balance sheet inventory account
2. Maintains no balance sheet inventory accounts
3. Maintains three balance sheet inventory accounts
4. Purchases products ready for resale
5. Designs and makes products for sale
6. Sells services
7. Determines the net cost of services sold

8. Includes the cost of goods manufactured in calculating cost of goods sold
9. Includes the cost of purchases in calculating cost of goods sold

LO3 **Missing Amounts—Manufacturing**

E 7. Presented below are incomplete inventory and income statement data for Trevor Corporation. Determine the missing amounts.

	Cost of Goods Sold	Cost of Goods Manufactured	Beginning Finished Goods Inventory	Ending Finished Goods Inventory
1.	$ 10,000	$12,000	$ 1,000	?
2.	$140,000	?	$45,000	$60,000
3.	?	$89,000	$23,000	$20,000

LO3 **Inventories, Cost of Goods Sold, and Net Income**

E 8. The data presented below are for a retail organization and a manufacturing organization.

1. Fill in the missing data for the retail organization:

	First Quarter	Second Quarter	Third Quarter	Fourth Quarter
Sales	$9	$e	$15	$k
Gross margin	a	4	5	l
Ending merchandise inventory	5	f	5	m
Beginning merchandise inventory	4	g	h	5
Net cost of purchases	b	7	9	n
Operating income	3	2	i	2
Operating expenses	c	2	2	4
Cost of goods sold	5	6	j	11
Cost of goods available for sale	d	12	15	15

2. Fill in the missing data for the manufacturing organization:

	First Quarter	Second Quarter	Third Quarter	Fourth Quarter
Ending finished goods inventory	$a	$3	$h	$6
Cost of goods sold	6	3	5	l
Operating income	1	3	1	m
Cost of finished goods available for sale	8	d	10	13
Cost of goods manufactured	5	e	i	8
Gross margin	4	f	j	7
Operating expenses	3	g	5	6
Beginning finished goods inventory	b	2	3	n
Sales	c	10	k	14

LO4 **Documentation**

E 9. Lisette Company manufactures music boxes. Seventy percent of its products are standard items produced in long production runs. The other 30 percent are special orders with specific requests for tunes. The latter cost from three to six times as much as the standard product because they require additional materials and labor.

Reza Seca, the controller, recently received a complaint memorandum from Iggy Paulo, the production supervisor, about the new network of source documents that has been added to the existing cost accounting system. The new documents include a purchase request, a purchase order, a receiving report, and a materials request. Paulo claims that the forms create extra work and interrupt the normal flow of production.

Prepare a written memorandum from Reza Seca to Iggy Paulo that fully explains the purpose of each type of document.

LO4   Cost Flows and Inventory Accounts

E 10. For each of the following activities, identify the inventory account (Materials Inventory, Work in Process Inventory, or Finished Goods Inventory), if any, that is affected. If an inventory account is affected, indicate whether the account balance will increase or decrease. (*Example*: Moved completed units to finished goods inventory. *Answer*: Increase Finished Goods Inventory; decrease Work in Process Inventory.) If no inventory account is affected, use "None of these" as your answer.

1. Moved materials requested by production
2. Sold units of product
3. Purchased and received direct materials for production
4. Used direct labor and overhead in the production process
5. Received payment from customer
6. Purchased office supplies and paid cash
7. Paid monthly office rent

LO5   Unit Cost Determination

E 11. The Pattia Winery is one of the finest wineries in the country. One of its famous products is a red wine called Old Vines. Recently, management has become concerned about the increasing cost of making Old Vines and needs to determine if the current selling price of $10 per bottle is adequate. The winery wants to achieve a 25 percent gross profit on the sale of each bottle. The following information is given to you for analysis:

Batch size	10,550 bottles
Costs	
Direct materials	
Olen Millot grapes	$22,155
Chancellor grapes	9,495
Bottles	5,275
Total direct materials costs	$36,925
Direct labor	
Pickers/loaders	$ 2,110
Crusher	422
Processors	8,440
Bottler	13,293
Total direct labor costs	$24,265
Overhead	
Depreciation, equipment	$2,743
Depreciation, building	5,275
Utilities	1,055
Indirect labor	6,330
Supervision	7,385
Supplies	9,917
Repairs	1,477
Miscellaneous	633
Total overhead costs	$34,815
Total production costs	$96,005

1. Compute the unit cost per bottle for materials, labor, and overhead.
2. How would you advise management regarding the price per bottle of wine?
3. Compute the prime costs per unit and the conversion costs per unit.

LO5 **Unit Costs in a Service Business**

E 12. Walden Green provides custom farming services to owners of five-acre wheat fields. In July, he earned $2,400 by cutting, turning, and baling 3,000 bales. In the same month, he incurred the following costs: gas, $150; tractor maintenance, $115; and labor, $600. His annual tractor depreciation is $1,500. What was Green's cost per bale? What was his revenue per bale? Should he increase the amount he charges for his services?

LO6, LO7 **Computation of Overhead Rate**

E 13. The overhead costs that Lucca Industries, Inc., used to compute its overhead rate for the past year are as follows:

Indirect materials and supplies	$ 79,200
Repairs and maintenance	14,900
Outside service contracts	17,300
Indirect labor	79,100
Factory supervision	42,900
Depreciation, machinery	85,000
Factory insurance	8,200
Property taxes	6,500
Heat, light, and power	7,700
Miscellaneous overhead	5,760
Total overhead costs	$346,560

The allocation base for the past year was 45,600 total machine hours. For the next year, all overhead costs except depreciation, property taxes, and miscellaneous overhead are expected to increase by 10 percent. Depreciation should increase by 12 percent, and property taxes and miscellaneous overhead are expected to increase by 20 percent. Plant capacity in terms of machine hours used will increase by 4,400 hours.

1. Compute the past year's overhead rate. (Carry your answer to three decimal places.)
2. Compute the overhead rate for next year. (Carry your answer to three decimal places.)

LO6, LO7 **Computation and Application of Overhead Rate**

E 14. Compumatics specializes in the analysis and reporting of complex inventory costing projects. Materials costs are minimal, consisting entirely of operating supplies (DVDs, inventory sheets, and other recording tools). Labor is the highest single expense, totaling $693,000 for 75,000 hours of work in 20x8. Overhead costs for 20x8 were $916,000 and were applied to specific jobs on the basis of labor hours worked. In 20x9, the company anticipates a 25 percent increase in overhead costs. Labor costs will increase by $130,000, and the number of hours worked is expected to increase by 20 percent.

1. Determine the total amount of overhead anticipated in 20x9.
2. Compute the overhead rate for 20x9. (Round your answer to the nearest cent.)

3. During April 20x9, 11,980 labor hours were worked. Calculate the overhead amount assigned to April production.

LO6, LO7   **Disposition of Overapplied Overhead**

E 15. At the end of 20x9, Compumatics had compiled a total of 89,920 labor hours worked. The actual overhead incurred was $1,143,400.

1. Using the overhead rate computed in **E 14**, determine the total amount of overhead applied to operations during 20x9.
2. Compute the amount of overapplied overhead for the year.
3. Will the Cost of Goods Sold account be increased or decreased to correct the over-application of overhead?

LO7, LO8   **Activities and Activity-Based Costing**

E 16. Zone Enterprises produces wireless components used in telecommunications equipment. One of the most important features of the company's new just-in-time production process is quality control. Initially, a traditional allocation method was used to assign the costs of quality control to products; all these costs were included in the plant's overhead cost pool and allocated to products based on direct labor dollars. Recently, the firm has implemented an activity-based costing system. The activities, cost drivers, and rates for the quality control function are summarized below, along with cost allocation information from the traditional method. Also shown is information related to one order, Order HL14. Compute the quality control cost that would be assigned to the order under both the traditional method and the activity-based costing method.

Traditional costing method:
Quality control costs were assigned at a rate of 12 percent of direct labor dollars. Order HL14 was charged with $9,350 of direct labor costs.

Activity-based costing method:

Activity	Activity Cost Driver	Activity Usage for Cost Rate	Order HL14
Incoming materials inspection	Types of materials used	$17.50 per type of material used	17 types of materials
In-process inspection	Number of products	$.06 per product	2,400 products
Tool and gauge control	Number of processes per cell	$26.50 per process per cell	11 processes
Product certification	Per order	$94.00 per order	1 order

Problems

LO3   **Statement of Cost of Goods Manufactured**

P 1. Dillo Vineyards, a large winery in Texas, produces a full line of varietal wines. The company, whose fiscal year begins on November 1, has just completed a record-breaking year. Its inventory account balances on October 31 of this year were Materials Inventory, $1,803,800; Work in Process Inventory, $2,764,500; and Finished Goods Inventory, $1,883,200. At the beginning of the year, the inventory account balances were Materials Inventory, $2,156,200; Work in Process Inventory, $3,371,000; and Finished Goods Inventory, $1,596,400.

During the fiscal year, the company's purchases of direct materials totaled $6,750,000. Direct labor hours totaled 142,500, and the average labor rate was $8.20 per hour. The following overhead costs were incurred during the year: depreciation, plant and equipment, $685,600; indirect labor, $207,300; property tax, plant and equipment, $94,200; plant maintenance, $83,700; small tools, $42,400; utilities, $96,500; and employee benefits, $76,100.

Required

Prepare a statement of cost of goods manufactured for the fiscal year ended October 31.

LO3   A Manufacturing Organization's Balance Sheet

P 2. The following information is from the balance sheet of Mills Manufacturing Company:

	Debit	Credit
Cash	$ 34,000	
Accounts receivable	27,000	
Materials inventory, ending	31,000	
Work in process inventory, ending	47,900	
Finished goods inventory, ending	54,800	
Production supplies	5,700	
Small tools	9,330	
Land	160,000	
Factory building	575,000	
Accumulated depreciation, factory building		$ 199,000
Factory equipment	310,000	
Accumulated depreciation, factory equipment		137,000
Patents	33,500	
Accounts payable		26,900
Insurance premiums payable		6,700
Income taxes payable		41,500
Mortgage payable		343,000
Common stock		200,000
Retained earnings		334,130
	$1,288,230	$1,288,230

Required

1. Manufacturing organizations use asset accounts that are not needed by retail organizations.
   a. List the titles of the asset accounts that are specifically related to manufacturing organizations.
   b. List the titles of the asset, liability, and equity accounts that you would see on the balance sheets of both manufacturing and retail organizations.
2. Assuming that the following information reflects the results of operations for the year, calculate the (a) gross margin, (b) cost of goods sold, (c) cost of goods available for sale, and (d) cost of goods manufactured:

Operating income	$138,130
Operating expenses	53,670
Sales	500,000
Finished goods inventory, beginning	50,900

3. **Manager Insight:** Does Mills Manufacturing use the periodic or perpetual inventory system?

LO5 Computation of Unit Cost

P 3. Carola Industries, Inc., manufactures discs for several of the leading recording studios in the United States and Europe. Department 60 is responsible for the electronic circuitry within each disc. Department 61 applies the plastic-like surface to the discs and packages them for shipment. Carola recently produced 4,000 discs for the Milo Company. In fulfilling this order, the departments incurred the following costs:

| | Department | |
	60	61
Direct materials used	$29,440	$3,920
Direct labor	6,800	2,560
Overhead	7,360	4,800

1. Compute the unit cost for each department.
2. Compute the total unit cost for the Milo Company order.
3. **Manager Insight:** The selling price for this order was $14 per unit. Was the selling price adequate? List the assumptions and/or computations upon which you based your answer. What suggestions would you make to Carola Industries' management about the pricing of future orders?
4. Compute the prime costs and conversion costs per unit for each department.

LO6, LO7 Allocation of Overhead

P 4. Natural Cosmetics Company applies overhead costs on the basis of machine hours. The overhead rate is computed by analyzing data from the previous year to determine the percentage change in costs. Thus, the 20x9 overhead rate will be based on the percentage change multiplied by the 20x8 costs. The controller prepared the overhead rate analysis for 20x9 using the following information:

	20x7	20x8
Machine hours	47,800	57,360
Overhead costs		
Indirect labor	$ 18,100	$ 23,530
Employee benefits	22,000	28,600
Manufacturing supervision	16,800	18,480
Utilities	10,350	14,490
Factory insurance	6,500	7,800
Janitorial services	11,000	12,100
Depreciation, factory and machinery	17,750	21,300
Miscellaneous overhead	5,750	7,475
Total overhead	$108,250	$133,775

In 20x9, the cost of utilities is expected to increase by 40 percent over the previous year; the cost of indirect labor, employee benefits, and miscellaneous overhead is expected to increase by 30 percent over the previous year; the cost of insurance and depreciation is expected to increase by 20 percent over the previous year; and the cost of supervision and janitorial services is expected to increase by 10 percent over the previous year. Machine hours are expected to total 68,832.

Required

1. Compute the projected costs and the overhead rate for 20x9, using the information about expected cost increases. (Carry your answer to three decimal places.)

2. Jobs completed during 20x9 and the machine hours used were as follows:

Job No.	Machine Hours
2214	12,300
2215	14,200
2216	9,800
2217	13,600
2218	11,300
2219	8,100

Determine the amount of overhead to be applied to each job and to total production during 20x9. (Round answers to whole dollars.)

3. Actual overhead costs for 20x9 were $165,845. Was overhead underapplied or overapplied? By how much? Should the Cost of Goods Sold account be increased or decreased to reflect actual overhead costs?

LO8 Activities and Activity-Based Costing

P 5. Byte Computer Company, a manufacturing organization, has just completed an order that Grater, Ltd., placed for 80 computers. Byte recently shifted from a traditional system of allocating costs to an activity-based costing system. Simone Faure, Byte's controller, wants to know the impact that the ABC system had on the Grater order. Direct materials, purchased parts, and direct labor costs for the Grater order are as follows:

Cost of direct materials	$36,750.00	Direct labor hours	220
Cost of purchased parts	$21,300.00	Average direct labor pay rate	$15.25

Other operating costs are as follows:

Traditional costing data:
Overhead costs were applied at a single, plantwide overhead rate of 270 percent of direct labor dollars.

Activity-based costing data:

Activity	Cost Driver	Activity Cost Rate	Activity Usage for Grater Order
Electrical engineering design	Engineering hours	$19.50 per engineering hour	32 engineering hours
Setup	Number of setups	$29.40 per setup	11 setups
Parts production	Machine hours	$26.30 per machine hour	134 machine hours
Product testing	Product testing hours	$32.80 per product testing hour	52 product testing hours
Packaging	Packaging hours	$17.50 per packaging hour	22 packaging hours
Building occupancy	Machine hours	$9.80 per machine hour	134 machine hours

Required

1. Using the traditional costing method, compute the total cost of the Grater order.
2. Using the activity-based costing method, compute the total cost of the Grater order.
3. **Manager Insight:** What difference in the amount of cost assigned to the Grater order resulted from the shift to activity-based costing? Was Byte's shift to activity-based costing a good management decision?

Alternate Problems

LO6, LO7 Allocation of Overhead

P 6. Lund Products, Inc., uses a predetermined overhead rate in its production, assembly, and testing departments. One rate is used for the entire company; it is based on machine hours. The rate is determined by analyzing data from the previous year to determine the percentage change in costs. Thus the 20x9 overhead rate will be based on the percentage change multiplied by the 20x8 costs. Lise Jensen is about to compute the rate for 20x9 using the following data:

	20x7	20x8
Machine hours	38,000	41,800
Overhead costs		
Indirect materials	$ 44,500	$ 57,850
Indirect labor	21,200	25,440
Supervision	37,800	41,580
Utilities	9,400	11,280
Labor-related costs	8,200	9,020
Depreciation, factory	9,800	10,780
Depreciation, machinery	22,700	27,240
Property taxes	2,400	2,880
Insurance	1,600	1,920
Miscellaneous overhead	4,400	4,840
Total overhead	$162,000	$192,830

In 20x9, the cost of indirect materials is expected to increase by 30 percent over the previous year. The cost of indirect labor, utilities, machinery depreciation, property taxes, and insurance is expected to increase by 20 percent over the previous year. All other expenses are expected to increase by 10 percent over the previous year. Machine hours for 20x9 are estimated at 45,980.

Required

1. Compute the projected costs and the overhead rate for 20x9 using the information about expected cost increases. (Round your answer to three decimal places.)
2. During 20x9, Lund Products completed the following jobs using the machine hours shown:

Job No.	Machine Hours	Job No.	Machine Hours
H–142	7,840	H–201	10,680
H–164	5,260	H–218	12,310
H–175	8,100	H–304	2,460

Determine the amount of overhead applied to each job. What was the total overhead applied during 20x9? (Round answers to the nearest dollar.)
3. Actual overhead costs for 20x9 were $234,485. Was overhead underapplied or overapplied in 20x9? By how much? Should the Cost of Goods Sold account be increased or decreased to reflect actual overhead costs?
4. At what point during 20x9 was the overhead rate computed? When was it applied? Finally, when was underapplied or overapplied overhead determined and the Cost of Goods Sold account adjusted to reflect actual costs?

LO8 Activities and Activity-Based Costing

P 7. Fraser Products, Inc., which produces copy machines for wholesale distributors in the Pacific Northwest, has just completed packaging an order from Kent Company for 150 Model 14 machines. Fraser recently switched from a traditional system of allocating costs to an activity-based costing system. Before the Kent order is shipped, the controller wants a unit cost analysis comparing the amounts computed under the traditional costing system with those computed under the ABC system. Direct materials, purchased parts, and direct labor costs for the Kent order are as follows:

Cost of direct materials	$17,450.00
Cost of purchased parts	$14,800.00
Direct labor hours	140
Average direct labor pay rate	$16.50

Other operating costs are as follows:

Traditional costing data:
Overhead costs were applied at a single, plantwide overhead rate of 240 percent of direct labor dollars.

Activity-based costing data:

Activity	Cost Driver	Activity Cost Rate	Activity Usage for Kent Order
Engineering systems design	Engineering hours	$28.00 per engineering hour	18 engineering hours
Setup	Number of setups	$42.00 per setup	8 setups
Parts production	Machine hours	$37.50 per machine hour	84 machine hours
Assembly	Assembly hours	$44.00 per assembly hour	36 assembly hours
Packaging	Packaging hours	$28.50 per packaging hour	28 packaging hours
Building occupancy	Machine hours	$10.40 per machine hour	84 machine hours

Required

1. Using the traditional costing approach, compute the total cost of the Kent order.
2. Using the activity-based costing approach, compute the total cost of the Kent order.
3. **Manager Insight:** What difference in the amount of cost assigned to the Kent order resulted from the shift to activity-based costing? Does the use of activity-based costing guarantee cost reduction for every product?

LO6, LO7, LO8 **Allocation of Overhead: Traditional and Activity-Based Costing Methods**

P 8. Sea Scout, Inc., manufactures two types of underwater vehicles. Oil companies use the vehicle called Rigger II to examine offshore oil rigs, and marine biology research foundations use the BioScout to study coastlines. The company's San Diego factory is not fully automated and requires some direct labor. Using estimated overhead costs of $220,000 and an estimated 16,000 hours of direct labor, Oz Parson, the company's controller, calculated a traditional overhead rate of $13.75 per direct labor hour. He used normal costing to calculate the product unit cost for both product lines, as shown in the following summary:

	Rigger II	BioScout
Product costs per unit		
Direct materials	$10,000.00	$12,000.00
Direct labor	1,450.00	1,600.00
Applied overhead	412.50*	550.00†
Product unit cost	$11,862.50	$14,150.00
Units of production	400	100
Direct labor hours	12,000	4,000

*$13.75 per Direct Labor Hour × 30 Direct Labor Hours per Unit = $412.50
†$13.75 per Direct Labor Hour × 40 Direct Labor Hours per Unit = $550

Parson believes that the product unit cost for the BioScout is too low. After carefully observing the production process, he has concluded that the BioScout requires much more attention than the Rigger II. Because of the BioScout's more intricate design, it requires more production activities, and fewer subassemblies can be produced by suppliers. He has therefore created four overhead activity pools, estimated the overhead costs of the activity pools, selected a cost driver for each pool, and estimated the cost driver levels for each product line, as shown in the following summary:

Activity Pool	Estimated Overhead Cost
Setup	$ 70,000
Inspection	20,000
Engineering	50,000
Assembly	80,0000
Total	$220,000

Cost Driver	Rigger II Driver Level	BioScout Driver Level	Total Driver Level
Number of setups	250	450	700
Number of inspections	150	350	500
Engineering hours	600	1,400	2,000
Machine hours	5,000	5,000	10,000

Required

1. Use activity-based costing to do the following:
   a. Calculate the activity cost rate for each activity pool.
   b. Compute the overhead costs applied to each product line by activity pool and in total.
   c. Calculate the product unit cost for each product line.
2. **Manager Insight:** What differences in the costs assigned to the two product lines resulted from the shift to activity-based costing?

ENHANCING Your Knowledge, Skills, and Critical Thinking

Conceptual Understanding Cases

LO1, LO2 **Comparison of Costs in Different Types of Businesses**

C 1. **H & R Block** is a service company that prepares tax returns; **Borders** is a retail company that sells books and CDs; **Indian Motorcycle Corporation** is a manufacturing company that makes motorcycles. Show that you understand how these companies differ by giving for each one an example of a direct and an indirect cost, a variable and a fixed cost, a value-adding and a nonvalue-adding cost, and a product and a period cost. Discuss the use of cost classifications in these three types of organizations.

LO6, LO7, LO8 **Comparison of Approaches to Developing Overhead Rates**

C 2. Both Matos Company and Stubee Corporation use predetermined overhead rates for product costing, inventory valuation, and sales quotations. The two businesses are about the same size, and they compete in the corrugated box industry. Because the overhead rate is an estimated measure, Matos Company's management believes that the controller's department should spend little effort in developing it. The company computes the rate annually based on an analysis of the previous year's costs. No one monitors its accuracy during the year. Stubee Corporation takes a different approach. One person in the controller's office is responsible for developing overhead rates on a monthly basis. All cost estimates are checked carefully to make sure they are realistic. Accuracy checks are done routinely at the end of each month, and forecasts of changes in business activity are taken into account.

Assume that Cooke Corporation, an East Coast manufacturer of corrugated boxes, has hired you as a consultant. Asimina Hiona, Cooke's controller, wants you to recommend the best method of developing overhead rates. Based on your knowledge of Matos's and Stubee's practices, write a memo to Hiona that answers the following questions:

1. What are the advantages and disadvantages of Matos's and Stubee's approaches to developing overhead rates?
2. Which company has taken the more cost-effective approach to developing overhead rates? Defend your answer.
3. Is an accurate overhead rate most important for product costing, inventory valuation, or sales quotations? Why?
4. What is activity-based costing (ABC)? Would it be better than the two approaches discussed above? Explain.

LO5   **Unit Costs in a Service Business**

C3. Municipal Hospital relies heavily on cost data to keep its pricing structures in line with those of its competitors. The hospital provides a wide range of services, including intensive care, intermediate care, and a neonatal nursery. Joo Young, the hospital's controller, is concerned about the profits generated by the 30-bed intensive care unit (ICU), so she is reviewing current billing procedures for that unit. The focus of her analysis is the hospital's billing per ICU patient day. This billing equals the per diem cost of intensive care plus a 40 percent markup to cover other operating costs and generate a profit. ICU patient costs include the following:

Doctors' care	2 hours per day @ $360 per hour (actual)
Special nursing care	4 hours per day @ $85 per hour (actual)
Regular nursing care	24 hours per day @ $28 per hour (average)
Medications	$237 per day (average)
Medical supplies	$134 per day (average)
Room rental	$350 per day (average)
Food and services	$140 per day (average)

One other significant ICU cost is equipment, which is about $185,000 per room. Young has determined that the cost per patient day for the equipment is $179.

Wiley Dix, the hospital director, has asked Young to compare the current billing procedure with another that uses industry averages to determine the billing per patient day.

1. Compute the cost per patient per day.
2. Compute the billing per patient day using the hospital's existing markup rate. (Round answers to whole dollars.)
3. Industry averages for markup rates are as follows:

Equipment	30%	Medications	50%
Doctors' care	50	Medical supplies	50
Special nursing care	40	Room rental	30
Regular nursing care	50	Food and services	25

Using these rates, compute the billing per patient day. (Round answers to the nearest whole dollars.)
4. Based on your findings in **2** and **3**, which billing procedure would you recommend? Why? Be prepared to discuss your response.

Interpreting Management Reports

LO3 **Financial Performance Measures**

C 4. Tarbox Manufacturing Company makes sheet metal products for heating and air conditioning installations. For the past several years, the company's income has been declining. Its statements of cost of goods manufactured and income statements for 20x9 and 20x8 follow. You have been asked to comment on why the ratios for Tarbox's profitability have deteriorated.

1. In preparing your comments, compute the following ratios for each year:
   a. Ratios of cost of direct materials used to total manufacturing costs, direct labor to total manufacturing costs, and total overhead to total manufacturing costs. (Round to one decimal place.)
   b. Ratios of sales salaries and commission expense, advertising expense, other selling expenses, administrative expenses, and total selling and administrative expenses to sales. (Round to one decimal place.)

Tarbox Manufacturing Company
Statements of Cost of Goods Manufactured
For the Years Ended December 31, 20x9 and 20x8

	20x9		20x8	
Direct materials used				
Materials inventory, beginning	$ 91,240		$ 93,560	
Direct materials purchased (net)	987,640		959,940	
Cost of direct materials available for use	$1,078,80		$1,053,500	
Less materials inventory, ending	95,020		91,240	
Cost of direct materials used		$ 983,860		$ 962,260
Direct labor		571,410		579,720
Overhead				
Indirect labor	$ 182,660		$ 171,980	
Power	34,990		32,550	
Insurance	22,430		18,530	
Supervision	125,330		120,050	
Depreciation	75,730		72,720	
Other overhead costs	41,740		36,820	
Total overhead		482,880		452,110
Total manufacturing costs		$2,038,150		$1,994,090
Add work in process inventory, beginning		148,875		152,275
Total cost of work in process during the period		$2,187,025		$2,146,365
Less work in process inventory, ending		146,750		148,875
Cost of goods manufactured		$2,040,275		$1,997,490

Tarbox Manufacturing Company
Income Statements
For the Years Ended December 31, 20x9 and 20x8

	20x9		20x8	
Sales		$2,942,960		$3,096,220
Cost of goods sold				
Finished goods inventory, beginning	$ 142,640		$ 184,820	
Cost of goods manufactured	2,040,275		1,997,490	
Cost of finished goods available for sale	$2,182,915		$2,182,310	
Less finished goods inventory, ending	186,630		142,640	
Total cost of goods sold		1,996,285		2,039,670
Gross margin		$ 946,675		$1,056,550
Selling and administrative expenses				
Sales salaries and commission expense	$ 394,840		$ 329,480	
Advertising expense	116,110		194,290	
Other selling expenses	82,680		72,930	
Administrative expenses	242,600		195,530	
Total selling and administrative expenses		836,230		792,230
Income from operations		$ 110,445		$ 264,320
Other revenues and expenses				
Interest expense		54,160		56,815
Income before income taxes		$ 56,285		$ 207,505
Income taxes expense		19,137		87,586
Net income		$ 37,148		$ 119,919

    c. Ratios of gross margin to sales and net income to sales. (Round to one decimal place.)

2. From your evaluation of the ratios computed in **1**, state the probable causes of the decline in net income.

3. What other factors or ratios do you believe should be considered in determining the cause of the company's decreased income?

Decision Analysis Using Excel

LO6, LO7, LO8   **Allocation of Overhead: Traditional and Activity-Based Costing Methods**

C 5. Refer to **P 8** in this chapter. Assume that Oz Parson, the controller of Sea Scout, Inc., has received some additional information from the production manager, Parvin Hrinda. Hrinda reported that robotic equipment has been installed on the factory floor to increase productivity. As a result, direct labor hours per unit will decrease by 20 percent. Depreciation and other machine costs for the robots will increase total overhead from $220,000 to $320,000 for the year, which will increase the assembly activity cost pool from $80,000 to $180,000. The cost driver level for the assembly cost pool will change from 5,000 machine hours to 2,000 machine hours for the Rigger II and from 5,000 machine hours to 8,000 machine hours for the BioScout. The cost driver levels and cost pool amounts for setup, inspection, and engineering activities will remain the same.

1. Use the traditional method of applying overhead costs to
   a. Calculate the overhead rate.
   b. Compute the amount of the total overhead costs applied to each product line.
   c. Calculate the product unit cost for each product line.
2. Use the activity-based costing method to
   a. Calculate the overhead activity cost rate for each activity pool.
   b. Compute the overhead costs applied to each product line by activity pool and in total.
   c. Calculate the product unit cost for each product line.
3. Complete the following table and discuss the differences in the costs assigned to the two product lines resulting from the additional information in this assignment:

Product unit cost	Rigger II	BioScout
Traditional		
Activity-based costing		
Difference: decrease (increase)		

Ethical Dilemma Case

LO5 **Preventing Pollution and the Costs of Waste Disposal**

C 6. Lake Weir Power Plant provides power to a metropolitan area of 4 million people. Sundeep Guliani, the plant's controller, has just returned from a conference on the Environmental Protection Agency's regulations concerning pollution prevention. She is meeting with Alton Guy, the president of the company, to discuss the impact of the EPA's regulations on the plant.

"Alton, I'm really concerned. We haven't been monitoring the disposal of the radioactive material we send to the Willis Disposal Plant. If Willis is disposing of our waste material improperly, we could be sued," said Guliani. "We also haven't been recording the costs of the waste as part of our product cost. Ignoring those costs will have a negative impact on our decision about the next rate hike."

"Sundeep, don't worry. I don't think we need to concern ourselves with the waste we send to Willis. We pay the company to dispose of it. The company takes it off our hands, and it's their responsibility to manage its disposal. As for the cost of waste disposal, I think we would have a hard time justifying a rate increase based on a requirement to record the full cost of waste as a cost of producing power. Let's just forget about waste and its disposal as a component of our power cost. We can get our rate increase without mentioning waste disposal," replied Guy.

What responsibility for monitoring the waste disposal practices at the Willis Disposal Plant does Lake Weir Power Plant have? Should Guliani take Guy's advice to ignore waste disposal costs in calculating the cost of power? Be prepared to discuss your response.

Internet Case

Identification of a Manufacturing Company's Costs

C 7. **Gateway, Inc.,** and **Dell Computer Corporation** assemble computers and sell them over the telephone or the Internet. Access the website of either of these companies. Become familiar with the products of the company you have chosen. For one of these products, such as a desktop or laptop computer, give examples of a direct and an indirect cost, a variable and a fixed cost, a value-adding and a nonvalue-adding cost, and a product and a period cost. Also give examples of the three elements of product cost: direct materials, direct labor, and overhead.

Group Activity Case

Management Information Needs

C 8. The H&W Pharmaceuticals Corporation manufactures most of its three pharmaceutical products in Indonesia. Inventory balances for March and April are as follows:

	March 31	April 30
Materials Inventory	$258,400	$228,100
Work in Process Inventory	138,800	127,200
Finished Goods Inventory	111,700	114,100

During April, purchases of direct materials, which include natural materials, basic organic compounds, catalysts, and suspension agents, totaled $612,600. Direct labor costs were $160,000, and actual overhead costs were $303,500. Sales of the company's three products for April totaled $2,188,400. General and administrative expenses were $362,000.

1. Prepare a statement of cost of goods manufactured and an income statement through operating income for the month ended April 30.
2. Why is it that the total manufacturing costs do not equal the cost of goods manufactured?
3. What additional information would you need to determine the profitability of each of the three product lines?
4. Indicate whether each of the following is a product cost or a period cost:
   a. Import duties for suspension agent materials
   b. Shipping expenses to deliver manufactured products to the United States
   c. Rent for manufacturing facilities in Jakarta
   d. Salary of the American production-line manager working at the Indonesian manufacturing facilities
   e. Training costs for an Indonesian accountant

Your instructor will divide the class into groups to work through the case. One student from each group should present the group's finding to the class.

Business Communication Cases

Management Decision About a Supporting Service Function

C 9. As the manager of grounds maintenance for Latchey, a large insurance company in Missouri, you are responsible for maintaining the grounds surrounding the company's three buildings, the six entrances to the property, and the recreational facilities, which include a golf course, a soccer field, jogging and bike paths, and tennis, basketball, and volleyball courts. Maintenance includes gardening (watering, planting, mowing, trimming, removing debris, and so on) and land improvements (e.g., repairing or replacing damaged or worn concrete and gravel areas).

Early in January, you receive a memo from the president of Latchey requesting information about the cost of operating your department for the last 12 months. She has received a bid from Xeriscape Landscapes, Inc., to perform the gardening activities you now perform. You are to prepare a cost report that will help her decide whether to keep gardening activities within the company or to outsource the work.

1. Before preparing your report, answer the following questions:
    a. What kinds of information do you need about your department?
    b. Why is this information relevant?
    c. Where would you go to obtain this information (sources)?
    d. When would you want to obtain this information?
2. Draft a report showing only headings and line items that best communicate the costs of your department. How would you change your report if the president asked you to reduce the costs of operating your department?
3. One of your department's cost accounts is the Maintenance Expense–Garden Equipment account.
    a. Is this a direct or an indirect cost?
    b. Is it a product or a period cost?
    c. Is it a variable or a fixed cost?
    d. Does the activity add value to Latchey's provision of insurance services?
    e. Is it a budgeted or an actual cost in your report?

Cost Classifications

C 10. Visit a local fast-food restaurant. Observe all aspects of the operation and take notes on the entire process. Describe the procedures used to take, process, and fill an order and deliver the food to the customer. Based on your observations, make a list of the costs incurred by the restaurant. Then create a table similar to Table 1 in the text, in which you classify the costs you have identified by their traceability (direct or indirect), cost behavior (variable or fixed), value attribute (value-adding or nonvalue-adding), and implications for financial reporting (product or period costs). Bring your notes and your table to class and be prepared to discuss your findings.

CHAPTER 3

Costing Systems: Job Order Costing

A product costing system is expected to provide unit cost information, to supply cost data for management decisions, and to furnish ending values for the Materials, Work in Process, and Finished Goods Inventory accounts. The appropriateness of a product costing system depends on the nature of the production process. Because the manufacture of custom orders and the manufacture of large quantities of similar products involve different processes, they generally require different types of costing systems. The two basic types are the job order costing system and the process costing system. In this chapter, we describe job order costing, including how to prepare job order cost cards and how to compute product unit cost. We also describe how job order costing differs from process costing. We return to the topic of process costing in Chapter 4.

LEARNING OBJECTIVES

LO1 Discuss the role that information about costs plays in the management process, and explain why unit cost is important.

LO2 Distinguish between the two basic types of product costing systems, and identify the information that each provides.

LO3 Explain the cost flow in a manufacturer's job order costing system.

LO4 Prepare a job order cost card, and compute a job order's product unit cost.

LO5 Apply job order costing to a service organization.

LO6 Distinguish between job order costing and project costing.

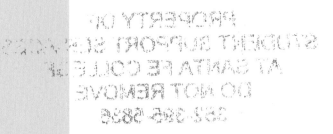

- Is the product costing system that is used for custom-made items appropriate for mass-produced items?

- What performance measures would be most useful in evaluating the results of each type of product?

However you like your ice cream, **Cold Stone Creamery** can create it for you. The personalized process begins on a frozen granite stone countertop with high-quality ice cream, which is freshly made every day, and your choice of mix-ins—chocolate, candy, nuts, fruit, and even homemade cake batter. Once the customer selects the mix-in, the server "spades" the ingredients together into one of three sizes—Like It, Love It, or Gotta Have It.

When the company was founded in Tempe, Arizona, in 1999, its management team set a tactical goal of opening 1,000 profitable stores by 2006. The team met its goal, and Cold Stone is now one of the fastest-growing privately owned companies.[1] So what is next for Cold Stone Creamery? The company has no immediate plans to create a product for sale in grocery stores or other retail establishments. But, as you will see in this chapter, if it did create such a product, it would need to adjust its product costing system, as well as its performance measures.

Product Cost Information and the Management Process

LO1 Discuss the role that information about costs plays in the management process, and explain why unit cost is important.

Managers depend on relevant and reliable information about costs to manage their organizations. Although they vary in their approaches to gathering, analyzing, and reporting information about costs, managers share the same basic concerns as they move through the management process. Figure I summarizes the management process and the concerns that managers address with relevant and timely information about costs.

Planning

When managers plan, they use information about costs to set performance expectations and estimate unit costs. In manufacturing companies, such as **Cold Stone Creamery**, **Toyota**, and **Levi Strauss & Co.**, managers use cost information to develop budgets, establish product prices, and plan production volumes. In service organizations, such as **Century 21**, **H&R Block**, and **Orkin Exterminating Company**, managers use cost information to develop budgets, establish prices, set sales goals, and determine human resource needs. During the planning process, having knowledge of unit costs helps managers of both manufacturing and service companies set reasonable selling prices and estimate the cost of their products or services.

Performing

Managers make decisions every day about controlling costs, managing the company's activity volume, ensuring quality, and negotiating prices. They use timely cost and volume information and actual unit costs to support their decisions. In manufacturing companies, managers use information about costs to decide whether to drop a product line, add a production shift, outsource the manufacture of a subassembly to another company, bid on a special order, or negotiate a selling price. In service organizations, managers use cost information to make decisions about bidding on jobs, dropping a current service, outsourcing a task to an independent contractor, adding staff, or negotiating a price.

All these day-to-day decisions can have far-reaching effects, including possible changes in unit cost or quality. When making such decisions, managers will want to consider whether they add value for all stakeholders and whether the decisions are ethical.

Evaluating

When managers evaluate results, they watch for changes in cost and quality. They compare actual and targeted total and unit costs and monitor relevant price and volume information. They analyze this information to evaluate their performance, and on the basis of this evaluation, they adjust their planning and decision-making strategies. For example, if a product's quality is suffering, managers may study the design, materials purchasing, and manufacturing processes to determine the source of the problem so that they can make changes that will assure the product's quality. If operating costs in a service

■ **FIGURE 1**
The Management Process: To-Do's for Managers

To-Do's for Managers

- Plan
  - Set performance expectations by developing budgets
  - Establish prices, plan sales and production volumes, and determine resource needs
  - Estimate unit costs of products or services

- Perform
  - Make decisions about controlling costs, managing the company's activity volume, ensuring quality, and negotiating contracts
  - Use timely cost, volume, and actual unit cost data

- Evaluate
  - Compare actual and targeted total and unit costs
  - Monitor relevant price and volume information
  - Analyze information to evaluate performance
  - Adjust plans and decision-making strategies

- Communicate
  - Prepare external reports, such as financial statements
  - Prepare internal performance evaluation reports comparing actual and targeted costs, analyzing nonfinancial measures of performance, and presenting data on whether goals for products or services are being achieved

business have risen too high, managers may break the unit cost of service down into its many components to analyze where costs can be cut or how the service can be performed more efficiently.

Communicating

When managers report to stakeholders, they prepare financial statements. In manufacturing companies, managers use product unit costs to determine inventory balances for the organization's balance sheet and the cost of goods sold for its income statement. In service organizations, managers use unit costs of services to determine cost of sales for the income statement. Managers also prepare performance evaluation reports for internal use. These reports compare actual unit costs with targeted costs, as well as actual and targeted nonfinancial measures of performance. Managers in both manufacturing and service organizations analyze the data in the performance evaluation reports to determine whether they are achieving cost goals for their organization's products or services.

Job Order Versus Process Costing

LO2 Distinguish between the two basic types of product costing systems, and identify the information that each provides.

For an organization to succeed, its managers must sell its products or services at prices that exceed the costs of creating and delivering them, thus ensuring a profit. To do so, managers need extensive information about such product-related costs as setup, production, and distribution. To meet managers' needs for cost information, it is necessary to have a highly reliable product costing system specifically designed to record and report the organization's operations.

A **product costing system** is a set of procedures used to account for an organization's product costs and to provide timely and accurate unit cost information for pricing, cost planning and control, inventory valuation, and financial statement preparation. The product costing system enables managers to track costs throughout the management process. It provides a structure for recording the revenue earned from sales and the costs incurred for direct materials, direct labor, and overhead.

Two basic types of product costing systems have been developed: job order costing systems and process costing systems. A **job order costing system** is used by companies that make unique or special-order products, such as personalized ice cream creations, specially built cabinets, made-to-order draperies, or custom-tailored suits. Such a system uses a single Work in Process Inventory account to record the costs of all job orders. It traces the costs of direct materials, direct labor, and overhead to a specific batch of products or a specific **job order** (i.e., a customer order for a specific number of specially designed, made-to-order products) by using a subsidiary ledger of job order cost cards. A **job order cost card** is the document on which all costs incurred in the production of a particular job order are recorded. The costs that a job order costing system gathers are used to measure the cost of each completed unit.

Companies that produce large amounts of similar products or liquid products or that have long, continuous production runs of identical products use a **process costing system**. Makers of paint, soft drinks, candy, bricks, paper, and gallon containers of ice cream would use such a system. A process costing sys-

Study Note

In job order costing, costs are traced to jobs; in process costing, costs are traced to production processes.

Businesses that make special order items, such as the kitchen cabinets shown here, use a job order costing system. With such a system, the costs of direct materials (e.g., the wood used in framing the cabinets), labor, and overhead (e.g., insurance and depreciation on tools and vehicles) are traced to a specific batch of products or a job order. All costs are tracked on a job order cost card.

 Study Note

The product cost arrived at by both job order and process costing systems is an average cost. Process costing usually averages cost over a greater volume of product.

tem first traces the costs of direct materials, direct labor, and overhead to processes, departments, or work cells and then assigns the costs to the products manufactured by those processes, departments, or work cells during a specific period. A process costing system uses several Work in Process Inventory accounts, one for each process, department, or work cell. Table 1 summarizes the characteristics of job order costing and process costing systems.

In reality, few production processes are a perfect match for either a job order costing system or a process costing system. The typical product costing system therefore combines parts of job order costing and process costing to create a hybrid system designed specifically for an organization's production process. For example, an automobile maker like **Toyota** or **General Motors** may use process costing to track the costs of manufacturing a standard car and

TABLE 1. Characteristics of Job Order Costing and Process Costing Systems

Job Order Costing System	Process Costing System
Traces manufacturing costs to a specific job order	Traces manufacturing costs to processes, departments, or work cells and then assigns the costs to products manufactured
Measures the cost of each completed unit	Measures costs in terms of units completed during a specific period
Uses a single Work in Process Inventory account to summarize the cost of all job orders	Uses several Work in Process Inventory accounts, one for each process, department, or work cell
Typically used by companies that make unique or special-order products, such as customized publications, built-in cabinets, or made-to-order draperies	Typically used by companies that make large amounts of similar products or liquid products or that have long, continuous production runs of identical products, such as makers of paint, soft drinks, candy, bricks, and paper

Why Does Toyota Use a Hybrid Product Costing System?

Thanks to its virtual production line, **Toyota** can now manufacture custom vehicles in five days. Computer software allows Toyota to calculate the exact number of parts needed at each precise point on its production line for a certain mix of cars. The mix can be modified up to five days in advance of actual production, allowing Toyota to modify a production run to include custom orders. When Toyota announced its hybrid approach, **General Motors** was taking 17 to 18 days to assemble a custom vehicle, and **DaimlerChrysler** needed an average of 10 to 12 days. Because most vehicles are mass-produced either in batches or on continuous flow assembly lines, manufacturers' process costing systems have not handled custom orders well. With its virtual production line and a hybrid product costing system, Toyota has gained a competitive advantage.[2]

job order costing to track the costs of customized features, such as a convertible top or a stick shift. Managers who know the terms and procedures related to both job order costing and process costing can help design product costing systems that fit their information needs in any operating environment.

In recent years, global competition, technology, and the shifting mix of materials, labor, and overhead in the manufacturing process have changed the way in which companies approach product costing. The use of multidisciplinary teams of managers has fostered the development of new management accounting practices that improve product costing. These new practices emphasize the elimination of waste, the importance of quality products and services, value-added processing, and increased customer satisfaction. We discuss some of the new practices, including the value chain, process value analysis, activity-based management, and the just-in-time operating environment, elsewhere in the text. In the rest of this chapter, we focus on the job order costing system.

S T O P • R E V I E W • A P P L Y

2-1. What is a product costing system?

2-2. What are the main similarities and differences between a job order costing system and a process costing system? (Focus on the characteristics of each type of system.)

2-3. What kind of product costing system do most companies use?

How Is the Value of a Thoroughbred Racehorse Tracked?

From the time a thoroughbred racehorse is conceived, job order costing is used to account for it. Financial performance measures, such as race winnings and the ratio of sales price to stud fee, and nonfinancial measures, such as lineage, food intake, and behavior in the pasture, are used to account for racehorses. Visit websites like www.juddmonte.com to view stallions, their race winnings, and their family trees; visit www.woodfordreservestables.com to learn more about the life and training of a racehorse; and visit www.ddfky.com to view equine business statistics.

Job Order Costing in a Manufacturing Company

LO3 Explain the cost flow in a manufacturer's job order costing system.

A job order costing system traces the costs of a specific order or batch of products to provide timely, accurate cost information and to facilitate the smooth and continuous flow of that information. Because such a system emphasizes cost flow, it is important to understand how costs are incurred, recorded, and transferred within the system. A basic part of a job order costing system is the set of procedures, documents, and accounts that a company uses when it incurs costs for materials, labor, and overhead. Job order cost cards and subsidiary ledgers for materials and finished goods inventories form the core of a job order costing system.

To study the cost flows in a job order costing system, let's look at how Joann Lytton, the owner of Augusta, Inc., operates her business. For the past few years, Lytton has been building both customized and general-purpose golf carts. The direct materials costs for a golf cart include the costs of a cart frame, wheels, upholstered seats, a windshield, a motor, and a rechargeable battery. Direct labor costs include the wages of the two production workers who assemble the golf carts. Overhead includes indirect materials costs for upholstery zippers, cloth straps to hold equipment in place, wheel lubricants, screws and fasteners, and silicon to attach the windshield. It also includes indirect labor costs for moving materials to the production area and inspecting a golf cart during its construction; depreciation on the manufacturing plant and equipment used to make the golf carts; and utilities, insurance, and property taxes related to the manufacturing plant. Exhibit 1 shows the flow of each of these costs.

Notice that all three inventory accounts have subsidiary ledgers backing up their totals. The beginning balance in the Materials Inventory account means that there are already direct and indirect materials in the materials storeroom. (The materials ledger contains cost information about individual materials.) The beginning balance in Work in Process Inventory means that Job CC is in production (with specifics given in the job order cost card). The zero beginning balance in Finished Goods Inventory means that all previously completed golf carts have been shipped.

Materials

When Augusta receives or expects to receive a sales order, the purchasing process begins with a request for specific quantities of direct and indirect materials that are needed for the order but are not currently available in the materials storeroom. When the new materials arrive at Augusta, the Accounting Department records the materials purchased by making an entry that debits or increases the balance of the Materials Inventory account and credits either the Cash or Accounts Payable account (depending on whether the purchase was for cash or credit):

Materials Inventory	XX	
Cash or Accounts Payable		XX

During the month, Augusta made two purchases on credit. In transaction **1**, the company purchased cart frames costing $572 and wheels costing $340 from

▼ EXHIBIT 1

The Job Order Costing System—Augusta, Inc.

MATERIALS INVENTORY

Beg. Bal.	1,230	Requests:	
(1) Purchases	912	Direct Materials	1,880 (3)
(2) Purchases	82	Indirect Materials	96 (3)
End. Bal.	248		

WORK IN PROCESS INVENTORY

Beg. Bal.	400		
(3) Direct			
Materials Used	1,880	Completed	3,880 (9)
(4) Direct Labor	1,640		
(8) Overhead	1,394		
End. Bal.	1,434		

FACTORY PAYROLL

Direct Labor	1,640 (4)
Indirect Labor	760 (5)

OVERHEAD

(3) Indirect		Applied	1,394 (8)
Materials Used	96		
(5) Indirect Labor	760		
(6) Other Indirect	295		
(7) Depreciation	240		
	1,391		1,394
(11) To close	3		
End. Bal.	—		

SUBSIDIARY LEDGERS

MATERIALS LEDGER

CART FRAMES

Beg. Bal.	830	Used	1,240 (3)
(1) Purchases	572		
End. Bal.	162		

WHEELS

Beg. Bal.	370	Used	640 (3)
(1) Purchases	340		
End. Bal.	70		

INDIRECT MATERIALS

Beg. Bal.	30	Used	96 (3)
(2) Purchases	82		
End. Bal.	16		

JOB ORDER COST CARDS

JOB CC

Costs from the Previous Period	400
Direct Materials	1,038
Direct Labor	1,320
Overhead	1,122
Completed Cost	3,880

JOB JB

Direct Materials	842
Direct Labor	320
Overhead	272
Ending Balance	1,434

one of its vendors. As shown in Exhibit 1, these purchases increase the debit balances in the Materials Inventory account and the corresponding accounts in the materials ledger. In transaction **2**, the company purchased indirect materials costing $82 from another vendor. This purchase also increases the debit balance in the Materials Inventory account as well as the balance in the Indirect Materials account in the materials ledger. Not shown in Exhibit 1 are the two credit entries to the Accounts Payable account.

FINISHED GOODS INVENTORY				COST OF GOODS SOLD			
Beg. Bal.	—			(10) Sold		Adjustment	3 (11)
(9) Completed		Sold	1,940 (10)	During			
During				Period	1,940		
Period	3,880			**End. Bal.**	**1,937**		
End. Bal.	**1,940**						

FINISHED GOODS LEDGER

JOB CC

Beg. Bal.	—	Sold	1,940 (10)
(9) Completed	3,880		
End. Bal.	**1,940**		

When golf carts are scheduled for production, requested materials are sent to the production area. To record the flow of direct materials requested from the Materials Inventory account into the Work in Process Inventory account, the entry is:

Work in Process Inventory	XX	
Materials Inventory		XX

To record the flow of indirect materials requested from the Materials Inventory account into the Overhead account, the entry is:

Overhead	XX	
Materials Inventory		XX

Transaction **3** shows the request for materials for the production of two jobs. Of the $1,880 of direct materials requested, the materials ledger shows that $1,240 was for cart frames and $640 was for wheels. Job CC, a batch run of two general-purpose golf carts already in production, required $1,038 of the additional direct materials. Job JB, a customized golf cart made to the specifications of an individual customer, required $842 of the direct materials. Notice that the $1,880 of direct materials requested appears as a debit in the Work in Process Inventory account because that account records the costs of partially completed units of product and as a credit in the Materials Inventory account. The cost of direct materials requested is also recorded on the corresponding job order cost cards. In addition, transaction **3** accounts for the $96 of indirect materials requested for production as a $96 debit to Overhead and a $96 credit to Materials Inventory. As you will see in our discussion of overhead, because the $96 was for indirect rather than direct materials, it flows into the Overhead account instead of to a Work in Process Inventory account for a specific job.

Labor

Every pay period, the payroll costs are recorded. In general, the payroll costs include salaries and wages for direct and indirect production labor as well as for nonproduction-related employees. As noted earlier, Augusta's two production employees assemble the golf carts. Several other employees support production by moving materials and inspecting the products. The following entry records the payroll:

Work in Process Inventory (direct labor costs)	XX	
Overhead (indirect labor costs)	XX	
Selling and Administrative Expenses	XX	
(non-production-related salary and wage costs)		
Factory Payroll		XX

Study Note

Parts of these transactions are not shown in Exhibit 1. Although complete debit and credit entries are necessary for an accurate balancing of the accounting records, some parts of the transactions do not deal directly with product costs. Exhibit 1 focuses only on the flow of product costs through the accounts.

Transactions **4** and **5** show the total production-related wages earned by these employees during the period. Job CC required direct labor of $1,320, and Job JB required direct labor of $320. The total direct labor cost of $1,640 ($1,320 + $320) is shown as a debit to the Work in Process Inventory account. The indirect labor cost of $760, shown in transaction **5**, flows to the Overhead account instead of to a particular job. The corresponding credit is to Augusta's Factory Payroll account.

Overhead

Thus far, indirect materials and indirect labor have been the only costs debited to the Overhead account. Other indirect production costs, such as utilities, property taxes, insurance, and depreciation, are also charged to the Overhead account as they are incurred during the period. In general, the entry appears as:

Overhead	XX	
Cash or Accounts Payable		XX
Accumulated Depreciation		XX

Transaction **6** shows that other indirect costs amounting to $295 were paid. Transaction **7** records the $240 of factory-related depreciation. The corresponding credits, not shown here, are to Augusta's Cash account for $295 and Accumulated Depreciation account for $240.

During the period, to recognize all product-related costs for a job, an overhead cost estimate is applied to a job using a predetermined rate. Based on its budget and past experience, Augusta currently uses a predetermined overhead rate of 85 percent of direct labor costs. The entry to apply overhead using a predetermined rate is:

Work in Process Inventory	XX	
Overhead		XX

In transaction **8**, total overhead of $1,394 is applied, with $1,122 going to Job CC (85 percent of $1,320) and $272 going to Job JB (85 percent of $320). Notice that the Work in Process Inventory account is debited for $1,394 (85 percent of $1,640; see transaction **4**), and the Overhead account is credited for the applied overhead of $1,394.

Completed Units

When a custom job or a batch of general-purpose golf carts is completed and ready for sale, the products are moved from the manufacturing area to the finished goods storeroom. To record the cost flow of completed products from the Work in Process Inventory account into the Finished Goods Inventory account, the entry is:

Finished Goods Inventory	XX	
Work in Process Inventory		XX

As shown in transaction **9**, when Job CC is completed and moved to the finished goods storeroom, its cost of $3,880 is transferred from the Work in Process Inventory account to the Finished Goods Inventory account by debiting Finished Goods Inventory for $3,880 and crediting Work in Process Inventory for $3,880. Its job order cost card is also completed and transferred to the finished goods file. Figure 2 shows the job order cost card for Job CC. Notice that the product unit cost for each of the two golf carts in the job is computed.

Sold Units

Study Note

In this example, the company uses a perpetual inventory system. In a periodic inventory system, the cost of goods sold is calculated at the end of the period.

When a company uses a perpetual inventory system, as Augusta does, two accounting entries are made when products are sold. One is prompted by the sales invoice and records the quantity and selling price of the products sold. The other entry, prompted by the delivery of products to a customer, records the quantity and cost of the products shipped. These two entries follow.

■ **FIGURE 2**
Job Order Cost Card for a Manufacturing Company

Job Order: _CC_

JOB ORDER COST CARD
Augusta, Inc.
Spring Hill, Florida

Customer: _Stock_   Batch: _X_   Custom: _____
Specifications: _Two general – purpose golf carts_
Date of Order: _2/26/xx_
Date of Completion: _3/6/xx_

Costs Charged to Job	Previous Months	Current Month	Cost Summary
Direct Materials	$165	$1,038	$1,203
Direct Labor	127	1,320	1,447
Overhead (85% of direct labor cost)	108	1,122	1,230
Totals	$400	$3,480	$3,880
Units Completed			2
Product Unit Cost			$1,940

Cash or Accounts Receivable (sales price × units sold)	XX	
Sales (sales price × units sold)		XX

Cost of Goods Sold (unit cost × units sold)	XX	
Finished Goods Inventory (unit cost × units sold)		XX

In transaction **10**, the $1,940 cost of the one general-purpose golf cart that was sold during the period is transferred from the Finished Goods Inventory account to the Cost of Goods Sold account. The sales entry for this golf cart is not shown in Exhibit 1. The Finished Goods Inventory account has an ending balance of $1,940 for the one remaining unsold cart.

Reconciliation of Overhead Costs

To prepare financial statements at the end of the accounting period, the Cost of Goods Sold account must reflect actual product costs, including actual overhead. Thus, the Overhead account must be reconciled every period. As you learned in a previous chapter, if at the end of the accounting period the actual overhead debit balance exceeds the applied overhead credit balance, then

Study Note

Why do financial statements require the reconciliation of overhead costs? Financial statements report actual cost information; therefore, estimated overhead costs applied during the accounting period must be adjusted to reflect actual overhead costs.

the Overhead account is said to be underapplied and the debit balance must be closed to the Cost of Goods Sold account. Here is the entry:

Cost of Goods Sold	XX	
Overhead		XX

Or, as is shown in transaction 11, if the actual overhead cost for the period ($1,391) is less than the estimated overhead that was applied during the period ($1,394), then the Overhead account is overapplied, and the $3 credit balance must be closed to the Cost of Goods Sold account. The entry is as follows:

Overhead	3	
Cost of Goods Sold		3

Because the applied overhead exceeded the actual overhead by $3, Cost of Goods Sold must be reduced by the amount of the overcharge. It will then reflect the actual overhead costs incurred. Given that the amount is minor, the company prefers to subtract it from the cost of the cart that was sold rather than tracing it back to the individual units worked on during the period. Thus, $3 is deducted from the Cost of Goods Sold account, making the ending balance of that account $1,937.

STOP • REVIEW • APPLY

3-1. What is the purpose of the Work in Process Inventory account?

3-2. Why is the Overhead account reconciled at the end of an accounting period?

T Account Analysis with Unknowns   Partial operating data for Sample Company are presented below. Sample Company's management has set the predetermined overhead rate for the current year at 60 percent of direct labor costs.

Account/Transaction	October
Beginning Materials Inventory	$ 4,000
Beginning Work in Process Inventory	6,000
Beginning Finished Goods Inventory	2,000
Direct materials used	16,000
Direct materials purchased	a
Direct labor costs	24,000
Overhead applied	b
Cost of units completed	c
Cost of Goods Sold	50,000
Ending Materials Inventory	3,000
Ending Work in Process Inventory	10,000
Ending Finished Goods Inventory	d

Using T accounts and the data provided, compute the unknown values. Show all your computations.

SOLUTION

MATERIALS INVENTORY

Beg. Bal.	4,000	Used	16,000
(a) Purchases	15,000		
End. Bal.	**3,000**		

WORK IN PROCESS INVENTORY

Beg. Bal.	6,000	(c) Completed During Period	50,400
Direct Materials Used	16,000		
Direct Labor	24,000		
(b) Overhead Applied	14,400*		
End. Bal.	**10,000**		

FINISHED GOODS INVENTORY

Beg. Bal.	2,000	Cost of Goods Sold	50,000
(c) Completed During Period	50,400		
(d) **End. Bal.**	**2,400**		

*$24,000 \times 60\% = \$14,400$

A Manufacturer's Job Order Cost Card and the Computation of Product Unit Cost

LO4 Prepare a job order cost card, and compute a job order's product unit cost.

As is evident from the preceding discussion, job order cost cards play a key role in a job order costing system. Because all manufacturing costs are accumulated in one Work in Process Inventory account, a separate accounting procedure is needed to trace those costs to specific jobs. The solution is the subsidiary ledger made up of job order cost cards. Each job being worked on has a job order cost card. As costs are incurred, they are classified by job and recorded on the appropriate card.

As you can see in Figure 2, a manufacturer's job order cost card has space for direct materials, direct labor, and overhead costs. It also includes the job order number, product specifications, the name of the customer, the date of the order, the projected completion date, and a cost summary. As a job incurs direct materials and direct labor costs, its job order cost card is updated. Overhead is also posted to the job order cost card at the predetermined rate. Job order cost cards for incomplete jobs make up the subsidiary ledger for the Work in Process Inventory account. To ensure correctness, the ending balance in the Work in Process Inventory account is compared with the total of the costs shown on the job order cost cards.

A job order costing system simplifies the calculation of product unit costs. When a job is finished, the costs of direct materials, direct labor, and overhead that have been recorded on its job order cost card are totaled. The product unit cost is computed by dividing the total costs for the job by the number of good (i.e., salable) units produced. The product unit cost is entered on the job order cost card and will be used to value items in inventory. The job order cost card in Figure 2 shows the costs for completed Job CC. Two golf carts were produced at a total cost of $3,880, so the product unit cost was $1,940.

STOP • REVIEW • APPLY

4-1. What is the purpose of a job order cost card?

4-2. How does a job order costing system simplify the computation of product unit costs?

Computation of Product Unit Cost Complete the following job order cost card for five custom-built cabinets:

Job Order 16

Job Order Cost Card
Unique Cupboards, LLP
Sample City, Oregon

Customer: Brian Tofer   Batch: ____   Custom: X
Specifications: 5 Custom cabinets
Date of Order: 5/4/xx   Date of Completion: 6/8/xx

Costs Charged to Job	Previous Months	Current Month	Cost Summary
Direct materials	$3,500	$2,800	$?
Direct labor	2,300	1,600	?
Overhead applied	1,150	800	?
Totals	$?	$?	$?
Units completed			÷ ?
Product unit cost			$?

SOLUTION

Job Order 16

Job Order Cost Card
Unique Cupboards, LLP
Sample City, Oregon

Customer: Brian Tofer   Batch: ____   Custom: X
Specifications: 5 Custom cabinets
Date of Order: 5/4/xx   Date of Completion: 6/8/xx

Costs Charged to Job	Previous Months	Current Month	Cost Summary
Direct materials	$3,500	$2,800	$ 6,300
Direct labor	2,300	1,600	3,900
Overhead applied	1,150	800	1,950
Totals	$6,950	$5,200	$12,150
Units completed			÷ 5
Product unit cost			$ 2,430

Job Order Costing in a Service Organization

LO5   Apply job order costing to a service organization.

Many service organizations use a job order costing system to compute the cost of rendering services. As we have pointed out elsewhere in the text, the costs of service organizations are different from those of a manufacturing organization in that they are not associated with a physical product that can be assembled, stored, and valued as inventory. Because these organizations sell services rather than making products for sale, the costs that they incur for materials are usually negligible. The most important cost for a service organization is labor, which is carefully accounted for through the use of time cards.

The cost flow of services is similar to the cost flow of manufactured products. Job order cost cards are used to keep track of the costs incurred for each job. Job costs include labor, materials and supplies, and service overhead. To cover these costs and earn a profit, many service organizations base jobs on **cost-plus contracts**. Such contracts require the customer to pay all costs incurred in performing the job plus a predetermined amount of profit, which is based on the amount of costs incurred. When the job is complete, the costs on the completed job order cost card become the cost of services. The cost of services is adjusted at the end of the accounting period for the difference between the applied service overhead costs and the actual service overhead costs.

To illustrate how a service organization uses a job order costing system, let's assume that a company called Gartner Landscaping Services employs 15 people and serves the San Francisco Bay area. Gartner earns its revenue by designing and installing landscapes for homes and offices. Figure 3 shows Gartner's job order cost card for the landscaping of Rico Corporation's corporate headquarters. Costs have been categorized into three separate activities: landscape design, landscape installation, and job-site cleanup.

Service organizations typically use job order cost cards to track the costs incurred for each job. Their most important cost is labor—such as the design work of the landscape architect shown here—and it is carefully tracked through the use of time cards.

■ **FIGURE 3**
Job Order Cost Card for a Service Organization

JOB ORDER COST CARD
Gartner Landscaping Services

Customer: _Rico Corporation_

Job Order Number: _____

Contract Type: _Cost-Plus_

Type of Service: _Landscape Corporate Headquarters_

Date Completed: _May 31, 20xx_

Costs Charged to Job	Previous Months	Current Month	Total Cost
Landscape Design			
Supplies	$ 100	$ —	$ 100
Design Labor	850	—	850
Service Overhead (40% of design labor)	340	—	340
Totals	$1,290	$ —	$1,290
Landscape Installation			
Planting Materials	$ 970	$1,200	$2,170
Installation Labor	400	620	1,020
Service Overhead (50% of installation labor)	200	310	510
Totals	$1,570	$2,130	$3,700
Job-Site Cleanup			
Janitorial Service Cost	$ 90	$ 320	$ 410
Totals	$2,950	$2,450	$5,400

Cost Summary to Date	Total Cost
Landscape Design	$ 1,290
Landscape Installation	3,700
Job-Site Cleanup	410
Totals	$ 5,400
Profit Margin (15%)	810
Contract Revenue	$ 6,210

Costs have been tracked to the Rico Corporation job throughout its duration, and now that the job is finished, it is time to complete the job order cost card. The service overhead cost for landscape design is 40 percent of design labor cost, and the service overhead cost for landscape installation is 50 percent of installation labor cost. Total costs incurred for this job were $5,400. Gartner's cost-plus contract with Rico has a 15 percent profit guarantee; therefore, $810 of profit margin is added to the total cost to arrive at the total contract revenue of $6,210, which is the amount billed to Rico.

S T O P • R E V I E W • A P P L Y

5-1. How do the costs of a service organization and a manufacturing organization differ? How do these differences affect the job order costing system of a service organization?

5-2. What is a cost-plus contract? How does this type of contract benefit a service organization?

Job Order Costing Versus Project Costing

LO6   Distinguish between job order costing and project costing.

Although the concept of a job order costing system that collects the costs of direct materials, direct labor, and overhead by specific job order for custom products or services remains valid, new approaches to costing are being developed. In today's business environment, many jobs take a long time to complete and require the talents of many departments, consultants, and subcontractors. These complex jobs have evolved into **projects**, jobs that are made up of many tasks and that take a broad, multidisciplinary approach to the production of goods or services. Examples of projects include the construction of a skyscraper and the development of a computer software program. At companies like **Industrial Light & Magic (ILM)**, discussed in the focus box in this section, effective project management requires a product costing system that accommodates today's environment of multidisciplinary work teams, networks of shared computer files, and integrated computer systems.

In the past, managers tended to focus on products or customer requests one at a time. Today, they often need to coordinate many jobs that are being performed at many different times in many different places. For that purpose, they may use project costing. In contrast to job order costing, which focuses on a specific job order, project costing links many different job orders and processes by transferring costs from one job or process to another, collecting and summarizing costs in a variety of ways, and providing appropriate internal controls to manage complicated projects. The detailed processes involved in project costing and project management are covered in more advanced accounting courses.

FOCUS ON BUSINESS PRACTICE

Who Uses Project Costing?

One company that uses project costing is **Industrial Light & Magic**. Founded by George Lucas in 1975, the special-effects company currently works on over a dozen film projects and more than 50 commercial projects a year. One cost shared by all the company's projects is that of the company's Computer Graphics Weeklies. At the weeklies (now held every six weeks), a project team shows how it solved a special-effects problem or asks for help from other teams. These hour-long forums encourage group learning and cross-pollination between ILM's projects and artists. They also enable the company to collectively celebrate its new ways of creating digital illusions and expanding cinematic boundaries.[3]

S T O P • R E V I E W • A P P L Y

6-1. How do projects differ from jobs?

6-2. Which of the following businesses is more likely to use project costing rather than job order costing: a developer of planned retirement communities or a planner of hotel's special events?

A LOOK BACK AT

COLD STONE CREAMERY, INC.

The Decision Point at the beginning of this chapter focused on **Cold Stone Creamery**, a company known for its method of making and serving ice cream. It posed these questions:

- **Is the product costing system that is used for custom-made items appropriate for mass-produced items?**
- **What performance measures would be most useful in evaluating the results of each type of product?**

Whether a product costing system is appropriate depends on the nature of the production process. Because the production of personalized creations and the manufacture of large quantities of retail products involve different processes, they generally require different costing systems. When a product is custom-made, it is possible to collect the costs of each order. When a product is mass-produced, the costs of a specific unit cannot be collected because there is a continuous flow of similar products; in this case, costs are collected by process, department, or work cell. Thus, if Cold Stone Creamery introduced a product for sale in grocery stores or other retail establishments, it would have to adjust its costing system to determine the product cost of a unit.

Performance measures would also differ if Cold Stone Creamery were to create a retail product line. Its management can now measure the profitability of each personalized order by comparing the order's cost and price. If a retail product were introduced, management would measure performance by comparing the budgeted and actual costs for a process, department, or work cell.

CHAPTER REVIEW

REVIEW of Learning Objectives

LO1 Discuss the role that information about costs plays in the management process, and explain why unit cost is important.

When managers plan, information about costs helps them develop budgets, establish prices, set sales goals, plan production volumes, estimate product or service unit costs, and determine human resource needs. Daily, managers use cost information to make decisions about controlling costs, managing the company's volume of activity, ensuring quality, and negotiating prices. When managers evaluate results, they analyze actual and targeted information to evaluate performance and make any necessary adjustments to their planning and decision-making strategies. When managers communicate with stakeholders, they use unit costs to determine inventory balances and the cost of goods or services sold for the financial statements. They also analyze internal reports that compare the organization's measures of actual and targeted performance to determine whether cost goals for products or services are being achieved.

LO2 Distinguish between the two basic types of product costing systems, and identify the information that each provides.

A job order costing system is a product costing system used by companies that make unique, custom, or special-order products. Such a system traces the costs of direct materials, direct labor, and overhead to a specific batch of products or to a specific job order. A job order costing system measures the cost of each complete unit and summarizes the cost of all jobs in a single Work in Process Inventory account that is supported by job order cost cards.

A process costing system is a product costing system used by companies that produce large amounts of similar products or liquid products or that have long, continuous production runs of identical products. Such a system first traces the costs of direct materials, direct labor, and overhead to processes, departments, or work cells and then assigns the costs to the products manufactured by those processes, departments, or work cells. A process costing system uses several Work in Process Inventory accounts, one for each department, process, or work cell.

LO3 Explain the cost flow in a manufacturer's job order costing system.

In a manufacturer's job order costing system, the costs of materials are first charged to the Materials Inventory account and to the respective materials accounts in the subsidiary ledger. The various actual overhead costs are debited to the Overhead account. As products are manufactured, the costs of direct materials and direct labor are debited to the Work in Process Inventory account and are recorded on each job's job order cost card. Overhead costs are applied and debited to the Work in Process Inventory account and credited to the Overhead account using a predetermined overhead rate. They too are recorded on the job order cost card. When products and jobs are completed, the costs assigned to them are transferred to the Finished Goods Inventory account. Then, when the products are sold and shipped, their costs are transferred to the Cost of Goods Sold account.

LO4 Prepare a job order cost card, and compute a job order's product unit cost.

All costs of direct materials, direct labor, and overhead for a particular job are accumulated on a job order cost card. When the job has been completed, those costs are totaled. The total is then divided by the number of good units produced to find the product unit cost for that order. The product unit cost is entered on the job order cost card and will be used to value items in inventory.

LO5 Apply job order costing to a service organization.

Many service organizations use a job order costing system to track the costs of labor, materials and supplies, and service overhead to specific customer jobs. Labor is an important cost for service organizations, but their materials costs are usually negligible. To cover their costs and earn a profit, service organizations often base jobs on cost-plus contracts, which require the customer to pay all costs incurred plus a predetermined amount of profit.

LO6 Distinguish between job order costing and project costing.

Projects are complex, time-consuming jobs that are made up of many tasks and that take a broad, multidisciplinary approach to the production of products or services. Unlike job order costing, which focuses on a specific job order, project costing links many job orders and processes by transferring costs from one job or process to another, collecting and summarizing costs in a variety of ways, and using appropriate internal controls to manage complicated projects.

REVIEW of Concepts and Terminology

The following concepts and terms were introduced in this chapter:

Cost-plus contracts: Job contracts that require the customer to pay all costs incurred in performing the job plus a predetermined amount of profit. **(LO5)**

Job order: A customer order for a specific number of specially designed, made-to-order products. **(LO2)**

Job order cost card: A document on which all costs incurred in the production of a particular job order are recorded; part of the subsidiary ledger for the Work in Process Inventory account. **(LO2)**

Job order costing system: A product costing system that traces the costs of direct materials, direct labor, and overhead to a specific batch of products or a specific job order; used by companies that make unique or special-order products. **(LO2)**

Process costing system: A product costing system that traces the costs of direct materials, direct labor,

and overhead to processes, departments, or work cells and then assigns the costs to the products manufactured by those processes, departments, or work cells; used by companies that produce large amounts of similar products or liquid products or that have long, continuous production runs of identical products. **(LO2)**

Product costing system: A set of procedures that is used to account for an organization's product costs and to provide timely and accurate unit cost information for pricing, cost planning and control, inventory valuation, and financial statement preparation. **(LO2)**

Projects: Complex jobs that are made up of many tasks and that take a broad, multidisciplinary approach to the production of products or services. **(LO6)**

Review Problem

LO4, LO5   **Job Order Costing in a Service Organization**

Sanibel Plumbing Company employs 30 people and serves the Fort Myers area. It earns roughly half its revenue from installing plumbing in newly constructed houses and half from plumbing repairs and remodeling jobs in older houses. It uses job order cost cards to keep track of the costs incurred on each job. Job costs (direct materials and supplies, direct labor, and service overhead) are categorized under three activities: plumbing system design, system installation, and job-site cleanup. The service overhead charge for plumbing system design is 30 percent of engineering labor costs, and the service overhead charge for system installation is 50 percent of direct labor cost.

Sanibel has tracked all costs of the Clary job, and now that the work is finished, it is time to complete the job order cost card. Its cost-plus contract with Clary has a 25 percent profit guarantee. The costs for the job are as follows:

Beginning Balances

Plumbing system design	$ 2,635
System installation	14,250
Job-site cleanup	75

Costs During October

Plumbing system design	
Supplies	$ 0
Engineering labor	250
System installation	
Materials	2,150
Direct labor	6,400
Job-site cleanup	
Janitorial service cost	525

Required

1. Create the job order cost card for the Clary job.
2. What amount will Sanibel Plumbing Company bill for the Clary job?
3. Using the format of the Work in Process Inventory account in Exhibit 1, reconstruct the beginning balance and costs for the current month.

Answer to Review Problem

1. Job order cost card for the Clary job:

Job Order Cost Card
Sanibel Plumbing Company

Customer: Clary
Job Order No.: 153
Contract Type: Cost-Plus
Type of Service: New Home Plumbing   Date of Completion: October 31, 20xx

Costs Charged to Job	Previous Months	Current Month	Total Cost
Plumbing system design			
Beginning balance	$ 2,635		$ 2,635
Current month's costs			
Supplies		$ 0	0
Engineering labor		250	250
Service overhead (30% of engineering labor)		75	75
Totals	$ 2,635	$ 325	$ 2,960
System installation			
Beginning balance	$14,250		$14,250
Current month's costs			
Materials		$ 2,150	2,150
Direct labor		6,400	6,400
Service overhead (50% of direct labor)		3,200	3,200
Totals	$14,250	$11,750	$26,000
Job-site cleanup			
Beginning balance	$ 75		$ 75
Current month's costs		$ 525	525
Totals	$ 75	$ 525	$ 600

Cost Summary to Date	Total Cost
Plumbing system design	$ 2,960
System installation	26,000
Job-site cleanup	600
Total	$29,560
Profit margin (25% of total cost)	7,390
Contract revenue	$36,950

2. Sanibel Plumbing will bill Clary $36,950 for this job.
3. Beginning balance for the current month and the current month's costs:

	A	B	C	D
1		**Work in Process Inventory**		
2	Beg. Bal.*	16,960	Completed	29,560
3	Plumbing System Design:			
4	Engineering Labor	250		
5	Overhead	75		
6	Systems Installation:			
7	Materials	2,150		
8	Direct Labor	6,400		
9	Overhead	3,200		
10	Job-Site Cleanup	525	—	
11	End. Bal.	—		
12				
13	*$2,635 + $14,250 + $75 = $16,960			

CHAPTER ASSIGNMENTS

BUILDING Your Basic Knowledge and Skills

Short Exercises

LO1 **Uses of Product Costing Information**

SE 1. Shelley's Kennel provides boarding for dogs and cats. Shelley, the owner of the kennel, must make several business decisions soon. Write *yes* or *no* to indicate whether knowing the cost to board one animal for one day (i.e., the product unit cost) can help Shelley answer these questions:

1. Is the boarding fee high enough to cover the kennel's costs?
2. How much profit will the kennel make if it boards an average of 10 dogs per day for 50 weeks?
3. What costs can be reduced to make the kennel's boarding fee competitive with that of its competitor?

LO2 **Companies That Use Job Order Costing**

SE 2. Write *yes* or *no* to indicate whether each of the following companies would typically use a job order costing system:

1. Soft drink producer
2. Jeans manufacturer

3. Submarine contractor
4. Office building contractor
5. Stuffed-toy maker

LO2   Job Order Versus Process Costing Systems

SE 3. State whether a job order costing system or a process costing system would typically be used to account for the costs of the following:

1. Manufacturing cat collars
2. Manufacturing custom-designed fencing for outdoor breeding kennels
3. Providing pet grooming
4. Manufacturing one-gallon aquariums
5. Manufacturing dog food
6. Providing veterinary services

LO3   Transactions in a Manufacturer's Job Order Costing System

SE 4. For each of the following transactions, state which account(s) would be debited and credited in a job order costing system:

1. Purchased materials on account, $12,890
2. Charged direct labor to production, $3,790
3. Requested direct materials for production, $6,800
4. Applied overhead to jobs in process, $3,570

LO3   Transactions in a Manufacturer's Job Order Costing System

SE 5. Enter the following transactions into T accounts:

1. Incurred $34,000 of direct labor and $18,000 of indirect labor
2. Applied overhead based on 12,680 labor hours @ $6.50 per labor hour

LO3   Accounts for Job Order Costing

SE 6. Identify the accounts in which each of the following transactions for Dom's Furniture, a custom manufacturer of oak tables and chairs, would be debited and credited:

1. Issued oak materials into production for Job ABC
2. Recorded direct labor time for the first week in February for Job ABC
3. Purchased indirect materials from a vendor on account
4. Received a production-related electricity bill
5. Applied overhead to Job ABC
6. Completed but did not yet sell Job ABC

LO4   Product Unit Cost

SE 7. Write *yes* or *no* to indicate whether each of the following costs is included in a product unit cost. Then explain your answers.

1. Direct materials costs
2. Fixed overhead costs
3. Variable selling costs
4. Fixed administrative costs
5. Direct labor costs
6. Variable overhead costs

LO4   Computation of Product Unit Cost

SE 8. Complete the following job order cost card for six custom-built computer systems:

Job Order 168

Job Order Cost Card
Keeper 3000
Apache City, North Dakota

Customer: Brian Patcher   Batch: _____   Custom: X

Specifications: 6 Custom-Built

Computer Systems

Date of Order: 4/4/xx   Date of Completion: 6/8/xx

Costs Charged to Job	Previous Months	Current Month	Cost Summary
Direct materials	$3,540	$2,820	$?
Direct labor	2,340	1,620	?
Overhead applied	2,880	2,550	?
Totals	$?	$?	$?
Units completed			÷ ?
Product unit cost			$?

LO5   Job Order Costing in a Service Organization

SE 9. For each of the following transactions, state which account(s) would be affected in a job order costing system for a desert landscaping business:

1. Charged customer for landscape design
2. Purchased cactus plants and gravel on credit for one job
3. Paid three employees to prepare soil for gravel
4. Paid for rental equipment to move gravel to job site

LO5   Job Order Costing with Cost-Plus Contracts

SE 10. Complete the following job order cost card for an individual tax return:

Job Order 20xx-A7

Job Order Cost Card
Doremus Tax Service
Puyallup, Washington

Customer: Arthur Farnsworth   Batch: _____   Custom: X

Specifications: Annual Individual Tax Return

Date of Order: 3/24/xx   Date of Completion: 4/8/xx

Costs Charged to Job	Previous Months	Current Month	Total Cost
Client interview			
Supplies	$ 10	$—	$?
Labor	50	60	?
Overhead (40% of interview labor costs)	20	24	?
Totals	$?	$?	$?

(Continued)

Preparation of return

Supplies	$—	$ 16	$?
Computer time	—	12	?
Labor	—	240	?
Overhead (50% of preparation labor costs)	—	120	?
Totals	$—	$?	$?

Delivery

Postage	$—	$ 12	$?
Totals	$—	$?	$?

Cost Summary to Date	Total Cost
Client interview	$?
Preparation of return	?
Delivery	?
Total	$?
Profit margin (25% of total cost)	?
Job revenue	$?

Exercises

LO2 **Product Costing**

E 1. Anniversary Printing Company specializes in wedding invitations. Anniversary needs information to budget next year's activities. Write *yes* or *no* to indicate whether each of the following costs is likely to be available in the company's product costing system:

1. Cost of paper and envelopes
2. Printing machine setup costs
3. Depreciation of printing machinery
4. Advertising costs
5. Repair costs for printing machinery
6. Costs to deliver stationery to customers
7. Office supplies costs
8. Costs to design a wedding invitation
9. Cost of ink
10. Sales commissions

LO2 **Costing Systems: Industry Linkage**

E 2. Which of the following products would typically be accounted for using a job order costing system? Which would typically be accounted for using a process costing system? (a) Paint, (b) jelly beans, (c) jet aircraft, (d) bricks, (e) tailor-made suit, (f) liquid detergent, (g) aluminum compressed-gas cylinders of standard size and capacity, and (h) aluminum compressed-gas cylinders with a special fiberglass wrap for a Mount Everest expedition.

LO2 **Costing Systems: Industry Linkage**

E 3. Which of the following products would typically be accounted for using a job order costing system? Which would typically be accounted for using a process costing system? (a) Standard nails, (b) television sets, (c) printed wedding invitations, (d) a limited edition of lithographs, (e) flea collars for pets, (f) high-speed lathes with special-order drill threads, (g) breakfast cereal, and (h) an original evening gown.

LO3 Job Order Cost Flow

E 4. The three product cost elements—direct materials, direct labor, and overhead—flow through a job order costing system in a structured, orderly fashion. Specific accounts and subsidiary ledgers are used to verify and record cost information. Write a paragraph describing the cost flow in a job order costing system.

LO3 Work in Process Inventory: T Account Analysis

E 5. On June 30, Specialty Company's Work in Process Inventory account showed a beginning balance of $29,400. The Materials Inventory account showed a beginning balance of $240,000. Production activity for July was as follows: Direct materials costing $238,820 were requested for production; total manufacturing payroll was $140,690, of which $52,490 was used to pay for indirect labor; indirect materials costing $28,400 were purchased and used; and overhead was applied at a rate of 150 percent of direct labor costs.

1. Record Specialty's materials, labor, and overhead costs for July in T accounts.
2. Compute the ending balance in the Work in Process Inventory account. Assume a transfer of $461,400 to the Finished Goods Inventory account during the period.

LO3 T Account Analysis with Unknowns

E 6. Partial operating data for Vue Picture Company are presented below. Management has set the predetermined overhead rate for the current year at 120 percent of direct labor costs.

Account/Transaction	June	July
Beginning Materials Inventory	a	e
Beginning Work in Process Inventory	$ 89,605	f
Beginning Finished Goods Inventory	79,764	$ 67,660
Direct materials requested	59,025	g
Materials purchased	57,100	60,216
Direct labor costs	48,760	54,540
Overhead applied	b	h
Cost of units completed	c	231,861
Cost of Goods Sold	166,805	i
Ending Materials Inventory	32,014	27,628
Ending Work in Process Inventory	d	j
Ending Finished Goods Inventory	67,660	30,515

Using T accounts and the data provided, compute the unknown values. Show all your computations.

LO3 T Account Analysis with Unknowns

E 7. Partial operating data for Starke Company are presented below. Starke Company's management has set the predetermined overhead rate for the current year at 80 percent of direct labor costs.

Account/Transaction	December
Beginning Materials Inventory	$ 42,000
Beginning Work in Process Inventory	66,000
Beginning Finished Goods Inventory	29,000
Direct materials used	168,000
Direct materials purchased	a
Direct labor costs	382,000
Overhead applied	b

Account/Transaction	December
Cost of units completed	c
Cost of Goods Sold	808,000
Ending Materials Inventory	38,000
Ending Work in Process Inventory	138,600
Ending Finished Goods Inventory	d

Using T accounts and the data provided, compute the unknown values. Show all your computations.

LO4 Job Order Cost Card and Computation of Product Unit Cost

E 8. In January, the Cabinet Company worked on six job orders for specialty kitchen cabinets. It began Job A-62 for Thomas Cabinets, Inc., on January 10 and completed it on January 24. Partial data for Job A-62 are as follows:

	Costs	Machine Hours Used
Direct materials		
Cedar	$7,900	
Pine	6,320	
Hardware	2,930	
Assembly supplies	988	
Direct labor		
Sawing	2,840	120
Shaping	2,200	220
Finishing	2,250	180
Assembly	2,890	50

The Cabinet Company produced a total of 34 cabinets for Job A-62. Its current predetermined overhead rate is $21.60 per machine hour. From the information given, prepare a job order cost card and compute the job order's product unit cost. (Round to whole dollars.)

LO4 Computation of Product Unit Cost

E 9. Using job order costing, determine the product unit cost based on the following costs incurred during March: liability insurance, manufacturing, $2,500; rent, sales office, $2,900; depreciation, manufacturing equipment, $6,100; direct materials, $32,650; indirect labor, manufacturing, $3,480; indirect materials, $1,080; heat, light, and power, manufacturing, $1,910; fire insurance, manufacturing, $2,600; depreciation, sales equipment, $4,250; rent, manufacturing, $3,850; direct labor, $18,420; manager's salary, manufacturing, $3,100; president's salary, $5,800; sales commissions, $8,250; and advertising expenses, $2,975. The Inspection Department reported that 48,800 good units were produced during March. Carry your answer to two decimal places.

LO4 Computation of Product Unit Cost

E 10. Wild Things, Inc., manufactures custom-made stuffed animals. Last month the company produced 4,540 stuffed bears with stethoscopes for the local children's hospital to sell at a fundraising event. Using job order costing, determine the product unit cost of a stuffed bear based on the following costs incurred during the month: manufacturing utilities, $500; depreciation on manufacturing equipment, $450; indirect materials, $300; direct materials, $1,300; indirect labor, $800; direct labor, $2,400; sales commissions, $3,000; president's salary, $4,000; insurance on manufacturing plant, $600; advertising expense, $500; rent on manufacturing plant, $5,000; rent on sales office, $4,000; and legal expense, $250. Carry your answer to two decimal places.

LO4 Computation of Product Unit Cost

E 11. Style Corporation manufactures specialty lines of women's apparel. During February, the company worked on three special orders: A-25, A-27, and B-14. Cost and production data for each order are as follows:

	Job A-25	Job A-27	Job B-14
Direct materials			
Fabric Q	$10,840	$12,980	$17,660
Fabric Z	11,400	12,200	13,440
Fabric YB	5,260	6,920	10,900
Direct labor			
Garment maker	8,900	10,400	16,200
Layout	6,450	7,425	9,210
Packaging	3,950	4,875	6,090
Overhead			
(120% of direct labor costs)	?	?	?
Number of units produced	700	775	1,482

1. Compute the total cost associated with each job. Show the subtotals for each cost category.
2. Compute the product unit cost for each job. (Round your computations to the nearest cent.)

LO5 Job Order Costing in a Service Organization

E 12. A job order cost card for Hal's Computer Services appears below. Complete the missing information. The profit factor in the organization's cost-plus contract is 30 percent of total cost.

Job Order Cost Card
Hal's Computer Services

Customer: James Lowe
Job Order No.:   8-324
Contract Type: Cost-Plus
Type of Service: Software Installation and Internet Interfacing
Date of Completion: October 6, 20xx

Costs Charged to Job	Total Cost
Software installation services	
Installation labor	$300
Service overhead (?% of installation labor costs)	?
Total	$450
Internet services	
Internet labor	$200
Service overhead (20% of Internet labor costs)	40
Total	$?

Cost Summary to Date	Total Cost
Software installation services	$?
Internet services	?
Total	$?
Profit margin (30% of total cost)	?
Contract revenue	$?

LO5 **Job Order Costing in a Service Organization**

E 13. A job order cost card for Miniblinds by Jenny appears below. Complete the missing information. The profit factor in the company's cost-plus contract is 50 percent of total cost.

Job Order Cost Card
Miniblinds by Jenny

Customer:	Carmen Sawyer
Job Order No.:	8-482
Contract Type:	Cost-Plus
Type of Service:	Miniblind Installation and Design
Date of Completion:	June 12, 20xx

Costs Charged to Job	Total Cost
Installation services	
Installation labor	$445
Service overhead (80% of installation labor costs)	?
Total	$?
Designer services	
Designer labor	$200
Service overhead (?% of designer labor costs)	?
Total	$400

Cost Summary to Date	Total Cost
Installation services	$?
Designer services	?
Total	$?
Profit margin (50% of total cost)	?
Contract revenue	$?

LO5 **Job Order Costing in a Service Organization**

E 14. Personal Shoppers, Inc., relieves busy women executives of the stress of shopping for clothes by taking an inventory of a client's current wardrobe and shopping for her needs for the next season or a special event. The company charges clients $30 per hour for the service plus the cost of the clothes purchased. It pays its employees various hourly wage rates.

During September, Personal Shoppers worked with three clients. It began Job 9-3, for Lucinda Mapley, on September 3 and completed the job on September 30. Using the partial data that follow, prepare the job order cost card. What amount of profit will Personal Shoppers make on this job?

Costs Charged to Job	Costs	Hours	Other
In-person consultation			
Supplies	$ 30		
Labor ($10 per hour)		4	
Overhead (10% of in-person labor costs)			

Costs Charged to Job	Costs	Hours	Other
Shopping			
Purchases	$560		
Labor ($15 per hour)		8	
Overhead (25% of shopping labor costs)			
Telephone consultations			
Cell phone calls ($1 per call)			6 calls
Labor ($6 per hour)		2	
Overhead (50% of telephone labor costs)			

LO5 **Job Order Costing in a Service Organization**

E 15. A job order cost card for Personal Trainers, Inc., appears below. Fill in the missing information.

Job Order **H.W.**

Job Order Cost Card
Personal Trainers, Inc.

Customer: Hillary White   Batch: _____   Custom: X _____
Specifications: Marathon Training
Date of Order: 4/2/xx   Date of Completion: 7/24/xx

Costs Charged to Job	Previous Months	Current Month	Total Cost
In-person consultation			
Training logbook	$ 20.00	$?	$20.00
Labor ($10 per hour)	20.00	?	50.00
Overhead (10% of in-person labor costs)	?	3.00	5.00
Total	$?	$?	$?
Training			
Bike rental	$ 30.00	$?	$60.00
Labor ($5 per hour)	150.00	300.00	?
Overhead (25% of training labor costs)	37.50	?	?
Total	$?	$?	$?
Telephone consultations			
Cell phone calls ($1 per call)	$ 30.00	$ 10.00	$?
Labor ($10 per hour)	10.00	10.00	?
Overhead (50% of telephone labor costs)	?	?	?
Total	$?	$?	$?
Total cost			$?

Job Revenue and Profit

Logbook and bike rental	?
Service fee: 97 hours × $30	?
Job revenue	$2,990.00
Less total cost	?
Profit	$2,222.50

Problems

LO3 **T Account Analysis with Unknowns**

P 1. Flagstaff Enterprises makes peripheral equipment for computers. Dana Dona, the company's new controller, can find only the following partial information for the past two months:

Account/Transaction	May	June
Beginning Materials Inventory	$ 36,240	$ e
Beginning Work in Process Inventory	56,480	f
Beginning Finished Goods Inventory	44,260	g
Materials purchased	a	96,120
Direct materials requested	82,320	h
Direct labor costs	b	72,250
Overhead applied	53,200	i
Cost of units completed	c	221,400
Cost of Goods Sold	209,050	j
Ending Materials Inventory	38,910	41,950
Ending Work in Process Inventory	d	k
Ending Finished Goods Inventory	47,940	51,180

The current year's predetermined overhead rate is 80 percent of direct labor cost.

Required

Using the data provided and T accounts, compute the unknown values.

LO3 **Job Order Costing: T Account Analysis**

P 2. Par Carts, Inc., produces special-order golf carts, so Par Carts uses a job order costing system. Overhead is applied at the rate of 90 percent of direct labor cost. The following is a list of transactions for January:

Jan. 1 Purchased direct materials on account, $215,400.

2 Purchased indirect materials on account, $49,500.

4 Requested direct materials costing $193,200 (all used on Job X) and indirect materials costing $38,100 for production.

10 Paid the following overhead costs: utilities, $4,400; manufacturing rent, $3,800; and maintenance charges, $3,900.

15 Recorded the following gross wages and salaries for employees: direct labor, $120,000 (all for Job X); indirect labor, $60,620.

15 Applied overhead to production.

19 Purchased indirect materials costing $27,550 and direct materials costing $190,450 on account.

21 Requested direct materials costing $214,750 (Job X, $178,170; Job Y, $18,170; and Job Z, $18,410) and indirect materials costing $31,400 for production.

31 Recorded the following gross wages and salaries for employees: direct labor, $132,000 (Job X, $118,500; Job Y, $7,000; Job Z, $6,500); indirect labor, $62,240.

31 Applied overhead to production.

31 Completed and transferred Job X (375 carts) and Job Y (10 carts) to finished goods inventory; total cost was $855,990.

31 Shipped Job X to the customer; total production cost was $824,520 and sales price was $996,800.

31 Recorded these overhead costs (adjusting entries): prepaid insurance expired, $3,700; property taxes (payable at year end), $3,400; and depreciation, machinery, $15,500.

Required

1. Record the entries for all transactions in January using T accounts for the following: Materials Inventory, Work in Process Inventory, Finished Goods Inventory, Overhead, Cash, Accounts Receivable, Prepaid Insurance, Accumulated Depreciation—Machinery, Accounts Payable, Factory Payroll, Property Taxes Payable, Sales, Cost of Goods Sold, and Selling and Administrative Expenses. Use job order cost cards for Job X, Job Y, and Job Z. Determine the partial account balances. Assume no beginning inventory balances. Also assume that when the payroll was recorded, entries were made to the Factory Payroll account.
2. Compute the amount of underapplied or overapplied overhead as of January 31 and transfer it to the Cost of Goods Sold account.
3. Why should the Overhead account's underapplied or overapplied overhead be transferred to the Cost of Goods Sold account?

LO3, LO4 **Job Order Cost Flow**

P 3. On May 31, the inventory balances of Abbey Designs, a manufacturer of high-quality children's clothing, were as follows: Materials Inventory, $21,360; Work in Process Inventory, $15,112; and Finished Goods Inventory, $17,120. Job order cost cards for jobs in process as of June 30 had these totals:

Job No.	Direct Materials	Direct Labor	Overhead
24-A	$1,596	$1,290	$1,677
24-B	1,492	1,380	1,794
24-C	1,984	1,760	2,288
24-D	1,608	1,540	2,002

The predetermined overhead rate is 130 percent of direct labor costs. Materials purchased and received in June were as follows:

June 4	$33,120
June 16	28,600
June 22	31,920

Direct labor costs for June were as follows:

June 15 payroll	$23,680
June 29 payroll	25,960

Direct materials requested by production during June were as follows:

June 6	$37,240
June 23	38,960

On June 30, Abbey Designs sold on account finished goods with a 75 percent markup over cost for $320,000.

Required

1. Using T accounts for Materials Inventory, Work in Process Inventory, Finished Goods Inventory, Overhead, Accounts Receivable, Factory Payroll, Sales, and Cost of Goods Sold, reconstruct the transactions in June.
2. Compute the cost of units completed during the month.
3. What was the total cost of goods sold during June?
4. Determine the ending inventory balances.
5. Jobs 24-A and 24-C were completed during the first week of July. No additional materials costs were incurred, but Job 24-A required $960 more of

direct labor, and Job 24-C needed an additional $1,610 of direct labor. Job 24-A was composed of 1,200 pairs of trousers; Job 24-C, of 950 shirts. Compute the product unit cost for each job. (Round your answers to two decimal places.

LO5   Job Order Costing in a Service Organization

P 4. Riggs & Associates is a CPA firm located in Clinton, Kansas. The firm deals primarily in tax and audit work. For billing of major audit engagements, it uses cost-plus contracts, and its profit factor is 25 percent of total job cost. Costs are accumulated for three primary activities: preliminary analysis, field work, and report development. Current service overhead rates based on billable hours are preliminary analysis, $12 per hour; field work, $20 per hour; and report development, $16 per hour. Supplies are treated as direct materials and are traceable to each engagement. Audits for three clients— Fulcrum, Inc., Rainy Day Bakeries, and Our Place Restaurants—are currently in process. During March 20xx, costs related to these projects were as follows:

	Fulcrum, Inc.	Rainy Day Bakeries	Our Place Restaurants
Beginning Balances			
Preliminary analysis	$1,160	$2,670	$2,150
Field work	710	1,980	3,460
Report development	—	1,020	420
Costs During March			
Preliminary analysis			
Supplies	$ 710	$ 430	$ 200
Labor: hours	60	10	12
dollars	$1,200	$ 200	$ 240
Field work			
Supplies	$ 450	$1,120	$ 890
Labor: hours	120	240	230
dollars	$4,800	$9,600	$9,200
Report development			
Supplies	$ 150	$ 430	$ 390
Labor: hours	30	160	140
dollars	$ 900	$4,800	$4,200

Required

1. Using the format shown in this chapter's Review Problem, create the job order cost card for each of the three audit engagements.
2. Riggs & Associates will complete the audits of Rainy Day Bakeries and Our Place Restaurants by the end of March. What will the billing amount for each of those audit engagements be?
3. What is the March ending balance of Riggs & Associates' Audit in Process account?

LO5   Job Order Costing in a Service Organization

P 5. Peruga Engineering Company specializes in designing automated characters and displays for theme parks. It uses cost-plus profit contracts, and its profit factor is 30 percent of total cost.

Peruga uses a job order costing system to track the costs of developing each job. Costs are accumulated for three primary activities: bid and proposal, design, and prototype development. Current service overhead rates based on engineering hours are as follows: bid and proposal, $18 per hour; design, $22 per hour; and prototype development, $20 per hour.

Supplies are treated as direct materials, traceable to each job. Peruga worked on three jobs, P-12, P-15, and P-19, during January. The following table shows the costs for those jobs:

	P-12	P-15	P-19
Beginning Balances			
Bid and proposal	$2,460	$2,290	$ 940
Design	1,910	460	—
Prototype development	2,410	1,680	—
Costs During January			
Bid and proposal			
Supplies	$ —	$ 280	$2,300
Labor: hours	12	20	68
dollars	$ 192	$ 320	$1,088
Design			
Supplies	$ 400	$ 460	$ 290
Labor: hours	64	42	26
dollars	$1,280	$ 840	$ 520
Prototype development			
Supplies	$6,744	$7,216	$2,400
Labor: hours	120	130	25
dollars	$2,880	$3,120	$ 600

Required

1. Using the format shown in this chapter's Review Problem, create the job order cost card for each of the three jobs.
2. Peruga completed Jobs P-12 and P-15, and the customers approved the prototype products. Customer A plans to produce 12 special characters using the design and specifications created by Job P-12. Customer B plans to make 18 displays from the design developed by Job P-15. What dollar amount will each customer use as the cost of design for each of those products (i.e., what is the product unit cost for Jobs P-12 and P-15)? Round to the nearest dollar.
3. What is the January ending balance of Peruga's Contract in Process account for the three jobs?
4. **Manager Insight:** Rank the jobs in order from most costly to least costly based on each job's total cost. From the rankings of cost, what observations can you make?
5. **Manager Insight:** Speculate on the price that Peruga should charge for such jobs.

Alternate Problems

LO3 **Job Order Costing: T Account Analysis**

P 6. Rothi Industries, Inc., the finest name in parking attendants' apparel, has been in business for over 30 years. Its colorful and stylish uniforms are special-ordered by luxury hotels all over the world. During September, Rothi Industries completed the following transactions:

Sept. 1 Purchased direct materials on account, $59,400.
3 Requested direct materials costing $26,850 for production (all for Job A).
4 Purchased indirect materials for cash, $22,830.
8 Issued checks for the following overhead costs: utilities, $4,310; manufacturing insurance, $1,925; and repairs, $4,640.

Sept. 10 Requested direct materials costing $29,510 (all used on Job A) and indirect materials costing $6,480 for production.

15 Recorded the following gross wages and salaries for employees: direct labor, $62,900 (all for Job A); indirect labor, $31,610; manufacturing supervision, $26,900; and sales commissions, $32,980.

15 Applied overhead to production at a rate of 120 percent of direct labor cost.

22 Paid the following overhead costs: utilities, $4,270; maintenance, $3,380; and rent, $3,250.

23 Recorded the purchase on account and receipt of $31,940 of direct materials and $9,260 of indirect materials.

27 Requested $28,870 of direct materials (Job A, $2,660; Job B, $8,400; Job C, $17,810) and $7,640 of indirect materials for production.

30 Recorded the following gross wages and salaries for employees: direct labor, $64,220 (Job A, $44,000; Job B, $9,000; Job C, $11,220); indirect labor, $30,290; manufacturing supervision, $28,520; and sales commissions, $36,200.

30 Applied overhead to production at a rate of 120 percent of direct labor cost.

30 Completed and transferred Job A (58,840 units) and Job B (3,525 units) to finished goods inventory; total cost was $322,400.

30 Shipped Job A to the customer; total production cost was $294,200, and sales price was $418,240.

30 Recorded the following adjusting entries: $2,680 for depreciation, manufacturing equipment; and $1,230 for property taxes, manufacturing, payable at month end.

Required

1. Record the entries for all Rothi's transactions in September using T accounts for the following: Materials Inventory, Work in Process Inventory, Finished Goods Inventory, Overhead, Cash, Accounts Receivable, Accumulated Depreciation–Manufacturing Equipment, Accounts Payable, Factory Payroll, Property Taxes Payable, Sales, Cost of Goods Sold, and Selling and Administrative Expenses. Use job order cost cards for Job A, Job B, and Job C. Determine the partial account balances. Assume no beginning inventory balances. Assume also that when payroll was recorded, entries were made to the Factory Payroll account. (Round your answers to the nearest whole dollar.)

2. Compute the amount of underapplied or overapplied overhead for September and transfer it to the Cost of Goods Sold account.

3. Why should the Overhead account's underapplied or overapplied overhead be transferred to the Cost of Goods Sold account?

LO3, LO4 **Job Order Cost Flow**

P 7. Dori Hatami is the chief financial officer of Gotham Industries, a company that makes special-order sound systems for home theaters. Her records for February revealed the following information:

Beginning inventory balances	
Materials Inventory	$27,450
Work in Process Inventory	22,900
Finished Goods Inventory	19,200
Direct materials purchased and received	
February 6	$ 7,200
February 12	8,110
February 24	5,890

Direct labor costs

February 14	$13,750
February 28	13,230

Direct materials requested for production

February 4	$ 9,080
February 13	5,940
February 25	7,600

Job order cost cards for jobs in process on February 28 had the following totals:

Job No.	Direct Materials	Direct Labor	Overhead
AJ-10	$3,220	$1,810	$2,534
AJ-14	3,880	2,110	2,954
AJ-15	2,980	1,640	2,296
AJ-16	4,690	2,370	3,318

The predetermined overhead rate for the month was 140 percent of direct labor costs. Sales for February totaled $152,400, which represented a 70 percent markup over the cost of production.

Required

1. Using T accounts for Materials Inventory, Work in Process Inventory, Finished Goods Inventory, Overhead, Accounts Receivable, Factory Payroll, Sales, and Cost of Goods Sold, reconstruct the transactions in February.
2. Compute the cost of units completed during the month.
3. What was the total cost of goods sold during February?
4. Determine the ending balances in the inventory accounts.
5. During the first week of March, Jobs AJ-10 and AJ-14 were completed. No additional direct materials costs were incurred, but Job AJ-10 needed $720 more of direct labor, and Job AJ-14 needed an additional $1,140 of direct labor. Job AJ-10 was 40 units; Job AJ-14, 55 units. Compute the product unit cost for each completed job (round to two decimal places).

LO5 **Job Order Costing in a Service Organization**

P 8. Locust Lodge, a restored 1920s lodge located in Arizona, caters and serves special events for businesses and social occasions. The company earns 60 percent of its revenue from weekly luncheon meetings of local clubs like Kiwanis. The remainder of its business comes from bookings for weddings and receptions.

Locust Lodge uses job order cost cards to keep track of the costs incurred. Job costs are separated into three categories: food and beverage, labor, and facility overhead. The facility overhead cost for weekly events is 10 percent of food and beverage costs, the facility overhead cost for sit-down receptions is 40 percent of food and beverage costs, and the facility overhead cost for stand-up receptions is 20 percent of food and beverage costs. Accumulated costs for three Locust Lodge clients in the current quarter are as follows:

	Food and Beverage	Labor	Facility Overhead
Tuesday Club meetings	Last month: $2,000 This month: $2,500	Last month: $ 200 This month: $ 250	Last month: ? This month: ?
Doar-Turner engagement and wedding parties	Last month: $3,000 This month: $8,000 Both sit-down affairs	Last month: $1,000 This month: $2,000	Last month: ? This month: ?
Reception for the new president	This month: $5,000 A stand-up affair	This month: $1,000	This month: ?

The number of attendees served at Tuesday Club meetings is usually 200 per month. The Doar-Turner parties paid for 500 guests. The organizers of the reception for the new president paid for 1,000 invitees.

Required

1. Using the format shown in this chapter's Review Problem, create a job order cost card for each of the three clients.
2. Calculate the total cost of each of the three jobs on its job order cost card.
3. Calculate the cost per attendee for each job.
4. **Manager Insight:** Rank the jobs in order from most costly to least costly based on each job's total cost and on the cost per attendee. From the rankings of cost, what observations are you able to make?
5. **Manager Insight:** Speculate on the price that Locust Lodge should charge for such jobs.

ENHANCING Your Knowledge, Skills, and Critical Thinking

Conceptual Understanding Cases

LO1 **Business Plans**

C 1. Fortune 500 companies continue to eliminate jobs; yet the U.S. economy keeps growing. New businesses have created most of the new employment. A key step in starting a new business is a realistic analysis of the people, opportunities, context, risks, and rewards of the venture and the formulation of a business plan. Note the similarities between the questions managers answer in the management process and the questions every great business plan should answer:

- Who is the new company's customer?
- How does the customer make decisions about buying this product or service?
- To what degree is the product or service a compelling purchase?
- How will the product or service be priced?
- How will the company reach all the identified customer segments?
- How much does it cost (in time and resources) to acquire a customer?
- How much does it cost to produce and deliver the product or service?
- How much does it cost to support a customer?
- How easy is it to retain a customer?

Assume that a new business has hired you as a consultant because of your knowledge of the management process. Write a memo that discusses how the nine questions listed above fit into the management process.

LO1, LO6 **Role of Cost Information in Software Development**

C 2. Software development companies frequently have a problem: When is "good enough" good enough? How many hours should be devoted to developing a new product? The industry's rule of thumb is that developing and shipping new software takes six to nine months. To be the first to market, a company must develop and ship products much more quickly than the industry norm. One performance measure that is used to answer the "good enough" question is a calculation based on the economic value (not cost) of what a company's developers create. The computation takes the estimated current market valuation of a firm and divides it by the number of product developers in the firm, to arrive at the market value created per developer. Some companies refine this calculation further to determine the value that each developer creates per workday. One company has estimated this value to be $10,000. Thus, for one software development company, "good enough" focuses on whether a new product's potential justifies an investment of time by someone who is worth $10,000 per day.

The salary cost of the company's developers is not used in the "good enough" calculation. Why is that cost not relevant?

LO1, LO2   **Design of a Product Costing System**

C3. The Al Khali Corporation's copper mines contain 63 percent of the 23.2 million tons of copper in Saudi Arabia. The owners of the mining operation are willing to invest millions of dollars in the latest pyrometallurgical copper-extraction process. Production managers are currently examining both batch and continuous versions of the new process. The method they choose will replace the hydrometallurgical process that is now in use.

What impact will the method that the production managers select have on the design of the product costing system? What impact would changing from hydrometallurgical to pyrometallurgical processing have on the design of the product costing system if both processes use continuous methods of extraction?

Interpreting Management Reports

LO1   **Interpreting Nonfinancial Data**

C4. Eagle Manufacturing supplies engine parts to Cherokee Cycle Company, a major U.S. manufacturer of motorcycles. Like all of Cherokee's suppliers, Eagle has always added a healthy profit margin to its cost when quoting selling prices to Cherokee. Recently, however, several companies have offered to supply engine parts to Cherokee for lower prices than Eagle has been charging.

Because Eagle Manufacturing wants to keep Cherokee Cycle Company's business, a team of Eagle's managers analyzed their company's product costs and decided to make minor changes in the company's manufacturing process. No new equipment was purchased, and no additional labor was required. Instead, the machines were rearranged, and some of the work was reassigned.

To monitor the effectiveness of the changes, Eagle introduced three new performance measures to its information system: inventory levels, lead time (total time required for a part to move through the production process), and productivity (number of parts manufactured per person per day). Eagle's goal was to reduce the quantities of the first two performance measures and to increase the quantity of the third.

A section of a recent management report, shown below, summarizes the quantities for each performance measure before and after the changes in the manufacturing process were made.

Measure	Before	After	Improvement
Inventory in dollars	$21,444	$10,772	50%
Lead time in minutes	17	11	35%
Productivity (parts per person per day)	515	1,152	124%

1. Do you believe that Eagle improved the quality of its manufacturing process and the quality of its engine parts? Explain your answer.
2. Can Eagle lower its selling price to Cherokee? Explain your answer.
3. Did the introduction of the new measures affect the design of the product costing system? Explain your answer.

4. Do you believe that the new measures caused a change in Eagle's cost per engine part? If so, how did they cause the change?

LO3, LO4 **Analysis of a Job Order Costing System**

C 5. Zavala Manufacturing Company is a small family-owned business that makes specialty plastic products. Since it was started three years ago, the company has grown quickly and now employs ten production people. Because of the nature of its products, it uses a job order costing system. The company's manual accounting system is falling behind in processing transactions.

Two months ago, in May, Zavala's accountant quit. You have been called in to help management. The following information is available to you:

Beginning Inventory Balances (December 31)

Materials Inventory	$50,420
Work in Process Inventory (Job K-2)	59,100
Finished Goods Inventory (Job K-1)	76,480

Direct Materials Requested by Production During the Year

Job K-2	$33,850
Job K-4	53,380
Job K-5	82,400

Direct Labor for the Year

Job K-2	$25,300
Job K-4	33,480
Job K-5	45,600

The company purchased materials only once (in February), for $126,500. All jobs use the same materials. For the current year, the company has used an overhead application rate of 150 percent of direct labor costs. So far this year, it has completed two jobs, K-2 and K-4, and has shipped Jobs K-1 and K-2 to customers. Job K-1 contained 3,200 units; Job K-2, 5,500 units; and Job K-4, 4,600 units. The beginning balance of Work in Process Inventory for Job K-2 consisted of $16,975 of direct materials, $16,850 of direct labor, and $25,275 of overhead.

1. Calculate the product unit costs for Jobs K-1, K-2, and K-4, and the costs so far for Job K-5.
2. From the information given, prepare job order cost cards for Jobs K-2, K-4, and K-5, and compute the current balances in the Materials Inventory, Work in Process Inventory, Finished Goods Inventory, and Cost of Goods Sold accounts.
3. Zavala's president has asked you to analyze the current job order costing system. Do you think the system should be changed? How? Why? Prepare an outline of your response to the president.

Decision Analysis Using Excel

LO5 **Job Order Costing in a Service Organization**

C 6. Refer to assignment **P 5** in this chapter. Peruga Engineering Company needs to analyze its jobs in process during the month of January.

1. Using Excel's Chart Wizard and the job order cost cards that you created for Jobs P-12, P-15, and P-19, prepare a bar chart that compares the bid and proposal costs, design costs, and prototype development costs of the jobs. The suggested format to use for the information table necessary to complete the bar chart is as follows:

A	P-12	P-15	P-19
1			
2 Bid and proposal			
3 Design			
4 Prototype development			
5 Total job cost			
6			

2. Examine the chart you prepared in 1. List some reasons for the differences between the costs of the various jobs.

Ethical Dilemma Case

LO3, LO5   **Costing Procedures and Ethics**

C 7. Kevin Rogers, the production manager of Stitts Metal Products Company, entered the office of controller Ed Harris and asked, "Ed, what gives here? I was charged for 330 direct labor hours on Job AD22, and my records show that we spent only 290 hours on that job. That 40-hour difference caused the total cost of direct labor and overhead for the job to increase by over $5,500. Are my records wrong, or was there an error in the direct labor assigned to the job?"

Harris replied, "Don't worry about it, Kevin. This job won't be used in your quarterly performance evaluation. Job AD22 was a federal government job, a cost-plus contract, so the more costs we assign to it, the more profit we make. We decided to add a few hours to the job in case there is some follow-up work to do. You know how fussy the feds are." What should Kevin Rogers do? Discuss Ed Harris's costing procedure.

Internet Case

LO1   **Evaluating Internet Shopping Sites**

C 8. Do a key word online search for clothing manufacturers or retailers. Select two companies that make or sell similar clothes and access their websites. Conduct an Internet shopping audit similar to the one P. Kelly Mooney does as the president and chief executive officer for **Resource Marketing, Inc.**, a technology marketing and communications company based in Columbus, Ohio. Mooney uses five principles to evaluate Internet shopping sites in such areas as prepurchase customer service, gift giving, special promotions, and postpurchase follow-through. She describes the five principles as follows:[4]

- *Don't just do it*: The website should be more than the company's catalogue loaded online.
- *Don't let your seams show*: Shopping, whether online or in a retail store, should be a seamless experience that guides customers according to their needs.
- *Own the customer experience*: The website should be intuitively easy to use and accessible. It should personalize service by asking customers about the types of information they want.
- *Avoid barriers to entry*: The website should center on the customer. It should have clear connection paths, quick-loading graphics, well-organized pages, crisp self-help features, and personal email responses that state all details of the shopping transaction in plain language.
- *Trust is a must*: The website should not follow a one-size-fits-all information-gathering approach. Rather, it should allow customers to personalize their approaches to browsing and buying so that they may come to view the company as a valued and trusted adviser.

Use Mooney's five principles to answer the following questions about the two companies you chose:

1. Identify the companies, their product lines, and their URLs. From a customer's perspective, what are your impressions of their websites and their products?
2. Compare the companies' order forms. Do the companies request the same measurements and other information? Are their prices for like items comparable? How do the order forms differ?
3. Assume you are the manager of each company you chose. Did your product unit cost influence your pricing decisions? What other factors had a significant effect on the prices you set?
4. If the companies' financial statements are available on their websites, review the figures for cost of goods sold and inventories. Describe your findings. Do the financial results agree with your previous impressions?

Group Activity Case

LO3 **Job Order Costing**

C 9. Many businesses accumulate costs for each job performed. Examples of businesses that use a job order costing system include print shops, car repair shops, health clinics, and kennels.

Visit a local business that uses job order costing, and interview the owner, manager, or accountant about the job order process and the documents the business uses to accumulate product costs. Write a paper that summarizes the information you obtained. Include the following in your summary:

1. The name of the business and the type of operations performed
2. The name and position of the individual you interviewed
3. A description of the process of starting and completing a job
4. A description of the accounting process and the documents used to track a job
5. Your responses to these questions:
   a. Did the person you interviewed know the actual amount of materials, labor, and overhead charged to a particular job? If the job includes some estimated costs, how are the estimates calculated? Do the costs affect the determination of the selling price of the product or service?
   b. Compare the documents discussed in this chapter with the documents used by the company you visited. How are they similar, and how are they different?
   c. In your opinion, does the business record and accumulate its product costs effectively? Explain.

Your instructor will divide the class into groups according to the type of business they selected to discuss this case. Summarize your group's discussion and select someone from the group to present the group's findings to the rest of the class.

Business Communication Case

LO1, LO2 **Product Costing Systems and Nonfinancial Data**

C 10. Refer to the information in **C 4**. Jordan Smith, the president of Eagle Manufacturing, wants to improve the quality of the company's operations and products. She believes waste exists in the design and manufacture of standard engine parts. To begin the improvement process, she has asked you to (1) identify the sources of such waste, (2) develop performance measures to account for the waste, and (3) estimate the current costs associated with the waste. She has asked you to submit a memo of your findings within two weeks so that she can begin strategic planning to revise the price at which Eagle sells engine parts to Cherokee.

You have identified two sources of costly waste. The Production Department is redoing work that was not done correctly the first time, and the Engineering Design Department is redesigning products that were not initially designed to customer specifications. Having improper designs has caused the company to buy parts that are not used in production. You have also obtained the following information from the product costing system:

Direct labor costs	$673,402
Engineering design costs	124,709
Indirect labor costs	67,200
Depreciation on production equipment	84,300
Supervisors' salaries	98,340
Direct materials costs	432,223
Indirect materials costs	44,332

1. In preparation for writing your memo, answer the following questions:
    a. For whom are you preparing the memo? What is the appropriate length of the memo?
    b. Why are you preparing the memo?
    c. What information is needed for the memo? Where can you get this information? What performance measure would you suggest for each activity? Is the accounting information sufficient for your memo?
    d. When is the memo due? What can be done to provide accurate and timely information?
2. Prepare an outline of the sections you would want to include in your memo.

4

Costing Systems: Process Costing

As we noted in Chapter 3, a product costing system is expected to provide unit cost information, to supply cost data for management decisions, and to furnish ending values for the Materials, Work in Process, and Finished Goods Inventory accounts. In that chapter, we described the job order costing system, which is appropriate for companies that make unique or special-order items. In this chapter, we focus on the other basic costing system: the process costing system, which is used by companies that make large amounts of similar products or liquid products or that have long, continuous production runs of identical products. We also describe product flow patterns, equivalent production, and the preparation of process cost reports.

LEARNING OBJECTIVES

LO1 Describe the process costing system, identify the reasons for its use, and discuss its role in the management process.

LO2 Relate the patterns of product flows to the cost flow methods in a process costing environment.

LO3 Explain the role of the Work in Process Inventory accounts in a process costing system.

LO4 Define *equivalent production,* and compute equivalent units.

LO5 Prepare a process cost report using the FIFO costing method.

LO6 Prepare a process cost report using the average costing method.

LO7 Evaluate operating performance using information about product cost.

- What type of product costing system will provide Intel's management with the best information about production costs?

- Why is a process costing system appropriate for Intel?

Intel Corporation, which introduced the microprocessor to the marketplace in 1971, is the world's largest manufacturer of computer chips, as well as a leading manufacturer of networking and communications products, including the flash memory used in cell phones. Because chips are becoming an off-the-shelf commodity, many of Intel's competitors have contracted to have their chips made by other companies. Intel, however, continues to manufacture chips. By using the latest manufacturing technology, the company is able to boost its operating performance and reduce production costs. Its costs per chip produced are some of the lowest among chipmakers.[1]

The Process Costing System

LO1 Describe the process costing system, identify the reasons for its use, and discuss its role in the management process.

As we noted earlier, a **process costing system** is a product costing system used by companies that make large amounts of similar products or liquid products or that have long, continuous production runs of identical products. Companies that produce paint, beverages, bricks, computer chips, milk, paper, and gallon containers of ice cream are typical users of a process costing system. Tracking costs to individual products in a continuous flow environment would be too difficult and too expensive and would not reveal significantly different product costs. One gallon of chocolate ice cream is identical to the next gallon; one computer chip looks just like the next one. Because the products are alike, they should cost the same amount to produce. A process costing system accumulates the costs of direct materials, direct labor, and overhead for each process, department, or work cell and assigns those costs to the products as they are produced during a particular period.

In the last chapter, we described how managers use the cost information that both job order costing and process costing systems yield. Figure 1 reviews those uses. When managers plan, they use information about past and projected product costing and customer preferences to decide what a product should cost and if that amount is reasonable. After they have determined a target number of units to be sold, all product-related costs for that targeted number of units can be computed and used in the budget. Each day, actual costs are incurred as units are produced, so actual unit costs can be computed. Managers use timely cost and volume information and actual unit costs to support their decision making and to add value for all of the company's stakeholders. When managers evaluate performance, they compare targeted costs with actual costs. If costs have exceeded expectations, managers analyze why this has occurred and adjust their planning and decision-making strategies. When managers communicate with external stakeholders, they use actual units produced and costs incurred to value inventory on the balance sheet and cost of goods sold on the income statement. Managers are also interested in internal reports on whether goals for product costs are being achieved.

> **Study Note**
>
> In process costing, costs are traced to production processes, whereas in job order costing, costs are traced to jobs.

Companies like Coca-Cola that produce large amounts of identical items in a continuous flow use a process costing system. With such a system, the manufacturing costs are traced to processes, departments, or work cells and are then assigned to the products manufactured during a specific period.

■ **FIGURE 1**
The Management Process: To-Do's for Managers

To-Do's for Managers

- Plan
  - Set performance expectations by developing budgets
  - Establish prices, plan sales and production volumes, and determine resource needs
  - Estimate unit costs of products or services

- Perform
  - Make decisions about controlling costs, managing the company's activity volume, ensuring quality, and negotiating contracts
  - Use timely cost, volume, and actual unit cost data

- Evaluate
  - Compare actual and targeted total and unit costs
  - Monitor relevant price and volume information
  - Analyze information to evaluate performance
  - Adjust plans and decision-making strategies

- Communicate
  - Prepare external reports, such as financial statements
  - Prepare internal performance evaluation reports comparing actual and targeted costs, analyzing nonfinancial measures of performance, and presenting data on whether goals for products or services are being achieved

FOCUS ON BUSINESS PRACTICE

What Kinds of Companies Use Process Costing?

Process costing is appropriate for companies in many types of industries. The following list provides some examples:

Industry	Company	Industry	Company
Aluminum	Alcoa, Inc.	Machinery	Caterpillar Inc.
Beverages	Coors	Manufacturing	Minnesota Mining & Manufacturing
Building materials	Owens Corning		
Chemicals	Engelhard Corporation	Oil and gas	Exxon
Computers	Apple Computer	Paper products	Boise Cascade
Containers	Crown Cork & Seal	Photography	Eastman Kodak
Electrical equipment	Emerson Electric	Plastic products	Tupperware
Foods	Kellogg Company	Soft drinks	Coca-Cola

S T O P • R E V I E W • A P P L Y

1-1. What types of businesses use process costing?

1-2. Are job order cost cards used in process costing?

Suggested answers to all Stop, Review, and Apply questions are available at http://college.hmco.com/accounting/needles/man_acc/8e/student_home.html.

Process Costing Versus Job Order Costing   Indicate whether the manufacturer of each of the following products should use a job order costing system or a process costing system to accumulate product costs:

a. Paper plates

b. Granola cereal

c. Nuclear submarines

d. Generic drugs

SOLUTION
a. Process
b. Process
c. Job order
d. Process

Patterns of Product Flows and Cost Flow Methods

LO2   Relate the patterns of product flows to the cost flow methods in a process costing environment.

During production in a process costing environment, products flow in a first-in, first-out (FIFO) fashion through several processes, departments, or work cells, and may undergo many different combinations of operations. Figure 2 illustrates two basic production flows. Example 1 shows a series of three processing steps, or departments. The completed product from one department becomes the direct materials for the next department. The product unit cost is the sum of the cost elements in all departments.

Example 2 in Figure 2 shows a different kind of production flow. Again there are three departments, but the product does not flow through all the departments in a simple 1–2–3 order. Instead, two separate products are developed: one in Department X and the other in Department Y. Both products then go to Department Z, where they are combined with a third direct material, Material AH. The unit cost transferred to the Finished Goods Inventory account when the products are completed includes cost elements from Departments X, Y, and Z.

At its simplest, product flow in a process costing environment uses a linear pattern. Because a linear approach illustrates all the concepts that are applied in both simple and complex environments, we present only that approach in this chapter. To illustrate a linear pattern of production flow, let's consider an

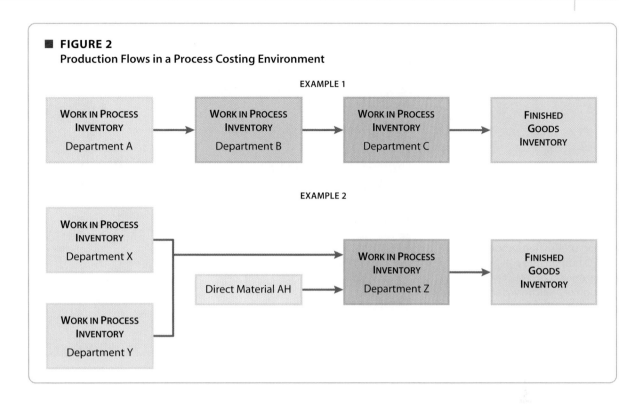

FIGURE 2
Production Flows in a Process Costing Environment

EXAMPLE 1

EXAMPLE 2

example from the computer industry. The following steps, which are illustrated in Figure 3, describe the production flow in a company like **Intel** during the manufacture of computer chips:

▶ *Producing the silicon wafer.* Silicon, which is extracted from sand and then purified, is the direct material from which computer chips are made. Through a process of crystallization, the refined, molten silicon is converted to a cylindrical ingot. The ingot is then sliced into wafers, and the wafers are polished

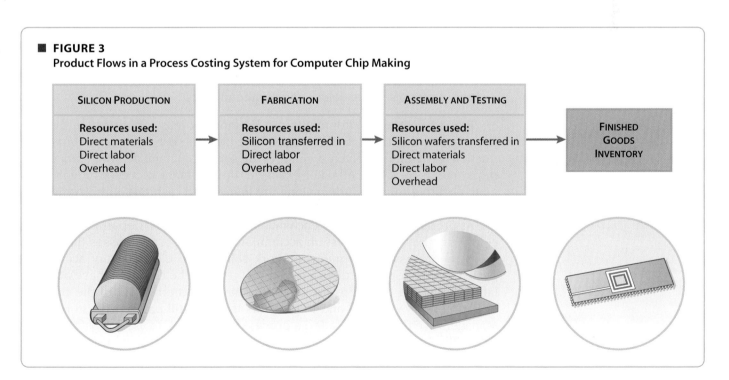

FIGURE 3
Product Flows in a Process Costing System for Computer Chip Making

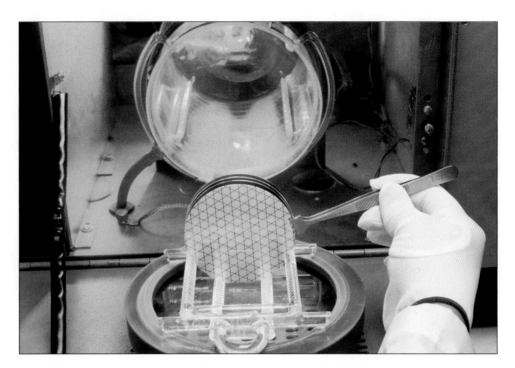

During production, products flow in a FIFO fashion through processes, departments, or work cells. The production of a silicon wafer is the first step in a production flow that results in a computer chip. The silicon wafer shown here is being tested for quality at a semiconductor plant.

to meet flatness and thickness specifications. The workers involved in these steps provide direct labor. Overhead includes the costs of the equipment that the workers use and the resources necessary to operate and maintain the equipment.

▶ *Fabricating the chips*. Fabrication includes photolithography, etching, ion implantation, and all the other steps needed to create the electronic circuits that make up each chip on a wafer. Additional direct labor and overhead costs are incurred during fabrication.

▶ *Final testing, assembly, and packaging of the chips*. Although the wafers are tested at each step in the fabrication process, each chip on a wafer is tested again when fabrication is complete. Those that pass this test are cut from the wafer, placed in metal or plastic packages, tested once again, and transferred to finished goods inventory in the warehouse. These steps incur additional direct materials, direct labor, and overhead costs.

Process costing environments can be more or less complex than the one we have just described, but even in simple process costing environments, production generally involves a number of separate manufacturing processes, departments, or work cells. For example, the separate processes involved in manufacturing sofas include making the frames and cushions, upholstering the frames, and assembling the frames and cushions into finished products.

As products pass through each manufacturing process, department, or work cell, the process costing system accumulates their costs and passes them on to the next process, department, or work cell. At the end of every accounting period, the system generates a report that assigns the costs that have accumulated during the period to the units that have transferred out of the process, department, or work cell and to the units that are still part of work in process. Managers use this report, called a **process cost report**, to assign costs by using a cost allocation method, such as the FIFO (first-in, first-out) costing method or the average costing method.

In the **FIFO costing method**, the cost flow follows the logical physical flow of production—that is, the costs assigned to the first materials processed are the first costs transferred out when those materials flow to the next process, department, or work cell. Thus, in Figure 3, the costs assigned to the production of the silicon wafers would be the first costs transferred to the fabrication of the chips. In contrast, the **average costing method** assigns an average cost to all products made during an accounting period; this method thus uses total cost averages and does not try to match cost flow with the physical flow of production. We discuss process cost reports that use the FIFO and average costing methods later in this chapter.

S T O P • R E V I E W • A P P L Y

2-1. What are the two process costing methods?

2-2. What are the similarities in the ways in which the job order costing system and the process costing system account for the costs of direct materials, direct labor, and overhead?

2-3. What are the differences in the ways in which the job order costing system and the process costing system assign costs to products?

Cost Flows Through the Work in Process Inventory Accounts

LO3 Explain the role of the Work in Process Inventory accounts in a process costing system.

As we pointed out in the last chapter, a job order costing system uses a single Work in Process Inventory account, whereas a process costing system has a separate Work in Process Inventory account for each process, department, or work cell. These accounts are the focal point of process costing. As products move from one process, department, or work cell to the next, the costs of the direct materials, direct labor, and overhead associated with them flow to the Work in Process Inventory account of that process, department, or work cell. The entry to record the transfer of product costs from one process, department, or work cell to another is:

Work in Process Inventory (next department)	XX	
Work in Process Inventory (this department)		XX

Once the products are completed, packaged, and ready for sale, their costs are transferred to the Finished Goods Inventory account. The entry to record the transfer of the completed product costs out of Work in Process Inventory into Finished Goods Inventory is:

Finished Goods Inventory	XX	
Work in Process Inventory		XX

As you will learn later in this chapter, the costs associated with these entries are the result of completing a process cost report for the process, department, or work cell.

To illustrate how costs flow through the Work in Process Inventory accounts in a process costing system, let's consider a company like **Nabisco**, which makes large quantities of identical cookies in a continuous flow. Such a company would have mixing, baking, and packaging departments. After the Mixing Department has prepared the cookie dough, the costs incurred for direct materials, direct labor, and overhead are transferred from that department's Work in Process Inventory account to the Work in Process Inventory account of the Baking Department. When the cookies are baked, the costs of the cookie dough and the baking costs are transferred from the Baking Department's Work in Process Inventory account to the Work in Process Inventory account of the Packaging Department. Once the cookies are packaged and ready for sale, all their costs—for dough, baking, and packaging—are transferred to the Finished Goods Inventory account. When the packages of cookies are sold, their costs are transferred from the Finished Goods Inventory account to the Cost of Goods Sold account.

Because the production of homogeneous products like packaged cookies, paint, or silicon chips is continuous, it would be impractical to try to assign their costs to a specific batch of products, as is done with a job order costing system. Instead, as we have noted, in a process costing system, a report prepared at the end of every accounting period assigns the costs that have accumulated in each Work in Process Inventory account to the units transferred out and to the units still in process. Notice that all costs incurred during production must be accounted for in the process cost report and that no costs are lost in the process. The report thus provides managers with an internal control over fraudulent reporting of production costs.

The process cost report uses a method like FIFO or average costing to compute the unit cost of all products worked on during the period. As a result, the product unit cost includes all costs from all processes, departments, or work cells.

STOP • REVIEW • APPLY

3-1. How many Work in Process Inventory accounts does a process costing system require?

3-2. What is the purpose of the Work in Process Inventory account?

Computing Equivalent Production

LO4 Define *equivalent production,* and compute equivalent units.

A process costing system makes no attempt to associate costs with particular job orders. Instead, it assigns the costs incurred in a process, department, or work cell to the units worked on during an accounting period by computing an average cost per unit. To compute the unit cost, the total cost of direct materials, direct labor, and overhead is divided by the total number of units worked on during the period. Thus, exactly how many units were worked on during the period is a critical question. Do we count only units started and completed during the period? Or should we include partially completed units in the beginning work in process inventory? And what about incomplete products in the ending work in process inventory?

These questions relate to the concept of equivalent production. **Equivalent production** (also called *equivalent units*) is a measure that applies a percentage-of-completion factor to partially completed units to calculate the equivalent number of whole units produced during a period for each type of input (i.e., direct materials, direct labor, and overhead). The number of equivalent units produced is the sum of (1) total units started and completed during the period and (2) an amount representing the work done on partially completed products in both the beginning and the ending work in process inventories.

Equivalent production must be computed separately for each type of input because of differences in the ways in which costs are incurred. Direct materials are usually added to production at the beginning of the process. The costs of direct labor and overhead are often incurred uniformly throughout the production process. Thus, it is convenient to combine direct labor and overhead when calculating equivalent units. These combined costs are called **conversion costs** (also called *processing costs*).

We will explain the computation of equivalent production by using a simplified example. Soda Products Company makes bottled soft drinks. As illustrated in Figure 4, the company started Week 2 with one half-completed drink in process. During Week 2, it started and completed three drinks, and at the end of Week 2, it had one drink that was three-quarters completed.

Equivalent Production for Direct Materials

At Soda Products, all direct materials, including liquids and bottles, are added at the beginning of production. Thus, the drink that was half-completed at the beginning of Week 2 had had all its direct materials added during the previous week, and no direct materials costs for this drink are included in the computation of Week 2's equivalent units for the beginning inventory units.

During Week 2, work began on four new drinks—the three drinks that were completed and the drink that was three-quarters completed at week's end. Because all direct materials are added at the beginning of the production process, all four drinks were 100 percent complete with regard to direct materials at the end of Week 2. Thus, for Week 2, the equivalent production for direct materials was 4.0 units. This figure includes direct materials for both the 3.0 units that were started and completed and the 1.0 unit that was three-quarters completed.

Equivalent Production for Conversion Costs

Because conversion costs at Soda Products are incurred uniformly throughout the production process, the equivalent production for conversion costs during

Study Note

Direct materials are sometimes added at stages of production other than the beginning (e.g., chocolate chips are added at the end of the mixing process).

Study Note

The number of units started and completed is not the same as the total number of units completed during the period. Total units completed include both units in beginning work in process inventory that were completed and units started and completed.

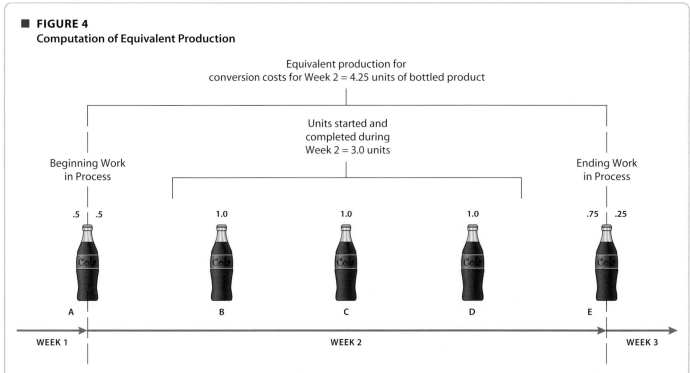

■ FIGURE 4
Computation of Equivalent Production

Note: Conversion costs (the cost of direct labor and overhead) are incurred uniformly as each physical unit of drink moves through production. Equivalent production for Week 2 is 4.25 units for conversion costs. But direct materials costs are all added to production at the beginning of the process. Because four physical units of drinks entered production in Week 2, equivalent production for the week is 4.0 units of effort for direct materials costs.

Study Note

Work in the current period is applied to three distinct product groups: units in beginning Work in Process Inventory, which must be completed; goods started and completed during the period; and goods started but not completed by the end of the accounting period.

Week 2 consists of three components: the cost to finish the half-completed unit in beginning work in process inventory (0.5), the cost to begin and finish three completed units (3.0), and the cost to begin work on the three-quarters-completed unit in ending work in process inventory (0.75). For Week 2, the total equivalent production for conversion costs was 4.25 (0.5 + 3.0 + 0.75) units.

In reality, Soda Products would make many more drinks during an accounting period and would have many more partially completed drinks in its beginning and ending work in process inventories. The number of partially completed drinks would be so great that it would be impractical to take a physical count of them. So, instead of taking a physical count, Soda Products would estimate an average percentage of completion for all drinks in process.

Summary of Equivalent Production

The following is a recap of the current equivalent production for direct materials and conversion costs for the period:

	Physical Units	Direct Materials		Conversion Costs	
Beginning inventory	1.00				
Units started this period	4.00				
Units to be accounted for	5.00				
Beginning inventory	1.00	—	0%	0.50	50%
Units started and completed	3.00	3.00	100%	3.00	100%
Ending inventory	1.00	1.00	100%	0.75	75%
Units accounted for	5.00	4.00		4.25	

S T O P • R E V I E W • A P P L Y

4-1. What is equivalent production (also called *equivalent units*)?

4-2. Why must actual unit data be changed to equivalent unit data to cost products in a process costing system?

4-3. What are *conversion costs*? Why does a process costing system compute conversion costs?

Equivalent Production   Sample Company adds direct materials at the beginning of its production process and adds conversion costs uniformly throughout the process. Given the following information from Sample Company's records for July, compute the current period's equivalent units of production:

Units in beginning inventory: 2,000

Units started during the period: 13,000

Units partially completed: 500

Percentage of completion of beginning inventory: 100% for direct materials; 40% for conversion costs

Percentage of completion of ending work in process inventory: 100% for direct materials; 70% for conversion costs

SOLUTION

Sample Company
For the Month Ended July 31

	Physical Units	Equivalent Units			
		Direct Materials		Conversion Costs	
Beginning inventory	2,000				
Units started this period	13,000				
Units to be accounted for	15,000				
Beginning inventory	2,000	—	0%	1,200	60%
Units started and completed	12,500	12,500	100%	12,500	100%
Ending inventory	500	500	100%	350	70%
Units accounted for	15,000	13,000		14,050	

Preparing a Process Cost Report Using the FIFO Costing Method

LO5   Prepare a process cost report using the FIFO costing method.

As we mentioned earlier, a process cost report, such as the one shown in Exhibit 1, is a report that managers use to track and analyze costs for a process, department, or work cell in a process costing system. In a process cost report that uses the FIFO costing method, the cost flow follows the

▼ **EXHIBIT 1**

Process Cost Report: FIFO Costing Method

Step 1:
Account for physical units.

Beginning inventory (units started last period)	6,200
Units started this period	57,500
Units to be accounted for	→ 63,700

Step 2:
Account for equivalent units.

	Physical Units	Direct Materials Materials	% Incurred During Period	Conversion Costs	% Incurred During Period
Beginning inventory (units completed this period)	6,200	0	0%	2,480	40%
Units started and completed this period	52,500	52,500	100%	52,500	100%
Ending inventory (units started but not completed this period)	5,000	5,000	100%	2,250	45%
Units accounted for	→ 63,700	57,500		57,230	

Step 3:
Account for costs.

Total Costs

Beginning inventory	→ $ 41,540	=	$ 20,150	+	$ 21,390
Current costs	510,238	=	189,750	+	320,488
Total costs	→ $551,778				

Step 4:
Compute cost per equivalent unit.

Current Costs			$189,750		$320,488
Equivalent Units			57,500		57,230
Cost per equivalent unit	$8.90	=	$3.30	+	$5.60

Step 5:
Assign costs to cost of goods manufactured and ending inventory.

Cost of goods manufactured and transferred out:					
From beginning inventory	→ $ 41,540				
Current costs to complete	13,888	=	0	+	(2,480 × $5.60)
Units started and completed this period	467,250	=	(52,500 × $3.30)	+	(52,500 × $5.60)
Cost of goods manufactured	$522,678	*(No rounding necessary)*			
Ending inventory	29,100	=	(5,000 × $3.30)	+	(2,250 × $5.60)
Total costs	→ $551,778				

WORK IN PROCESS INVENTORY ACCOUNT: COST RECAP

Beg. Bal.	41,540	522,678 (Cost
Direct materials	189,750	of goods
Conversion costs	320,488	manufactured and transferred out)
End. Bal.	**29,100**	

WORK IN PROCESS INVENTORY ACCOUNT: UNIT RECAP

Beg. Bal.	6,200	58,700 (FIFO units transferred
Units started	57,500	out from the 6,200 in beginning inventory plus the 52,500 started and completed)
End. Bal.	**5,000**	

Study Note

The FIFO method focuses on the work done in the current period only.

logical physical flow of production—that is, the costs assigned to the first products processed are the first costs transferred out when those products flow to the next process, department, or work cell.

As illustrated in Exhibit 1, the preparation of a process cost report involves five steps. The first two steps account for the units of product being processed; the next two steps account for the costs of the direct materials, direct labor, and overhead being incurred; and the final step assigns costs to products being transferred out of the area and to those remaining behind in ending work in process inventory.

Accounting for Units

Managers must account for the physical flow of products through their areas (Step 1) before they can compute equivalent production for the accounting period (Step 2). To continue with the Soda Products example, assume the following facts for the accounting period of February:

- The beginning work in process inventory consists of 6,200 partially completed units (60 percent processed in the previous period).

- During the period, the 6,200 units in beginning inventory were completed, and 57,500 units were started into production.

- Of the 57,500 units started during the period, 52,500 units were completed. The other 5,000 units remain in ending work in process inventory and are 45 percent complete.

Study Note

The percentage of completion for beginning work in process inventory is the amount of work completed during the previous period. Under FIFO, the amount of effort required to complete beginning work in process inventory is the relevant percentage.

In Step 1 of Exhibit 1, Soda Products' department manager computes the total units to be accounted for by adding the 6,200 units in beginning inventory to the 57,500 units started into production during this period. These 63,700 units are the actual physical units that the manager is responsible for during the period.

Step 2 continues accounting for physical units. As shown in Exhibit 1, the 6,200 units in beginning inventory that were completed during the period, the 52,500 units that were started and finished in the period, and the 5,000 units remaining in the department at the end of the period are summed, and the total is listed as "units accounted for." (Note that the "units accounted for" in Step 2 must equal the "units to be accounted for" in Step 1.) These amounts are used to compute equivalent production for the department's direct materials and conversion costs for the month, as described below.

Study Note

Units in beginning work in process inventory represent work accomplished in the previous accounting period that has already been assigned a certain portion of its total cost. Those units must be completed in the current period, incurring additional costs.

Beginning Inventory   Because all direct materials are added at the beginning of the production process, the 6,200 partially completed units that began February as work in process were already 100 percent complete in regard to direct materials. They were 60 percent complete in regard to conversion costs on February 1. The remaining 40 percent of their conversion costs were incurred as they were completed during the month. Thus, as shown in the "Conversion Costs" column of Exhibit 1, the equivalent production for their conversion costs is 2,480 units (6,200 × 40%).

Units Started and Completed During the Period   All the costs of the 52,500 units started and completed during February were incurred during this accounting period. Thus, the full amount of 52,500 is entered as the equivalent units for both direct materials costs and conversion costs.

Ending Inventory Because the materials for the 5,000 drinks still in process at the end of February were added when the drinks went into production during the month, the full amount of 5,000 is entered as the equivalent units for direct materials costs. However, these drinks are only 45 percent complete in terms of conversion costs. Thus, as shown in the "Conversion Costs" column of Exhibit 1, the equivalent production for their conversion costs is 2,250 units (5,000 × 45%).

Totals Step 2 is completed by summing all the physical units to be accounted for, all equivalent units for direct materials costs, and all equivalent units for conversion costs. Exhibit 1 shows that for February, Soda Products accounted for 63,700 units. Equivalent units for direct materials costs totaled 57,500, and equivalent units for conversion costs totaled 57,230. Once Soda Products knows February's equivalent unit amounts, it can complete the remaining three steps in the preparation of a process cost report.

Accounting for Costs

Thus far, we have focused on accounting for units of productive output—in our example, bottled soft drinks. We now turn our focus to cost information. Step 3 in preparing a process cost report involves accumulating and analyzing all costs charged to the Work in Process Inventory account of each production process, department, or work cell. In Step 4, the cost per equivalent unit for direct materials costs and conversion costs is computed. The following information about Soda Products' manufacture of soft drinks during February enables us to complete Steps 3 and 4:

WORK IN PROCESS INVENTORY		
Costs from beginning inventory:		
Direct materials costs	$ 20,150	
Conversion costs	21,390	
Current period costs:		
Direct materials costs	189,750	
Conversion costs	320,488	

As shown in Step 3 of Exhibit 1, all costs for the period are accumulated in the Total Costs column. Beginning inventory's direct materials costs of $20,150 are added to its conversion costs of $21,390 to determine the total cost of beginning inventory ($41,540). Current period costs for direct materials ($189,750) are added to conversion costs ($320,488) to determine the total current manufacturing costs ($510,238). The grand total of $551,778 is the sum of beginning inventory costs ($41,540) and current period costs ($510,238). Notice that only the Total Costs column is totaled. Because only the current period costs for direct materials and conversion are used in Step 4, there is no need to find the total costs of the direct materials and conversion costs columns in Step 3.

In Step 4, the direct materials costs and conversion costs for the current period are divided by their respective units of equivalent production to arrive at the cost per equivalent unit. Prior period costs attached to units in beginning inventory are not included in these computations because the FIFO costing method uses a separate costing analysis for each accounting period. (The FIFO method treats the costs of beginning inventory separately, in Step 5.) Exhibit 1 shows that the total current cost of $8.90 per equivalent unit consists

Study Note

The cost per equivalent unit using the FIFO method measures the current cost divided by current effort. Notice in Exhibit 1 that the cost of beginning work in process inventory is omitted.

FOCUS ON BUSINESS PRACTICE

How Do Businesses Today Handle the Costs of Scrap and Rework?

Traditional product costing approaches, which trace actual costs incurred to products produced, were developed at a time when businesses believed that it was efficient to anticipate scrap and rework. The costs of machine and worker downtime were part of the product cost, and significant amounts of managerial time and dollars were spent tracking those costs and analyzing differences between actual and budgeted costs. Businesses worldwide no longer tolerate defects in the production process, and the importance of scrap and rework in product costing has

therefore diminished. To cost out their products, many managers now use "engineered" costs, which exclude the costs of scrap and rework. Engineered costs are computed by determining the resources needed to manufacture a product and assigning anticipated costs to those resources. All similar products are given the same product cost. Using engineered costs frees managers to focus on nonfinancial measures, such as product throughput time and costs of quality, rather than on traditional cost-based measures that tolerate scrap and rework.

of $3.30 per equivalent unit for direct materials costs ($189,750 ÷ 57,500 equivalent units) plus $5.60 per equivalent unit for conversion costs ($320,488 ÷ 57,230 equivalent units). (Note that the equivalent units are taken from Step 2 of Exhibit 1.)

Assigning Costs

Study Note

The process cost report is developed for the purpose of assigning a value to one transaction: the transfer of goods from one department to another or to finished goods inventory. The ending balance in the Work in Process Inventory account represents the costs that remain after this transfer.

Step 5 in the preparation of a process costing report uses information from Steps 2 and 4 to assign costs, as shown in Exhibit 1. This final step determines the costs that are transferred out either to the next production process, department, or work cell or to the Finished Goods Inventory account (i.e., the cost of goods manufactured), as well as the costs that remain in the ending balance in the Work in Process Inventory account. The total costs assigned to units completed and transferred out and to ending inventory must equal the total costs in Step 3.

Cost of Goods Manufactured and Transferred Out Step 5 in Exhibit 1 shows that the costs transferred to the Finished Goods Inventory account include the $41,540 in direct materials and conversion costs for completing the 6,200 units in beginning inventory. Step 2 in the exhibit shows that 2,480 equivalent units of conversion costs were required to complete these 6,200 units. Because the equivalent unit conversion cost for February is $5.60, the cost to complete the units carried over from January is $13,888 (2,480 units × $5.60).

Each of the 52,500 units started and completed in February cost $8.90 to produce. Their combined cost of $467,250 is added to the $41,540 and $13,888 of costs required to produce the 6,200 units from beginning inventory to arrive at the total of $522,678 that is transferred to the Finished Goods Inventory account. The entry resulting from doing the process cost report for February is:

Study Note

All costs must be accounted for, including both costs from beginning inventory and costs incurred during the current period. All costs must be assigned to either ending inventory or the goods transferred out.

Finished Goods Inventory	522,678	
Work in Process Inventory		522,678

Ending Inventory All costs remaining in Soda Products Company's Work in Process Inventory account after the cost of goods manufactured has been transferred out represent the costs of the drinks still in production at the end of February. As shown in Step 5 of Exhibit 1, the balance of $29,100 in the ending Work in Process Inventory is made up of $16,500 of direct materials costs (5,000 units × $3.30 per unit) and $12,600 of conversion costs (5,000 × 45% × $5.60 per unit).

Rounding Differences

Rounding Differences   As you perform Step 5 in any process cost report, remember that the total costs in Steps 3 and 5 must always be the same number. In Exhibit 1, for example, they are both $551,778. If the numbers are not the same, first check for omission of any costs and for calculation errors. If that does not solve the problem, check whether any rounding was necessary in computing the costs per equivalent unit in Step 4. If rounding was done in Step 4, rounding differences will occur when assigning costs in Step 5. In that case, adjust the total costs transferred out for any rounding difference so that the total costs in Step 5 equal the total costs in Step 3.

> **Study Note**
>
> Rounding product unit costs to even dollars may lead to a significant difference in total costs, giving the impression that costs have been miscalculated. Carry product unit costs to two decimal places where appropriate.

Recap of Work in Process Inventory Account   When the process cost report is complete, an account recap may be prepared to show the effects of the report on the Work in Process Inventory account for the period. Two recaps of Soda Products' Work in Process Inventory account for February—one for costs and one for units—appear at the end of Exhibit 1.

Process Costing for Two or More Production Departments

Because Soda Products Company has only one production department, it needs only one Work in Process Inventory account. However, a company that has more than one production department must have a Work in Process Inventory account for each department. For instance, a soft drink maker that has a production department for formulation, another for bottling, and another for packaging needs three Work in Process Inventory accounts. When products flow from the Formulation Department to the Bottling Department, their costs flow from the Formulation Department's Work in Process Inventory account to the Bottling Department's Work in Process Inventory account. The costs transferred into the Bottling Department's Work in Process Inventory account are treated in the same way as the cost of direct materials added at the beginning of the production process. When production flows to the Packaging Department, the accumulated costs (incurred in the two previous departments) are transferred to that department's Work in Process Inventory account. At the end of the accounting period, a separate process cost report is prepared for each department.

5-1. What five steps does a process cost report entail?

5-2. What are the purposes of accounting for costs in a process cost report?

5-3. What two important dollar amounts come from the assignment of costs in Step 5 of a process cost report? How do they relate to the year-end financial statements?

5-4. How many process cost reports are prepared each period?

Preparing a Process Cost Report Using the Average Costing Method

LO6 Prepare a process cost report using the average costing method.

When a process cost report uses the average costing method, cost flows do not follow the logical physical flow of production as they do when the FIFO method is used. Instead, the costs in beginning inventory are averaged with current period costs to compute the product unit costs. Preparing a process cost report using the average costing method involves the same five steps as preparing one using the FIFO method, but the procedures for completing the steps differ. We now return to the example of Soda Products Company, but this time we assume that Soda Products uses the average costing method of process costing.

Accounting for Units

Step 1 of a process cost report, which accounts for the physical units in a production process, department, or work cell during an accounting period, is identical for the average costing and FIFO costing methods. The physical units in beginning inventory are added to the physical units started during the period to arrive at "units to be accounted for." In Step 1 of Exhibit 2, Soda Products' department manager computes the 63,700 total units to be accounted for by adding the 6,200 units in beginning inventory to the 57,500 units started into production in this period.

Step 2 also accounts for production during the period in terms of units. After the number of units completed and transferred to finished goods inventory and the number of units in ending inventory have been added to arrive at "units accounted for," the equivalent units in terms of direct materials costs and conversion costs are computed, as described below.

Units Completed and Transferred Out   As you can see in Exhibit 2, the average costing method treats both the direct materials costs and the conversion costs of the 58,700 units completed in February (6,200 units from beginning inventory + 52,500 started this period) as if they were incurred in the current period. Thus, the full amount of 58,700 is entered as the equivalent

▼ **EXHIBIT 2**

Process Cost Report: Average Costing Method

Step 1:
Account for physical units.

Beginning inventory (units started last period)	6,200
Units started this period	57,500
Units to be accounted for	63,700

Step 2:
Account for equivalent units.

	Physical Units	Direct Materials Materials	% Incurred During Period	Conversion Costs	% Incurred During Period
Units completed and transferred out	58,700	58,700	100%	58,700	100%
Ending inventory (units started but not completed this period)	5,000	5,000	100%	2,250	45%
Units accounted for	63,700	63,700		60,950	

Step 3:
Account for costs.

	Total Costs		Direct Materials		Conversion Costs
Beginning inventory	$ 41,540	=	$ 20,150	+	$ 21,390
Current costs	510,238	=	189,750	+	320,488
Total costs	$551,778		$209,900		$341,878

Step 4:
Compute cost per equivalent unit.

			Direct Materials		Conversion Costs
Total Costs			$209,900		$341,878
Equivalent Units			63,700		60,950
Cost per equivalent unit	$8.91	=	$3.30*	+	$5.61*

*Rounded to nearest cent   *Rounded to nearest cent

Step 5:
Assign costs to cost of goods manufactured and ending inventory.

			Direct Materials		Conversion Costs
Cost of goods manufactured and transferred out	$522,655 (Less rounding, $362)	=	(58,700 × $3.30)	+	(58,700 × $5.61)
Ending inventory	29,123* *Rounded.	=	(5,000 × $3.30)	+	(2,250 × $5.61)
Total costs	$551,778				

WORK IN PROCESS INVENTORY ACCOUNT: COST RECAP

Beg. Bal.	41,540	$522,655 (cost of goods manufactured and transferred out)
Direct materials	189,750	
Conversion costs	320,488	
End. Bal.	**29,123**	

WORK IN PROCESS INVENTORY ACCOUNT: UNIT COST RECAP

Beg. Bal.	6,200	58,700 units goods transferred out
Units started	57,500	
End. Bal.	**5,000**	

units for these costs. In contrast, as shown in Exhibit 1, the FIFO costing method disregards the previous period costs of units started in the last period and calculates only the equivalent units required in the current period to complete the units in beginning inventory.

Ending Inventory   The average costing method treats ending inventory in exactly the same way as the FIFO costing method. Because all direct materials are added at the beginning of the production process, the full amount of 5,000 is entered as the equivalent units for direct materials cost. Because the 5,000 units in ending inventory are only 45 percent complete in terms of conversion costs, the amount of equivalent units is 2,250 (5,000 × 45%).

Totals   Whether the FIFO costing method or the average costing method is used, Step 2 in a process cost report is completed by summing all the physical units to be accounted for, all equivalent units for direct materials costs, and all equivalent units for conversion costs. Exhibit 2 shows that for the month of February, Soda Products accounted for 63,700 physical units. Equivalent units for direct materials costs totaled 63,700, and equivalent units for conversion costs totaled 60,950.

Accounting for Costs

As we noted in our discussion of process cost reports that use the FIFO method, Step 3 of the report accumulates and analyzes all costs in the Work in Process Inventory account, and Step 4 computes the cost per equivalent unit for direct materials costs and conversion costs. You may recall from that discussion that the costs of Soda Products' beginning inventory were $20,150 for direct materials and $21,390 for conversion. Current period costs were $189,750 for direct materials and $320,488 for conversion.

If you compare Exhibit 2 with Exhibit 1, you will see that the average costing and FIFO costing methods deal with Step 3 in the same manner. All direct materials costs and conversion costs for beginning inventory and the current period are accumulated in the Total Costs column. The total of $551,778 consists of $209,900 in direct materials costs and $341,878 in conversion costs.

Step 4 computes the cost per equivalent unit for direct materials costs and conversion costs by dividing the total of these costs by their respective equivalent units. The $8.91 total cost per equivalent unit consists of $3.30 per equivalent unit for direct materials ($209,900 ÷ 63,700 equivalent units) plus $5.61 per equivalent unit for conversion ($341,878 ÷ 60,950 equivalent units). Notice that the cost per equivalent unit for both direct materials and conversion costs has been rounded to the nearest cent. In this text, any rounding differences are assigned to the units transferred out in Step 5. Notice also that the average costing and FIFO costing methods use different numerators and denominators in Step 4. Average costing divides *total* cost by *total* equivalent units, whereas FIFO divides *current* costs by *current* equivalent units.

Assigning Costs

Using information from Steps 2 and 4, Step 5 of a process cost report assigns direct materials and conversion costs to the units transferred out and to the units still in process at the end of the period. As noted above, any rounding issues that arise in completing Step 5 are included in units completed and transferred out. Soda Products completes Step 5 as described next.

Cost of Goods Manufactured and Transferred Out As shown in Exhibit 2, the costs of the units completed and transferred out are assigned by multiplying the equivalent units for direct materials and conversion costs (accounted for in Step 2) by their respective cost per equivalent unit (computed in Step 4) and then totaling these assigned values. Thus, the $522,655 assigned to cost of goods manufactured and transferred out includes $193,710 of direct materials costs (58,700 equivalent units × $3.30 cost per equivalent unit) plus $329,307 of conversion costs (58,700 equivalent units × $5.61 cost per equivalent unit). In this case, because the costs per equivalent unit were rounded in Step 4, a rounding difference of $362 has been deducted from the total cost. The $522,655 of transferred costs will go to the Finished Goods Inventory account, since the goods are ready for sale. The entry resulting from doing the process cost report for February is:

Finished Goods Inventory	522,655	
Work in Process Inventory		522,655

Ending Inventory The costs of the units in ending work in process inventory are assigned in the same way as the costs of cost of goods manufactured and transferred out. As you can see in Exhibit 2, the total of $29,123 assigned to ending inventory includes $16,500 of direct materials costs (5,000 equivalent units × $3.30 cost per equivalent unit) plus $12,623 of conversion costs (2,250 equivalent units × $5.61 cost per equivalent unit). The $29,123 (rounded) will appear as the ending balance in this department's Work in Process Inventory account.

Rounding Differences Because the costs per equivalent unit computed in Step 4 were rounded to the nearest cent, rounding differences occurred when costs were assigned in Step 5. Thus, in Step 5, a $362 deduction was made to cost of goods manufactured and transferred out so that total costs in Step 5 would equal total costs in Step 3.

Recap of Work in Process Inventory Account As we noted earlier, when a process cost report is complete, an account recap may be prepared to show the effects of the report on the Work in Process Inventory account for the period. Exhibit 2 includes a cost recap and a unit recap of Soda Products' Work in Process Inventory account for February.

S T O P • R E V I E W • A P P L Y

6-1. Briefly describe the similarities and differences in process cost reports that use the FIFO and average costing methods.

6-2. Explain the average costing method of assigning costs to products in a process costing system.

6-3. In Step 4, how do the average costing and FIFO costing methods differ in computing the cost per equivalent unit for direct materials costs and conversion costs?

Equivalent Production: Average Costing Method Sample Company adds direct materials at the beginning of its production process and adds conversion costs uniformly throughout the process. Given the following information from Sample Company's records for July, compute the current period's equivalent units of production:

Units in beginning inventory: 2,000

Units started during the period: 13,000

Units partially completed: 500

Percentage of completion of beginning inventory: 100% for direct materials; 40% for conversion costs

Percentage of completion of ending work in process inventory: 100% for direct materials; 70% for conversion costs

SOLUTION

Sample Company
For the Month Ended July 31

	Physical Units	Direct Materials		Conversion Costs	
		Equivalent Units			
Beginning inventory	2,000				
Units started this period	13,000				
Units to be accounted for	15,000				
Beginning inventory	2,000				
Units started and completed	14,500	14,500	100%	14,500	100%
Ending inventory	500	500	100%	350	70%
Units accounted for	15,000	15,000		14,850	

Using Information About Product Cost to Evaluate Performance

LO7 Evaluate operating performance using information about product cost.

Study Note

Performance measures are quantitative tools that help managers assess the performance of a specific process or expected outcome.

A product costing system—whether it's a job order or a process costing system—provides managers with valuable information. As we have noted, managers use the information that such a system provides in determining a product's price and in computing the balances in the Materials Inventory, Work in Process Inventory, and Finished Goods Inventory accounts on the balance sheet and the Cost of Goods Sold account on the income statement. Managers also use product cost information to evaluate operating performance. Such an analysis may include consideration of the following:

▶ Cost trends for a product or product line

▶ Units produced per time period

▶ Materials usage per unit produced

▶ Labor cost per unit produced

▶ Special needs of customers

▶ Cost-effectiveness of changing to a more advanced production process

Cost trends can be developed from product cost data over several time periods. Such trends help managers identify areas of rising costs or areas in which cost-effectiveness has improved. Tracking units produced per time period, a figure easily pulled from a product cost analysis, can help managers evaluate operating efficiency.

Direct materials and labor costs are significant parts of a product's cost and should be monitored constantly. Trends in direct materials usage and labor costs per unit produced can help managers determine optimal resource usage.

Anticipating customers' needs is very important to managers. By tracking the size, cost, and type of products ordered by customers, managers can see which customers are increasing or reducing their orders and take action to improve customer relations.

Finally, decisions to purchase new machinery and equipment are often based on the savings that the change is expected to produce. Information from a product costing system helps managers make such decisions in that it enables them to estimate unit costs for the new equipment and to compare them with cost trends for the existing equipment.

STOP • REVIEW • APPLY

7-1. How can information about product cost help managers evaluate operating performance?

7-2. What type of operating performance can be evaluated with the information that a product costing system provides about (a) units produced per time period, (b) labor cost per unit produced, and (c) special needs of customers?

A LOOK BACK AT

INTEL CORPORATION

The Decision Point at the beginning of this chapter focused on **Intel Corporation**, a company known as a leader in the field of silicon technology. It posed these questions:

- **What type of product costing system will provide Intel's management with the best information about production costs?**
- **Why is a process costing system appropriate for Intel?**

Because there is a continuous flow of similar products during most of the chip-making process, the most appropriate costing system for Intel is a process costing system. Such a system accumulates costs by process, department, or work cell and assigns them to the products as they pass through the production system. Use of the process costing system does not imply that every finished product is exactly the same. For instance, some computer chips are more complex than others and are therefore more difficult and costly to produce. Intel's management has created a system for tracking the activities involved in chip production. All costs connected with processing activities are assigned to a batch of chips based on the types of activities involved in production. This process costing system provides the information that Intel's management needs to make sound product decisions.

CHAPTER REVIEW

REVIEW of Learning Objectives

LO1 Describe the process costing system, identify the reasons for its use, and discuss its role in the management process.

A process costing system is a product costing system used by companies that produce large amounts of similar products or liquid products or that have long, continuous production runs of identical products. Because these companies have a continuous production flow, it would be impractical for them to use a job order costing system, which tracks costs to a specific batch of products or a specific job order. In contrast to a job order costing system, a process costing system accumulates the costs of direct materials, direct labor, and overhead for each process, department, or work cell and assigns those costs to the products as they are produced during a particular period.

The product costs provided by a process costing system play a key role in the management process. When managers plan, they use past and projected information about product costs to set selling prices and prepare budgets. Each day, managers use cost information to make decisions about controlling costs, managing the company's volume of activity, ensuring quality, and negotiating prices. Actual costs are incurred as units are produced, so actual unit costs can be computed. When managers evaluate performance results, they compare targeted costs with actual costs. When managers communicate with external stakeholders, they use actual units produced and costs incurred to value inventory on the balance sheet and cost of goods sold on the income statement. They also analyze internal reports that compare the organization's measures of actual and targeted performance to determine whether cost goals for products or services are being achieved.

LO2 Relate the patterns of product flows to the cost flow methods in a process costing environment.

During production in a process costing environment, products flow in a first-in, first-out (FIFO) fashion through several processes, departments, or work cells. As they do, the process costing system accumulates their costs and passes them on to the next process, department, or work cell. At the end of every accounting period, the system generates a report that assigns the costs that have accumulated during the period to the units that have transferred out of the process, department, or work cell and to the units that are still work in process. The process cost report may assign costs by using the FIFO costing method—in which the costs assigned to the first products processed are the first costs transferred out when those products flow to the next process, department, or work cell—or the average costing method, which assigns an average cost to all products made during an accounting period.

LO3 Explain the role of the Work in Process Inventory accounts in a process costing system.

The Work in Process Inventory accounts are the focal point of a process costing system. Each production process, department, or work cell has its own Work in Process Inventory account. All costs charged to that process, department, or work cell flow into its Work in Process Inventory account. A process cost report prepared at the end of every accounting period assigns the costs that have accumulated during the period to the units that have flowed out of the process, department, or work cell (the cost of goods transferred out) and to the units that are still in process (the cost of ending inventory).

LO4 Define *equivalent production,* and compute equivalent units.

Equivalent production is a measure that applies a percentage-of-completion factor to partially completed units to compute the equivalent number of whole units produced in an accounting period for each type of input. Equivalent units are computed from (1) units in the beginning work in process inventory and their percentage of completion, (2) units started and completed during the period, and (3) units in the ending work in process inventory and their percentage of completion. The computation of equivalent units differs depending on whether the FIFO method or the average costing method is used.

LO5 Prepare a process cost report using the FIFO costing method.

In a process cost report that uses the FIFO costing method, the cost flow follows the logical physical flow of production—that is, the costs assigned to the first products processed are the first costs transferred when those products flow to the next process, department, or work cell. Preparation of a process cost report involves five steps. Steps 1 and 2 account for the physical flow of products and compute the equivalent units of production. Once equivalent production has been determined, the focus of the report shifts to accounting for costs. In Step 3, all direct materials costs and conversion costs for the current period are added to arrive at total costs. In Step 4, the cost per equivalent unit for both direct materials costs and conversion costs is found by dividing those costs by their respective equivalent units. In Step 5, costs are assigned to the units completed and transferred out during the period, as well as to the ending work in process inventory. The costs assigned to units completed and transferred out include the costs incurred in the preceding period and the conversion costs that were needed to complete those units during the current period. That amount is added to the total cost of producing all units started and completed during the period. The result is the total cost transferred out for the units completed during the period. Step 5 also assigns costs to units still in process at the end of the period by multiplying their direct materials costs and conversion costs by their respective equivalent units. The total equals the balance in the Work in Process Inventory account at the end of the period.

LO6 Prepare a process cost report using the average costing method.

The average costing method is an alternative method of accounting for production costs in a manufacturing environment characterized by a continuous production flow. The difference between a process costing report that uses the FIFO method and one that uses the average costing method is that the latter does not differentiate when work was done on inventory. When the average costing method is used, the costs in beginning inventory are averaged with the current period costs to compute the product unit costs. These costs are used to value the ending balance in Work in Process Inventory and the goods completed and transferred out of the process, department, or work cell.

LO7 Evaluate operating performance using information about product cost.

Both the job order and process costing systems supply information that managers can use to evaluate operating performance. Such an analysis may include consideration of the cost trends for a product or product line, units produced per time period, materials usage per unit produced, labor cost per unit produced, special needs of customers, and the cost-effectiveness of changing to a more advanced production process.

REVIEW of Concepts and Terminology

The following concepts and terms were introduced in this chapter:

Average costing method: A process costing method that assigns an average cost to all products made during an accounting period. **(LO2)**

Conversion costs: The combined costs of direct labor and overhead. Also called *processing costs*. **(LO4)**

Equivalent production: A measure that applies a percentage-of-completion factor to partially completed units to compute the equivalent number of whole units produced during a period for each type of input. Also called *equivalent units*. **(LO4)**

FIFO costing method: A process costing method in which the cost flow follows the actual flow of production, so that the costs assigned to the first products processed are the first costs transferred out when those products flow to the next process, department, or work cell. **(LO2)**

Process costing system: A product costing system that traces the costs of direct materials, direct labor, and overhead to processes, departments, or work cells and then assigns the costs to the products

manufactured by those processes, departments, or work cells; used by companies that produce large amounts of similar products or liquid products or that have long, continuous production runs of identical products. **(LO1)**

Process cost report: A report that managers use to track and analyze costs in a process costing system. **(LO2)**

≡ REVIEW Problem

LO5, LO6 **Process Costing Using the FIFO Costing and Average Costing Methods**

Pop Chewing Gum Company produces several flavors of bubble gum. Two basic direct materials, gum base and flavored sweetener, are blended at the beginning of the manufacturing process. No materials are lost in the process, so one kilogram of materials input produces one kilogram of bubble gum. Direct labor and overhead costs are incurred uniformly throughout the blending process. On June 30, 16,000 units were in process. All direct materials had been added, but the units were only 70 percent complete in regard to conversion costs. Direct materials costs of $8,100 and conversion costs of $11,800 were attached to the beginning inventory. During July, 405,000 kilograms of materials were used at a cost of $202,500. Direct labor charges were $299,200, and overhead costs applied during July were $284,000. The ending work in process inventory was 21,600 kilograms. All direct materials have been added to those units, and 25 percent of the conversion costs have been assigned. Output from the Blending Department is transferred to the Packaging Department.

Required

1. Prepare a process cost report using the FIFO costing method for the Blending Department for July.
2. Identify the amount that should be transferred out of the Work in Process Inventory account, and state where those dollars should be transferred. What is the journal entry?
3. Repeat 1 using the average costing method.
4. Repeat 2 using the average costing method.

Answer to Review Problem

1. Process cost report using the FIFO costing method:

Pop Chewing Gum Company
Blending Department
Process Cost Report: FIFO Method
For the Month Ended July 31

Step 1:

Account for physical units.	Beginning inventory	
	(units started last period)	16,000
	Units started this period	405,000
	Units to be accounted for	421,000

(Continued)

		Physical Units	Direct Materials Costs	% Incurred During Period	Conversion Costs	% Incurred During Period
Step 2:						
Account for equivalent units.	Beginning inventory (units completed this period)	16,000	0	0%	4,800	30%
	Units started and completed this period	383,400	383,400	100%	383,400	100%
	Ending inventory (units started but not completed this period)	21,600	21,600	100%	5,400	25%
	Units accounted for	421,000	405,000		393,600	

		Total Costs				
Step 3:						
Account for costs.	Beginning inventory	$ 19,900	=	$ 8,100	+	$ 11,800
	Current costs	785,700	=	202,500	+	583,200
	Total costs	$805,600				

Step 4:	Current Costs		$202,500		$583,200
Compute cost per equivalent unit.	Equivalent Units		405,000		393,600
	Cost per equivalent unit	$1.98	=	$.50	+	$1.48*

*Rounded to nearest cent

Step 5:					
Assign costs to cost of goods manufactured and ending inventory.	Cost of goods manufactured and transferred out:				
	From beginning inventory	$ 19,900			
	Current costs to complete	7,104	=	0	+	(4,800 × $1.48)
	Units started and completed this period	759,132	=	(383,400 × $.50)	+	(383,400 × $1.48)
	Cost of goods manufactured	$786,808 *(Add rounding, $672)*				
	Ending inventory	18,792	=	(21,600 × $.50)	+	(5,400 × $1.48)
	Total costs	$805,600				

WORK IN PROCESS INVENTORY ACCOUNT: COST RECAP			
Beg. Bal.	19,900	786,808 (cost of	
Direct materials	202,500	goods manufactured	
Conversion costs	583,200	and transferred out)	
End. Bal.	**18,792**		

WORK IN PROCESS INVENTORY ACCOUNT: UNIT RECAP			
Beg. Bal.	16,000	399,400 (FIFO units transferred	
Units started	405,000	out from the 16,000 in	
		beginning inventory plus the	
		383,400 started and completed)	
End. Bal.	**21,600**		

2. The amount of $786,808 should be transferred to the Work in Process Inventory account of the Packaging Department. The journal entry is:

Work in Process Inventory (Packaging Department)	786,808	
Work in Process Inventory (Blending Department)		786,808

3. Process cost report using the average costing method:

Pop Chewing Gum Company
Blending Department
Process Cost Report: Average Costing Method
For the Month Ended July 31

Step 1:
Account for physical units.

Beginning inventory (units started last period)	16,000	
Units started this period	405,000	
Units to be accounted for	421,000	

Step 2:
Account for equivalent units.

	Physical Units	Direct Materials Costs	% Incurred During Period	Conversion Costs	% Incurred During Period
Units completed and transferred out	399,400	399,400	100%	399,400	100%
Ending inventory (units started but not completed this period)	21,600	21,600	100%	5,400	25%
Units accounted for	421,000	421,000		404,800	

Step 3:
Account for costs.

	Total Costs		Direct Materials		Conversion
Beginning inventory	$ 19,900	=	$ 8,100	+	$ 11,800
Current costs	785,700	=	202,500	+	583,200
Total costs	$805,600		$210,600		$595,000

Step 4:
Compute cost per equivalent unit.

Total Costs			$210,600		$595,000
Equivalent Units			421,000		404,800
Cost per equivalent unit	$1.97	=	$.50	+	$1.47*

*Rounded to nearest cent   *Rounded to nearest cent

Step 5:
Assign costs to cost of goods manufactured inventory.

Cost of goods manufactured and transferred out	$786,862	=	(399,400 × $.50) + (399,400 × $1.47)
			(Add rounding $44)
Ending inventory	18,738	=	(21,600 × $.50) + (5,400 × $1.47)
Total costs	$805,600		

WORK IN PROCESS INVENTORY ACCOUNT: COST RECAP

Beg. Bal.	19,900	$786,862 (cost of	
Direct materials	202,500	goods manufactured	
Conversion costs	583,200	and transferred out)	
End. Bal.	**18,738**		

WORK IN PROCESS INVENTORY ACCOUNT: UNIT RECAP

Beg. Bal.	16,000	399,400 units goods	
Units started	405,000	transferred out	
End. Bal.	**21,600**		

4. The amount of $786,862 should be transferred to the Work in Process Inventory account of the Packaging Department. The entry is:

Work in Process Inventory (Packaging Department)	786,862	
Work in Process Inventory (Blending Department)		786,862

CHAPTER ASSIGNMENTS

BUILDING Your Basic Knowledge and Skills

Short Exercises

LO1   **Process Costing Versus Job Order Costing**

SE 1. Indicate whether the manufacturer of each of the following products should use a job order costing system or a process costing system to accumulate product costs:

1. Plastics
2. Ocean cruise ships
3. Cereal
4. Medical drugs for veterinary practices

LO1   **Process Costing Versus Job Order Costing**

SE 2. Indicate whether each of the following is a characteristic of job order costing or of process costing:

1. Several Work in Process Inventory accounts are used, one for each department or work cell in the process.
2. Costs are grouped by process, department, or work cell.
3. Costs are measured for each completed job.
4. Only one Work in Process Inventory account is used.
5. Costs are measured in terms of units completed in specific time periods.
6. Costs are assigned to specific jobs or batches of product.

LO3   **Process Costing and a Work in Process Inventory Account**

SE 3. Prue Chemical uses an automated mixing machine in its Mixing Department to combine three raw materials into a product called Triogo. On the average, each unit of Triogo contains $3 of Material X, $6 of Material Y, $9 of Material Z, $2 of direct labor, and $12 of overhead. Total costs charged to the Mixing Department's Work in Process Inventory account during the month were $208,000. There were no units in beginning or ending work in process inventory. How many units were completed and transferred to Finished Goods Inventory during the month?

LO4   **Equivalent Production: FIFO Costing Method**

SE 4. Blue Blaze adds direct materials at the beginning of its production process and adds conversion costs uniformly throughout the process. Given the following information from Blue Blaze's records for July and using Steps 1 and 2 of the FIFO costing method, compute the equivalent units of production:

Units in beginning inventory	3,000
Units started during the period	17,000
Units partially completed	2,500
Percentage of completion of ending work in process inventory	100% for direct materials; 70% for conversion costs
Percentage of completion of beginning inventory	100% for direct materials; 40% for conversion costs

LO5   **Determining Unit Cost: FIFO Costing Method**

SE 5. Using the information from **SE 4** and the following data, compute the total cost per equivalent unit:

	Costs for the Period	Beginning Work in Process
Direct materials costs	$20,400	$7,600
Conversion costs	32,490	2,545

LO5 **Assigning Costs: FIFO Costing Method**

SE 6. Using the data in **SE 4** and **SE 5**, assign costs to the units transferred out and to the units in ending inventory for July.

LO6 **Equivalent Production: Average Costing Method**

SE 7. Using the same data as in **SE 4** but Steps 1 and 2 of the average costing method, compute the equivalent units of production for the month.

LO6 **Determining Unit Cost: Average Costing Method**

SE 8. Using the average costing method and the information from **SE 4**, **SE 5**, and **SE 7**, compute the total cost per equivalent unit.

LO6 **Assigning Costs: Average Costing Method**

SE 9. Using the data in **SE 4**, **SE 5**, **SE 7**, and **SE 8** and assuming that Blue Blaze uses the average costing method, assign costs to the units completed and transferred out and to the units in ending inventory for July.

LO7 **Measuring Performance with Product Costing Data**

SE 10. The following table presents the weekly average of direct materials costs per unit for two products. How could the manager of the department that makes these products use this information?

Week	Product A	Product B
1	$45.20	$23.90
2	46.10	23.80
3	48.30	23.80
4	49.60	23.60

Exercises

LO1 **Process Costing Versus Job Order Costing**

E 1. Indicate whether the manufacturer of each of the following products should use a job order costing system or a process costing system to accumulate product costs:

1. Paint
2. Fruit juices
3. Tailor-made suits
4. Milk
5. Coffee cups printed with your school insignia
6. Paper
7. Roller coaster for a theme park
8. Posters for a fundraising event

LO2 **Use of Process Costing Information**

E 2. Tom's Bakery makes a variety of cakes, cookies, and pies for distribution to five major chains of grocery stores in the Quad-City area. The company uses a standard manufacturing process for all items except special-order cakes. It currently uses a process costing system. Tom, the owner of the company, has some urgent questions, which are listed on the next page. Which of these questions can be answered using information from a process costing system? Which can be best answered using information from a job order costing system? Explain your answers.

1. How much does it cost to make one chocolate cheesecake?
2. Did the cost of making special-order cakes exceed the cost budgeted for this month?
3. What is the value of the pie inventory at the end of June?
4. What were the costs of the cookies sold during June?
5. At what price should Tom's Bakery sell its famous brownies to the grocery store chains?
6. Were the planned production costs of $3,000 for making pies in June exceeded?

LO3 **Work in Process Inventory Accounts in Process Costing Systems**

E 3. Gilbert, Inc., which uses a process costing system, makes a chemical used as a food preservative. The manufacturing process involves Departments A and B. The company had the following total costs and unit costs for completed production last month, when it manufactured 10,000 pounds of the chemical. Neither Department A nor Department B had any beginning or ending work in process inventories.

	Total Cost	Unit Cost
Department A		
Direct materials	$10,000	$1.00
Direct labor	2,600	0.26
Overhead	1.300	0.13
Total costs	$13,900	$1.39
Department B		
Direct materials	$ 3,000	$0.30
Direct labor	700	0.07
Overhead	1,000	0.10
Total costs	$ 4,700	$0.47
Totals	$18,000	$1.86

1. How many Work in Process Inventory accounts would Gilbert use?
2. What dollar amount of the chemical's production cost was transferred from Department A to Department B last month?
3. What dollar amount was transferred from Department B to the Finished Goods Inventory account?
4. What dollar amount is useful in determining a selling price for one pound of the chemical?

LO4 **Equivalent Production: FIFO Costing Method**

E 4. McCabe Stone Company produces bricks. Although the company has been in operation for only 12 months, it already enjoys a good reputation. During its first twelve months, it put 600,000 bricks into production and completed and transferred 586,000 bricks to finished goods inventory. The remaining bricks were still in process at the end of the year and were 60 percent complete.

The company's process costing system adds all direct materials costs at the beginning of the production process; conversion costs are incurred uniformly throughout the process. From this information, compute the equivalent units of production for direct materials and conversion costs for the company's first year, which ended December 31. Use the FIFO costing method.

LO4   **Equivalent Production: FIFO Costing Method**

E 5. Olivares Enterprises makes Rainberry Shampoo for professional hair stylists. On July 31, it had 5,200 liters of shampoo in process, which were 80 percent complete in regard to conversion costs and 100 percent complete in regard to direct materials costs. During August, it put 212,500 liters of direct materials into production. Data for work in process inventory on August 31 were as follows: shampoo, 4,500 liters; stage of completion, 60 percent for conversion costs and 100 percent for direct materials. From this information, compute the equivalent units of production for direct materials and conversion costs for the month. Use the FIFO costing method.

LO4   **Equivalent Production: FIFO Costing Method**

E 6. Cunningham Paper Corporation produces wood pulp that is used in making paper. The following data pertain to the company's production of pulp during September:

	Tons	Percentage Complete Direct Materials	Percentage Complete Conversion Costs
Work in process, Aug. 31	40,000	100%	60%
Placed into production	250,000	—	—
Work in process, Sept. 30	80,000	100%	40%

Compute the equivalent units of production for direct materials and conversion costs for September using the FIFO costing method.

LO5   **Work in Process Inventory Accounts: Total Unit Cost**

E 7. Scientists at Anschultz Laboratories, Inc., have just perfected Dentalite, a liquid substance that dissolves tooth decay. The substance, which is generated by a complex process involving five departments, is very expensive. Cost and equivalent unit data for the latest week are as follows (units are in ounces):

Dept.	Direct Materials Costs Dollars	Direct Materials Costs Equivalent Units	Conversion Costs Dollars	Conversion Costs Equivalent Units
A	$12,000	1,000	$33,825	2,050
B	21,835	1,985	13,065	1,005
C	23,896	1,030	20,972	2,140
D	—	—	22,086	2,045
E	—	—	15,171	1,945

From these data, compute the unit cost for each department and the total unit cost of producing one ounce of Dentalite.

LO5   **Determining Unit Cost: FIFO Costing Method**

E 8. Turner's Pots, Inc., manufactures sets of heavy-duty cookware. It has just completed production for August. At the beginning of August, its Work in Process Inventory account showed direct materials costs of $31,700 and conversion costs of $29,400. The cost of direct materials used in August was $275,373; conversion costs were $175,068. During the month, the company started and completed 15,190 sets. For August, a total of 16,450 equivalent sets for direct materials and 16,210 equivalent sets for conversion costs have been computed.

From this information, determine the cost per equivalent set for August. Use the FIFO costing method.

LO5   **Assigning Costs: FIFO Costing Method**

E 9. The Beach Bakery produces Healthnut coffee bread. It uses a process costing system. In March, its beginning inventory was 450 units, which were 100 percent complete for direct materials costs and 10 percent complete for conversion costs. The cost of beginning inventory was $655. Units started and completed during the month totaled 14,200. Ending inventory was 410 units, which were 100 percent complete for direct materials costs and 70 percent complete for conversion costs. Costs per equivalent unit for March were $1.40 for direct materials costs and $.80 for conversion costs.

From this information, compute the cost of goods transferred to the Finished Goods Inventory account, the cost remaining in the Work in Process Inventory account, and the total costs to be accounted for. Use the FIFO costing method.

LO6   **Equivalent Production: Average Costing Method**

E 10. Using the data in **E 4** and assuming that the company uses the average costing method, compute the equivalent units of production for direct materials and conversion costs for the year ended December 31.

LO6   **Equivalent Production: Average Costing Method**

E 11. Using the data in **E 5** and assuming that the company uses the average costing method, compute the equivalent units of production for direct materials and conversion for August.

LO6   **Equivalent Production: Average Costing Method**

E 12. Using the data in **E 6** and assuming that the company uses the average costing method, compute the equivalent units of production for direct materials and conversion for September.

LO6   **Determining Unit Cost: Average Costing Method**

E 13. Using the data in **E 8** and the average costing method, determine the cost per equivalent set for August. Assume equivalent sets are 16,900 for direct materials costs and 17,039 for conversion costs.

LO6   **Process Cost Report: Average Costing Method**

E 14. Toy Country Corporation produces children's toys using a liquid plastic formula and a continuous production process. In the company's toy truck work cell, the plastic is heated and fed into a molding machine. The molded toys are then cooled and trimmed and sent to the packaging work cell. All direct materials are added at the beginning of the process. In November, the beginning work in process inventory was 420 units, which were 40 percent complete; the ending balance was 400 units, which were 70 percent complete.

During November, 15,000 units were started into production. The Work in Process Inventory account had a beginning balance of $937 for direct materials costs and $370 for conversion costs. In the course of the month, $35,300 of direct materials were added to the process, and $31,760 of conversion costs were assigned to the work cell. Using the average costing method, prepare a process cost report that computes the equivalent units for November, the product unit cost for the toys, and the ending balance in the Work in Process Inventory account.

LO7   **Measuring Performance with Nonfinancial Product Data**

E 15. During December, Carola Products Company conducted a study of the productivity of its metal-trimming operation, which requires the use of three machines. The data were condensed into product units per hour so that managers could analyze the productivity of the three workers who operate the machines. The target output established for the year was 125 units per hour. From the following data, analyze the productivity of the three machine operators:

Week	Operator 1	Operator 2	Operator 3
1	119 per hour	129 per hour	124 per hour
2	120 per hour	127 per hour	124 per hour
3	122 per hour	125 per hour	123 per hour
4	124 per hour	122 per hour	124 per hour

Problems

LO5 **Process Costing: FIFO Costing Method**

P 1. Lightning Industries specializes in making Flash, a high-moisture, low-alkaline wax used to protect and preserve skis. The company began producing a new, improved brand of Flash on January 1. Materials are introduced at the beginning of the production process. During January, 15,300 pounds were used at a cost of $46,665. Direct labor of $17,136 and overhead costs of $25,704 were incurred uniformly throughout the month. By January 31, 13,600 pounds of Flash had been completed and transferred to the finished goods inventory (one pound of input equals one pound of output). Since no spoilage occurred, the leftover materials remained in production and were 40 percent complete on average.

Required

1. Using the FIFO costing method, prepare a process cost report for January.
2. From the information in the process cost report, identify the amount that should be transferred out of the Work in Process Inventory account, and state where those dollars should be transferred.

LO5 **Process Costing: FIFO Costing Method**

P 2. Liquid Extracts Company produces a line of fruit extracts for home use in making wine, jams and jellies, pies, and meat sauces. Fruits enter the production process in pounds; the product emerges in quarts (one pound of input equals one quart of output). On May 31, 4,250 units were in process. All direct materials had been added, and the units were 70 percent complete for conversion costs. Direct materials costs of $4,607 and conversion costs of $3,535 were attached to the units in beginning work in process inventory. During June, 61,300 pounds of fruit were added at a cost of $71,108. Direct labor for the month totaled $19,760, and overhead costs applied were $31,375. On June 30, 3,400 units remained in process. All direct materials for these units had been added, and 50 percent of conversion costs had been incurred.

Required

1. Using the FIFO costing method, prepare a process cost report for June.
2. From the information in the process cost report, identify the amount that should be transferred out of the Work in Process Inventory account, and state where those dollars should be transferred.

LO5 **Process Costing: FIFO Costing Method**

P 3. Canned fruits and vegetables are the main products made by Good Foods, Inc. All direct materials are added at the beginning of the Mixing Department's process. When the ingredients have been mixed, they go to the Cooking Department. There the mixture is heated to 100° Celsius and simmered for 20 minutes. When cooled, the mixture goes to the Canning Department for final processing. Throughout the operations, direct labor and overhead costs are incurred uniformly. No direct materials are added in the Cooking Department. Cost data and other information for the Mixing Department for January are as follows:

Production Cost Data	Direct Materials Costs	Conversion Costs
Mixing Department		
Beginning inventory	$ 28,560	$ 5,230
Current period costs	$450,000	$181,200
Work in process inventory		
Beginning inventory		
Mixing Department (40% complete)	5,000 liters	
Ending inventory		
Mixing Department (60% complete)	6,000 liters	
Unit production data		
Units started during January	90,000 liters	
Units transferred out during January	89,000 liters	

Assume that no spoilage or evaporation loss took place during January.

Required

1. Using the FIFO costing method, prepare a process cost report for the Mixing Department for January.
2. **Manager Insight:** Explain how the analysis for the Cooking Department will differ from the analysis for the Mixing Department.

LO5 **Process Costing: One Process and Two Time Periods—FIFO Costing Method**

P 4. Wash Clean Laboratories produces biodegradable liquid detergents that leave no soap film. The production process has been automated, so the product can now be produced in one operation instead of in a series of heating, mixing, and cooling operations. All direct materials are added at the beginning of the process, and conversion costs are incurred uniformly throughout the process. Operating data for July and August are as follows:

	July	August
Beginning work in process inventory		
Units (pounds)	2,300	3,050
Direct materials costs	$ 4,699	?*
Conversion costs	$ 1,219	?*
Production during the period		
Units started (pounds)	31,500	32,800
Direct materials costs	$65,520	$66,912
Conversion costs	$54,213	$54,774
Ending work in process inventory		
Units (pounds)	3,050	3,600

*From calculations at end of July.

The beginning work in process inventory was 30 percent complete for conversion costs. The ending work in process inventory for July was 60 percent complete; for August, it was 50 percent complete. Assume that the loss from spoilage and evaporation was negligible.

Required

1. Using the FIFO costing method, prepare a process cost report for July.

2. From the information in the process cost report, identify the amount that should be transferred out of the Work in Process Inventory account, and state where those dollars should be transferred.

3. Repeat **1** and **2** for August.

LO6 **Process Costing: Average Costing Method**

P 5. Hurricane Products, Inc., makes high-vitamin, calorie-packed wafers that are popular among professional athletes because they supply quick energy. The company produces the wafers in a continuous flow, and it uses a process costing system based on the average costing method. It recently purchased several automated machines so that the wafers can be produced in a single department. All direct materials are added at the beginning of the process. The costs for the machine operators' labor and production-related overhead are incurred uniformly throughout the process.

In February, the company put a total of 231,200 liters of direct materials into production at a cost of $294,780. Two liters of direct materials were used to produce one unit of output (one unit = 144 wafers). Direct labor costs for February were $60,530, and overhead was $181,590. The beginning work in process inventory for February was 14,000 units, which were 100 percent complete for direct materials and 20 percent complete for conversion costs. The total cost of those units was $55,000, $48,660 of which was assigned to the cost of direct materials. The ending work in process inventory of 12,000 units was fully complete for direct materials but only 30 percent complete for conversion costs.

Required

1. Using the average costing method and assuming no loss due to spoilage, prepare a process cost report for February.

2. From the information in the process cost report, identify the amount that should be transferred out of the Work in Process Inventory account, and state where those dollars should be transferred.

Alternate Problems

LO5, LO6 **Process Costing: FIFO Costing and Average Costing Methods**

P 6. Sunshine Soda Company manufactures and sells several different kinds of soft drinks. Direct materials (sugar syrup and artificial flavor) are added at the beginning of production in the Mixing Department. Direct labor and overhead costs are applied to products throughout the process. For August, beginning inventory for the citrus flavor was 2,400 gallons, 80 percent complete. Ending inventory was 3,600 gallons, 50 percent complete. Production data show 240,000 gallons started during August. A total of 238,800 gallons was completed and transferred to the Bottling Department. Beginning inventory costs were $600 for direct materials and $676 for conversion costs. Current period costs were $57,600 for direct materials and $83,538 for conversion costs.

Required

1. Using the FIFO costing method, prepare a process cost report for the Mixing Department for August.

2. From the information in the process cost report, identify the amount that should be transferred out of the Work in Process Inventory account, and state where those dollars should be transferred.

3. Repeat **1** and **2** using the average costing method.

LO5 **Process Costing: One Process and Two Time Periods—FIFO Costing Method**

P 7. Honey Dews Company produces organic honey, which it sells to health food stores and restaurants. The company owns thousands of beehives. No direct materials other than honey are used. The production operation is a simple one. Impure honey is added at the beginning of the process and flows through a series of filterings, leading to a pure finished product. Costs of labor and overhead are incurred uniformly throughout the filtering process. Production data for April and May are as follows:

	April	May
Beginning work in process inventory		
Units (liters)	7,100	12,400
Direct materials costs	$ 2,480	?*
Conversion costs	$ 5,110	?*
Production during the period		
Units started (liters)	288,000	310,000
Direct materials costs	$100,800	$117,800
Conversion costs	$251,550	$277,281
Ending work in process inventory		
Units (liters)	12,400	16,900

*From calculations at end of April.

The beginning work in process inventory for April was 80 percent complete for conversion costs, and ending work in process inventory was 20 percent complete. The ending work in process inventory for May was 30 percent complete for conversion costs. Assume that there was no loss from spoilage or evaporation.

Required

1. Using the FIFO method, prepare a process cost report for April.
2. From the information in the process cost report, identify the amount that should be transferred out of the Work in Process Inventory account, and state where those dollars should be transferred.
3. Repeat **1** and **2** for May.

LO6 **Process Costing: Average Costing Method**

P 8. Many of the products made by Wireless Plastics Company are standard replacement parts for telephones that require long production runs and are produced continuously. A unit for Wireless Plastics is a box of parts. During April, direct materials for 25,250 units were put into production. Total cost of direct materials used during April was $2,273,000. Direct labor costs totaled $1,135,000, and overhead was $2,043,000. The beginning work in process inventory contained 1,600 units, which were 100 percent complete for direct materials costs and 60 percent complete for conversion costs. Costs attached to the units in beginning inventory totaled $232,515, which included $143,500 of direct materials costs. At the end of the month, 1,250 units were in ending inventory; all direct materials had been added, and the units were 70 percent complete for conversion costs.

Required

1. Using the average costing method and assuming no loss due to spoilage, prepare a process cost report for April.
2. From the information in the process cost report, identify the amount that should be transferred out of the Work in Process Inventory account, and state where those dollars should be transferred.

ENHANCING Your Knowledge, Skills, and Critical Thinking

Conceptual Understanding Cases

LO1   **Concept of Process Costing Systems**

C 1. For more than 60 years, **Dow Chemical Company** has made and sold a tasteless, odorless, and calorie-free substance called Methocel. When heated, this liquid plastic (methyl cellulose) has the unusual characteristic (for plastics) of becoming a gel that resembles cooked egg whites. It is used in over 400 food products, including gravies, soups, and puddings. It was also used as wampa drool in *The Empire Strikes Back* and dinosaur sneeze in *Jurassic Park*. What kind of costing system is most appropriate for the manufacture of Methocel? Why is that system most appropriate? Describe the system, and include in the description a general explanation of how costs are determined.

LO2, LO3   **Changing the Accounting System**

C 2. Transnational Cablecom produces several types of communications cable. Since the manufacturing process is continuous, the company uses a process costing system to develop product costs. Until recently, costs were accumulated monthly, and revised product costs were made available to management by the tenth of the following month. Because the company has installed a computer-integrated manufacturing (CIM) system, cost information is now available as soon as each production run is finished. The production superintendent has asked the controller to change the accounting system so that product unit costs are available the day after a production run ends.

Prepare a memorandum to the corporate vice president justifying the proposed change in the accounting system. Identify reasons that the controller can use to support the production superintendent's request. What benefits would be obtained from the proposed modification?

LO1, LO3   **Process Costing and Work in Process Inventory Accounts**

C 3. SvenskStål, AB, is a steel-producing company located in Solentuna, Sweden. The company originally produced only specialty steel products that were made to order for customers. A job order product costing system has been used for the made-to-order products. This year, after purchasing three continuous processing work cells, the company created a new division that produces three types of sheet steel in continuous rolls. Ingrid Bjorn, the company controller, has redesigned the management accounting system to accommodate these changes and has installed a process costing system for the new division.

At a recent meeting of the firm's executive committee, Bjorn explained that the new product costing system uses three Work in Process Inventory accounts, one for each of the three new work cells. The production superintendent questioned the need to change product costing approaches and asked why so many new Work in Process Inventory accounts were necessary.

Why did Bjorn install a process costing system? Was a new division necessary, or could the three work cells have been merged with the old production facilities? Why were three Work in Process Inventory accounts required? Could the single Work in Process Inventory account used for the specialty orders have tracked and accumulated the costs incurred in the new work cells?

Interpreting Management Reports

LO4, LO5   **Analysis of Product Cost**

C 4. Ready Tire Corporation makes several lines of automobile and truck tires. The company operates in a competitive marketplace, so it relies heavily on cost data from its FIFO-based process costing system. It uses that information to set prices for its most competitive tires. The company's radial line has lost some of its market share during each of the past four years. Management believes that price breaks allowed by the company's three biggest competitors are the main reason for the decline in sales.

The company controller, Sara Birdsong, has been asked to review the product costing information that supports pricing decisions on the radial line. In preparing her report, she collected the following data for 20x8, the most recent full year of operations:

		Units	Dollars
Equivalent units:	Direct materials costs	84,200	
	Conversion costs	82,800	
Manufacturing costs:	Direct materials		$1,978,700
	Direct labor		800,400
	Overhead		1,600,800
Unit cost data:	Direct materials costs		23.50
	Conversion costs		29.00
Work in process inventory:			
Beginning (70% complete)		4,200	
Ending (30% complete)		3,800	

Units started and completed during 20x8 totaled 80,400. Attached to the beginning Work in Process Inventory account were direct materials costs of $123,660 and conversion costs of $57,010. Birdsong found that little spoilage had occurred. The proper cost allowance for spoilage was included in the predetermined overhead rate of $2 per direct labor dollar. The review of direct labor cost revealed, however, that $90,500 had been charged twice to the production account, the second time in error. This resulted in overly high overhead costs being charged to the production account.

So far in 20x9, the radial has been selling for $92 per tire. This price was based on the 20x8 unit data plus a 75 percent markup to cover operating costs and profit. During 20x9, the company's three main competitors have been charging about $87 for a tire of comparable quality. The company's process costing system adds all direct materials at the beginning of the process, and conversion costs are incurred uniformly throughout the process.

1. Identify what inaccuracies in costs, inventories, and selling prices result from the company's cost-charging error.
2. Prepare a revised process cost report for 20x8. Round unit costs to two decimal places. Round total costs to whole dollars.
3. What should have been the minimum selling price per tire in 20x9?
4. Suggest ways of preventing such errors in the future.

LO5 ### Setting a Selling Price

C 5. For the past four years, three companies have dominated the soft drink industry, holding a combined 85 percent of market share. Wonder Cola, Inc., ranks second nationally in soft drink sales. Its management is thinking about introducing a new low-calorie drink called Null Cola.

Wonder soft drinks are processed in a single department. All ingredients are added at the beginning of the process. At the end of the process, the beverage is poured into bottles that cost $.24 per case produced. Direct labor and overhead costs are applied uniformly throughout the process.

Corporate controller Adam Daneen believes that costs for the new cola will be very much like those for the company's Cola Plus drink. Last year (20x9), he collected the following data about Cola Plus:

	Units*	Costs
Work in process inventory		
December 31, 20x8[†]	2,200	
Direct materials costs		$ 2,080
Conversion costs		620
December 31, 20x9[‡]	2,000	
Direct materials costs		1,880
Conversion costs		600
Units started during 20x9	458,500	
Costs for 20x9		
Liquid materials added		430,990
Direct labor and overhead		229,400
Bottles		110,068

*Each unit is a 24-bottle case.
[†]50% complete.
[‡]60% complete.

The company's variable general administrative and selling costs are $1.10 per unit. Fixed administrative and selling costs are assigned to products at the rate of $.50 per unit. Each of Wonder Cola's two main competitors is already market- ing a diet cola. Company A's product sells for $4.10 per unit; Company B's, for $4.05. All costs are expected to increase by 10 percent in the next three years. Wonder Cola tries to earn a profit of at least 15 percent on the total unit cost.

1. What factors should Wonder Cola, Inc., consider in setting a unit selling price for a case of Null Cola?
2. Using the FIFO costing method, compute (a) equivalent units for direct materials, cases of bottles, and conversion costs; (b) the total production cost per unit; and (c) the total cost per unit of Cola Plus for 20x9.
3. What is the expected unit cost of Null Cola for 20x9?
4. Recommend a unit selling price range for Null Cola for 20x9 and give the reason(s) for your choice.

Decision Analysis Using Excel

LO6, LO7 **Average Process Costing: Two Time Periods**

C 6. Lid Corporation produces a line of beverage lids. The production process has been automated, so the product can now be produced in one operation rather than in the three operations that were needed before the company pur- chased the automated machinery. All direct materials are added at the begin- ning of the process, and conversion costs are incurred uniformly throughout the process. Operating data for May and June are as follows:

	May	June
Beginning work in process inventory		
Units (May: 40% complete)	220,000	?
Direct materials costs	$ 3,440	$ 400
Conversion costs	$ 6,480	$ 420
Production during the month		
Units started	24,000,000	31,000,000
Direct materials costs	$45,000	$93,200
Conversion costs	$66,000	$92,796
Ending work in process inventory		
Units (May: 70% complete; June: 60% complete)	200,000	320,000

1. Using the average costing method, prepare process cost reports for May and June. (Round unit costs to three decimal places; round all other costs to the nearest dollar.)
2. From the information in the process cost report for May, identify the amount that should be transferred out of the Work in Process Inventory account, and state where those dollars should be transferred.
3. Compare the product costing results for June with the results for May. What is the most significant change? What are some of the possible causes of this change?

LO1, LO2   ## Ethical Dilemma Case

Continuing Professional Education

C 7. Paula Woodward is the head of the Information Systems Department at Moreno Manufacturing Company. Roland Randolph, the company's controller, is meeting with her to discuss changes in data gathering that relate to the company's new flexible manufacturing system. Woodward opens the conversation by saying, "Roland, the old job order costing methods just will not work with the new flexible manufacturing system. The new system is based on continuous product flow, not batch processing. We need to change to a process costing system for both data gathering and product costing. Otherwise, our product costs will be way off, and it will affect our pricing decisions. I found out about the need for this change at a professional seminar I attended last month. You should have been there with me."

Randolph responds, "Paula, who is the accounting expert here? I know what product costing approach is best for this situation. Job order costing has provided accurate information for this product line for more than 15 years. Why should we change just because we've purchased a new machine? We've purchased several machines for this line over the years. And as for your seminar, I don't need to learn about costing methods. I was exposed to them all when I studied management accounting back in the late 1970s."

Is Randolph's behavior ethical? If not, what has he done wrong? What can Woodward do if Randolph continues to refuse to update the product costing system?

LO1   ## Internet Case

Comparison of Companies That Use Process Costing Systems

C 8. A Focus on Business Practice box in this chapter lists many companies for which process costing systems are appropriate. Access the websites of at least two of these companies. Find as much information as you can about the products the companies make and how they make them, including the manufacturing processes involved. For which products would process costing be most appropriate? For which products would it be inappropriate? Identify differences in the nature of the business conducted by the companies you chose. Do you think those differences have any bearing on the type of product costing system the company uses? Explain your reasoning. Do the companies make any products that might require a costing system other than process costing?

LO1   ## Group Activity Case

Process Costing Systems

C 9. Locate an article about a company that you believe would use a process costing system. Conduct your search using an Internet search engine or a business periodical, such as T*he Wall Street Journal*. Prepare a short report describing the product(s) the company makes, its production process, and why it would probably use a process costing system. Bring this information to class to share with your classmates. Be sure to include the company's name and identify the article's title, author(s), and publication date.

Your instructor will divide the class into groups. Summarize your group's discussion, and select someone from the group to present the group's findings to the rest of the class.

Business Communication Case

LO2, LO4, LO5   **Using the Process Costing System**

C 10. You are the production manager for Great Grain Corporation, a manufacturer of four cereal products. The company's best-selling product is Smackaroos, a sugar-coated puffed rice cereal. Yesterday, Clark Winslow, the controller, reported that the production cost for each box of Smackaroos has increased approximately 22 percent in the last four months. Because the company is unable to increase the selling price for a box of Smackaroos, the increased production costs will reduce profits significantly.

Today, you received a memo from Gilbert Rom, the company president, asking you to review your production process to identify inefficiencies or waste that can be eliminated. Once you have completed your analysis, you are to write a memo presenting your findings and suggesting ways to reduce or eliminate the problems. The president will use your information during a meeting with the top management team in ten days.

You are aware of previous problems in the Baking Department and the Packaging Department. Winslow has provided you with process cost reports for the two departments. He has also given you the following detailed summary of the cost per equivalent unit for a box of Smackaroos cereal:

	April	May	June	July
Baking Department				
Direct materials	$1.25	$1.26	$1.24	$1.25
Direct labor	.50	.61	.85	.90
Overhead	.25	.31	.34	.40
Department totals	$2.00	$2.18	$2.43	$2.55
Packaging Department				
Direct materials	$ .35	$ .34	$ .33	$ .33
Direct labor	.05	.05	.04	.06
Overhead	.10	.16	.15	.12
Department totals	$ .50	$ .55	$ .52	$ .51
Total cost per equivalent unit	$2.50	$2.73	$2.95	$3.06

1. In preparation for writing your memo, answer the following questions:
   a. For whom are you preparing the memo? Does this affect the length of the memo? Explain.
   b. Why are you preparing the memo?
   c. What actions should you take to gather information for the memo? What information is needed? Is the information that Winslow provided sufficient for analysis and reporting?
   d. When is the memo due? What can be done to provide accurate, reliable, and timely information?
2. Based on your analysis of the information that Winslow provided, where is the main problem in the production process?
3. Prepare an outline of the sections you would want in your memo.

Activity-Based Systems: ABM and JIT

To remain competitive in today's changing business environment, companies have had to rethink their organizational processes and basic operating methods. Managers focus on creating value for their customers. They design their internal value chain and external supply chain to provide customer-related, activity-based information; to track costs; and to eliminate waste and inefficiencies. In this chapter, we describe two systems that help managers improve operating processes and make better decisions: activity-based management and the just-in-time operating philosophy.

LEARNING OBJECTIVES

LO1 Explain the role of managers in activity-based systems.

LO2 Define *activity-based management (ABM)* and discuss its relationship to the supply chain and the value chain.

LO3 Distinguish between value-adding and nonvalue-adding activities, and describe process value analysis.

LO4 Define *activity-based costing* and explain how a cost hierarchy and a bill of activities are used.

LO5 Define the *just-in-time (JIT) operating philosophy* and identify the elements of a JIT operating environment.

LO6 Identify the changes in product costing that result when a firm adopts a JIT operating environment.

LO7 Define and apply *backflush costing*, and compare the cost flows in traditional and backflush costing.

LO8 Compare ABM and JIT as activity-based systems.

- How have ABM and JIT helped La-Z-Boy improve its production processes and reduce delivery time?

- How do the managers of La-Z-Boy plan to remain the industry's leading marketer and manufacturer of upholstered products?

A critical factor in the success of **La-Z-Boy, Inc.,** is the speed of its value chain. La-Z-Boy makes about 11,000 built-to-order sofas and chairs each week in its Tennessee plant, and it generally delivers them less than three weeks after customers have placed their orders with a retailer. This is quite a feat, especially since the company offers 85 styles of sofas and a choice of 550 fabrics. It also gives La-Z-Boy a competitive advantage.[1]

Activity-Based Systems and Management

LO1 Explain the role of managers in activity-based systems.

Many companies, including **La-Z-Boy, Inc.**, operate in volatile business environments that are strongly influenced by customer demands. Managers know that customers buy value, usually in the form of quality products or services that are delivered on a timely basis for a reasonable price. Companies generate revenue when customers see value and buy their products or services. Thus, companies measure value as revenue (customer value = revenue generated).

Value exists when some characteristic of a product or service satisfies customers' wants or needs. For example, customers who appreciate comfort are an important market segment for La-Z-Boy. In response to their needs, La-Z-Boy creates value and increases revenue by selling recliners and customized sofas that include the patented La-Z-Boy mechanism, the strongest frame, the most reclining positions, a secure locking footrest, and total body and lumbar support.

Creating value by satisfying customers' needs for quality, reasonable price, and timely delivery requires that managers do the following:

- Work with suppliers and customers.

- View the organization as a collection of value-adding activities.

- Use resources for value-adding activities.

- Reduce or eliminate nonvalue-adding activities.

- Know the total cost of creating value for a customer.

If an organization's business plan focuses on providing products or services that customers esteem, then managers will work with suppliers and customers to find ways of improving quality, reducing costs, and shortening delivery time. Managers will also focus their attention internally to find the best ways of using resources to create and maintain the value of their products or services. This requires matching resources to the operating activities that add value to a product or service. Managers will examine all business activities, including research and development, purchasing, production, storing, selling, shipping, and customer service, so that they can allocate resources effectively.

In addition, managers need to know the **full product cost**, which includes not only the costs of direct materials and direct labor, but also the costs of all production and nonproduction activities required to satisfy the customer. For example, the full product cost of a La-Z-Boy recliner or sofa includes the cost of the frame and upholstery, as well as the costs of taking the sales order, processing the order, packaging and shipping the furniture, and providing subsequent customer service for warranty work. If the activities are executed well and in agreement with the business plan, and if costs are assigned fairly, the company can improve its product pricing and quality, increase productivity, and generate revenues (value) and profits.

Activity-Based Systems

Organizations that focus on their customers design their accounting information systems to provide customer-related, activity-based information.

Activity-based systems are information systems that provide quantitative information about an organization's activities. They create opportunities to improve the cost information supplied to managers. They also help managers view their organization as a collection of activities. Activity-based cost information helps managers improve operating processes and make better pricing decisions.

Activity-based systems developed because traditional accounting systems failed to produce the types of information that today's managers need for decision making. Traditional systems focused primarily on the measurements needed for financial reporting and auditing, such as the measurement of cost of goods sold and the valuation of inventory. Because they were not designed to capture data on activities or to trace the full cost of a product, these systems could not isolate the cost of unnecessary activities, penalize for overproduction, or quantify measures that improved quality or reduced throughput time.

In this chapter, we explore two types of activity-based systems—activity-based management (ABM) and the just-in-time (JIT) operating environment—and consider how they affect product costing. Both systems help organizations manage activities, not costs, but by managing activities, organizations can reduce or eliminate many nonvalue-adding activities, which leads to reduced costs and hence to increased income.

Study Note

ABM and JIT focus on value-adding activities—not costs—to increase income.

Using Activity-Based Cost Information

In this section, we look at the ways in which managers use activity-based cost information. Figure 1 summarizes these uses.

Planning When managers plan, they want answers to questions like "Which activities add value to a product or service?" "What resources are needed to perform those activities?" and "How much should the product or service cost?" By examining their company's value-adding activities and the related costs, managers can ensure that the company is offering quality products or services at the lowest cost. With budgeted costs prepared for each activity, they can not only better allocate resources to cost objects (such as product or service lines, customer groups, or sales territories) and estimate product or service unit cost more accurately, but also measure operating performance. If managers assume that resource-consuming activities cause costs and that products and services incur costs through the activities that they require, the estimated unit cost will be more accurate.

Performing During the period in which managers are performing their duties, they want an answer to the question "What is the actual cost of making our product or providing our service?" They want to know what activities are being performed, how well they are being performed, and what resources they are consuming. Although managers focus on the activities that create the most value for customers, they also monitor some nonvalue-adding activities that have been reduced but not completely eliminated. An activity-based accounting information system measures actual quantities of activity (a quantitative nonfinancial measure) and accumulates related activity costs (a quantitative financial measure). Gathering quantitative information at the activity level gives managers the flexibility to create cost pools for different types of cost objects. For example, the costs of the selling activity can be assigned to a customer, a sales territory, or a product or service line.

■ **FIGURE 1**
The Management Process: To-Do's for Managers

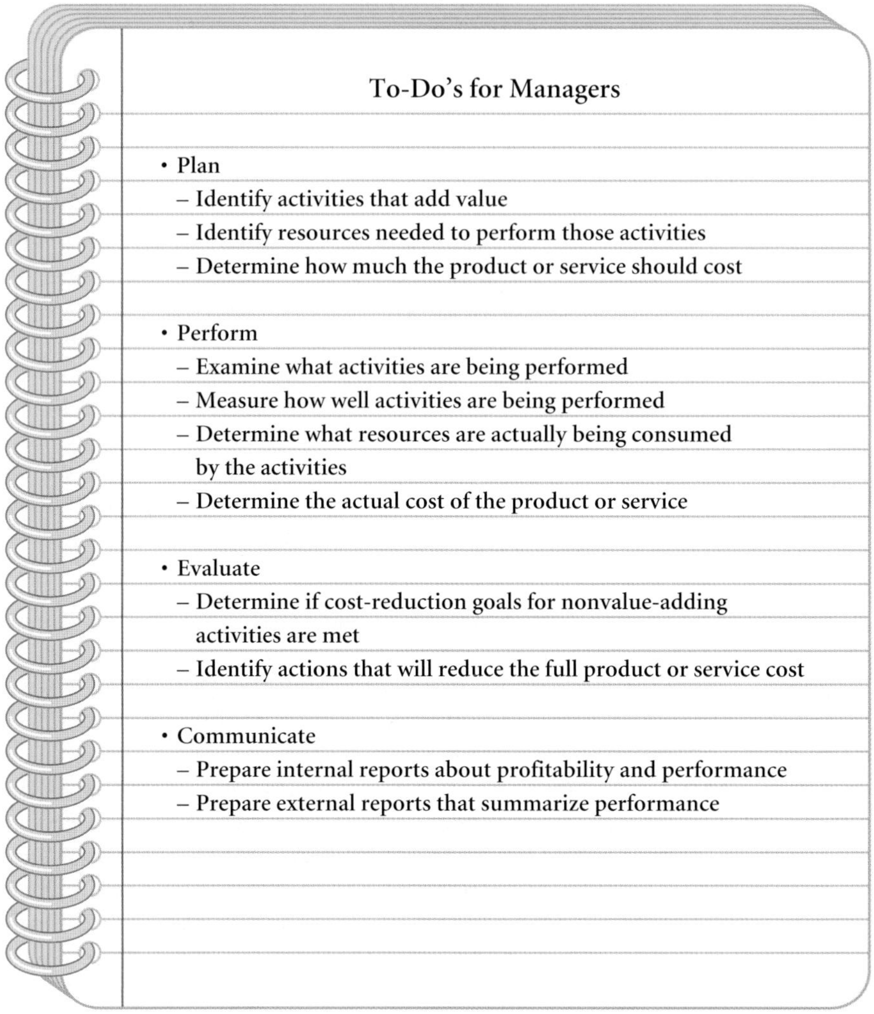

To-Do's for Managers

- Plan
  - Identify activities that add value
  - Identify resources needed to perform those activities
  - Determine how much the product or service should cost

- Perform
  - Examine what activities are being performed
  - Measure how well activities are being performed
  - Determine what resources are actually being consumed
    by the activities
  - Determine the actual cost of the product or service

- Evaluate
  - Determine if cost-reduction goals for nonvalue-adding
    activities are met
  - Identify actions that will reduce the full product or service cost

- Communicate
  - Prepare internal reports about profitability and performance
  - Prepare external reports that summarize performance

Evaluating When managers evaluate performance, they want answers to the questions "What actions will reduce the full product and service cost?" and "Did we meet our cost-reduction goals for nonvalue-adding activities?" Managers measure an activity's performance by reviewing the difference between its actual and budgeted costs. With this information, they can analyze the variances in activity levels, identify waste and inefficiencies, and take action to improve processes and activities. They can also continue to monitor the costs of nonvalue-adding activities to see if the company met its goals of reducing or eliminating those costs. Careful review and analysis will increase value for the customer by improving product quality and reducing costs and cycle time.

Communicating Managers communicate plans and performance results when they prepare reports about the company's performance for internal and external use. Internal reports show the application of the costs of activities to cost objects, which results in a better measurement of profitability, as we discuss later in the chapter. External reports summarize past performance and answer such questions as "Did the company earn a profit?" and "Were company resources utilized efficiently and effectively?"

S T O P • R E V I E W • A P P L Y

1-1. How do companies measure customer value? What do managers do to create value and satisfy customers' needs?

1-2. What is the main focus of an activity-based system?

1-3. What is the value of gathering quantitative information at the activity level?

Suggested answers to all Stop, Review, and Apply questions are available at http://college.hmco.com/accounting/needles/man_acc/8e/student_home.html.

Activity-Based Management

LO2 Define *activity-based management (ABM)* and discuss its relationship to the supply chain and the value chain.

As you may recall from an earlier chapter, **activity-based management (ABM)** is an approach to managing an organization that identifies all major operating activities, determines the resources consumed by each activity and the cause of the resource usage, and categorizes the activities as either adding value to a product or service or not adding value. ABM focuses on reducing or eliminating nonvalue-adding activities. Because it provides financial and performance information at the activity level, ABM is useful both for strategic planning and for making operational decisions about business segments, such as product lines, market segments, and customer groups. It also helps managers eliminate waste and inefficiencies and redirect resources to activities that add value to the product or service. Activity-based costing (ABC) is the tool used in an ABM environment to assign activity costs to cost objects. ABC helps managers make better pricing decisions, inventory valuations, and profitability decisions.

Value Chains and Supply Chains

As we noted earlier in the text, a **value chain** is a sequence of activities inside the organization, also known as *primary processes*, that add value to a company's product or service; the value chain also includes support services, such as management accounting, that facilitate the primary processes. ABM enables managers to see their organization's internal value chain as part of a larger system that includes the value chains of suppliers and customers. This larger

FOCUS ON BUSINESS PRACTICE
How Can a Changing Economy Cause Strategy Shifts in a Company's Value Chain?

When the economy took a downturn a few years ago, high-tech companies like **Oracle** and **SAP** experienced overcapacity. They therefore shifted the emphasis of their value chains from marketing to customer service. Measures that had been used to gauge the performance of an aggressive sales force, such as sales volume, were now irrelevant and were replaced by measures of customer satisfaction and retention.[2]

Each company in a supply chain is a customer of an earlier supplier. The furniture maker shown here would be a customer of a metal manufacturer, a caning supplier, a supplier of high-quality wood, and perhaps a leather manufacturer. His customer might be a furniture wholesaler or retail store. The retail store, which sells the furniture to customers, is the final link in the supply chain.

system is the **supply chain**—the path that leads from the suppliers of the materials from which a product is made to the final customer. The supply chain (also called the *supply network*) includes both suppliers and suppliers' suppliers, and customers and customers' customers. It links businesses together in a relationship chain of business to business to business.

As Figure 2 shows, in the supply chain for a furniture company like **La-Z-Boy**, a metal manufacturer supplies metal to the recliner mechanism manufacturer, which supplies recliner mechanisms to the furniture manufacturer. The furniture manufacturer supplies furniture to furniture stores, which in turn supply furniture to the final customers. Each organization in this supply chain is a customer of an earlier supplier, and each has its own value chain. The sequence of primary processes in the value chain varies from company to company depending on a number of factors, including the size of the company and the types of products or services that it sells. Figure 2 also shows the primary processes that add value for a furniture manufacturer—marketing, research and development, purchasing, production, sales, shipping, and customer service.

Understanding value chains and supply chains gives managers a better grasp of their company's internal and external operations. Managers who understand the supply chain and how their company's value-adding activities fit into their suppliers' and customers' value chains can see their company's role in the overall process of creating and delivering products or services. Such an understanding can also make a company more profitable. By working with suppliers and customers across the entire supply chain, managers may be able to reduce the total cost of making a product, even though costs for a particular activity may increase.

For example, La-Z-Boy places computers for online order entry in its licensed furniture galleries. The computers streamline the processing of orders and make the orders more accurate. In this case, even though La-Z-Boy incurs the cost of the computers, the total cost of making and delivering furniture decreases because the cost of order processing decreases. When organizations work cooperatively with others in their supply chain, they can develop new processes that reduce the total costs of their products or services.

■ **FIGURE 2**
The Supply Chain and Value Chain in a Manufacturing Company

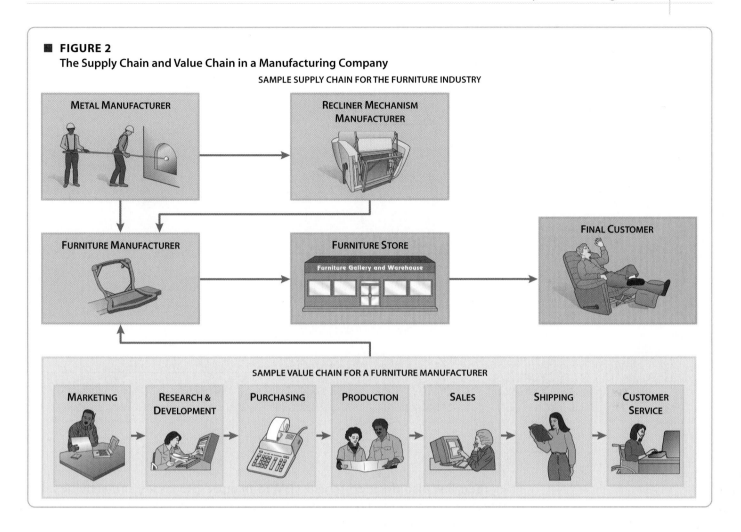

SAMPLE SUPPLY CHAIN FOR THE FURNITURE INDUSTRY

METAL MANUFACTURER

RECLINER MECHANISM MANUFACTURER

FURNITURE MANUFACTURER

FURNITURE STORE

Furniture Gallery and Warehouse

FINAL CUSTOMER

SAMPLE VALUE CHAIN FOR A FURNITURE MANUFACTURER

MARKETING · RESEARCH & DEVELOPMENT · PURCHASING · PRODUCTION · SALES · SHIPPING · CUSTOMER SERVICE

ABM in a Service Organization

To illustrate how a service organization can use ABM, let's assume that a firm called Direct Ads, Inc. (DAI), offers database marketing strategies to help companies like La-Z-Boy increase their sales. DAI's basic package of services includes the design of a mailing piece (either a Direct Mailer or a Store Mailer), creation and maintenance of marketing databases containing information about the client's target group, and a production process that prints a promotional piece and prepares it for mailing. In its marketing strategies, DAI targets working women ages 25 to 54 who are married with children and who have an annual household income in excess of $50,000.

In preparing DAI's business plan, Fran Teerlink, the owner and manager of DAI, reviewed the company's supply chain. As Figure 3 shows, this supply chain includes suppliers, DAI as a service provider, one customer group (licensed furniture galleries), and the customer group's customers. DAI has a number of suppliers, including office supply companies, printers, and computer stores. Teerlink chose licensed furniture galleries as the supply chain's primary customer group because they represent a sizable percentage of revenues. The customers of the furniture galleries are included in the supply chain because they receive the mailing pieces that DAI prepares. Based on his review of the supply chain, Teerlink concluded that DAI's strategy to work with suppliers and the licensed furniture galleries to improve DAI's services was sound.

■ **FIGURE 3**
The Supply Chain and Value Chain in a Service Organization

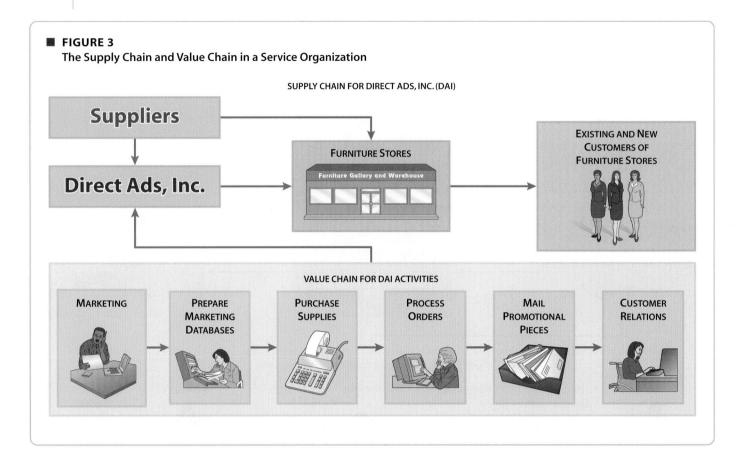

SUPPLY CHAIN FOR DIRECT ADS, INC. (DAI)

Teerlink also decided to use ABM to manage processes and activities. He developed a value chain of activities for DAI so that he could identify all major operating activities, the resources each activity consumes, and the cause of the resource usage. As shown in Figure 3, the activities that add value to DAI's services are marketing, preparing marketing databases, purchasing supplies, processing orders, mailing promotional pieces, and customer relations.

S T O P • R E V I E W • A P P L Y

2-1. What is activity-based management (ABM)? How is ABM useful for strategic planning and operational decision making?

2-2. How does the focus of a supply chain differ from that of a value chain?

Value-Adding and Nonvalue-Adding Activities and Process Value Analysis

LO3 Distinguish between value-adding and nonvalue-adding activities, and describe process value analysis.

An important element of activity-based management is the identification of value-adding and nonvalue-adding activities. A **value-adding activity** is one that adds value to a product or service as perceived by the customer. Examples include designing the components of a new recliner, assem-

bling the recliner, and upholstering it. A **nonvalue-adding activity** is one that adds cost to a product or service but does not increase its market value. ABM focuses on eliminating nonvalue-adding activities that are not essential to an organization and on reducing the costs of those that are essential, such as legal services, management accounting, machine repair, materials handling, and building maintenance. The costs of both value-adding and nonvalue-adding activities are accumulated to measure performance and to determine whether the goal of reducing the cost of nonvalue-adding activities has been achieved.

To minimize costs, managers continuously seek to improve processes and activities. To manage the cost of an activity, they can reduce the activity's frequency or eliminate it entirely. For example, inspection costs can be reduced if an inspector samples one of every three reclining mechanisms received from a supplier rather than inspecting every mechanism. If the supplier is a reliable source of high-quality mechanisms, such a reduction in inspection activity is appropriate. Another way to reduce costs is to outsource an activity—that is, to have it done by another company that is more competent at the work and can perform it at a lower cost. Many companies outsource purchasing, accounting, and the maintenance of their information systems.

Some activities can be eliminated completely if business processes are changed. For example, when a company adopts a just-in-time operating philosophy, it can eliminate some recordkeeping activities. Because it purchases materials just in time for production and manufactures products just in time for customer delivery, it no longer needs to accumulate costs as the product is made.

Value-Adding and Nonvalue-Adding Activities in a Service Organization

To illustrate how service organizations deal with value-adding and nonvalue-adding activities, let's suppose that Fran Teerlink, the owner and manager of DAI, has examined the activities related to the design, processing, and mailing of his company's Direct Mailers and has drawn up the list of value-adding activities shown in Table 1. When Teerlink's customers ask for database marketing

TABLE 1. Value-Adding Activities for a Service Organization

Direct Ads, Inc.
Value-Adding Activities for the Direct Mailers

Value-Adding Activities	How the Activity Adds Value
Designing the mailer	Enhances the effectiveness of the communication
Creating a database of customers' names and addresses sorted in ZIP code order	Increases the probability that the client will efficiently and effectively reach the targeted customer group
Verifying the conformity of mailings with USPS requirements	Ensures that the client's mailing will receive the best postal rate
Processing the job: A computer prints a personalized mailer A machine folds the mailer, inserts it and other information into an envelope, prints the address on the envelope, and seals and meters the envelope	Creates the client mailing
Delivering the mailers to the post office	Begins the delivery process

services, these are the activities they pay for. Teerlink has also identified the following nonvalue-adding activities:

▶ Preparing a job order form and scheduling the job

▶ Ordering, receiving, inspecting, and storing paper, envelopes, and other supplies

▶ Setting up machines to process a specific letter size

▶ Logging the total number of items processed in a batch

▶ Billing the client and recording and depositing payments from the client

After reviewing the list of nonvalue-adding activities, Teerlink arranged with his suppliers to have paper, envelopes, and other supplies delivered the day a job is performed. This helped reduce DAI's storage costs. Teerlink was also able to reduce the costs of some value-adding activities. For example, he reduced the cost of the labor involved in verifying the conformity of mailings with United States Postal Service (USPS) requirements by purchasing computer software that verifies addresses, determines postage, and automatically sorts the letters.

Process Value Analysis

Process value analysis (PVA) is a technique that managers use to identify and link all the activities involved in the value chain. It analyzes business processes by relating activities to the events that prompt those activities and to the resources that the activities consume. PVA forces managers to look critically at all phases of their operations. Managers who use ABM find it an effective way of reducing nonvalue-adding activities and their costs. PVA improves cost traceability and results in significantly more accurate product costs, which in turn improves management decisions and increases profitability.

By using PVA to identify nonvalue-adding activities, companies can reduce their costs and redirect their resources to value-adding activities. For example, PVA has enabled companies like **Westinghouse Electric**, **Pepsi-Cola North America**, and **Land O'Lakes** to reduce the processing costs of purchasing and accounts payable. After identifying the nonvalue-adding activities involved in small-dollar purchases (e.g., recording and paying small bills, setting up accounts, and establishing credit with seldom-used suppliers) and their costs, managers of these companies decided to stop performing such activities internally. Instead, they chose the less expensive alternative of using a special credit card known as a procurement (or purchasing) card from Visa, MasterCard, or American Express to handle large volumes of small-dollar purchases.

FOCUS ON BUSINESS PRACTICE
What Is VBM?

Value-based management (VBM) is a long-term strategy that many businesses use to reward managers who create and sustain shareholder wealth and value. In other words, VBM encourages managers to think like business owners. Three elements are essential for a successful VBM program. First, VBM must have the full support of top management. Second, performance and compensation must be linked, because "what gets measured and rewarded gets done." Finally, everyone involved must understand the what, why, and how of the program. Since a variety of VBM approaches exist, each company can tailor its VBM performance metrics and implementation strategy to meet its particular needs.[3]

S T O P • R E V I E W • A P P L Y

3-1. Are customers willing to pay for nonvalue-adding activities?

3-2. Define process value analysis.

Activity-Based Costing

LO4 Define *activity-based costing* and explain how a cost hierarchy and a bill of activities are used.

 Study Note

With ABC, indirect costs like overhead are assigned to cost objects using an appropriate allocation scheme.

As access to value chain data has improved, managers have refined the issue of how to assign costs fairly to products or services to determine unit costs. You may recall from an earlier chapter that traditional methods of allocating overhead costs to products use such cost drivers as direct labor hours, direct labor costs, or machine hours. In the mid-1980s, organizations began realizing that these methods did not assign overhead costs to their product lines accurately and that the resulting inaccuracy in product unit costs was causing poor pricing decisions. In their search for more accurate product costing, many organizations embraced activity-based costing.

Activity-based costing (ABC) is a method of assigning costs that calculates a more accurate product cost than traditional methods. It does so by categorizing all indirect costs by activity, tracing the indirect costs to those activities, and assigning those costs to products using a cost driver related to the cause of the cost.

Activity-based costing is an important tool of activity-based management because it improves the allocation of activity-driven costs to cost objects. To implement activity-based costing, managers

1. Identify and classify each activity.

2. Estimate the cost of resources for each activity.

3. Identify a cost driver for each activity and estimate the quantity of each cost driver.

4. Calculate an activity cost rate for each activity.

5. Assign costs to cost objects based on the level of activity required to make the product or provide the service.

FOCUS ON BUSINESS PRACTICE

A Simpler and More Time-Focused ABC

Full-scale implementation of ABC has historically been difficult, since much of the data were gathered by employee surveys. In a revised ABC model called Time-Driven Activity-Based Costing, managers can estimate how much it costs per time unit of capacity to supply resources to an activity, and how long it takes to carry out one unit of each activity. Time-Driven ABC is easier to adopt and use because it requires only two measures and time equations to reflect the complexity of what is done for specific orders or customers.[4]

The Cost Hierarchy and the Bill of Activities

Two tools used in implementing ABC are a cost hierarchy and a bill of activities.

Cost Hierarchy A **cost hierarchy** is a framework for classifying activities according to the level at which their costs are incurred. Many companies use this framework to allocate activity-based costs to products or services. In a manufacturing company, the cost hierarchy typically has four levels: the unit level, the batch level, the product level, and the facility level.

- **Unit-level activities** are performed each time a unit is produced and are generally considered variable costs. For example, when a furniture manufacturer like **La-Z-Boy** installs a recliner mechanism in a chair, unit-level activities include the direct cost of the recliner mechanism and connecting the mechanism to the chair frame. Because each chair contains only one mechanism, these activities have a direct correlation to the number of chairs produced.

- **Batch-level activities** are performed each time a batch or production run of goods is produced. Examples of batch-level activities include setup, inspection, scheduling, and materials handling for the production run of a certain style of recliner. These activities vary with the number of batches prepared or production runs completed.

- **Product-level activities** are performed to support a particular product line. Examples of product-level activities include implementing engineering or marketing changes for a particular brand of product and redesigning the installation process for that product line.

- **Facility-level activities** are performed to support a facility's general manufacturing process and are generally fixed costs. Examples for a furniture manufacturer include maintaining, lighting, securing, and insuring the factory.

Note that the frequency of activities varies across levels and that the cost hierarchy includes both value-adding and nonvalue-adding activities. Service organizations can also use a cost hierarchy to group their activities; the four levels typically are the unit level, the batch level, the service level, and the operations level. Table 2 lists examples of activities in the cost hierarchies of a manufacturing company and a service organization.

TABLE 2. Sample Activities in Cost Hierarchies		
Activity Level	**Furniture Manufacturer: Recliner Mechanism Installation**	**Direct Mail Service: Preparing a Mailing to Store Customers**
Unit level	Install mechanism Test mechanism	Print and fold letter Insert letter and other information into envelope
Batch level	Set up installation process Move mechanisms Inspect mechanisms	Retool machines Verify correct postage Bill client
Product or service level	Redesign installation process	Train employees Develop and maintain computer systems and databases
Facility or operations level	Provide facility maintenance, lighting, and security	Provide facility maintenance, lighting, and security

▼ **EXHIBIT 1**

Bill of Activities for a Service Organization

Direct Ads, Inc.
Bill of Activities for Direct Mailers and Store Mailers
For the Month Ended May 31, 20x9

Activity	Activity Cost Rate	Direct Mailers (110,000 mailers)		Store Mailers (48,000 mailers)	
		Cost Driver Level	Activity Cost	Cost Driver Level	Activity Cost
Unit level					
Process mailers	$20 per machine hour	300 machine hours	$ 6,000	90 machine hours	$ 1,800
Batch level					
Prepare databases	$85 per 1,000 names	50,000 names	4,250	20,000 names	1,700
Set up machines	$10 per direct labor hour	220 direct labor hours	2,200	100 direct labor hours	1,000
Inspect for USPS compliance	$12 per inspection hour	100 inspection hours	1,200	80 inspection hours	960
Service level					
Develop databases	$25 per design hour	118 design hours	2,950	81 design hours	2,025
Solicit new customers	$3 per solicitation	300 solicitations	900	95 solicitations	285
Operations level					
Provide utilities and space	$15 per machine hour	300 machine hours	$ 4,500	90 machine hours	1,350
Total activity costs assigned to services			$22,000		$ 9,120
Total volume			÷110,000		÷48,000
Activity costs per unit (total activity costs ÷ total volume)			$ 0.20		$ 0.19
Cost summary					
Direct materials cost			$ 7,700		$ 5,280
Postage costs			17,600		7,680
Activity costs (includes labor and overhead)			22,000		$ 9,120
Total costs for month			$47,300		$22,080
Product unit cost (total costs for month ÷ total volume)			$ 0.43		$ 0.46

Study Note

A bill of activities summarizes costs relating to a product or service and supports the calculation of the product or service unit cost.

Bill of Activities Once managers have created the cost hierarchy, they group the activities into the specified levels and prepare a summary of the activity costs assigned to the selected cost objects. A **bill of activities** is a list of activities and related costs that is used to compute the costs assigned to activities and the product unit cost. More complex bills of activities group activities into activity pools and include activity cost rates and the cost driver levels used to assign costs to cost objects. A bill of activities may be used as the primary document or as a supporting schedule to calculate the product unit cost in both job order and process costing systems and in both manufacturing and service businesses. Exhibit 1 shows a bill of activities for DAI.

Fran Teerlink uses the bill of activities to see how activity costs contribute to unit costs. As Exhibit 1 shows, DAI produces two types of mailing pieces, the Direct Mailer and the Store Mailer.

▶ Preparing the Direct Mailer involves printing, folding, and collating letters and other materials, inserting them into a printed, addressed envelope, and then metering and sealing the envelope. The cost of the Direct Mailer includes the costs of direct materials (envelopes, letters, and other materials), postage, and service overhead.

▶ The Store Mailer is a one-page solicitation that can be refolded and returned to the store's address. Its cost includes the costs of direct materials (a single piece of paper for each mailer), postage, and service overhead.

The volume of mailings for a customer like **La-Z-Boy** can vary from 150 to 20,000 addresses in a single mailing. The sizes of the databases that are prepared and the number of machine setups and inspection hours also vary from job to job. The service overhead costs for the activities identified in the cost hierarchy are assigned using ABC. The activity costs are calculated for the service overhead related to each type of mailing piece. These are then added to the costs of direct materials and postage to calculate a unit cost.

Teerlink grouped activities by unit, batch, service, and operations levels:

▶ At the unit level, Teerlink included the costs of all activities needed to process each Direct Mailer and Store Mailer. He used machine hours as the cost driver.

▶ At the batch level, for each job, he included the costs of all activities required to prepare the database of names and addresses for mailing, to set up the machines, and to inspect the letters for compliance with postal regulations. He used the number of names in the database, direct labor hours, and inspection hours as the cost drivers.

▶ At the service level, he included the costs of all activities required to develop databases for new clients and to solicit new business for DAI. He used design hours and number of solicitations as the cost drivers.

▶ At the operations level, he included the costs of all activities related to providing utilities and space. He used machine hours as the cost driver.

Teerlink prepared a bill of activities for one month ending May 31, 20x9. He supported each activity's cost with information about the activity cost rate and the cost driver level. He also calculated the total activity costs and the activity cost per unit for each type of mailing piece. At the bottom of the bill of activities for the month, he prepared a summary of the total costs of the mailings and calculated the unit cost for each type (the total costs divided by the number of units mailed).

The cost information gathered in the bill of activities helped Teerlink estimate the company's profits by allowing him to compare costs with revenues. To be competitive, he is currently offering the Direct Mailer for $.50 per letter and the Store Mailer for $.45 per mailer. The Direct Mailer is generating a positive gross margin of $.07 ($.50 − $.43) per letter, but the Store Mailer shows a negative gross margin of $.01 ($.45 − $.46) per mailer. Teerlink must find ways to increase fee revenue, reduce costs, or increase volume for the Store Mailer. ABC can help him reduce costs because the activity costs, including labor and overhead, are categorized by activities and grouped into activity levels. Teerlink can examine those activities to identify and reduce or eliminate some of the company's nonvalue-adding activities.

Activity-Based Costing for Selling and Administrative Activities

Activity-based costing can also be used to assign the costs of selling and administrative activities. The costs of these activities include salaries, benefits, depreciation on buildings and equipment, sales commissions, and utilities. ABC groups such costs into activity pools and assigns them to cost objects using cost drivers like the number of sales calls, sales orders, invoices, or billings. The cost objects might be products, services, customers, or sales territories. Because it is difficult to assign costs to individual customers, many companies treat similar customers, such as distributors or retailers, as a single group.

Because customer groups and sales territories differ in their complexity and diversity, each should support its related costs. For example, some customers place larger or more frequent orders than others, and a larger portion of the costs of selling and administrative activities can therefore be traced to them. Sales territories differ in size and in the number of customers served; thus, some sales territories may require more support services than others.

Exhibit 2 presents a customer-related income statement for DAI. A similar format can be used to create an income statement for any cost object. Service organizations typically group clients according to significant characteristics, such as the length of time required to perform the service or the frequency of the service. In our example, Fran Teerlink can use the ABC information to review the profitability of each customer or customer group. He can also use it to compare selling and administrative costs across customer groups and as a basis for making changes in selling and administrative activities that will increase his company's profitability.

EXHIBIT 2 ▶

Income Statement for a Cost Object

Direct Ads, Inc.
Customer-Related Income Statement
Muncie Furniture Gallery
For the Month Ended May 31, 20x9

Fee revenue ($.50 × 12,000 Direct Mailers)	$6,000
Cost of processing order ($.43 × 12,000 Direct Mailers)	5,160
Gross margin	$ 840
Less: Selling and administrative activity costs	726
Operating income contributed by Muncie Furniture Gallery	$ 114

Activity	Activity Cost Rate	Cost Driver Level	Activity Cost
Make sales calls	$12 per sales call	10 sales calls	$120
Prepare sales orders	$6 per sales order	25 sales orders	150
Handle inquiries	$.50 per minute	120 minutes	60
Process credits	$20 per notice	1 notice	20
Process invoices	$10 per invoice	12 invoices	120
Follow-ups	$8 per follow-up	20 follow-ups	160
Process billings and collections	$4 per billing	24 billings	96
Total selling and administrative activity costs			$726

S T O P • R E V I E W • A P P L Y

4-1. Why have many organizations turned to activity-based costing?

4-2. What are the five steps involved in implementing activity-based costing?

4-3. List and define the four levels in the cost hierarchy for a company.

4-4. How does a bill of activities differ from a job order cost card?

The New Operating Environment and JIT Operations

LO5 Define the *just-in-time (JIT) operating philosophy* and identify the elements of a JIT operating environment.

To remain competitive in today's changing business environment, companies have had to rethink their organizational processes and basic operating methods. One of the operating philosophies that managers have devised for the new operating environment is JIT. The **just-in-time (JIT) operating philosophy** requires that all resources—materials, personnel, and facilities—be acquired and used only as needed. Its objectives are to enhance productivity, eliminate waste, reduce costs, and improve product quality.

Traditionally, a company operated with large amounts of inventory, including finished goods stored in anticipation of customers' orders; purchased materials infrequently but in large amounts; had long production runs with infrequent setups; manufactured large batches of products; and trained each member of its work force to perform a limited number of tasks. Managers determined that changes in this process were necessary because

 *Study Note*

Traditional environments emphasize *functional* departments that tend to group similar activities together (e.g., a typing pool).

▶ Large amounts of an organization's space and money were tied up in inventory.

▶ The source of poor-quality materials, products, or services was hard to pinpoint.

▶ The number of nonvalue-adding manufacturing activities was growing.

▶ Accounting for the manufacturing process was becoming ever more complex.

To achieve JIT's objectives, a company must redesign its operating systems, plant layout, and basic management methods to conform to several basic concepts:

▶ Simple is better.

▶ The quality of the product or service is critical.

▶ The work environment must emphasize continuous improvement.

▶ Maintaining large inventories wastes resources and may hide poor work.

▶ Activities or functions that do not add value to a product or service should be eliminated or reduced.

FOCUS ON BUSINESS PRACTICE

Just-in-Time Who's Who

- Eli Whitney perfected the concept of interchangeable parts in 1799, when he produced 10,000 muskets for the U.S. Army for the low price of $13.40 per musket.

- In the late 1890s, Frederick W. Taylor used his ideas of scientific management to standardize work through time studies.

- In the early twentieth century, Frank and Lillian Galbraith (parents of the authors of *Cheaper by the Dozen*) focused on eliminating waste by studying worker motivation and using motion studies and process charting.

- Starting in 1910, Henry Ford and Charles E. Sorensen arranged all the elements of manufacturing into a continuous system called the *production line*.

- After World War II, Taichii Ohno and Shigeo Shingo recognized the importance of inventory management, and they perfected the Toyota production system, also known as the *just-in-time system (JIT)*.[5]

▶ Goods should be produced only when needed.

▶ Workers must be multiskilled and must participate in improving efficiency and product quality.

Application of these concepts creates a JIT operating environment. Here, we describe the elements used in a JIT operating environment to enhance productivity, eliminate waste, reduce costs, and improve product quality.

Minimum Inventory Levels

Maintaining minimum inventory levels is fundamental to the JIT operating philosophy. In the traditional manufacturing environment, parts, materials, and supplies are purchased far in advance and stored until the production department needs them. In contrast, in a JIT environment, materials and parts are

A basic rule in a JIT operating environment is to keep inventory at a minimum. Doing so has many advantages, including reducing the amount of storage space needed, the amount of materials handling, and the amount of capital tied up in inventory. Maintaining minimum inventory levels does, however, increase the risk of stock depletions, so employees must keep a careful eye on inventory. The employee shown here is checking inventory in an electronics warehouse.

purchased and received only when they are needed. The JIT system lowers costs by reducing the space needed for inventory storage, the amount of materials handling, and the amount of inventory obsolescence. It also reduces the need for inventory control facilities, personnel, and recordkeeping. In addition, it significantly decreases the amount of work in process inventory and the amount of working capital tied up in all inventories.

Maintaining minimum inventory levels does increase the risk of stock depletions and downtime, which can be costly and can result in late revenues. Before adopting the JIT operating philosophy, managers need to plan for such risks.

Pull-Through Production

Study Note

Pull-through production represents a change in concept. Instead of producing goods in anticipation of customers' needs, customers' orders trigger the production process.

A JIT operating environment requires **pull-through production**, a system in which a customer's order triggers the purchase of materials and the scheduling of production for the products that have been ordered. In contrast, with the **push-through method** used in traditional manufacturing operations, products are manufactured in long production runs and stored in anticipation of customers' orders. With pull-through production, the size of a customer's order determines the size of a production run, and the company purchases materials and parts as needed. Inventory levels are kept low, but machines must be set up more frequently, resulting in more work stoppages.

Quick Setup and Flexible Work Cells

Study Note

In the JIT environment, normal operating activities—setup, production, and maintenance—still take place. But the timing of those activities is altered to promote smoother operations and to minimize downtime.

In the past, managers felt that it was more cost-effective to produce large batches of goods because producing small batches increases the number of machine setups. The success of JIT has disproved this. By placing machines in more efficient locations, setup time can be minimized. In addition, when workers perform frequent setups, they become more efficient at it.

In a traditional factory layout, similar machines are grouped together, forming functional departments. Products are routed through these departments in sequence, so that all necessary operations are completed in order. This process can take several days or weeks, depending on the size and complexity of the job. By changing the factory layout so that all the machines needed for sequential processing are placed together, the JIT operating environment may cut the manufacturing time of a product from days to hours, or from weeks to days. The new cluster of machinery forms a flexible **work cell**, an autonomous production line that can perform all required operations efficiently and continuously. The flexible work cell handles a "family of products"—that is, products of similar shape or size. Product families require minimal setup changes as workers move from one job to the next. The more flexible the work cell is, the greater its potential to minimize total production time.

A Multiskilled Work Force

In the flexible work cells of a JIT environment, one worker may be required to operate several types of machines simultaneously. The worker may have to set up and retool the machines and even perform routine maintenance on them. A JIT operating environment thus requires a multiskilled work force, and multiskilled workers have been very effective in contributing to high levels of productivity.

High Levels of Product Quality

JIT operations result in high-quality products since high-quality direct materials are used and because inspections are made throughout the production process. According to the JIT philosophy, inspection as a separate step does not add value to a product, so inspection is incorporated into ongoing operations. A JIT machine operator inspects the products as they pass through the manufacturing process. If the operator detects a flaw, he or she shuts down the work cell to prevent the production of similarly flawed products while the cause of the problem is being determined. The operator either fixes the problem or helps the engineer or quality control person find a way to correct it. This integrated inspection procedure, combined with high-quality materials, produces high-quality finished goods.

Effective Preventive Maintenance

When a company rearranges its machinery into flexible work cells, each machine becomes an integral part of its cell. If one machine breaks down, the entire work cell stops functioning, and the product cannot easily be routed to another machine while the malfunctioning machine is being repaired. Continuous JIT operations therefore require an effective system of preventive maintenance. Preventing machine breakdowns is considered more important and more cost-effective than keeping machines running continuously. Machine operators are trained to perform minor repairs when they detect problems. Machines are serviced regularly—much as an automobile is—to help guarantee continued operation. The machine operator conducts routine maintenance during periods of downtime between orders. (Remember that in a JIT setting, the work cell does not operate unless there is a customer order for the product. Machine operators take advantage of such downtime to perform routine maintenance.)

Continuous Improvement of the Work Environment

A JIT environment fosters loyalty among workers, who are likely to see themselves as part of a team because they are so deeply involved in the production process. Machine operators must have the skills to run several types of machines, detect defective products, suggest measures to correct problems, and maintain the machinery within their work cells. In addition, each worker is encouraged to suggest improvements to the production process. Companies with a JIT operating environment receive thousands of employee suggestions and implement a high percentage of them, and they reward workers for suggestions that improve the process. Such an environment fosters workers' initiative and benefits the company.

S T O P • R E V I E W • A P P L Y

5-1. What are the objectives of a JIT operating environment?

5-2. What is pull-through production, and how is it different from the push-through method?

5-3. How does the inspection function change in a JIT operating environment?

Accounting for Product Costs in the New Operating Environment

LO6 Identify the changes in product costing that result when a firm adopts a JIT operating environment.

When a firm shifts to the new operating environment, managers must take a new approach to evaluating costs and controlling operations. The changes in the operations will affect how costs are determined and what measures are used to monitor performance.

When a company adopts a JIT operating environment, the work cells and the goal of reducing or eliminating nonvalue-adding activities change the way costs are classified and assigned. In this section, we examine those changes.

Classifying Costs

The traditional production process can be divided into five time frames:

Processing time	The actual amount of time spent working on a product
Inspection time	The time spent looking for product flaws or reworking defective units
Moving time	The time spent moving a product from one operation or department to another
Queue time	The time a product spends waiting to be worked on once it arrives at the next operation or department
Storage time	The time a product spends in materials inventory, work in process inventory, or finished goods inventory

In product costing under JIT, costs associated with processing time are classified as either direct materials costs or conversion costs. **Conversion costs** are the sum of the direct labor costs and overhead costs incurred by a production department, work cell, or other work center. According to the JIT philosophy, costs associated with inspection, moving, queue, and storage time should be reduced or eliminated because they do not add value to the product.

Assigning Costs

In a JIT operating environment, managers focus on **throughput time**, the time it takes to move a product through the entire production process. Measures of product movement, such as machine time, are used to apply conversion costs to products.

Sophisticated computer monitoring of the work cells allows many costs to be traced directly to the cells in which products are manufactured. As Table 3 shows, several costs that in a traditional environment are treated as indirect costs and applied to products using an overhead rate are treated as the direct costs of a JIT work cell. Because the products that a work cell manufactures are similar in nature, direct materials and conversion costs should be nearly uniform for each product in a cell. The costs of repairs and maintenance, materials handling, operating supplies, utilities, and supervision can be traced directly to work cells as they are incurred. Depreciation charges are based on units of output, not on time, so depreciation can be charged directly to work cells based on the number of units produced. Building occupancy costs, insurance premiums, and property taxes remain indirect costs and must be assigned to the work cells for inclusion in the conversion cost.

TABLE 3. Direct and Indirect Costs in Traditional and JIT Environments

	Costs in a Traditional Environment	Costs in a JIT Environment
Direct materials	Direct	Direct
Direct labor	Direct	Direct
Repairs and maintenance	Indirect	Direct to work cell
Materials handling	Indirect	Direct to work cell
Operating supplies	Indirect	Direct to work cell
Utilities costs	Indirect	Direct to work cell
Supervision	Indirect	Direct to work cell
Depreciation	Indirect	Direct to work cell
Supporting service functions	Indirect	Mostly direct to work cell
Building occupancy	Indirect	Indirect
Insurance and taxes	Indirect	Indirect

S T O P • R E V I E W • A P P L Y

6-1. Which time frame in the production process is value-adding?

6-2. How do JIT operations affect the classification of costs?

Backflush Costing

LO7 Define and apply *backflush costing,* and compare the cost flows in traditional and backflush costing.

Study Note

Backflush costing eliminates the need to make journal entries during the period to track cost flows through the production process as the product is made.

Managers in a just-in-time operating environment are continuously seeking ways of reducing wasted resources and wasted time. So far, we have focused on how they can trim waste from operations, but they can reduce waste in other areas as well, including the accounting process. Because a JIT environment reduces labor costs, the accounting system can combine the costs of direct labor and overhead into the single category of conversion costs, and because materials arrive just in time to be used in the production process, there is little reason to maintain a separate Materials Inventory account. Thus, by simplifying cost flows through the accounting records, a JIT environment makes it possible to reduce the time it takes to record and account for the costs of the manufacturing process.

A JIT organization can also streamline its accounting process by using backflush costing. In **backflush costing**, all product costs are first accumulated in the Cost of Goods Sold account; at the end of the accounting period, they are "flushed back," or worked backward, into the appropriate inventory accounts. By having all product costs flow straight to a final destination and working back to determine the proper balances for the inventory accounts at the end of the period, this method saves recording time. As illustrated in Figure 4, it eliminates the need to record several transactions that must be recorded in traditional operating environments.

■ **FIGURE 4**
Comparison of Cost Flows in Traditional and Backflush Costing

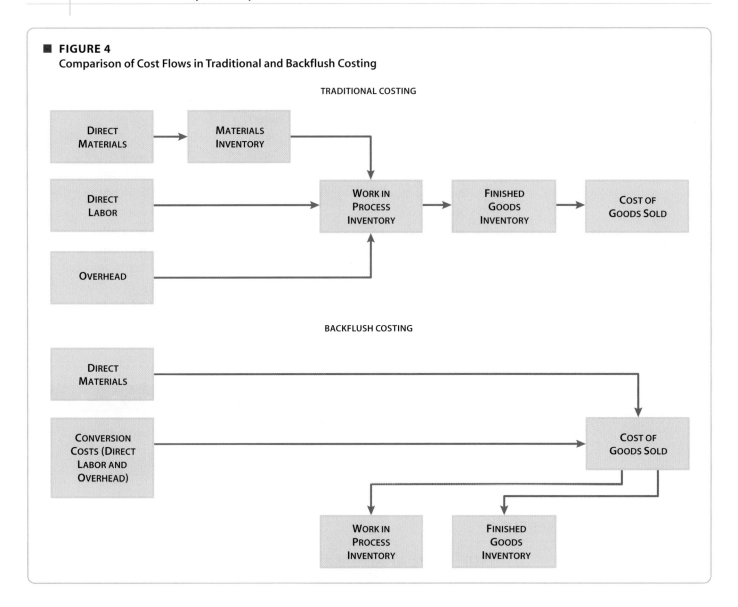

Study Note

In backflush costing, entries to the Work in Process Inventory and Finished Goods Inventory accounts are made at the end of the period.

When direct materials arrive at a factory in which traditional costing methods are used, their costs flow into the Materials Inventory account. Then, when the direct materials are requisitioned into production, their costs flow into the Work in Process Inventory account. When direct labor is used, its costs are added to the Work in Process Inventory account. Overhead is applied to production using a base like direct labor hours, machine hours, or number of units produced and is added to the other costs in the Work in Process Inventory account. At the end of the manufacturing process, the costs of the finished units are transferred to the Finished Goods Inventory account, and when the units are sold, their costs are transferred to the Cost of Goods Sold account.

In a JIT setting, direct materials arrive just in time to be placed into production. As you can see in Figure 4, when backflush costing is used, the direct materials costs and the conversion costs (direct labor and overhead) are immediately charged to the Cost of Goods Sold account. At the end of the period, the costs of goods in work in process inventory and in finished goods inventory are determined, and those costs are flushed back to the Work in Process Inventory account and the Finished Goods Inventory account. Once those costs have been flushed back, the Cost of Goods Sold account contains only the costs of units completed and sold during the period.

■ **FIGURE 5**
Cost Flows Through T Accounts in Traditional and Backflush Costing

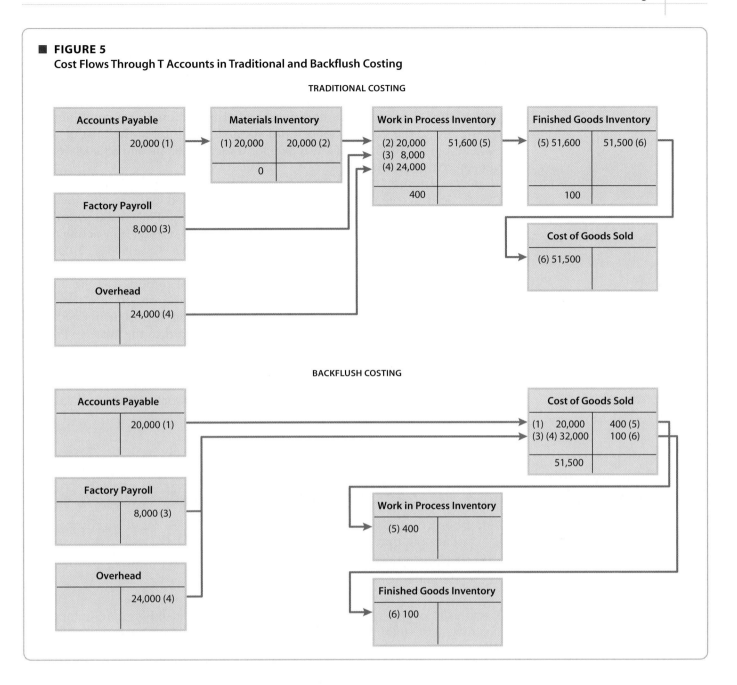

To illustrate, assume that the following transactions occurred at one of La-Z-Boy's factories last month:

1. Purchased $20,000 of direct materials on account.

2. Used all of the direct materials in production during the month.

3. Incurred direct labor costs of $8,000.

4. Applied $24,000 of overhead to production.

5. Completed units costing $51,600 during the month.

6. Sold units costing $51,500 during the month.

The top diagram in Figure 5 shows how these transactions would be entered in T accounts when traditional product costing is used. You can trace the flow of each cost by following its transaction number.

The bottom diagram in Figure 5 shows how backflush costing in a JIT environment would treat the same transactions. The cost of direct materials (Transaction 1) is charged directly to the Cost of Goods Sold account. Transaction 2, which is included in the traditional method, is not included when backflush costing is used because there is no Materials Inventory account. The costs of direct labor (Transaction 3) and overhead (Transaction 4) are combined and transferred to the Cost of Goods Sold account. The total in the Cost of Goods Sold account is then $52,000 ($20,000 for direct materials and $32,000 for conversion costs).

Once all product costs for the period have been entered in the Cost of Goods Sold account, the amounts to be transferred back to the inventory accounts are calculated. The amount transferred to the Finished Goods Inventory account is the difference between the cost of units sold (Transaction 6) and the cost of completed units (Transaction 5) ($51,600 − $51,500 = $100). The remaining difference in the Cost of Goods Sold account represents the cost of the work that is still in production at the end of the period. It is the amount charged to the Cost of Goods Sold account during the period less the actual cost of goods finished during the period (Transaction 5) [($20,000 + $8,000 + $24,000) − $51,600 = $400]; this amount is transferred to the Work in Process Inventory account.

Notice that the ending balance in the Cost of Goods Sold account, $51,500, is the same as the ending balance when traditional costing is used. The difference is that backflush costing enabled us to use fewer accounts and to avoid recording several transactions.

S T O P • R E V I E W • A P P L Y

7-1. Does JIT or ABM use backflush costing? How does backflush costing reduce the time spent on recordkeeping?

7-2. How is the ending balance in the Finished Goods Inventory account determined when backflush costing is used?

Backflush Costing For work done during August, Plush Furniture Company incurred direct materials costs of $123,450 and conversion costs of $265,200. The company employs a just-in-time operating philosophy and backflush costing.

At the end of August, it was determined that the Work in Process Inventory account had been assigned $980 of costs, and the ending balance of the Finished Goods Inventory account was $1,290. There were no beginning inventory balances. How much was charged to the Cost of Goods Sold account during August? What was the ending balance of the Cost of Goods Sold account?

SOLUTION
A total of $388,650 ($123,450 + $265,200) was charged to the Cost of Goods Sold account during August. The ending balance of Cost of Goods Sold was $386,380 ($388,650 − $980 − $1,290).

Comparison of ABM and JIT

Study Note

ABM's primary goal is to calculate product or service cost accurately. JIT's primary goal is to simplify and standardize business processes.

ABM and JIT have several things in common. As activity-based systems, both analyze processes and identify value-adding and nonvalue-adding activities. Both seek to eliminate waste and reduce nonvalue-adding activities to improve product or service quality, reduce costs, and improve an organization's efficiency and productivity. Both improve the quality of the information that managers use to make decisions about bidding, pricing, product lines, and outsourcing. However, the two systems differ in their methods of costing and cost assignment.

ABM's tool, ABC, calculates product or service cost by using cost drivers to assign the indirect costs of production to cost objects. ABC affects only the assignment of overhead costs to products or services; the costs of direct materials and direct labor are traced directly to products or services and are unaffected by ABC. ABC is often a fairly complex accounting method used with job order and process costing systems. Note that the ABC method can also be used to examine nonproduction-related activities, such as marketing and shipping.

JIT reorganizes many activities so that they are performed within work cells. The costs of those activities become direct costs of the work cell and of the products made in that cell. The total production costs within the cell can then be assigned by using simple cost drivers, such as process hours or direct materials cost. Companies that have implemented JIT manufacturing may use backflush costing rather than job order costing or process costing. This approach focuses on the output at the end of the production process and simplifies the accounting system. Table 4 summarizes the characteristics of ABM and JIT.

TABLE 4.   Comparison of ABM and JIT Activity-Based Systems

	ABM	JIT
Primary purpose	To eliminate or reduce nonvalue-adding activities	To eliminate or reduce waste
Cost assignment	Uses ABC to assign overhead costs to the product cost by using appropriate cost drivers	Reorganizes activities so that they are performed within work cells; overhead costs incurred in the work cell become direct costs of the products made in that cell
Costing method	Integrates ABC with job order or process costing to calculate product costs	May use backflush costing to calculate product costs when the products are completed

A company can use both ABM and JIT. ABM and ABC will improve the accuracy of the company's product or service costing and help it to reduce or eliminate business activities that do not add value for its customers. It can apply the JIT operating philosophy to simplify processes, use resources effectively, and eliminate waste. To remain competitive in today's fast-changing business environment, many organizations rely on both of these activity-based systems.

S T O P • R E V I E W • A P P L Y

8-1. How do ABM and JIT differ in their approaches to product costing?

8-2. Can a business use both ABM and JIT?

A LOOK BACK AT

LA-Z-BOY, INC.

In this chapter's Decision Point, we asked the following questions:

- **How have ABM and JIT helped La-Z-Boy improve its production processes and reduce delivery time?**

- **How do the managers of La-Z-Boy plan to remain the industry's leading marketer and manufacturer of upholstered products?**

La-Z-Boy's managers use activity-based management (ABM) and a just-in-time (JIT) operating environment to identify and reduce or eliminate activities that do not add value to the company's products. These systems focus on minimizing waste, reducing costs, improving the allocation of resources, and ensuring that suppliers deliver materials just at the time the company needs them. They help managers make better decisions about costing and pricing products, adding or dropping product styles, changing production and delivery systems, and contracting with suppliers. The continuous flow of information that ABM and JIT provide has enabled La-Z-Boy's managers to improve the company's production processes and act in an ethical, responsible manner. They are able to adjust their labor needs each week to meet order requirements; to schedule timely deliveries from suppliers, thus maintaining appropriate inventory levels; and to keep track of the company's fleet of delivery trucks.

La-Z-Boy's disciplined monitoring of order, production, and delivery activities gives the company a competitive edge. By using ABM and JIT, La-Z-Boy has achieved higher productivity than other furniture manufacturers, is able to offer more than 40,000 product variations, and has cut its delivery time to its licensed furniture galleries by one-half to one-third.[6]

CHAPTER REVIEW

REVIEW of Learning Objectives

LO1 Explain the role of managers in activity-based systems.

Activity-based systems are information systems that provide quantitative information about an organization's activities. They help managers view the organization as a collection of related activities. Activity-based cost information enables managers to improve operating processes and make better pricing decisions. When managers plan, activity-based systems help them identify value-adding activities, determine the resources needed for those activities, and estimate product costs. As managers manage and evaluate operating performance, these systems help them determine the full product or service cost, identify actions that will reduce that cost, and establish whether cost-reduction goals for nonvalue-adding activities were reached. Activity-based systems also help managers communicate the cost of inventory and determine the degree to which product goals were achieved.

LO2 Define *activity-based management (ABM)* and discuss its relationship to the supply chain and the value chain.

Activity-based management (ABM) is an approach to managing an organization that identifies all major operating activities, determines the resources consumed by each activity and the cause of the resource usage, and categorizes the activities as either adding value to a product or service or not adding value. ABM enables managers to see their organization as a collection of value-creating activities (a value chain) that operates as part of a larger system that includes suppliers' and customers' value chains (a supply chain). This perspective helps managers work cooperatively both inside and outside their organizations to reduce costs by eliminating waste and inefficiencies and by redirecting resources toward value-adding activities.

LO3 Distinguish between value-adding and nonvalue-adding activities, and describe process value analysis.

A value-adding activity adds value to a product or service as perceived by the customer. Examples include designing the components of a new recliner, assembling the recliner frame, and upholstering it. A nonvalue-adding activity adds cost to a product or service but does not increase its market value. Examples include legal services, management accounting, machine repair, materials handling, and building maintenance. PVA is a technique that managers use to identify and link all the activities involved in the value chain. It analyzes business processes by relating activities to the events that prompt the activities and to the resources that the activities consume.

LO4 Define *activity-based costing* and explain how a cost hierarchy and a bill of activities are used.

Activity-based costing (ABC) is a method of assigning costs that calculates a more accurate product cost than traditional methods do. It does so by categorizing all indirect costs by activity, tracing the indirect costs to those activities, and assigning those costs to products using a cost driver related to the cause of the cost. To implement ABC, managers (1) identify and classify each activity, (2) estimate the cost of resources for each activity, (3) identify a cost driver for each activity and estimate the quantity of each cost driver, (4) calculate an activity cost rate for each activity, and (5) assign costs to cost objects based on the level of activity required to make the product or provide the service.

Two tools—a cost hierarchy and a bill of activities—help in the implementation of ABC. To create a cost hierarchy, managers classify activities into four levels. Unit-level activities are performed each time a unit is produced. Batch-level activities are performed each time a batch of goods is produced. Product-level activities are performed to support a particular product line or brand. Facility-level activities are performed to support a facility's general manufacturing process. A bill of activities is then used to compute the costs assigned to activities and the product or service unit cost.

LO5   Define the *just-in-time (JIT) operating philosophy* and identify the elements of a JIT operating environment.

The just-in-time (JIT) operating philosophy is a management philosophy that requires that all resources—materials, personnel, and facilities—be acquired and used only as needed. Its objectives are to enhance productivity, eliminate waste, reduce costs, and improve product quality. The elements in a JIT operating environment that are designed to achieve those objectives are minimum inventory levels, pull-through production, quick setup and flexible work cells, a multiskilled work force, high levels of product quality, effective preventive maintenance, and continuous improvement of the work environment.

LO6   Identify the changes in product costing that result when a firm adopts a JIT operating environment.

In product costing under JIT, processing costs are classified as either direct materials costs or conversion costs. The costs associated with inspection time, moving time, queue time, and storage time are reduced or eliminated. With computerized monitoring of the work cells, many costs that are treated as indirect or overhead costs in traditional manufacturing settings, such as the costs of utilities and operating supplies, can be traced directly to work cells. The only costs that remain indirect costs and must be assigned to the work cells for inclusion in the overhead cost are those associated with building occupancy, insurance, and property taxes.

LO7   Define and apply *backflush costing*, and compare the cost flows in traditional and backflush costing.

In backflush costing, all product costs are first accumulated in the Cost of Goods Sold account; at the end of the accounting period, they are "flushed back," or worked backward, into the appropriate inventory accounts. Backflush costing is commonly used to account for product costs in a JIT operating environment. It differs from the traditional costing approach, which records the costs of materials purchased in the Materials Inventory account and uses the Work in Process Inventory account to record the costs of direct materials, direct labor, and overhead during the production process. The objective of backflush costing is to save recording time, which cuts costs.

LO8   Compare ABM and JIT as activity-based systems.

As activity-based systems, both ABM and JIT seek to eliminate waste and reduce nonvalue-adding activities. However, they differ in their approaches to cost assignment and calculation of product cost. ABM uses ABC to assign indirect costs to products using cost drivers; JIT reorganizes activities so that they are performed within work cells, and the overhead costs incurred in a work cell become direct costs of the products made in that cell. ABM uses job order or process costing to calculate product costs, whereas JIT may use backflush costing.

REVIEW of Concepts and Terminology

The following concepts and terms were introduced in this chapter:

Activity-based costing: A method of assigning costs that calculates a more accurate product cost than traditional methods by categorizing all indirect costs by activity, tracing the indirect costs to those activities, and assigning those costs to products using a cost driver related to the cause of the cost. **(LO4)**

Activity-based management (ABM): An approach to managing an organization that identifies all major operating activities, determines the resources consumed by each activity and the cause of the resource usage, categorizes the activities as either adding value to a product or service or not adding value, and seeks to reduce or eliminate nonvalue-adding activities. **(LO2)**

Activity-based systems: Information systems that provide quantitative information about an organization's activities. **(LO1)**

Backflush costing: A product costing approach in which all product costs are first accumulated in the Cost of Goods Sold account and at the end of the period are "flushed back," or worked backward, into the appropriate inventory accounts. **(LO7)**

Batch-level activities: Activities performed each time a batch of goods is produced. **(LO4)**

Bill of activities: A list of activities and related costs that is used to compute the costs assigned to activities and the product unit cost. **(LO4)**

Conversion costs: The sum of the direct labor costs and overhead costs incurred by a production department, work cell, or other work center. **(LO6)**

Cost hierarchy: A framework for classifying activities according to the level at which their costs are incurred. **(LO4)**

Facility-level activities: Activities performed to support a facility's general manufacturing process. **(LO4)**

Full product cost: A cost that includes not only the costs of direct materials and direct labor, but also the costs of all production and nonproduction activities required to satisfy the customer. **(LO1)**

Inspection time: The time spent looking for product flaws or reworking defective units. **(LO6)**

Just-in-time (JIT) operating philosophy: An operating philosophy that requires that all resources—materials, personnel, and facilities—be acquired and used only as needed; it focuses on eliminating or reducing waste. **(LO5)**

Moving time: The time spent moving a product from one operation or department to another. **(LO6)**

Nonvalue-adding activity: An activity that adds cost to a product or service but does not increase its market value. **(LO3)**

Processing time: The actual amount of time spent working on a product. **(LO6)**

Process value analysis (PVA): A technique that analyzes business processes by relating activities to the events that prompt those activities and to the resources that the activities consume. **(LO3)**

Product-level activities: Activities performed to support a particular product line. **(LO4)**

Pull-through production: A production system in which a customer's order triggers the purchase of materials and the scheduling of production for the required products. **(LO5)**

Push-through method: A production system in which products are manufactured in long production runs and stored in anticipation of customers' orders. **(LO5)**

Queue time: The time a product spends waiting to be worked on once it enters a new operation or department. **(LO6)**

Storage time: The time a product spends in materials storage, work in process inventory, or finished goods inventory. **(LO6)**

Supply chain: The path that leads from the suppliers of the materials from which a product is made to the final customer. **(LO2)**

Throughput time: The time it takes to move a product through the entire production process. **(LO6)**

Unit-level activities: Activities performed each time a unit is produced. **(LO4)**

Value-adding activity: An activity that adds value to a product or service as perceived by the customer. **(LO3)**

Value chain: A sequence of activities, or primary processes, that add value to a product or service; also includes support services that facilitate these activities. **(LO2)**

Work cell: An autonomous production line that can perform all required operations efficiently and continuously. **(LO5)**

REVIEW Problem

LO4   Activity-Based Costing

Quality Sofas Corporation produces more than a dozen styles of sofas and upholstered furniture. The eight-piece modular seating group is the most difficult to produce and the most expensive. The reclining sofa, which is the company's leading seller, is the easiest to produce. The other styles increase in difficulty of production as the number of pieces increases. Stylemaker Stores recently ordered 175 of the six-piece modular seating group. Because Quality Sofas Corporation is considering a shift to activity-based costing, its controller, Sam Overstreet, is interested in using this order to compare ABC with traditional costing. Costs directly traceable to the Stylemaker Stores order are as follows:

Direct materials	$57,290
Purchased parts	$76,410
Direct labor hours	1,320
Average direct labor pay rate per hour	$ 14.00

With the traditional costing approach, Sam Overstreet applies overhead costs at a rate of 320 percent of direct labor costs.

For activity-based costing of the Stylemaker Stores order, Overstreet uses the following data:

Activity	Cost Driver	Activity Cost Rate	Activity Usage
Product design	Engineering hours	$62 per engineering hour	76 engineering hours
Work cell setup	Number of setups	$90 per setup	16 setups
Parts production	Machine hours	$38 per machine hour	380 machine hours
Assembly	Assembly labor hours	$40 per assembly labor hour	500 assembly labor hours
Product simulation	Testing hours	$90 per testing hour	28 testing hours
Packaging and shipping	Product units	$26 per unit	175 units
Building occupancy	Direct labor cost	125% of direct labor cost	$18,480 direct labor cost

Required

1. Use the traditional costing approach to compute the total cost and product unit cost of the Stylemaker Stores order.
2. Using the cost hierarchy for manufacturing companies, classify each activity of the Stylemaker Stores order according to the level at which it occurs.
3. Prepare a bill of activities for the operating costs.
4. Use ABC to compute the total cost and product unit cost.
5. What is the difference between the product unit cost you computed using the traditional approach and the one you computed using ABC? Does the use of ABC guarantee cost reduction for every order?

Answer to Review Problem

1. Traditional costing approach:

Direct materials	$ 57,290
Purchased parts	76,410
Direct labor	18,480
Overhead (320% of direct labor cost)	59,136
Total cost of order	$211,316
Product unit cost (total cost ÷ 175 units)	$1,207.52

2. Activities classified by level of the manufacturing cost hierarchy:

Unit level:	Parts production
	Assembly
	Packaging and shipping
Batch level:	Work cell setup
Product level:	Product design
	Product simulation
Facility level:	Building occupancy

3, 4. Bill of activities and total cost and product unit cost computed with ABC:

Quality Sofas Corporation
Bill of Activities
Stylemaker Stores Order

Activity	Activity Cost Rate	Cost Driver Level	Activity Cost
Unit level			
Parts production	$38 per machine hour	380 machine hours	$ 14,440
Assembly	$40 per assembly labor hour	500 assembly labor hours	20,000
Packaging and shipping	$26 per unit	175 units	4,550
Batch level			
Work cell setup	$90 per setup	16 setups	1,440
Product level			
Product design	$62 per engineering hour	76 engineering hours	4,712
Product simulation	$90 per testing hour	28 testing hours	2,520
Facility level			
Building occupancy	125% of direct labor cost	$18,480 direct labor cost	23,100
Total activity costs assigned to job			$ 70,762
Total job units			÷175
Activity costs per unit (total activity costs ÷ total units)			$ 404.35
Cost summary			
Direct materials			$ 57,290
Purchased parts			76,410
Activity costs (includes labor and overhead)			70,762
Total cost of order			$ 204,462
Product unit cost (total cost of order ÷ 175 units)			$1,168.35

5. Product unit cost using traditional costing approach: $1,207.52
   Product unit cost using activity-based costing approach: 1,168.35
   Difference: $ 39.17

   Although the product unit cost computed using ABC is lower than the one computed using the traditional costing approach, ABC does not guarantee cost reduction for every product. It does improve cost traceability, which often identifies products that are undercosted or overcosted by a traditional product costing system.

CHAPTER ASSIGNMENTS

BUILDING Your Basic Knowledge and Skills

Short Exercises

LO1   Activity-Based Systems

SE 1. Amber Lutz started a retail clothing business two years ago. Lutz's first year was very successful, but sales dropped 50 percent in the second year. A friend who is a business consultant analyzed Lutz's business and came up with two basic reasons for the decline in sales: (1) Lutz has been placing orders late in each season, and (2) shipments of clothing have been arriving late and in poor condition. What measures can Lutz take to improve her business and persuade customers to return?

LO2   The Value Chain

SE 2. Which of the following activities would be part of the value chain of a manufacturing company? Which activities do not add value?

1. Product inspection
2. Machine drilling
3. Materials storage
4. Product engineering
5. Product packing
6. Cost accounting
7. Moving work in process
8. Inventory control

LO2   The Supply Chain

SE 3. Thom DuBois is developing plans to open a restaurant called Ribs 'n Slaw. He has located a building and will lease all the furniture and equipment he needs for the restaurant. Food Servers, Inc., will supply all the restaurant's personnel. Identify the components of Ribs 'n Slaw's supply chain.

LO3   Value-Adding and Nonvalue-Adding Activities

SE 4. Indicate whether the following activities of a submarine sandwich shop are value-adding (V) or nonvalue-adding (NV):

1. Purchasing sandwich ingredients
2. Storing condiments
3. Making sandwiches
4. Cleaning up the shop
5. Making home deliveries
6. Accounting for sales and costs

LO4   The Cost Hierarchy

SE 5. Engineering design is an activity that is vital to the success of any motor vehicle manufacturer. Identify the level at which engineering design would be classified in the cost hierarchy used with ABC for each of the following:

1. A maker of unique editions of luxury automobiles
2. A maker of built-to-order city and county emergency vehicles (orders are usually placed for 10 to 12 identical vehicles)
3. A maker of a line of automobiles sold throughout the world

LO4   The Cost Hierarchy

SE 6. Match the four levels of the cost hierarchy to the following activities of a blue jeans manufacturer that uses activity-based management:

1. Routine maintenance of sewing machines
2. Designing a pattern for a new style

3. Sewing seams on a garment
4. Producing 100 jeans of a certain style in a certain size

LO5 Elements of a JIT Operating Environment

SE 7. Maintaining minimum inventory levels and using pull-through production are important elements of a just-in-time operating environment. How does pull-through production help minimize inventories?

LO6 Product Costing Changes in a JIT Environment

SE 8. Aromatherapy Products Company is in the process of adopting the just-in-time operating philosophy for its lotion-making operations. Indicate which of the following overhead costs are nonvalue-adding costs (NVA) and which can be traced directly to the new lotion-making work cell (D):

1. Storage containers for work in process inventory
2. Inspection labor
3. Machine electricity
4. Machine repairs
5. Depreciation of the storage container moving equipment
6. Machine setup labor

LO7 Backflush Costing

SE 9. For work done during August, Pansey Company incurred direct materials costs of $120,000 and conversion costs of $260,000. The company employs a just-in-time operating philosophy and backflush costing. At the end of August, it was determined that the Work in Process Inventory account had been assigned $900 of costs, and the ending balance of the Finished Goods Inventory account was $1,300. There were no beginning inventory balances. How much was charged to the Cost of Goods Sold account during August? What was the ending balance of that account?

LO8 Comparison of ABM and JIT

SE 10. Hwang Corp. recently installed three just-in-time work cells in its screen-making division. The work cells will make large quantities of products for major window and door manufacturers. Should Hwang use JIT and backflush costing or ABM and ABC to account for product costs? Defend your choice of activity-based system.

Exercises

LO1 Management Reports

E 1. The reports that follow are from a department in an insurance company. Which report would be used for financial purposes, and which would be used for activity-based decision making? Why?

Salaries	$ 1,400	Enter claims into system	$ 2,000
Equipment	1,200	Analyze claims	1,000
Travel expenses	8,000	Suspend claims	1,500
Supplies	300	Receive inquiries	1,500
Use and occupancy	3,000	Resolve problems	400
		Process batches	3,000
		Determine eligibility	4,000
		Make copies	200
		Write correspondence	100
		Attend training	200
Total	$13,900	Total	$13,900

LO2 The Supply Chain and Value Chain

E 2. Indicate which of the following persons and activities associated with a lawn and garden nursery are part of the supply chain (S) and which are part of the value chain (V):

1. Plant and tree vendor
2. Purchasing potted trees
3. Computer and software company
4. Creating marketing plans
5. Advertising company
6. Scheduling delivery trucks
7. Customer service

LO2 The Supply Chain and Value Chain

E 3. The items in the following list are associated with a hotel. Indicate which are part of the supply chain (S) and which are part of the value chain (V).

1. Travel agency
2. Housekeeping supplies
3. Special events and promotions
4. Customer service
5. Travel bureau website
6. Tour agencies

LO3 Value Analysis

E 4. Libbel Enterprises has been in business for 30 years. Last year, the company purchased Chemcraft Laboratory and entered the chemical processing business. Libbel's controller prepared a process value analysis of the new operation and identified the following activities:

New product research	Product sales	Product bottling process
Solicitation of vendor bids	Packaging process	Product warranty work
Materials storage	Materials inspection	Product engineering
Product curing process	New product marketing	Purchasing of direct materials
Product scheduling	Product inspection	Finished goods storage
Product spoilage	Product delivery	Cleanup of processing areas
Customer follow-up	Materials delivery	Product mixing process

Identify the value-adding activities in this list, and classify them into the activity areas of the value chain illustrated in Figure 2 in this chapter. Prepare a separate list of the nonvalue-adding activities.

LO3 Value-Adding Activities

E 5. When Courtney Tybee prepared a process value analysis for her company, she identified the following primary activities. Identify the value-adding activities.

1. Production scheduling
2. Customer follow-up
3. Materials moving
4. Product inspection
5. Engineering design
6. Product marketing
7. Product sales
8. Materials storage

LO4 The Cost Hierarchy

E 6. Copia Electronics makes speaker systems. Its customers range from new hotels and restaurants that need specifically designed sound systems to nationwide retail outlets that order large quantities of similar products. The following activities are part of the company's operating process:

New retail product design	Purchasing of materials	Assembly labor
Retail product marketing	Building repair	Assembly line setup

Unique system design   Retail sales commissions   Building security
Unique system   Bulk packing of orders   Facility supervision
  packaging

Classify each activity as unit level (UL), batch level (BL), product level (PL), or facility level (FL).

LO4   Bill of Activities

E 7. Lake Corporation has received an order for handheld computers from Union, LLC. A partially complete bill of activities for that order appears below. Fill in the missing data.

Lake Corporation
Bill of Activities for Union, LLC
Order Form

Activity	Activity Cost Rate	Cost Driver Level	Activity Cost
Unit level			
Parts production	$50 per machine hour	200 machine hours	$?
Assembly	$20 per direct labor hour	100 direct labor hours	?
Packaging and shipping	$12.50 per unit	400 units	?
Batch level			
Work cell setup	$100 per setup	16 setups	?
Product level			
Product design	$60 per engineering hour	80 engineering hours	?
Product simulation	$80 per testing hour	30 testing hours	?
Facility level			
Building occupancy	200% of assembly labor cost	?	?
Total activity costs assigned to job			$?
Total job units			400
Activity costs per unit (total activity costs ÷ total units)			$?
Cost summary			
Direct materials			$60,000
Purchased parts			80,000
Activity costs			?
Total cost of order			$?
Product unit cost (total cost ÷ 400 units)			$?

LO4   Activity Cost Rates

E 8. Compute the activity cost rates for materials handling, assembly, and design based on these data:

Materials

Cloth	$26,000
Fasteners	4,000
Purchased parts	40,000

Materials handling

Labor	$8,000
Equipment depreciation	5,000
Electrical power	2,000
Maintenance	6,000

Assembly

Machine operators	5,000

Design

Labor	5,000
Electrical power	1,000
Overhead	8,000

Output totaled 40,000 units. Each unit requires three machine hours of effort. Materials handling costs are allocated to the products based on direct materials cost. Design costs are allocated based on units produced. Assembly costs are allocated based on 500 machine operator hours.

LO5   Elements of a JIT Operating Environment

E 9. The numbered items below are concepts that underlie activity-based systems, such as ABM and JIT. Match each concept to the related lettered element(s) of a JIT operating environment.

1. Business processes are simplified.
2. The quality of the product or service is critical.
3. Employees are cross-trained.
4. Large inventories waste resources and may hide bad work.
5. Goods should be produced only when needed.
6. Equipment downtime is minimized.

a. Minimum inventory levels
b. Pull-through production
c. Quick machine setups and flexible work cells
d. A multiskilled work force
e. High levels of product quality
f. Effective preventive maintenance

LO5   Comparison of Traditional Manufacturing Environments and JIT

E 10. Identify which of the following exist in a traditional manufacturing environment and which exist in a JIT environment:

1. Large amounts of inventory
2. Complex manufacturing processes
3. A multiskilled labor force
4. Flexible work cells
5. Push-through production methods
6. Materials purchased infrequently but in large lot sizes
7. Infrequent setups

LO6   Direct and Indirect Costs in JIT and Traditional Manufacturing Environments

E 11. The cost categories in this list are typical of many manufacturing operations:

Direct materials:	Direct labor	Depreciation, machinery
Sheet steel	Engineering labor	Supervisory salaries
Iron castings	Indirect labor	Electrical power
Assembly parts:	Operating supplies	Insurance and taxes, plant
Part 24RE6	Small tools	President's salary
Part 15RF8	Depreciation, plant	Employee benefits

Identify each cost as direct or indirect, assuming that it was incurred in (1) a traditional manufacturing setting and (2) a JIT environment. State the reasons for changes in classification.

LO7 Backflush Costing

E 12. Conda Products Company implemented a JIT work environment in its trowel division eight months ago, and the division has been operating at near capacity since then. At the beginning of May, Work in Process Inventory and Finished Goods Inventory had zero balances. The following transactions took place last week:

May 28 Ordered, received, and used handles and sheet metal costing $11,340.
29 Direct labor costs incurred, $5,400.
29 Overhead costs incurred, $8,100.
30 Completed trowels costing $24,800.
31 Sold trowels costing $24,000.

Using backflush costing, calculate the ending balance in the Work in Process Inventory and Finished Goods Inventory accounts.

LO7 Backflush Costing

E 13. Good Morning Enterprises produces digital alarm clocks. It has a just-in-time assembly process and uses backflush costing to record production costs. Overhead is assigned at a rate of $17 per assembly labor hour. There were no beginning inventories in March. During March, the following operating data were generated:

Cost of direct materials purchased and used	$53,200
Direct labor costs incurred	$27,300
Overhead costs assigned	?
Assembly hours worked	3,840 hours
Ending work in process inventory	$1,050
Ending finished goods inventory	$960

Using T accounts, show the flow of costs through the backflush costing system. What is the total cost of goods sold in March?

LO8 Comparison of ABM and JIT

E 14. Identify each of the following as a characteristic of ABM or JIT:

1. Backflush costing
2. ABC used to assign overhead costs to the product cost
3. ABC integrated with job order or process costing systems
4. Complexity reduced by using work cells, minimizing inventories, and reducing or eliminating nonvalue-adding activities
5. Activities reorganized so that they are performed within work cells

LO8 Comparison of ABM and JIT

E 15. The following are excerpts from a conversation between two managers about their companies' activity-based systems. Identify the manager who works for a company that emphasizes ABM and the one who works for a company that emphasizes a JIT system.

Manager 1: We try to manage our resources effectively by monitoring operating activities. We analyze all major operating activities, and we focus on reducing or eliminating the ones that don't add value to our products.

Manager 2: We're very concerned with eliminating waste. We've designed our operations to reduce the time it takes to move, store, queue, and inspect materials. We've also reduced our inventories by buying and using materials only when we need them.

Problems

LO2, LO3 **The Value Chain and Process Value Analysis**

P 1. Lindstrom Industries, Inc., produces chain saws, weed whackers, and lawn mowers for major retail chains. Lindstrom makes these products to order in large quantities for each customer. It has adopted activity-based management, and its controller is in the process of developing an ABC system. The controller has identified the following primary activities of the company:

Product delivery	Production—assembly
Customer follow-up	Engineering design
Materials and parts purchasing	Product inspection
Materials storage	Processing areas cleanup
Materials inspection	Product marketing
Production—drilling	Building maintenance
Product packaging	Product sales
New product testing	Product rework
Finished goods storage	Production—grinding
Production—machine setup	Personnel services
Materials moving	Production scheduling

Required

1. Identify the activities that do not add value to Lindstrom's products.
2. Assist the controller's analysis by grouping the value-adding activities into the activity areas of the value chain shown in Figure 2 of this chapter.
3. **Manager Insight:** State whether each nonvalue-adding activity is necessary or unnecessary. Suggest how each unnecessary activity could be reduced or eliminated.

LO4 **Activity-Based Costing**

P 2. Boulware Products, Inc., produces printers for wholesale distributors. It has just completed packaging an order from Shawl Company for 150 printers. Before the order is shipped, the controller wants to compare the unit costs computed under the company's new activity-based costing system with the unit costs computed under its traditional costing system. Boulware's traditional costing system assigned overhead costs at a rate of 240 percent of direct labor cost.

Data for the Shawl order are as follows: direct materials, $17,552; purchased parts, $14,856; direct labor hours, 140; and average direct labor pay rate per hour, $17.

Data for activity-based costing related to processing direct materials and purchased parts for the Shawl order are as follows:

Activity	Cost Driver	Activity Cost Rate	Activity Usage
Engineering systems design	Engineering hours	$28 per engineering hour	18 engineering hours
Setup	Number of setups	$36 per setup	12 setups
Parts production	Machine hours	$37 per machine hour	82 machine hours
Product assembly	Assembly hours	$42 per assembly hour	96 assembly hours
Packaging	Number of packages	$5.60 per package	150 packages
Building occupancy	Machine hours	$10 per machine hour	82 machine hours

Required

1. Use the traditional costing approach to compute the total cost and the product unit cost of the Shawl order.
2. Using the cost hierarchy, identify each activity as unit level, batch level, product level, or facility level.
3. Prepare a bill of activities for the activity costs.
4. Use ABC to compute the total cost and product unit cost of the Shawl order.
5. **Manager Insight:** What is the difference between the product unit cost you computed using the traditional approach and the one you computed using ABC? Does the use of ABC guarantee cost reduction for every order?

LO4 **Activity Cost Rates**

P 3. Noir Company produces four versions of its model J17-21 bicycle seat. The four versions have different shapes, but their processing operations and production costs are identical. During July, these costs were incurred:

Direct materials	
Leather	$25,430
Metal frame	39,180
Bolts	3,010
Materials handling	
Labor	8,232
Equipment depreciation	4,410
Electrical power	2,460
Maintenance	5,184
Assembly	
Direct labor	13,230
Engineering design	
Labor	4,116
Electrical power	1,176
Engineering overhead	7,644
Overhead	
Equipment depreciation	7,056
Indirect labor	30,870
Supervision	17,640
Operating supplies	4,410
Electrical power	10,584
Repairs and maintenance	21,168
Building occupancy overhead	52,920

July's output totaled 29,400 units. Each unit requires three machine hours of effort. Materials handling costs are allocated to the products based on direct materials cost, engineering design costs are allocated based on units produced, and overhead is allocated based on machine hours. Assembly costs are allocated based on direct labor hours, which are estimated at 882 for July.

During July, Noir Company completed 500 bicycle seats for Job 142. The activity usage for Job 142 was as follows: direct materials, $1,150; direct labor hours, 15.

Required

1. Compute the following activity cost rates: (a) materials handling cost rate; (b) assembly cost rate, (c) engineering design cost rate, and (d) overhead rate.

2. Prepare a bill of activities for Job 142.
3. Use activity-based costing to compute the job's total cost and product unit cost.

LO6 Direct and Indirect Costs in JIT and Traditional Manufacturing Environments

P 4. Funz Company, which produces wooden toys, is about to adopt a JIT operating environment. In anticipation of the change, Letty Hernando, Funz's controller, prepared the following list of costs for December:

Wood	$3,200	Insurance, plant	$ 324
Bolts	32	President's salary	4,000
Small tools	54	Engineering labor	2,700
Depreciation, plant	450	Utilities	1,250
Depreciation, machinery	275	Building occupancy	1,740
Direct labor	2,675	Supervision	2,686
Indirect labor	890	Operating supplies	254
Purchased parts	58	Repairs and maintenance	198
Materials handling	74	Employee benefits	2,654

Required

1. Identify each cost as direct or indirect, assuming that it was incurred in a traditional manufacturing setting.
2. Identify each cost as direct or indirect, assuming that it was incurred in a just-in-time (JIT) environment.
3. Assume that the costs incurred in the JIT environment are for a work cell that completed 1,250 toy cars in December. Compute the total direct cost and the direct cost per unit for the cars produced.

LO7 Backflush Costing

P 5. Automotive Parts Company produces 12 parts for car bodies and sells them to three automobile assembly companies in the United States. The company implemented just-in-time operating and costing procedures three years ago. Overhead is applied at a rate of $26 per work cell hour used. All direct materials and purchased parts are used as they are received.

One of the company's work cells produces automotive fenders that are completely detailed and ready to install when received by the customer. The cell is operated by four employees and involves a flexible manufacturing system with 14 workstations. Operating details for February for this cell are as follows:

Beginning work in process inventory	—
Beginning finished goods inventory	$420
Cost of direct materials purchased on account and used	$213,400
Cost of parts purchased on account and used	$111,250
Direct labor costs incurred	$26,450
Overhead costs assigned	?
Work cell hours used	8,260
Costs of goods completed during February	$564,650
Ending work in process inventory	$1,210
Ending finished goods inventory	$670

Required

1. Using T accounts, show the cost flows through a backflush costing system.

2. Using T accounts, show the cost flows through a traditional costing system.
3. What is the total cost of goods sold for the month?

Alternate Problems

LO4 **Activity-Based Costing**

P 6. Kaui Company produces cellular phones. It has just completed an order for 80 phones placed by Many Hands, Ltd. Kaui recently shifted to an activity-based costing system, and its controller is interested in the impact that the ABC system had on the Many Hands order. Data for that order are as follows: direct materials, $36,950; purchased parts, $21,100; direct labor hours, 220; average direct labor pay rate per hour, $15.

Under Kaui's traditional costing system, overhead costs were assigned at a rate of 270 percent of direct labor cost.

Data for activity-based costing for the Many Hands order are as follows:

Activity	Cost Driver	Activity Cost Rate	Activity Usage
Electrical engineering design	Engineering hours	$19 per engineering hour	32 engineering hours
Setup	Number of setups	$29 per setup	11 setups
Parts production	Machine hours	$26 per machine hour	134 machine hours
Product testing	Number of tests	$32 per test	52 tests
Packaging	Number of packages	$4.675 per package	80 packages
Building occupancy	Machine hours	$9.80 per machine hour	134 machine hours
Assembly	Direct labor hours	$15 per direct labor hour	220 direct labor hours

Required

1. Use the traditional costing approach to compute the total cost and the product unit cost of the Many Hands order.
2. Using the cost hierarchy, identify each activity as unit level, batch level, product level, or facility level.
3. Prepare a bill of activities for the activity costs.
4. Use ABC to compute the total cost and product unit cost of the Many Hands order.
5. Manager Insight: What is the difference between the product unit cost you computed using the traditional approach and the one you computed using ABC? Does the use of ABC guarantee cost reduction for every order?

LO4 **Activity Cost Rates**

P 7. Alligood Company produces three models of aluminum skateboards. The models have minor differences, but their processing operations and production costs are identical. During June, these costs were incurred:

Direct materials	
Aluminum frame	$162,524
Bolts	3,876
Purchased parts	
Wheels	74,934
Decals	5,066

Materials handling (assigned based on direct materials cost)

Labor	$17,068
Utilities	4,438
Maintenance	914
Depreciation	876

Assembly line (assigned based on labor hours)

Labor	46,080

Setup (assigned based on number of setups)

Labor	6,385
Supplies	762
Overhead	3,953

Product testing (assigned based on number of tests)

Labor	2,765
Supplies	435

Building occupancy (assigned based on machine hours)

Insurance	5,767
Depreciation	2,452
Repairs and maintenance	3,781

For June, output totaled 32,000 skateboards. Each board required 1.5 machine hours of effort. During June, Alligood's assembly line worked 2,304 hours, performed 370 setups and 64,000 product tests, and completed an order for 1,000 skateboards placed by Executive Toys Company. The job incurred costs of $5,200 for direct materials and $2,500 for purchased parts. It required 3 setups, 2,000 tests, and 72 assembly line hours.

Required

1. Compute the following activity cost rates:
   a. Materials handling cost rate
   b. Assembly line cost rate
   c. Setup cost rate
   d. Product testing cost rate
   e. Building occupancy cost rate
2. Prepare a bill of activities for the Executive Toys job.
3. Use activity-based costing to compute the job's total cost and product unit cost. (Round your answer to two decimal places.)

LO7 **Backflush Costing**

P 8. Reilly Corporation produces metal fasteners using six work cells, one for each of its product lines. It implemented just-in-time operations and costing methods two years ago. Overhead is assigned using a rate of $14 per machine hour for the Machine Snap Work Cell. There were no beginning inventories on April 1. All direct materials and purchased parts are used as they are received. Operating details for April for the Machine Snap Work Cell are as follows:

Cost of direct materials purchased on account and used	$104,500
Cost of parts purchased on account and used	$78,900
Direct labor costs incurred	$39,000
Overhead costs assigned	?
Machine hours used	12,220
Costs of goods completed during April	$392,540

| Ending work in process inventory | $940 |
| Ending finished goods inventory | $1,020 |

Required

1. Using T accounts, show the flow of costs through a backflush costing system.
2. Using T accounts, show the flow of costs through a traditional costing system.
3. What is the total cost of goods sold for April using a traditional costing system?

ENHANCING Your Knowledge, Skills, and Critical Thinking

Conceptual Understanding Cases

LO5 **JIT in a Service Business**

C 1. The initiation banquet for new members of your business club is being held at an excellent restaurant. You are sitting next to two college students who are majoring in marketing. In discussing the accounting course they are taking, they mention that they are having difficulty understanding the just-in-time philosophy. They have read that the elements of a company's JIT operating system support the concepts of simplicity, continuous improvement, waste reduction, timeliness, and efficiency. They realize that to understand JIT in a complex manufacturing environment, they must first understand JIT in a simpler context. They ask you to explain the philosophy and provide an example.

Briefly explain the JIT philosophy. Apply the elements of a JIT operating system to the restaurant where the banquet is being held. Do you believe the JIT philosophy applies in all restaurant operations? Explain your answer.

LO2, LO3 **Adding Value**

C 2. In a new business model called "zero time," time is the primary focus that drives everything else in an organization. According to this model, instantaneous, or "zero-time," Internet access to relevant information allows a company to add value for customers at every point along its value chain—marketing, research and development, purchasing, production, sales, shipping, and customer service.[7]

1. Identify and comment on the primary focus of traditional business models, such as job order or process costing.
2. Speculate on how focusing on time would add value for customers throughout an organization's value chain.

LO3, LO5, LO6 **Activities, Cost Drivers, and JIT**

C 3. Fifteen years ago, Bruce Sable, together with 10 financial supporters, founded Sable Corporation. Located in Atlanta, the company originally manufactured roller skates, but 12 years ago, on the advice of its marketing department, it switched to making skateboards. More than 4 million skateboards later, Sable Corporation finds itself an industry leader in both volume and quality. To retain market share, it has decided to automate its manufacturing process. It has ordered flexible manufacturing systems for wheel assembly and board shaping. Manual operations will be retained for board decorating because some hand painting is involved. All operations will be converted to a just-in-time environment.

Bruce Sable wants to know how the JIT approach will affect the company's product costing practices and has called you in as a consultant.

1. Summarize the elements of a JIT environment.
2. How will the automated systems change product costing?
3. What are some cost drivers that the company should employ? In what situations should it employ them?

Interpreting Management Reports

LO3, LO4 **ABC and Selling and Administrative Expenses**

C 4. Sandy Star, the owner of Star Bakery, wants to know the profitability of each of her bakery's customer groups. She is especially interested in the State Institutions customer group, which is one of the company's largest customer groups. Currently, the bakery is selling doughnuts and snack foods to ten state institutions in three states. The controller has prepared the following income statement for the State Institutions customer group:

Star Bakery
Income Statement for State Institutions Customer Group
For the Year Ended December 31, 20x8

Sales ($5 per case × 50,000 cases)	$250,000
Cost of goods sold ($3.50 per case × 50,000 cases)	175,000
Gross margin	$ 75,000
Less: Selling and administrative activity costs	94,750
Operating income (loss) contributed by State Institutions customer group	($19,750)

Activity	Activity Cost Rate	Actual Cost Driver Level	Activity Cost
Make sales calls	$60 per sales call	60 sales calls	$ 3,600
Prepare sales orders	$10 per sales order	900 sales orders	9,000
Handle inquiries	$5 per minute	1,000 minutes	5,000
Ship products	$1 per case sold	50,000 cases	50,000
Process invoices	$20 per invoice	950 invoices	19,000
Process credits	$20 per notice	40 notices	800
Process billings and collections	$7 per billing	1,050 billings	7,350
Total selling and administrative activity costs			94,750

The controller has also provided budgeted information about selling and administrative activities for the State Institutions customer group. For 20x8, the planned activity cost rates and the annual cost driver levels for each selling and administrative activity are as follows:

Activity	Activity Cost Rate	Planned Annual Cost Driver Level
Make sales calls	$60 per sales call	59 sales calls
Prepare sales orders	$10 per sales order	850 sales orders
Handle inquiries	$5.10 per minute	1,000 minutes
Ship products	$.60 per case sold	50,000 cases
Process invoices	$1 per invoice	500 invoices
Process credits	$10 per notice	5 notices
Process billings and collections	$4 per billing	600 billings

You have been called in as a consultant on the State Institutions customer group.

1. Calculate the planned activity cost for each activity.
2. Calculate the differences between the planned activity cost and the State Institutions customer group's activity costs for 20x8.
3. From your evaluation of the differences calculated in **2** and your review of the income statement, identify the nonvalue-adding activities and state which selling and administrative activities should be examined.
4. What actions might the company take to reduce the costs of nonvalue-adding selling and administrative activities?

Decision Analysis Using Excel

LO3, LO4 **ABC in Planning and Control**

C 5. Refer to the income statement in **C 4** for the State Institutions customer group for the year ended December 31, 20x8. Sandy Star, the owner of Star Bakery, is in the process of budgeting income for 20x9. She has asked the controller to prepare a budgeted income statement for the State Institutions customer group. She estimates that the selling price per case, the number of cases sold, the cost of goods sold per case, and the activity costs for making sales calls, preparing sales orders, and handling inquiries will remain the same for 20x9. She has contracted with a new freight company to ship the 50,000 cases at $.60 per case sold. She has also analyzed the procedures for invoicing, processing credits, billing, and collecting and has decided that it would be less expensive for a customer service agency to do the work. The agency will charge the bakery 1.5 percent of the total sales revenue.

1. Prepare a budgeted income statement for the State Institutions customer group for the year ended December 31, 20x9.
2. Refer to the information in **C 4**. Assuming that the planned activity cost rate and planned annual cost driver level for each selling and administrative activity remain the same in 20x9, calculate the planned activity cost for each activity.
3. Calculate the differences between the planned activity costs (determined in requirement **2**) and the State Institutions customer group's budgeted activity costs for 20x9 (determined in **1**).
4. Evaluate the results of changing freight companies and outsourcing the customer service activities.

Ethical Dilemma Case

LO5 **Ethics and JIT Implementation**

C 6. For almost a year, Traki Company has been changing its manufacturing process from a traditional to a JIT approach. Management has asked for employees' assistance in the transition and has offered bonuses for suggestions that cut time from the production operation. Deb Hinds and Jack Snow each identified a time-saving opportunity and turned in their suggestions to their manager, Randall Soder.

Soder sent the suggestions to the committee charged with reviewing employees' suggestions, which inadvertently identified them as being Soder's own. The committee decided that the two suggestions were worthy of reward and voted a large bonus for Soder. When notified of this, Soder could not bring himself to identify the true authors of the suggestions.

When Hinds and Snow heard about Soder's bonus, they confronted him with his fraudulent act and expressed their grievances. He told them that he needed the recognition to be eligible for an upcoming promotion and promised that if they kept quiet about the matter, he would make sure that they both received significant raises. Prepare written responses to the following questions so that you can discuss them in class:

1. Should Hinds and Snow keep quiet? What other options are open to them?
2. How should Soder have dealt with Hinds's and Snow's complaints?

Internet Case

LO3 **Value-Adding and Nonvalue-Adding Activities**

C 7. **Levi Strauss & Co.** has been making jeans since 1853. Today, it manufactures different types of jeans for different market segments. For example, **Wal-Mart** sells Levi Strauss's Signature brand of jeans for about $15 less than department stores sell the company's Levi's brand.[8]

Visit the Levi Strauss website to learn more about the company's brands. What value-adding production and nonproduction activities do you think might account for the higher price of the Levi's brand? Which of these activities do you think Levi Strauss would eliminate for the less costly Signature brand? (By visiting the website, you can also discover what Levi Strauss called jeans when it first sold them 150 years ago, as well as the year in which the company officially changed the name to "jeans.")

Group Activity Case

LO4 **ABM and ABC in a Service Business**

C 8. Kendle and Watson, a CPA firm, has provided audit and tax services to businesses in the London area for over 50 years. Recently, the firm decided to use ABM and activity-based costing to assign its overhead costs to those service functions. Bellamy Kendle is interested in seeing how the change from the traditional to the activity-based costing approach affects the average cost per audit job. The following information has been provided to assist in the comparison:

Total direct labor costs	£400,000
Other direct costs	120,000
Total direct costs	£520,000

The traditional costing approach assigned overhead costs at a rate of 120 percent of direct labor costs.

Data for activity-based costing of the audit function are as follows:

Activity	Cost Driver	Activity Cost Rate	Activity Usage
Professional development	Number of employees	£2,000 per employee	50 employees
Administration	Number of jobs	£1,000 per job	50 jobs
Client development	Number of new clients	£5,000 per new client	29 new clients

1. Using direct labor cost as the cost driver, calculate the total costs for the audit function. What is the average cost per job?
2. Using activity-based costing to assign overhead, calculate the total costs for the audit function. What is the average cost per job?

3. Calculate the difference in total costs between the two approaches. Why would activity-based costing be the better approach for assigning overhead to the audit function?

4. Your instructor will divide the class into groups to work through the case. One student from each group should present the group's findings to the class.

Business Communication Cases

LO5 **JIT Production**

C 9. To compete for new domestic and foreign business, many large, multinational companies, as well as many smaller firms, have installed automated just-in-time production processes. Locate an article about a company that has recently installed a JIT system or an annual report from such a company. Conduct your search using an Internet search engine like Google and a business periodical like *The Wall Street Journal.*

Choose a source that describes the changes the company made to its plant to increase product quality and to compete as a world-class manufacturer. Prepare a one-page description of those changes. Include in your report the name of the company, its location, the name of the chief executive officer and/or president, and, if available, the dollar amount of the company's total sales for the most recent year. Be prepared to present your findings in class.

LO5 **Manufacturing Processes**

C 10. Classic Clubs, Inc., manufactures professional golf clubs in a continuous manufacturing process. Demand has been so great that the company has built a special plant that makes only custom-crafted clubs. The clubs are shaped by machines but vary according to the customer's sex, height, weight, and arm length. Ten basic sets of clubs are produced, five for females and five for males. Slight variations in machine setup produce the differences in the club weights and lengths.

In the past six months, several problems have developed. Even though a computer-controlled machine is used in the manufacturing process, the company's backlog is growing rapidly, and customers are complaining that delivery is too slow. Quality is declining because clubs are being pushed through production without proper inspection. Working capital is tied up in excessive amounts of inventory and storage space. Workers are complaining about the pressure to produce the backlogged orders. Machine breakdowns are increasing. Production control reports are not useful because they are not timely and contain irrelevant information. The company's profitability and cash flow are suffering.

Classic Clubs has hired you as a consultant to analyze its problems and suggest a solution. Denise Rodeburg, the president, asks that you complete your work within a month so that she can prepare a plan to present to the board of directors at the midyear board meeting.

1. In memo form, prepare a report for Rodeburg recommending specific changes in the manufacturing processes.
2. In preparing the report, answer the following questions:
   a. Why are you preparing the report? What is its purpose?
   b. Who is the audience for this report?
   c. What kinds of information do you need to prepare the report, and where will you find it (i.e., what sources will you use)?
   d. When do you need to obtain the information?

Cost Behavior Analysis

Knowing how costs will behave is essential knowledge for managers as they chart their organization's course and make ethical decisions on behalf of all the organization's stakeholders. Managers commonly analyze alternative courses of action using cost behavior information so they can select the course that will best generate income for an organization's owners, maintain liquidity for its creditors, and use the organization's resources responsibly. Thus, analysis of cost behavior is important not only in achieving profitability, but also in using resources wisely.

LEARNING OBJECTIVES

LO1 Define *cost behavior* and explain how managers use this concept.

LO2 Identify variable, fixed, and mixed costs, and separate mixed costs into their variable and fixed components.

LO3 Define *cost-volume-profit (C-V-P) analysis* and discuss how managers use it as a tool for planning and control.

LO4 Define *breakeven point* and use contribution margin to determine a company's breakeven point for multiple products.

LO5 Use C-V-P analysis to project the profitability of products and services.

- How does Kraft decide which products to offer?
- Why do Kraft's managers analyze cost behavior to project the profitability of the company's core sectors?

Kraft, Philadelphia, Maxwell House, Nabisco, Oscar Mayer, Jell-O, and Post are among the brands that **Kraft Foods** brings to households around the world. The company has five core sectors—snacks and cereals, beverages, cheese, grocery, and convenience meals—and locations in more than 155 countries around the globe. Kraft's 98,000 employees work to make food a simpler, easier, and more enjoyable part of life by adding innovative products and optimizing line and geographic extensions of current offerings.[1]

The types and numbers of products that Kraft makes and sells vary from year to year depending on shoppers' preferences. The challenge for Kraft's management is to offer a product mix that excites consumers and allows the company to charge higher prices at the supermarket.

Cost Behavior and Management

LO1 Define *cost behavior* and explain how managers use this concept.

Cost behavior—the way costs respond to changes in volume or activity—is a factor in almost every decision managers make. Managers commonly use it to analyze alternative courses of action so they can select the course that will best generate income for an organization's owners and maintain liquidity for its creditors. Figure 1 shows how managers use cost behavior to plan, perform, evaluate, and communicate.

Planning

When managers plan, they use cost behavior to determine how many units of products or services must be sold to generate a targeted amount of profit and how changes in planned operating, investing, and financing activities will affect operating income. For example, when **Kraft's** managers launched a product

■ FIGURE 1
The Management Process: To-Do's for Managers

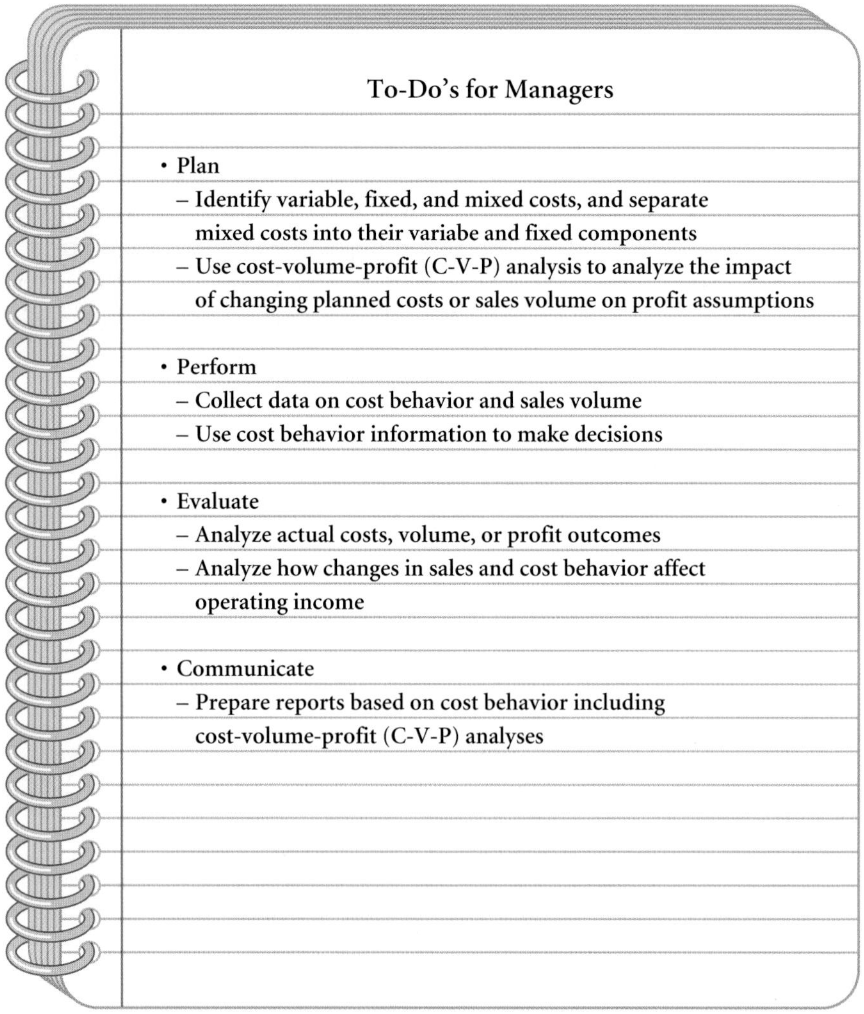

To-Do's for Managers

- Plan
  - Identify variable, fixed, and mixed costs, and separate mixed costs into their variabe and fixed components
  - Use cost-volume-profit (C-V-P) analysis to analyze the impact of changing planned costs or sales volume on profit assumptions

- Perform
  - Collect data on cost behavior and sales volume
  - Use cost behavior information to make decisions

- Evaluate
  - Analyze actual costs, volume, or profit outcomes
  - Analyze how changes in sales and cost behavior affect operating income

- Communicate
  - Prepare reports based on cost behavior including cost-volume-profit (C-V-P) analyses

called Boca, they used cost behavior to analyze how offering two flavors of this soy-based burger would contribute to the organization's operating income.

Service-based businesses like **Google** also find cost behavior analyses useful to determine the optimal mix of services to offer. For example, Google's managers analyze cost behavior of new products like Writely, a free Web-based word processor, or Gmail, an email program with upward of two to six gigabytes of storage space in their online Google Labs to gather user data and feedback before officially deciding to add a new feature.

Performing

As we have noted, managers use information about cost behavior in almost every decision they make. Throughout the year, managers at **Kraft** and at service businesses like **Google, Sprint,** and **Verizon** must understand and anticipate cost behavior to determine the impact of their actions on operating income. For example, Google's managers must understand the changes in income that can result from buying new, more productive servers or launching an online advertising product like AdWords or AdSense.

Evaluating and Communicating

When evaluating operations and preparing reports for various product or service lines or geographic regions, managers in all types of organizations, including businesses like **Kraft, Google, Federal Express,** and **UPS,** need to understand cost behavior. As you will learn later in the chapter, cost-volume-profit reports, such as a contribution margin income statement (sometimes referred to as a variable costing income statement), are commonly used to analyze how changes in cost and sales affect the profitability of product lines, sales territories, customers, departments, and other segments. Other reports based on cost behavior are used when deciding whether to eliminate a product line, accept a special order, or outsource services.

The Behavior of Costs

LO2   Identify variable, fixed, and mixed costs, and separate mixed costs into their variable and fixed components.

Although our focus in this chapter is on cost behavior as it relates to products and services, cost behavior can also be observed in selling, administrative, and general activities. For example, increases in the number of shipments affect shipping costs; the number of units sold or total sales revenue affects the cost of sales commissions; and the number of customers billed or the number of hours needed to bill affects total billing costs. If managers can predict how costs behave, then costs become manageable.

Some costs vary with volume or operating activity (variable costs). Others remain fixed as volume changes (fixed costs). Between those two extremes are costs that exhibit characteristics of each type (mixed costs).

Variable Costs

Total costs that change in direct proportion to changes in productive output (or any other measure of volume) are called **variable costs**. To explore how variable costs work, consider the tire costs of Land Rover, a maker of off-road vehicles. Each new vehicle has four tires, and each tire costs $48. The total cost of tires, then, is $192 for one vehicle, $384 for two, $960 for five, $1,920 for ten, $19,200 for one hundred, and so on. In the production of off-road vehicles, the total cost of tires is a variable cost. On a per unit basis, however, a variable cost remains constant. In this case, the cost of tires per vehicle is $192 whether the automaker produces one vehicle or one hundred vehicles. True, the cost of tires will vary depending on the number purchased if discounts are available for purchases of large quantities. But once the purchase has been made, the cost per tire is established.

Figure 2 illustrates other examples of variable costs. All those costs—whether incurred by a manufacturer like **Kraft, La-Z-Boy,** or **Intel**, a service business like **Google,** or a merchandiser like **Wal-Mart**—are variable based on either productive output or total sales.

Operating Capacity   Because variable costs increase or decrease in direct proportion to volume or output, it is important to know an organization's operating capacity. **Operating capacity** is the upper limit of an organization's

Study Note

Variable costs change in *direct proportion* to changes in activity; that is, they increase *in total* with an increase in volume and decrease *in total* with a decrease in volume, but they remain the same on a *per unit* basis.

■ FIGURE 2
Examples of Variable, Fixed, and Mixed Costs

Costs	Manufacturing Company—Tire Manufacturer	Merchandising Company—Department Store	Service Company—Bank
VARIABLE	Direct materials Direct labor (hourly) Indirect labor (hourly) Operating supplies Small tools	Merchandise to sell Sales commissions Shelf stockers (hourly)	Computer equipment leasing (based on usage) Computer operators (hourly) Operating supplies Data storage disks

FIXED	Depreciation, machinery
	  and building
	Insurance premiums
	Labor (salaried)
	Supervisory salaries
	Property taxes (on machinery
	  and building)
		Depreciation, building
		Insurance premiums
		Buyers (salaried)
		Supervisory salaries
		Property taxes (on equipment
		  and building)
			Depreciation, furniture and fixtures
			Insurance premiums
			Salaries:
			  Programmers
			  Systems designers
			  Bank administrators
			Rent, buildings

MIXED	Electrical power Telephone Heat	Electrical power Telephone Heat	Electrical power Telephone Heat

productive output capability, given its existing resources. It describes just what an organization can accomplish in a given period. Operating capacity can be expressed in several ways, including total labor hours, total machine hours, and total units of output. Any increase in volume or activity over operating capacity requires additional expenditures for buildings, machinery, personnel, and operations. When additional operating capacity is added, cost behavior patterns can change. In our discussion of those patterns, we assume that operating capacity is constant and that all activity occurs within the limits of current operating capacity.

There are three common measures, or types, of operating capacity: theoretical, or ideal, capacity; practical capacity; and normal capacity. **Theoretical (ideal) capacity** is the maximum productive output for a given period in which all machinery and equipment are operating at optimum speed, without interruption. In a just-in-time operating environment, the long-term goal is to approach theoretical capacity through continuous improvement; however, no company ever actually operates at such an ideal level. **Practical capacity** is theoretical capacity reduced by normal and expected work stoppages, such as machine breakdowns; downtime for retooling, repairs, and maintenance; and employees' breaks. Although theoretical capacity and practical capacity are

⌐─⟩Study Note

In a just-in-time operating environment, theoretical (ideal) capacity is used as a benchmark, a relatively constant reference point against which to measure improvement.

useful when estimating maximum production levels, neither measure is realistic when planning operations. Practical capacity is sometimes called *engineering capacity*.

When planning operations, managers use **normal capacity**, which is the average annual level of operating capacity needed to meet expected sales demand. The sales demand figure is adjusted for seasonal changes and industry and economic cycles. Normal capacity is therefore a realistic measure of what an organization is *likely* to produce, not what it *can* produce. Each variable cost should be related to an appropriate measure of normal capacity, but often more than one measure of normal capacity applies. Operating costs can be related to machine hours used or total units produced. Sales commissions, on the other hand, usually vary in direct proportion to total sales dollars.

The basis for measuring the activity of variable costs should be carefully selected for two reasons. First, an appropriate activity base simplifies cost planning and control. Second, managers must combine (aggregate) many variable costs with the same activity base so that the costs can be analyzed in a reasonable way. Such aggregation also provides information that allows management to predict future costs.

The general guide for selecting an activity base is to relate costs to their most logical or causal factor. For example, machinery setup costs should be considered variable in relation to the number of setups needed for a particular job. This will allow machinery setup costs to be budgeted and controlled more effectively.

Linear Relationships and the Relevant Range The traditional definition of a variable cost assumes that costs go up or down as volume increases or decreases, as demonstrated by the linear relationship in the tire example we cited earlier. Figure 3 shows a similar straight-line relationship. There, each unit of output requires $2.50 of labor cost. Total labor costs grow in direct proportion to the increase in units of output. For two units, total labor costs are $5.00; for six units, the organization incurs $15.00 in labor costs.

Many costs, however, vary with operating activity in a nonlinear fashion. Graph A in Figure 4 shows the behavior of power costs as usage increases and the unit cost of power consumption falls. Graph B shows the behavior of rental

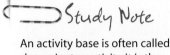

Study Note

An activity base is often called *denominator activity*; it is the activity for which relationships are established. The basic relationships should not change greatly if activity fluctuates around the level of denominator activity.

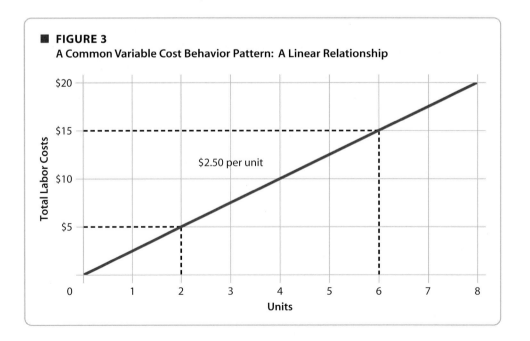

■ **FIGURE 3**
A Common Variable Cost Behavior Pattern: A Linear Relationship

$2.50 per unit

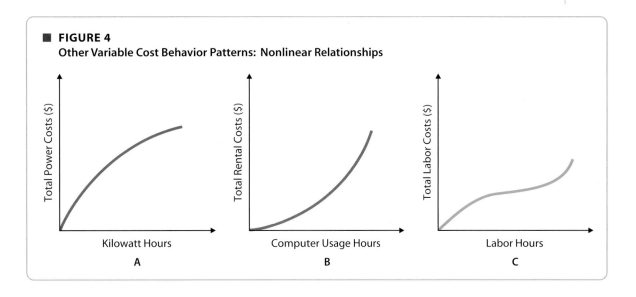

■ FIGURE 4
Other Variable Cost Behavior Patterns: Nonlinear Relationships

costs when each additional hour of computer usage costs more than the previous hour. Graph C shows how labor costs vary as efficiency increases and decreases. These three nonlinear cost patterns are variable in nature, but they differ from the linear variable cost pattern shown in Figure 3.

Variable costs with linear relationships to a volume measure are easy to analyze and project for cost planning and control. Nonlinear variable costs are not easy to use. But all costs must be included in an analysis if the results are to be useful to management. To simplify cost analysis procedures and make variable costs easier to use, accountants have developed a method of converting nonlinear variable costs into linear variable costs. Called *linear approximation*, this method relies on the concept of relevant range. **Relevant range** is the span of activity in which a company expects to operate. Within the relevant range, it is assumed that both total fixed costs and per unit variable costs are constant. Under that assumption, many nonlinear costs can be estimated using the linear approximation approach illustrated in Figure 5. Those estimated costs can then be treated as part of the other variable costs.

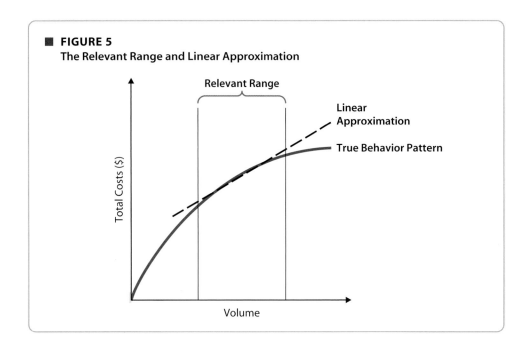

■ FIGURE 5
The Relevant Range and Linear Approximation

A linear approximation of a nonlinear variable cost is not a precise measure, but it allows the inclusion of nonlinear variable costs in cost behavior analysis, and the loss of accuracy is usually not significant. The goal is to help management estimate costs and prepare budgets, and linear approximation helps accomplish that goal.

Fixed Costs

Fixed costs behave very differently from variable costs. **Fixed costs** are total costs that remain constant within a relevant range of volume or activity—that is, the range in which actual operations are likely to occur. Look back at Figure 2 for examples of fixed costs. The manufacturer, the department store, and the bank all incur depreciation costs and fixed annual insurance premiums. In addition, all salaried personnel have fixed earnings for a particular period. The manufacturer and the department store own their buildings and pay annual property taxes, and the bank pays an annual fixed rental charge for the use of its building.

According to economic theory, all costs tend to be variable in the long run; thus, as the examples in Figure 2 suggest, a cost is fixed only within a limited period. A change in plant capacity, machinery, labor needs, or other production factors causes fixed costs to increase or decrease. For planning, management usually considers a one-year period, and fixed costs are expected to be constant within that period.

Of course, fixed costs change when activity exceeds the relevant range. For example, assume that a manufacturer of aluminum cans needs one supervisor for an eight-hour work shift. Production can range from zero to 500,000 units (cans) per month per shift. The relevant range, then, is from zero to 500,000 units. The supervisor's salary is $4,000 per month. The cost behavior analysis is as follows:

Units of Output per Month	Total Supervisory Salaries per Month
0–500,000	$4,000
Over 500,000–1,000,000	$8,000

If a maximum of 500,000 units can be produced per month per shift, output over 500,000 units would require another shift and another supervisor. Like all fixed costs, the new fixed cost remains constant in total within the new relevant range.

What about unit costs? Fixed unit costs vary inversely with activity or volume. On a per unit basis, fixed costs go down as volume goes up, as long as a firm is operating within the relevant range of activity. Look at how supervisory costs per unit fall as the volume of activity increases within the relevant range:

Volume of Activity	Supervisory Cost per Unit
100,000 units	$4,000 ÷ 100,000 = $.0400
300,000 units	$4,000 ÷ 300,000 = $.0133
500,000 units	$4,000 ÷ 500,000 = $.0080
600,000 units	$8,000 ÷ 600,000 = $.0133

At 600,000 units, the activity level is above the relevant range, which means another shift must be added and another supervisor must be hired; thus, the per unit cost increases to $.0133.

Figure 6 shows this behavior pattern. The fixed supervisory costs for the first 500,000 units of production are $4,000. Those costs hold steady at $4,000

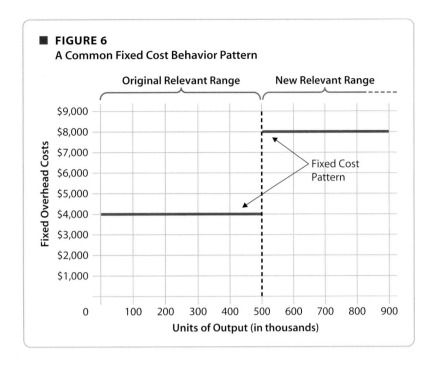

■ FIGURE 6
A Common Fixed Cost Behavior Pattern

for any level of output within the relevant range. But if output goes above 500,000 units, another supervisor must be hired, pushing fixed supervisory costs to $8,000.

Mixed Costs

Mixed costs have both variable and fixed cost components. Part of a mixed cost changes with volume or usage, and part is fixed over a particular period. Monthly electricity costs are an example. Such costs include charges per kilowatt hour used plus a basic monthly service charge. The kilowatt-hour charges are variable because they depend on the amount of use; the monthly service charge is a fixed cost.

Graph A in Figure 7 depicts an organization's total electricity costs. The monthly bill begins with a fixed service charge and increases as kilowatt hours

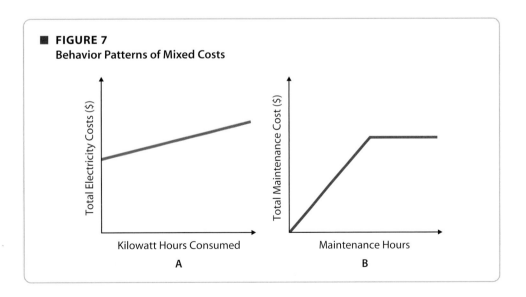

■ FIGURE 7
Behavior Patterns of Mixed Costs

Like most businesses, the U.S. Postal Service is concerned about delivery time. To determine how many deliveries a postal worker should be able to make within a certain period, it conducts periodic audits using the engineering method (a type of analysis that is also known as a *time and motion study*). To speed delivery time, it has provided some of its workers with Segways, such as the one shown here.

are consumed. Graph B illustrates a special contractual arrangement. Here, the annual cost of equipment maintenance provided by an outside company increases for each maintenance hour worked, up to a maximum amount per period. After the maximum is reached, additional maintenance is done at no cost.

For cost planning and control purposes, mixed costs must be divided into their variable and fixed components. The separate components can then be grouped with other variable and fixed costs for analysis. Four methods are commonly used to separate costs into their variable and fixed components: the engineering, scatter diagram, high-low, and statistical methods. Because the results yielded by each of these methods are likely to differ, managers often use multiple approaches before determining the best possible estimate for a mixed cost.

The Engineering Method
The **engineering method** of separating costs measures the work required by performing a step-by-step analysis of the tasks, costs, and processes involved. It is generally used to estimate the cost of activities and new products. For example, the U.S. Postal Service conducts periodic audits of how many letters a postal worker should be able to deliver on a particular mail route within a certain period. This type of analysis is sometimes called a *time and motion study*. The engineering method is expensive to use because it is so detailed. In addition, this method requires the expertise of engineers to determine the cost of a new product or activity for which no prior data exist.

The Scatter Diagram Method
When there is doubt about the behavior pattern of a particular cost, especially a mixed cost, it helps to plot past costs and related measures of volume in a scatter diagram. A **scatter diagram** is a chart of plotted points that helps determine whether a linear relationship exists between a cost item and its related activity measure. It is a form of linear approximation. If the diagram suggests a linear relationship, a cost line can be imposed on the data by either visual means or statistical analysis.

Suppose, for example, that the Piedmont Corporation's Park Division incurred the following machine hours and electricity costs last year:

Month	Machine Hours	Electricity Costs
January	6,250	$ 24,000
February	6,300	24,200
March	6,350	24,350
April	6,400	24,600
May	6,300	24,400
June	6,200	24,300
July	6,100	23,900
August	6,050	23,600
September	6,150	23,950
October	6,250	24,100
November	6,350	24,400
December	6,450	24,700
Totals	$75,150	$290,500

Figure 8 shows a scatter diagram of these data. The diagram suggests a linear relationship between machine hours and the cost of electricity. If we were to add a line to the diagram to represent the linear relationship, the estimated fixed electricity cost would occur at the point at which the line intersects the vertical axis. The variable cost per unit can be estimated by determining the slope of the line, much as is done in Step 1 of the high-low method.

The High-Low Method   The **high-low method** is a common, three-step approach to determining the variable and fixed components of a mixed cost. It is based on the premise that only two data points are necessary to define a linear cost-volume relationship. It is a relatively crude method since it uses only the high and low data observations to predict cost behavior. The disadvantage of this method is that if one or both data points are not representative of the remaining data set, the estimate of variable and fixed costs may not be accurate. Its advantage is that it can be used when only limited data are available. The method involves three steps.

Study Note

A scatter diagram shows how closely volume and costs are correlated. A tight, closely associated group of data is better for linear approximation than a random or circular pattern of data points.

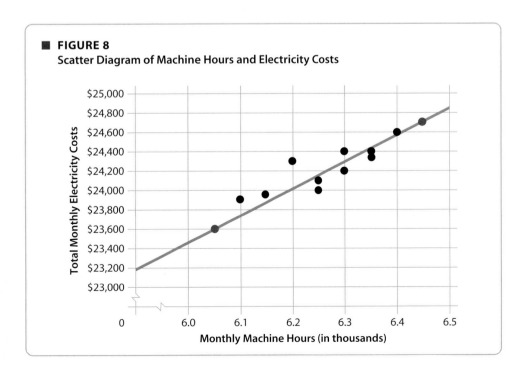

■ **FIGURE 8**
Scatter Diagram of Machine Hours and Electricity Costs

Step 1. *Calculate the variable cost per activity base.* Select the periods of highest and lowest activity within the accounting period. In our example, the Park Division experienced its highest machine-hour activity in December and its lowest machine-hour activity in August. Find the difference between the highest and lowest amounts for both the machine hours and their related electricity costs:

Volume	Month	Activity Level	Cost
Highest	December	6,450 machine hours	$24,700
Lowest	August	6,050 machine hours	23,600
Difference		400 machine hours	$ 1,100

To determine the variable cost per machine hour, divide the difference in cost by the difference in machine hours:

$$\text{Variable Cost per Machine Hour} = \$1,100 \div 400 \text{ Machine Hours}$$
$$= \$2.75 \text{ per Machine Hour}$$

Step 2. *Calculate the total fixed costs.* Compute total fixed costs for a month by selecting the information from the month with either the highest or the lowest volume. Here, we use the month with the highest volume:

$$\text{Total Fixed Costs} = \text{Total Costs} - \text{Total Variable Costs}$$
$$\text{Total Fixed Costs for December} = \$24,700.00 - (6,450 \times \$2.75) = \$6,962.50$$

You can check your answer by recalculating total fixed costs using the month with the lowest activity. Total fixed costs will be the same:

$$\text{Total Fixed Costs for August} = \$23,600.00 - (6,050 \times \$2.75) = \$6,962.50$$

Step 3. *Calculate the formula to estimate the total costs within the relevant range:*

$$\text{Total Costs per Month} = \$6,962.50 + \$2.75 \text{ per Machine Hour}$$

Remember that the cost formula will work only within the relevant range. In this example, the formula would work for amounts between 6,050 machine hours and 6,450 machine hours. To estimate the electricity costs for machine hours outside the relevant range (in this case, below 6,050 machine hours or above 6,450 machine hours), a new cost formula must be calculated.

Statistical Methods Statistical methods, such as **regression analysis**, mathematically describe the relationship between costs and activities. Because all data observations are used, the resulting linear equation is more representative of cost behavior than either the high-low or scatter diagram methods. Regression analysis can be performed using one or more activities to predict costs. For example, overhead costs can be predicted using only machine hours (a simple regression analysis), or they can be predicted using both machine hours and labor hours (a multiple regression analysis) because both activities affect overhead. We leave further description of regression analysis to statistics courses, which provide detailed coverage of this method.

STOP • REVIEW • APPLY

2-1. What is normal capacity? Why is normal capacity considered more relevant and useful than either theoretical or practical capacity?

2-2. What does relevant range of activity mean?

2-3. "Fixed costs remain constant in total but decrease per unit as productive output increases." Explain this statement.

2-4. What is a mixed cost? Give an example.

The High-Low Method   Using the high-low method and the information below, compute the monthly variable cost per kilowatt hour and the monthly fixed electricity cost for GLE Corporation.

Month	Kilowatt Hours Used	Electricity Expenses
April	90	$450
May	80	430
June	70	420

SOLUTION

Volume	Month	Activity Level	Cost
High	April	90 hours	$450
Low	June	70 hours	420
Difference		20 hours	$ 30

Variable cost per kilowatt hour   = $30 ÷ 20 hours
                                    = $1.50 per hour

Fixed costs for April: $450 − (90 × $1.50) = $315
Fixed costs for June: $420 − (70 × $1.50) = $315

Cost-Volume-Profit Analysis

LO3   Define *cost-volume-profit (C-V-P) analysis* and discuss how managers use it as a tool for planning and control.

ike **Kraft Foods**, many companies produce and distribute a variety of products and services. For example, a division of **Sony Corporation,** Sony Records, makes compact disks (CDs). Producing these CDs is a complex process that requires hiring and organizing hundreds of people, including

To make and market its compact disks, Sony Records has to hire and organize hundreds of people, including singers like Joss Stone, who is shown here posing for photographs at the Sony Studios in New York. To determine how many CDs it must sell just to break even and what the profit will be if the CD is a hit, Sony uses cost-volume-profit analysis. C-V-P analysis is also an important tool in setting sales targets.

Study Note

One of the important benefits of C-V-P analysis is that it allows managers to adjust different variables and to evaluate how these changes affect profit.

musicians, and maintaining studios and offices. The company hopes, of course, that all its CDs will be hits, but the reality is that only some will be. At the least, the company wants to break even—that is, not lose any money—on each CD. Cost-volume-profit analysis is an important tool that enables Sony's managers to determine how many CDs they must sell to avoid losing money and what their profit will be if they have a hit. It is also an important tool in setting sales targets.

Cost-volume-profit (C-V-P) analysis is an examination of the cost behavior patterns that underlie the relationships among cost, volume of output, and profit. C-V-P analysis usually applies to a single product, product line, or division of a company. For that reason, *profit*, which is only part of an entire company's operating income, is the term used in the C-V-P equation. The equation is expressed as

$$\text{Sales Revenue} - \text{Variable Costs} - \text{Fixed Costs} = \text{Profit}$$

or as

$$S - VC - FC = P$$

In cases involving the income statement of an entire company, the term *operating income* is more appropriate than *profit*. In the context of C-V-P analysis, however, *profit* and *operating income* mean the same thing.

C-V-P analysis is a tool for both planning and control. The techniques and the problem-solving procedures involved in the process express relationships among revenue, sales mix, cost, volume, and profit. Those relationships provide a general model of financial activity that managers can use for short-range planning and for evaluating performance and analyzing alternative courses of action.

For planning, managers can use C-V-P analysis to calculate net income when sales volume is known, or they can determine the level of sales needed to reach a targeted amount of net income. C-V-P analysis is used extensively in budgeting as well. C-V-P analysis is also a way of measuring how well an organization's departments are performing. At the end of a period, sales volume and related actual costs are analyzed to find actual net income. A department's performance is measured by comparing actual costs with expected costs—

costs that have been computed by applying C-V-P analysis to actual sales volume. The result is a performance report on which managers can base the control of operations.

In addition, managers use C-V-P analysis to measure the effects of alternative courses of action, such as changing variable or fixed costs, expanding or contracting sales volume, and increasing or decreasing selling prices. C-V-P analysis is useful in making decisions about product pricing, product mix (when an organization makes more than one product or offers more than one service), adding or dropping a product line, and accepting special orders.

C-V-P analysis has many applications, all of which managers use to plan and control operations effectively. However, it is useful only under certain conditions and only when certain assumptions hold true. Those conditions and assumptions are as follows:

1. The behavior of variable and fixed costs can be measured accurately.

2. Costs and revenues have a close linear approximation. For example, if costs rise, revenues rise proportionately.

3. Efficiency and productivity hold steady within the relevant range of activity.

4. Cost and price variables also hold steady during the period being planned.

5. The sales mix does not change during the period being planned.

6. Production and sales volume are roughly equal.

If one or more of these conditions and assumptions are absent, the C-V-P analysis may be misleading.

S T O P • R E V I E W • A P P L Y

3-1. Define cost-volume-profit analysis.

3-2. Identify two uses of C-V-P analysis and explain their significance to management.

3-3. What conditions must be met for C-V-P computations to be accurate?

Breakeven Analysis

> **LO4** Define *breakeven point* and use contribution margin to determine a company's breakeven point for multiple products.

Breakeven analysis uses the basic elements of cost-volume-profit relationships. The **breakeven point** is the point at which total revenues equal total costs. It is thus the point at which an organization can begin to earn a profit. When a new venture or product line is being planned, the likelihood of the project's success can be quickly measured by finding its breakeven point. If, for instance, the breakeven point is 24,000 units and the total market is only 25,000 units, the margin of safety would be very low, and the idea should be considered carefully. The **margin of safety** is the number of sales units or amount of sales dollars by which actual sales can fall below planned sales without resulting in a loss—in this example, 1,000 units.

Sales (S), variable costs (VC), and fixed costs (FC) are used to compute the breakeven point, which can be stated in terms of sales units or sales dollars. The general equation for finding the breakeven point is as follows:

$$S - VC - FC = \$0$$

Suppose, for example, that a company called Valley Metal Products, Inc., makes ornamental iron plant stands. Variable costs are $50 per unit, and fixed costs average $20,000 per year. Each plant stand sells for $90. Given this information, we can compute the breakeven point for this product in sales units (x equals sales units):

$$S - VC - FC = \$0$$
$$\$90x - \$50x - \$20,000 = \$0$$
$$\$40x = \$20,000$$
$$x = 500 \text{ Units}$$

We can also compute it in sales dollars:

$$\$90 \times 500 \text{ Units} = \$45,000$$

In addition, we can make a rough estimate of the breakeven point using a scatter graph. This method is less exact, but it does yield meaningful data. Figure 9 shows a breakeven graph for Valley Metal Products. As you can see there, the graph has five parts:

1. A horizontal axis for units of output

2. A vertical axis for dollars

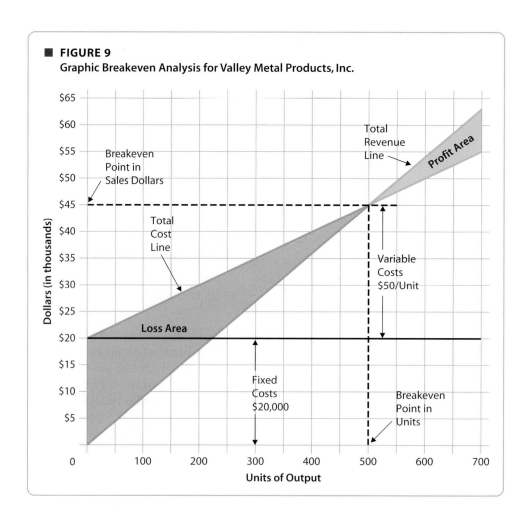

■ **FIGURE 9**
Graphic Breakeven Analysis for Valley Metal Products, Inc.

3. A line running horizontally from the vertical axis at the level of fixed costs

4. A total cost line that begins at the point where the fixed cost line crosses the vertical axis and slopes upward to the right (The slope of the line depends on the variable cost per unit.)

5. A total revenue line that begins at the origin of the vertical and horizontal axes and slopes upward to the right (The slope depends on the selling price per unit.)

At the point at which the total revenue line crosses the total cost line, revenues equal total costs. The breakeven point, stated in either sales units or dollars of sales, is found by extending broken lines from this point to the axes. As Figure 9 shows, Valley Metal Products will break even when it has sold 500 plant stands for $45,000.

Using Contribution Margin to Determine the Breakeven Point

Study Note

Contribution margin equals sales minus variable costs, whereas gross margin equals sales minus the cost of goods sold.

A simpler method of determining the breakeven point uses contribution margin. **Contribution margin (CM)** is the amount that remains after all variable costs are subtracted from sales:

$$S - VC = CM$$

A product line's contribution margin represents its net contribution to paying off fixed costs and earning a profit. Profit (P) is what remains after fixed costs are paid and subtracted from the contribution margin:

$$CM - FC = P$$

Study Note

The maximum contribution a unit of product or service can make is its selling price. After paying for itself (variable costs), a product or service provides a contribution margin to help pay total fixed costs and then earn a profit.

The example that follows uses contribution margin to determine the profitability of Valley Metal Products.

		Units Produced and Sold		
Symbols		250	500	750
S	Sales revenue ($90 per unit)	$22,500	$45,000	$67,500
VC	Less variable costs ($50 per unit)	12,500	25,000	37,500
CM	Contribution margin ($40 per unit)	$10,000	$20,000	$30,000
FC	Less fixed costs	20,000	20,000	20,000
P	Profit (loss)	($10,000)	$ 0	$10,000

FOCUS ON BUSINESS PRACTICE
Supersizing Value Meals

Understanding their costs helps fast-food restaurants like McDonald's increase their profitability in at least two ways. One way is to encourage customers to buy "value meals"—combinations of three products, such as sandwich, drink, and fries—by offering them at a lower price than the three items purchased separately. Although the contribution margin of a value meal is lower than the combined contribution margins of the three products sold separately, fast-food restaurants know from experience that value meals lead to higher total sales.

Another way fast-food restaurants increase profitability is by offering "supersized" orders for only a few cents more than the price of a regular order. Supersizing increases the total contribution margin because the additional variable cost of the larger size is very small. Profitability is enhanced even though revenue increases by only a small amount. Selling larger sizes is so important to a fast-food restaurant's profitability that a common performance measure in the industry is the percentage of value meals that are supersized.

The breakeven point (BE) can be expressed as the point at which contribution margin minus total fixed costs equals zero (or the point at which contribution margin equals total fixed costs). In terms of units of product, the equation for the breakeven point looks like this:

$$(CM \text{ per Unit} \times BE \text{ Units}) - FC = \$0$$

It can also be expressed like this:

$$BE \text{ Units} = \frac{FC}{CM \text{ per unit}}$$

To show how the formula works, we use the data for Valley Metal Products:

$$BE = \frac{FC}{CM \text{ per unit}} = \frac{\$20,000}{\$90 - \$50} = \frac{\$20,000}{\$40} = 500 \text{ Units}$$

The breakeven point in total sales dollars may be determined by multiplying the breakeven point in units by the selling price (SP) per unit:

$$BE \text{ Dollars} = SP \times BE \text{ Units} = \$90 \times 500 \text{ Units} = \$45,000$$

An alternative way of determining the breakeven point in total sales dollars is to divide the fixed costs by the contribution margin ratio. The contribution margin ratio is the contribution margin divided by the selling price:

$$CM \text{ Ratio} = \frac{CM}{SP} = \frac{\$40}{\$90} = .444, \text{ or } 4/9$$

$$BE \text{ Dollars} = \frac{FC}{CM \text{ Ratio}} = \frac{\$20,000}{.444} = \$45,045^*$$

*Difference due to rounding up.

The Breakeven Point for Multiple Products

To satisfy the needs of different customers, many manufacturers sell a variety of products, which often have different variable and fixed costs and different selling prices. To calculate the breakeven point for each product, its unit contribution margin must be weighted by the sales mix. The **sales mix** is the proportion of each product's unit sales relative to the company's total unit sales.

Let's assume that Valley Metal Products sells two types of plant stands: a floor stand model and a smaller tabletop model. If the company sells 500 units, of which 300 units are floor stands and 200 are tabletops, the sales mix would be 3:2. For every three floor stands sold, two tabletops are sold. The sales mix can also be stated in percentages. Of the 500 units sold, 60 percent (300 ÷ 500) are floor stand sales, and 40 percent (200 ÷ 500) are tabletop sales (see Figure 10).

The breakeven point for multiple products can be computed in three steps. To illustrate, we will use Valley Metal Products' sales mix of 60 percent floor stands to 40 percent tabletops and total fixed costs of $32,000; the selling price, variable cost, and contribution margin per unit for each product line are shown in Step 1 below.

Step 1. *Compute the weighted-average contribution margin.* To do so, multiply the contribution margin for each product by its percentage of the sales mix, as follows:

 Study Note

A company's sales mix can be very dynamic—as, for example, with both Kraft and Google. If the mix is constantly changing, an assumption of stability may undermine the C-V-P analysis.

	Selling Price		Variable Costs		Contribution Margin (CM)		Percentage of Sales Mix		Weighted-Average CM
Floor stand	$90	−	$50	=	$40	×	60%	=	$24
Tabletop	$40	−	$20	=	$20	×	40%	=	8
Weighted-average contribution margin									$32

■ **FIGURE 10**
Sales Mix for Valley Metal Products, Inc.

Step 2. *Calculate the weighted-average breakeven point.* Divide total fixed costs by the weighted-average contribution margin:

Weighted-Average Breakeven Point = Total Fixed Costs ÷ Weighted-Average
Contribution Margin
= $32,000 ÷ $32
= 1,000 Units

Step 3. *Calculate the breakeven point for each product.* Multiply the weighted-average breakeven point by each product's percentage of the sales mix:

	Weighted-Average Breakeven Point		Sales Mix		Breakeven Point
Floor stand	1,000 units	×	60%	=	600 units
Tabletop	1,000 units	×	40%	=	400 units

To verify, determine the contribution margin of each product and subtract the total fixed costs:

Contribution margin		
Floor stand	600 × $40 =	$24,000
Tabletop	400 × $20 =	8,000
Total contribution margin		$32,000
Less fixed costs		32,000
Profit		$ 0

S T O P • R E V I E W • A P P L Y

4-1. Define *breakeven point.* Why is information about the breakeven point important to managers?

4-2. Define *contribution margin,* and describe its use in breakeven analysis.

4-3. Why does the total revenue line in a breakeven graph start at the origin (zero units, zero dollars) while the total cost line usually starts higher on the vertical axis?

Using C-V-P Analysis to Plan Future Sales, Costs, and Profits

LO5 Use C-V-P analysis to project the profitability of products and services.

The primary goal of a business venture is not to break even; it is to generate profits. C-V-P analysis adjusted for targeted profit can be used to estimate the profitability of a venture. This approach is excellent for "what-if" analysis, in which managers select several scenarios and compute the profit that may be anticipated from each. For instance, what if sales increase by 17,000 units? What effect will the increase have on profit? What if sales increase by only 6,000 units? What if fixed costs are reduced by $14,500? What if the variable unit cost increases by $1.40? Each scenario generates a different amount of profit or loss.

Applying C-V-P to a Manufacturing Business

To illustrate how a manufacturing business can apply C-V-P analysis, assume that Van Bryce, the president of Valley Metal Products, Inc., has set $4,000 in profit as this year's goal for the plant stands. If all the data in our earlier example remain the same, how many plant stands must Valley Metal Products sell to reach the targeted profit? Again, x equals the number of units.

$$S = VC + FC + P$$
$$\$90x = \$50x + \$20,000 + \$4,000$$
$$\$40x = \$24,000$$
$$x = 600 \text{ Units}$$

To check the answer, insert all known data into the equation:

$$S - VC - FC = P$$
$$(600 \times \$90) - (600 \times \$50) - \$20,000 = \$4,000$$
$$\$54,000 - \$30,000 - \$20,000 = \$4,000$$

The contribution margin approach can also be used for profit planning. To do so, simply add the targeted profit to the numerator of the contribution margin breakeven equation:

$$\text{Targeted Sales Units} = \frac{FC + P}{CM \text{ per Unit}}$$

The number of sales units Valley Metal Products needs to generate $4,000 in profit is computed this way:

$$\text{Targeted Sales Units} = \frac{FC + P}{CM \text{ per Unit}} = \frac{\$20,000 + \$4,000}{\$40} = \frac{\$24,000}{\$40} = 600 \text{ Units}$$

Contribution income statements (sometimes referred to as *variable costing income statements*), which are prepared for internal use, are also useful to managers in planning and making decisions about their company's operations. As you can see in the contribution income statement for Valley Metal Products that appears below, the focus of such a statement is on cost behavior, *not* cost function. All variable costs related to production, selling, and administration are subtracted from sales to determine the total contribution margin. All fixed costs related to production, selling, and administration are subtracted from the total contribution margin to determine operating income. (As we noted earlier, in income statements involving an entire company, the term *operating income* is more appropriate than *profit*.)

Valley Metal Products, Inc.
Contribution Income Statement
For the Year Ended December 31

	Per Unit	Total for 600 Units
Sales revenue	$90	$54,000
Less variable costs	50	30,000
Contribution margin	$40	$24,000
Less fixed costs		20,000
Operating income		$ 4,000

Van Bryce wants Valley Metal Products' planning team to consider three alternatives to the original plan shown in the contribution income statement. In the following sections, we examine each of these alternatives and its impact on operating income. In the summary, we review our work and analyze the different breakeven points.

Alternative 1: Decrease Variable Costs, Increase Sales Volume

The planning team worked with production, purchasing, and sales employees to determine what operating income would be if the company purchased and used aluminum rather than iron to make the plant stands. If aluminum were used, the direct materials cost per unit would decrease by $3 to $47. If the company painted the aluminum to meet the needs of a new customer group, it would increase sales volume by 10 percent to 660 units. What is the estimated operating income for this alternative? How does this alternative affect operating income?

	Per Unit	Total for 660 units
Sales revenue	$90	$59,400
Less variable costs	47	31,020
Contribution margin	$43	$28,380
Less fixed costs		20,000
Operating income		$ 8,380
Increase in operating income ($8,380 − $4,000)		$ 4,380

A different way to determine the impact of changes in selling price, cost, or sales volume on operating income is to analyze only the data that change between the original plan and the proposed alternative. If Alternative 1 is used, variable costs will decrease by $3 (from $50 to $47), which will increase the contribution margin per unit by $3 (from $40 to $43). This will increase the total contribution margin and operating income by $1,800 ($3 × 600). In addition, a sales increase of 60 units (.10 × 600) will increase the total contribution margin and operating income by $2,580 ($43 × 60). The total increase in operating income due to the decrease in variable costs and the increase in sales volume will be $4,380.

Analysis of Changes Only

Increase in contribution margin from	
Planned sales [($43 − $40) × 600 units]	$1,800
Additional sales ($43 × 60 units)	2,580
Increase in operating income	$4,380

Alternative 2: Increase Fixed Costs, Increase Sales Volume

Instead of changing the direct materials, the Marketing Department suggested that a $500 increase in advertising costs would increase sales volume by 5 percent. What is the estimated operating income for this alternative? How does this alternative affect operating income?

	Per Unit	Total for 630 Units
Sales revenue	$ 90	$56,700
Less variable costs	50	31,500
Contribution margin	$ 40	$25,200
Less fixed costs		20,500
Operating income		$ 4,700
Increase in operating income ($4,700 − $4,000)		$ 700

Additional advertising costs will affect both sales volume and fixed costs. The sales volume will increase by 30 plant stands, from 600 units to 630 units (600 × 1.05), which increases the total contribution margin and operating income by $1,200 (from $24,000 to $25,200). Fixed costs will increase from $20,000 to $20,500, which decreases operating income by $500. The increase in operating income will be $700 ($1,200 − $500).

Analysis of Changes Only

Increase in contribution margin from additional units sold [($40 × (600 × .05)]	$1,200
Less increase in fixed costs	500
Increase in operating income	$ 700

Alternative 3: Increase Selling Price, Decrease Sales Volume

Van Bryce asked the planning team to evaluate the impact of a $10 increase in selling price on the company's operating income. If the selling price is increased, the team estimates that the sales volume will decrease by 15 percent to 510 units. What is the estimated operating income for this alternative? How does this alternative affect operating income?

	Per Unit	Total for 510 Units
Sales revenue	$ 100	$51,000
Less variable costs	50	25,500
Contribution margin	$ 50	$25,500
Less fixed costs		20,000
Operating income		$ 5,500
Increase in operating income ($5,500 − $4,000)		$ 1,500

Analysis of Changes Only

Increase in contribution margin from increase in selling price ($10 increase in selling price × 510 units sold)	$5,100
Decrease in contribution margin from decrease in sales volume ($40 contribution margin per unit × 90 sales units lost)	(3,600)
Increase in operating income	$1,500

Comparative Summary In preparation for a meeting with Van Bryce, the planning team at Valley Metal Products compiled the summary presented in Exhibit 1. It compares the three alternatives with the original plan and shows how changes in variable and fixed costs, selling price, and sales volume affect the breakeven point.

Note that the decrease in variable costs (direct materials) proposed in Alternative 1 increases the contribution margin per unit (from $40 to $43), which reduces the breakeven point. Because fewer sales dollars are required to cover variable costs, the breakeven point is reached sooner than in the original plan—at a sales volume of 466 units rather than at 500 units. In Alternative 2, the increase in fixed costs has no effect on the contribution margin per unit, but it does require the total contribution margin to cover more fixed costs before reaching the breakeven point. Thus, the breakeven point is higher than in the original plan—513 units as opposed to 500. The increase in selling price in Alternative 3 increases the contribution margin per unit, which reduces the breakeven point. Because more sales dollars are available to cover fixed costs,

EXHIBIT 1 ▶ **Comparative Summary of Alternatives at Valley Metal Products, Inc.**

	Original Plan	Alternative 1	Alternative 2	Alternative 3
	Totals For 600 Units	Decrease Direct Materials Costs for 660 Units	Increase Advertising Costs for 630 Units	Increase Selling Price for 510 Units
Sales revenue	$54,000	$59,400	$56,700	$51,000
Less variable costs	30,000	31,020	31,500	25,500
Contribution margin	$24,000	$28,380	$25,200	$25,500
Less fixed costs	20,000	20,000	20,500	20,000
Operating income	$ 4,000	$ 8,380	$ 4,700	$ 5,500

Breakeven point in whole units (FC ÷ CM)

$20,000 ÷ $40 =	500			
$20,000 ÷ $43 =		466*		
$20,500 ÷ $40 =			513*	
$20,000 ÷ $50 =				400

*Rounded up to next whole unit.

the breakeven point of 400 units is lower than the breakeven point in the original plan.

Which plan should Bryce choose? If he wants the highest operating income, he will choose Alternative 1. If, however, he wants the company to begin generating operating income more quickly, he will choose the plan with the lowest breakeven point, Alternative 3. Remember that the breakeven point provides a rough estimate of the number of units that must be sold to cover the total costs.

Additional qualitative information may help Bryce make a better decision. Will customers perceive that the quality of the plant stands is lower if the company uses aluminum rather than iron, as proposed in Alternative 1? Will increased expenditures on advertising yield a 5 percent increase in sales volume, as Alternative 2 suggests? Will the increase in selling price suggested in Alternative 3 create more than a 15 percent decline in unit sales?

Quantitative information is essential for planning, but managers must also be sensitive to qualitative factors, such as product quality, reliability and quality of suppliers, and availability of human and technical resources.

Applying C-V-P Analysis to a Service Business

In this section, we look at how a service business can use C-V-P analysis in planning its operations. Assume that Glenda Haley, the manager of the Appraisal Department at Edmunds Mortgage Company, wants to plan the home appraisal activities that each mortgage loan application requires. She estimates that over the next year, her department will perform an average of 100 appraisals per month and service fee revenue will be $400 per appraisal. Other estimated data for the year are as follows:

Variable costs: direct professional labor, $160 per appraisal; county survey map fee, $99 per appraisal

Mixed costs (monthly service overhead):

Volume	Month	Activity Level	Cost
Highest	March	180 appraisals	$23,380
Lowest	February	98 appraisals	$20,018

Estimating Service Overhead Costs

Haley wants to estimate the total service overhead cost of appraisals for next year. She uses the high-low method to do so:

Step 1. *Calculate the variable service overhead cost per appraisal.*

$$\frac{\text{Variable Service Overhead}}{\text{Cost per Appraisal}} = \frac{(\text{Highest Cost} - \text{Lowest Cost}) \div}{(\text{Highest Volume} - \text{Lowest Volume})}$$
$$= (\$23,380 - \$20,018) \div (180 - 98)$$
$$= \$3,362 \div 82 \text{ Appraisals} = \$41$$

Step 2. *Calculate the total fixed service overhead costs.*

Total Fixed Service Overhead Costs = Total Service Overhead Costs − Total Variable Service Overhead Costs

Total Fixed Service Overhead Costs for March = $23,380 − ($41 × 180)
= $16,000

Step 3. *Calculate the total service overhead costs for one month.*

Total Service   = Total Fixed Service Overhead Costs +
Overhead Costs   (Variable Rate $\times$ Estimated Number of Appraisals)
        = \$16,000 + (\$41 per Appraisal $\times$ Number of Appraisals)

Step 4. *Calculate the total service overhead costs for one month assuming that 100 appraisals will be made.*

Total Overhead Service Costs = \$16,000 + (\$41 $\times$ 100) = \$20,100

Determining the Breakeven Point
Glenda Haley also wants to know how many appraisals her department must perform each month to cover the fixed and variable appraisal costs. She calculates the breakeven point as follows:

Let x = Number of Appraisals per Month at Breakeven Point
$$S - VC - FC = 0$$
$$\$400x - \$300x - \$16,000 = 0$$
$$\$100x = \$16,000$$
$$x = 160 \text{ Appraisals per Month}$$

The variable rate of \$300 per appraisal includes the variable service overhead rate, the direct professional labor, and the county survey map fee (\$41 + \$160 + \$99).

Determining the Effect of a Change in Operating Costs
Haley is worried because her department can perform an average of only 100 appraisals each month, but the estimated breakeven point is 160 appraisals per month. Because of strong competition, increasing the appraisal fee is not an option; to make the appraisals profitable, the mortgage company has asked Haley to find ways of reducing costs. In reviewing the situation, Haley has determined that improved scheduling of appraisals will reduce appraisers' travel time. Travel time is included in the current professional labor cost of \$160 per appraisal (four hours of an appraiser's time at \$40 per hour). By scheduling the jobs according to location, Haley can reduce the appraisers' travel time enough to reduce the total time required by 50 percent, thus cutting the professional labor cost to \$80 per appraisal [(.50 $\times$ 4 hours) $\times$ \$40 per hour]. The new scheduling process will increase fixed costs by \$200 per month. Given these circumstances, what will the breakeven point be?

Let x = Number of Appraisals per Month at Breakeven Point
$$S - VC - FC = 0$$
$$\$400x - \$220x - \$16,200 = 0$$
$$\$180x = \$16,200$$
$$x = 90 \text{ Appraisals per Month}$$

Variable costs become \$220 (\$300 − \$80) per appraisal due to the reduced labor costs. This change increases the contribution margin by \$80 per appraisal. Fixed costs increase from \$16,000 to \$16,200. The increase in the contribution margin is greater than the increase in the fixed costs, so the breakeven point decreases from 160 appraisals per month to 90 appraisals per month.

Achieving a Targeted Profit
How many appraisals would Glenda Haley's department have to perform each month to achieve a targeted profit of \$18,000 per month?

$$\text{Let } x = \text{Targeted Sales in Units}$$
$$S - VC - FC = P$$
$$\$400x - \$220x - \$16,200 = \$18,000$$
$$\$180x = \$34,200$$
$$x = 190 \text{ Appraisals per Month}$$

STOP • REVIEW • APPLY

5-1. State the equation that uses fixed costs, targeted profit, and contribution margin per unit to determine targeted sales units.

5-2. Give three examples of the ways in which a service business can use C-V-P analysis.

5-3. What are the differences and similarities in C-V-P analysis for manufacturing organizations and service organizations?

A LOOK BACK AT

KRAFT FOODS

The Decision Point at the beginning of this chapter focused on **Kraft Foods,** a company whose five key sectors produce brands sold around the world. It posed these questions:

- **How does Kraft decide which products to offer?**
- **Why do Kraft's managers analyze cost behavior to project the profitability of the company's core sectors?**

Kraft's managers must consider the variable and fixed costs of making products when determining the profitability of the company's sales mix and projecting the operating results of its core sectors. They use cost information to determine selling prices that cover both fixed and variable costs and that take into account the variability of demand for the company's brands. For example, the variable costs of the direct materials and direct labor the company uses to make each one-pound package of cheese are roughly the same, but the total cost of direct materials will vary according to the number of packages produced in any one year. Similarly, the fixed costs of operating the factories and of the manufacturing equipment used in making the cheese will not change significantly from year to year in relation to the number of pounds produced. However, the portion of those costs applied to each pound of product will vary depending on the number of pounds actually produced. In short, to project the profitability of a brand or one of its five key sectors for a particular year, Kraft's managers must take into account both the selling price and the estimated production and sales mix of products and the effects those estimates have on a brand's unit cost.

CHAPTER REVIEW

REVIEW of Learning Objectives

LO1 Define *cost behavior* and explain how managers use this concept.

Cost behavior is the way costs respond to changes in volume or activity. When managers plan, they use cost behavior to determine how many units of products or services must be sold to generate a targeted amount of profit and how changes in planned activities will affect operating income. During the period, managers must understand and anticipate cost behavior to determine the impact of their decisions on operating income. When managers evaluate performance and communicate results, they analyze how changes in cost and sales affect the profitability of product lines, sales territories, customers, departments, and other business segments by preparing reports using variable costing.

LO2 Identify variable, fixed, and mixed costs, and separate mixed costs into their variable and fixed components.

Some costs vary in relation to volume or operating activity; other costs remain fixed as volume changes. Cost behavior depends on whether the focus is total costs or cost per unit. Total costs that change in direct proportion to changes in productive output (or any other volume measure) are called *variable costs*. They include hourly wages, the cost of operating supplies, direct materials costs, and the cost of merchandise. Total *fixed costs* remain constant within a relevant range of volume or activity. They change only when volume or activity exceeds the relevant range—for example, when new equipment or new buildings must be purchased, higher insurance premiums and property taxes must be paid, or additional supervisory personnel must be hired to accommodate increased activity. A *mixed cost*, such as the cost of electricity, has both variable and fixed cost components. For cost planning and control, mixed costs must be separated into their variable and fixed components. To separate them, managers use a variety of methods, including the engineering, scatter diagram, high-low, and statistical methods.

LO3 Define *cost-volume-profit (C-V-P) analysis* and discuss how managers use it as a tool for planning and control.

Cost-volume-profit analysis is an examination of the cost behavior patterns that underlie the relationships among cost, volume of output, and profit. It is a tool for both planning and control. The techniques and problem-solving procedures involved in C-V-P analysis express relationships among revenue, sales mix, cost, volume, and profit. Those relationships provide a general model of financial activity that management can use for short-range planning and for evaluating performance and analyzing alternatives.

LO4 Define *breakeven point* and use contribution margin to determine a company's breakeven point for multiple products.

The *breakeven point* is the point at which total revenues equal total costs—in other words, the point at which net sales equal variable costs plus fixed costs. Once the number of units needed to break even is known, the number can be multiplied by the product's selling price to determine the breakeven point in sales dollars. *Contribution margin* is the amount that remains after all variable costs have been subtracted from sales. A product's contribution margin represents its net contribution to paying off fixed costs and earning a profit. The breakeven point in units can be computed by using the following formula:

$$\text{BE Units} = \frac{\text{FC}}{\text{CM per Unit}}$$

Sales mix is used to calculate the breakeven point for each product when a company sells more than one product.

LO5   Use C-V-P analysis to project the profitability of products and services.

The addition of targeted profit to the breakeven equation makes it possible to plan levels of operation that yield the targeted profit. The formula in terms of contribution margin is

$$\text{Targeted Sales Units} = \frac{FC + P}{CM \text{ per Unit}}$$

C-V-P analysis, whether used by a manufacturing company or a service organization, enables managers to select several "what if" scenarios and evaluate the outcome of each to determine which will generate the desired amount of profit.

REVIEW of Concepts and Terminology

The following concepts and terms were introduced in this chapter:

Breakeven point: The point at which total revenues equal total costs. **(LO4)**

Contribution margin (CM): The amount that remains after all variable costs are subtracted from sales. **(LO4)**

Cost behavior: The way costs respond to changes in volume or activity. **(LO1)**

Cost-volume-profit (C-V-P) analysis: An examination of the cost behavior patterns that underlie the relationships among cost, volume of output, and profit. **(LO3)**

Engineering method: A method that separates costs into their fixed and variable components by performing a step-by-step analysis of the tasks, costs, and processes involved in completing an activity or product. **(LO2)**

Fixed costs: Total costs that remain constant within a relevant range of volume or activity. **(LO2)**

High-low method: A three-step approach to separating a mixed cost into its variable and fixed components. **(LO2)**

Margin of safety: The number of sales units or amount of sales dollars by which actual sales can fall below planned sales without resulting in a loss. **(LO4)**

Mixed costs: Costs that have both variable and fixed components. **(LO2)**

Normal capacity: The average annual level of operating capacity needed to meet expected sales demand. **(LO2)**

Operating capacity: The upper limit of an organization's productive output capability, given its existing resources. **(LO2)**

Practical capacity: Theoretical capacity reduced by normal and expected work stoppages. **(LO2)**

Regression analysis: A mathematical approach to separating a mixed cost into its variable and fixed components. **(LO2)**

Relevant range: The span of activity in which a company expects to operate. **(LO2)**

Sales mix: The proportion of each product's unit sales relative to the company's total unit sales. **(LO4)**

Scatter diagram: A chart of plotted points that helps determine whether a linear relationship exists between a cost item and its related activity measure. **(LO2)**

Theoretical (ideal) capacity: The maximum productive output for a given period in which all machinery and equipment are operating at optimum speed, without interruption. **(LO2)**

Variable costs: Total costs that change in direct proportion to changes in productive output or any other measure of volume. **(LO2)**

REVIEW Problem

LO4, LO5   **Breakeven Analysis and Profitability Planning**

Olympia, Inc., is a major producer of golf clubs. Its oversized putter has a large potential market. The following is a summary of data from the company's operations this year:

Selling price per unit: $95

Overhead	$195,000
Advertising	55,000
Administrative expense	68,000
Total fixed costs	$318,000

Direct materials	$23
Direct labor	8
Overhead	6
Selling expense	5
Variable costs per unit	$42

Required

1. Compute the breakeven point in units for the year.
2. Olympia sold 6,500 putters this year. How much profit did it realize?
3. To improve profitability next year, management is considering the four alternative courses of action indicated below. (In performing the required steps, use the figures from items **1** and **2** and treat each alternative independently.)

   a. Calculate the number of units Olympia must sell to generate a targeted profit of $95,400. Assume that costs and selling price remain constant.
   b. Calculate the operating income if the company increases the number of units sold by 20 percent and cuts the selling price by $5 per unit.
   c. Determine the number of units that must be sold to break even if advertising costs are increased by $47,700.
   d. Find the number of units that must be sold to generate a targeted profit of $120,000 if variable costs are cut by 10 percent.

Answer to Review Problem

1. Breakeven point in units for this year:

$$\text{Breakeven Units} = \frac{\text{FC}}{\text{CM per Unit}} = \frac{\$318,000}{\$95 - \$42} = \frac{\$318,000}{\$53} = 6,000 \text{ Units}$$

2. Profit from sale of 6,500 units:

Units sold	6,500
Units required to break even	6,000
Units over breakeven	500

Profit = $53 per unit × 500 = $26,500

   Contribution margin equals sales minus all variable costs. Contribution margin per unit equals the amount left to cover fixed costs and earn a profit after variable costs have been subtracted from sales dollars. If all fixed costs have been absorbed by the time breakeven is reached, the entire contribution margin of each unit sold in excess of breakeven represents profit.

3. a. Number of units that must be sold to generate a targeted profit of $95,400:

$$\text{Targeted Sales Units} = \frac{\text{FC} + \text{P}}{\text{CM per Unit}}$$

$$\frac{\$318,000 + \$95,400}{\$53} = \frac{\$413,400}{\$53} = 7,800 \text{ Units}$$

b. Operating income if unit sales increase 20 percent and unit selling price decreases by $5:

Sales revenue [7,800 (6,500 × 1.20) units at $90 per unit]	$702,000
Less variable costs (7,800 units × $42)	327,600
Contribution margin	$374,400
Less fixed costs	318,000
Operating income	$ 56,400

c. Number of units needed to break even if advertising costs (fixed costs) increase by $47,700:

$$\text{BE Units} = \frac{FC}{CM \text{ per Unit}}$$

$$\frac{\$318,000 + \$47,700}{\$53} = \frac{\$365,700}{\$53} = 6,900 \text{ Units}$$

d. Number of units that must be sold to generate a targeted profit of $120,000 if variable costs decrease by 10 percent:

$$CM \text{ per Unit} = \$95.00 - (\$42.00 \times .90) = \$95.00 - \$37.80 = \$57.20$$

$$\text{Targeted Sales Units} = \frac{FC + P}{CM \text{ per Unit}}$$

$$\frac{\$318,000 + \$120,000}{\$57.20} = \frac{\$438,000}{\$57.20} = 7,658 \text{ Units*}$$

*Note that the answer is rounded up to the next whole unit.

CHAPTER ASSIGNMENTS

BUILDING Your Basic Knowledge and Skills

Short Exercises

LO1 **Concept of Cost Behavior**

SE 1. Dapper Hat Makers is in the business of designing and producing specialty hats. The material used for derbies costs $4.50 per unit, and Dapper pays each of its two full-time employees $250 per week. If Employee A makes 15 derbies in one week, what is the variable cost per derby, and what is this worker's fixed cost per derby? If Employee B makes only 12 derbies in one week, what are this worker's variable and fixed costs per derby? (Round to two decimal places where necessary.)

LO2 **Identification of Variable, Fixed, and Mixed Costs**

SE 2. Identify the following as (a) fixed costs, (b) variable costs, or (c) mixed costs:

1. Direct materials
2. Electricity
3. Operating supplies
4. Personnel manager's salary
5. Factory building rent

LO2 **Mixed Costs: High-Low Method**

SE 3. Using the high-low method and the information below, compute the monthly variable cost per telephone hour and total fixed costs for Sadiko Corporation.

Month	Telephone Hours Used	Telephone Costs
April	96	$4,350
May	93	4,230
June	105	4,710

LO3 **C-V-P Analysis**

SE 4. DeLuca, Inc., wants to make a profit of $20,000. It has variable costs of $80 per unit and fixed costs of $12,000. How much must it charge per unit if 4,000 units are sold?

LO4 **Breakeven Analysis**

SE 5. How many units must Braxton Company sell to break even if the selling price per unit is $8.50, variable costs are $4.30 per unit, and fixed costs are $3,780? What is the breakeven point in total dollars of sales?

LO4 **Contribution Margin**

SE 6. Using the contribution margin approach, find the breakeven point in units for Norcia Consumer Products if the selling price per unit is $11, the variable cost per unit is $6, and the fixed costs are $5,500.

LO4 **Contribution Margin Ratio**

SE 7. Using the information in **SE 6** and the contribution margin ratio, compute the breakeven point in total sales dollars.

LO4 **Breakeven Analysis for Multiple Products**

SE 8. Using the contribution margin approach, find the breakeven point in units for Sardinia Company's two products. Product A's selling price per unit is $10, and its variable cost per unit is $4. Product B's selling price per unit is $8, and its variable cost per unit is $5. Fixed costs are $15,000, and the sales mix of Product A to Product B is 2:1.

LO4, LO5 **Contribution Margin and Projected Profit**

SE 9. If Oui Watches sells 300 watches at $48 per watch and has variable costs of $18 per watch and fixed costs of $4,000, what is the projected profit?

LO5 **Cost Behavior in a Service Business**

SE 10. Guy Spy, a private investigation firm, has the following costs for December:

Direct labor: $190 per case

Service overhead

Salary for director of investigations	$ 4,800
Telephone	930
Depreciation	8,300
Legal advice	2,300
Supplies	590
Advertising	360
Utilities	1,560
Wages for clerical personnel	2,000
Total service overhead	$20,840

Service overhead for October was $21,150; for November, it was $21,350. The number of cases investigated during October, November, and December was 93, 97, and 91, respectively. Compute the variable and fixed cost components of service overhead. Then determine the variable and fixed costs per case for December. (Round to nearest dollar where necessary.)

Exercises

LO2 **Identification of Variable and Fixed Costs**

E 1. Indicate whether each of the following costs of productive output is usually (a) variable or (b) fixed:

1. Packing materials for stereo components
2. Real estate taxes
3. Gasoline for a delivery truck
4. Property insurance
5. Depreciation expense of buildings (calculated with the straight-line method)
6. Supplies
7. Indirect materials
8. Bottles used to package liquids
9. License fees for company cars
10. Wiring used in radios
11. Machine helper's wages
12. Wood used in bookcases
13. City operating license
14. Machine depreciation based on machine hours used
15. Machine operator's hourly wages
16. Cost of required outside inspection of each unit produced

LO2 **Variable Cost Analysis**

E 2. Zero Time Oil Change has been in business for six months. The company pays $0.50 per quart for the oil it uses in servicing cars. Each job requires an average of four quarts of oil. The company estimates that in the next three months, it will service 240, 288, and 360 cars.

1. Compute the cost of oil for each of the three months and the total cost for all three months.

Month	Cars to Be Serviced	Required Quarts/Car	Cost/Quart	Total Cost/Month
1	240	4	$0.50	_____
2	288	4	0.50	_____
3	360	4	0.50	_____
Three-month total	888			_____

2. Complete the following sentences by choosing the words that best describe the cost behavior at Zero Time Oil Change:
   a. Cost per unit (increased, decreased, remained constant).
   b. Total variable cost per month (increased, decreased) as the quantity of oil used (increased, decreased).

LO2 **Mixed Costs: High-Low Method**

E 3. Whitehouse Company manufactures major appliances. Because of growing interest in its products, it has just had its most successful year. In preparing the budget for next year, its controller compiled these data:

Month	Volume in Machine Hours	Electricity Cost
July	6,000	$ 60,000
August	5,000	53,000
September	4,500	49,500
October	4,000	46,000
November	3,500	42,500
December	3,000	39,000
Six month total	26,000	$290,000

Using the high-low method, determine (1) the variable electricity cost per machine hour, (2) the monthly fixed electricity cost, and (3) the total variable electricity costs and fixed electricity costs for the six-month period.

LO2 **Mixed Costs: High-Low Method**

E 4. When Jerome Company's monthly costs were $75,000, sales were $80,000; when its monthly costs were $60,000, sales were $50,000. Use the high-low method to develop a monthly cost formula for Jerome's coming year.

LO4 **Contribution Margin**

E 5. Senora Company manufactures a single product that sells for $110 per unit. The company projects sales of 500 units per month. Projected costs are as follows:

Type of Cost	Manufacturing	Nonmanufacturing
Variable	$10,000	$5,000
Nonvariable	$12,500	$7,500

1. What is the company's contribution margin per unit?
2. What is the contribution margin ratio?
3. What volume, in terms of units, must the company sell to break even?

LO4, LO5 **Breakeven Point and C-V-P Analysis**

E 6. Using the data in the contribution income statement for Sedona, Inc., that appears below, calculate (1) selling price per unit, (2) variable costs per unit, and (3) breakeven point in sales dollars.

Sedona, Inc.
Contribution Income Statement
For the Year Ended December 31

Sales (10,000 units)		$16,000,000
Less variable costs		
Cost of goods sold	$8,000,000	
Selling, administrative, and general	4,000,000	
Total variable costs		12,000,000
Contribution margin		$ 4,000,000
Less fixed costs		
Overhead	$1,200,000	
Selling, administrative, and general	800,000	
Total fixed costs		2,000,000
Operating income		$ 2,000,000

LO4 **Graphic Breakeven Analysis**

E 7. Identify the letter of the point, line segment, or area of the breakeven graph shown below that correctly completes each of the following statements:

1. The maximum possible operating loss is
   a. A.   c. B.
   b. D.   d. F.
2. The breakeven point in sales dollars is
   a. C.   c. A.
   b. D.   d. G.
3. At volume F, total contribution margin is
   a. C.   c. E.
   b. D.   d. G.
4. Net income is represented by area
   a. KDL.   c. BDC.
   b. KCJ.   d. GCJ.
5. At volume J, total fixed costs are represented by
   a. H.   c. I.
   b. G.   d. J.
6. If volume increases from F to J, the change in total costs is
   a. HI minus DE.   c. BC minus DF.
   b. DF minus HJ.   d. AB minus DE.

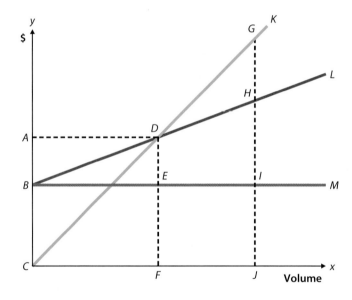

LO4 **Breakeven Analysis**

E 8. Techno Designs produces head covers for golf clubs. The company expects to generate a profit next year. It anticipates fixed manufacturing costs of $126,500 and fixed general and administrative expenses of $82,030 for the year. Variable manufacturing and selling costs per set of head covers will be $4.65 and $2.75, respectively. Each set will sell for $13.40.

1. Compute the breakeven point in sales units.
2. Compute the breakeven point in sales dollars.
3. If the selling price is increased to $14 per unit and fixed general and administrative expenses are cut by $33,465, what will the new breakeven point be in units?
4. Prepare a graph to illustrate the breakeven point computed in **2**.

LO4, LO5 **Breakeven Analysis and Pricing**

E 9. McLennon Company has a plant capacity of 100,000 units per year, but its budget for this year indicates that only 60,000 units will be produced and sold. The entire budget for this year is as follows:

Sales (60,000 units at $4)		$240,000
Less cost of goods produced (based on production of 60,000 units)		
Direct materials (variable)	$60,000	
Direct labor (variable)	30,000	
Variable overhead costs	45,000	
Fixed overhead costs	75,000	
Total cost of goods produced		210,000
Gross margin		$ 30,000
Less selling and administrative expenses		
Selling (fixed)	$24,000	
Administrative (fixed)	36,000	
Total selling and administrative expenses		60,000
Operating income (loss)		($ 30,000)

1. Given the budgeted selling price and cost data, how many units would McLennon have to sell to break even? (**Hint:** Be sure to consider selling and administrative expenses.)
2. Market research indicates that if McLennon were to drop its selling price to $3.80 per unit, it could sell 100,000 units. Would you recommend the drop in price? What would the new operating income or loss be?

LO4 **Breakeven Point for Multiple Products**

E 10. Saline Aquarium, Inc., manufactures and sells aquariums, water pumps, and air filters. The sales mix is 1:2:2 (i.e., for every one aquarium sold, two water pumps and two air filters are sold). Using the contribution margin approach, find the breakeven point in units for each product. The company's fixed costs are $26,000. Other information is as follows:

	Selling Price per Unit	Variable Costs per Unit
Aquariums	$60	$25
Water pumps	20	12
Air filters	10	3

LO4 **Sales Mix Analysis**

E 11. Ella Mae Simpson is the owner of a hairdressing salon in Palm Coast, Florida. Her salon provides three basic services: shampoo and set, permanents, and cut and blow dry. The following are its operating results from the past quarter:

Type of Service	Number of Customers	Total Sales	Contribution Margin Dollars
Shampoo and set	1,200	$24,000	$14,700
Permanents	420	21,000	15,120
Cut and blow dry	1,000	15,000	10,000
	2,620	$60,000	$39,820
Total fixed costs			30,000
Profit			$ 9,820

Compute the breakeven point in units based on the weighted-average contribution margin for the sales mix.

LO4, LO5 **Contribution Margin and Profit Planning**

E 12. Target Systems, Inc., makes heat-seeking missiles. It has recently been offered a government contract from which it may realize a profit. The contract purchase price is $130,000 per missile, but the number of units to be purchased has not yet been decided. The company's fixed costs are budgeted at $3,973,500, and variable costs are $68,500 per unit.

1. Compute the number of units the company should agree to make at the stated contract price to earn a profit of $1,500,000.
2. Using a lighter material, the variable unit cost can be reduced by $1,730, but total fixed overhead will increase by $27,500. How many units must be produced to make $1,500,000 in profit?
3. Given the figures in **2**, how many additional units must be produced to increase profit by $1,264,600?

LO5 **Planning Future Sales**

E 13. Short-term automobile rentals are the specialty of ASAP Auto Rentals, Inc. Average variable operating costs have been $12.50 per day per automobile. The company owns 60 cars. Fixed operating costs for the next year are expected to be $145,500. Average daily rental revenue per automobile is expected to be $34.50. Management would like to earn a profit of $47,000 during the year.

1. Calculate the total number of daily rentals the company must have during the year to earn the targeted profit.
2. On the basis of your answer to **1**, determine the average number of days each automobile must be rented.
3. Determine the total revenue needed to achieve the targeted profit of $47,000.
4. What would the total rental revenue be if fixed operating costs could be lowered by $5,180 and the targeted profit increased to $70,000?

LO5 **Cost Behavior in a Service Business**

E 14. Luke Ricci, CPA, is the owner of a firm that provides tax services. The firm charges $50 per return for the direct professional labor involved in preparing standard short-form tax returns. In January, the firm prepared 850 such returns; in February, 1,000; and in March, 700. Service overhead (telephone and utilities, depreciation on equipment and building, tax forms, office supplies, and wages of clerical personnel) for January was $18,500; for February, $20,000; and for March, $17,000.

1. Determine the variable and fixed cost components of the firm's Service Overhead account.
2. What would the estimated total cost per tax return be if the firm prepares 825 standard short-form tax returns in April?

LO5 **C-V-P Analysis in a Service Business**

E 15. Flossmoor Inspection Service specializes in inspecting cars that have been returned to automobile leasing companies at the end of their leases. Flossmoor's charge for each inspection is $50; its average cost per inspection is $15. Tony Lomangeno, Flossmoor's owner, wants to expand his business by hiring another employee and purchasing an automobile. The fixed costs of the new employee and automobile would be $3,000 per month. How many inspections per month would the new employee have to perform to earn Lomangeno a profit of $1,200?

Problems

LO2, LO5 **Cost Behavior and Projection**

P 1. Luster Auto, Inc., specializes in "detailing" automobile exteriors—that is, revitalizing them so the cars look as if they had just rolled off the showroom floor. The company charges $100 for a full exterior detailing. It has just completed its first year of business and has asked its accountants to analyze the operating results. Management wants costs divided into variable, fixed, and mixed components and would like them projected for the coming year. Anticipated volume for next year is 1,100 jobs. The process used to detail a car's exterior is as follows:

1. One $20-per-hour employee spends 20 minutes cleaning the car's exterior.
2. One can per car of Bugg-Off, a cleaning compound, is used on trouble spots.
3. A chemical compound called Buff Glow is used to remove oxidants from the paint surface and restore the natural oils to the paint.
4. Poly Wax is applied by hand, allowed to sit for 10 minutes, and then buffed off.
5. The final step is an inspection to see that all wax and debris have been removed.

On average, two hours are spent on each car, including cleaning time and drying time for the wax. Operating information for Luster Auto's first year is as follows:

Number of automobiles detailed	840
Labor per auto	2 hours at $20.00 per hour
Containers of Bugg-Off consumed	840 at $3.50 per can
Pounds of Buff Glow consumed	105 pounds at $32.00 per pound
Pounds of Poly Wax consumed	210 pounds at $8.00 per pound
Rent	$1,400.00 per month

During the year, utilities costs ranged from $800 for 40 jobs in March to $1,801 for 110 jobs in August.

Required

1. Classify the costs as variable, fixed, or mixed.
2. Using the high-low method, separate the mixed costs into their variable and fixed components. Use number of jobs as the basis.
3. Project the same costs for next year, assuming that the anticipated increase in activity will occur and that fixed costs will remain constant.
4. Compute the unit cost per job for next year.
5. Manager Insight: Given your answer to **4**, should the price remain at $100 per job?

LO4, LO5 **Breakeven Analysis**

P 2. Luce & Morgan, a law firm in downtown Jefferson City, is considering opening a legal clinic for middle- and low-income clients. The clinic would bill at a rate of $18 per hour. It would employ law students as paraprofessional help and pay them $9 per hour. Other variable costs are anticipated to be $5.40 per hour, and annual fixed costs are expected to total $27,000.

Required

1. Compute the breakeven point in billable hours.

2. Compute the breakeven point in total billings.
3. Find the new breakeven point in total billings if fixed costs should go up by $2,340.
4. Using the original figures, compute the breakeven point in total billings if the billing rate decreases by $1 per hour, variable costs decrease by $0.40 per hour, and fixed costs go down by $3,600.

LO4, LO5   **Planning Future Sales: Contribution Margin Approach**

P 3. Icon Industries is considering a new product for its Trophy Division. The product, which would feature an alligator, is expected to have global market appeal and to become the mascot for many high school and university athletic teams. Expected variable unit costs are as follows: direct materials, $18.50; direct labor, $4.25; production supplies, $1.10; selling costs, $2.80; and other, $1.95. Annual fixed costs are depreciation, building and equipment, $36,000; advertising, $45,000; and other, $11,400. Icon Industries plans to sell the product for $55.00.

Required

1. Using the contribution margin approach, compute the number of units the company must sell to (a) break even and (b) earn a profit of $70,224.
2. Using the same data, compute the number of units that must be sold to earn a profit of $139,520 if advertising costs rise by $40,000.
3. Using the original information and sales of 10,000 units, compute the selling price the company must use to make a profit of $131,600. (**Hint:** Calculate contribution margin per unit first.)
4. **Manager Insight:** According to the vice president of marketing, Albert Flora, the most optimistic annual sales estimate for the product would be 15,000 units, and the highest competitive selling price the company can charge is $52 per unit. How much more can be spent on fixed advertising costs if the selling price is $52, if the variable costs cannot be reduced, and if the targeted profit for 15,000 unit sales is $251,000?

LO4, LO5   **Breakeven Analysis and Planning Future Sales**

P 4. Write Company has a maximum capacity of 200,000 units per year. Variable manufacturing costs are $12 per unit. Fixed overhead is $600,000 per year. Variable selling and administrative costs are $5 per unit, and fixed selling and administrative costs are $300,000 per year. The current sales price is $23 per unit.

Required

1. What is the breakeven point in (a) sales units and (b) sales dollars?
2. How many units must Write Company sell to earn a profit of $240,000 per year?
3. A strike at one of the company's major suppliers has caused a shortage of materials, so the current year's production and sales are limited to 160,000 units. To partially offset the effect of the reduced sales on profit, management is planning to reduce fixed costs to $841,000. Variable cost per unit is the same as last year. The company has already sold 30,000 units at the regular selling price of $23 per unit.

   a. What amount of fixed costs was covered by the total contribution margin of the first 30,000 units sold?
   b. What contribution margin per unit will be needed on the remaining 130,000 units to cover the remaining fixed costs and to earn a profit of $210,000 this year?

LO2, LO5   Cost Behavior and Projection for a Service Business

P 5. Power Brite Painting Company specializes in refurbishing exterior painted surfaces that have been hard hit by humidity and insect debris. It uses a special technique, called pressure cleaning, before priming and painting the surface. The refurbishing process involves the following steps:

1. Unskilled laborers trim all trees and bushes within two feet of the structure.
2. Skilled laborers clean the building with a high-pressure cleaning machine, using about six gallons of chlorine per job.
3. Unskilled laborers apply a coat of primer.
4. Skilled laborers apply oil-based exterior paint to the entire surface.

On average, skilled laborers work 12 hours per job, and unskilled laborers work 8 hours. The refurbishing process generated the following operating results during the year on 628 jobs:

Skilled labor	$20 per hour
Unskilled labor	$8 per hour
Gallons of chlorine used	3,768 gallons at $5.50 per gallon
Paint primer	7,536 gallons at $15.50 per gallon
Paint	6,280 gallons at $16 per gallon
Depreciation of paint spraying equipment	$600 per month depreciation
Lease of two vans	$800 per month total
Rent on storage building	$450 per month

Data on utilities for the year are as follows:

Month	Number of Jobs	Cost	Hours Worked
January	42	$ 3,950	840
February	37	3,550	740
March	44	4,090	880
April	49	4,410	980
May	54	4,720	1,080
June	62	5,240	1,240
July	71	5,820	1,420
August	73	5,890	1,460
September	63	5,370	1,260
October	48	4,340	960
November	45	4,210	900
December	40	3,830	800
Totals	628	$55,420	12,560

Required

1. Classify the costs as variable, fixed, or mixed.
2. Using the high-low method, separate mixed costs into their variable and fixed components. Use total hours worked as the basis.
3. Compute the average cost per job for the year. (**Hint:** Divide the total of all costs for the year by the number of jobs completed.)
4. Project the average cost per job for next year if variable costs per job increase 20 percent.

Alternate Problems

LO4, LO5   Breakeven Analysis

P 6. At the beginning of each year, the Accounting Department at Moon Glow Lighting, Ltd., must find the point at which projected sales revenue will equal total budgeted variable and fixed costs. The company produces custom-made, low-voltage outdoor lighting systems. Each system sells for an average of $435. Variable costs per unit are $210. Total fixed costs for the year are estimated to be $166,500.

Required

1. Compute the breakeven point in sales units.
2. Compute the breakeven point in sales dollars.
3. Find the new breakeven point in sales units if the fixed costs go up by $10,125.
4. Using the original figures, compute the breakeven point in sales units if the selling price decreases to $425 per unit, fixed costs go up by $15,200, and variable costs decrease by $15 per unit.

Planning Future Sales: Contribution Margin Approach

P 7. Garden Marbles manufactures birdbaths, statues, and other decorative items, which it sells to florists and retail home and garden centers. Its Design Department has proposed a new product, a statue of a frog, that it believes will be popular with home gardeners. Expected variable unit costs are direct materials, $9.25; direct labor, $4.00; production supplies, $0.55; selling costs, $2.40; and other, $3.05. The following are fixed costs: depreciation, building and equipment, $33,000; advertising, $40,000; and other, $6,000. Management plans to sell the product for $29.25.

LO4, LO5 **Required**

1. Using the contribution margin approach, compute the number of statues the company must sell to (a) break even and (b) earn a profit of $50,000.
2. Using the same data, compute the number of statues that must be sold to earn a profit of $70,000 if advertising costs rise by $20,000.
3. Using the original data and sales of 15,000 units, compute the selling price the company must charge to make a profit of $100,000.
4. **Manager Insight:** According to the vice president of marketing, Yvonne Palmer, if the price of the statues is reduced and advertising is increased, the most optimistic annual sales estimate is 25,000 units. How much more can be spent on fixed advertising costs if the selling price is reduced to $28.00 per statue, if the variable costs cannot be reduced, and if the targeted profit for sales of 25,000 statues is $120,000?

Planning Future Sales for a Service Business

P 8. Lending Hand Financial Corporation is a subsidiary of Gracey Enterprises. Its main business is processing loan applications. Last year, Bettina Brent, the manager of the corporation's Loan Department, established a policy of charging a $250 fee for every loan application processed. Next year's variable costs have been projected as follows: loan consultant's wages, $15.50 per hour (a loan application takes five hours to process); supplies, $2.40 per application; and other variable costs, $5.60 per application. Annual fixed costs include depreciation of equipment, $8,500; building rental, $14,000; promotional costs, $12,500; and other fixed costs, $8,099.

LO5 **Required**

1. Using the contribution margin approach, compute the number of loan applications the company must process to (a) break even and (b) earn a profit of $14,476.
2. Using the same approach and assuming promotional costs increase by $5,662, compute the number of applications the company must process to earn a profit of $20,000.

3. Assuming the original information and the processing of 500 applications, compute the loan application fee the company must charge if the targeted profit is $41,651.

4. **Manager Insight:** Brent's staff can handle a maximum of 750 loan applications. How much more can be spent on promotional costs if the highest fee tolerable to the customer is $280, if variable costs cannot be reduced, and if the targeted profit for the loan applications is $50,000?

ENHANCING Your Knowledge, Skills, and Critical Thinking

Conceptual Understanding Cases

LO1, LO2 **Concept of Cost Behavior**

C 1. Gulf Coast Shrimp Company is a small company. It owns an icehouse and processing building, a refrigerated van, and three shrimp boats. Bob Jones inherited the company from his father three months ago. The company employs three boat crews of four people each and five processing workers. Trey Goodfellow of Bayou Accountants, a local accounting firm, has kept the company's financial records for many years. In his last analysis of operations, Goodfellow stated that the company's fixed cost base of $100,000 is satisfactory for its type and size of business. However, variable costs have averaged 70 percent of sales over the last two years, which is too high for the volume of business. Last year, only 30 percent of the sales revenue of $300,000 contributed to covering fixed costs. As a result, the company reported a $10,000 operating loss.

Jones wants to improve the company's net income, but he is confused by Goodfellow's explanation of the fixed and variable costs. Prepare a response to Jones from Goodfellow in which you explain the concept of cost behavior as it relates to Gulf Coast's operations. Include ideas for improving the company's net income based on changes in fixed and variable costs.

LO5 **Comparison of Cost Behavior**

C 2. Allstate Insurance Co. and **USAA** are two well-known insurers of motorists. Allstate has agents and offices all over the country. USAA sells only through the mail and over the telephone or Internet. In addition to offering collision and liability coverage for automobiles, each company offers life insurance and homeowners' insurance. When a motorist buys auto insurance from Allstate, the agent generally offers life insurance and homeowners' insurance as well—a strategy that helps increase Allstate's profitability. Although USAA usually sells its policies at lower prices than Allstate does, it is a very profitable company.

Identify and discuss the role that fixed costs, sales mix, and contribution margin can play in increasing profitability. Suggest a performance measure that could be used to evaluate agents who sell auto insurance. What is the role of variable costs? What is it about the relationship of USAA's fixed and variable costs that allows the company to sell policies at lower prices than Allstate and yet remain profitable?

LO2 **Mixed Costs**

C 3. Officials of the Hidden Hills Golf and Tennis Club are in the process of preparing a budget for the year ending December 31. Because Ramon Saud, the club treasurer, has had difficulty with two expense items, the process has been delayed by more than four weeks. The two items are mixed costs—expenses for electricity and for repairs and maintenance—and Saud has been having trouble breaking them down into their variable and fixed components.

An accountant friend has suggested that he use the high-low method to divide the costs into their variable and fixed parts. The spending patterns and activity measures related to each cost during the past year are as follows:

	Electricity Expense		Repairs and Maintenance	
Month	Amount	Kilowatt Hours	Amount	Labor Hours
January	$ 7,500	210,000	$ 7,578	220
February	8,255	240,200	7,852	230
March	8,165	236,600	7,304	210
April	8,960	268,400	7,030	200
May	7,520	210,800	7,852	230
June	7,025	191,000	8,126	240
July	6,970	188,800	8,400	250
August	6,990	189,600	8,674	260
September	7,055	192,200	8,948	270
October	7,135	195,400	8,674	260
November	8,560	252,400	8,126	240
December	8,415	246,600	7,852	230
Totals	$92,550	2,622,000	$96,416	2,840

1. Using the high-low method, compute the variable cost rates used last year for each expense. What was the monthly fixed cost for electricity and for repairs and maintenance?
2. Compute the total variable cost and total fixed cost for each expense category for last year.
3. Saud believes that in the coming year, the electricity rate will increase by $0.005 and the repairs rate, by $1.20. Usage of all items and their fixed cost amounts will remain constant. Compute the projected total cost for each category. How will the cost increases affect the club's profits and cash flow?

LO3 C-V-P Analysis and Decision Making

C 4. The Goslar Corporation cuts granite, marble, and sandstone for use in building and restoring cathedrals throughout Europe. The German-based company has operations in Italy and Switzerland. Gunder Shillar, the controller, recently determined that the breakeven point was €325,000 in sales. For a quarterly planning meeting, Shillar must provide information about the following six proposals, which the planning team will discuss individually:

a. Increase the selling price of marble slabs by 10 percent.
b. Change the sales mix to respond to an increased demand for marble slabs—that is, increase production and sales of marble slabs and decrease the production and sales of sandstone slabs, the least profitable product.
c. Increase fixed production costs by €40,000 annually to cover depreciation on new stone-cutting equipment.
d. Increase variable costs by 1 percent to cover higher export duties on foreign sales.
e. Decrease the sales volume of sandstone slabs because of a reduction in demand in Eastern Europe.
f. Decrease the number of days a customer can defer payment without being charged interest.

1. For each proposal, determine whether cost-volume-profit (C-V-P) analysis would provide useful financial information.
2. Indicate how each proposal that lends itself to C-V-P analysis would affect profit.

LO3, LO4 **C-V-P Analysis**

C 5. Based in Italy, Datura, Ltd., is an international importer-exporter of pottery with distribution centers in the United States, Europe, and Australia. The company was very successful in its early years, but its profitability has since declined. As a member of a management team selected to gather information for Datura's next strategic planning meeting, you have been asked to review its most recent contribution income statement, which appears below.

Datura, Ltd.
Contribution Income Statement
For the Year Ended December 31, 20x7

Sales revenue		€13,500,000
Less variable costs		
Purchases	€6,000,000	
Distribution	2,115,000	
Sales commissions	1,410,000	
Total variable costs		9,525,000
Contribution margin		€ 3,975,000
Less fixed costs		
Distribution	€ 985,000	
Selling	1,184,000	
General and administrative	871,875	
Total fixed costs		3,040,875
Operating income		€ 934,125

In 20x7, Datura sold 15,000 sets of pottery.

1. For each set of pottery sold in 20x7, calculate the (a) selling price, (b) variable purchases cost, (c) variable distribution cost, (d) variable sales commission, and (e) contribution margin.
2. Calculate the breakeven point in units and in sales euros.
3. Historically, Datura's variable costs have been about 60 percent of sales. What was the ratio of variable costs to sales in 20x7? List three actions Datura could take to correct the difference.
4. How would fixed costs have been affected if Datura had sold only 14,000 sets of pottery in 20x7?

Interpreting Management Reports

LO4, LO5 **Planning Future Sales and Costs**

C 6. In a recent annual report, read management's letter to the stockholders. This section of an annual report typically discusses initiatives or actions that the company implemented during the year as part of its strategic plan. Identify at least three such initiatives or actions that you believe affected the company's annual sales or costs. Also identify one initiative or action the company is planning for the coming year that you believe will affect revenue or expenses.

Decision Analysis Using Excel

LO5 **Planning Future Sales**

C 7. As noted in **C 5**, Datura, Ltd., sold 15,000 sets of pottery in 20x7. In 20x8, Datura's strategic planning team targeted sales of 15,000 sets of pottery, reduced the selling price to £890 per set, increased sales commissions to 12 percent of the selling price, and decreased fixed distribution costs by 10 percent and variable distribution costs by 4 percent. It was assumed that all other costs would stay the same.

Based on an analysis of these changes, Sophia Callas, Datura's president, is concerned that the proposed strategic plan will not meet her goal of increasing Datura's operating income by 10 percent over last year's income and that the operating income will be less than last year's income. She has come to you for spreadsheet analysis of the proposed strategic plan and for analysis of a special order she just received from an Australian distributor for 4,500 sets of pottery. The order's selling price, variable purchases cost per unit, sales commission, and total fixed costs will be the same as for the rest of the business, but the variable distribution costs will be €160 per unit.

Using an Excel spreadsheet, complete the following tasks:

1. Calculate the targeted operating income for 20x8 using just the proposed strategic plan.
2. Prepare a budgeted contribution income statement for 20x8 based on just the strategic plan. Do you agree with Datura's president that the company's projected operating income for 20x8 will be less than the operating income for 20x7? Explain your answer.
3. Calculate the total contribution margin from the Australian sales.
4. Prepare a revised budgeted contribution income statement for 20x8 that includes the Australian order. (**Hint:** Combine the information from **2** and **3** above.)
5. Does Datura need the Australian sales to achieve its targeted operating income for 20x8?

Ethical Dilemma Case

LO4   **Breaking Even and Ethics**

C 8. Lesley Chomski is the supervisor of the New Product Division of MCO Corporation. Her annual bonus is based on the success of new products and is computed on the number of sales that exceed each new product's projected breakeven point. In reviewing the computations supporting her most recent bonus, Chomski found that although an order for 7,500 units of a new product called R56 had been refused by a customer and returned to the company, the order had been included in the calculations. She later discovered that the company's accountant had labeled the return an overhead expense and had charged the entire cost of the returned order to the plantwide Overhead account. The result was that product R56 appeared to exceed breakeven by more than 5,000 units and Chomski's bonus from this product amounted to over $800. What actions should Chomski take? Be prepared to discuss your response in class.

Internet Case

LO4, LO5   **Planning Future Sales and Costs**

C 9. The video rental business is changing as more customers are downloading movies from the Internet rather than renting them through the mail from online sites like **Netflix** or from stores like **Blockbuster**. Go to Blockbuster's and Netflix's websites and review the initiatives or actions that these companies are implementing as part of their strategic plan to address the changing nature of their business (see Management's Discussion in their annual reports).

1. Identify at least two initiatives or actions that one of these companes is implementing that you believe will affect revenue or expenses.
2. Identify the variable costs and fixed costs of these companies.
3. Speculate on how the changes that these companies are making will affect their breakeven point in units (movie rentals).

Group Activity Case

LO2, LO4 **Cost Behavior and Contribution Margin**

C 10. Visit a local fast-food restaurant. Observe all aspects of the operation and take notes on the entire process. Describe the procedures used to take, process, and fill an order and deliver the order to the customer. Based on your observations, make a list of the costs incurred by the operation. Identify at least three variable costs and three fixed costs. Can you identify any potential mixed costs? Why is the restaurant willing to sell a large drink for only a few cents more than a medium drink? How is the restaurant able to offer a "value meal" (e.g., sandwich, drink, and fries) for considerably less than those items would cost if they were bought separately? Bring your notes to class and be prepared to discuss your findings.

Your instructor will divide the class into groups to discuss the case. Summarize your group's discussion and ask one member of the group to present the summary to the rest of the class.

Business Communication Case

LO5 **C-V-P Analysis Applied**

C 11. Refer to the information in **C 5**. In January 20x8, Sophia Callas, the president of Datura, Ltd., conducted a strategic planning meeting. During the meeting, Phillipe Mazzeo, vice president of distribution, noted that because of a new contract with an international shipping line, the company's fixed distribution costs for 20x8 would be reduced by 10 percent and its variable distribution costs by 4 percent. Gino Roma, vice president of sales, offered the following information:

> We plan to sell 15,000 sets of pottery again in 20x8, but based on review of the competition, we are going to lower the selling price to €890 per set. To encourage increased sales, we will raise sales commissions to 12 percent of the selling price.

Sophia Callas is concerned that the changes described by Roma and Mazzeo may not improve operating income sufficiently in 20x8. If operating income does not increase by at least 10 percent, she will want to find other ways to reduce the company's costs. She asks you to evaluate the situation in a written report. Because it is already January of 20x8 and changes need to be made quickly, she requests your report within five days.

1. Prepare a budgeted contribution income statement for 20x8. Your report should show the budgeted (estimated) operating income based on the information provided above and in **C 5**. Will the changes improve operating income sufficiently? Explain.
2. In preparation for writing your report, answer the following questions:
   a. Why are you preparing the report?
   b. Who needs the report?
   c. What sources of information will you use?
   d. When is the report due?

The Budgeting Process

Budgeting is not only an essential part of planning; it also helps managers control, evaluate, and report on operations. When managers develop budgets, they match their organizational goals with the resources necessary to accomplish those goals. During the budgeting process, they evaluate operational, tactical, value chain, and capacity issues; assess how resources for operating, investing, and financing activities are currently being used and how they can be efficiently used in the future; and develop contingency budgets as business conditions change. Managers also use budget information to control daily operations, measure and report on performance outcomes, and allocate resources wisely. In this chapter, we describe the budgeting process, identify the elements of a master budget, and demonstrate how managers prepare operating budgets and financial budgets.

LEARNING OBJECTIVES

LO1 Define *budgeting,* and explain management's role in the budgeting process.

LO2 Identify the elements of a master budget in different types of organizations and the guidelines for preparing budgets.

LO3 Prepare the operating budgets that support the financial budgets.

LO4 Prepare a budgeted income statement, a cash budget, and a budgeted balance sheet.

- How is Johnson & Johnson's budgeting process linked to the company's long-term goals and objectives?

- How does Johnson & Johnson's budgeting process work?

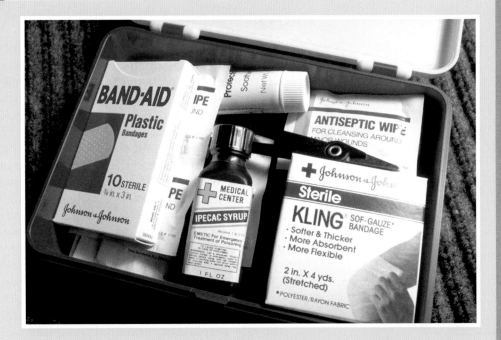

With products that range from baby powder, Band-Aids, Tylenol, and contact lenses to diagnostic and surgical devices, Johnson & Johnson is the largest and most diversified manufacturer of health care products in the world. It has had affiliated companies operating in Latin America, Europe, Africa, and Australia for more than fifty years. Today, it is a global family of over two hundred decentralized companies. Unifying the strategic planning of these companies' management teams are the common values and ethical principles expressed in Johnson & Johnson's credo, or mission statement. The strategic direction and major developments of the various companies are discussed at board meetings throughout the year and at meetings between management and board members. This ongoing dialogue provides managers with insight into the activities and direction of the company's businesses and is the basis for Johnson & Johnson's budgeting decisions.[1]

The Budgeting Process

Johnson&Johnson

Budgeting is the process of identifying, gathering, summarizing, and communicating financial and nonfinancial information about an organization's future activities. It is an essential part of the continuous planning that an organization must do to accomplish its long-term goals and intermediate objectives. The budgeting process provides managers of all types of organizations—including for-profit organizations, such as **Johnson & Johnson** and **Merck**, and not-for-profit organizations, such as the United Way and the United Nations—the opportunity to match their organizational goals with the resources necessary to accomplish those goals. As part of the ongoing budgeting process, managers evaluate operational, tactical, value chain, and capacity issues; assess how resources for operating, investing, and financing activities are currently being used and how they can be efficiently used in the future; and develop contingency budgets as business conditions change.

Budgets—plans of action based on forecasted transactions, activities, and events—are synonymous with managing an organization. They are essential to accomplishing the goals articulated in an organization's strategic plan. They are used to communicate information, coordinate activities and resource usage, motivate employees, and evaluate performance. For example, a board of directors may use budgets to determine managers' areas of responsibility and to measure managers' performance in those areas. Budgets are, of course, also used to manage and account for cash. Such budgets establish minimum or targeted levels of cash receipts and limits on the spending of cash for particular purposes.

Study Note

For-profit organizations often use the term *profit planning* rather than *budgeting.*

Budgets come in many forms. For example, a cash budget focuses on financial information; it shows, among other things, how cash resources will be allotted to operating, investing, and financing activities over a future period. A production budget, on the other hand, focuses on nonfinancial information; it shows planned production in units and identifies the activities needed to meet certain requirements or standards established during the planning process.

To compete successfully in today's global market, an organization must ensure that its managers have continuously updated operating data against which to measure performance. Thus, an ongoing budgeting process is especially important in the current business environment.

FOCUS ON BUSINESS PRACTICE

A Global Look at Leadership

The number of women in corporate leadership positions is increasing. For example, the president of **Southwest Airlines** is a woman, and before **Albertson's** was sold, the grocery chain's board of directors was predominantly female.

A survey of women serving on the corporate boards that govern the world's 200 largest companies reveals widely different participation rates among countries. Nor-

way has the greatest number of women serving on corporate boards, with a 33.3 percent participation rate, followed by the United States, with 17.5 percent; the United Kingdom, with 12.5 percent; and Malaysia and Finland, with 12.5 percent each. The countries in which the smallest number of women serve on corporate boards are Japan, with 0.7 percent; Spain, with 1.8 percent; Italy, with 1.8 percent; and China, with 2.7 percent.[2]

Shown here at an opening bell ceremony of the New York Stock Exchange are some of the women whom *Fortune* magazine named as the 50 most powerful women in business. The number of women in corporate leadership positions varies widely among countries. Norway has the largest number of women serving on corporate boards—a 33 percent participation rate—and it will soon have even more. A Norwegian law requires that by 2008, women make up 40 percent of the board membership of the country's corporations.

Budgeting and Goals

Long-Term Goals

Strategic planning is the process by which management establishes an organization's long-term goals. These goals define the strategic direction that an organization will take over a five- to ten-year period and are the basis for making annual operating plans and preparing budgets. You may recall from an earlier chapter that long-term goals should take into consideration economic and industry forecasts, employee-management relations, the structure and role of management, value chain considerations, organizational capacity, and any other operational and tactical issues facing the organization, such as the expected quality of products or services, growth rates, and desired market share.

Long-term goals cannot be vague; they must set specific tactical targets and timetables and assign responsibility for achieving the goals to specific personnel. For example, a long-term goal for a company that currently holds only 4 percent of its product's market share might specify that the vice president of marketing is to develop strategies to ensure that the company controls 10 percent of the market in five years and 15 percent by the end of ten years. An organization's strategic plan should include a range of long-term goals and give direction to its efforts to achieve those goals. It should include profit projections and describe new products or services in general terms.

Short-Term Goals

Annual operating plans involve every part of an enterprise and are much more detailed than long-term strategic plans. To formulate an annual operating plan, an organization must restate its long-term goals in terms of what it needs to accomplish during the next year. The process entails making decisions about sales and profit targets, human resource needs, and the introduction of new products or services. The short-term goals identified in an annual operating plan are the basis of an organization's operating budgets for the year.

Once management has established short-term goals, the organization's controller plays a central role in coordinating the budgeting process. This person designs a complete set of budget-development directions, including a timetable complete with deadlines for all parts of the year's operating plan,

Study Note

As plans are formulated for time periods closer to the current date, they become more specific and quantified. The annual budget is a very specific plan of action.

A recent survey of 1,000 leading U.K. companies has suggested that to keep pace with today's fast-changing business environment, managers would like more frequent budget revisions. The survey asked participants how often they revise their budgets and how often they believe budget revisions should be done. The survey results, summarized in the table to the right, show a trend toward more frequent revisions.[3]

Frequency	Current Practice	Desired Practice
Daily	—	1%
Weekly	—	4%
Monthly	24%	44%
Quarterly	36%	33%
Twice a year	15%	17%
Once a year	15%	—
No revision	10%	1%

and assigns clearly defined responsibilities for carrying out each part of the budget's development to specific individuals or management teams.

Depending on organizational practice, a budget may be reviewed and revised during the year. As pointed out in the focus box above, there is a growing trend toward more frequent budget revisions.

The Importance of Participation

Because an organization's main activities—such as production, sales, and employee training—take place at its lower levels, the information necessary for establishing a budget flows from the supervisors of those activities through middle managers to senior executives. Each person in this chain of communication thus plays a role in developing a budget, as well as in implementing it. If these individuals feel that they have a voice in setting the budget targets, they will be motivated to ensure that their departments attain those targets and stay within the budget. If they do not feel that they have a role in the budgeting process, motivation will suffer. The key to a successful budget is therefore **participative budgeting**, a process in which personnel at all levels of an organization actively engage in making decisions about the budget.

Because the controller is at the center of the budgeting process, collecting and distributing information and coordinating all budgeting activities, that person has considerable influence over the nature of the budgeting process. Participative budgeting depends on joint decision making, and to foster a climate in which that can take place, a controller must be able to communicate and negotiate effectively with people at all levels of an organization—from the senior executives who formulate the organization's long- and short-term goals to the middle managers and supervisors responsible for daily operations.

Senior executives also play a central role in determining the nature of the budgeting process. If they dictate targets instead of allowing middle managers and supervisors a voice in setting them, the budgeting process will be authoritative rather than participative. Without input from personnel at operational levels, the targets may be unrealistic and impossible to attain, which will further undermine the motivation of the managers and supervisors whose cooperation is essential for successful budget implementation. Problems may also arise if senior executives allow the controller to develop the budget without consulting other managers. In that case, managers may feel that budgeting is not a top priority and that budgets need not be taken seriously. Such difficulties can be avoided if senior executives recognize the importance of allowing personnel at all levels to play meaningful roles in the budgeting process.

Budget Implementation

As we have noted, an organization's controller plays a central role in designing and coordinating the budgeting process. The controller is part of a **budget committee** that has overall responsibility for budget implementation. This committee oversees each stage in the preparation of the organization's overall budget, mediates any departmental disputes that may arise in the process, and gives final approval to the budget. Other top managers who are part of the budget committee include the company's president and the vice presidents in charge of various functional areas, such as production, purchasing, marketing, and human resources. The make-up of the committee ensures that the budgeting process has a companywide perspective.

A budget may have to go through many revisions before it includes all planning decisions and has the approval of the budget committee. Once the committee approves the budget, periodic reports from department managers allow the committee to monitor the company's progress in attaining budget targets.

Successful budget implementation depends on two factors—clear communication and the support of top management. To ensure their cooperation in implementing the budget, all key persons involved must know what roles they are expected to play and must have specific directions on how to achieve their performance goals. Thus, the controller and other members of the budget committee must be very clear in communicating performance expectations and budget targets. Equally important, top management must show support for the budget and encourage its implementation. The process will succeed only if middle- and lower-level managers are confident that top management is truly interested in the outcome and is willing to reward personnel for meeting the budget targets. Today, many organizations have employee incentive plans that tie the achievement of budget targets to bonuses or other types of compensation.

 Study Note

Because good communication can eliminate many of the problems that typically arise in the budgeting process, companywide dialogue is extremely important.

Managers and the Budgeting Process

As Figure 1 shows, budgeting helps managers do their jobs. To illustrate the relationship between budgeting and managers, we will refer to the budgeting activities of Framecraft Company, a manufacturer specializing in high-quality plastic picture frames. Framecraft's sole stockholder, Chase Vitt, believes that the future growth of his company depends on a good budgeting process.

Planning   Budgets put managers' plans into operation. They reflect an organization's long- and short-term plans for achieving key success factors, such as high-quality products, reasonable costs, and timely delivery. Chase Vitt believes that by distributing workloads carefully and allotting resources to specific products, departments, and sales territories, budgets help his managers orchestrate short-term activities to accomplish long-term goals. Because

FOCUS ON BUSINESS PRACTICE
What Can Cause the Planning Process to Fail?

When chief financial officers were asked what caused their planning process to fail, these were the six factors they most commonly cited:[4]

- An inadequately defined strategy
- No clear link between strategy and the operational budget

- Lack of individual accountability for results
- Lack of meaningful performance measures
- Inadequate pay for performance
- Lack of appropriate data

■ **FIGURE 1**
The Management Process: To-Do's for Managers

To-Do's for Managers

• Plan
  – Review strategic, tactical, and operating objectives
  – Analyze and forecast sales
  – Analyze costs and determine cost formulas
  – Prepare operating budgets
  – Prepare financial budgets
  – Analyze effects of alternative scenarios on the budget
  – Finalize and approve budget

• Perform
  – Implement budget

• Evaluate
  – Compare actual results with budget, revise budget if needed

• Communicate
  – Prepare internal budget reports
  – Prepare comparative analyses of budget to actual results

⌐⌐⌐ Study Note

Budgeting is not only an essential part of planning; it also helps in controlling operations.

Vitt recognizes the benefits of participative budgeting, he includes personnel from all levels of the company in the budgeting process. To motivate employees to achieve the targets set forth in the budget, Framecraft Company awards bonuses for good performance. As measures of performance, managers have selected profits, number of units sold, number of defective units, and cycle time (the time to obtain, manufacture, and ship an order).

Performing Managers use budget information to control daily operations, measure performance outcomes, and allocate resources. The managers of Framecraft Company use budget information daily, weekly, and monthly to communicate expectations about performance, to measure performance and motivate employees, and to coordinate activities and allot resources among various departments. For example, Geoff Kovic, the production manager, uses the units of production specified in the budget as an operating target for his workers and the number of defective units as a performance measure to motivate them to manufacture high-quality products. Chase Vitt uses standard product costs, generated in the planning process, to submit bids and estimate profits.

Evaluating   When managers assess performance results, they look for variances between planned and actual performance and create solutions for the variances they detect. As we have already indicated, Framecraft Company's managers use the targets established in the planning stage as targets for actual performance. When Vitt and Kovic review Framecraft's results, they compare planned performance with actual performance. If they identify variances, they focus on finding solutions to the problems, which promotes continuous improvement of the company's products and processes. Framecraft Company's managers review their budgets on a regular basis because doing so helps them evaluate past performance and chart the course of future operations.

Communicating   Because budgets are plans of action based on forecasts of transactions, activities, and events, they serve as a reference point for many kinds of reports. For example, performance reports that support bonuses and promotions are based on budget information. Other budget-based reports support operating decisions. To provide continuous feedback about an organization's operating, investing, and financing activities, managers prepare and distribute reports based on budget information throughout the year.

S T O P • R E V I E W • A P P L Y

1-1. What is a budget? What types of information does a budget include?

1-2. How do long-term strategic plans and annual operating plans differ?

1-3. Who are the people responsible for ensuring that budget implementation is successful? What are their responsibilities?

Suggested answers to all Stop, Review, and Apply questions are available at http://college.hmco.com/accounting/needles/man_acc/8e/student_home.html.

The Master Budget

LO2   Identify the elements of a master budget in different types of organizations and the guidelines for preparing budgets.

A **master budget** consists of a set of operating budgets and a set of financial budgets that detail an organization's financial plans for a specific accounting period, generally a year. When a master budget covers an entire year, some of the operating and financial budgets may show planned results by month or by quarter. As the term implies, **operating budgets** are plans used in daily operations. They are also the basis for preparing the **financial budgets**, which are projections of financial results for the accounting period. Financial budgets include a budgeted income statement, a capital expenditures budget, a cash budget, and a budgeted balance sheet.

The budgeted financial statements—that is, the budgeted income statement and budgeted balance sheet—are also called **pro forma statements**, meaning that they show projections rather than actual results. Pro forma statements are often used to communicate business plans to external parties. If, for example, you wanted to obtain a bank loan so that you could start a new business, you would have to present the bank with a pro forma, or budgeted,

Study Note

Budgeted financial statements are often referred to as *forecasted financial statements, pro forma statements,* or *forward-looking statements.*

■ **FIGURE 2**
Preparation of a Master Budget for a Manufacturing Organization

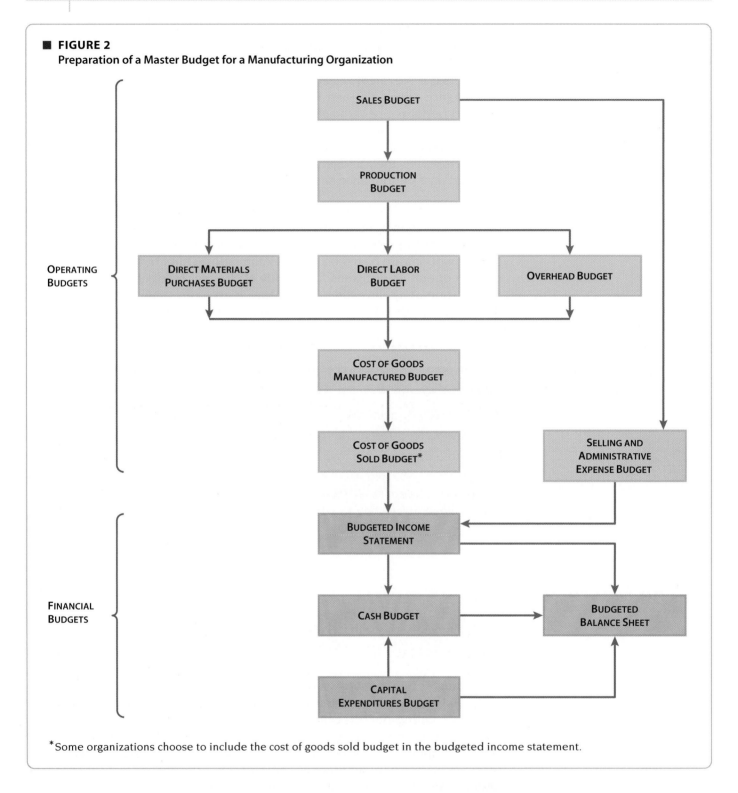

*Some organizations choose to include the cost of goods sold budget in the budgeted income statement.

income statement and balance sheet showing that you could repay the loan with cash generated by profitable operations.

Suppose you have started your own business. Whether it is a manufacturing, retail, or service organization, to manage it effectively, you would prepare a master budget each period. A master budget provides the information needed to match long-term goals to short-term activities and to plan the resources needed to ensure an organization's profitability and liquidity.

Figures 2, 3, and 4 display the elements of a master budget for a manufacturing organization, a retail organization, and a service organization, respec-

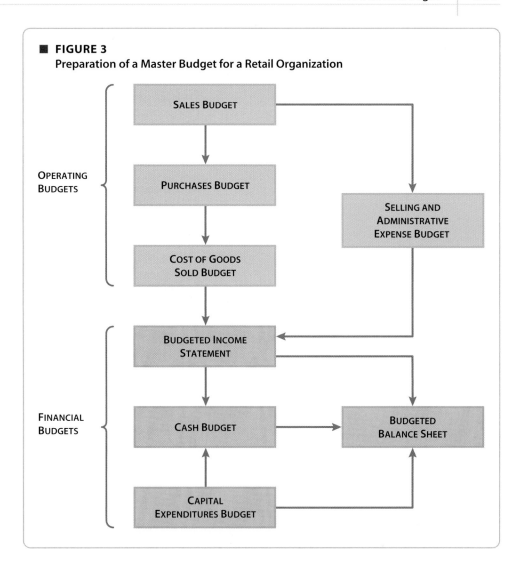

■ FIGURE 3
Preparation of a Master Budget for a Retail Organization

tively. As these illustrations indicate, the process of preparing a master budget is similar in all three types of organizations in that each prepares a set of operating budgets that serve as the basis for preparing the financial budgets. The process differs mainly in the kinds of operating budgets that each type of organization prepares.

The operating budgets of manufacturing organizations, such as **Johnson & Johnson**, **Intel**, and **John Deere**, include budgets for sales, production, direct materials, direct labor, overhead, selling and administrative expenses, and cost of goods manufactured. Retail organizations, such as **Nordstrom**, **Talbots**, and **Lowe's**, prepare a sales budget, a purchases budget, a selling and administrative expense budget, and a cost of goods sold budget. The operating budgets of service organizations, such as **Enterprise Rent-A-Car**, **UPS**, and **Amtrak**, include budgets for revenue (sales), labor, overhead, and selling and administrative expenses.

The sales budget (or, in service organizations, the service revenue budget) is prepared first because it is used to estimate sales volume and revenues. Once managers know the quantity of products or services to be sold and how many sales dollars to expect, they can develop other budgets that will enable them to manage their organization's resources so that they generate profits on those sales.

For example, in a retail organization, the purchases budget provides managers with information about the quantity of merchandise needed to meet the

■ **FIGURE 4**
Preparation of a Master Budget for a Service Organization

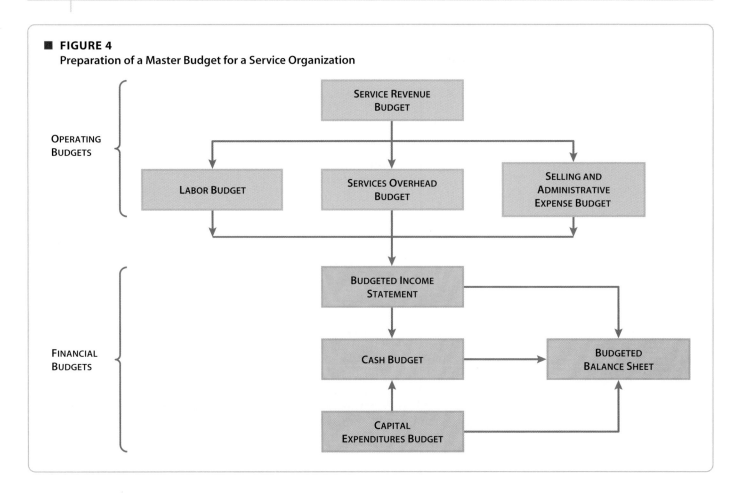

sales demand and yet maintain a minimum level of inventory. In a service organization, the labor budget provides information about the labor hours and labor rates needed to provide services and generate the revenues planned for each period; managers use this information in scheduling services and setting prices.

Because procedures for preparing budgets vary from organization to organization, there is no standard format for budget preparation. The only universal requirement is that budgets communicate the appropriate information to the reader in a clear and understandable manner. By keeping that in mind and using the following guidelines, managers can improve the quality of budgets in any type of organization:

1. Know the purpose of the budget.

2. Identify the user group and its information needs.

3. Identify sources of accurate, meaningful budget information. Such information may be gathered from documents or from interviews with employees, suppliers, or managers who work in the related areas.

4. Establish a clear format for the budget. A budget should begin with a clearly stated heading that includes the organization's name, the type of budget, and the accounting period under consideration. The budget's components should be clearly labeled, and the unit and financial data should be listed in an orderly manner.

5. Use appropriate formulas and calculations in deriving the quantitative information.

6. Revise the budget until it includes all planning decisions. Several revisions may be required before the final version is ready for distribution.

S T O P • R E V I E W • A P P L Y

2-1. What is a master budget? What is its purpose?

2-2. In what ways are the master budgets of manufacturing, retail, and service organizations similar?

2-3. List the guidelines for preparing a budget.

Operating Budgets

LO3 Prepare the operating budgets that support the financial budgets.

Although procedures for preparing operating budgets vary, the tools used in the process do not. They include cost behavior analysis, cost-volume-profit (C-V-P) analysis, and a product costing method. In this section, we use Framecraft Company to illustrate how a manufacturing organization prepares its operating budgets. Because Framecraft makes only one product—a plastic picture frame—it prepares only one of each type of operating budget. Organizations that manufacture a variety of products or provide many types of services may prepare either separate operating budgets or one comprehensive budget for each product or service.

The Sales Budget

Study Note

The sales budget is the only budget based on an estimate of customer demand. Other budgets for the period are prepared from it and are based on the numbers it provides.

As we indicated earlier, the first step in preparing a master budget is to prepare a sales budget. A **sales budget** is a detailed plan, expressed in both units and dollars, that identifies the sales expected during an accounting period. Sales managers use this information to plan sales- and marketing-related activities and to determine their human, physical, and technical resource needs. Accountants use the information to determine estimated cash receipts for the cash budget.

The following equation is used to determine the total budgeted sales:

$$\begin{array}{c} \text{Total} \\ \text{Budgeted} \\ \text{Sales} \end{array} = \begin{array}{c} \text{Estimated} \\ \text{Selling Price} \\ \text{per Unit} \end{array} \times \begin{array}{c} \text{Estimated} \\ \text{Sales in} \\ \text{Units} \end{array}$$

Although the calculation is easy, selecting the best estimates for the selling price per unit and the sales demand in units can be difficult. An estimated selling price below the current selling price may be needed if competitors are currently selling the same product or service at lower prices or if the organization wants to increase its share of the market. On the other hand, if the organization has improved the quality of its product or service by using more expensive materials or processes, the estimated selling price may have to be higher than the current price.

The estimated sales volume is very important because it will affect the level of operating activities and the amount of resources needed for operations. The resources needed for production, packing, shipping, accounting,

EXHIBIT 1 ▶ | **Sales Budget**

Framecraft Company
Sales Budget
For the Year Ended December 31, 20x9

	Quarter				
	1	**2**	**3**	**4**	**Year**
Sales in units	10,000	30,000	10,000	40,000	90,000
× Selling price per unit	× $5	× $5	× $5	× $5	× $5
Total sales	$50,000	$150,000	$50,000	$200,000	$450,000

purchasing, selling, and administrative activities will increase in varying degrees with increases in the estimated sales volume. To help estimate sales volume, managers often use a **sales forecast**, which is a projection of sales demand (the estimated sales in units) based on an analysis of external and internal factors. The external factors include

1. The state of the local and national economies

2. The state of the industry's economy

3. The nature of the competition and its sales volume and selling price

Internal factors taken into consideration in a sales forecast include

1. The number of units sold in prior periods

2. The organization's credit policies

3. The organization's collection policies

4. The organization's pricing policies

5. Any new products that the organization plans to introduce to the market

6. The capacity of the organization's manufacturing facilities

Exhibit 1 illustrates Framecraft Company's sales budget for the year 20x9. The budget shows the estimated number of unit sales and dollar revenue amounts for each quarter and for the entire year. Because a sales forecast indicated a highly competitive marketplace, Framecraft's managers have estimated a selling price of $5 per unit. The sales forecast also indicated highly seasonal sales activity; the estimated sales volume therefore varies from 10,000 to 40,000 per quarter.

The Production Budget

A **production budget** is a detailed plan showing the number of units that a company must produce to meet budgeted sales and inventory needs. Production managers use this information to plan for the materials and human resources that production-related activities will require. To prepare a production budget, managers must know the budgeted number of unit sales (which is specified in the sales budget) and the desired level of ending finished goods inventory for each period in the budget year. That level is often stated as a percentage of the next period's budgeted unit sales. For example, Framecraft

EXHIBIT 2 ▶ | Production Budget

Framecraft Company
Production Budget
For the Year Ended December 31, 20x9

	Quarter				
	1	2	3	4	Year
Sales in units	10,000	30,000	10,000	40,000	90,000
Plus desired units of ending finished goods inventory	3,000	1,000	4,000	1,500	1,500
Desired total units	13,000	31,000	14,000	41,500	91,500
Less desired units of beginning finished goods inventory	1,000	3,000	1,000	4,000	1,000
Total production units	12,000	28,000	13,000	37,500	90,500

Company's desired level of ending finished goods inventory is 10 percent of the next quarter's budgeted unit sales. (Its desired level of beginning finished goods inventory is 10 percent of the current quarter's budgeted unit sales.)

The following formula identifies the production needs for each accounting period:

$$\begin{matrix} \text{Total} \\ \text{Production} \\ \text{Units} \end{matrix} = \begin{matrix} \text{Budgeted} \\ \text{Sales in} \\ \text{Units} \end{matrix} + \begin{matrix} \text{Desired Units of} \\ \text{Ending Finished} \\ \text{Goods Inventory} \end{matrix} - \begin{matrix} \text{Desired Units of} \\ \text{Beginning} \\ \text{Finished Goods} \\ \text{Inventory} \end{matrix}$$

Exhibit 2 shows Framecraft Company's production budget for 20x9. Notice that each quarter's desired total units of ending finished goods inventory become the next quarter's desired total units of beginning finished goods inventory. Because unit sales of 15,000 are budgeted for the first quarter of 201x, the ending finished goods inventory for the fourth quarter of 20x9 is 1,500 units (.10 × 15,000 units), which is the same as the desired number of units of ending finished goods inventory for the entire year. Similarly, the number of desired units for the first quarter's beginning finished goods inventory—1,000—is the same as the desired number of units of beginning finished goods inventory for the entire year.

The Direct Materials Purchases Budget

A **direct materials purchases budget** is a detailed plan that identifies the quantity of purchases required to meet budgeted production and inventory needs and the costs associated with those purchases. A purchasing department uses this information to plan purchases of direct materials. Accountants use the same information to estimate cash payments to suppliers.

To prepare a direct materials purchases budget, managers must know what production needs will be in each accounting period in the budget; this information is provided by the production budget. They must also know the desired level of the direct materials inventory for each period and the per-unit cost of direct materials. The desired level of ending direct materials inventory is usually stated as a percentage of the next period's production needs. Framecraft's desired level of ending direct materials inventory is 20 percent of the

EXHIBIT 3 ▶   **Direct Materials Purchases Budget**

Framecraft Company
Direct Materials Purchases Budget
For the Year Ended December 31, 20x9

	Quarter				
	1	2	3	4	Year
Total production units	12,000	28,000	13,000	37,500	90,500
× 10 ounces per unit	× 10	× 10	× 10	× 10	× 10
Total production needs in ounces	120,000	280,000	130,000	375,000	905,000
Plus desired ounces of ending direct materials inventory	56,000	26,000	75,000	30,000	30,000
	176,000	306,000	205,000	405,000	935,000
Less desired ounces of beginning direct materials inventory	24,000	56,000	26,000	75,000	24,000
Total ounces of direct materials to be purchased	152,000	250,000	179,000	330,000	911,000
× Cost per ounce	× $.05	× $.05	× $.05	× $.05	× $.05
Total cost of direct materials purchases	$ 7,600	$ 12,500	$ 8,950	$ 16,500	$ 45,550

next quarter's budgeted production needs. (Its desired level of beginning direct materials inventory is 20 percent of the current quarter's budgeted production needs.)

The first step in preparing a direct materials purchases budget is to calculate each period's total production needs in units of direct materials. Plastic is the only direct material used in Framecraft Company's picture frames; each frame requires 10 ounces of plastic. Framecraft's managers therefore calculate units of production needs in ounces; they multiply the number of frames budgeted for production in a quarter by the 10 ounces of plastic that each frame requires.

In the second step, the following formula is used to determine the quantity of direct materials to be purchased during each accounting period in the budget:

$$\begin{matrix} \text{Total Units of} \\ \text{Direct} \\ \text{Materials to} \\ \text{Be Purchased} \end{matrix} = \begin{matrix} \text{Total Production} \\ \text{Needs in} \\ \text{Units of Direct} \\ \text{Materials} \end{matrix} + \begin{matrix} \text{Desired Units of} \\ \text{Ending Direct} \\ \text{Materials} \\ \text{Inventory} \end{matrix} - \begin{matrix} \text{Desired Units of} \\ \text{Beginning Direct} \\ \text{Materials} \\ \text{Inventory} \end{matrix}$$

The third step is to calculate the cost of the direct materials purchases by multiplying the total number of unit purchases by the direct materials cost. Framecraft's Purchasing Department has estimated the cost of the plastic used in the picture frames at $.05 per ounce.

Exhibit 3 shows Framecraft's direct materials purchases budget for 20x9. Notice that each quarter's desired units of ending direct materials inventory become the next quarter's desired units of beginning direct materials inventory. The company's budgeted number of units for the first quarter of 201x is 150,000 ounces; its ending direct materials inventory for the fourth quarter of 20x9 is therefore 30,000 ounces (.20 × 150,000 ounces), which is the same as the number of desired units of ending direct materials inventory for the entire year. Similarly, the number of desired units for the first quarter's beginning direct materials inventory—24,000 ounces—is the same as the beginning amount for the entire year.

The Direct Labor Budget

A **direct labor budget** is a detailed plan that estimates the direct labor hours needed during an accounting period and the associated costs. Production managers use estimated direct labor hours to plan how many employees will be required during the period and the hours that each will work, and accountants use estimated direct labor costs to plan for cash payments to the workers. Managers of human resources use the information in a direct labor budget in deciding whether to hire new employees or reduce the existing work force, and also as a guide in training employees and preparing schedules of employee fringe benefits.

The first step in preparing a direct labor budget is to estimate the total direct labor hours by multiplying the estimated direct labor hours per unit by the anticipated units of production (see Exhibit 2). The second step in preparing such a budget is to calculate the total budgeted direct labor cost by multiplying the estimated total direct labor hours by the estimated direct labor cost per hour. A company's human resources department provides an estimate of the hourly labor wage.

$$\begin{array}{c}\text{Total Budgeted} \\ \text{Direct Labor Costs}\end{array} = \begin{array}{c}\text{Estimated Total Direct} \\ \text{Labor Hours}\end{array} \times \begin{array}{c}\text{Estimated Direct} \\ \text{Labor Cost per Hour}\end{array}$$

Exhibit 4 shows how Framecraft Company uses these formulas to estimate the total direct labor cost. Framecraft's Production Department needs an estimated one-tenth (.10) of a direct labor hour to complete one unit. Its Human Resources Department estimates a direct labor cost of $6 per hour.

EXHIBIT 4 ▶

Direct Labor Budget

Framecraft Company
Direct Labor Budget
For the Year Ended December 31, 20x9

	Quarter				
	1	2	3	4	Year
Total production units	12,000	28,000	13,000	37,500	90,500
× Direct labor hours per unit	× .1	× .1	× .1	× .1	× .1
Total direct labor hours	1,200	2,800	1,300	3,750	9,050
× Direct labor cost per hour	× $6	× $6	× $6	× $6	× $6
Total direct labor cost	$ 7,200	$16,800	$ 7,800	$22,500	$54,300

EXHIBIT 5 ▶ | Overhead Budget

Framecraft Company
Overhead Budget
For the Year Ended December 31, 20x9

			Quarter		
	1	2	3	4	Year
Variable overhead costs					
Factory supplies	$ 2,160	$ 5,040	$ 2,340	$ 6,750	$ 16,290
Employee benefits	2,880	6,720	3,120	9,000	21,720
Inspection	1,080	2,520	1,170	3,375	8,145
Maintenance and repair	1,920	4,480	2,080	6,000	14,480
Utilities	3,600	8,400	3,900	11,250	27,150
Total variable overhead costs	$11,640	$27,160	$12,610	$36,375	$ 87,785
Fixed overhead costs					
Depreciation, machinery	$ 2,810	$ 2,810	$ 2,810	$ 2,810	$ 11,240
Depreciation, building	3,225	3,225	3,225	3,225	12,900
Supervision	9,000	9,000	9,000	9,000	36,000
Maintenance and repair	2,150	2,150	2,150	2,150	8,600
Other overhead expenses	3,175	3,175	3,175	3,175	12,700
Total fixed overhead costs	$20,360	$20,360	$20,360	$20,360	$ 81,440
Total overhead costs	$32,000	$47,520	$32,970	$56,735	$169,225

The Overhead Budget

An **overhead budget** is a detailed plan of anticipated manufacturing costs, other than direct materials and direct labor costs, that must be incurred to meet budgeted production needs. It has two purposes: to integrate the overhead cost budgets developed by the managers of production and production-related departments, and to group information for the calculation of overhead rates for the next accounting period. The format for presenting information in an overhead budget is flexible. Grouping information by activities is useful for organizations that use activity-based costing. This approach makes it easier for accountants to determine the application rates for each cost pool.

As Exhibit 5 shows, Framecraft Company prefers to group information into variable and fixed costs to facilitate C-V-P analysis. The single overhead rate is the estimated total overhead costs divided by the estimated total direct labor hours. Framecraft's predetermined overhead rate for 20x9 is $18.70 per direct labor hour ($169,225 ÷ 9,050 direct labor hours), or $1.87 per unit produced ($18.70 per direct labor hour × .10 direct labor hour per unit). The variable portion of the overhead rate is $9.70 per direct labor hour ($87,785 ÷ 9,050 direct labor hours), which includes factory supplies, $1.80; employee benefits, $2.40; inspection, $.90; maintenance and repair, $1.60; and utilities, $3.00.

The Selling and Administrative Expense Budget

A **selling and administrative expense budget** is a detailed plan of operating expenses, other than those related to production, that are needed to support

EXHIBIT 6 ▶

Selling and Administrative Expense Budget

Framecraft Company
Selling and Administrative Expense Budget
For the Year Ended December 31, 20x9

	Quarter				
	1	2	3	4	Year
Variable selling and administrative expenses					
Delivery expenses	$ 800	$ 2,400	$ 800	$ 3,200	$ 7,200
Sales commissions	1,000	3,000	1,000	4,000	9,000
Accounting	700	2,100	700	2,800	6,300
Other administrative expenses	400	1,200	400	1,600	3,600
Total variable selling and administrative expenses	$ 2,900	$ 8,700	$ 2,900	$11,600	$ 26,100
Fixed selling and administrative expenses					
Sales salaries	$ 4,500	$ 4,500	$ 4,500	$ 4,500	$ 18,000
Executive salaries	12,750	12,750	12,750	12,750	51,000
Depreciation–office equipment	925	925	925	925	3,700
Taxes and insurance	1,700	1,700	1,700	1,700	6,800
Total fixed selling and administrative expenses	$19,875	$19,875	$19,875	$19,875	$ 79,500
Total selling and administrative expenses	$22,775	$28,575	$22,775	$31,475	$105,600

 Study Note

Remember that selling and administrative expenses are period costs, not product costs.

sales and overall operations during an accounting period. Accountants use this budget to estimate cash payments for products or services not used in production-related activities.

Framecraft Company's selling and administrative expense budget for 20x9 appears in Exhibit 6. The company groups its selling and administrative expenses into variable and fixed components for purposes of cost behavior analysis, C-V-P analysis, and profit planning. Framecraft Company's estimated variable selling and administrative expense rate for 20x9 is $.29 per unit sold, which includes delivery expenses, $.08; sales commissions, $.10; accounting, $.07; and other administrative expenses, $.04.

The Cost of Goods Manufactured Budget

A **cost of goods manufactured budget** is a detailed plan that summarizes the estimated costs of production during an accounting period. The sources of information for total manufacturing costs are the direct materials, direct labor, and overhead budgets. Most manufacturing organizations anticipate some work in process at the beginning or end of the period covered by a budget. However, Framecraft Company has a policy of no work in process on December 31 of any year. Exhibit 7 summarizes the company's estimated costs of

EXHIBIT 7 ▶

Cost of Goods Manufactured Budget			

		Framecraft Company **Cost of Goods Manufactured Budget** **For the Year Ended December 31, 20x9**	**Sources of Data**
Direct materials used			
Direct materials inventory, December 31, 20x8	$ 1,200*		**Exhibit 3**
Purchases for 20x9	45,550		**Exhibit 3**
Cost of direct materials available for use	$46,750		
Less direct materials inventory, December 31, 20x9	1,500*		**Exhibit 3**
Cost of direct materials used		$45,250	
Direct labor costs		54,300	**Exhibit 4**
Overhead costs		169,225	**Exhibit 5**
Total manufacturing costs		$268,775	
Work in process inventory, December 31, 20x8		—†	
Less work in process inventory, December 31, 20x9		—†	
Cost of goods manufactured		$268,775	

* The desired direct materials inventory balance at December 31, 20x8, is $1,200 (24,000 ounces × $.05 per ounce); at December 31, 20x9, it is $1,500 (30,000 ounces × $.05 per ounce).
† It is the company's policy to have no units in process at the beginning or end of the year.

production in 20x9. (The right-hand column of the exhibit shows the sources of key data.) The budgeted, or standard, product unit cost for one picture frame is rounded to $2.97 ($268,775 ÷ 90,500 units).

S T O P • R E V I E W • A P P L Y

3-1. What is a sales forecast? What internal and external factors does a sales forecast take into consideration?

3-2. What are the three steps in preparing a direct materials purchases budget?

3-3. What are the two steps in preparing a direct labor budget?

3-4. Why does a selling and administrative expense budget use units sold rather than units produced?

Production Budget Sample Company is preparing a production budget for the year. The company's policy is to maintain a finished goods inventory equal to one-half of the next month's sales. Sales of 4,000 units are budgeted for April. Use the following monthly production budget for the first quarter to determine how many units should be produced in January, February, and March:

	January	February	March
Sales in units	3,000	2,400	6,000
Add desired units of ending finished goods inventory	——	——	——
Desired total units			
Less desired units of beginning finished goods inventory	——	——	——
Total production units	═══	═══	═══

SOLUTION

	January	February	March
Sales in units	3,000	2,400	6,000
Add desired units of ending finished goods inventory	1,200	3,000	2,000
Desired total units	4,200	5,400	8,000
Less desired units of beginning finished goods inventory	1,500	1,200	3,000
Total production units	2,700	4,200	5,000

Financial Budgets

LO4 Prepare a budgeted income statement, a cash budget, and a budgeted balance sheet.

With revenues and expenses itemized in the operating budgets, an organization's controller is able to prepare the financial budgets, which, as we noted earlier, are projections of financial results for the accounting period. Financial budgets include a budgeted income statement, a capital expenditures budget, a cash budget, and a budgeted balance sheet.

The Budgeted Income Statement

A **budgeted income statement** projects an organization's net income for an accounting period based on the revenues and expenses estimated for that period. Exhibit 8 shows Framecraft Company's budgeted income statement for 20x9. The company's expenses include 8 percent interest paid on a $70,000 note payable and income taxes paid at a rate of 30 percent.

Information about projected sales and costs comes from several operating budgets, as indicated by the right-hand column of Exhibit 8, which identifies the sources of key data and makes it possible to trace how Framecraft company's budgeted income statement was developed. At this point, you can review the overall preparation of the operating budgets and the budgeted income statement by comparing the preparation flow in Figure 2 with the budgets in Exhibits 1 through 8. You will notice that Framecraft Company has no budget for cost of goods sold; that information is included in its budgeted income statement.

The Capital Expenditures Budget

A **capital expenditures budget** is a detailed plan outlining the anticipated amount and timing of capital outlays for long-term assets during an accounting period. Managers rely on the information in a capital expenditures budget

EXHIBIT 8 ▶

Budgeted Income Statement

Framecraft Company
Budgeted Income Statement
For the Year Ended December 31, 20x9

			Sources of Data
Sales		$450,000	**Exhibit 1**
Cost of goods sold			
Finished goods inventory, December 31, 20x8	$ 2,970		**Exhibit 2**
Cost of goods manufactured	268,775		**Exhibit 7**
Cost of finished goods available for sale	$271,745		
Less finished goods inventory, December 31, 20x9	4,455		**Exhibit 2**
Cost of goods sold		267,290	
Gross margin		$182,710	
Selling and administrative expenses		105,600	**Exhibit 6**
Income from operations		$ 77,110	
Interest expense (8% × $70,000)		5,600	
Income before income taxes		$ 71,510	
Income taxes expense (30%)		21,453	
Net income		$ 50,057	

Note: Finished goods inventory balances assume that product unit costs were the same in 20x8 and 20x9:

December 31, 20x8	December 31, 20x9
1,000 units (Exhibit 2)	1,500 units (Exhibit 2)
× $2.97*	× $2.97*
$2,970	$4,455

*$268,775 ÷ 90,500 units (Exhibits 7 and 2)

when making decisions about such matters as buying equipment, building a new plant, purchasing and installing a materials handling system, or acquiring another business. Framecraft Company's capital expenditures budget for 20x9 includes $30,000 for the purchase of a new extrusion machine. The company plans to pay $15,000 in the first quarter of 20x9, when the order is placed, and $15,000 in the second quarter of 20x9, when it receives the extrusion machine. This information is necessary for preparing the company's cash budget. We discuss capital expenditures in more detail in another chapter.

The Cash Budget

A **cash budget** is a projection of the cash that an organization will receive and the cash that it will pay out during an accounting period. It summarizes the cash flow prospects of all transactions considered in the master budget. The information that the cash budget provides enables managers to plan for short-term loans when the cash balance is low and for short-term investments when the cash balance is high. Table 1 shows how the elements of a cash budget relate to operating, investing, and financing activities.

A cash budget excludes planned noncash transactions, such as depreciation expense, amortization expense, issuance and receipt of stock dividends, uncollectible accounts expense, and gains and losses on sales of assets. Some

A worker oversees a newspaper being printed out on a large press. A printing press like this is a long-term asset and would be included in a company's capital expenditures budget. This budget is a detailed plan outlining the amount and timing of capital outlays for long-term assets during an accounting period.

organizations also exclude deferred taxes and accrued interest from the cash budget.

The following formula is useful in preparing a cash budget:

$$\begin{matrix} \text{Estimated} \\ \text{Ending Cash} \\ \text{Balance} \end{matrix} = \begin{matrix} \text{Total} \\ \text{Estimated} \\ \text{Cash Receipts} \end{matrix} - \begin{matrix} \text{Total} \\ \text{Estimated} \\ \text{Cash Payments} \end{matrix} + \begin{matrix} \text{Estimated} \\ \text{Beginning Cash} \\ \text{Balance} \end{matrix}$$

Estimates of cash receipts are based on information from several sources. Among these sources are the sales budget, the budgeted income statement, cash budgets from previous periods, cash collection records and analyses of collection trends, and records pertaining to notes, stocks, and bonds. Information used in estimating cash payments comes from the operating budgets, the

TABLE 1.	Elements of a Cash Budget	
Activities	**Cash Receipts From**	**Cash Payments For**
Operating	Cash sales	Purchases of direct materials
	Cash collections on credit sales	Purchases of indirect materials
	Interest income from investments	Direct labor
	Cash dividends from investments	Overhead expenses
		Selling expenses
		Administrative expenses
		Interest expense
		Income taxes
Investing	Sale of investments	Purchases of investments
	Sale of long-term assets	Purchases of long-term assets
Financing	Proceeds from loans	Loan repayments
	Proceeds from issue of stock	Cash dividends to stockholders
	Proceeds from issue of bonds	Purchases of treasury stock
		Retirement of bonds

Note: Classifications of cash receipts and cash payments correspond to those in a statement of cash flows.

EXHIBIT 9 ▶ | **Schedule of Expected Cash Collections from Customers**

Framecraft Company
Schedule of Expected Cash Collections from Customers
For the Year Ended December 31, 20x9

	Quarter				
	1	2	3	4	Year
Accounts receivable, Dec. 31, 20x8	$38,000	$ 10,000	$ —	$ —	$ 48,000
Cash sales	10,000	30,000	10,000	40,000	90,000
Collections of credit sales					
First quarter ($40,000)	24,000	12,000	4,000		40,000
Second quarter ($120,000)		72,000	36,000	12,000	120,000
Third quarter ($40,000)			24,000	12,000	36,000
Fourth quarter ($160,000)				96,000	96,000
Total cash to be collected from customers	$72,000	$124,000	$74,000	$160,000	$430,000

budgeted income statement, the capital expenditures budget, the previous year's financial statements, and loan records.

In estimating cash receipts and cash payments for the cash budget, many organizations prepare supporting schedules. For example, Framecraft Company's controller converts credit sales to cash inflows and purchases made on credit to cash outflows, and then discloses those conversions on schedules that support the cash budget. The schedule in Exhibit 9 shows the cash that Framecraft Company expects to collect from customers in 20x9. Cash sales represent 20 percent of the company's expected sales; the other 80 percent are credit sales. Experience has shown that Framecraft collects payments for 60 percent of all credit sales in the quarter of sale, 30 percent in the quarter following sale, and 10 percent in the second quarter following sale.

As you can see in Exhibit 9, Framecraft's balance of accounts receivable was $48,000 at December 31, 20x8. The company expects to collect $38,000 of that amount in the first quarter of 20x9 and the remaining $10,000 in the second quarter. At December 31, 20x9, the estimated ending balance of accounts receivable is $68,000—that is, $4,000 from the third quarter's credit sales [($50,000 × .80) × .10] plus $64,000 from the fourth quarter's sales [($200,000 × .80) × .40]. The expected cash collections for each quarter and for the year appear in the total cash receipts section of the cash budget.

Exhibit 10 shows Framecraft's schedule of expected cash payments for direct materials in 20x9. This information is summarized in the first line of the cash payments section of the company's cash budget. Framecraft pays 50 percent of the invoices it receives in the quarter of purchase and the other 50 percent in the following quarter. The beginning balance of accounts payable for the first quarter is $4,200. At December 31, 20x9, the estimated ending balance of accounts payable is $8,250 (50 percent of the $16,500 of direct materials purchases in the fourth quarter).

EXHIBIT 10 ▶ | **Schedule of Expected Cash Payments for Direct Materials**

Framecraft Company
Schedule of Expected Cash Payments for Direct Materials
For the Year Ended December 31, 20x9

	Quarter				
	1	2	3	4	Year
Accounts payable, Dec. 31, 20x8	$4,200	$ —	$ —	$ —	$ 4,200
First quarter ($7,600)	3,800	$ 3,800			7,600
Second quarter ($12,500)		6,250	$ 6,250		12,500
Third quarter ($8,950)			4,475	$ 4,475	8,950
Fourth quarter ($16,500)				8,250	8,250
Total cash payments for direct materials	$8,000	$10,050	$10,725	$12,725	$41,500

Framecraft's cash budget for 20x9 appears in Exhibit 11. It shows the estimated cash receipts and cash payments for the period, as well as the cash increase or decrease. The cash increase or decrease plus the period's beginning cash balance equals the ending cash balance anticipated for the period. As you can see in Exhibit 11, the beginning cash balance for the first quarter is $20,000. This amount is also the beginning cash balance for the year. Note that each quarter's budgeted ending cash balance becomes the next quarter's beginning cash balance. Also note that equal income tax payments are made quarterly. You can trace the development of this budget by referring to the data sources listed in the exhibit.

Many organizations maintain a minimum cash balance to provide a margin of safety against uncertainty. If the ending cash balance on the cash budget falls below the minimum level required, short-term borrowing may be necessary to cover planned cash payments during the year. If the ending cash balance is significantly larger than the organization needs, it may invest the excess cash in short-term securities to generate additional income. For example, if Framecraft Company wants a minimum of $10,000 cash available at the end of each quarter, its balance of $7,222 at the end of the first quarter indicates that there is a problem. Framecraft's management has several options for handling this problem. It can borrow cash to cover the first quarter's cash needs, delay purchasing the new extrusion machine until the second quarter, or reduce some of the operating expenses. On the other hand, the balance at the end of the fourth quarter may be higher than the company wants, in which case management might invest a portion of the idle cash in short-term securities.

FOCUS ON BUSINESS PRACTICE
Does Budgeting Lead to a Breakdown in Corporate Ethics?

When budgets are used to force performance results, as they were at **WorldCom**, breaches in corporate ethics can occur. One former WorldCom employee described the situation at that company as follows: "You would have a budget, and he [WorldCom CEO Bernard Ebbers] would mandate that you had to be 2% under budget. Nothing else was acceptable."[5] This type of restrictive budget policy appears to have been a factor in many of the recent corporate scandals.

▼ **EXHIBIT 11**

Cash Budget

						Sources of Data
Framecraft Company						
Cash Budget						
For the Year Ended December 31, 20x9						

	Quarter					
	1	**2**	**3**	**4**	**Year**	
Cash receipts						
Cash collections						
from customers	$ 72,000	$124,000	$74,000	$160,000	$430,000	**Exhibit 9**
Total cash receipts	$ 72,000	$124,000	$74,000	$160,000	$430,000	
Cash payments						
Direct materials	$ 8,000	$ 10,050	$10,725	$ 12,725	$ 41,500	**Exhibit 10**
Direct labor	7,200	16,800	7,800	22,500	54,300	**Exhibit 4**
Factory supplies	2,160	5,040	2,340	6,750	16,290	
Employee benefits	2,880	6,720	3,120	9,000	21,720	
Inspection	1,080	2,520	1,170	3,375	8,145	
Variable maintenance and repair	1,920	4,480	2,080	6,000	14,480	
Utilities	3,600	8,400	3,900	11,250	27,150	**Exhibit 5**
Supervision	9,000	9,000	9,000	9,000	36,000	
Fixed maintenance and repair	2,150	2,150	2,150	2,150	8,600	
Other overhead expenses	3,175	3,175	3,175	3,175	12,700	
Delivery expenses	800	2,400	800	3,200	7,200	
Sales commissions	1,000	3,000	1,000	4,000	9,000	
Accounting	700	2,100	700	2,800	6,300	
Other administrative expenses	400	1,200	400	1,600	3,600	**Exhibit 6**
Sales salaries	4,500	4,500	4,500	4,500	18,000	
Executive salaries	12,750	12,750	12,750	12,750	51,000	
Taxes and insurance	1,700	1,700	1,700	1,700	6,800	
Capital expenditures*	15,000	15,000			30,000	
Interest expense	1,400	1,400	1,400	1,400	5,600	**Exhibit 8**
Income taxes	5,363	5,363	5,363	5,364	21,453	
Total cash payments	$ 84,778	$117,748	$74,073	$123,239	$399,838	
Cash increase (decrease)	$(12,778)	$ 6,252	$ (73)	$ 36,761	$ 30,162	
Beginning cash balance	20,000	7,222	13,474	13,401	20,000	
Ending cash balance	$ 7,222	$ 13,474	$13,401	$ 50,162	$ 50,162	

*The company plans to purchase an extrusion machine costing $30,000 and to pay for it in two installments of $15,000 each in the first and second quarters of 20x9.

The Budgeted Balance Sheet

A **budgeted balance sheet** projects an organization's financial position at the end of an accounting period. It uses all estimated data compiled in the course of preparing a master budget and is the final step in that process. Exhibit 12 presents Framecraft Company's budgeted balance sheet at December 31, 20x9. Again, the data sources are listed in the exhibit. The beginning balances for Land, Notes Payable, Common Stock, and Retained Earnings were $50,000, $70,000, $150,000, and $50,810, respectively.

EXHIBIT 12 ▶ | Budgeted Balance Sheet

Framecraft Company
Budgeted Balance Sheet
December 31, 20x9

				Sources of Data
Assets				
Current assets				
Cash			$ 50,162	Exhibit 11
Accounts receivable			68,000[a]	Exhibit 9
Direct materials inventory			1,500	Exhibit 7
Work in process inventory			—	Exhibit 7, Note
Finished goods inventory			4,455	Exhibit 8, Note
Total current assets			$124,117	
Property, plant, and equipment				
Land			$ 50,000	
Plant and equipment[b]		$200,000		
Less accumulated depreciation[c]		45,000	155,000	
Total property, plant, and equipment			205,000	
Total assets			$329,117	
Liabilities				
Current liabilities				
Accounts payable			$ 8,250[d]	Exhibit 10
Total current liabilities			$ 8,250	
Long-term liabilities				
Notes payable			70,000	
Total liabilities			$ 78,250	
Stockholders' Equity				
Contributed capital				
Common stock		$150,000		
Retained earnings[e]		100,867		
Total stockholders' equity			250,867	
Total liabilities and stockholders' equity			$329,117	

[a] The accounts receivable balance at December 31, 20x9, is $68,000: $4,000 from the third quarter's sales [($50,000 × .80) × .10] plus $64,000 from the fourth quarter's sales [($200,000 × .80) × .40].
[b] The plant and equipment balance includes the $30,000 purchase of an extrusion machine.
[c] The accumulated depreciation balance includes depreciation expense of $27,840 for machinery, building, and office equipment ($11,240, $12,900, and $3,700, respectively).
[d] At December 31, 20x9, the estimated ending balance of accounts payable is $8,250 (50 percent of the $16,500 of direct materials purchases in the fourth quarter).
[e] The retained earnings balance at December 31 equals the beginning retained earnings balance plus the net income projected for 20x9 ($50,810 and $50,057, respectively).

S T O P • R E V I E W • A P P L Y

4-1. How is the cash budget related to the master budget? What are the purposes of preparing a cash budget?

4-2. What is the final step in developing a master budget?

4-3. Why must a cash budget be prepared before a budgeted balance sheet can be completed?

Computing Retained Earnings from Balance Sheet Information Sample Corporation's budgeted balance sheet for the coming year shows total assets of $5,000,000 and total liabilities of $2,000,000. Common stock and retained earnings make up the entire stockholders' equity section of the balance sheet. Common stock remains at its beginning balance of $1,500,000. The projected net income for the year is $350,000. The company pays no cash dividends. What is the balance of retained earnings at the beginning and end of the year?

> **SOLUTION**
> Using the accounting equation (A=L+OE) and the information given, the beginning balance sheet would show assets of $5,000,000 equaling liabilities of $2,000,000 plus common stock of $1,500,000 plus beginning retained earnings. Thus, the beginning balance of retained earnings is $1,500,000. To compute the ending retained earnings, add the beginning retained earnings of $1,500,000 and the net income for the year of $350,000. Because no dividends were paid, there is no subtraction. Thus, at the end of the year, retained earnings are $1,850,000.

A LOOK BACK AT

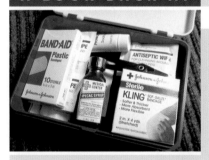

JOHNSON & JOHNSON

The budgeting process can be a highly effective way of linking strategic planning to operations, especially when it is coupled with ongoing discussions about a company's activities and direction. In this chapter's Decision Point, we pointed out that such discussions are the basis for **Johnson & Johnson's** budgeting decisions; we also asked these questions:

- **How is Johnson & Johnson's budgeting process linked to the company's long-term goals and objectives?**

- **How does Johnson & Johnson's budgeting process work?**

Like all corporate budgets, Johnson & Johnson's budget sets forth the company's goals and long-term objectives in concrete terms. It thus enables managers and employees to act in ways that will attain those objectives, and it also gives them a means of monitoring the results of their actions.

Johnson & Johnson's budgeting process is as follows:

- Sales and marketing teams from the decentralized companies develop sales budgets by product, geographic territory, and distribution channel. Senior management and staff then review the sales budgets to see that they meet the goals of Johnson & Johnson's strategic plan.

- Scheduling teams prepare production and shipping schedules to coordinate activities at the different manufacturing plants.
- Managers responsible for functional areas (such as research and development, production, marketing, distribution, and customer service) prepare cost and expense budgets.
- The accounting group reviews all budgets from the decentralized companies and analyzes their contents to determine whether they are in accordance with the overall strategic plan.
- The controller prepares a complete set of companywide budgeted financial statements and submits them to the budget committee and top corporate leaders for approval.

At Johnson & Johnson, the budgeting process and ongoing dialogue about strategy foster rapid improvements in productivity and customer service, as well as innovation in product and market development.

CHAPTER REVIEW

REVIEW of Learning Objectives

LO1 Define *budgeting,* and explain management's role in the budgeting process.

Budgeting is the process of identifying, gathering, summarizing, and communicating financial and nonfinancial information about an organization's future activities. When managers plan, budgeting helps them relate an organization's long-term and intermediate goals to short-term activities, plan the distribution of resources, and establish performance measures. When managers perform, they use budget information to communicate expectations, measure performance, motivate employees, coordinate activities, and allot resources. When managers evaluate performance results, they check for variances between planned and actual performance and create solutions to the problems that they detect. To provide continuous feedback about an organization's operating, investing, and financing activities, managers prepare and distribute reports based on budget information throughout the year.

Participative budgeting, a process in which personnel at all levels actively engage in making decisions about the budget, is key to a successful budget. The controller has considerable influence over the nature of the budgeting process, and to ensure that budgeting is participative, that person must be able to communicate and negotiate effectively with people at all levels of the organization. Senior executives also play a central role in determining whether budgeting is participative.

A budget committee made up of top management has overall responsibility for budget implementation. The committee oversees each stage in the preparation of the master budget, mediates any departmental disputes that may arise during the process, and gives final approval to the budget. After the committee approves the master budget, periodic reports from department managers enable it to monitor the progress the company is making in attaining budget targets. To ensure the cooperation of personnel in implementing the budget, top managers must clearly communicate performance expectations and budget targets. They must also show their support for the budget and encourage its implementation.

LO2 Identify the elements of a master budget in different types of organizations and the guidelines for preparing budgets.

A master budget consists of a set of operating budgets and a set of financial budgets that detail an organization's financial plans for a specific accounting period. The operating budgets serve as the basis for preparing the financial budgets, which include a budgeted income statement, a capital expenditures budget, a cash budget, and a budgeted balance sheet.

The operating budgets of a manufacturing organization include budgets for sales, production, direct materials purchases, direct labor, overhead, selling and administrative expenses, and cost of goods manufactured. The operating budgets of a retail organization include budgets for sales, purchases, selling and administrative expenses, and cost of goods sold. The operating budgets of a service organization include budgets for service revenue, labor, services overhead, and selling and administrative expenses.

The guidelines for preparing budgets include identifying the purpose of the budget, the user group and its information needs, and the sources of budget information; establishing a clear format for the budget; and using appropriate formulas and calculations to derive the quantitative information.

LO3 Prepare the operating budgets that support the financial budgets.

The initial step in preparing a master budget in any type of organization is to prepare a sales budget. Once sales have been estimated, the manager of a manufacturing organization's production department is able to prepare a budget that shows how many units of products must be manufactured to meet the projected sales volume. With that information in hand, other managers are able to prepare budgets for direct materials purchases, direct labor, overhead, selling and administrative expenses, and cost of goods manufactured. A cost of goods sold budget may be prepared separately, or it may be included in the cost of goods manufactured budget. The operating budgets supply the information needed to prepare the financial budgets.

LO4 Prepare a budgeted income statement, a cash budget, and a budgeted balance sheet.

With estimated revenues and expenses itemized in the operating budgets, a controller is able to prepare the financial budgets. A budgeted income statement projects an organization's net income for a specific accounting period. A capital expenditures budget estimates the amount and timing of the organization's capital outlays during the period. A cash budget projects its cash receipts and cash payments for the period. Estimates of cash receipts and payments are needed to prepare a cash budget. Information about cash receipts comes from several sources, including the sales budget, the budgeted income statement, and various financial records. Sources of information about cash payments include the operating budgets, the budgeted income statement, and the capital expenditures budget. The difference between the total estimated cash receipts and total estimated cash payments is the cash increase or decrease anticipated for the period. That total plus the period's beginning cash balance equals the ending cash balance. The final step in developing a master budget is to prepare a budgeted balance sheet, which projects the organization's financial position at the end of the accounting period. All budgeted data are used in preparing this statement.

REVIEW of Concepts and Terminology

The following concepts and terms were introduced in this chapter:

Budget committee: A committee made up of top management that has overall responsibility for budget implementation. **(LO1)**

Budgeted balance sheet: A statement that projects an organization's financial position at the end of an accounting period. **(LO4)**

Budgeted income statement: A projection of an organization's net income for an accounting period based on the revenues and expenses estimated for that accounting period. **(LO4)**

Budgeting: The process of identifying, gathering, summarizing, and communicating financial and nonfinancial information about an organization's future activities. **(LO1)**

Budgets: Plans of action based on forecasted transactions, activities, and events. **(LO1)**

Capital expenditures budget: A detailed plan outlining the anticipated amount and timing of capital outlays for long-term assets during an accounting period. **(LO4)**

Cash budget: A projection of the cash that an organization will receive and the cash that it will pay out during an accounting period. **(LO4)**

Cost of goods manufactured budget: A detailed plan that summarizes the estimated costs of production during an accounting period. **(LO3)**

Direct labor budget: A detailed plan that estimates the direct labor hours needed during an accounting period and the associated costs. **(LO3)**

Direct materials purchases budget: A detailed plan that identifies the quantity of purchases required to meet budgeted production and inventory needs and the costs associated with those purchases. **(LO3)**

Financial budgets: Budget projections of the financial results for an accounting period. **(LO2)**

Master budget: A set of operating budgets and a set of financial budgets that detail an organization's financial plans for a specific accounting period. **(LO2)**

Operating budgets: Budget plans used in daily operations. **(LO2)**

Overhead budget: A detailed plan of anticipated manufacturing costs, other than direct materials and direct labor costs, that must be incurred to meet budgeted production needs. **(LO3)**

Participative budgeting: A process in which personnel at all levels of an organization actively engage in making decisions about a budget. **(LO1)**

Production budget: A detailed plan showing the number of units that a company must produce to meet budgeted sales and inventory needs. **(LO3)**

Pro forma statements: Financial statements that show projections rather than actual results and that are often used to communicate business plans to external parties. **(LO2)**

Sales budget: A detailed plan, expressed in both units and dollars, that identifies the product (or

service) sales expected during an accounting period. **(LO3)**

Sales forecast: A projection of sales demand based on an analysis of external and internal factors. **(LO3)**

Selling and administrative expense budget: A detailed plan of operating expenses, other than those related to production, that are needed to support sales and overall operations during an accounting period. **(LO3)**

Strategic planning: The process by which management establishes an organization's long-term goals. **(LO1)**

REVIEW Problem

LO4

Preparing a Cash Budget

Info Processing Company provides database management services. It uses state-of-the-art equipment and employs five information specialists. Each specialist works an average of 160 hours a month. Info Processing's controller has compiled the following information:

	Actual Data for 20x8		Forecasted Data for 20x9		
	November	December	January	February	March
Client billings (sales)	$25,000	$35,000	$25,000	$20,000	$40,000
Selling and administrative expenses	12,000	13,000	12,000	11,000	12,500
Operating supplies	2,500	3,500	2,500	2,500	4,000
Processing overhead	3,200	3,500	3,000	2,500	3,500

Of the client billings, 60 percent are cash sales collected during the month of sale, 30 percent are collected in the first month following the sale, and 10 percent are collected in the second month following the sale. Operating supplies are paid for in the month of purchase. Selling and administrative expenses and processing overhead are paid in the month following the cost's incurrence.

The company has a bank loan of $12,000 at a 12 percent annual interest rate. Interest is paid monthly, and $2,000 of the loan principal is due on February 28, 20x9. Income taxes of $4,550 for calendar year 20x8 are due and payable on March 15, 20x9. The information specialists earn $8.50 an hour, and all payroll-related employee benefit costs are included in processing overhead. The company anticipates no capital expenditures for the first quarter of the coming year. It expects its cash balance on December 31, 20x8, to be $13,840.

Required

Prepare a monthly cash budget for Info Processing Company for the three-month period ended March 31, 20x9. Comment on whether the ending cash balances are adequate for Info Processing's cash needs.

Answer to Review Problem

	A	B	C	D	E
1		Info Processing Company			
2		Monthly Cash Budget			
3		For the Three-Month Period Ended March 31, 20x9			
4					
5		January	February	March	Totals
6	Cash receipts				
7	Client billings	$28,000	$23,000	$32,500	$83,500
8	Cash payments				
9	Operating supplies	$ 2,500	$ 2,500	$ 4,000	$ 9,000
10	Direct labor	6,800	6,800	6,800	20,400
11	Selling and administrative				
12	Expenses	13,000	12,000	11,000	36,000
13	Processing overhead	3,500	3,000	2,500	9,000
14	Interest expense	120	120	100	340
15	Loan payment	—	2,000	—	2,000
16	Income tax payment	—	—	4,550	4,550
17	Total cash payments	$25,920	$26,420	$28,950	$81,290
18	Cash increase (decrease)	$ 2,080	($ 3,420)	$ 3,550	$ 2,210
19	Beginning cash balance	13,840	15,920	12,500	13,840
20	Ending cash balance	$15,920	$12,500	$16,050	$16,050
21					

The details supporting the individual computations in this cash budget are as follows:

	January	February	March
Client billings			
November	$ 2,500	—	—
December	10,500	$ 3,500	—
January	15,000	7,500	$ 2,500
February	—	12,000	6,000
March	—	—	24,000
	$28,000	$23,000	$32,500
Operating supplies			
Paid for in the month purchased	$ 2,500	$ 2,500	$ 4,000
Direct labor			
5 employees × 160 hours a month × $8.50 an hour	6,800	6,800	6,800
Selling and administrative expenses			
Paid in the month following incurrence	13,000	12,000	11,000
Processing overhead			
Paid in the month following incurrence	3,500	3,000	2,500
Interest expense			
January and February = 1% of $12,000	120	120	—
March = 1% of $10,000	—	—	100
Loan payment	—	2,000	—
Income tax payment	—	—	4,550

The ending cash balances of $15,920, $12,500, and $16,050 for January, February, and March 20x9, respectively, appear to be comfortable but not too large for Info Processing Company.

CHAPTER ASSIGNMENTS

BUILDING Your Basic Knowledge and Skills

Short Exercises

LO1   Budgeting in a Retail Organization

SE 1. Sam Zubac is the manager of the shoe department in a discount department store. During a recent meeting, Zubac and his supervisor agreed that Zubac's goal for the next year would be to increase the number of pairs of shoes sold by 20 percent. The department sold 8,000 pairs of shoes last year. Two salespersons currently work for Zubac. What types of budgets should Zubac use to help him achieve his sales goal? What kinds of information should those budgets provide?

LO1   Budgetary Control

SE 2. Toby Andres owns a tree nursery. She analyzes her business's results by comparing actual operating results with figures budgeted at the beginning of the year. When the business generates large profits, she often overlooks the differences between actual and budgeted data. But when profits are low, she spends many hours analyzing the differences. If you owned Andres's business, would you use her approach to budgetary control? If not, what changes would you make?

LO2, LO3   Components of a Master Budget

SE 3. A master budget is a compilation of forecasts for the coming year or operating cycle made by various departments or functions within an organization. What is the most important forecast made in a master budget? List the reasons for your answer. Which budgets must managers prepare before they can prepare a direct materials purchases budget?

LO3   Production Budget

SE 4. Isobel Law, the controller for Aberdeen Lock Company, is preparing a production budget for the year. The company's policy is to maintain a finished goods inventory equal to one-half of the following month's sales. Sales of 7,000 locks are budgeted for April. Complete the monthly production budget for the first quarter:

	January	February	March
Sales in units	5,000	4,000	6,000
Add desired units of ending finished goods inventory	2,000	?	?
Desired total units	7,000		
Less desired units of beginning finished goods inventory	?	?	?
Total production units	4,500	?	?

LO3   Preparing an Operating Budget

SE 5. Quester Company expects to sell 50,000 units of its product in the coming year. Each unit sells for $45. Sales brochures and supplies for the year are expected to cost $7,000. Three sales representatives cover the southeast region. Each representative's base salary is $20,000, and each earns a sales commission of 5 percent of the selling price of the units he or she sells. The sales representatives supply their own transportation;

they are reimbursed for travel at a rate of $.40 per mile. The company estimates that the sales representatives will drive a total of 75,000 miles next year. From the information provided, calculate Quester Company's budgeted selling expenses for the coming year.

LO3, LO4   **Budgeted Gross Margin**

SE 6. Operating budgets for the DiPaolo Company reveal the following information: net sales, $450,000; beginning materials inventory, $23,000; materials purchased, $185,000; beginning work in process inventory, $64,700; beginning finished goods inventory, $21,600; direct labor costs, $34,000; overhead applied, $67,000; ending work in process inventory, $61,200; ending materials inventory, $18,700; and ending finished goods inventory, $16,300. Compute DiPaolo Company's budgeted gross margin.

LO4   **Estimating Cash Collections**

SE 7. KD Insurance Company specializes in term life insurance contracts. Cash collection experience shows that 20 percent of billed premiums are collected in the month before they are due, 60 percent are paid in the month in which they are due, and 16 percent are paid in the month following their due date. Four percent of the billed premiums are paid late (in the second month following their due date) and include a 10 percent penalty payment. Total billing notices in January were $58,000; in February, $62,000; in March, $66,000; in April, $65,000; in May, $60,000; and in June, $62,000. How much cash does the company expect to collect in May?

LO4   **Cash Budget**

SE 8. The projections of direct materials purchases that follow are for the Stromboli Corporation.

	Purchases on Account	Cash Purchases
December 20x8	$40,000	$20,000
January 20x9	60,000	30,000
February 20x9	50,000	25,000
March 20x9	70,000	35,000

The company pays for 60 percent of purchases on account in the month of purchase and 40 percent in the month following the purchase. Prepare a monthly schedule of expected cash payments for direct materials for the first quarter of 20x9.

LO4   **Cash Budget**

SE 9. Alberta Limited needs a cash budget for the month of November. The following information is available:

a. The cash balance on November 1 is $6,000.
b. Sales for October and November are $80,000 and $60,000, respectively. Cash collections on sales are 30 percent in the month of sale and 65 percent in the month after the sale; 5 percent of sales are uncollectible.
c. General expenses budgeted for November are $25,000 (depreciation represents $2,000 of this amount).
d. Inventory purchases will total $30,000 in October and $40,000 in November. The company pays for half of its inventory purchases in the month of purchase and for the other half the month after purchase.
e. The company will pay $4,000 in cash for office furniture in November. Sales commissions for November are budgeted at $12,000.

    f. The company maintains a minimum ending cash balance of $4,000 and can borrow from the bank in multiples of $100. All loans are repaid after 60 days.

Prepare a cash budget for Alberta Limited for the month of November.

LO4 **Budgeted Balance Sheet**

SE 10. Wellman Corporation's budgeted balance sheet for the coming year shows total assets of $4,650,000 and total liabilities of $1,900,000. Common stock and retained earnings make up the entire stockholders' equity section of the balance sheet. Common stock remains at its beginning balance of $1,500,000. The projected net income for the year is $349,600. The company pays no cash dividends. What is the balance of retained earnings at the beginning of the budget period?

Exercises

LO1 **Characteristics of Budgets**

E 1. You recently attended a workshop on budgeting and overheard the following comments as you walked to the refreshment table:

1. "Budgets are the same regardless of the size of an organization or management's role in the budgeting process."
2. "Budgets can include financial or nonfinancial data. In our organization, we plan the number of hours to be worked and the number of customer contacts we want our salespeople to make."
3. "All budgets are complicated. You have to be an expert to prepare one."
4. "Budgets don't need to be highly accurate. No one in our company stays within a budget anyway."

Do you agree or disagree with each comment? Explain your answers.

LO1 **Budgeting and Goals**

E 2. Effective planning of long- and short-term goals has contributed to the success of Multitasker Calendars, Inc. Described below are the actions that the company's management team took during a recent planning meeting. Indicate whether the goals related to those actions are short-term or long-term.

1. In forecasting the next 10-year period, the management team considered economic and industry forecasts, employee-management relationships, and the structure and role of management.
2. Based on the 10-year forecast, the team made decisions about next year's sales and profit targets.

LO1 **Budgeting and Goals**

E 3. Assume that you work in the accounting department of a small wholesale warehousing company. Inspired by a recent seminar on budgeting, the company's president wants to develop a budgeting system and has asked you to direct it. Identify the points concerning the initial steps in the budgeting process that you should communicate to the president. Concentrate on principles related to long-term goals and short-term goals.

LO2, LO3, LO4 **Components of a Master Budget**

E 4. Identify the order in which the following budgets are prepared. Use the letter *a* to indicate the first budget to be prepared, *b* for the second, and so on.

1. Production budget
2. Direct labor budget
3. Direct materials purchases budget
4. Sales budget
5. Budgeted balance sheet
6. Cash budget
7. Budgeted income statement

LO3   Sales Budget

E 5. Quarterly and annual sales for 20x8 for Steen Manufacturing Company follow. Prepare a sales budget for 20x9 for the company. Show both quarterly and annual totals for each product class.

Steen Manufacturing Company
Actual Sales Revenue
For the Year Ended December 31, 20x8

Product Class	January– March	April– June	July– September	October– December	Annual Totals	Estimated 20x9 Percent Increases by Product Class
Marine products	$ 44,500	$ 45,500	$ 48,200	$ 47,900	$ 186,100	10%
Mountain products	36,900	32,600	34,100	37,200	140,800	5%
River products	29,800	29,700	29,100	27,500	116,100	30%
Hiking products	38,800	37,600	36,900	39,700	153,000	15%
Running products	47,700	48,200	49,400	49,900	195,200	25%
Biking products	65,400	65,900	66,600	67,300	265,200	20%
Totals	$263,100	$259,500	$264,300	$269,500	$1,056,400	

LO3   Production Budget

E 6. Santa Fe Corporation produces and sells a single product. Expected sales for September are 12,000 units; for October, 15,000 units; for November, 9,000 units; for December, 10,000 units; and for January, 14,000 units. The company's desired level of ending finished goods inventory at the end of a month is 10 percent of the following month's sales in units. At the end of August, 1,200 units were on hand. How many units need to be produced in the fourth quarter?

LO3   Direct Materials Purchases Budget

E 7. The U-Z Door Company manufactures garage door units. The units include hinges, door panels, and other hardware. Prepare a direct materials purchases budget for the first quarter of the year based on budgeted production of 16,000 garage door units. Sandee Morton, the controller, has provided the information that follows.

Hinges	4 sets per door	$11.00 per set
Door panels	4 panels per door	$27.00 per panel
Other hardware	1 lock per door	$31.00 per lock
	1 handle per door	$22.50 per handle
	2 roller tracks per door	$16.00 per set of 2 roller tracks
	8 rollers per door	$4.00 per roller

Assume no beginning or ending quantities of direct materials inventory.

LO3 Direct Materials Purchases Budget

E 8. Hard Corporation projects sales of $230,000 in May, $250,000 in June, $260,000 in July, and $240,000 in August. Since the dollar value of the company's cost of goods sold is generally 65 percent of total sales, cost of goods sold is $149,500 in May, $162,500 in June, $169,000 in July, and $156,000 in August. The dollar value of its desired ending inventory is 25 percent of the following month's cost of goods sold. Compute the total purchases in dollars budgeted for June and the total purchases in dollars budgeted for July.

LO3 Direct Labor Budget

E 9. Paige Metals Company has two departments—Cutting and Grinding—and manufactures three products. Budgeted unit production for the coming year is 21,000 of Product T, 36,000 of Product M, and 30,000 of Product B. The company is currently analyzing direct labor hour requirements for the coming year. Data for each department are as follows:

	Cutting	Grinding
Estimated hours per unit		
Product T	1.1	.5
Product M	.6	2.9
Product B	3.2	1.0
Hourly labor rate	$9	$7

Prepare a direct labor budget for the coming year that shows the budgeted direct labor costs for each department and for the company as a whole.

LO3 Overhead Budget

E 10. Carole Dahl is chief financial officer of the Phoenix Division of Dahl Corporation, a multinational company with three operating divisions. As part of the budgeting process, Dahl's staff is developing the overhead budget for next year. The division estimates that it will manufacture 50,000 units during the year. The budgeted cost information is as follows:

	Variable Rate per Unit	Total Fixed Costs
Indirect materials	$1.00	
Indirect labor	4.00	
Supplies	.40	
Repairs and maintenance	3.00	$ 40,000
Electricity	.10	20,000
Factory supervision		180,000
Insurance		25,000
Property taxes		35,000
Depreciation, machinery		82,000
Depreciation, building		72,000

Using these data, prepare the division's overhead budget for next year.

Cash Collections

E 11. Dacahr Bros., Inc., is an automobile maintenance and repair company with outlets throughout the western United States. Henley Turlington, the company controller, is starting to assemble the cash budget for the fourth quarter. Projected sales for the quarter are as follows:

	On Account	Cash
October	$452,000	$196,800
November	590,000	214,000
December	720,500	218,400

Cash collection records pertaining to sales on account indicate the following collection pattern:

Month of sale	40%
First month following sale	30%
Second month following sale	28%
Uncollectible	2%

Sales on account during August were $346,000. During September, sales on account were $395,000.

Compute the amount of cash to be collected from customers during each month of the fourth quarter.

Cash Collections

E 12. XYZ Company collects payment on 50 percent of credit sales in the month of sale, 40 percent in the month following sale, and 5 percent in the second month following the sale. Its sales budget is as follows:

Month	Cash Sales	Credit Sales
May	$20,000	$ 40,000
June	40,000	60,000
July	60,000	80,000
August	80,000	100,000

Compute XYZ Company's total cash collections in July and its total cash collections in August.

Cash Budget

E 13. SABA Enterprises needs a cash budget for the month of June. The following information is available:

a. The cash balance on June 1 is $4,000.
b. Sales for May and June are $50,000 and $40,000, respectively. Cash collections on sales are 40 percent in the month of sale and 50 percent in the month after the sale; 10 percent of sales are uncollectible.
c. General expenses budgeted for June are $20,000 (depreciation represents $1,000 of this amount).
d. Inventory purchases will total $40,000 in May and $30,000 in June. The company pays for half of its inventory purchases in the month of purchase and for the other half the month after purchase.
e. The company will pay $5,000 in cash for office furniture in June. Sales commissions for June are budgeted at $6,000.
f. The company maintains a minimum ending cash balance of $4,000 and can borrow from the bank in multiples of $100. All loans are repaid after 60 days.

Prepare a cash budget for SABA Enterprises for the month of June.

LO4 **Cash Budget**

E 14. Tex Kinkaid's dream was to develop the biggest produce operation with the widest selection of fresh fruits and vegetables in northern Texas. Within three years of opening Minigarden Produce, Inc., Kincaid accomplished his objective. Kinkaid has asked you to prepare monthly cash budgets for Minigarden Produce for the quarter ended September 30.

Credit sales to retailers in the area constitute 80 percent of Minigarden Produce's business; cash sales to customers at the company's retail outlet make up the other 20 percent. Collection records indicate that Minigarden Produce collects payment on 50 percent of all credit sales during the month of sale, 30 percent in the month after the sale, and 20 percent in the second month after the sale.

The company's total sales in May were $66,000; in June, they were $67,500. Anticipated sales in July are $69,500; in August, $76,250; and in September, $84,250. The company's purchases are expected to total $43,700 in July, $48,925 in August, and $55,725 in September. The company pays for all purchases in cash.

Projected monthly costs for the quarter include $1,040 for heat, light, and power; $375 for bank fees; $1,925 for rent; $1,120 for supplies; $1,705 for depreciation of equipment; $1,285 for equipment repairs; and $475 for miscellaneous expenses. Other projected costs for the quarter are salaries and wages of $18,370 in July, $19,200 in August, and $20,300 in September.

The company's cash balance at June 30 was $2,745. It has a policy of maintaining a minimum monthly cash balance of $1,500.

1. Prepare a monthly cash budget for Minigarden Produce, Inc., for the quarter ended September 30.
2. Should Minigarden Produce anticipate taking out a loan during the quarter? If so, how much should it borrow, and when?

LO4 **Budgeted Income Statement**

E 15. Delft House, Inc., a multinational company based in Amsterdam, organizes and coordinates art shows and auctions throughout the world. Its budgeted and actual costs for last year are as follows:

	Budgeted Cost	Actual Cost
Salaries expense, staging	€ 480,000	€ 512,800
Salaries expense, executive	380,000	447,200
Travel costs	640,000	652,020
Auctioneer services	540,000	449,820
Space rental costs	251,000	246,580
Printing costs	192,000	182,500
Advertising expense	169,000	183,280
Insurance, merchandise	84,800	77,300
Insurance, liability	64,000	67,100
Home office costs	209,200	219,880
Shipping costs	105,000	112,560
Miscellaneous	25,000	25,828
Total operating expenses	€3,140,000	€3,176,868
Net receipts	€6,200,000	€6,369,200

Delft House, Inc., has budgeted the following fixed costs for the coming year: executive salaries, €440,000; advertising expense, €190,000; merchandise insurance, €80,000; and liability insurance, €68,000. Additional information pertaining to the operations of Delft House, Inc., in the coming years is as follows:

a. Net receipts are estimated at €6,400,000.
b. Salaries expense for staging will increase 20 percent over the actual figures for the last year.
c. Travel costs are expected to be 11 percent of net receipts.
d. Auctioneer services will be billed at 9.5 percent of net receipts.
e. Space rental costs will be 20 percent higher than the amount budgeted in the last year.
f. Printing costs are expected to be €190,000.
g. Home office costs are budgeted for €230,000.
h. Shipping costs are expected to be 20 percent higher than the amount budgeted in the last year.
i. Miscellaneous expenses for the coming year will be budgeted at €28,000.

   Because the company sells only services, it has expenses only and no cost of sales. (Net receipts equal gross margin.)

1. Using a 34 percent income tax rate, prepare the company's budgeted income statement for the coming year.
2. Should the budget committee be worried about the trend in the company's operations? Explain your answer.

Problems

LO3   Preparing Operating Budgets

P 1. The principal product of Yangsoo Enterprises, Inc., is a multipurpose hammer that carries a lifetime guarantee. Listed below are cost and production data for the Yangsoo hammer.

Direct materials
   Anodized steel: 2 kilograms per hammer at $1.60 per kilogram
   Leather strapping for the handle: .5 square meter per hammer at $4.40 per square meter

Direct labor
   Forging operation: $12.50 per labor hour; 6 minutes per hammer
   Leather-wrapping operation: $12.00 per direct labor hour; 12 minutes per hammer

Overhead
   Forging operation: rate equals 70 percent of department's direct labor dollars
   Leather-wrapping operation: rate equals 50 percent of department's direct labor dollars

In October, November, and December, Yangsoo Enterprises expects to produce 108,000, 104,000, and 100,000 hammers, respectively. The company has no beginning or ending balances of direct materials inventory or work in process inventory for the year.

Required

1. For the three-month period ending December 31, prepare monthly production cost information for the Yangsoo hammer. Classify the costs as direct materials, direct labor, or overhead and show your computations.

2. Prepare a cost of goods manufactured budget for the hammer. Show monthly cost data and combined totals for the quarter for each cost category.

LO3, LO4 **Preparing a Comprehensive Budget**

P 2. Bertha's Bathworks began manufacturing hair and bath products in 20x1. Its biggest customer is a national retail chain that specializes in such products. Bertha Jackson, the owner of Bertha's Bathworks, would like to have an estimate of the company's net income in 20x9.

Required

Calculate Bertha's Bathworks' net income in 20x9 by completing the operating budgets and budgeted income statement that follow.

1. Sales budget:

Bertha's Bathworks
Sales Budget
For the Year Ended December 31, 20x9

	Quarter				
	1	2	3	4	Year
Sales in units	4,000	3,000	5,000	5,000	17,000
× Selling price per unit	× $5	× ?	× ?	× ?	× ?
Total sales	$20,000	?	?	?	?

2. Production budget:

Bertha's Bathworks
Production Budget
For the Year Ended December 31, 20x9

	Quarter				
	1	2	3	4	Year
Sales in units	4,000	?	?	?	?
Plus desired units of ending finished goods inventory*	300	?	?	600	600
Desired total units	4,300				
Less desired units of beginning finished goods inventory†	400	?	?	?	400
Total production units	3,900	?	?	?	?

*Desired units of ending finished goods inventory = 10% of next quarter's budgeted sales.
†Desired units of beginning finished goods inventory = 10% of current quarter's budgeted sales.

3. Direct materials purchases budget:

Bertha's Bathworks
Direct Materials Purchases Budget
For the Year Ended December 31, 20x9

	Quarter				
	1	2	3	4	Year
Total production units	3,900	3,200	5,000	5,100	17,200
× 3 ounces per unit	× 3	× ?	× ?	× ?	× ?
Total production needs in ounces	11,700	?	?	?	?
Plus desired ounces of ending direct materials inventory*	1,920	?	?	3,600	3,600
	13,620	?	?	?	?
Less desired ounces of beginning direct materials inventory†	2,340	?	?	?	2,340
Total ounces of direct materials to be purchased	11,280	?	?	?	?
× Cost per ounce	× $.10	× ?	× ?	× ?	× ?
Total cost of direct materials purchases	$1,128	?	?	?	?

*Desired ounces of ending direct materials inventory = 20% of next quarter's budgeted production needs in ounces.
†Desired ounces of beginning direct materials inventory = 20% of current quarter's budgeted production needs in ounces.

4. Direct labor budget:

Bertha's Bathworks
Direct Labor Budget
For the Year Ended December 31, 20x9

	Quarter				
	1	2	3	4	Year
Total production units	3,900	?	?	?	?
× Direct labor hours per unit	× .1	× ?	× ?	× ?	× ?
Total direct labor hours	390	?	?	?	?
× Direct labor cost per hour	× $7	× ?	× ?	× ?	× ?
Total direct labor cost	$2,730	?	?	?	?

5. Overhead budget:

Bertha's Bathworks
Overhead Budget
For the Year Ended December 31, 20x9

	Quarter				
	1	2	3	4	Year
Variable overhead costs					
Factory supplies ($.05)	$ 195	?	?	?	?
Employee benefits ($.25)	975	?	?	?	?
Inspection ($.10)	390	?	?	?	?
Maintenance and repair ($.15)	585	?	?	?	?
Utilities ($.05)	195	?	?	?	?
Total variable overhead costs	$2,340	?	?	?	?
Fixed overhead costs					
Depreciation, machinery	$ 500	?	?	?	?
Depreciation, building	700	?	?	?	?
Supervision	1,800	?	?	?	?
Maintenance and repair	400	?	?	?	?
Other overhead expenses	600	?	?	?	?
Total fixed overhead costs	$4,000	?	?	?	?
Total overhead costs	$6,340	?	?	?	?

Note: The figures in parentheses are variable costs per unit.

6. Selling and administrative expense budget:

Bertha's Bathworks
Selling and Administrative Expense Budget
For the Year Ended December 31, 20x9

	Quarter				
	1	2	3	4	Year
Variable selling and administrative expenses					
Delivery expenses ($.10)	$ 400	?	?	?	?
Sales commissions ($.15)	600	?	?	?	?
Accounting ($.05)	200	?	?	?	?
Other administrative expenses ($.20)	800	?	?	?	?
Total variable selling and administrative expenses	$2,000	?	?	?	?
Fixed selling and administrative expenses					
Sales salaries	$5,000	?	?	?	?
Depreciation, office equipment	900	?	?	?	?
Taxes and insurance	1,700	?	?	?	?
Total fixed selling and administrative expenses	$7,600	?	?	?	?
Total selling and administrative expenses	$9,600	?	?	?	?

Note: The figures in parentheses are variable costs per unit.

7. Cost of goods manufactured budget:

Bertha's Bathworks
Cost of Goods Manufactured Budget
For the Year Ended December 31, 20x9

Direct materials used		
Direct materials inventory, December 31, 20x8	?	
Purchases for 20x9	?	
Cost of direct materials available for use	?	
Less direct materials inventory, December 31, 20x9	?	
Cost of direct materials used		?
Direct labor costs		?
Overhead costs		?
Total manufacturing costs		?
Work in process inventory, December 31, 20x8*		?
Less work in process inventory, December 31, 20x9*		?
Cost of goods manufactured		?
Manufactured Cost per Unit = Cost of Goods Manufactured ÷ Units Produced		?

*It is the company's policy to have no units in process at the end of the year.

8. Budgeted income statement:

Bertha's Bathworks
Budgeted Income Statement
For the Year Ended December 31, 20x9

Sales		?
Cost of goods sold		
Finished goods inventory, December 31, 20x8	?	
Cost of goods manufactured	?	
Cost finished of goods available for sale	?	
Less finished goods inventory, December 31, 20x9	?	
Cost of goods sold		?
Gross margin		?
Selling and administrative expenses		?
Income from operations		?
Income taxes expense (30%)*		?
Net income		?

*The figure in parentheses is the company's income tax rate.

LO4   **Basic Cash Budget**

P 3. Felasco Nurseries, Inc., has been in business for six years and has four divisions. Ethan Poulis, the corporation's controller, has been asked to prepare a cash budget for the Southern Division for the first quarter. Projected data supporting this budget follow.

Sales (60 percent on credit)		Purchases	
November	$160,000	December	$ 86,800
December	200,000	January	124,700
January	120,000	February	99,440
February	160,000	March	104,800
March	140,000		

Collection records of accounts receivable have shown that 30 percent of all credit sales are collected in the month of sale, 60 percent in the month following the sale, and 8 percent in the second month following the sale; 2 percent of the sales are uncollectible. All purchases are paid for in the month after the purchase. Salaries and wages are projected to be $25,200 in January, $33,200 in February, and $21,200 in March. Estimated monthly costs are utilities, $4,220; collection fees, $1,700; rent, $5,300; equipment depreciation, $5,440; supplies, $2,480; small tools, $3,140; and miscellaneous, $1,900.

Each of the corporation's divisions maintains a $6,000 minimum cash balance. As of December 31, the Southern Division had a cash balance of $9,600.

Required

1. Prepare a monthly cash budget for Felasco Nurseries' Southern Division for the first quarter.
2. **Manager Insight:** Should Felasco Nurseries anticipate taking out a loan for the Southern Division during the quarter? If so, how much should it borrow, and when?

LO4 **Cash Budget**

P 4. Security Services Company provides security monitoring services. It employs five security specialists. Each specialist works an average of 160 hours a month. The company's controller has compiled the following information:

	Actual Data for Last Year		Forecasted Data for Next Year		
	November	December	January	February	March
Security billings (sales)	$30,000	$35,000	$25,000	$20,000	$30,000
Selling and administrative expenses	10,000	11,000	9,000	8,000	10,500
Operating supplies	2,500	3,500	2,500	2,000	3,000
Service overhead	3,000	3,500	3,000	2,500	3,000

Sixty percent of the client billings are cash sales collected during the month of sale; 30 percent are collected in the first month following the sale; and 10 percent are collected in the second month following the sale. Operating supplies are paid for in the month of purchase. Selling and administrative expenses and service overhead are paid in the month following the cost's incurrence.

The company has a bank loan of $12,000 at a 12 percent annual interest rate. Interest is paid monthly, and $2,000 of the loan principal is due on February 28. Income taxes of $4,500 for last calendar year are due and payable on March 15. The five security specialists each earn $8.50 an hour, and all payroll-related employee benefit costs are included in service overhead. The company anticipates no capital expenditures for the first quarter of the coming year. It expects its cash balance on December 31 to be $13,000.

Required

Prepare a monthly cash budget for Security Services Company for the three-month period ended March 31.

LO4   **Budgeted Income Statement and Budgeted Balance Sheet**

P 5. Moontrust Bank has asked the president of Wishware Products, Inc., for a budgeted income statement and budgeted balance sheet for the quarter ended June 30. These pro forma statements are needed to support Wishware Products' request for a loan.

Wishware Products routinely prepares a quarterly master budget. The operating budgets prepared for the quarter ending June 30 have provided the following information: Projected sales for April are $220,400; for May, $164,220; and for June, $165,980. Direct materials purchases for the period are estimated at $96,840; direct materials usage, at $102,710; direct labor expenses, at $71,460; overhead, at $79,940; selling and administrative expenses, at $143,740; capital expenditures, at $125,000 (to be spent on June 29); cost of goods manufactured, at $252,880; and cost of goods sold, at $251,700.

Balance sheet account balances at March 31 were as follows: Accounts Receivable, $26,500; Materials Inventory, $23,910; Work in Process Inventory, $31,620; Finished Goods Inventory, $36,220; Prepaid Expenses, $7,200; Plant, Furniture, and Fixtures, $498,600; Accumulated Depreciation, Plant, Furniture, and Fixtures, $141,162; Patents, $90,600; Accounts Payable, $39,600; Notes Payable, $105,500; Common Stock, $250,000; and Retained Earnings, $207,158.

Projected monthly cash balances for the second quarter are as follows: April 30, $20,490; May 31, $35,610; and June 30, $45,400. During the quarter, accounts receivable are expected to increase by 30 percent, patents to go up by $6,500, prepaid expenses to remain constant, and accounts payable to go down by 10 percent (Wishware Products will make a $5,000 payment on a note payable, $4,100 of which is principal reduction). The federal income tax rate is 34 percent, and the second quarter's tax is paid in July. Depreciation for the quarter will be $6,420, which is included in the overhead budget. The company will pay no dividends.

Required

1. Prepare a budgeted income statement for the quarter ended June 30. Round answers to the nearest dollar.
2. Prepare a budgeted balance sheet as of June 30.

Alternate Problems

LO3, LO4   **Preparing a Comprehensive Budget**

P 6. The Bottled Water Company has been bottling and selling water since 1940. Ginnie Adams, the current owner of The Bottled Water Company, would like to know how a new product would affect the company's net income in the coming year.

Required

Calculate The Bottled Water Company's net income for the new product in the coming year by completing the operating budgets and budgeted income statement that follow.

1. Sales budget:

The Bottled Water Company
Sales Budget
For the Year Ended December 31

| | Quarter | | | | |
	1	2	3	4	Year
Sales in units	40,000	30,000	50,000	55,000	175,000
× Selling price per unit	× $1	× ?	× ?	× ?	× ?
Total sales	$40,000	?	?	?	?

2. Production budget:

The Bottled Water Company
Production Budget
For the Year Ended December 31

| | Quarter | | | | |
	1	2	3	4	Year
Sales in units	40,000	?	?	?	?
Plus desired units of ending finished goods inventory*	3,000	?	?	6,000	6,000
Desired total units	43,000				
Less desired units of beginning finished goods inventory†	4,000	?	?	?	4,000
Total production units	39,000	?	?	?	?

*Desired units of ending finished goods inventory = 10% of next quarter's budgeted sales.
†Desired units of beginning finished goods inventory = 10% of current quarter's budgeted sales.

3. Direct materials purchases budget:

The Bottled Water Company
Direct Materials Purchases Budget
For the Year Ended December 31

	Quarter				
	1	2	3	4	Year
Total production units	39,000	32,000	50,500	55,500	?
× 20 ounces per unit	× 20	× ?	× ?	× ?	× ?
Total production needs in ounces	780,000	?	?	?	?
Plus desired ounces of ending direct materials inventory*	128,000	?	?	240,000	240,000
	908,000	?	?	?	?
Less desired ounces of beginning direct materials inventory†	156,000	?	?	?	156,000
Total ounces of direct materials to be purchased	752,000	?	?	?	?
× Cost per ounce	× $.01	× ?	× ?	× ?	× ?
Total cost of direct materials purchases	$ 7,520	?	?	?	?

*Desired ounces of ending direct materials inventory = 20% of next quarter's budgeted production needs in ounces.
†Desired ounces of beginning direct materials inventory = 20% of current quarter's budgeted production needs in ounces.

4. Direct labor budget:

The Bottled Water Company
Direct Labor Budget
For the Year Ended December 31

	Quarter				
	1	2	3	4	Year
Total production units	39,000	?	?	?	?
× Direct labor hours per unit	× .001	× ?	× ?	× ?	× ?
Total direct labor hours	39	?	?	?	?
× Direct labor cost per hour	× $8	× ?	× ?	× ?	× ?
Total direct labor cost	$312	?	?	?	?

5. Overhead budget:

The Bottled Water Company
Overhead Budget
For the Year Ended December 31

	Quarter				
	1	2	3	4	Year
Variable overhead costs					
Factory supplies ($.01)	$ 390	?	?	?	?
Employee benefits ($.05)	1,950	?	?	?	?
Inspection ($.01)	390	?	?	?	?
Maintenance and repair ($.02)	780	?	?	?	?
Utilities ($.01)	390	?	?	?	?
Total variable overhead costs	$3,900	?	?	?	?
Total fixed overhead costs	1,500	?	?	?	?
Total overhead costs	$5,400	?	?	?	?

Note: The figures in parentheses are variable costs per unit.

6. Selling and administrative expense budget:

The Bottled Water Company
Selling and Administrative Expense Budget
For the Year Ended December 31

	Quarter				
	1	2	3	4	Year
Variable selling and administrative expenses					
Delivery expenses ($.01)	$ 400	?	?	?	?
Sales commissions ($.02)	800	?	?	?	?
Accounting ($.01)	400	?	?	?	?
Other administrative expenses ($.01)	400	?	?	?	?
Total variable selling and administrative expenses	$2,000	?	?	?	?
Total fixed selling and administrative expenses	5,000	?	?	?	?
Total selling and administrative expenses	$7,000	?	?	?	?

Note: The figures in parentheses are variable costs per unit.

7. Cost of goods manufactured budget:

The Bottled Water Company
Cost of Goods Manufactured Budget
For the Year Ended December 31

Direct materials used		
Direct materials inventory, beginning	?	
Purchases	?	
Cost of direct materials available for use	?	
Less direct materials inventory, ending		?
Cost of direct materials used		?
Direct labor costs		?
Overhead costs		?
Total manufacturing costs		?
Work in process inventory, beginning*		0
Less work in process inventory, ending*		0
Cost of goods manufactured		?
Manufactured Cost per Unit = Cost of Goods Manufactured ÷ Units Produced		?

*It is the company's policy to have no units in process at the end of the year.

8. Budgeted income statement:

The Bottled Water Company
Budgeted Income Statement
For the Year Ended December 31

Sales		?
Cost of goods sold		
Finished goods inventory, beginning	?	
Cost of goods manufactured	?	
Cost of finished goods available for sale	?	
Less finished goods inventory, ending	?	
Cost of goods sold		?
Gross margin		?
Selling and administrative expenses		?
Income from operations		?
Income taxes expense (30%)*		?
Net income		?

*The figure in parentheses is the company's income tax rate.

LO4 **Comprehensive Cash Budget**

P 7. Located in Telluride, Colorado, Wellness Centers, Inc., emphasizes the benefits of regular workouts and the importance of physical examinations. The corporation operates three fully equipped fitness centers, as well as a medical center that specializes in preventive medicine. The data that follow pertain to the corporation's first quarter.

Cash Receipts

Memberships: December, 870; January, 880; February, 910; March, 1,030

Membership dues: $90 per month, payable on the 10th of the month (80 percent collected on time; 20 percent collected one month late)

Medical examinations: January, $35,610; February, $41,840; March, $45,610

Special aerobics classes: January, $4,020; February, $5,130; March, $7,130

High-protein food sales: January, $4,890; February, $5,130; March, $6,280

Cash Payments

Salaries and wages:

Corporate officers: 2 at $12,000 per month

Physicians: 2 at $7,000 per month

Nurses: 3 at $2,900 per month

Clerical staff: 2 at $1,500 per month

Aerobics instructors: 3 at $1,100 per month

Clinic staff: 6 at $1,700 per month

Maintenance staff: 3 at $900 per month

Health-food servers: 3 at $750 per month

Purchases:

Muscle-toning machines: January, $14,400; February, $13,800 (no purchases in March)

Pool supplies: $520 per month

Health food: January, $3,290; February, $3,460; March, $3,720

Medical supplies: January, $10,400; February, $11,250; March, $12,640

Medical uniforms and disposable garments: January, $7,410; February, $3,900; March, $3,450

Medical equipment: January, $11,200; February, $3,400; March $5,900

Advertising: January, $2,250; February, $1,190; March, $2,450

Utilities expense: January, $5,450; February, $5,890; March, $6,090

Insurance:

Fire: January, $3,470

Liability: March, $3,980

Property taxes: $3,760 due in January

Federal income taxes: Last year's taxes of $21,000 due in March

Miscellaneous: January, $2,625; February, $2,800; March, $1,150

Wellness Centers' controller anticipates that the beginning cash balance on January 1 will be $9,840.

Required

Prepare a cash budget for Wellness Centers, Inc., for the first quarter of the year. Use **January**, **February**, **March**, and **Quarter** as the column headings.

LO4 **Budgeted Income Statement and Budgeted Balance Sheet**

P 8. Whatever Video Company, Inc., produces and markets two popular video games, "High Range" and "Star Boundary." The closing account balances on the company's balance sheet for last year are as follows: Cash, $18,735; Accounts Receivable, $19,900; Materials Inventory, $18,510; Work in Process Inventory, $24,680; Finished Goods Inventory, $21,940; Prepaid Expenses, $3,420; Plant and Equipment, $262,800; Accumulated Depreciation, Plant and Equipment, $55,845; Other Assets, $9,480; Accounts Payable, $52,640; Mortgage Payable, $70,000; Common Stock, $90,000; and Retained Earnings, $110,980.

Operating budgets for the first quarter of the coming year show the following estimated costs: direct materials purchases, $58,100; direct materials usage, $62,400; direct labor expense, $42,880; overhead, $51,910; selling expenses, $35,820; general and administrative expenses, $60,240; cost of goods manufactured, $163,990; and cost of goods sold, $165,440. Estimated ending cash balances are as follows: January, $34,610; February, $60,190; and March, $54,802. The company will have no capital expenditures during the quarter.

Sales are projected to be $125,200 in January, $105,100 in February, and $112,600 in March. Accounts receivable are expected to double during the quarter, and accounts payable are expected to decrease by 20 percent. Mortgage payments for the quarter will total $6,000, of which $2,000 will be interest expense. Prepaid expenses are expected to go up by $20,000, and other assets are projected to increase by 50 percent over the budget period. Depreciation for plant and equipment (already included in the overhead budget) averages 5 percent of total plant and equipment per year. Federal income taxes (34 percent of profits) are payable in April. The company pays no dividends.

Required

1. Prepare a budgeted income statement for the quarter ended March 31.
2. Prepare a budgeted balance sheet as of March 31.

ENHANCING Your Knowledge, Skills, and Critical Thinking

Conceptual Understanding Cases

LO4 **Budgeting for Cash Flows**

C 1. The nature of a company's business affects its need to budget for cash flows. **H&R Block** is a service company whose main business is preparing tax returns. Most tax returns are prepared after January 31 and before April 15. For a fee and interest, the company will advance cash to clients who are due refunds. The clients are expected to repay the cash advances when they receive their refunds. Although H&R Block has some revenues throughout the year, it devotes most of the nontax season to training potential employees in tax preparation procedures and to laying the groundwork for the next tax season.

Toys "R" Us is a toy retailer whose sales are concentrated in October, November, and December of one year and January of the next year. Sales continue at a steady but low level during the rest of the year. The company purchases most of its inventory between July and September.

Johnson & Johnson sells the many health care products that it manufactures to retailers, and the retailers sell them to the final customer. Johnson & Johnson offers retailers credit terms.

Discuss the nature of cash receipts and cash disbursements over a calendar year in the three companies we have just described. What are some key estimates that the management of these companies must make when preparing a cash budget?

LO4 **Goals and the Cash Budget**

C 2. The products of **Minnesota Mining and Manufacturing Company (3M)** range from office supplies, duct tape, and road reflectors to laser imagers for CAT scanners. One of the company's goals is to accelerate sales and product development. Toward that end, it spends over $1 billion a year on research and development (R&D) and related investment activities. It has also redesigned many of its products to satisfy the needs of its three international operations groups.[6] Suppose the manager of 3M's Asia-Pacific group is preparing the cash budget for next year's operations. Explain how R&D expenses would affect the cash receipts and cash payments in that cash budget.

LO1, LO2 **Policies for Budget Development**

C 3. Hector Corporation is a manufacturing company with annual sales of $25 million. Its budget committee has created the following policy that the company uses each year in developing its master budget for the following calendar year:

May	The company's controller and other members of the budget committee meet to discuss plans and objectives for next year. The controller conveys all relevant information from this meeting to division managers and department heads.
June	Division managers, department heads, and the controller meet to discuss the corporate plans and objectives for next year. They develop a timetable for developing next year's budget data.
July	Division managers and department heads develop budget data. The vice president of sales provides them with final sales estimates, and they complete monthly sales estimates for each product line.
August	Estimates of next year's monthly production activity and inventory levels are completed. Division managers and department heads communicate these estimates to the controller, who distributes them to other operating areas.
September	All operating areas submit their revised budget data. The controller integrates their labor requirements, direct materials requirements, unit cost estimates, cash requirements, and profit estimates into a preliminary master budget.
October	The budget committee meets to discuss the preliminary master budget and to make any necessary corrections, additions, or deletions. The controller incorporates all authorized changes into a final draft of the master budget.
November	The controller submits the final draft to the budget committee for approval. If the committee approves it, it is distributed to all corporate officers, division managers, and department heads.

1. Comment on this policy.
2. What changes would you recommend?

Interpreting Management Reports

LO1, LO4 **Budgeting Procedures**

C 4. Since Rood Enterprises inaugurated participative budgeting 10 years ago, everyone in the organization—from maintenance personnel to the president's staff—has had a voice in the budgeting process. Until recently, participative budgeting has worked in the best interests of the company as a whole. Now, however, it is becoming evident that some managers are using the practice solely to benefit their own divisions. The budget committee has therefore asked you, the company's controller, to analyze this year's divisional budgets carefully before incorporating them into the company's master budget.

The Motor Division was the first of the company's six divisions to submit its budget request for 20x9. The division's budgeted income statement follows.

Rood Enterprises
Motor Division
Budgeted Income Statement
For the Years Ended December 31, 20x8 and 20x9

	Budget 12/31/x8	Budget 12/31/x9	Increase (Decrease)
Net sales			
Radios	$ 850,000	$ 910,000	$ 60,000
Appliances	680,000	740,000	60,000
Telephones	270,000	305,000	35,000
Miscellaneous	84,400	90,000	5,600
Net sales	$1,884,400	$2,045,000	$160,600
Less cost of goods sold	750,960	717,500*	(33,460)
Gross margin	$1,133,440	$1,327,500	$194,060
Operating expenses			
Wages			
Warehouse	$ 94,500	$ 102,250	$ 7,750
Purchasing	77,800	84,000	6,200
Delivery/shipping	69,400	74,780	5,380
Maintenance	42,650	45,670	3,020
Salaries			
Supervisory	60,000	92,250	32,250
Executive	130,000	164,000	34,000
Purchases, supplies	17,400	20,500	3,100
Merchandise moving equipment			
Maintenance	72,400	82,000	9,600
Depreciation	62,000	74,750†	12,750
Building rent	96,000	102,500	6,500
Sales commissions	188,440	204,500	16,060
Insurance			
Fire	12,670	20,500	7,830
Liability	18,200	20,500	2,300
Utilities	14,100	15,375	1,275
Taxes			
Property	16,600	18,450	1,850
Payroll	26,520	41,000	14,480
Miscellaneous	4,610	10,250	5,640
Total operating expenses	$1,003,290	$1,173,275	$169,985
Income from operations	$ 130,150	$ 154,225	$ 24,075

*Less expensive merchandise will be purchased in 20x9 to boost profits.
†Depreciation is increased because additional equipment must be bought to handle increased sales.

1. Recast the Motor Division's budgeted income statement in the following format (round percentages to two places):

	Budget for 12/31/x8		Budget for 12/31/x9	
Account	Amount	Percentage of Net Sales	Amount	Percentage of Net Sales

2. Actual results for 20x8 revealed the following information about revenues and cost of goods sold:

	Amount	Percentage of Sales
Net sales		
Radios	$ 780,000	43.94
Appliances	640,000	36.06
Telephones	280,000	15.77
Miscellaneous	75,000	4.23
Net sales	$1,775,000	100.00
Less cost of goods sold	763,425	43.01
Gross margin	$1,011,575	56.99

On the basis of this information and your analysis in requirement 1, what do you think the budget committee should say to the managers of the Motor Division? Identify any specific areas of the budget that may need to be revised and explain why the revision is needed.

Decision Analysis Using Excel

LO3, LO4 **The Budgeting Process**

C 5. Refer to our development of Framecraft Company's master budget for 20x9 in this chapter. Suppose that because of a new customer in Canada, Chase Vitt has decided to increase budgeted sales in the first quarter of 20x9 by 5,000 units. The expenses for this sale will include direct materials, direct labor, variable overhead, and variable selling and administrative expenses. The delivery expense for the Canadian customer will be $.18 per unit rather than the regular $.08 per unit. The desired units of beginning finished goods inventory will remain at 1,000 units.

1. Using an Excel spreadsheet, revise Framecraft Company's budgeted income statement and the operating budgets that support it to reflect the changes described above. (Round manufactured cost per unit to three decimals.)
2. What was the change in income from operations? Would you recommend accepting the order from the Canadian customer? If so, why?

Ethical Dilemma Case

LO1, LO3 **Ethical Considerations in Budgeting**

C 6. Javier Gonzales is the manager of the Repairs and Maintenance Department of JG Industries. He is responsible for preparing his department's annual budget. Most managers in the company inflate their budget numbers by at least 10 percent because their bonuses depend upon how much below budget their departments operate. Gonzales turned in the following information for his department's 20x9 budget to the company's budget committee:

	Budget 20x8	Actual 20x8	Budget 20x9
Supplies	$ 20,000	$ 16,000	$ 24,000
Labor	80,000	82,000	96,000
Utilities	8,500	8,000	10,200
Tools	12,500	9,000	15,000
Hand-carried equipment	25,000	16,400	30,000
Cleaning materials	4,600	4,200	5,520
Miscellaneous	2,000	2,100	2,400
Totals	$152,600	$137,700	$183,120

Because the figures for 20x9 are 20 percent above those in the 20x8 budget, the budget committee questioned them. Gonzales defended them by saying that he expects a significant increase in activity in his department in 20x9.

What do you think are the real reasons for the increase in the budgeted amounts? What ethical considerations enter into this situation?

Internet Case

The Budgeting Process

LO1 **C 7.** Some corporate websites include areas specifically designed for student needs. Search the student area of Johnson & Johnson's website (www.jnj.com/ student_resources/index.htm). What kinds of information does it provide? How does the information apply to the material discussed in this chapter?

Group Activity Case

The Budgeting Process

LO1, LO2 **C 8.** Many people believe that the budgeting process is wasteful and ineffective. They maintain that managers spend too much time focusing on the mechanics of budgeting and not enough time on strategic issues. They believe that this emphasis on the budgeting process causes managers to neglect more important matters, such as eliminating nonvalue-adding activities that waste resources. Critics of the budgeting process also maintain that the information and formats that managers use in budgets fail to communicate the short-term business activities needed to achieve long-term goals. Place yourself in the role of a company's controller and search the Internet for articles on budgeting. Based on your research, prepare a memorandum to your company's owner that (1) justifies the use of budgeting and (2) suggests ways of making the budgeting process, the budget information, and the budgets themselves efficient, effective, and meaningful.

After you complete this part of the assignment, your instructor will divide the class into groups. Group members will compare their memorandums and prepare a summary statement, which one member of the group will present to the rest of the class.

Business Communication Case

Financial Budgets

LO1, LO2, LO4 **C 9.** Suppose you have just signed a partnership agreement with your cousin Eddie to open a bookstore near your college. You believe that the store will be able to provide excellent service and undersell the local competition. To fund operations, you and Eddie have applied for a loan from the Small Business Administration. The loan application requires you to submit two financial budgets—a pro forma income statement and a pro forma balance sheet—within six weeks. Because of your expertise in accounting and business, Eddie has asked you to prepare the financial budgets.

1. How do the four *w*'s of preparing an accounting report apply in this situation—that is, *why* are you preparing these financial budgets, *who* needs them, *what* information do you need to prepare for them, and *when* are they due?
2. If you obtain the loan and open the bookstore, how can you and Eddie use the pro forma statements that you prepared?

8

Performance Management and Evaluation

If managers want satisfactory results, they must understand the cause and effect relationships between their actions and their organization's overall performance. By measuring and tracking the relationships that they are responsible for, managers can improve performance and thereby add value for all of their organization's stakeholders. In this chapter, we describe the role of the balanced scorecard, responsibility accounting, and economic value added as they relate to performance management and evaluation. We also point out how managers can use a wide range of financial and nonfinancial data to manage and evaluate performance more effectively.

LEARNING OBJECTIVES

LO1 Describe how the balanced scorecard aligns performance with organizational goals.

LO2 Discuss performance measurement, and identify the issues that affect management's ability to measure performance.

LO3 Define *responsibility accounting,* and describe the role that responsibility centers play in performance management and evaluation.

LO4 Prepare performance reports for cost centers using flexible budgets and for profit centers using variable costing.

LO5 Prepare performance reports for investment centers using the traditional measures of return on investment and residual income and the newer measure of economic value added.

LO6 Explain how properly linked performance incentives and measures add value for all stakeholders in performance management and evaluation.

- **How do managers at Vail Resorts link performance measures and set performance targets to achieve performance objectives?**

- **How do they use the PEAKS system and its integrated database to improve performance management and evaluation?**

Vail Resorts includes five Colorado vacation spots: Vail, Breckenridge, Keystone, Heavenly, and Beaver Creek. To help guests enjoy all the activities that these places offer, Vail Resorts instituted its PEAKS system. PEAKS is an all-in-one card that guests at the five resort areas can use to pay for lift tickets, skiing and snowboarding lessons, equipment rentals, dining, and more.

Guests like the PEAKS system's convenience and its program for earning points toward free or reduced-rate lift tickets, dining, and lodging. They enroll in the system by filling out a one-page form that asks for their name, home address, email address, phone number, date of birth, credit card number, and a signature to authorize charge privileges. Data for up to eight family members can be integrated in one membership account. All family members receive a bar-coded picture identification card that is scanned each time they ride the ski lifts, attend ski school, or charge purchases, meals, or lodging.[1]

Managers at Vail Resorts like the PEAKS system because it enables them to collect huge amounts of information—both financial and nonfinancial—in a simple way and because the data have so many uses. New data are entered in the system each time a guest's card is scanned. Those data then become part of an integrated management information system that managers use to measure and evaluate the performance of their resorts in many ways.

Organizational Goals and the Balanced Scorecard

LO1 Describe how the balanced scorecard aligns performance with organizational goals.

The **balanced scorecard**, developed by Robert S. Kaplan and David P. Norton, is a framework that links the perspectives of an organization's four basic stakeholder groups—financial (investors), learning and growth (employees), internal business processes, and customers—with the organization's mission and vision, performance measures, strategic and tactical plans, and resources. To succeed, an organization must add value for all groups in both the short and the long term. Thus, an organization will determine each group's objectives and translate them into performance measures that have specific, quantifiable performance targets. Ideally, managers should be able to see how their actions contribute to the achievement of organizational goals and understand how their compensation is related to their actions. The balanced scorecard assumes that an organization will get only what it measures.

The Balanced Scorecard and Management

VAIL RESORTS®

Just Another Day In Paradise™

To illustrate how managers use the balanced scorecard, we will refer to **Vail Resorts'** PEAKS system, which we described in the Decision Point.

Planning During the planning stage, the balanced scorecard provides a framework that enables managers to translate their organization's vision and strategy into operational terms. Managers evaluate the company's vision from the perspective of each stakeholder group and seek to answer one key question for each group:

- **Financial (investors):** To achieve our organization's vision, how should we appear to our shareholders?

- **Learning and growth (employees):** To achieve our organization's vision, how should we sustain our ability to improve and change?

- **Internal business processes:** To succeed, in which business processes must our organization excel?

- **Customers:** To achieve our organization's vision, how should we appeal to our customers?

These key questions align the organization's strategy from all perspectives. The answers to the questions result in performance objectives that are mutually beneficial to all stakeholders. Once the organization's objectives are set, managers can select performance measures and set performance targets to translate the objectives into an action plan.

FOCUS ON BUSINESS PRACTICE

Risky Business

The balanced scorecard provides a platform for managing business risk. It fits well with enterprise risk management systems (ERMs), which identify events that may affect a business and help manage them so that they are deemed ethical and provide reasonable assurance that the business will achieve its objectives. The linking of goals, measures, and targets from multiple perspectives is the key.[2]

Study Note

The alignment of an organization's strategy with all the perspectives of the balanced scorecard results in performance objectives that benefit all stakeholders.

For example, if Vail Resorts' collective vision and strategy is to please guests, its managers might establish the following overall objectives:

Perspective	Objective
Financial (investors)	Increase guests' spending at the resorts.
Learning and growth (employees)	Continually cross-train employees in each other's duties to sustain premium-quality service for guests.
Internal business processes	Leverage market position by introducing and improving innovative marketing and technology-driven advances that clearly benefit guests.
Customers	Create new premium-price experiences and facilities for vacations in all seasons.

These overall objectives are then translated into specific performance objectives and measures for managers. For example, a ski lift manager's performance objectives might be measured in terms of the following:

- **Financial (investors):** hourly lift cost, lift ticket sales in dollars and in units

- **Learning and growth (employees):** number of cross-trained tasks per employee, employee turnover

- **Internal business processes:** number of accident-free days, number and cost of mechanical breakdowns, average lift cycle time (that is, the time between getting in line to ride the ski lift and completing the ski run)

- **Customers:** average number of ski runs per daily lift ticket, number of repeat customers, number of PEAKS points redeemed

Figure 1 summarizes how Vail Resorts' managers might link their organization's vision and strategy to objectives, then link the objectives to logical performance measures, and, finally, set performance targets. As a result, a ski lift manager will have a variety of performance measures that balance the perspectives and needs of all stakeholders.

Performing Managers use the mutually agreed-upon strategic and tactical objectives for the entire organization as the basis for decision making within their individual areas of responsibility. This practice ensures that they consider the needs of all stakeholder groups and shows how measuring and managing performance for some stakeholder groups can lead to improved performance for another stakeholder group. Specifically, improving the performance of leading indicators like internal business processes and learning and growth will create improvements for customers, which in turn will result in improved financial performance (a lagging indicator). For example, when making decisions about available ski lift capacity, the ski lift manager at Vail Resorts will balance such factors as lift ticket sales, snow conditions, equipment reliability, trained staff availability, and length of wait for ski lifts.

When managers understand the causal and linked relationship between their actions and their company's overall performance, they can see new ways to be more effective. For example, a ski lift manager may hypothesize that shorter waiting lines for the ski lifts would improve customer satisfaction and lead to more visits to the ski lift. The manager could test this possible cause-and-effect relationship by measuring and tracking the length of ski lift waiting lines and the number of visits to the ski lift. If a causal relationship exists, the

■ **FIGURE 1**
Sample Balanced Scorecard of Linked Objectives, Performance Measures, and Targets

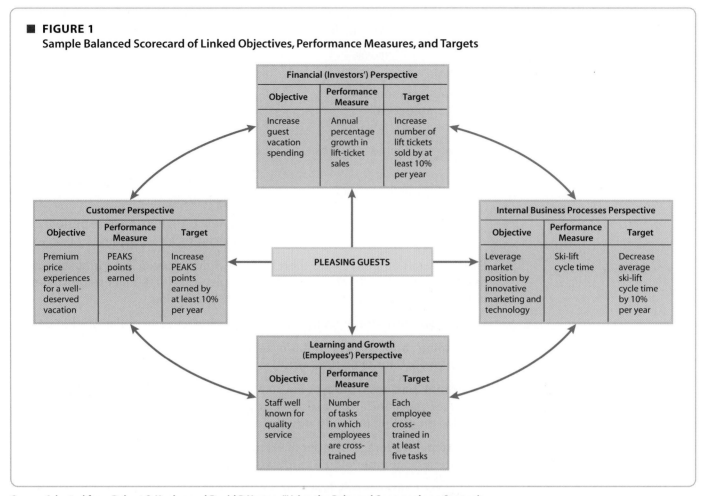

Source: Adapted from Robert S. Kaplan and David P. Norton, "Using the Balanced Scorecard as a Strategic Management System," *Harvard Business Review*, January–February 1996.

manager can improve the performance of the ski lift operation by doing everything possible to ensure that waiting lines are short because a quicker ride to the top will result in improved results for the operation and for other perspectives as well.

Evaluating Managers review financial and nonfinancial results frequently during the year, at year end, and over longer periods to evaluate their strategies for meeting the objectives and performance targets set during the planning stage. They compare performance objectives and targets with actual results to determine if the targets were met, what measures need to be changed, and what strategies or objectives need revision. For example, the ski lift manager at Vail Resorts would analyze the reasons for performance gaps and make recommendations to improve the performance of the ski lift area.

Communicating Finally, during the communication stage of the management process, a variety of reports are prepared. For example, the database makes it possible to prepare financial performance reports, customer PEAKS statements, internal business process reports for targeted performance measures and results, and performance appraisals of individual employees. Such reports enable managers to monitor and evaluate performance measures that add value for stakeholder groups.

■ **FIGURE 2**
The Management Process: To-Do's for Managers

To-Do's for Managers

- Plan
  - Translate organizational mission and vision into operational objectives from multiple stakeholders' perspectives
  - Select performance measures for objectives
  - Establish targets for each performance measure

- Perform
  - Balance needs of all stakeholders when making management decisions
  - Improve performance by tracking causal relationships between objectives, measures, and targets

- Evaluate
  - Compare financial and nonfinancial results with performance measurement targets
  - Analyze results and take corrective actions

- Communicate
  - Prepare reports of interest to stakeholder groups

As you can see in Figure 2, the balanced scorecard adds dimension to a manager's to do list. Managers plan, perform, evaluate, and communicate the organization's performance from multiple perspectives. By balancing the needs of all stakeholders, managers are more likely to achieve their objectives in both the short and the long term.

S T O P ● R E V I E W ● A P P L Y

1-1. What four basic stakeholder groups are included in the balanced scorecard?

1-2. On which perspective do most businesses focus?

1-3. Why is it important for managers to see the causal relationships between their actions and the company's overall performance?

Suggested answers to all Stop, Review, and Apply questions are available at http://college.hmco.com/accounting/needles/man_acc/8e/student_home.html.

Performance Measurement

As a company's management philosophy changes, so must the measures in its performance management and evaluation system. A **performance management and evaluation system** is a set of procedures that account for and report on both financial and nonfinancial performance, so that a company can identify how well it is doing, where it is going, and what improvements will make it more profitable.

What to Measure, How to Measure

Performance measurement is the use of quantitative tools to gauge an organization's performance in relation to a specific goal or an expected outcome. For performance measurement to succeed, managers must be able to distinguish between what is being measured and the actual measures used to monitor performance. For instance, product or service quality is *not* a performance measure. It is part of a management strategy: Management wants to produce the highest-quality product or service possible, given the resources available. Product or service quality thus is what management *wants* to measure. To measure product or service quality, managers must collaborate with other managers to develop a group of measures, such as the balanced scorecard, that will identify changes in product or service quality and help employees determine what needs to be done to improve quality.

Other Measurement Issues

Each organization must develop a set of performance measures that is appropriate to its situation. In addition to answering the basic questions of what to measure and how to measure, management must consider a variety of other issues, including the following:

▶ What performance measures can be used?

▶ How can managers monitor the level of product or service quality?

▶ How can managers monitor production and other business processes to identify areas that need improvement?

▶ How can managers measure customer satisfaction?

Study Note

What a manager is measuring—for example, quality—is not the same thing as the actual measures used to monitor performance—for example, the number of defective units per hour.

FOCUS ON BUSINESS PRACTICE

"Old" Doesn't Mean "Out-of-Date"

The *tableau de bord*, or "dashboard," was developed by French engineers around 1900 as a concise performance measurement system that helped managers understand the cause-and-effect relationships between their decisions and the resulting performance. The indicators, both financial and nonfinancial, allowed managers at all levels to monitor their progress in terms of the mission and objectives of their unit and of their company overall. Like a set of nested Russian dolls, each unit's key success factors and key performance indicators were integrated with those of other units. The dashboard continues to encourage a performance measurement system that focuses on and supports an organization's strategic plan.[3]

How can managers monitor financial performance?

Are there other stakeholders to whom a manager is accountable?

What performance measures do government entities impose on the company?

How can a manager measure the company's effect on the environment?

S T O P • R E V I E W • A P P L Y

2-1. What is a performance management and evaluation system?

2-2. When managers make changes in how work should be done, should performance measures be reviewed?

Responsibility Accounting

LO3 Define *responsibility accounting,* and describe the role that responsibility centers play in performance management and evaluation.

As part of their performance management systems, many organizations assign resources to specific areas of responsibility and track how the managers of those areas use those resources. For example, **Vail Resorts** assigns resources to its Lodging, Dining, Retail and Rental, Ski School, and Real Estate divisions and holds the managers of those divisions responsible for generating revenue and managing costs. In addition, the company may give the managers resources to invest in assets that will support the growth of their divisions. Within each division, other managers are assigned responsibility for such areas as Children and Adult Ski School, Snowboard School, or Private Lessons. All managers at all levels are then evaluated in terms of their ability to manage their areas of responsibility in keeping with the organization's goals.

To assist in performance management and evaluation, many organizations use responsibility accounting. **Responsibility accounting** is an information system that classifies data according to areas of responsibility and reports each area's activities by including only the revenue, cost, and resource categories that the assigned manager can control. A **responsibility center** is an organizational unit whose manager has been assigned the responsibility of managing a portion of the organization's resources. The activities of a responsibility center dictate the extent of a manager's responsibility.

Types of Responsibility Centers

There are five types of responsibility centers: (1) cost centers, (2) discretionary cost centers, (3) revenue centers, (4) profit centers, and (5) investment centers. The key characteristics of the five types of responsibility centers are summarized in Table 1.

Cost Centers   A responsibility center whose manager is accountable only for controllable costs that have well-defined relationships between the center's resources and certain products or services is called a **cost center**. Manufacturing companies like **Coach, Inc.**, **DaimlerChrysler**, **Apple Computer**, and **Kraft** use cost centers to manage assembly plants, where the relationship

TABLE 1. Types of Responsibility Centers

Responsibility Center	Manager Accountable For	How Performance Is Measured	Examples
Cost center	Only controllable costs, where there are well-defined links between the costs of resources and the resulting products or services	Compare actual costs with flexible and master budget costs Analyze resulting variances	Product: Manufacturing assembly plants Service: Food service for hospital patients
Discretionary cost center	Only controllable costs; the links between the costs of resources and the resulting products or services are *not* well defined	Compare actual noncost-based measures with targets Determine compliance with preapproved budgeted spending limits	Product or service: Administrative activities such as accounting, human resources, and research and development
Revenue center	Revenue generation	Compare actual revenue with budgeted revenue Analyze resulting variances	Product: Phone or ecommerce sales for pizza delivery Service: National car rental reservation center
Profit center	Operating income resulting from controllable revenues and costs	Compare actual variable costing income statement with the budgeted income statement	Product or service: Local store of a national chain
Investment center	Controllable revenues, costs, and the investment of resources to achieve organizational goals	Return on investment Residual income Economic value added	Product: A division of a multinational corporation Service: A national office of a multinational consulting firm

between the costs of resources (direct material, direct labor) and the resulting products is well defined.

Nonmanufacturing organizations use cost centers to manage activities in which resources are clearly linked with a service that is provided at no additional charge. For example, in nursing homes and hospitals, there is a clear relationship between the costs of food and direct labor and the number of inpatient meals served.

The performance of a cost center is usually evaluated by comparing an activity's actual cost with its budgeted cost and analyzing the resulting variances. You will learn more about this performance evaluation process in the chapter on standard costing.

Shown here at the Monsanto Research Centre in Bangalore, India, is a scientist engaged in mapping the rice genome. Research and development units are a type of discretionary cost center, in which a manager is accountable for costs only and the relationship between resources and products or services produced is not well defined. A common performance measure used to evaluate research and development activities is the number of patents obtained.

Discretionary Cost Centers   A responsibility center whose manager is accountable for costs only and in which the relationship between resources and the products or services produced is not well defined is called a **discretionary cost center**. Units that perform administrative activities, such as accounting, human resources, and legal services, are typical examples of discretionary cost centers. These centers, like cost centers, have approved budgets that set spending limits.

Because the spending and use of resources in discretionary cost centers are not clearly linked to the production of a product or service, cost-based measures usually cannot be used to evaluate performance (although such centers are penalized if they exceed their approved budgets). For example, among the performance measures used to evaluate the research and development activities at manufacturing companies such as **DaimlerChrysler**, **Monsanto**, and **Intel** are the number of patents obtained and the number of cost-saving innovations that are developed. At service organizations, such as the **United Way**, a common measure of administrative activities is how low their costs are as a percentage of total contributions.

Revenue Centers   A responsibility center whose manager is accountable primarily for revenue and whose success is based on its ability to generate revenue is called a **revenue center**. Examples of revenue centers are **Hertz**'s national car reservation center and the clothing retailer **Nordstrom**'s ecommerce order department. A revenue center's performance is usually evaluated by comparing its actual revenue with its budgeted revenue and analyzing the resulting variances. Performance measures at both manufacturing and service organizations may include sales dollars, number of customer sales, or sales revenue per minute.

Profit Centers   A responsibility center whose manager is accountable for both revenue and costs and for the resulting operating income is called a **profit center**. A good example is a local store of a national chain, such as **Wal-Mart**, **Coach, Inc.**, or **Jiffy Lube**. The performance of a profit center is usually evaluated by comparing the figures in its actual income statement with the figures in its master or flexible budget income statement.

Investment Centers   A responsibility center whose manager is accountable for profit generation and can also make significant decisions about the resources that the center uses is called an **investment center**. For example, the president of **DaimlerChrysler's** Jeep Division, the president of **Harley-Davidson's** Buell subsidiary, and the president of **Brinker International's** Chili's Grill and Bar can control revenues, costs, and the investment of assets to achieve organizational goals. The performance of these centers is evaluated using such measures as return on investment, residual income, and economic value added. These measures are used in all types of organizations, both manufacturing and nonmanufacturing, and are discussed later in this chapter.

Organizational Structure and Performance Management

Much can be learned about an organization by examining how its managers organize activities and resources. A company's organizational structure formalizes its lines of managerial authority and control. An **organization chart** is a visual representation of an organization's hierarchy of responsibility for the purposes of management control. Within an organization chart, the five types of responsibility centers are arranged by level of management authority and control.

A responsibility accounting system establishes a communications network within an organization that is ideal for gathering and reporting information about the operations of each area of responsibility. The system is used to prepare budgets by responsibility area and to report the actual results of each responsibility center. The report for a responsibility center should contain only the costs, revenues, and resources that the manager of that center can control. Such costs and revenues are called **controllable costs and revenues** because they are the result of a manager's actions, influence, or decisions. A responsibility accounting system ensures that managers will not be held responsible for items that they cannot change.

Shown here is the interior of a Chili's Grill and Bar. Each restaurant in the Chili's chain is a profit center for Brinker International. Typically, in a corporate division like Chili's, restaurant managers report to vice presidents, who report to the president of the restaurant division. The division president's office is an investment center because capital investment decisions are made at this level.

■ **FIGURE 3**
Partial Organization Chart of Café Cubano, a Restaurant Chain

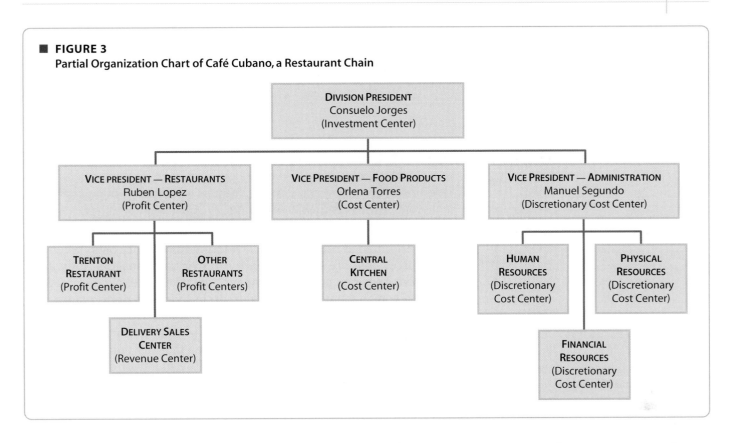

By examining a typical corporate organization chart, you can see how a responsibility accounting system works. Figure 3 shows part of the management structure for Café Cubano, a multiconcept restaurant chain like **Brinker International, Inc.**, and **Carlson Restaurants Worldwide Inc.** Typically, several vice presidents report to the president of a restaurant division like Chili's or T.G.I. Friday's U.S.A. Notice that the figure shows examples of all five types of responsibility centers. The office of Consuelo Jorges, the division president, is an investment center because capital investment decisions are made at the division level. The vice president–restaurants, Ruben Lopez, manages both profit and revenue centers. The vice president–administration, Manuel Segundo, supervises three discretionary cost centers, and the vice president–food products, Orlena Torres, is responsible for the operation of the central kitchen, a cost center.

In a responsibility accounting system, the performance reports for each level of management are tailored to each manager's individual needs for information. Because the system provides a report for every manager and lower-level managers report to higher-level managers, the same information may appear in varying formats in several different reports. When information about lower-level operations appears in upper-level managers' reports, it is usually condensed. Performance reporting by responsibility level enables an organization to trace the source of a cost, revenue, or resource to the manager who controls it and to evaluate that manager's performance accordingly.

S T O P • R E V I E W • A P P L Y

3-1. Define responsibility accounting.

3-2. Describe a responsibility center.

3-3. How should managers' performance be evaluated?

3-4. How does a company's organizational structure affect its responsibility accounting system?

Performance Evaluation of Cost Centers and Profit Centers

LO4 Prepare performance reports for cost centers using flexible budgets and for profit centers using variable costing.

Because performance reports contain information about costs, revenues, and resources that are controllable by individual managers, they allow comparisons between actual performance and budget expectations. Such comparisons allow management to evaluate an individual's performance with respect to responsibility center objectives and companywide objectives and to recommend changes. It is important to emphasize that performance reports should contain only costs, revenues, and resources that the manager can control. If a performance report includes items that the manager cannot control, the credibility of the entire responsibility accounting system can be called into question. It is up to management to structure and interpret the performance results fairly.

The content and format of a performance report depend on the nature of the responsibility center. Let us take a closer look at the performance reports for cost centers and profit centers.

Study Note

Only controllable items should be included on a manager's performance report.

Evaluating Cost Center Performance Using Flexible Budgeting

Orlena Torres, the vice president–food products at Café Cubano, is responsible for the central kitchen, where the food products that the restaurants sell are prepared. The central kitchen is a cost center because its costs have well-defined relationships with the resulting products. To ensure that the central kitchen is meeting its performance goals, Torres has decided to evaluate the performance of each food item produced. She will prepare a separate report for each product that compares its actual costs with the corresponding amounts from the budget. The performance report for Café Cubano's House Dressing, one of the chain's signature menu items, is presented in Exhibit 1.

The performance report in Exhibit 1 compares data from the master budget (prepared at the beginning of the period) with the actual results for the period. As you can see, actual costs exceeded budgeted costs. Most managers would consider such a cost overrun significant. But was there really a cost overrun? The amounts budgeted in the master budget are based on an output of 1,000 units of dressing; however, the actual output was 1,200 units of dressing. To judge the central kitchen's performance accurately, the company's managers must change the budgeted data in the master budget to reflect an output of 1,200 units. They can do this by using a flexible budget.

A **flexible budget** (also called a *variable budget*) is a summary of expected costs for a range of activity levels. Unlike a static budget, a flexible budget provides forecasted data that can be adjusted for changes in the level of output. A flexible budget is derived by multiplying actual unit output by predetermined unit costs for each cost item in the report. The flexible budget is used primarily

EXHIBIT 1 ►

Central Kitchen's Performance Report on Café Cubano's House Dressing						
	Actual Results	**Variance**	**Flexible Budget**	**Variance**	**Master Budget**	
Gallons produced	1,200	0	1,200	200 (F)	1,000	
Center costs						
Direct materials ($.25 per gallon)	$312	$12 (U)	$300	$50 (U)	$250	
Direct labor ($.05 per gallon)	72	12 (U)	60	10 (U)	50	
Variable overhead ($.03 per gallon)	33	3 (F)	36	6 (U)	30	
Fixed overhead	2	3 (F)	5	0	5	
Total cost	$419	$18 (U)	$401	$66 (U)	$335	
Performance measures						
Defect-free gallons to total produced	.98	.01 (U)	N/A	N/A	.99	
Average throughput time per gallon	11 minutes	1 minute (F)	N/A	N/A	12 minutes	

as a cost control tool in evaluating performance at the end of a period, as in Exhibit 1.

In another chapter, you will learn that favorable (positive, or F) and unfavorable (negative, or U) variances between actual costs and the flexible budget can be further examined by using standard costing to compute specific variances for direct materials, direct labor, and variable and fixed overhead. Also, you will use the flexible budget as a cost control tool to evaluate performance and derive a flexible budget by multiplying actual unit output by the standard unit costs. Refer to the chapter on standard costing for further information on performance evaluation using variances or the flexible budget.

Evaluating Profit Center Performance Using Variable Costing

Ruben Lopez, the vice president–restaurants, oversees many restaurants. Because the restaurants are profit centers, each is accountable for its own revenues and costs and for the resulting operating income. A profit center's performance is usually evaluated by comparing its actual income statement results to its budgeted income statement.

Variable costing is a method of preparing profit center performance reports that classifies a manager's controllable costs as either variable or fixed. Variable costing produces a variable costing income statement instead of a traditional income statement (also called a *full costing* or *absorption costing income statement*), which is used for external reporting purposes. A variable costing income statement is the same as a contribution income statement, the format of which you may recall from its use in cost-volume-profit analysis. Such an income statement is useful in performance management and evaluation because it focuses on cost variability and the profit center's contribution to operating income.

When variable costing is used to evaluate profit center performance, the variable cost of goods sold and the variable selling and administrative

EXHIBIT 2 ▶

Variable Costing Income Statement Versus Traditional Income Statement for Trenton Restaurant

Variable Costing Income Statement		Traditional Income Statement	
Sales	$2,500	Sales	$2,500
Variable cost of goods sold	1,575	Cost of goods sold	1,745
Variable selling expenses	325	($1,575 + $170 = $1,745)	
Contribution margin	$ 600	Gross margin	$ 755
Fixed manufacturing costs	170	Variable selling expenses	325
Fixed selling expenses	230	Fixed selling expenses	230
Profit center income	$ 200	Profit center income	$ 200

expenses are subtracted from sales to arrive at the contribution margin for the center. All the controllable fixed costs of a profit center, including those from manufacturing, selling, and administrative activities, are subtracted from the contribution margin to determine the operating income.

The variable costing income statement differs from the traditional income statement prepared for financial reporting, as shown by the two income statements in Exhibit 2 for Trenton Restaurant, part of the Café Cubano restaurant chain. In the traditional income statement, all manufacturing costs are assigned to cost of goods sold; in the variable costing income statement, only the variable manufacturing costs are included. Under variable costing, direct materials costs, direct labor costs, and variable overhead costs are the only cost elements used to compute variable cost of goods sold. Fixed manufacturing costs are considered costs of the current accounting period. Notice that fixed manufacturing costs are listed with fixed selling expenses after the contribution margin has been computed.

▼ **EXHIBIT 3**

Performance Report Based on Variable Costing and Flexible Budgeting for Trenton Restaurant

	Actual Results	Variance	Flexible Budget	Variance	Master Budget
Meals served	750	0	750	250 (U)	1,000
Sales (average meal $2.85)	$2,500.00	$362.50 (F)	$2,137.50	$712.50 (U)	$2,850.00
Controllable variable costs					
Variable cost of goods sold ($1.50)	1,575.00	450.00 (U)	1,125.00	375.00 (F)	1,500.00
Variable selling expenses ($.40)	325.00	25.00 (U)	300.00	100.00 (F)	400.00
Contribution margin	$ 600.00	$112.50 (U)	$ 712.50	$237.50 (U)	$ 950.00
Controllable fixed costs					
Fixed manufacturing expenses	170.00	30.00 (F)	200.00	0.00	200.00
Fixed selling expenses	230.00	20.00 (F)	250.00	0.00	250.00
Profit center income	$ 200.00	$ 62.50 (U)	$ 262.50	$237.50 (U)	$ 500.00
Other nonfinancial performance measures					
Number of orders processed	300	50 (F)	N/A	N/A	250
Average sales order	$8.34	$3.06 (U)	N/A	N/A	$11.40

The manager of a profit center may also want to measure and evaluate non-financial information. For example, Ruben Lopez of Café Cubano may want to track the number of food orders processed and the average amount of a sales order at Trenton Restaurant. The resulting report, based on variable costing and flexible budgeting, is shown in Exhibit 3.

Although performance reports vary in format depending on the type of responsibility center, they have some common themes. For example, all responsibility center reports compare actual results to budgeted figures and focus on the differences. Often, comparisons are made to a flexible budget as well as to the master budget. Only the items that the manager can control are included in the performance report. Nonfinancial measures are also examined to achieve a more balanced view of the manager's responsibilities.

STOP • REVIEW • APPLY

4-1. What types of information are in performance reports?

4-2. When is a flexible budget prepared?

4-3. What are some similarities among the performance reports for the various kinds of responsibility centers?

Performance Evaluation of Investment Centers

LO5 Prepare performance reports for investment centers using the traditional measures of return on investment and residual income and the newer measure of economic value added.

The evaluation of an investment center's performance requires more than a comparison of controllable revenues and costs with budgeted amounts. Because the managers of investment centers also control resources and invest in assets, other performance measures must be used to hold them accountable for revenues, costs, and the capital investments that they control. In this section, we focus on the traditional performance evaluation measures of return on investment and residual income and the relatively new performance measure of economic value added.

Return on Investment

Traditionally, the most common performance measure that takes into account both operating income and the assets invested to earn that income is **return on investment (ROI)**. Return on investment is computed as follows:

$$\text{Return on Investment (ROI)} = \frac{\text{Operating Income}}{\text{Assets Invested}}$$

In this formula, *assets invested* is the average of the beginning and ending asset balances for the period.

Properly measuring the income and the assets specifically controlled by a manager is critical to the quality of this performance measure. Using ROI, it is

EXHIBIT 4 ▶

	Actual Results	Variance	Master Budget
Performance Report Based on Return on Investment for the Café Cubano Restaurant Division			
Operating income	$610	$280 (U)	$ 890
Assets invested	$800	$200 (F)	$1,000
Performance measure			
ROI	76%	13% (U)	89%

ROI = Operating Income ÷ Assets Invested
$890 ÷ $1,000 = .89 = 89%
$610 ÷ $800 = .76 = 76%

possible to evaluate the manager of any investment center, whether it is an entire company or a unit within a company, such as a subsidiary, division, or other business segment. For example, assume that the Café Cubano Restaurant Division had actual operating income of $610 and that the average assets invested were $800. The master budget called for $890 in operating income and $1,000 in invested assets. As shown in Exhibit 4, the budgeted ROI for Consuelo Jorges, the president of the division, would be 89 percent, and the actual ROI would be 76 percent. The actual ROI was lower than the budgeted ROI because the division's actual operating income was lower than expected relative to the actual assets invested.

For investment centers, the ROI computation is really the aggregate measure of many interrelationships. The basic ROI equation, Operating Income ÷ Assets Invested, can be rewritten to show the many elements within the aggregate ROI number that a manager can influence. Two important indicators of performance are profit margin and asset turnover. **Profit margin** is the ratio of operating income to sales; it represents the percentage of each sales dollar that results in profit. **Asset turnover** is the ratio of sales to average assets invested; it indicates the productivity of assets, or the number of sales dollars generated by each dollar invested in assets. Return on investment is equal to profit margin multiplied by asset turnover:

$$\text{ROI} = \text{Profit Margin} \times \text{Asset Turnover}$$

$$\text{ROI} = \frac{\text{Operating Income}}{\text{Sales}} \times \frac{\text{Sales}}{\text{Assets Invested}} = \frac{\text{Operating Income}}{\text{Assets Invested}}$$

Study Note

Profit margin focuses on the income statement, and asset turnover focuses on the balance sheet aspects of ROI.

Profit margin and asset turnover help explain changes in return on investment for a single investment center or differences in return or investment among investment centers. Therefore, the formula ROI = Profit Margin × Asset Turnover is useful for analyzing and interpreting the elements that make up a business's overall return on investment.

Du Pont, one of the first organizations to recognize the many interrelationships that affect ROI, designed a formula similar to the one diagrammed in Figure 4. You can see that ROI is affected by a manager's decisions about pricing, product sales mix, capital budgeting for new facilities, product sales volume, and other financial matters. In essence, a single ROI number is a composite index of many cause-and-effect relationships and interdependent financial elements. A manager can improve ROI by increasing sales, decreasing costs, or decreasing assets.

■ **FIGURE 4**
Factors Affecting the Computation of Return on Investment

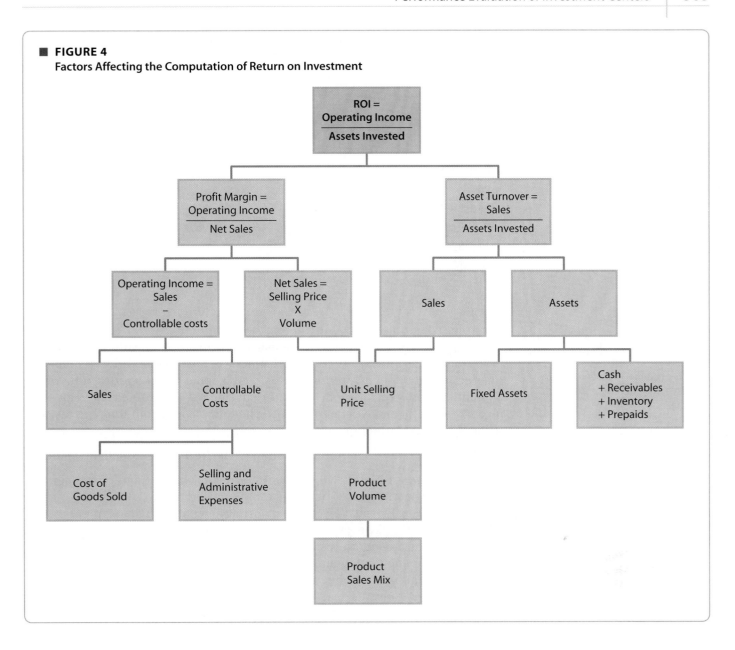

Because of the many factors that affect ROI, management should use this measure cautiously in evaluating performance. If ROI is overemphasized, investment center managers may react by making business decisions that favor their personal ROI performance at the expense of companywide profits or the long-term success of other investment centers. To avoid such problems, other performance measures should always be used in conjunction with ROI—for example, comparisons of revenues, costs, and operating income with budget amounts or past trends; sales growth percentages; market share percentages; or other key variables in the organization's activity. ROI should also be compared with budgeted goals and with past ROI trends because changes in this ratio over time can be more revealing than any single number.

Residual Income

Because of the pitfalls of using return on investment as a performance measure, other approaches to evaluating investment centers have evolved. For

EXHIBIT 5 ▶

Performance Report Based on Residual Income for the Café Cubano Restaurant Division			
	Actual Results	Variance	Master Budget
Operating income	$610	$280 (U)	$ 890
Assets invested	$800	$200 (F)	$1,000
Desired ROI			20%
Performance measures			
ROI	76%	13% (U)	89%
Residual income	$450	$240 (U)	$ 690

Residual Income = Operating Income − (Desired ROI × Assets Invested)
$890 − 20%($1,000) = $690
$610 − 20%($800) = $450

Study Note

ROI is expressed as a percentage, and residual income is expressed in dollars.

example, companies like **General Motors**, **General Electric**, **Coca-Cola**, and **UPS** now use residual income to measure performance. **Residual income (RI)** is the operating income that an investment center earns above a minimum desired return on invested assets. Residual income is not a ratio, but a dollar amount: the amount of profit left after subtracting a predetermined desired income target for an investment center. The formula for computing the residual income of an investment center is:

Residual Income = Operating Income − (Desired ROI × Assets Invested)

As in the computation of ROI, assets invested is the average of the center's beginning and ending asset balances for the period.

The desired RI will vary from investment center to investment center depending on the type of business and the level of risk assumed. The performance report based on residual income for Consuelo Jorges, the president of the Café Cubano Restaurant Division, is shown in Exhibit 5. Assume that the president's residual income performance target is to exceed a 20 percent return on assets invested in the division. Note that the division's residual income is $450, which was lower than the $690 that was projected in the master budget.

Comparisons with other residual income figures will strengthen the analysis. To add context to the analysis of the division and its manager, questions such as the following need to be answered: How did the division's residual income this year compare with its residual income in previous years? Did the actual residual income exceed the budgeted residual income? How did this division's residual income compare with the amounts generated by other investment centers of the company?

Caution is called for when using residual income to compare investment centers within a company. For their residual income figures to be comparable, all investment centers must have equal access to resources and similar asset investment bases. Some managers may be able to produce larger residual incomes simply because their investment centers are larger rather than because their performance is better. Like ROI, RI has some flaws.

Economic Value Added

More and more businesses are using the shareholder wealth created by an investment center, or the **economic value added (EVA)**, as an indicator of per-

EXHIBIT 6 ▶

	Performance Report Based on Economic Value Added for the Café Cubano Restaurant Division			
		Actual Results	Variance	Master Budget
	Performance measures			
	ROI	76%	13% (U)	89%
	Residual income	$450	$240 (U)	$690
	Economic value added	$334		
	Economic Value Added = After-Tax Operating Income −			
	[Cost of Capital × (Total Assets − Current Liabilities)]			
	$400 − 12% ($800 − $250) = $334			

formance. The calculation of EVA, a registered trademark of the consulting firm **Stern Stewart & Company,** can be quite complex because it makes various cost of capital and accounting principles adjustments. You will learn more about the cost of capital in the chapter that discusses capital investment decisions. However, for the purposes of computing EVA, the **cost of capital** is the minimum desired rate of return on an investment, such as the assets invested in an investment center.

Basically, the computation of EVA is similar to the computation of residual income, except that after-tax operating income is used instead of pretax operating income, and a cost of capital percentage is multiplied by the center's invested assets less current liabilities instead of a desired ROI percentage being multiplied by invested assets. Also, like residual income, the economic value added is expressed in dollars. The formula is:

$$EVA = \text{After-Tax Operating Income} - \text{Cost of Capital in Dollars}$$

$$EVA = \text{After-Tax Operating Income} - [\text{Cost of Capital} \times (\text{Total Assets} - \text{Current Liabilities})]$$

A very basic computation of economic value added for Consuelo Jorges, the president of the Café Cubano Restaurant Division, is shown in Exhibit 6. The report assumes that the division's after-tax operating income is $400, its cost of capital is 12 percent, its total assets are $800, and its current liabilities are $250.

The report shows that the division has added $334 to its economic value after taxes and cost of capital. In other words, the division produced after-tax profits of $334 in excess of the cost of capital required to generate those profits.

Because many factors affect the economic value of an investment center, management should be cautious when drawing conclusions about performance. The evaluation will be more meaningful if the current economic value added is compared to EVAs from previous periods, target EVAs, and EVAs from other investment centers.

The factors that affect the computation of economic value added are illustrated in Figure 5. An investment center's economic value is affected by managers' decisions on pricing, product sales volume, taxes, cost of capital, capital investments, and other financial matters. In essence, the EVA number is a composite index drawn from many cause-and-effect relationships and interdependent financial elements. A manager can improve the economic value of an investment center by increasing sales, decreasing costs, decreasing assets, or lowering the cost of capital.

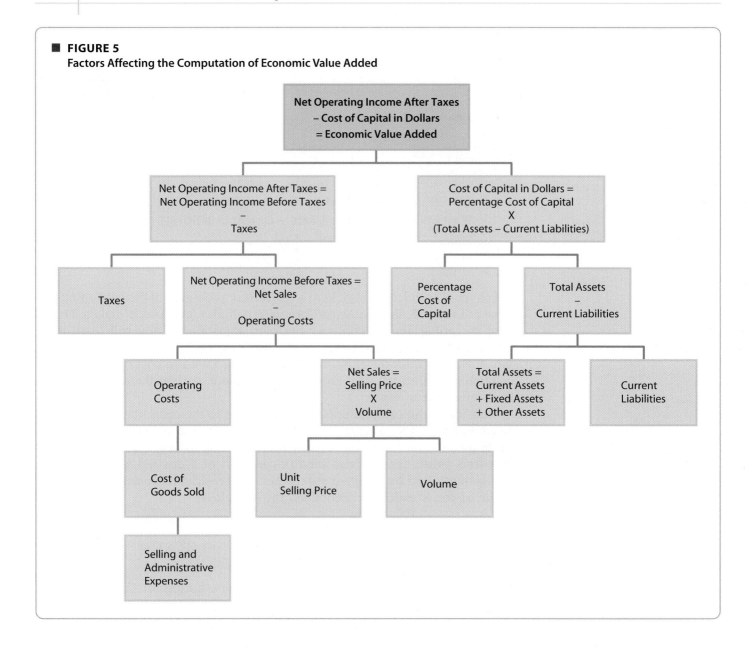

■ **FIGURE 5**
Factors Affecting the Computation of Economic Value Added

The Importance of Multiple Performance Measures

In summary, to be effective, a performance management system must consider both operating results and multiple performance measures, such as return on investment, residual income, and economic value added. Comparing actual results to budgeted figures adds meaning to the evaluation. Performance measures such as ROI, RI, and EVA indicate whether an investment center is effective in coordinating its own goals with companywide goals because these measures take into account both operating income and the assets used to produce that income. However, all three measures are limited by their focus on short-term financial performance. To obtain a fuller picture, management needs to break these three measures down into their components, analyze such information as responsibility center income over time, and compare current results to the targeted amounts in the flexible or master budget. In addition, the analysis of such nonfinancial performance indicators as average through-put time, employee turnover, and number of orders processed will ensure a more balanced view of a business's well-being and how to improve it.

5-1. Why is return on investment more than a ratio of two numbers?

5-2. What are the similarities and differences between RI and EVA?

Performance Measures Brew Mountain Company sells coffee and hot beverages. Its Coffee Cart Division sells to skiers as they come off the mountain. The balance sheet for the Coffee Cart Division showed that the company had invested assets of $30,000 at the beginning of the year and $50,000 at the end of the year. During the year, the division's operating income was $80,000 on sales of $120,000.

a. Compute the division's residual income if the desired ROI is 20 percent.

b. Compute the return on investment for the division.

c. Compute the economic value added for Brew Mountain Company if total corporate assets are $600,000, current liabilities are $80,000, after-tax operating income is $70,000, and the cost of capital is 12 percent.

SOLUTION
a. $80,000 − [20% × ($30,000 + $50,000) ÷ 2] = $72,000
b. $80,000 ÷ [($30,000 + $50,000) ÷ 2] = 200%
c. $70,000 − [12% × ($600,000 − $80,000)] = $7,600

Performance Incentives and Goals

LO6 Explain how properly linked performance incentives and measures add value for all stakeholders in performance management and evaluation.

The effectiveness of a performance management and evaluation system depends on how well it coordinates the goals of responsibility centers, managers, and the entire company. Two factors are key to the successful coordination of goals: the logical linking of goals to measurable objectives and targets, and the tying of appropriate compensation incentives to the achievement of the targets, that is, performance-based pay.

Linking Goals, Performance Objectives, Measures, and Performance Targets

The causal links between an organization's goals, performance objectives, measures, and targets must be apparent. For example, if a company seeks to be an environmental steward, as **Vail Resorts** does, it may choose the following linked goal, objective, measure, and performance target:

Goal	Objective	Measure	Performance Target
To be an environmental steward	To reduce, reuse, and recycle	Number of tons recycled per year	To recycle at least one pound per guest

You may recall that the balanced scorecard also links objectives, measures,
and targets, as shown in Figure 1 earlier in this chapter.

Performance-Based Pay

The tying of appropriate compensation incentives to performance targets
increases the likelihood that the goals of responsibility centers, managers, and
the entire organization will be well coordinated. Unfortunately, this linkage
does not always happen. Responsibility center managers are more likely to
achieve their performance targets if their compensation depends on it.
Performance-based pay is the linking of employee compensation to the
achievement of measurable business targets.

Cash bonuses, awards, profit-sharing plans, and stock programs are common types of incentive compensation. Cash bonuses are usually given to
reward an individual's short-term performance. A bonus may be stated as a
fixed dollar amount or as a percentage of a target figure, such as 5 percent of
operating income or 10 percent of the dollar increase in operating income. An
award may be a trip or some other form of recognition for desirable individual
or group performance. For example, many companies sponsor a trip for all
managers who have met their performance targets during a specified period.
Other companies award incentive points that employees may redeem for
goods or services. (Notice that awards can be used to encourage both short-
term and long-term performance.) Profit-sharing plans reward employees with
a share of the company's profits. Employees often receive company stock as
recognition of their contribution to a profitable period. Using stock as a reward
encourages employees to think and act as investors as well as employees and
encourages a stable work force. In terms of the balanced scorecard, employees
assume two stakeholder perspectives and take both a short- and a long-term
viewpoint. Companies use stock to motivate employees to achieve financial
targets that increase the company's stock price.

The Coordination of Goals

What performance incentives and measures should a company use to manage
and evaluate performance? What actions and behaviors should an organization
reward? Which incentive compensation plans work best? The answers to such
questions depend on the facts and circumstances of each organization. Something that promotes the coordination of goals for one organization may not do
so for another. To be effective, incentive plans must be developed with input
from all employees. All must understand the causal links between goals, objectives, measures, and performance targets. To determine the right performance
incentives for their organization, employees and managers must answer several questions:

FOCUS ON BUSINESS PRACTICE
Aligning Incentives Among Supply Chain Partners

A study of more than 50 supply networks found that misaligned performance incentives are often the cause of inventory buildups or shortages, misguided sales efforts, and poor customer relations. A supply chain works only if the partners work together effectively by adopting revenue-sharing contracts, using technology to track shared information, and/or working with intermediaries to build trust. Such incentives among supply chain partners must be reassessed periodically, as business conditions change.[5]

▶ When should the reward be given: now or sometime in the future?

▶ Whose performance should be rewarded: that of responsibility centers, individual managers, or the entire company?

▶ How should the reward be computed?

▶ On what should the reward be based?

▶ What performance criteria should be used?

▶ Does our performance incentive plan address the interests of all stakeholders?

The effectiveness of a performance management and evaluation system relies on the coordination of responsibility center, managerial, and company goals. Performance can be optimized by linking goals to measurable objectives and targets and by tying appropriate compensation incentives to the achievement of the targets. Common types of incentive compensation are cash bonuses, awards, profit-sharing plans, and stock programs. Each organization's unique circumstances will determine the correct mix of measures and compensation incentives for that organization. If management values the perspectives of all of its stakeholder groups, its performance management and evaluation system will balance and benefit all interests.

STOP • REVIEW • APPLY

6-1. Why do incentive plans use performance-based pay?

6-2. Which performance incentives work best?

A LOOK BACK AT

VAIL RESORTS

In this chapter's Decision Point, we asked these questions:

- **How do managers at Vail Resorts link performance measures and set performance targets to achieve performance objectives?**
- **How do they use the PEAKS system and its integrated database to improve performance management and evaluation?**

Managers at **Vail Resorts** link their organization's vision and strategy to their performance objectives; they then link the objectives to logical performance measures; and, finally, they set performance targets. A balanced scorecard approach enables them to consider the perspectives of all the organization's stakeholders: financial (investors), learning and growth (employees), internal business processes, and customers.

As we indicated in the Decision Point, Vail Resorts' managers like the PEAKS all-in-one-card system because it enables them to quickly and easily collect huge amounts of valuable and highly versatile information. Whenever a guest's card is scanned, new data enter the system and become part of an integrated management information system that allows managers to measure and control costs, quality, and performance in all resort areas. The system's ability to store both financial and nonfinancial data about all aspects of the resorts enables managers to learn about and balance the interests of all the organization's stakeholders: The managers can then use the information to answer traditional financial questions about such matters as the cost of sales and the value of inventory (e.g., food ingredients in the resorts' restaurants and the merchandise in their shops) and to obtain performance data about the resorts' activities, products, services, and customers. In addition, managers and employees receive timely feedback about their performance, and this encourages continuous improvement.

CHAPTER REVIEW

REVIEW of Learning Objectives

LO1 Describe how the balanced scorecard aligns performance with organizational goals.

The balanced scorecard is a framework that links the perspectives of an organization's four basic stakeholder groups—financial, learning and growth, internal business processes, and customers—with its mission and vision, performance measures, strategic and tactical plans, and resources. Ideally, managers should see how their actions help to achieve organizational goals and understand how their compensation is linked to their actions. The balanced scorecard assumes that an organization will get what it measures.

LO2 Discuss performance measurement, and identify the issues that affect management's ability to measure performance.

An effective performance measurement system accounts for and reports on both financial and nonfinancial performance so that an organization can ascertain how well it is doing, where it is going, and what improvements will make it more profitable. Each organization must develop a unique set of performance measures that are appropriate to its specific situation. Besides answering basic questions about what to measure and how to measure, management must consider a variety of other issues. Managers must collaborate to develop a group of measures, such as the balanced scorecard, that will help them determine how to improve performance.

LO3 Define *responsibility accounting,* and describe the role that responsibility centers play in performance management and evaluation.

Responsibility accounting classifies data according to areas of responsibility and reports each area's activities by including only the revenue, cost, and resource categories that the assigned manager can control. There are five types of responsibility centers: cost, discretionary cost, revenue, profit, and investment. Performance reporting by responsibility center allows the source of a cost, revenue, or resource to be traced to the manager who controls it and thus makes it easier to evaluate a manager's performance.

LO4 Prepare performance reports for cost centers using flexible budgets and for profit centers using variable costing.

Performance reports contain information about the costs, revenues, and resources that individual managers can control. The content and format of a performance report depend on the nature of the responsibility center.

The performance of a cost center can be evaluated by comparing its actual costs with the corresponding amounts in the flexible and master budgets. A flexible budget is a summary of anticipated costs for a range of activity levels. It provides forecasted cost data that can be adjusted for changes in the level of output. A flexible budget is derived by multiplying actual unit output by predetermined standard unit costs for each cost item in the report. As you will learn in another chapter, the resulting variances between actual costs and the flexible budget can be examined further by using standard costing to compute specific variances for direct materials, direct labor, and overhead.

The performance of a profit center is usually evaluated by comparing the profit center's actual income statement results with its budgeted income statement. When variable costing is used, the controllable costs of the profit center's manager are classified as variable or fixed. The resulting performance report takes the form of a contribution income statement instead of a traditional income statement. The variable costing income statement is useful because it focuses on cost variability and the profit center's contribution to operating income.

LO5 Prepare performance reports for investment centers using the traditional measures of return on investment and residual income and the newer measure of economic value added.

Traditionally, the most common performance measure has been return on investment (ROI). The basic formula is ROI = Operating Income ÷ Assets Invested. Return on investment can also be examined in terms of profit margin and asset turnover. In this case, ROI = Profit Margin × Asset Turnover, where Profit Margin = Operating Income ÷ Sales, and Asset Turnover = Sales ÷ Assets Invested. Residual income (RI) is the operating income that an investment center earns above a minimum desired return on invested assets. It is expressed as a dollar amount: Residual Income = Operating Income − (Desired ROI × Assets Invested). It is the amount of profit left after subtracting a predetermined desired income target for an investment. Today, businesses are increasingly using the shareholder wealth created by an investment center, or economic value added (EVA), as a performance measure. The calculation of economic value added can be quite complex because of the various adjustments it involves. Basically, it is similar to the calculation of residual income: EVA = After-Tax Operating Income − Cost of Capital in Dollars. A manager can improve the economic value of an investment center by increasing sales, decreasing costs, decreasing assets, or lowering the cost of capital.

LO6 Explain how properly linked performance incentives and measures add value for all stakeholders in performance management and evaluation.

The effectiveness of a performance management and evaluation system depends on how well it coordinates the goals of responsibility centers, managers, and the entire company. Performance can be optimized by linking goals to measurable objectives and targets and tying appropriate compensation incentives to the achievement of those targets. Common types of incentive compensation are cash bonuses, awards, profit-sharing plans, and stock programs. If management values the perspectives of all of its stakeholder groups, its performance management and evaluation system will balance and benefit all interests.

REVIEW of Concepts and Terminology

The following concepts and terms were introduced in this chapter:

Asset turnover: The productivity of assets, or the number of sales dollars generated by each dollar invested in assets; Sales ÷ Assets Invested. **(LO5)**

Balanced scorecard: A framework that links the perspectives of an organization's four basic stakeholder groups—financial (investors), learning and growth (employees), internal business processes, and customers—with the organization's mission and vision, performance measures, strategic plan, and resources. **(LO1)**

Controllable costs and revenues: Costs and revenues that are the result of a manager's actions, influence, or decisions. **(LO3)**

Cost center: A responsibility center whose manager is accountable only for controllable costs that have well-defined relationships between the center's resources and certain products or services. **(LO3)**

Cost of capital: The minimum desired rate of return on an investment, such as assets invested in an investment center. **(LO5)**

Discretionary cost center: A responsibility center whose manager is accountable for costs only and in which the relationship between resources and the products or services produced is not well defined. **(LO3)**

Economic value added (EVA): The shareholder wealth created by an investment center; Economic Value Added = After-Tax Operating Income − Cost of Capital in Dollars. **(LO5)**

Flexible budget: A summary of expected costs for a range of activity levels. Also called a *variable budget*. **(LO4)**

Investment center: A responsibility center whose manager is accountable for profit generation and can also make significant decisions about the resources the center uses. **(LO3)**

Organization chart: A visual representation of an organization's hierarchy of responsibility for the purposes of management control. **(LO3)**

Performance-based pay: The linking of employee compensation to the achievement of measurable business targets. **(LO6)**

Performance management and evaluation system: A set of procedures that account for and report on both financial and nonfinancial performance, so that a company can identify how well it is doing, where it is going, and what improvements will make it more profitable. **(LO2)**

Performance measurement: The use of quantitative tools to gauge an organization's performance in relation to a specific goal or an expected outcome. **(LO2)**

Profit center: A responsibility center whose manager is accountable for both revenue and costs and for the resulting operating income. **(LO3)**

Profit margin: The percentage of each sales dollar that results in profit; Operating Income ÷ Sales. **(LO5)**

Residual income (RI): The operating income that an investment center earns above a minimum desired return on invested assets; Residual Income = Investment Center's Operating Income − (Desired ROI × Assets Invested). **(LO5)**

Responsibility accounting: An information system that classifies data according to areas of responsibility and reports each area's activities by including only the categories that the manager can control. **(LO3)**

Responsibility center: An organizational unit whose manager has been assigned the responsibility of managing a portion of the organization's resources. The five types of responsibility centers are a cost center, discretionary cost center, revenue center, profit center, and investment center. **(LO3)**

Return on investment (ROI): A traditional performance measure that takes into account both operating income and the assets invested to produce that income; ROI = Operating Income ÷ Assets Invested. ROI can also be expressed as Profit Margin × Asset Turnover. **(LO5)**

Revenue center: A responsibility center whose manager is accountable primarily for revenue and whose success is based on its ability to generate revenue. **(LO3)**

Variable costing: A method of preparing profit center performance reports that classifies a manager's controllable costs as either fixed or variable and produces a contribution income statement. **(LO4)**

REVIEW Problem

LO3, LO4, LO5   **Evaluating Profit Center and Investment Center Performance**

Winter Wonderland is a full-service resort and spa. Mary Fortenberry, the resort's general manager, is responsible for guest activities, administration, and food and lodging. In addition, she is solely responsible for the resort's capital investments. The organization chart below shows the resort's various activities and the levels of authority that Fortenberry has established:

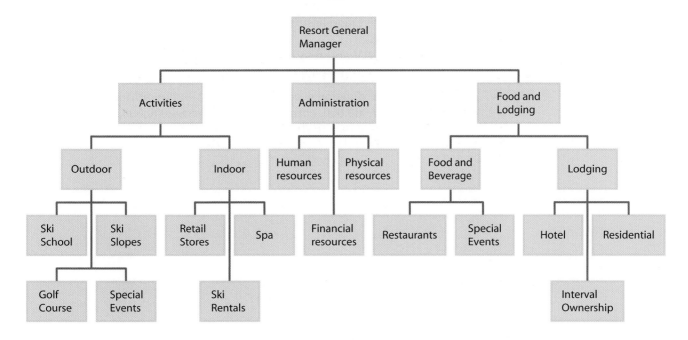

Three divisional managers receive compensation based on their division's performance and have the authority to make employee compensation decisions for their division. Alexandra Patel manages the Food and Lodging Division. The Food and Lodging Division's master budget and actual results for the year ended June 30 follow.

		Master Budget	Actual Results
	Winter Wonderland		
	Food and Lodging Division		
	For the Year Ended June 30		
	(Dollar amounts in thousands)		
		Master	**Actual**
		Budget	**Results**
Guest days		4,000	4,100
Sales		$38,000	$40,000
Variable cost of sales		24,000	25,000
Variable selling and administrative expenses		4,000	4,250
Fixed cost of sales		2,000	1,800
Fixed selling and administrative expenses		2,500	2,500

Required

1. What types of responsibility centers are Administration, Food and Lodging, and Resort General Manager?
2. Assume that Food and Lodging is a profit center. Prepare a performance report using variable costing and flexible budgeting. Determine the variances between actual results and the corresponding figures in the flexible budget and the master budget.
3. Assume that the divisional managers have been assigned responsibility for capital expenditures and that their divisions are thus investment centers. Food and Lodging is expected to generate a desired ROI of at least 30 percent on average assets invested of $10,000,000.

    a. Compute the division's return on investment and residual income using the average assets invested in both the actual and the budget calculations.
    b. Using the ROI and residual income, evaluate Alexandra Patel's performance as divisional manager.

4. Compute the division's actual economic value added if the division's assets are $12,000,000, current liabilities are $3,000,000, after-tax operating income is $4,500,000, and the cost of capital is 20 percent.

Answer to Review Problem

1. Administration: discretionary cost center; Food and Lodging: profit center; Resort General Manager: investment center.
2. Performance report:

			Actual Results	Variance		Flexible Budget	Variance		Master Budget

Winter Wonderland
Food and Lodging Division
For the Year Ended June 30
(Dollar amounts in thousands)

	Actual Results	Variance		Flexible Budget	Variance		Master Budget
Guest days	4,100	—		4,100	100	(F)	4,000
Sales	$40,000	$1,050	(F)	$38,950	$950	(F)	$38,000
Controllable variable costs							
Variable cost of sales	25,000	400	(U)	24,600	600	(U)	24,000
Variable selling and							
administrative							
expenses	4,250	150	(U)	4,100	100	(U)	4,000
Contribution margin	$10,750	$ 500	(F)	$10,250	$250	(F)	$10,000
Controllable fixed costs							
Fixed cost of sales	1,800	200	(F)	2,000	—		2,000
Fixed selling and							
administrative							
expenses	2,500	—		2,500	—		2,500
Division operating income	$ 6,450	$ 700	(F)	$ 5,750	$250	(F)	$ 5,500

3. a. **Return on investment**
    Actual results: $6,450,000 ÷ $10,000,000 = 64.50%
    Flexible budget: $5,750,000 ÷ $10,000,000 = 57.50%
    Master budget: $5,500,000 ÷ $10,000,000 = 55.00%

    Residual income
    Actual results: $6,450,000 − 30%($10,000,000) = $3,450,000
    Flexible budget: $5,750,000 − 30%($10,000,000) = $2,750,000
    Master budget: $5,500,000 − 30%($10,000,000) = $2,500,000

   b. Alexandra Patel's performance as the divisional manager of Food and Lodging exceeds company performance expectations. Actual ROI was 64.5 percent, whereas the company expected an ROI of 30 percent and the flexible budget and the master budget showed projections of 57.5 percent and 55.0 percent, respectively. Residual income also exceeded expectations. The Food and Lodging Division generated $3,450,000 in residual income when the flexible budget and master budget had projected RIs of $2,750,000 and $2,500,000, respectively. The performance report for the division shows 100 more guest days than had been anticipated and a favorable controllable fixed cost variance. As a manager, Patel will investigate the unfavorable variances associated with her controllable variable costs.

4. Economic value added:
    $4,500,000 − 20%($12,000,000 − $3,000,000) = $2,700,000

CHAPTER ASSIGNMENTS

BUILDING Your Basic Knowledge and Skills

Short Exercises

LO1 **Balanced Scorecard**

SE 1. One of your college's overall goals is customer satisfaction. In light of that goal, match each of the following stakeholders' perspectives with the appropriate objective:

Perspective	Objective
1. Financial (investors)	a. Customer satisfaction means that the faculty engages in cutting-edge research.
2. Learning and growth (employees)	
3. Internal business processes	b. Customer satisfaction means that students receive their degrees in four years.
4. Customers	c. Customer satisfaction means that the college has a winning athletics program.
	d. Customer satisfaction means that fundraising campaigns are successful.

LO3 **Responsibility Centers**

SE 2. Identify each of the following as a cost center, a discretionary cost center, a revenue center, a profit center, or an investment center:

1. The manager of center A is responsible for generating cash inflows and incurring costs with the goal of making money for the company. The manager has no responsibility for assets.
2. Center B produces a product that is not sold to an external party.
3. The manager of center C is responsible for the telephone order operations of a large retailer.
4. Center D designs, produces, and sells products to external parties. The manager makes both long-term and short-term decisions.
5. Center E provides human resource support for the other centers in the company.

LO3 **Controllable Costs**

SE 3. Adana Kim is the manager of the Paper Cutting Department in the Northwest Division of Williams Paper Products. Identify each of the following costs as either controllable or not controllable by Kim:

1. Salaries of cutting machine workers
2. Cost of cutting machine parts
3. Cost of electricity for the Northwest Division
4. Lumber Department hauling costs
5. Vice president's salary

LO4 **Cost Center Performance Report**

SE 4. Complete the following performance report for cost center C for the month ended December 31:

	Actual Results	Variance	Flexible Budget	Variance	Master Budget
Units produced	80	0	?	(20) U	100
Center costs					
Direct materials	$ 84	$?	$ 80	$?	$100
Direct labor	150	?	?	40 (F)	200
Variable overhead	?	20 (U)	240	?	300
Fixed overhead	280	?	250	?	250
Total cost	$?	$44 (U)	$?	$120 (F)	$850
Performance measures					
Defect-free units to total produced	75%	?	N/A	N/A	90%
Average throughput time per unit	12 minutes	?	N/A	N/A	10 minutes

LO4   Profit Center Performance Report

SE 5. Complete the following performance report for profit center P for the month ended December 31:

	Actual Results	Variance	Master Budget
Sales	$?	$20 (F)	$120
Controllable variable costs			
Variable cost of goods sold	25	10 (U)	?
Variable selling and administrative expenses	15	?	5
Contribution margin	$100	$?	$100
Controllable fixed costs	?	$10 (F)	60
Profit center income	$ 50	$10 (F)	$?
Performance measures			
Number of orders processed	50	20 (F)	?
Average daily sales	$?	$.66 (F)	$4.00
Number of units sold	100	40 (F)	?

LO5   Return on Investment

SE 6. Complete the profit margin, asset turnover, and return on investment calculations for investment centers D and V:

	Subsidiary D	Subsidiary V
Total sales	$1,650	$2,840
Operating income	$ 180	$ 210
Average assets invested	$ 940	$1,250
Profit margin	?	7.39%
Asset turnover	1.76 times	?
ROI	?	?

LO5   Return on Investment

SE 7. Complete the average assets invested, profit margin, asset turnover, and return on investment calculations for investment centers J and K on the next page.

	Subsidiary J	Subsidiary K
Total sales	$2,000	$2,000
Operating income	$ 500	$ 800
Beginning assets invested	$4,000	$ 500
Ending assets invested	$6,000	$1,500
Average assets invested	$?	$?
Profit margin	25%	?
Asset turnover	?	2 times
ROI	?	?

LO5 Residual Income

SE 8. Complete the operating income, ending assets invested, average assets invested, and residual income calculations for investment centers H and F:

	Subsidiary H	Subsidiary F
Total sales	$20,000	$25,000
Operating income	$ 1,500	$?
Beginning assets invested	$ 4,000	$ 500
Ending assets invested	$ 6,000	$?
Average assets invested	$?	$ 1,000
Desired ROI	20%	20%
Residual income	$?	$ 600

LO5 Economic Value Added

SE 9. Complete the current liabilities, total assets − current liabilities, and economic value added calculations for investment centers M and N:

	Subsidiary M	Subsidiary N
Total sales	$15,000	$18,000
After-tax operating income	$ 1,000	$ 1,100
Total assets	$ 4,000	$ 5,000
Current liabilities	$ 1,000	$?
Total assets − current liabilities	$?	$ 3,500
Cost of capital	15%	15%
Economic value added	$?	$?

LO6 Coordination of Goals

SE 10. One of your college's goals is customer satisfaction. In view of that goal, identify each of the following as a linked objective, a measure, or a performance target:

1. To have successful fund-raising campaigns
2. Number of publications per year per tenure-track faculty
3. To increase the average donation by 10 percent
4. Average number of dollars raised per donor
5. To have faculty engage in cutting-edge research
6. To increase the number of publications per faculty member by at least one per year

Exercises

LO1 Balanced Scorecard

E 1. Biggs Industries is considering adopting the balanced scorecard and has compiled the following list of possible performance measures. Select the balanced scorecard perspective that best matches each performance measure.

Performance Measure	Balanced Scorecard Perspective
1. Residual income	a. Financial (investors)
2. Customer satisfaction rating	b. Learning and growth (employees)
3. Employee absentee rate	c. Internal business processes
4. Growth in profits	d. Customers
5. On-time deliveries	
6. Manufacturing process time	

LO1 Balanced Scorecard

E 2. Virtual Online Products is considering adopting the balanced scorecard and has compiled the following list of possible performance measures. Select the balanced scorecard perspective that best matches each performance measure.

Performance Measure	Balanced Scorecard Perspective
1. Economic value added	a. Financial (investors)
2. Employee turnover	b. Learning and growth (employees)
3. Average daily sales	c. Internal business processes
4. Defect-free units	d. Customers
5. Number of repeat customer visits	
6. Employee training hours	

LO2 Performance Measures

E 3. Eva Washington wants to measure her division's product quality. Link an appropriate performance measure with each balanced scorecard perspective:

Product Quality	Possible Performance Measures
1. Financial (investors)	a. Number of defective products returned
2. Learning and growth (employees)	b. Number of products failing inspection
3. Internal business processes	c. Increased market share
4. Customers	d. Savings from employee suggestions

LO2 Performance Measures

E 4. Monty Sams wants to measure customer satisfaction within his region. Link an appropriate performance measure with each balanced scorecard perspective:

Customer Satisfaction	Possible Performance Measures
1. Financial (investors)	a. Number of cross-trained staff
2. Learning and growth (employees)	b. Customer satisfaction rating
3. Internal business processes	c. Time lapse from order to delivery
4. Customers	d. Dollar sales to repeat customers

LO3 Responsibility Centers

E 5. Identify the most appropriate type of responsibility center for each of the following organizational units:

1. A pizza store in a pizza chain
2. The ticket sales center of a major airline
3. The South American division of a multinational company

4. A subsidiary of a business conglomerate
5. The information technology area of a company
6. A manufacturing department of a large corporation
7. An eye clinic in a community hospital
8. The food service function at a nursing home
9. The food preparation plant of a large restaurant chain
10. The catalog order department of a retailer

LO3 **Controllable Costs**

E 6. Angel Sweets produces pies. The company has the following three-tiered manufacturing structure:

Vice President–Production
↑
Plant Manager
↑
Production Supervisors

Identify the manager responsible for each of the following costs:

1. Repair and maintenance costs
2. Materials handling costs
3. Direct labor
4. Supervisors' salaries
5. Maintenance of plant grounds
6. Depreciation, equipment
7. Plant manager's salary
8. Cost of materials used
9. Storage of finished goods
10. Property taxes, plant
11. Depreciation, plant

LO3 **Organization Chart**

E 7. Hooper Industries wants to formalize its management structure by designing an organization chart. The company has a president, a board of directors, and two vice presidents. Four discretionary cost centers—Financial Resources, Human Resources, Information Resources, and Physical Resources—report to one of the vice presidents. The other vice president has one manufacturing plant with three subassembly areas reporting to her. Draw the company's organization chart.

LO4 **Performance Reports**

E 8. Jackie Jefferson, a new employee at Handown, Inc., is learning about the various types of performance reports. Describe the typical contents of a performance report for each type of responsibility center.

LO4 **Variable Costing Income Statement**

E 9. Vegan, LLC, owns a chain of gourmet vegetarian take-out markets. Last month, Store P generated the following information: sales, $890,000; direct materials, $220,000; direct labor, $97,000; variable overhead, $150,000; fixed overhead, $130,000; variable selling and administrative expenses, $44,500; and fixed selling expenses, $82,300. There were no beginning or ending inventories. Average daily sales (25 business days) were $35,600. Customer orders processed totaled 15,000. Vegan had budgeted monthly sales of $900,000; direct materials, $210,000; direct labor, $100,000; variable overhead, $140,000; fixed overhead, $140,000; variable selling and administrative expenses, $45,000; and fixed selling expenses, $85,000. Store P had been projected to do $36,000 in daily sales and process 16,000 customer orders. Using this information, prepare a performance report for Store P.

LO4 **Variable Costing Income Statement**

E 10. The income statement in the traditional reporting format for Green Products, Inc., for the year ended December 31, is as follows:

Green Products, Inc.
Income Statement
For the Year Ended December 31

Sales	$296,400
Cost of goods sold	112,750
Gross margin	$183,650
Operating expenses	
Selling expenses	
Variable	69,820
Fixed	36,980
Administrative expenses	27,410
Operating income	$ 49,440

Total fixed manufacturing costs for the year were $16,750. All administrative expenses are considered to be fixed.

Using this information, prepare an income statement for Green Products, Inc., for the year ended December 31, using the variable costing format.

LO4 Performance Report for a Cost Center

E 11. Archer, LLC, owns a blueberry processing plant. Last month, the plant generated the following information: blueberries processed, 50,000 pounds; direct materials, $50,000; direct labor, $10,000; variable overhead, $12,000; and fixed overhead, $13,000. There were no beginning or ending inventories. Average daily pounds processed (25 business days) were 2,000. Average rate of processing was 250 pounds per hour. At the beginning of the month, Archer had budgeted costs of blueberries, $45,000; direct labor, $10,000; variable overhead, $14,000; and fixed overhead, $14,000. The monthly master budget was based on producing 50,000 pounds of blueberries each month. This means that the plant had been projected to process 2,000 pounds daily at the rate of 240 pounds per hour.

Using this information, prepare a performance report for the month for the blueberry processing plant. Include a flexible budget and a computation of variances in your report. Indicate whether the variances are favorable (F) or unfavorable (U) to the performance of the plant.

LO5 Investment Center Performance

E 12. Momence Associates is evaluating the performance of three divisions: Maple, Oaks, and Juniper. Using the following data, compute the return on investment and residual income for each division, compare the divisions' performance, and comment on the factors that influenced performance:

	Maple	Oaks	Juniper
Sales	$100,000	$100,000	$100,000
Operating income	$ 10,000	$ 10,000	$ 20,000
Assets invested	$ 25,000	$ 12,500	$ 25,000
Desired ROI	40%	40%	40%

LO5 Economic Value Added

E 13. Leesburg, LLP, is evaluating the performance of three divisions: Lake, Sumter, and Poe. Using the data that appear on the next page, compute the economic value added by each division, and comment on each division's performance.

	Lake	Sumter	Poe
Sales	$100,000	$100,000	$100,000
After-tax operating income	$ 10,000	$ 10,000	$ 20,000
Total assets	$ 25,000	$ 12,500	$ 25,000
Current liabilities	$ 5,000	$ 5,000	$ 5,000
Cost of capital	15%	15%	15%

LO6 **Performance Incentives**

E 14. Dynamic Consulting is advising Solid Industries on the short-term and long-term effectiveness of cash bonuses, awards, profit sharing, and stock as performance incentives. Prepare a chart identifying the effectiveness of each incentive as either long-term or short-term or both.

LO6 **Goal Congruence**

E 15. Necessary Toys, Inc., has adopted the balanced scorecard to motivate its managers to work toward the companywide goal of leading its industry in innovation. Identify the four stakeholder perspectives that would link to the following objectives, measures, and targets:

Perspective	Objective	Measure	Target
	Profitable new products	New product ROI	New product ROI of at least 75 percent
	Work force with cutting-edge skills	Percentage of employees cross-trained on work-group tasks	100 percent of work group cross-trained on new tasks within 30 days
	Agile product design and production processes	Time to market (the time between a product idea and its first sales)	Time to market less than one year for 80 percent of introductions
	Successful product introductions	New product market share	Capture 80 percent of new product market within one year

Problems

LO3, LO4 **Evaluating Cost Center Performance**

P 1. Beverage Products, LLC, manufactures metal beverage containers. The division that manufactures soft drink beverage cans for the North American market has two plants that operate 24 hours a day, 365 days a year. The plants are evaluated as cost centers. Small tools and plant supplies are considered variable overhead. Depreciation and rent are considered fixed overhead. The master budget for a plant and the operating results of the two North American plants, East Coast and West Coast, are as follows:

	Master Budget	East Coast	West Coast
Center costs			
Rolled aluminum ($.01)	$4,000,000	$3,492,000	$5,040,000
Lids ($.005)	2,000,000	1,980,000	2,016,000
Direct labor ($.0025)	1,000,000	864,000	1,260,000
Small tools and supplies ($.0013)	520,000	432,000	588,000
Depreciation and rent	480,000	480,000	480,000
Total cost	$8,000,000	$7,248,000	$9,384,000

Performance measures

Cans processed per hour	45,662	41,096	47,945
Average daily pounds of scrap metal	5	6	7
Cans processed (in millions)	400	360	420

Required

1. Prepare a performance report for the East Coast plant. Include a flexible budget and variance analysis.
2. Prepare a performance report for the West Coast plant. Include a flexible budget and variance analysis.
3. Compare the two plants, and comment on their performance.
4. **Manager Insight:** Explain why a flexible budget should be prepared.

LO4 **Traditional and Variable Costing Income Statements**

P 2. Roofing tile is the major product of the Tops Corporation. The company had a particularly good year, as shown by its operating data. It sold 88,400 cases of tile. Variable cost of goods sold was $848,640; variable selling expenses were $132,600; fixed overhead was $166,680; fixed selling expenses were $152,048; and fixed administrative expenses were $96,450. Selling price was $18 per case. There were no partially completed jobs in process at the beginning or the end of the year. Finished goods inventory had been used up at the end of the previous year.

Required

1. Prepare the calendar year-end income statement for the Tops Corporation using the traditional reporting format.
2. Prepare the calendar year-end income statement for the Tops Corporation using the variable costing format.

LO3, LO4, LO5 **Evaluating Profit and Investment Center Performance**

P 3. Bobbie Howell, the managing partner of the law firm Howell, Bagan, and Clark, LLP, makes asset acquisition and disposal decisions for the firm. As managing partner, she supervises the partners in charge of the firm's three branch offices. Those partners have the authority to make employee compensation decisions. The partners' compensation depends on the profitability of their branch office. Victoria Smith manages the City Branch, which has the following master budget and actual results for the year:

	Master Budget	Actual Results
Billed hours	5,000	4,900
Revenue	$250,000	$254,800
Controllable variable costs		
Direct labor	120,000	137,200
Variable overhead	40,000	34,300
Contribution margin	$ 90,000	$ 83,300
Controllable fixed costs		
Rent	30,000	30,000
Other administrative expenses	45,000	42,000
Branch operating income	$ 15,000	$ 11,300

Required

1. Assume that the City Branch is a profit center. Prepare a performance report that includes a flexible budget. Determine the variances between actual results, the flexible budget, and the master budget.
2. Evaluate Victoria Smith's performance as manager of the City Branch.

3. Assume that the branch managers are assigned responsibility for capital expenditures and that the branches are thus investment centers. City Branch is expected to generate a desired ROI of at least 30 percent on average invested assets of $40,000.

a. Compute the branch's return on investment and residual income.

b. **Manager Insight:** Using the ROI and residual income, evaluate Victoria Smith's performance as branch manager.

LO5 **Return on Investment and Residual Income**

P 4. The financial results for the past two years for Ornamental Iron, a division of the Iron Foundry Company, follow.

Iron Foundry Company
Ornamental Iron Division
Balance Sheet
December 31, 20x8 and 20x7

	20x8	20x7
Assets		
Cash	$ 5,000	$ 3,000
Accounts receivable	10,000	8,000
Inventory	30,000	32,000
Other current assets	600	600
Plant assets	128,300	120,300
Total assets	$173,900	$163,900
Liabilities and Stockholders' Equity		
Current liabilities	$ 13,900	$ 10,000
Long-term liabilities	90,000	93,900
Stockholders' equity	70,000	60,0006
Total liabilities and stockholders' equity	$173,900	$163,900

Iron Foundry Company
Ornamental Iron Division
Income Statement
For the Years Ended December 31, 20x8 and 20x7

	20x8	20x7
Sales	$180,000	$160,000
Cost of goods sold	100,000	90,000
Selling and administrative expenses	27,500	26,500
Operating income	$ 52,500	$ 43,500
Income taxes	17,850	14,790
After-tax operating income	$ 34,650	$ 28,710

Required

1. Compute the division's profit margin, asset turnover, and return on investment for 20x8 and 20x7. Beginning total assets for 20x7 were $157,900. Round to two decimal places.

2. The desired return on investment for the division has been set at 12 percent. Compute Ornamental Iron's residual income for 20x8 and 20x7.

3. The cost of capital for the division is 8 percent. Compute the division's economic value added for 20x8 and 20x7.

4. **Manager Insight:** Before drawing conclusions about this division's performance, what additional information would you want?

LO5 **Return on Investment and Economic Value Added**

P 5. The balance sheet for the New Products Division of NuBone Corporation showed invested assets of $200,000 at the beginning of the year and $300,000 at the end of the year. During the year, the division's operating income was $12,500 on sales of $500,000.

Required

1. Compute the division's residual income if the desired ROI is 6 percent.

2. Compute the following performance measures for the division: (a) profit margin, (b) asset turnover, and (c) return on investment

3. Recompute the division's ROI under each of the following independent assumptions:
   a. Sales increase from $500,000 to $600,000, causing operating income to rise from $12,500 to $30,000.
   b. Invested assets at the beginning of the year are reduced from $200,000 to $100,000.
   c. Operating expenses are reduced, causing operating income to rise from $12,500 to $20,000.

4. Compute NuBone's EVA if total corporate assets are $500,000, current liabilities are $80,000, after-tax operating income is $50,000, and the cost of capital is 8 percent.

Alternate Problems

LO4 **Traditional and Variable Costing Income Statements**

P 6. Interior designers often use the deluxe carpet products of Lux Mills, Inc. The Maricopa blend is the company's top product line. In March, Lux produced and sold 174,900 square yards of Maricopa blend. Factory operating data for the month included variable cost of goods sold of $2,623,500 and fixed overhead of $346,875. Other expenses were variable selling expenses, $166,155; fixed selling expenses, $148,665; and fixed general and administrative expenses, $231,500. Total sales revenue equaled $3,935,250. All production took place in March, and there was no work in process at month end. Goods are usually shipped when completed.

Required

1. Prepare the March income statement for Lux Mills, Inc., using the traditional reporting format.

2. Prepare the March income statement for Lux Mills, Inc., using the variable costing format.

LO3, LO4, LO5 **Return on Investment and Residual Income**

P 7. Portia Carter is the president of a company that owns six multiplex movie theaters. Carter has delegated decision-making authority to the theater managers for all decisions except those relating to capital expenditures and film selection. The theater managers' compensation depends on the profitability of their theaters. Max Burgman, the manager of the Park Theater, had the following master budget and actual results for the month:

	Master Budget	Actual Results
Tickets sold	120,000	480,000
Revenue–tickets	$ 840,000	$ 880,000
Revenue–concessions	480,000	330,000
Total Revenue	$1,320,000	$1,210,000
Controllable variable costs		
Concessions	120,000	99,000
Direct labor	420,000	330,000
Variable overhead	540,000	550,000
Contribution margin	$ 240,000	$ 231,000
Controllable fixed costs		
Rent	55,000	55,000
Other administrative expenses	45,000	50,000
Theater operating income	$ 140,000	$ 126,000

Required

1. Assuming that the theaters are profit centers, prepare a performance report for the Park Theater. Include a flexible budget. Determine the variances between actual results, the flexible budget, and the master budget.
2. Evaluate Burgman's performance as manager of the Park Theater.
3. Assume that the managers are assigned responsibility for capital expenditures and that the theaters are thus investment centers. Park Theater is expected to generate a desired ROI of at least 6 percent on average invested assets of $2,000,000.
   a. Compute the theater's return on investment and residual income.
   b. **Manager Insight:** Using the ROI and residual income, evaluate Burgman's performance as manager.

LO5 Return on Investment and Economic Value Added

P 8. Micanopy Company makes replicas of Indian artifacts. The balance sheet for the Arrowhead Division showed that the company had invested assets of $300,000 at the beginning of the year and $500,000 at the end of the year. During the year, Arrowhead Division's operating income was $80,000 on sales of $1,200,000.

Required

1. Compute Arrowhead Division's residual income if the desired ROI is 20 percent.
2. Compute the following performance measures for the division: (a) profit margin, (b) asset turnover, and (c) return on investment.
3. Compute Micanopy Company's economic value added if total corporate assets are $6,000,000, current liabilities are $800,000, after-tax operating income is $750,000, and the cost of capital is 12 percent.

ENHANCING Your Knowledge, Skills, and Critical Thinking

LO3 Conceptual Understanding Cases

Comparison of Business Types Using Responsibility Accounting

C 1. The structure of an organization affects its responsibility accounting system. **Accenture**, a major management consulting firm, organizes its consultants by industry and location. **Target**, a retailer, has over 1,300 stores in 47 states, including more than 140 SuperTarget stores, as well as an online business. **Monsanto**, a manufacturer, structures its organization into two segments: Seeds and Genomics, and Agricultural Productivity (which includes Roundup and other herbicides).

What is a responsibility accounting system, what is it based on, and what is the criterion for including an item in a manager's operating report? Discuss the general effects that organizational structure has on the creation of a responsibility reporting system, and give an example of a cost center, a profit center, and an investment center at Accenture, Target, and Monsanto.

LO2, LO3, LO4, LO6   **Types of Responsibility Centers**

C 2. Yuma Foods acquired Aldo's Tortillas several years ago. Aldo's has continued to operate as an independent company, except that Yuma Foods has exclusive authority over capital investments, production quantity, and pricing decisions because Yuma has been Aldo's only customer since the acquisition. Yuma uses return on investment to evaluate the performance of Aldo's manager. The most recent performance report is as follows:

Yuma Foods
Performance Report for Aldo's Tortillas
For the Year Ended June 30

Sales	$6,000
Variable cost of goods sold	3,000
Variable administrative expenses	1,000
Variable corporate expenses (% of sales)	600
Contribution margin	$1,400
Fixed overhead (includes depreciation of $100)	400
Fixed administrative expenses	500
Operating income	$ 500
Average assets invested	$5,500
Return on investment	9.09%

1. Analyze the items listed in the performance report and identify the items that Aldo controls and those that Yuma controls. In your opinion, what type of responsibility center is Aldo's Tortillas? Explain your response.
2. Prepare a revised performance report for Aldo's Tortillas and an accompanying memo to the president of Yuma Foods that explains why it is important to change the content of the report. Cite some basic principles of responsibility accounting to support your recommendation.

LO2, LO5, LO6   **Economic Value Added and Performance**

C 3. Sevilla Consulting offers environmental consulting services worldwide. The managers of branch offices are rewarded for superior performance with bonuses based on the economic value that the office adds to the company. Last year's operating results for the entire company and for its three offices, expressed in millions of U.S. dollars, are as follows:

	Worldwide	Europe	Americas	Asia
Cost of capital	9%	10%	8%	12%
Total assets	$210	$70	$70	$70
Current liabilities	80	10	40	30
After-tax operating income	15	5	5	5

1. Compute the economic value added for each office worldwide. What factors affect each office's economic value added? How can an office improve its economic value added?
2. If managers' bonuses are based on economic value added to office performance, what specific actions will managers be motivated to take?
3. Is economic value added the only performance measure needed to evaluate investment centers adequately? Explain your response.

Interpreting Management Reports

LO1   **Balanced Scorecard Results**

C 4. IT, Inc., has adopted the balanced scorecard approach to motivate the managers of its product divisions to work toward the companywide goal of leading its industry in innovation. The corporation's selected performance measures and scorecard results are as follows:

Measure	Division A	B	C	Performance Target
New product ROI	80%	75%	70%	75%
Employees cross-trained in new tasks within 30 days	95	96	94	100
New product's time to market less than one year	85	90	86	80
New product's market share one year after introduction	50	100	80	80

Can you effectively compare the performance of the three divisions against the targets? What other measures mentioned in this chapter are needed to evaluate performance effectively?

LO2, LO3   **Responsibility Centers**

C 5. Wood4Fun makes wooden playground equipment for the institutional and consumer markets. The company strives for low-cost, high-quality production because it operates in a highly competitive market in which product price is set by the marketplace and is not based on production costs. The company is organized into responsibility centers. The vice president of manufacturing is responsible for three manufacturing plants. The vice president of sales is responsible for four sales regions. Recently, these two vice presidents began to disagree about whether the manufacturing plants are cost centers or profit centers. The vice president of manufacturing views the plants as cost centers because the managers of the plants control only product-related costs. The vice president of sales believes the plants are profit centers because product quality and product cost strongly affect company profits.

1. Identify the controllable performance that Wood4Fun values and wants to measure. Give at least three examples of performance measures that Wood4Fun could use to monitor such performance.
2. For the manufacturing plants, what type of responsibility center is most consistent with the controllable performance Wood4Fun wants to measure?
3. For the sales regions, what type of responsibility center is most appropriate?

Decision Analysis Using Excel

LO5   **Return on Investment and Residual Income**

C 6. Tina Patel, the manager of the Food and Lodging Division at Winter Wonderland, has hired you as a consultant to help her examine her division's performance under several different circumstances.

1. Type the data that follow into an Excel spreadsheet to compute the division's actual return on investment and residual income. (Data are from parts **3** and **4** of this chapter's Review Problem.) Match your data entries to the rows and columns shown below. (**Hint:** When entering a formula, begin with "= SUM," and enclose the formula in parentheses. The spreadsheet will then know to compute the answer. Remember to format each cell for the type of numbers it holds, such as percentage, currency, or general.)

	A	B	C	D
1				**Investment Center**
2				**Food and Lodging Division**
3				**Actual Results**
4	Sales			$40,000,000
5	Operating income			$ 6,450,000
6	Average assets invested			$10,000,000
7	Desired ROI			30%
8	Return on Investment			=SUM(D5/D6)
9	Profit Margin			=SUM(D5/D4)
10	Asset Turnover			=SUM(D4/D6)
11	Residual Income			=SUM(D5-(D7*D6))
12				

2. Patel would like to know how the figures would change if Food and Lodging had a desired ROI of 40 percent and average assets invested of $10,000,000. Revise your spreadsheet from requirement **1** to compute the division's return on investment and residual income under those conditions.
3. Patel also wants to know how the figures would change if Food and Lodging had a desired ROI of 30 percent and average assets invested of $12,000,000. Revise your spreadsheet from requirement **1** to compute the division's return on investment and residual income under those conditions.
4. Does the use of formatted spreadsheets simplify the computation of ROI and residual income? Do such spreadsheets make it easier to perform "what-if" analyses?

Ethical Dilemma Case

LO5   Effects of Manager's Decisions on ROI

C7. Cooper Huntington is the manager of the upstate store of a large retailer of farm products. His company is a stable, consistently profitable member of the farming industry. The upstate store is doing fine despite severe drought conditions in the area. At the first of the year, corporate headquarters set a targeted return on investment for the store of 20 percent. The upstate store currently averages $140,000 in invested assets (beginning invested assets, $130,000; ending invested assets, $150,000) and is projected to have an operating income of $30,800. Huntington is considering whether to take one or both of the following actions before year end:

- Hold off recording and paying $5,000 in bills owed until the start of the next fiscal year.

- Write down $3,000 in store inventory (nonperishable emergency flood supplies) to zero value because Huntington was unable to sell the items all year.

Currently, Huntington's bonus is based on store profits. Next year, corporate headquarters is changing its performance incentive program so that bonuses will be based on a store's actual return on investment.

1. What effect would each of Huntington's possible actions have on the store's operating income this year? (**Hint:** Use Figure 4 in this chapter to trace the effects.) In your opinion, is either action unethical?
2. Independent of question 1, if corporate headquarters changes its performance incentive plan for store managers, how will the inventory write-down affect next year's income and return on investment if the items are sold for $4,000 next year? In your opinion, does Huntington have an ethical dilemma?

Internet Case

LO6 **Top Executive Compensation**

C 8. Are top executives paid too much? Do the companies run by the most highly paid executives perform better than other companies? Do U.S. executives make more money than their foreign counterparts? These are some of the questions asked routinely in articles and surveys about executive compensation. Moreover, the Securities and Exchange Commission is calling for better disclosure of pay packages for a company's top five executives.

Use the Internet to locate the top executive salary rankings compiled annually by business publications and other sources. Study the rankings and select several U.S. and foreign companies in the same industry for comparison. You can access this type of information on the Internet in several ways. One way is to do key word searches using terms like *executive compensation* or *executive salary survey*. Another way is to go to the website of a business publication, such as www.forbes.com, and do key word searches of articles. You can also access corporate websites and read their annual reports. Some corporate websites are searchable by key word; you might use a phrase like *compensation discussion and analysis*.

1. In your review of top executive compensation, what types of incentives did you find included in annual compensation?
2. Are the companies with the highest-paid executives the best performers in their industry?
3. Do U.S. executives receive higher pay than their foreign counterparts? If so, do the U.S. companies perform better than their foreign counterparts?

Group Activity Case

LO1, LO2 **Performance Measures and the Balanced Scorecard**

C 9. Working in a group of four to six students, select a local business. The group should become familiar with the background of the business by interviewing its manager or accountant. Each group member should identify several performance measures for the business and link each measure with a specific stakeholder's perspective from the balanced scorecard. (Select at least one performance measure for each perspective.) For each measure, ask yourself, "If you were the manager of the business, how would you set performance targets for each measure?" Then prepare an email stating the business's name, location, and activities and your linked performance measures and perspectives.

In class, members of the group should compare their individual emails and compile them into a group report by having each group member assume a different stakeholder perspective (add government and community if you want more than four perspectives). Each group should be ready to present all perspectives and the group's report in class.

Business Communication Case

LO2, LO4, LO6

Earnings Management

C 10. Many large multinational companies have recently taken a large one-time write-off (known as a "big bath") or used other downsizing accounting practices that have affected the measurement of the company's performance for only one year. Conduct a search for information about a company that has recently taken a sizable reduction in income for just one year. Do a key word search on the Internet, using terms like *big bath* or *earnings management*. Prepare a one-page description of your findings. Include the name of the company, the reason for the large decrease in income, and the probable effect on the company's ROI. Be prepared to present your findings in class.

9

Standard Costing and Variance Analysis

S tandard costs are useful tools for management because they are based on realistic estimates of operating costs. Managers use them to develop budgets, to control costs, and to prepare reports. Because of their usefulness in comparing planned and actual costs, standard costs have usually been most closely associated with the performance evaluation of cost centers. In this chapter, we describe how standard costs are computed and how managers use the variances between standard and actual costs to evaluate performance and control costs.

LEARNING OBJECTIVES

LO1 Define *standard costs*, and describe how managers use these costs.

LO2 Explain how standard costs are developed, and compute a standard unit cost.

LO3 Prepare a flexible budget, and describe how managers use variance analysis to control costs.

LO4 Compute and analyze direct materials variances.

LO5 Compute and analyze direct labor variances.

LO6 Compute and analyze overhead variances.

LO7 Explain how variances are used to evaluate managers' performance.

- How does setting performance standards help managers control costs?

- How do Coach's managers use standard costs to control costs?

- How do they use standard costs to evaluate the performance of cost centers?

The durability of a well-crafted baseball glove was the inspiration for the high-quality leather goods that **Coach** began making more than 50 years ago. Now sold worldwide, the company's products include not only leather goods, such as handbags and luggage, but also fine accessories and gifts for men and women. Coach's managers value a by-the-numbers approach to business. They keep Coach highly profitable by using design specifications to set standard costs for the company's product lines.[1] Managers use these figures as performance targets and as benchmarks against which to measure actual spending trends and continuously monitor changes in business conditions.

☰ Standard Costing

S tandard costs are realistic estimates of costs based on analyses of both past and projected operating costs and conditions. They are usually stated in terms of cost per unit. They provide a standard, or predetermined, performance level for use in **standard costing**, a method of cost control that also includes a measure of actual performance and a measure of the difference, or **variance**, between standard and actual performance. This method of measuring and controlling costs differs from the actual and normal costing methods in that it uses estimated costs exclusively to compute all three elements of product cost—direct materials, direct labor, and overhead. Standard costing is especially effective for managing cost centers. You may recall that a cost center is a responsibility center in which there are well-defined links between the cost of the resources (direct materials, direct labor, and overhead) and the resulting products or services.

Using standard costing can be expensive because the estimated costs are based not just on past costs, but also on engineering estimates, forecasted demand, worker input, time and motion studies, and type and quality of direct materials. However, this method can be used in any type of business. Both manufacturers and service businesses can use standard costing in conjunction with a job order costing, process costing, or activity-based costing system.

Standard Costs and Managers

As shown in Figure 1, standard costs are useful tools for management. Managers use them to develop budgets, to control costs, and to prepare reports. Because of their usefulness in comparing planned and actual costs, standard costs have usually been most closely associated with the performance evaluation of cost centers.

Planning After managers have projected sales and production targets for the next accounting period, standard costs can be used in developing budgets for direct materials, direct labor, and variable overhead. These estimated operating costs not only serve as targets for product costing, but are also useful in making decisions about product distribution and pricing.

Performing As actual costs for direct materials, direct labor, and overhead are incurred and recorded, managers apply standard costs to the work in process. By using these standards as yardsticks for measuring expenditures, they can control product costs as those costs occur. For example, when the

Study Note

Standard costs are necessary for planning and control. Budgets are developed from standard costs, and performance is measured against them.

FOCUS ON BUSINESS PRACTICE
Why Go on a Factory Tour?

If you've had some manufacturing experience, you probably understand the importance of standard costing and variance analysis. If you haven't had any manufacturing experience, you can gain insight into the importance of cost planning and control by visiting a factory. Consult your local chamber of commerce for factory tours near you. You can also tour factories online. Check out the virtual production tour of jelly beans at www.jellybelly.com or see how chocolate is made at www.hersheys.com.[2]

■ **FIGURE 1**
The Management Process: To-Do's for Managers

To-Do's for Managers

- Plan
  - Determine standard costs and prepare budgets
  - Establish cost-based goals for products or services

- Perform
  - Apply cost standards as work is performed in cost centers
  - Collect actual cost data

- Evaluate
  - Use flexible budgets to evaluate managers' performance
  - Calculate variances between standard and actual costs
    for direct materials, direct labor, variable overhead,
    and fixed overhead
  - Determine their causes and take corrective action

- Communicate
  - Prepare cost center performance reports using standard
    costing
  - Prepare comparative analyses of flexible budget to actual
    results for materials, labor and overhead

price that a vendor offers is higher than the standard cost, a manager may decide to take the company's business elsewhere.

Evaluating   At the end of an accounting period—whether it is a day, a week, a month, or a quarter—managers compare the actual costs incurred for direct materials, direct labor, variable overhead, and fixed overhead with standard costs and compute the variances. Variances provide measures of performance that can be used to control costs. In evaluating a variance, managers compute its amount, and if the amount is significant, they analyze what is causing it. Their analysis of significant unfavorable variances may reveal operating problems of the cost center, such as inefficient functions within a department or work cell, which they can then act to correct. Managers also investigate significant favorable variances to determine why and how the positive performance occurred. Favorable variances may indicate desirable practices that should be implemented elsewhere or a need to revise the existing standards. Both favorable and unfavorable variances from standard costs can be used to evaluate a cost center and its individual manager's performance.

Communicating Managers use standard costs to report on cost center operations and managerial performance. A variance report tailored to a manager's specific responsibilities provides useful information about how well cost center operations are proceeding and how well the manager is controlling them.

The Relevance of Standard Costing in Today's Business Environment

In recent years, the increasing automation of manufacturing processes has caused a significant decrease in direct labor costs and a corresponding decline in the importance of labor-related standard costs and variances. As a result, **Coach** and other manufacturing companies, such as **Kraft Foods** and **Boeing**, which once used standard costing for all three elements of product cost, may now apply this method only to direct materials and overhead.

Today, many service organizations, including **Bank of America** and **Liberty Mutual Insurance Company**, also use standard costing. Although a service organization has no direct materials costs, labor and overhead costs are very much a part of providing services, and standard costing is an effective way of planning and controlling them.

S T O P • R E V I E W • A P P L Y

1-1. What are standard costs?

1-2. What is a variance?

1-3. Can a service organization use standard costing? Explain your answer.

Suggested answers to all Stop, Review, and Apply questions are available at http://college.hmco.com/accounting/needles/man_acc/8e/student_home.html.

Computing Standard Costs

> **LO2** Explain how standard costs are developed, and compute a standard unit cost.

A fully integrated standard costing system uses standard costs for all the elements of product cost: direct materials, direct labor, and overhead. Inventory accounts for materials, work in process, and finished goods, as well as the Cost of Goods Sold account, are maintained and reported in terms of standard costs, and standard unit costs are used to compute account balances. Actual costs are recorded separately so that managers can compare what should have been spent (the standard costs) with the actual costs incurred in the cost center.

A standard unit cost for a manufactured product has the following six elements: a price standard for direct materials, a quantity standard for direct materials, a standard for direct labor rate, a standard for direct labor time, a standard for variable overhead rate, and a standard for fixed overhead rate. To compute a standard unit cost, it is necessary to identify and analyze each of these elements. (A standard unit cost for a service includes only the elements that relate to direct labor and overhead.)

Standard Direct Materials Cost

The **standard direct materials cost** is found by multiplying the price standard for direct materials by the quantity standard for direct materials. If the price standard for a certain item is $2.75 and a specific job calls for a quantity standard of eight of the items, the standard direct materials cost for that job is computed as follows:

$$\begin{array}{ccc} \text{Standard Direct} \\ \text{Materials Cost} \end{array} = \begin{array}{c} \text{Direct Materials} \\ \text{Price Standard} \end{array} \times \begin{array}{c} \text{Direct Materials} \\ \text{Quantity Standard} \end{array}$$
$$\$22.00 = \$2.75 \times 8$$

The **direct materials price standard** is a careful estimate of the cost of a specific direct material in the next accounting period. An organization's purchasing agent or its purchasing department is responsible for developing price standards for all direct materials and for making the actual purchases. When estimating a direct materials price standard, the purchasing agent or department must take into account all possible price increases, changes in available quantities, and new sources of supply.

The **direct materials quantity standard** is an estimate of the amount of direct materials, including scrap and waste, that will be used in an accounting period. It is influenced by product engineering specifications, the quality of direct materials, the age and productivity of machinery, and the quality and experience of the work force. Production managers or management accountants usually establish and monitor standards for direct materials quantity, but engineers, purchasing agents, and machine operators may also contribute to the development of these standards.

Standard Direct Labor Cost

The **standard direct labor cost** for a product, task, or job order is calculated by multiplying the standard wage for direct labor by the standard hours of direct labor. If the standard direct labor rate is $8.40 per hour and a product takes 1.5 standard direct labor hours to produce, the product's standard direct labor cost is computed as follows:

$$\begin{array}{ccc} \text{Standard Direct} \\ \text{Labor Cost} \end{array} = \begin{array}{c} \text{Direct Labor} \\ \text{Rate Standard} \end{array} \times \begin{array}{c} \text{Direct Labor} \\ \text{Time Standard} \end{array}$$
$$\$12.60 = \$8.40 \times 1.5 \text{ hours}$$

The **direct labor rate standard** is the hourly direct labor rate that is expected to prevail during the next accounting period for each function or job classification. Although rate ranges are established for each type of worker and rates vary within those ranges according to each worker's experience and length of service, an average standard rate is developed for each task. Even if the person making the product is paid more or less than the standard rate, the standard rate is used to calculate the standard direct labor cost. Standard labor rates are fairly easy to develop because labor rates are either set by a labor union contract or defined by the company.

The **direct labor time standard** is the expected labor time required for each department, machine, or process to complete the production of one unit or one batch of output. In many cases, standard time per unit is a small fraction of an hour. Current time and motion studies of workers and machines, as well as records of their past performance, provide the data for developing this standard. The direct labor time standard should be revised whenever a machine is replaced or the quality of the labor force changes.

Standard Overhead Cost

The **standard overhead cost** is the sum of the estimates of variable and fixed overhead costs in the next accounting period. It is based on standard overhead rates that are computed in much the same way as the predetermined overhead rate that we discussed in an earlier chapter. Unlike that rate, however, the standard overhead rate has two parts, one for variable costs and one for fixed costs. The reason for computing the standard variable and fixed overhead rates separately is that their cost behavior differs.

The **standard variable overhead rate** is computed by dividing the total budgeted variable overhead costs by an expression of capacity, such as the number of standard machine hours or standard direct labor hours. (Other bases may be used if machine hours or direct labor hours are not good predictors, or drivers, of variable overhead costs.) Using standard machine hours as the base, the formula is as follows:

$$\frac{\text{Standard Variable}}{\text{Overhead Rate}} = \frac{\text{Total Budgeted Variable Overhead Costs}}{\text{Expected Number of Standard Machine Hours}}$$

The **standard fixed overhead rate** is computed by dividing the total budgeted fixed overhead costs by an expression of capacity, usually normal capacity in terms of standard hours or units. The denominator is expressed in the same terms as the variable overhead rate. Using normal capacity in terms of standard machine hours as the denominator, the formula is as follows:

$$\frac{\text{Standard Fixed}}{\text{Overhead Rate}} = \frac{\text{Total Budgeted Fixed Overhead Costs}}{\text{Normal Capacity in Terms of Standard Machine Hours}}$$

Recall that normal capacity is the level of operating capacity needed to meet expected sales demand. Using it as the application base ensures that all fixed overhead costs have been applied to units produced by the time normal capacity is reached.

Total Standard Unit Cost

Using standard costs eliminates the need to calculate unit costs from actual cost data every week or month or for each batch of goods produced. Once standard costs for direct materials, direct labor, and variable and fixed overhead have been developed, a total standard unit cost can be computed at any time.

To illustrate how standard costs are used to compute total unit cost, let's suppose that a company called Remember When, Inc., recently updated the standards for its line of watches. Direct materials price standards are now $9.20 per square foot for casing materials and $2.17 for each movement mechanism. Direct materials quantity standards are .025 square foot of casing materials per watch and one movement mechanism per watch. Direct labor time standards are .01 hour per watch for the Case Stamping Department and .05 hour per watch for the Watch Assembly Department. Direct labor rate standards are $8.00 per hour for the Case Stamping Department and $10.20 per hour for the Watch Assembly Department. Standard manufacturing overhead rates are $12.00 per direct labor hour for the standard variable overhead rate and $9.00 per direct labor hour for the standard fixed overhead rate. The standard cost of making one watch would be computed in the following manner:

An employee at a German watch-making company works on a partially assembled watch. The total standard cost of producing a watch like this represents the desired production cost. It is based on the standards established for direct materials costs, direct labor costs, and variable and fixed overhead.

Study Note

The total standard cost of $4.25 represents the *desired* cost of producing one watch.

Direct materials costs:	
Casing ($9.20 per sq. ft. × .025 sq. ft.)	$ .23
One movement mechanism	2.17
Direct labor costs:	
Case Stamping Department ($8.00 per hour × .01 hour per watch)	.08
Watch Assembly Department ($10.20 per hour × .05 hour per watch)	.51
Variable overhead ($12.00 per hour × .06 hour per watch)	.72
Total standard variable cost of one watch	$3.71
Fixed overhead ($9.00 per hour × .06 hour per watch)	.54
Total standard cost of one watch	$4.25

S T O P • R E V I E W • A P P L Y

2-1. Explain the following statement: "Standard costing is a total unit cost concept in that standard unit costs are determined for direct materials, direct labor, and overhead."

2-2. What do a standard overhead rate and a predetermined overhead rate have in common? How do they differ?

2-3. Name the six elements used to compute a standard unit cost.

Computing a Standard Unit Cost   Using the following information, compute the standard unit cost of a five-pound bag of sugar:

Direct materials quantity standard	5 pounds per unit
Direct materials price standard	$.05 per pound
Direct labor time standard	.01 hour per unit
Direct labor rate standard	$10.00 per hour
Variable overhead rate standard	$.15 per machine hour
Fixed overhead rate standard	$.10 per machine hour
Machine hour standard	.5 hour per unit

SOLUTION

Direct materials cost	
($0.05 × 5 pounds)	$0.25
Direct labor cost	
($10.00 × 0.01 hour)	0.10
Variable overhead	
($0.15 × 0.5 machine hour)	0.08
Fixed overhead	
($0.10 × 0.5 machine hour)	0.05
Total standard unit cost	$0.48

Variance Analysis

LO3 Prepare a flexible budget, and describe how managers use variance analysis to control costs.

Managers in all types of organizations constantly compare the costs of what was expected to happen with the costs of what actually did happen. By examining the differences, or variances, between standard and actual costs, they can gather much valuable information. **Variance analysis** is the process of computing the differences between standard costs and actual costs and identifying the causes of those differences. In this section, we look at how managers use flexible budgets to improve the accuracy of variance analysis and how they use variance analysis to control costs.

The Role of Flexible Budgets in Variance Analysis

The accuracy of variance analysis depends to a large extent on the type of budget that managers use when comparing variances. *Static*, or fixed, budgets forecast revenues and expenses for just one level of sales and just one level of output. The budgets that make up a master budget are usually based on a single level of output, but many things can happen over an accounting period that will cause actual output to differ from the estimated output. If a company produces more products than predicted, total production costs will almost always be greater than predicted. When that is the case, a comparison of actual production costs with fixed budgeted costs will inevitably show variances.

The performance report in Exhibit 1 compares data from Remember When's static master budget with the actual costs of its Watch Division for the

FOCUS ON BUSINESS PRACTICE

Why Complicate the Flexible Budget?

Because of the database capabilities of enterprise resource management (ERM) systems and the principles of resource consumption accounting (RCA), the flexible budget has become more complicated. This new and more complex version of a flexible budget is called *authorized reporting*. Authorized reporting is like a flexible budget in that it restates an accounting period's costs in terms of different levels of output, but it enhances cost restatement by taking into account all the factors that can influence a cost's behavior. With its sophisticated cost analyses, authorized reporting is a more relevant yardstick for cost comparison and control than the traditional flexible budget.[3]

EXHIBIT 1 ▶ | **Performance Report Using Data from a Static Budget**

Remember When, Inc.
Performance Report—Watch Division
For the Year Ended December 31

Cost Category	Budgeted Costs*	Actual Costs†	Difference Under (Over) Budget
Direct materials	$42,000	$46,000	($4,000)
Direct labor	10,325	11,779	(1,454)
Variable overhead			
Indirect materials	3,500	3,600	(100)
Indirect labor	5,250	5,375	(125)
Utilities	1,750	1,810	(60)
Other	2,100	2,200	(100)
Fixed overhead			
Supervisory salaries	4,000	3,500	500
Depreciation	2,000	2,000	—
Utilities	450	450	—
Other	3,000	3,200	(200)
Totals	$74,375	$79,914	($5,539)

*Budgeted costs are based on an output of 17,500 units.
†Actual output was 19,100 units.

year ended December 31. As you can see, actual costs exceeded budgeted costs by $5,539, or 7.4 percent. On the face of it, most managers would consider such a cost overrun significant. But was there really a cost overrun? The budgeted amounts are based on an output of 17,500 units; however, the actual output was 19,100 units. To judge the division's performance accurately, the company's managers must change the budgeted data to reflect an output of 19,100 units. They can do this by using a flexible budget. A **flexible budget** (also called a *variable budget*) is a summary of expected costs for a range of activity levels. Unlike a static budget, a flexible budget provides forecasted data that can be adjusted for changes in the level of output. The flexible budget is used primarily as a cost control tool in evaluating performance at the end of a period.

A flexible budget for Remember When's Watch Division appears in Exhibit 2. It shows the estimated costs for 15,000, 17,500, and 20,000 units of output. The total cost of a variable cost item is found by multiplying the number of units produced by the item's per-unit cost. For example, if the Watch Division produces 15,000 units, direct materials will cost $36,000 (15,000 units × $2.40). An important element in this exhibit is the **flexible budget formula**, an equation that determines the expected, or budgeted, cost for any level of output. Its components include a per-unit amount for variable costs and a total amount for fixed costs. (In Exhibit 2, the $3.71 variable cost per unit is computed in the far right column, and the $9,450 is found in the section on fixed overhead costs.) Using the flexible budget formula, you can create a budget for the Watch Division for any level of output in the range of levels given.

The performance report in Exhibit 3 is based on data from the flexible budget shown in Exhibit 2. Variable unit costs have been multiplied by the 19,100 units actually produced to arrive at the total budgeted costs, and fixed

Study Note

Flexible budgets allow managers to compare budgeted and actual costs at the same level of output.

EXHIBIT 2 ▶ **Flexible Budget for Evaluation of Overall Performance**

Remember When, Inc.
Flexible Budget—Watch Division
For the Year Ended December 31

Cost Category	Units Produced* 15,000	17,500	20,000	Variable Cost per Unit†
Direct materials	$36,000	$42,000	$48,000	$2.40
Direct labor	8,850	10,325	11,800	.59
Variable overhead				
Indirect materials	3,000	3,500	4,000	.20
Indirect labor	4,500	5,250	6,000	.30
Utilities	1,500	1,750	2,000	.10
Other	1,800	2,100	2,400	.12
Total variable costs	$55,650	$64,925	$74,200	$3.71
Fixed overhead				
Supervisory salaries	$ 4,000	$ 4,000	$ 4,000	
Depreciation	2,000	2,000	2,000	
Utilities	450	450	450	
Other	3,000	3,000	3,000	
Total fixed overhead costs	$ 9,450	$ 9,450	$ 9,450	
Total costs	$65,100	$74,375	$83,650	

Flexible budget formula:

Total Budgeted Costs = (Variable Cost per Unit × Number of Units Produced)
+ Budgeted Fixed Costs
= ($3.71 × Units Produced) + $9,450

*Flexible budgets are commonly used only for overhead costs; when they are, machine hours or direct labor hours are used in place of units produced.
†Computed by dividing the dollar amount in any column by the respective level of output.

overhead information has been carried over from Exhibit 2. In this report, actual costs are $397 less than the amount budgeted. In other words, when we use a flexible budget at the end of the period, we find that the performance of the Watch Division in this period actually exceeded budget targets by $397.

Using Variance Analysis to Control Costs

As Figure 2 shows, using variance analysis to control costs is a four-step process. First, managers compute the amount of the variance. If the amount is insignificant—meaning that actual operating results are close to those anticipated—no corrective action is needed. If the amount is significant, then managers analyze the variance to identify its cause. In identifying the cause, they are usually able to pinpoint the activities that need to be monitored. They then select performance measures that will enable them to track those activities, analyze the results, and determine the action needed to correct the problem. Their final step is to take the appropriate corrective action.

While computing the amount of a variance is important, it is also important to remember that this computation does nothing to prevent the variance from

EXHIBIT 3 ▶ | **Performance Report Using Data from a Flexible Budget**

Remember When, Inc.
Performance Report—Watch Division
For the Year Ended December 31

Cost Category (Variable Unit Cost)	Budgeted Costs*	Actual Costs	Difference Under (Over) Budget
Direct materials ($2.40)	$45,840	$46,000	($160)
Direct labor ($.59)	11,269	11,779	(510)
Variable overhead			
Indirect materials ($.20)	3,820	3,600	220
Indirect labor ($.30)	5,730	5,375	355
Utilities ($.10)	1,910	1,810	100
Other ($.12)	2,292	2,200	92
Fixed overhead			
Supervisory salaries	4,000	3,500	500
Depreciation	2,000	2,000	—
Utilities	450	450	—
Other	3,000	3,200	(200)
Totals	$80,311	$79,914	$397

*Budgeted costs are based on an output of 19,100 units.

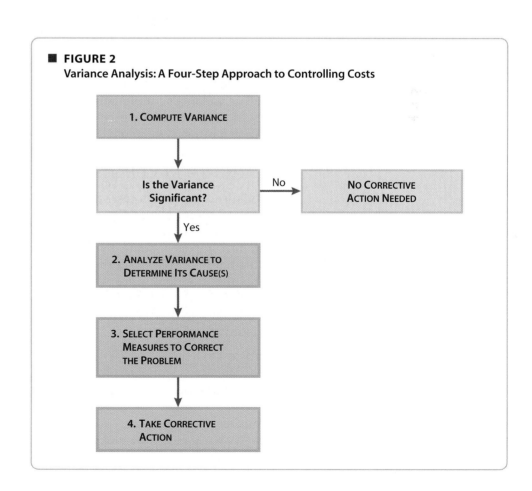

■ **FIGURE 2**
Variance Analysis: A Four-Step Approach to Controlling Costs

1. COMPUTE VARIANCE

Is the Variance Significant? —No→ NO CORRECTIVE ACTION NEEDED

Yes

2. ANALYZE VARIANCE TO DETERMINE ITS CAUSE(S)

3. SELECT PERFORMANCE MEASURES TO CORRECT THE PROBLEM

4. TAKE CORRECTIVE ACTION

recurring. To control costs, managers must determine the cause of the variance and select performance measures that will help them track the problem and find the best solution for it.

As we focus on the computation and analysis of cost center variances in the next sections, we follow the steps outlined in Figure 2. We limit our analysis to eight variances, two for each of the cost categories of direct materials, direct labor, variable overhead, and fixed overhead. We give examples of operating problems that might cause each of these variances to occur. We also identify some financial and nonfinancial performance measures that can be used to track the cause of a variance and that can be helpful in correcting it.

S T O P • R E V I E W • A P P L Y

3-1. "Performance is evaluated by comparing what did happen with what should have happened." What does this statement mean? How does it relate to cost control?

3-2. What is a flexible budget? What is its purpose?

3-3. What are the components of the flexible budget formula? How are they related?

Computing and Analyzing Direct Materials Variances

LO4 Compute and analyze direct materials variances.

To control cost center operations, managers compute and analyze variances for whole cost categories, such as total direct materials costs, as well as variances for elements of those categories, such as the price and quantity of each direct material. The more detailed their analysis of direct materials variances is, the more effective they will be in controlling costs.

Computing Direct Materials Variances

The **total direct materials cost variance** is the difference between the standard cost and actual cost of direct materials used to produce the salable units; it is also referred to as the *good units produced*. To illustrate how this variance is computed, let us assume that a manufacturer called Cambria Company makes leather bags. Each bag should use four feet of leather (standard quantity), and the standard price of leather is $6.00 per foot. During August, Cambria Company purchased 760 feet of leather costing $5.90 per foot and used the leather to produce 180 bags. The total direct materials cost variance is calculated as follows:

Standard cost

$$\text{Standard price} \times \text{standard quantity} =$$
$$\$6.00 \text{ per foot} \times (180 \text{ bags} \times 4 \text{ feet per bag}) =$$
$$\$6.00 \text{ per foot} \times 720 \text{ feet} = \$4,320$$

Less actual cost

$$\text{Actual price} \times \text{actual quantity} =$$
$$\$5.90 \text{ per foot} \times 760 \text{ feet} = \underline{4,484}$$
$$\text{Total direct materials cost variance} \quad \underline{\$\ \ 164}\ (U)$$

A worker assembles a Louis Vuitton bag at the company's leather goods factory in Ducey, France. To control costs in a factory like this, managers compute and analyze variances for cost categories, such as the quantity of direct materials. For example, if more leather is used in the production of Louis Vuitton handbags than the standard quantity the company expected to use, the variance is said to be unfavorable, and the managers will take corrective action.

 Study Note

It is just as important to identify whether a variance is favorable or unfavorable as it is to compute the variance. This information is necessary for analyzing the variance and taking corrective action.

Study Note

The direct materials price variance measures the difference between the standard cost and the actual cost of purchased materials. It is not concerned with the quantity of materials used in the production process.

Here, actual cost exceeds standard cost. The situation is unfavorable, as indicated by the *U* in parentheses after the dollar amount. An *F* means a favorable situation.

To find the area or people responsible for the variance, the total direct materials cost variance must be broken down into two parts: the direct materials price variance and the direct materials quantity variance. The **direct materials price variance** (also called the *direct material spending* or *rate variance*) is the difference between the standard price and the actual price per unit multiplied by the actual quantity purchased. For Cambria Company, the direct materials price variance is computed as follows:

Standard price	$6.00
Less actual price	5.90
Difference per foot	$ .10 (F)

$$\text{Direct Materials Price Variance} = (\text{Standard Price} - \text{Actual Price}) \times \text{Actual Quantity}$$
$$= \$.10 \times 760 \text{ feet}$$
$$= \underline{\$76} \text{ (F)}$$

Because the price that the company paid for the direct materials was less than the standard price it expected to pay, the variance is favorable.

The **direct materials quantity variance** (also called the *direct material efficiency* or *usage variance*) is the difference between the standard quantity allowed and the actual quantity used multiplied by the standard price. It is computed as follows:

Standard quantity allowed (180 bags × 4 feet per bag)	720 feet
Less actual quantity	760 feet
Difference	40 feet (U)

$$\text{Direct Materials Quantity Variance} = \text{Standard Price} \times (\text{Standard Quantity Allowed} - \text{Actual Quantity})$$
$$= \$6 \times 40 \text{ feet}$$
$$= \underline{\$240} \text{ (U)}$$

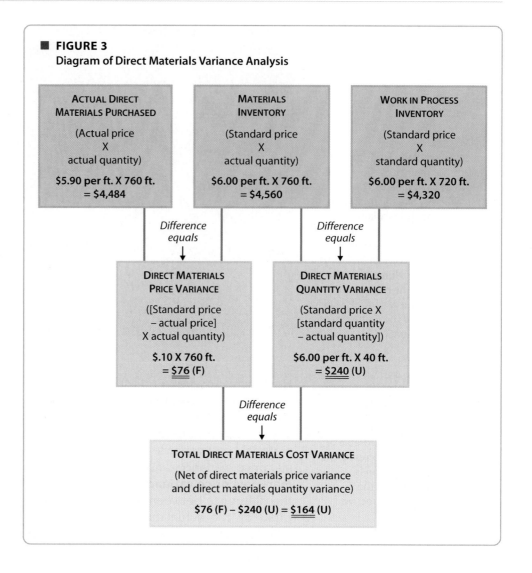

■ **FIGURE 3**
Diagram of Direct Materials Variance Analysis

Because more leather than the standard quantity was used in the production process, the direct materials quantity variance is unfavorable.

If the calculations are correct, the net of the direct materials price variance and the direct materials quantity variance should equal the total direct materials cost variance. The following check shows that the variances were computed correctly:

Direct materials price variance	$ 76 (F)
Direct materials quantity variance	240 (U)
Total direct materials cost variance	$164 (U)

Variance analyses are sometimes easier to interpret in diagram form. Figure 3 illustrates our analysis of Cambria Company's direct materials variances. Notice that although direct materials are purchased at actual cost, they are entered in the Materials Inventory account at standard price; thus, the direct materials price variance of $76 (F) is obvious when the costs are recorded. As Figure 3 shows, the standard price multiplied by the standard quantity is the amount entered in the Work in Process Inventory account.

Analyzing and Correcting Direct Materials Variances

Cambria Company's managers were concerned because the company had been experiencing direct materials price variances and quantity variances for some time; moreover, as our analysis shows, the price variances were always favorable, and the quantity variances were always unfavorable. By tracking the purchasing activity for three months, the managers discovered that the company's purchasing agent, without any authorization, had been purchasing a lower grade of leather at a reduced price. After careful analysis, the engineering manager determined that the substitute leather was not appropriate and that the company should resume purchasing the grade of leather originally specified. In addition, an analysis of scrap and rework revealed that the inferior quality of the substitute leather was causing the unfavorable quantity variance. By tracking the purchasing activity, Cambria's managers were able to solve the problems the company had been having with direct materials variances.

S T O P • R E V I E W • A P P L Y

4-1. How would you interpret an unfavorable direct materials price variance?

4-2. Can an unfavorable direct materials quantity variance be caused, at least in part, by a favorable direct materials price variance? Explain your answer.

Direct Materials Variances Using the following information, compare the actual and standard cost and usage data for the production of five-pound bags of sugar, and compute the direct materials price and direct materials quantity variances using formulas or diagram form:

Direct materials quantity standard	5 pounds per unit
Direct materials price standard	$.05 per pound
Direct materials purchased and used	55,100 pounds
Price paid for direct materials	$.04 per pound
Number of good units produced	11,000 units

SOLUTION

Direct Materials Price Variance = (Standard Price − Actual Price) × Actual Quantity

= ($0.05 − $0.04) × 55,100 pounds

= $0.01 × 55,100 pounds = $551 (F)

Direct Materials Quantity Variance = Standard Price × (Standard Quantity − Actual Quantity)

= $0.05 × [(11,000 × 5 pounds) − 55,100 pounds]

= $0.05 × (55,000 pounds − 55,100 pounds) = $5.00 (U)

Diagram Form:

	Actual Price × Actual Quantity		Standard Price × Actual Quantity		Standard Price × Standard Quantity
Direct Materials	$2,204[a]	Price Variance	$2,755[b]	Quantity Variance	$2.750[c]
		$551 (F)		$5 (U)	

[a] $0.04 × 55,100 = $2,204
[b] $0.05 × 55,100 = $2,755
[c] $0.05 × (11,000 × 5) = $2,750

Computing and Analyzing Direct Labor Variances

LO5 Compute and analyze direct labor variances.

The procedure for computing and analyzing direct labor cost variances parallels the procedure for finding direct materials variances. Again, the more detailed the analysis is, the more effective managers will be in controlling costs.

Computing Direct Labor Variances

The **total direct labor cost variance** is the difference between the standard direct labor cost for good units produced and actual direct labor costs. (*Good units* are the total units produced less units that are scrapped or need to be reworked—in other words, the salable units.) At Cambria Company, each leather bag requires 2.4 standard direct labor hours, and the standard direct labor rate is $8.50 per hour. During August, 450 direct labor hours were used to make 180 bags at an average pay rate of $9.20 per hour. The total direct labor cost variance is computed as follows:

Standard Cost
Standard rate × standard hours allowed	=	
$8.50 × (180 bags × 2.4 hours per bag)	=	
$8.50 × 432 hours	=	$3,672

Less Actual Cost
Actual rate × actual hours = $9.20 × 450 hours	=	4,140
Total direct labor cost variance		$ 468 (U)

Both the actual direct labor hours per bag and the actual direct labor rate varied from the standard. For effective performance evaluation, management must know how much of the total cost arose from different direct labor rates and how much from different numbers of direct labor hours. This information is found by computing the direct labor rate variance and the direct labor efficiency variance.

The **direct labor rate variance** (also called the *direct labor spending variance*) is the difference between the standard direct labor rate and the actual direct labor rate multiplied by the actual direct labor hours worked. It is computed as follows:

Standard rate	$8.50
Less actual rate	9.20
Difference per hour	$ .70 (U)

$$\text{Direct Labor Rate Variance} = (\text{Standard Rate} - \text{Actual Rate}) \times \text{Actual Hours}$$
$$= \$.70 \times 450 \text{ hours}$$
$$= \$315 \text{ (U)}$$

The **direct labor efficiency variance** (also called the *direct labor quantity* or *usage variance*) is the difference between the standard direct labor hours allowed for good units produced and the actual direct labor hours worked multiplied by the standard direct labor rate. It is computed this way:

Standard hours allowed (180 bags × 2.4 hours per bag)	432 hours
Less actual hours	450 hours
Difference	18 hours (U)

 Study Note

The computation of the direct labor rate variance is very similar to the computation of the direct materials price variance. Computations of the direct labor efficiency variance and the direct materials quantity variance are also similar.

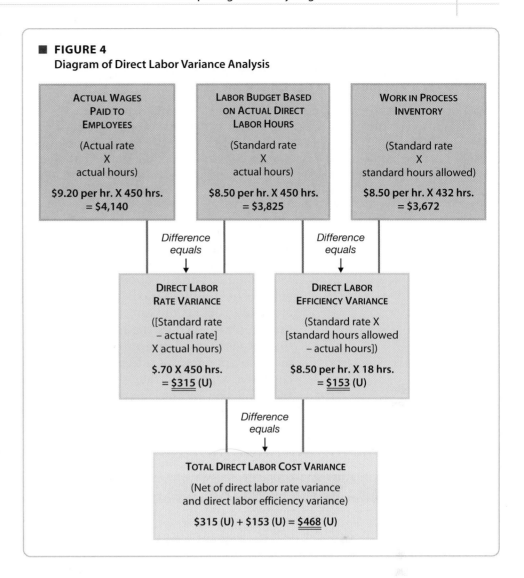

■ FIGURE 4
Diagram of Direct Labor Variance Analysis

Direct Labor Efficiency Variance = Standard Rate $\times$ (Standard Hours Allowed $-$ Actual Hours)

$$= \$8.50 \times 18 \text{ hours}$$
$$= \underline{\$153} \text{ (U)}$$

If the calculations are correct, the net of the direct labor rate variance and the direct labor efficiency variance should equal the total direct labor cost variance. The following check shows that the variances were computed correctly:

Direct labor rate variance	$315 (U)
Direct labor efficiency variance	153 (U)
Total direct labor cost variance	$468 (U)

Figure 4 summarizes our analysis of Cambria Company's direct labor variances. Unlike direct materials variances, the direct labor rate and efficiency variances are usually computed and recorded at the same time.

Analyzing and Correcting Direct Labor Variances

Because Cambria Company's direct labor rate variance and direct labor efficiency variance were unfavorable, its managers investigated the causes of these variances. An analysis of employee time cards revealed that the Bag Assembly Department had replaced an assembly worker who was ill with a machine operator from another department. The machine operator made $9.20 per hour, whereas the assembly worker earned the standard $8.50 per hour rate. When questioned about the unfavorable efficiency variance, the assembly supervisor identified two causes. First, the machine operator had had to learn assembly skills on the job, so his assembly time was longer than the standard time per bag. Second, the materials handling people were partially responsible because they delivered parts late on five different occasions. Because the machine operator was a temporary replacement, Cambria's managers took no corrective action, but they decided to keep a close eye on the materials handling function by tracking delivery times and number of delays for the next three months. Once they have collected and analyzed the new data, they will take whatever action is needed to correct the scheduling problem.

S T O P • R E V I E W • A P P L Y

5-1. Identify two possible causes of a direct labor rate variance, and describe the measures used to track performance in those areas. Then do the same for a direct labor efficiency variance.

5-2. If the direct labor rate variance is unfavorable, will the direct labor efficiency variance also be unfavorable?

Direct Labor Variances   Using the following information, compare the standard cost and usage data for the production of five-pound bags of sugar, and compute the direct labor rate and direct labor efficiency variances using formulas or diagram form:

Direct labor time standard	.01 hour per unit
Direct labor rate standard	$10.00 per hour
Direct labor hours used	100 hours
Total cost of direct labor	$1,010
Number of good units produced	11,000 units

SOLUTION

Direct Labor Rate Variance = (Standard Rate − Actual Rate) × Actual Hours

$= [\$10.00 − (\$1,010 ÷ 100 \text{ hours})] × 100 \text{ hours}$

$= (\$10.00 − \$10.10) × 100 \text{ hours}$

$= \$0.10 × 100 \text{ hours} = \underline{\underline{\$10.00}} \text{ (U)}$

Direct Labor
Efficiency = Standard Rate × (Standard Hours Allowed − Actual Hours)
Variance

= $10.00 × [(11,000 × 0.01 hour) − 100 hours]
= $10.00 × (110 hours − 100 hours)
= $10.00 × (10 hours) = ($100.00) (F)

Diagram Form:

	Actual Rate × Actual Hours		Standard Rate × Actual Hours		Standard Rate × Standard Hours
Direct Labor	$1,010[a]	Rate Variance	$1,000[b]	Efficiency Variance	$1,100[c]
		$10.00 (U)		($100.00) (F)	

[a] $10.10 × 100 = $1,010
[b] $10.00 × 100 = $1,000
[c] $10.00 × (11,000 × 0.01 hour) = $1,100

Computing and Analyzing Overhead Variances

LO6 Compute and analyze overhead variances.

Many types of variable and fixed overhead costs may contribute to variances from standard costs. Controlling these costs is more difficult than controlling direct materials and direct labor costs because the responsibility for overhead costs is hard to assign. Fixed overhead costs may be unavoidable past costs, such as depreciation and lease expenses; they are therefore not under the control of any department manager. If variable overhead costs can be related to departments or activities, however, some control is possible.

Using a Flexible Budget to Analyze Overhead Variances

Earlier in the chapter, we described the flexible budget that the managers of Remember When, Inc., use to evaluate overall performance. That budget, shown in Exhibit 2, is based on units of output. Cambria Company's managers also use a flexible budget, but to analyze overhead costs only. As you can see in Exhibit 4, Cambria's flexible budget uses direct labor hours as the expression of activity. Thus, variable costs vary with the number of direct labor hours worked. Total fixed overhead costs remain constant. The flexible budget formula in such cases is as follows:

Total Budgeted Overhead Costs = (Variable Costs per Direct Labor Hour
× Number of Direct Labor Hours)
+ Budgeted Fixed Overhead Costs

When applied to Cambria Company's data, the flexible budget formula is as follows:

Total Budgeted Overhead Costs = ($5.75 × Number of Direct
Labor Hours) + $1,300

EXHIBIT 4 ▶ | **Flexible Budget for Evaluation of Overhead Costs**

Cambria Company
Flexible Budget—Overhead
Bag Assembly Department
For an Average One-Month Period

Cost Category	Direct Labor Hours (DLH) 400	432	500	Variable Cost per DLH
Budgeted variable overhead				
Indirect materials	$ 600	$ 648	$ 750	$1.50
Indirect labor	800	864	1,000	2.00
Supplies	300	324	375	.75
Utilities	400	432	500	1.00
Other	200	216	250	.50
Total budgeted variable overhead costs	$2,300	$2,484	$2,875	$5.75
Budgeted fixed overhead				
Supervisory salaries	$ 600	$ 600	$ 600	
Depreciation	400	400	400	
Other	300	300	300	
Total budgeted fixed overhead costs	$1,300	$1,300	$1,300	
Total budgeted overhead costs	$3,600	$3,784	$4,175	

Flexible budget formula (based on a normal capacity of 400 direct labor hours):

Total Budgeted Overhead Costs = (Variable Costs per Direct Labor Hour
  × Number of DLH) + Budgeted Fixed Overhead
  Costs
  = ($5.75 × number of DLH) + $1,300

Cambria's flexible budget shows monthly overhead costs for 400, 432, and 500 direct labor hours. To find the total monthly flexible budgeted overhead costs for the 180 bags produced, you simply insert the direct labor hours allowed in the flexible budget formula—for example, ($5.75 × 432 direct labor hours) + $1,300 = $3,784.

Computing Overhead Variances

Analyses of overhead variances differ in degree of detail. The basic approach is to compute the **total overhead variance**, which is the difference between actual overhead costs and standard overhead costs applied. You may recall from a previous chapter how overhead was applied to production by using a standard overhead rate.

A standard overhead rate has two parts: a variable rate and a fixed rate. For Cambria Company, the standard variable rate is $5.75 per direct labor hour (from the flexible budget). The standard fixed overhead rate is found by dividing total budgeted fixed overhead ($1,300) by normal capacity set by the master budget at the beginning of the period. (Cambria's normal capacity is 400 direct labor hours.) The result is a fixed overhead rate of $3.25 per direct labor hour ($1,300 ÷ 400 hours). So, Cambria's total standard overhead rate is $9.00 per direct labor hour ($5.75 + $3.25).

Cambria Company's total overhead variance would be computed as follows:

Standard overhead costs applied to good units produced	
$9.00 per direct labor hour × (180 bags × 2.4 hr. per bag)	$3,888
Less actual overhead costs	4,100
Total overhead variance	$ 212 (U)

This amount can be divided into variable overhead variances and fixed overhead variances.

Variable Overhead Variances

The **total variable overhead variance** is the difference between actual variable overhead costs and the standard variable overhead costs that are applied to good units produced using the standard variable rate. The procedure for finding this variance is similar to the procedure for finding direct materials and labor variances.

Figure 5 shows an analysis of Cambria Company's variable overhead variances. At Cambria, each leather bag requires 2.4 standard direct labor hours,

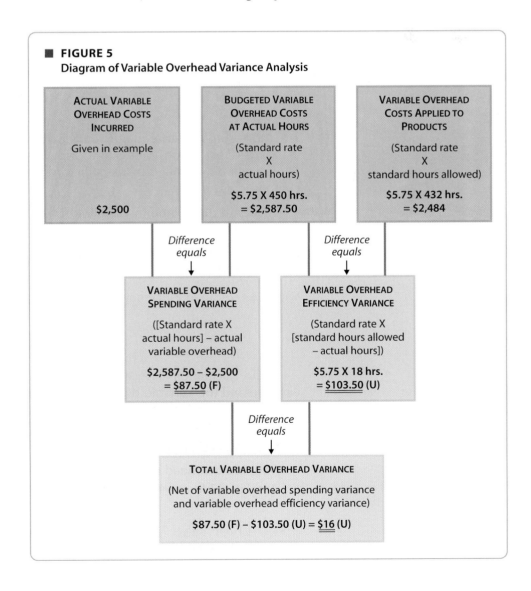

■ FIGURE 5
Diagram of Variable Overhead Variance Analysis

ACTUAL VARIABLE OVERHEAD COSTS INCURRED	BUDGETED VARIABLE OVERHEAD COSTS AT ACTUAL HOURS	VARIABLE OVERHEAD COSTS APPLIED TO PRODUCTS
Given in example	(Standard rate X actual hours)	(Standard rate X standard hours allowed)
	$5.75 X 450 hrs. = $2,587.50	$5.75 X 432 hrs. = $2,484
$2,500		

Difference equals

Difference equals

VARIABLE OVERHEAD SPENDING VARIANCE	VARIABLE OVERHEAD EFFICIENCY VARIANCE
([Standard rate X actual hours] – actual variable overhead)	(Standard rate X [standard hours allowed – actual hours])
$2,587.50 – $2,500 = $87.50 (F)	$5.75 X 18 hrs. = $103.50 (U)

Difference equals

TOTAL VARIABLE OVERHEAD VARIANCE

(Net of variable overhead spending variance and variable overhead efficiency variance)

$87.50 (F) – $103.50 (U) = $16 (U)

and the standard variable overhead rate is $5.75 per direct labor hour. During August, the company incurred $2,500 of variable overhead costs. The total variable overhead cost variance is computed as follows:

Overhead applied to good units produced
Standard variable rate × standard labor hours allowed =
$5.75 per hour × (180 bags × 2.4 hours per bag)   =
$5.75 × 432 hours   = $2,484
Less actual cost   2,500
Total variable overhead cost variance $ 16 (U)

Both the actual variable overhead and the direct labor hours per bag may vary from the standard. For effective performance evaluation, managers must know how much of the total cost arose from variable overhead spending deviations and how much from variable overhead application deviations (i.e., applied and actual direct labor hours). This information is found by computing the variable overhead spending variance and the variable overhead efficiency variance.

The **variable overhead spending variance** (also called the *variable overhead rate variance*) is computed by multiplying the actual hours worked by the difference between actual variable overhead costs and the standard variable overhead rate, as follows:

Variable Overhead Spending Variance = (Standard Variable Rate × Actual Hours Worked) − Actual Variable Overhead Cost
= ($5.75 × 450 hours) − $2,500
= $2,587.50 − $2,500
= $87.50 (F)

The **variable overhead efficiency variance** is the difference between the standard direct labor hours allowed for good units produced and the actual hours worked multiplied by the standard variable overhead rate per hour. It is computed as follows:

Standard direct labor hours allowed (180 bags × 2.4 hours
  per bag)   432 hours
Less actual hours   450 hours
Difference   18 hours (U)

Variable Overhead Efficiency Variance = Standard Variable Rate × (Standard Hours Allowed − Actual Hours)
= $5.75 × 18 hours
= $103.50 (U)

If the calculations are correct, the net of the variable overhead spending variance and the variable overhead efficiency variance should equal the total variable overhead variance. The following check shows that these variances have been computed correctly:

Variable overhead spending variance $ 87.50 (F)
Variable overhead efficiency variance   103.50 (U)
Total variable overhead cost variance $ 16.00 (U)

Fixed Overhead Variances

The **total fixed overhead variance** is the difference between actual fixed overhead costs and the standard fixed over-

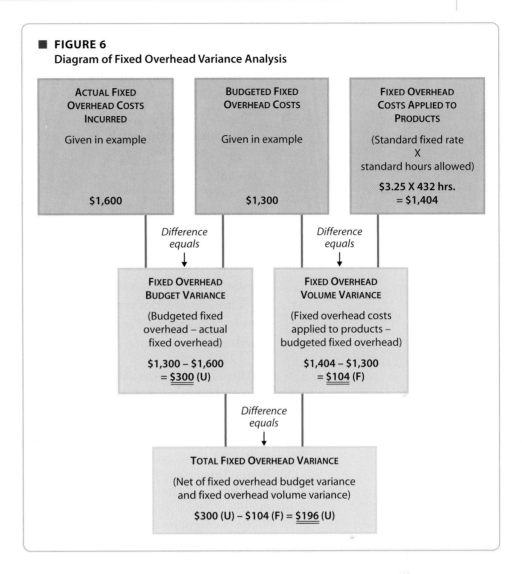

■ **FIGURE 6**
Diagram of Fixed Overhead Variance Analysis

head costs that are applied to good units produced using the standard fixed overhead rate. The procedure for finding this variance differs from the procedure used for finding direct materials, direct labor, and variable overhead variances.

Figure 6 shows an analysis of fixed overhead variances for Cambria Company. At Cambria, each bag requires 2.4 standard direct labor hours, and the standard fixed overhead rate is $3.25 per direct labor hour. As we noted earlier, the standard fixed overhead rate is found by dividing budgeted fixed overhead ($1,300) by normal capacity, which was set by the master budget at the beginning of the period. In this case, because normal capacity is 400 direct labor hours, the fixed overhead rate is $3.25 per direct labor hour ($1,300 ÷ 400 hours).

During August, Cambria incurred $1,600 of actual fixed overhead costs. The total fixed overhead variance is computed as follows:

Overhead applied to the good units produced
Standard fixed rate × standard direct labor hours allowed =
$3.25 × (180 bags × 2.4 hours per bag) =
$3.25 × 432 hours = $1,404

Less actual cost	1,600
Total fixed overhead cost variance	$ 196 (U)

For effective performance evaluation, managers break down the total fixed overhead variance into two additional variances: the fixed overhead budget variance and the fixed overhead volume variance.

The **fixed overhead budget variance** (also called the *budgeted fixed overhead variance*) is the difference between budgeted and actual fixed overhead costs, computed as follows:

$$\begin{aligned}\text{Fixed Overhead Budget Variance} &= \text{Budgeted Fixed Overhead} - \\ &\quad\ \text{Actual Fixed Overhead} \\ &= \$1,300 - \$1,600 \\ &= \$300 \text{ (U)}\end{aligned}$$

The **fixed overhead volume variance** is the difference between budgeted fixed overhead costs and the overhead costs that are applied to production using the standard fixed overhead rate. The fixed overhead volume variance is computed as follows:

Standard fixed overhead applied to good units produced	
$3.25 per direct labor hour × (180 bags × 2.4 hours per bag)	$1,404
Less total budgeted fixed overhead	1,300
Fixed overhead volume variance	$ 104 (F)

Because the fixed overhead volume variance measures the use of existing facilities and capacity, a volume variance will occur if more or less than normal capacity is used. At Cambria Company, 400 direct labor hours are considered normal use of facilities. Because fixed overhead costs are applied on the basis of standard hours allowed, Cambria Company's overhead was applied on the basis of 432 hours, even though the fixed overhead rate was computed using 400 hours. Thus, more fixed costs would be applied to products than were budgeted. When capacity exceeds the expected amount, the result is a favorable overhead volume variance because fixed overhead was overapplied.

When a company operates at a level below the normal capacity in units, the result is an unfavorable volume variance. Not all of the fixed overhead costs will be applied to units produced. In other words, fixed overhead is underapplied, and the cost of goods produced does not include the full budgeted cost of fixed overhead.

Summary of Overhead Variances   If our calculations of variable and fixed overhead variances are correct, the net of these variances should equal the total overhead variance. Checking the computations, we find that the variable and fixed overhead variances do equal the total overhead variance:

Variable overhead spending variance	$ 87.50 (F)
Variable overhead efficiency variance	103.50 (U)
Fixed overhead budget variance	300.00 (U)
Fixed overhead volume variance	104.00 (F)
Total overhead variance	$212.00 (U)

Figures 5 and 6 summarize our analysis of overhead variances. The total overhead variance is also the amount of overapplied or underapplied overhead. You may recall from an earlier chapter that actual variable and fixed overhead costs are recorded as they occur, that variable and fixed overhead are applied to products as they are produced, and that the overapplied or underapplied overhead is computed and reconciled at the end of each accounting period. By breaking down the total overhead variance into variable and fixed variances, managers can more accurately control costs and reconcile their causes. An analysis of these two overhead variances will help explain why the amount of overhead applied to units produced is different from the actual overhead costs incurred.

Analyzing and Correcting Overhead Variances

In analyzing the unfavorable total overhead variance of $212, the manager of Cambria Company's Bag Assembly Department found causes for the variances that contributed to it. Although the variable overhead spending variance was favorable ($87.50 less than expected because of savings on purchases), the inefficiency of the machine operator who substituted for an assembly worker created unfavorable variances for both direct labor efficiency and variable overhead efficiency. As a result, the manager is going to consider the feasibility of implementing a program for cross-training employees.

After reviewing the fixed overhead costs, the manager of the Bag Assembly Department concluded that higher than anticipated factory insurance premiums were the reason for the unfavorable fixed overhead budget variance and were the result of an increase in the number of insurance claims filed by employees. To obtain more specific information, the manager will study the insurance claims filed over a three-month period.

Finally, since the 432 standard hours were well above the normal capacity of 400 direct labor hours, fixed overhead was overapplied, and it resulted in a $104(F) volume variance. The overutilization of capacity was traced to high seasonal demand that pressed the company to use almost all its capacity. Management decided not to do anything about the fixed overhead volume variance because it fell within an anticipated seasonal range.

S T O P • R E V I E W • A P P L Y

6-1. Can the variable overhead efficiency variance have the same causes as the direct labor efficiency variance?

6-2. Distinguish between the fixed overhead budget variance and the fixed overhead volume variance.

6-3. If standard hours allowed exceed normal hours, will the period's fixed overhead volume variance be favorable or unfavorable? Explain your answer.

Using Cost Variances to Evaluate Managers' Performance

LO7   Explain how variances are used to evaluate managers' performance.

How effectively and fairly a manager's performance is evaluated depends on human factors—the people doing the evaluating—as well as on company policies. The evaluation process becomes more accurate when managerial performance reports include variances from standard costs.

To ensure that the evaluation of a manager's performance is effective and fair, a company's policies should be based on input from managers and employees and should specify the procedures that managers are to use when doing the following:

- Preparing operational plans
- Assigning responsibility for carrying out the operational plans
- Communicating the operational plans to key personnel
- Evaluating performance in each area of responsibility
- Identifying the causes of significant variances from the operational plan
- Taking corrective action to eliminate problems

Because variance analysis provides detailed data about differences between standard and actual costs and thus helps identify the causes of those differences, it is usually more effective at pinpointing efficient and inefficient operating areas than are basic comparisons of budgeted and actual data. A managerial performance report based on standard costs and related variances should identify the causes of each significant variance, the personnel involved, and the corrective actions taken. It should be tailored to the cost center manager's specific areas of responsibility and explain clearly how the manager's department met or did not meet operating expectations. Managers should be held accountable only for the cost areas under their control.

Exhibit 5 shows a performance report for the manager of Cambria Company's Bag Assembly Department. The report summarizes all cost data and variances for direct materials, direct labor, and overhead. In addition, it identifies the causes of the variances and the corrective actions taken. Such a report would enable a supervisor to review a cost center manager's actions and evaluate his or her performance.

A point to remember is that the mere occurrence of a variance does not indicate that a manager of a cost center has performed poorly. However, if a variance occurs consistently, and no cause is identified and no corrective action is taken, it may well indicate poor managerial performance.

Exhibit 5 shows that the causes of the variances have been identified and corrective actions have been taken, indicating that the manager of the Cambria Company's Bag Assembly Department has the operation under control.

STOP • REVIEW • APPLY

7-1. Why should evaluations of the performance of cost center managers not follow a set pattern?

7-2. What should a managerial performance report based on standard costs and related variances include? How should it be prepared?

EXHIBIT 5 ▼

Managerial Performance Report Using Variance Analysis

Cambria Company
Managerial Performance Report
Bag Assembly Department
For the Month Ended August 31

Productivity Summary:

Normal capacity in units	167 bags
Normal capacity in direct labor hours (DLH)	400 DLH
Good units produced	180 bags
Performance level (standard hours allowed for good units produced)	432 DLH

Cost and Variance Analysis:

	Standard Costs	Actual Costs	Total Variance	Variance Breakdown Amount	Variance Breakdown Type
Direct materials	$ 4,320	$ 4,484	$164 (U)	$ 76.00 (F)	Direct materials price variance
				240.00 (U)	Direct materials quantity variance
Direct labor	3,672	4,140	468 (U)	315.00 (U)	Direct labor rate variance
				153.00 (U)	Direct labor efficiency variance
Variable overhead	2,484	2,500	16 (U)	87.50 (F)	Variable overhead spending variance
				103.50 (U)	Variable overhead efficiency variance
Fixed overhead	1,404	1,600	196 (U)	300.00 (U)	Fixed overhead budget variance
				104.00 (F)	Fixed overhead volume variance
Totals	$11,880	$12,724	$844 (U)	$844.00 (U)	

Causes of Variances	**Actions Taken**
Direct materials price variance: New direct materials purchased at reduced price	New direct materials deemed inappropriate; resumed purchasing materials originally specified
Direct materials quantity variance: Poor quality of new direct materials	New direct materials deemed inappropriate; resumed using direct materials originally specified
Direct labor rate variance: Machine operator who had to learn assembly skills	Temporary replacement; no action taken on the job
Direct labor efficiency variance: Machine operator who had to learn assembly skills	Temporary replacement; no action taken on the job
Late delivery of parts to assembly floor	Material delivery times and number of delays being tracked
Variable overhead spending variance: Cost savings on purchases	No action necessary
Variable overhead efficiency variance: Machine operator who had to learn assembly skills on the job	A cross-training program for employees now under consideration
Fixed overhead budget variance: Large number of factory insurance claims	Study of insurance claims being conducted
Fixed overhead volume variance: High number of orders caused by seasonal demand	No action necessary

A LOOK BACK AT

COACH, INC.

The Decision Point at the beginning of this chapter focused on Coach, Inc., a manufacturer of high-quality leather goods and fine gifts and accessories. It asked these questions:

- How does setting performance standards help managers control costs?
- How do Coach's managers use standard costs to control costs?
- How do they use standard costs to evaluate the performance of cost centers?

Managers at Coach base standard costs on realistic estimates of operating costs. They use these figures as performance targets and as benchmarks against which they measure actual spending trends. By analyzing variances between standard and actual costs, they gain insight into the causes of those differences. Once they have identified an operating problem that is causing a cost variance, they can devise a solution to the problem and better control costs.

When evaluating the performance of cost centers, managers use standard costs to prepare flexible budgets, which will improve the accuracy of their variance analysis. This comparison of actual costs and a budget based on actual output provides Coach's managers with objective data that they can use to assess the center's performance in terms of its key success factor—cost.

CHAPTER REVIEW

REVIEW of Learning Objectives

LO1 Define *standard costs,* and describe how managers use these costs.

Standard costs are realistic estimates of costs based on analyses of both past and projected operating costs and conditions. They provide a standard, or predetermined, performance level for use in standard costing, a method of cost control that also includes a measure of actual performance and a measure of the variance between standard and actual performance. When managers plan, they use standard costs to develop budgets for direct materials, direct labor, and variable overhead. These estimated costs not only serve as targets for product costing, but are also useful in making decisions about product distribution and pricing. During an accounting period, as managers perform, they use standard costs to measure expenditures and to control costs as they occur. At the end of the period, managers evaluate performance by comparing actual costs with standard costs and computing the variances. The variances provide measures of performance that can be used to control costs. Managers also use standard cost reports to communicate about operations and managerial performance.

LO2 Explain how standard costs are developed, and compute a standard unit cost.

A standard unit cost has six elements. The direct materials price standard is based on a careful estimate of all possible price increases, changes in available quantities, and new sources of supply in the next accounting period. The direct materials quantity standard is based on product engineering specifications, the quality of direct materials, the age and productivity of the machines, and the quality and experience of the work force. Labor union contracts or company policies define the direct labor rate standard. Current time and motion studies of workers and machines and records of their past performance provide the data for developing the direct labor time standard. Standard variable and fixed overhead rates are found by dividing total budgeted variable and fixed overhead costs by an appropriate application base, such as normal capacity. A total standard unit cost is computed by adding the following costs: direct materials costs (direct materials price standard times direct materials quantity standard), direct labor costs (direct labor rate standard times direct labor time standard), and overhead costs (standard variable and standard fixed overhead rate times standard direct labor hours allowed per unit).

LO3 Prepare a flexible budget, and describe how managers use variance analysis to control costs.

A flexible budget is a summary of anticipated costs for a range of activity levels. It provides forecasted cost data that can be adjusted for changes in level of output. The variable cost per unit and total fixed costs presented in a flexible budget are components of the flexible budget formula, an equation that determines the budgeted cost for any level of output. A flexible budget improves the accuracy of variance analysis, which is a four-step approach to controlling costs. First, managers compute the amount of the variance. If the amount is insignificant, no corrective action is needed. If the amount is significant, managers then analyze the variance to identify its cause. In identifying the cause, they are usually able to pinpoint the activities that need to be monitored. They then select performance measures that will enable them to track those activities, analyze the results, and determine the action needed to correct the problem. Their final step is to take the appropriate corrective action.

LO4 Compute and analyze direct materials variances.

The direct materials price variance is computed by finding the difference between the standard price and the actual price per unit and multiplying it by the actual quantity purchased. The direct materials quantity variance is the difference between the standard quantity that should have been used and the actual quantity used, multiplied by the standard price. An analysis of these variances enables managers to identify what is causing them and to formulate plans for correcting related operating problems.

LO5 Compute and analyze direct labor variances.

The direct labor rate variance is computed by determining the difference between the standard direct labor rate and the actual rate and multiplying it by the actual direct labor hours worked. The direct labor efficiency variance is the difference between the standard hours allowed for the number of good units produced and the actual hours worked multiplied by the standard direct labor rate. Managers analyze these variances to find the causes of differences between standard direct labor costs and actual direct labor costs.

LO6 Compute and analyze overhead variances.

The total overhead variance is equal to the amount of under- or overapplied overhead costs for an accounting period. An analysis of the variable and fixed overhead variances will help explain why the amount of overhead applied to units produced differs from the actual overhead costs incurred. The total overhead variance can be broken down into a variable overhead spending variance, a variable overhead efficiency variance, a fixed overhead budget variance, and a fixed overhead volume variance.

LO7 Explain how variances are used to evaluate managers' performance.

How effectively and fairly a manager's performance is evaluated depends on human factors—the people doing the evaluating—as well as on company policies. To ensure that performance evaluation is effective and fair, a company's evaluation policies should be based on input from managers and employees and should be specific about the procedures that managers are to follow. The evaluation process becomes more accurate when managerial performance reports for cost centers include variances from standard costs. A managerial performance report based on standard costs and related variances should identify the causes of each significant variance, along with the personnel involved and the corrective actions taken. It should be tailored to the cost center manager's specific areas of responsibility.

REVIEW of Concepts and Terminology

The following concepts and terms were introduced in this chapter:

Direct labor efficiency variance: The difference between the standard direct labor hours allowed for good units produced and the actual direct labor hours worked multiplied by the standard direct labor rate. Also called *direct labor quantity* or *usage variance*. **(LO5)**

Direct labor rate standard: The hourly direct labor rate that is expected to prevail during the next accounting period for each function or job classification. **(LO2)**

Direct labor rate variance: The difference between the standard direct labor rate and the actual direct labor rate multiplied by the actual direct labor hours worked. Also called *direct labor spending variance*. **(LO5)**

Direct labor time standard: The expected labor time required for each department, machine, or process to complete the production of one unit or one batch of output. **(LO2)**

Direct materials price standard: A careful estimate of the cost of a specific direct material in the next accounting period. **(LO2)**

Direct materials price variance: The difference between the standard price and the actual price per unit multiplied by the actual quantity purchased. Also called *direct materials spending* or *rate variance*. **(LO4)**

Direct materials quantity standard: An estimate of the amount of direct materials, including scrap and waste, that will be used in an accounting period. **(LO2)**

Direct materials quantity variance: The difference between the standard quantity allowed and the actual quantity used multiplied by the standard price. Also called *direct materials efficiency* or *usage variance*. **(LO4)**

Fixed overhead budget variance: The difference between budgeted and actual fixed overhead costs. Also called *budgeted fixed overhead variance*. **(LO6)**

Fixed overhead volume variance: The difference between budgeted fixed overhead costs and the overhead costs that are applied to production using the standard fixed overhead rate. **(LO6)**

Flexible budget: A summary of expected costs for a range of activity levels. Also called *variable budget*. **(LO3)**

Flexible budget formula: An equation that determines the expected, or budgeted, cost for any level of output. **(LO3)**

Standard costing: A method of cost control with three components: a standard, or predetermined, performance level; a measure of actual performance; and a measure of the difference, or variance, between standard and actual performance. **(LO1)**

Standard costs: Realistic estimates of costs based on analyses of both past and projected operating costs and conditions. **(LO1)**

Standard direct labor cost: The standard wage for direct labor multiplied by the standard hours of direct labor. **(LO2)**

Standard direct materials cost: The standard price for direct materials multiplied by the standard quantity for direct materials. **(LO2)**

Standard fixed overhead rate: Total budgeted fixed overhead costs divided by an expression of capacity, usually normal capacity in terms of standard hours or units. **(LO2)**

Standard overhead cost: The sum of the estimates of variable and fixed overhead costs in the next accounting period. **(LO2)**

Standard variable overhead rate: Total budgeted variable overhead costs divided by an expression of capacity, such as the expected number of standard machine hours or standard direct labor hours. **(LO2)**

Total direct labor cost variance: The difference between the standard direct labor cost for good units produced and actual direct labor costs. **(LO5)**

Total direct materials cost variance: The difference between the standard cost and actual cost of direct materials. Also called *good units produced*. **(LO4)**

Total fixed overhead variance: The difference between actual fixed overhead costs and the standard fixed overhead costs that are applied to good units produced using the standard fixed overhead rate. **(LO6)**

Total overhead variance: The difference between actual overhead costs and standard overhead costs applied. **(LO6)**

Total variable overhead variance: The difference between actual variable overhead costs and the standard variable overhead costs that are applied to good units produced using the standard variable overhead rate. **(LO6)**

Variable overhead efficiency variance: The difference between the standard direct labor hours allowed for good units produced and the actual hours worked multiplied by the standard variable overhead rate per hour. **(LO6)**

Variable overhead spending variance: The difference between actual variable overhead costs and the standard variable overhead rate multiplied by the actual hours used. Also called the *variable overhead rate variance*. **(LO6)**

Variance: The difference between a standard cost and an actual cost. **(LO1)**

Variance analysis: The process of computing the differences between standard costs and actual costs and identifying the causes of those differences. **(LO3)**

REVIEW Problem

LO2, LO4, LO5, LO6   **Variance Analysis**

Leather Goods Company has a standard costing system and keeps all its cost standards up to date. The company's main product is a leather briefcase, which is made in a single cost center. The standard variable costs for one unit are as follows:

Direct materials (3 sq. meters @ $12.50 per sq. meter)	$37.50
Direct labor (1.2 hours @ $9.00 per hour)	10.80
Variable overhead (1.2 hours @ $5.00 per direct labor hour)	6.00
Standard variable cost per unit	$54.30

The company's master budget was based on its normal capacity of 15,000 direct labor hours. Its budgeted fixed overhead costs for the year were $54,000. During the year, it produced and sold 12,200 units, and it purchased and used 37,500 square meters of direct materials; the purchase cost was $12.40 per square meter. The average labor rate was $9.20 per hour, and 15,250 direct labor hours were worked. The company's actual variable overhead costs for the year were $73,200, and its fixed overhead costs were $55,000.

Required

Using the data given, compute the following using formulas or diagram form:

1. Standard hours allowed for good output
2. Standard fixed overhead rate
3. Direct materials cost variances:
   a. Direct materials price variance
   b. Direct materials quantity variance
   c. Total direct materials variance
4. Direct labor cost variances:
   a. Direct labor rate variance
   b. Direct labor efficiency variance
   c. Total direct labor variance
5. Variable overhead cost variances:
   a. Variable overhead spending variance
   b. Variable overhead efficiency variance
   c. Total variable overhead variance
6. Fixed overhead cost variances:
   a. Fixed overhead budget variance
   b. Fixed overhead volume variance
   c. Total fixed overhead variance

Answer to Review Problem

1. Standard Hours Allowed = Good Units Produced × Standard Direct Labor Hours per Unit
   = 12,200 Units × 1.2 Direct Labor Hours per Unit
   = 14,640 Hours

2. Standard Fixed Overhead Rate = $\dfrac{\text{Budgeted Fixed Overhead Cost}}{\text{Normal Capacity}}$
   = $\dfrac{\$54,000}{15,000 \text{ Direct Labor Hours}}$
   = $3.60 per Direct Labor Hour

3. Direct materials cost variances:
   a. Direct materials price variance

Price difference:		
Standard price	$12.50	
Less actual price	12.40	
Difference	$ .10 (F)	

   Direct Materials Price Variance = (Standard Price − Actual Price) × Actual Quantity
   = $.10 × 37,500 Sq. Meters
   = $3,750 (F)

b. Direct materials quantity variance

Quantity difference: Standard quantity

(12,200 units × 3 sq. meters)	36,600	Sq. Meters
Less actual quantity	37,500	Sq. Meters
Difference	900	Sq. Meters (U)

Direct Materials Quantity Variance = Standard Price × (Standard
Quantity − Actual Quantity)
= $12.50 per Sq. Meter ×
900 Sq. Meters
= $11,250 (U)

c. Total direct materials cost variance:

Total Direct Materials Cost Variance = Net of Direct Materials Price
Variance and Direct Materials
Quantity Variance
= $3,750 (F) − $11,250 (U)
= $7,500 (U)

Diagram Form:

	Actual Price × Actual Quantity		Standard Price × Actual Quantity		Standard Price × Standard Quantity
Direct Materials	$12.40 × 37,500 = $465,000	**Price Variance**	$12.50 × 37,500 = $468,750	**Quantity Variance**	$12.50 × (12,200 × 3) = $457,500
		$3,750 (F)	**Total Direct Materials Cost Variance**	$11,250 (U)	
			$7,500 (U)		

4. Direct labor cost variances:
    a. Direct labor rate variance:

Rate difference: Standard labor rate	$9.00
Less actual labor rate	9.20
Difference	$ .20 (U)

Direct Labor Rate Variance = (Standard Rate − Actual Rate) ×
Actual Hours
= $.20 × 15,250 hours
= $3,050 (U)

b. Direct labor efficiency variance:

Difference in hours: Standard hours allowed	14,640	hours*
Less actual hours	15,250	hours
Difference	610	hours (U)

Direct Labor Efficiency Variance = Standard Rate × (Standard Hours
Allowed − Actual Hours)
= $9.00 per hour × 610 hours (U)
= $5,490 (U)

---

*12,200 units produced × 1.2 hours per unit = 14,640 hours.

c. Total direct labor cost variance:

$$\text{Total Direct Labor Cost Variance} = \text{Net of Direct Labor Rate Variance}$$
$$\text{and Direct Labor Efficiency Variance}$$
$$= \$3,050 \text{ (U)} + \$5,490 \text{ (U)}$$
$$= \underline{\underline{\$8,540 \text{ (U)}}}$$

Diagram Form:

	Actual Rate × Actual Hours		Standard Rate × Actual Hours		Standard Rate × Standard Hours
Direct Labor	$9.20 × 15,250 = $140,300	Rate Variance	$9.00 × 15,250 = $137,250	Efficiency Variance	$9.00 × (12,200 × 1.2) = $131,760
		$3,050 (U)	Total Direct Labor Cost Variance	$5,490 (U)	
			$8,540 (U)		

5. Variable overhead cost variances:
   a. Variable overhead spending variance:

Standard variable rate × actual hours worked ($5.00 per hour × 15,250 labor hours)	$76,250	
Less actual variable overhead costs incurred	73,200	
Variable overhead spending variance	$ 3,050 (F)	

   b. Variable overhead efficiency variance:

Variable overhead applied to good units produced (14,640 hours* × $5.00 per hour)	$73,200	
Less budgeted variable overhead for actual hours (15,250 hours × $5.00 per hour)	76,250	
Variable overhead efficiency variance	$ 3,050 (U)	

   ---
   *12,200 units produced × 1.2 hours per unit = 14,640 hours.

   c. Total variable overhead cost variance:

   $$\text{Total Variable Overhead Cost Variance} = \text{Net of Variable Overhead}$$
   $$\text{Spending Variance and}$$
   $$\text{Variable Overhead Efficiency}$$
   $$\text{Variance}$$
   $$= \$3,050 \text{ (F)} - \$3,050 \text{ (U)}$$
   $$= \$0$$

Diagram Form:

	Actual Variable Overhead Costs		Standard Rate × Actual Hours		Standard Rate × Standard Hours
Variable Overhead	$73,200	Spending Variance	$5.00 × 15,250 = $76,250	Efficiency Variance	$5.00 × (12,200 × 1.2) = $73,200
		$3,050 (F)	Total Variable Overhead Cost Variance	$3,050 (U)	
			$0		

6. Fixed overhead cost variances:
   a. Fixed overhead budget variance:

Budgeted fixed overhead	$54,000
Less actual fixed overhead	55,000
Fixed overhead budget variance	$ 1,000 (U)

   b. Fixed overhead volume variance:

Standard fixed overhead applied (14,640 labor hours × $3.60* per hour)	$52,704
Less total budgeted fixed overhead	54,000
Fixed overhead volume variance	$ 1,296 (U)

   c. Total fixed overhead cost variance:

   Total Fixed Overhead Cost Variance = Net of Fixed Overhead Budget Variance and Fixed Overhead Volume Variance
   = $1,000 (U) + $1,296 (U)
   = $2,296 (U)

   _____
   *From answer to Requirement 2.

Diagram Form:

	Actual Fixed Overhead Costs		Budgeted Fixed Overhead Costs		Standard Rate × Standard Hours
Fixed Overhead	$55,000	Budget Variance	$54,000	Volume Variance	$3.60 × (12,200 × 1.2) = $52,704
		$1,000 (U)	Total Fixed Overhead Variance	$1,296 (U)	
			$2,296 (U)		

CHAPTER ASSIGNMENTS

BUILDING Your Basic Knowledge and Skills

Short Exercises

LO1 **Uses of Standard Costs**

SE 1. Lago Corporation is considering adopting the standard costing method. Dan Sarkis, the manager of the Ohio Division, attended a corporate meeting at which Leah Rohr, the controller, discussed the proposal. Sarkis asked, "Leah, how will this new method benefit me? How will I use it?" Prepare Rohr's response to Sarkis.

LO1 **Purposes of Standard Costs**

SE 2. Suppose you are a management consultant and a client asks you why companies include standard costs in their cost accounting systems. Prepare your response, listing several purposes for using standard costs.

LO2 **Computing a Standard Unit Cost**

SE 3. Using the information that follows, compute the standard unit cost of Product JLT.

Direct materials quantity standard	5 pounds per unit
Direct materials price standard	$10.20 per pound
Direct labor time standard	.4 hour per unit
Direct labor rate standard	$10.75 per hour
Variable overhead rate standard	$7.00 per machine hour
Fixed overhead rate standard	$11.00 per machine hour
Machine hour standard	2 hours per unit

LO3 **Analyzing Cost Variances**

SE 4. Garden Metal Works produces lawn sculptures. The company analyzes only variances that differ by more than 5 percent from the standard cost. The controller computed the following direct labor efficiency variances for March:

	Direct Labor Efficiency Variance	Standard Direct Labor Cost
Product 4	$1,240 (U)	$26,200
Product 6	3,290 (F)	41,700
Product 7	2,030 (U)	34,300
Product 9	1,620 (F)	32,560
Product 12	2,810 (U)	59,740

For each product, determine the variance as a percentage of the standard cost (round to one decimal place). Then identify the products whose variances should be analyzed and suggest possible causes for the variances.

LO3 **Preparing a Flexible Budget**

SE 5. Prepare a flexible budget for 10,000, 12,000, and 14,000 units of output, using the following information:

Variable costs	
Direct materials	$8.00 per unit
Direct labor	$2.50 per unit
Variable overhead	$6.00 per unit
Total budgeted fixed overhead	$81,200

LO4 **Direct Materials Variances**

SE 6. Using the standard costs in **SE 3** and the following actual cost and usage data, compute the direct materials price and direct materials quantity variances:

Direct materials purchased and used	55,000 pounds
Price paid for direct materials	$10.00 per pound
Number of good units produced	11,000 units

LO5 **Direct Labor Variances**

SE 7. Using the standard costs in **SE 3** and the following actual cost and usage data, compute the direct labor rate and direct labor efficiency variances:

Direct labor hours used	4,950 hours
Total cost of direct labor	$53,460
Number of good units produced	11,000 units

LO6 **Overhead Variances**

SE 8. Sutherland Products uses standard costing. The following information about overhead was generated during August:

Standard variable overhead rate	$2 per machine hour
Standard fixed overhead rate	$3 per machine hour
Actual variable overhead costs	$443,200

Actual fixed overhead costs	$698,800
Budgeted fixed overhead costs	$700,000
Standard machine hours per unit produced	12
Good units produced	18,940
Actual machine hours	228,400

Compute the variable overhead spending and efficiency variances and the fixed overhead budget and volume variances.

LO6 **Fixed Overhead Rate and Variances**

SE 9. To the Point Manufacturing Company uses the standard costing method. The company's main product is a fine-quality fountain pen that normally takes 2.5 hours to produce. Normal annual capacity is 30,000 direct labor hours, and budgeted fixed overhead costs for the year were $15,000. During the year, the company produced and sold 14,000 units. Actual fixed overhead costs were $19,000. Compute the fixed overhead rate per direct labor hour and determine the fixed overhead budget and volume variances.

LO7 **Evaluating Managerial Performance**

SE 10. Gina Rolando, the controller at WAWA Industries, gave Jason Ponds, the production manager, a report containing the following information:

	Actual Cost	Standard Cost	Variance
Direct materials	$38,200	$36,600	$1,600 (U)
Direct labor	19,450	19,000	450 (U)
Variable overhead	62,890	60,000	2,890 (U)

Rolando asked for a response. If you were Ponds, how would you respond? What additional information might you need to prepare your response?

Exercises

LO1 **Uses of Standard Costs**

E 1. Summer Diaz has just assumed the duties of controller for Market Research Company. She is concerned that the company's methods of cost planning and control do not accurately track the operations of the business. She plans to suggest to the company's president, Sydney Tyson, that the company start using standard costing for budgeting and cost control. The new method could be incorporated into the existing accounting system. The anticipated cost of adopting it and training managers is around $7,500. Prepare a memo from Summer Diaz to Sydney Tyson that defines standard costing and outlines its uses and benefits.

LO2 **Computing Standard Costs**

E 2. Normal Corporation uses standard costing and is in the process of updating its direct materials and direct labor standards for Product 20B. The following data have been accumulated:

Direct materials

In the previous period, 20,500 units were produced, and 32,800 square yards of direct materials at a cost of $122,344 were used to produce them.

Direct labor

During the previous period, 57,400 direct labor hours were worked—34,850 hours on machine H and 22,550 hours on machine K. Machine H operators earned $9.40 per hour, and machine K operators earned $9.20

per hour last period. A new labor union contract calls for a 10 percent increase in labor rates for the coming period.

Using this information as the basis for the new standards, compute the direct materials quantity and price standards and the direct labor time and rate standards for each machine for the coming accounting period.

LO2 **Computing a Standard Unit Cost**

E 3. Weather Aerodynamics, Inc., makes electronically equipped weather-detecting balloons for university meteorology departments. Because of recent nationwide inflation, the company's management has ordered that standard costs be recomputed. New direct materials price standards are $600 per set for electronic components and $13.50 per square meter for heavy-duty canvas. Direct materials quantity standards include one set of electronic components and 100 square meters of heavy-duty canvas per balloon. Direct labor time standards are 26 hours per balloon for the Electronics Department and 19 hours per balloon for the Assembly Department. Direct labor rate standards are $11 per hour for the Electronics Department and $10 per hour for the Assembly Department. Standard overhead rates are $16 per direct labor hour for the standard variable overhead rate and $12 per direct labor hour for the standard fixed overhead rate. Using these production standards, compute the standard unit cost of one weather balloon.

LO3 **Preparing a Flexible Budget**

E 4. Keel Company's fixed overhead costs for the year are expected to be as follows: depreciation, $72,000; supervisory salaries, $92,000; property taxes and insurance, $26,000; and other fixed overhead, $14,500. Total fixed overhead is thus expected to be $204,500. Variable costs per unit are expected to be as follows: direct materials, $16.50; direct labor, $8.50; operating supplies, $2.60; indirect labor, $4.10; and other variable overhead costs, $3.20. Prepare a flexible budget for the following levels of production: 18,000 units, 20,000 units, and 22,000 units. What is the flexible budget formula for the year ended December 31?

LO4 **Direct Materials Price and Quantity Variances**

E 5. SITO Elevator Company manufactures small hydroelectric elevators with a maximum capacity of ten passengers. One of the direct materials used is heavy-duty carpeting for the floor of the elevator. The direct materials quantity standard for April was 8 square yards per elevator. During April, the purchasing agent purchased this carpeting at $11 per square yard; the standard price for the period was $12. Ninety elevators were completed and sold during the month; the Production Department used an average of 8.5 square yards of carpet per elevator. Calculate the company's direct materials price and quantity variances for carpeting for April.

LO4 **Direct Materials Variances**

E 6. Diekow Productions manufactured and sold 1,000 products at $11,000 each during the past year. At the beginning of the year, production had been set at 1,200 products; direct materials standards had been set at 100 pounds of direct materials at $2 per pound for each product produced. During the year, the company purchased and used 98,000 pounds of direct materials; the cost was $2.04 per pound. Calculate Diekow Production's direct materials price and quantity variances for the year.

LO5   Direct Labor Variances

E 7. At the beginning of last year, Diekow Productions set direct labor standards of 20 hours at $15 per hour for each product produced. During the year, 20,500 direct labor hours were actually worked at an average cost of $16 per hour. Using this information and the applicable information in **E 6**, calculate Diekow Production's direct labor rate and efficiency variances for the year.

LO5   Direct Labor Rate and Efficiency Variances

E 8. NEO Foundry, Inc., manufactures castings that other companies use in the production of machinery. For the past two years, NEO's best-selling product has been a casting for an eight-cylinder engine block. Standard direct labor hours per engine block are 1.8 hours. A labor union contract requires that the company pay all direct labor employees $14 per hour. During June, NEO produced 16,500 engine blocks. Actual direct labor hours and costs for the month were 29,900 hours and $433,550, respectively.

1. Compute the direct labor rate variance for eight-cylinder engine blocks during June.
2. Using the same data, compute the direct labor efficiency variance for eight-cylinder engine blocks during June. Check your answer, assuming that the total direct labor cost variance is $17,750 (U).

LO6   Variable Overhead Variances

E 9. At the beginning of last year, Diekow Productions set variable overhead standards of 10 machine hours at a rate of $10 per hour for each product produced. During the year, 10,800 machine hours were used at a cost of $10.20 per hour. Using this information and the applicable information in **E 6**, calculate Diekow Production's variable overhead spending and efficiency variances for the year.

Fixed Overhead Variances

LO6 **E 10.** At the beginning of last year, Diekow Productions set budgeted fixed overhead costs at $456,000. During the year, actual fixed overhead costs were $500,000. Using this information and the applicable information in **E 6**, calculate Diekow Production's fixed overhead budget and volume variances for the year. Assume that fixed overhead is applied based on units of product.

LO6   Variable Overhead Variances for a Service Business

E 11. Design Architects, LLP, billed clients for 6,000 hours of design work for the month. Actual variable overhead costs for the month were $315,000, and 6,250 hours were worked. At the beginning of the year, a variable overhead standard of $50 per design hour had been developed based on a budget of 5,000 design hours each month. Calculate Design Architects' variable overhead spending and efficiency variances for the month.

LO6   Fixed Overhead Variances for a Service Business

E 12. Engineering Associates billed clients for 11,000 hours of engineering work for the month. Actual fixed overhead costs for the month were $435,000, and 11,850 hours were worked. At the beginning of the year, a fixed overhead standard of $40 per engineering hour had been developed based on a budget of 10,000 engineering hours each month. Calculate Engineering Associates' fixed overhead budget and volume variances for the month.

LO6 Overhead Variances

E 13. Cedar Key Company produces handmade clamming buckets and sells them to distributors along the Gulf Coast of Florida. The company incurred $9,400 of actual overhead costs ($8,000 variable; $1,400 fixed) in May. Budgeted standard overhead costs for May were $4 of variable overhead costs per direct labor hour and $1,500 of fixed overhead costs. Normal capacity was set at 2,000 direct labor hours per month. In May, the company produced 10,100 clamming buckets by working 1,900 direct labor hours. The time standard is .2 direct labor hour per clamming bucket. Compute (1) the variable overhead spending and efficiency variances and (2) the fixed overhead budget and volume variances for May.

LO6 Overhead Variances

E 14. Suncoast Industries uses standard costing and a flexible budget for cost planning and control. Its monthly budget for overhead costs is $200,000 of fixed costs plus $5.20 per machine hour. Monthly normal capacity of 100,000 machine hours is used to compute the standard fixed overhead rate. During December, employees worked 105,000 machine hours. Only 98,500 standard machine hours were allowed for good units produced during the month. Actual overhead costs incurred during December totaled $441,000 of variable costs and $204,500 of fixed costs. Compute (1) the under- or overapplied overhead during December and (2) the variable overhead spending and efficiency variances and the fixed overhead budget and volume variances.

LO7 Evaluating Managerial Performance

E 15. Ron LaTulip oversees projects for ACE Construction Company. Recently, the company's controller sent him a performance report regarding the construction of the Campus Highlands Apartment Complex, a project that LaTulip supervised. Included in the report was an unfavorable direct labor efficiency variance of $1,900 for roof structures. What types of information does LaTulip need to analyze before he can respond to this report?

Problems

LO2 Computing and Using Standard Costs

P 1. Prefabricated houses are the specialty of Affordable Homes, Inc., of Corsicana, Texas. Although Affordable Homes produces many models, the company's best-selling model is the Welcome Home, a three-bedroom, 1,400-square-foot house with an impressive front entrance. Last year, the standard costs for the six basic direct materials used in manufacturing the entrance were as follows: wood framing materials, $2,140; deluxe front door, $480; door hardware, $260; exterior siding, $710; electrical materials, $580; and interior finishing materials, $1,520. Three types of direct labor are used to build the entrance: carpenter, 30 hours at $12 per hour; door specialist, 4 hours at $14 per hour; and electrician, 8 hours at $16 per hour. Last year, the company used an overhead rate of 40 percent of total direct materials cost.

This year, the cost of wood framing materials is expected to increase by 20 percent, and a deluxe front door will cost $496. The cost of the door hardware will increase by 10 percent, and the cost of electrical materials will increase by 20 percent. Exterior siding cost should decrease by $16 per unit. The cost of interior finishing materials is expected to remain the same. The carpenter's wages will increase by $1 per hour, and the door specialist's wages should remain the same. The electrician's wages will increase by $.50 per hour. Finally, the overhead rate will decrease to 25 percent of total direct materials cost.

Required

1. Compute the total standard cost of direct materials per entrance for last year.
2. Using your answer to item 1, compute the total standard unit cost per entrance for last year.
3. Compute the total standard unit cost per entrance for this year.

LO3 **Preparing a Flexible Budget and Evaluating Performance**

P 2. Home Products Company manufactures a complete line of kitchen glass-ware. The Beverage Division specializes in 12-ounce drinking glasses. Erin Fisher, the superintendent of the Beverage Division, asked the controller to prepare a report of her division's performance in April. The following report was handed to her a few days later:

Cost Category (Variable Unit Cost)	Budgeted Costs*	Actual Costs	Difference Under (Over) Budget
Direct materials ($.10)	$ 5,000	$ 4,975	$ 25
Direct labor ($.12)	6,000	5,850	150
Variable overhead			
Indirect labor ($.03)	1,500	1,290	210
Supplies ($.02)	1,000	960	40
Heat and power ($.03)	1,500	1,325	175
Other ($.05)	2,500	2,340	160
Fixed overhead			
Heat and power	3,500	3,500	—
Depreciation	4,200	4,200	—
Insurance and taxes	1,200	1,200	—
Other	1,600	1,600	—
Totals	$28,000	$27,240	$760

*Based on normal capacity of 50,000 units.

In discussing the report with the controller, Fisher stated, "Profits have been decreasing in recent months, but this report indicates that our pro-duction process is operating efficiently."

Required

1. Prepare a flexible budget for the Beverage Division using production lev-els of 45,000 units, 50,000 units, and 55,000 units.
2. What is the flexible budget formula?
3. Assume that the Beverage Division produced 46,560 units in April and that all fixed costs remained constant. Prepare a revised performance report similar to the one above, using actual production in units as a basis for the budget column.
4. **Manager Insight:** Which report is more meaningful for performance evalu-ation, the original one above or the revised one? Why?

LO4, LO5 **Direct Materials and Direct Labor Variances**

P 3. Winners Trophy Company produces a variety of athletic awards, most of them in the form of trophies. Its deluxe trophy stands three feet tall above the base. The company's direct materials standards for the deluxe trophy include one pound of metal and eight ounces of wood for the base. Standard prices for the year were $3.30 per pound of metal and $.45 per ounce of wood. Direct labor standards for the deluxe trophy specify .2 hour of direct labor in the Molding Department and .4 hour in the Trimming/Finishing Department. Standard direct labor rates are $10.75 per hour in the Molding Department and $12.00 per hour in the Trimming/Finishing Department.

During January, the company made 16,400 deluxe trophies. Actual production data are as follows:

Direct materials	
Metal	16,640 pounds @ $3.25 per pound
Wood	131,400 ounces @ $.48 per ounce
Direct labor	
Molding	3,400 hours @ $10.60 per hour
Trimming/Finishing	6,540 hours @ $12.10 per hour

Required

1. Compute the direct materials price and quantity variances for metal and wood.
2. Compute the direct labor rate and efficiency variances for the Molding and the Trimming/Finishing Departments.

LO4, LO5, LO6 **Direct Materials, Direct Labor, and Overhead Variances**

P 4. The Doormat Division of Clean Sweep Company produces all-vinyl mats. Each doormat calls for .4 meter of vinyl material; the material should cost $3.10 per meter. Standard direct labor hours and labor cost per doormat are .2 hour and $1.84 (.2 hour $\times$ $9.20 per hour), respectively. Currently, the division's standard variable overhead rate is $1.50 per direct labor hour, and its standard fixed overhead rate is $.80 per direct labor hour.

In August, the division manufactured and sold 60,000 doormats. During the month, it used 25,200 meters of vinyl material; the total cost of the material was $73,080. The total actual overhead costs for August were $28,200, of which $18,200 was variable. The total number of direct labor hours worked was 10,800, and the factory payroll for direct labor for the month was $95,040. Budgeted fixed overhead for August was $9,280. Normal monthly capacity for the year was set at 58,000 doormats.

Required

1. Compute for August the (a) direct materials price variance, (b) direct materials quantity variance, (c) direct labor rate variance, (d) direct labor efficiency variance, (e) variable overhead spending variance, (f) variable overhead efficiency variance, (g) fixed overhead budget variance, and (h) fixed overhead volume variance.
2. **Manager Insight:** Prepare a performance report based on your variance analysis and suggest possible causes for each variance.

LO6 **Overhead Variances**

P 5. Celine Corporation's accountant left for vacation before completing the monthly cost variance report. George Celine, the corporation's president, has asked you to complete the report. The following data are available to you (capacities are expressed in machine hours):

Actual machine hours	17,100
Standard machine hours allowed	17,500
Actual variable overhead	**a**

Standard variable overhead rate	$2.50
Variable overhead spending variance	$250 (F)
Variable overhead efficiency variance	b
Actual fixed overhead	c
Budgeted fixed overhead	$153,000
Fixed overhead budget variance	$1,300 (U)
Fixed overhead volume variance	$4,500 (F)
Normal capacity in machine hours	d
Standard fixed overhead rate	e
Fixed overhead applied	f

Required

Analyze the data and fill in the missing amounts. (**Hint:** Use the structure of Figures 5 and 6 in this chapter to guide your analysis.)

Alternate Problems

LO2   **Computing Standard Costs for Direct Materials**

P 6. TickTock, Ltd., assembles clock movements for grandfather clocks. Each movement has four components: the clock facing, the clock hands, the time movement, and the spring assembly. For the current year, the company used the following standard costs: clock facing, $15.90; clock hands, $12.70; time movement, $66.10; and spring assembly, $52.50.

Prices of materials are expected to change next year. TickTock will purchase 60 percent of the facings from Company A at $18.50 each and the other 40 percent from Company B at $18.80 each. The clock hands, which are produced for TickTock by Hardware, Inc., will cost $15.50 per set next year. TickTock will purchase 30 percent of the time movements from Company Q at $68.50 each, 20 percent from Company R at $69.50 each, and 50 percent from Company S at $71.90 each. The manufacturer that supplies TickTock with spring assemblies has announced that it will increase its prices by 20 percent.

Required

1. Determine the total standard direct materials cost per unit for next year.
2. Suppose that because TickTock has guaranteed Hardware, Inc., that it will purchase 2,500 sets of clock hands next year, the cost of a set of clock hands has been reduced by 20 percent. Find the standard direct materials cost per clock.
3. Manager Insight: Suppose that to avoid the increase in the cost of spring assemblies, TickTock purchased substandard ones from a different manufacturer at $50 each; 20 percent of them turned out to be unusable and could not be returned. Assuming that all other data remain the same, compute the standard direct materials unit cost. Spread the cost of the defective materials over the good units produced.

LO4, LO5   **Direct Materials and Direct Labor Variances**

P 7. Fruit Packaging Company makes plastic baskets for food wholesalers. Each basket requires .8 gram of liquid plastic and .6 gram of an additive that includes color and hardening agents. The standard prices are $.15 per gram of liquid plastic and $.09 per gram of additive. Two kinds of direct labor—molding and trimming/packing—are required to make the baskets. The direct labor time and rate standards for a batch of 100 baskets are as follows: molding, 1.0 hour per batch at an hourly rate of $12; and trimming/packing, 1.2 hours per batch at $10 per hour.

During the year, the company produced 48,000 baskets. It used 38,600 grams of liquid plastic at a total cost of $5,404 and 28,950 grams of additive at $2,895. Actual direct labor included 480 hours for molding at a total cost of $5,664 and 560 hours for trimming/packing at $5,656.

Required

1. Compute the direct materials price and quantity variances for both the liquid plastic and the additive.
2. Compute the direct labor rate and efficiency variances for the molding and trimming/packing processes.

LO4, LO5, LO6   **Computing Variances and Evaluating Performance**

P 8. Last year, Biomed Laboratories, Inc., researched and perfected a cure for the common cold. Called Cold-Gone, the product sells for $28.00 per package, each of which contains five tablets. Standard unit costs for this product were developed late last year for use this year. Per package, the standard unit costs were as follows: chemical ingredients, 6 ounces at $1.00 per ounce; packaging, $1.20; direct labor, .8 hour at $14.00 per hour; standard variable overhead, $4.00 per direct labor hour; and standard fixed overhead, $6.40 per direct labor hour. Normal capacity is 46,875 units per week.

In the first quarter of this year, demand for the new product rose well beyond the expectations of management. During those three months, the peak season for colds, the company produced and sold over 500,000 packages of Cold-Gone. During the first week in April, it produced 50,000 packages but used materials for 50,200 packages costing $60,240. It also used 305,000 ounces of chemical ingredients costing $292,800. The total cost of direct labor for the week was $579,600; direct labor hours totaled 40,250. Total variable overhead was $161,100, and total fixed overhead was $242,000. Budgeted fixed overhead for the week was $240,000.

Required

1. Compute for the first week of April (a) all direct materials price variances, (b) all direct materials quantity variances, (c) the direct labor rate variance, (d) the direct labor efficiency variance, (e) the variable overhead spending variance, (f) the variable overhead efficiency variance, (g) the fixed overhead budget variance, and (h) the fixed overhead volume variance.
2. **Manager Insight:** Prepare a performance report based on your variance analysis and suggest possible causes for each significant variance.

ENHANCING Your Knowledge, Skills, and Critical Thinking

Conceptual Understanding Cases

LO1, LO2   **Cost Standards for Service Companies: A Comparison**

C 1. Both **ChemLawn** and **United Parcel Service (UPS)** use truck drivers to deliver services to clients. ChemLawn's drivers use a hose connected to the tanks on their trucks to spray liquid fertilizers and weed killers on clients' lawns. Drivers of UPS trucks deliver packages to residences and businesses. If you were setting cost standards for ChemLawn and UPS, what standards would you set that apply to the drivers, and what cost components would you use? What measures would you use to evaluate the drivers' performance? How would cost standards for these two service companies be similar, and how would they differ? How do cost standards for service companies differ from those of manufacturing companies?

LO5, LO6 **Standard Costing in a Service Company**

C 2. Annuity Life Insurance Company (ALIC) markets several types of life insurance policies, but P20A—a permanent, 20-year life annuity policy—is its most popular. This policy sells in $10,000 increments and features variable percentages of whole life insurance and single-payment annuities, depending on the policyholder's needs and age. ALIC devotes an entire department to supporting and marketing the P20A policy. Because both the support staff and the salespersons contribute to each P20A policy, ALIC categorizes them as direct labor for purposes of variance analysis, cost control, and performance evaluation. For unit costing, each $10,000 increment is considered one unit; thus, a $90,000 policy is counted as nine units. Standard unit cost information for January is as follows:

Direct labor	
Policy support staff	
3 hours at $12.00 per hour	$ 36.00
Policy salesperson	
8.5 hours at $14.20 per hour	120.70
Operating overhead	
Variable operating overhead	
11.5 hours at $26.00 per hour	299.00
Fixed operating overhead	
11.5 hours at $18.00 per hour	207.00
Standard unit cost	$662.70

Actual costs incurred for the 265 units sold during January were as follows:

Direct labor	
Policy support staff	
848 hours at $12.50 per hour	$10,600
Policy salespersons	
2,252.5 hours at $14.00 per hour	31,535
Operating overhead	
Variable operating overhead	78,440
Fixed operating overhead	53,400

Normal monthly capacity is 260 units, and the budgeted fixed operating overhead for January was $53,820.

1. Compute the standard hours allowed in January for policy support staff and policy salespersons.
2. What should the total standard costs for January have been? What were the total actual costs that the company incurred in January? Compute the total cost variance for the month.
3. Compute the direct labor rate and efficiency variances for policy support staff and policy salespersons.
4. Compute the variable and fixed operating overhead variances for January.
5. Identify possible causes for each variance and suggest possible solutions.

LO3, LO4, LO5 **Variance Analysis**

C 3. Ying Zsoa recently became the controller of a joint venture in Hong Kong. He has been using standard costing to plan and control the company's activities. In a meeting with the budget team, which includes managers and employees from purchasing, engineering, and production, Zsoa asked the team members to share any operating problems that they had encountered during the last quarter. He explained that his staff would use this information in analyzing the causes of significant cost variances that had occurred in the quarter.

For each of the following situations, identify the direct materials and/or direct labor variance(s) that could be affected and indicate whether the variances are favorable or unfavorable:

1. The production department used highly skilled, higher-paid workers.
2. Machines were improperly adjusted.
3. Direct labor personnel worked more carefully to manufacture the product.
4. The product design engineer substituted a direct material that was less expensive and of lower quality.
5. The Purchasing Department bought higher-quality materials at a higher price.
6. A major supplier used a less-expensive mode of transportation to deliver the raw materials.
7. Work was halted for two hours because of a power disruption.

Interpreting Management Reports

LO3 **Flexible Budgets and Performance Evaluation**

C 4. Cassen Realtors, Inc., specializes in the sale of residential properties. It earns its revenue by charging a percentage of the sales price. Commissions for salespersons, listing agents, and listing companies are its main costs. Business has improved steadily over the last ten years. Bonnie Cassen, the managing partner of Cassen Realtors, receives a report summarizing the company's performance each year. The report for the most recent year appears below.

Cassen Realtors, Inc.
Performance Report
For the Year Ended December 31

	Budgeted*	Actual†	Difference Under (Over) Budget
Total selling fees	$2,052,000	$2,242,200	($190,200)
Variable costs			
Sales commissions	$1,102,950	$1,205,183	($102,233)
Automobile	36,000	39,560	(3,560)
Advertising	93,600	103,450	(9,850)
Home repairs	77,400	89,240	(11,840)
General overhead	656,100	716,970	(60,870)
	$1,966,050	$2,154,403	($188,353)
Fixed costs			
General overhead	60,000	62,300	(2,300)
Total costs	$2,026,050	$2,216,703	($190,635)
Operating income	$ 25,950	$ 25,497	$ 453

*Budgeted data are based on 180 units sold.
†Actual data for 200 units sold.

1. Analyze the performance report. What does it say about the company's performance? Is the performance report reliable? Explain your answer.
2. Calculate the budgeted selling fee and budgeted variable costs per home sale.
3. Prepare a performance report using a flexible budget based on the actual number of home sales.

4. Analyze the report you prepared in **3.** What does it say about the company's performance? Is the report reliable? Explain your answer.
5. What recommendations would you make to improve the company's performance next year?

Decision Analysis Using Excel

LO3, LO6   **Developing a Flexible Budget and Analyzing Overhead Variances**

C 5. Ezelda Marva is the controller at FH Industries. She has asked you, her new assistant, to analyze the following data related to projected and actual overhead costs for October:

	Standard Variable Costs per Machine Hour (MH)	Actual Variable Costs in October
Indirect materials and supplies	$1.10	$ 2,380
Indirect machine setup labor	2.50	5,090
Materials handling	1.40	3,950
Maintenance and repair	1.50	2,980
Utilities	.80	1,490
Miscellaneous	.10	200
Totals	$7.40	$16,090

	Budgeted Fixed Overhead	Actual Fixed Overhead in October
Supervisory salaries	$ 3,630	$ 3,630
Machine depreciation	8,360	8,580
Other	1,210	1,220
Totals	$13,200	$13,430

For October, the number of good units produced was used to compute the 2,100 standard machine hours allowed.

1. Prepare a monthly flexible budget for operating activity at 2,000 machine hours, 2,200 machine hours, and 2,500 machine hours.
2. Develop a flexible budget formula.
3. The company's normal operating capacity is 2,200 machine hours per month. Compute the fixed overhead rate at this level of activity. Then break the rate down into rates for each element of fixed overhead.
4. Prepare a detailed comparative cost analysis for October. Include all variable and fixed overhead costs. Format your analysis by using columns for the following five elements: cost category, cost per machine hour, costs applied, actual costs incurred, and variance.
5. Develop an overhead variance analysis for October that identifies the variable overhead spending and efficiency variances and the fixed overhead budget and volume variances.
6. Prepare an analysis of the variances. Could a manager control some of the fixed costs? Defend your answer.

Ethical Dilemma Case

LO1, LO2   **An Ethical Question Involving Standard Costs**

C 6. Taylor Industries, Inc., develops standard costs for all its direct materials, direct labor, and overhead costs. It uses these costs to price products, cost inventories, and evaluate the performance of purchasing and production managers. It updates the standard costs whenever costs, prices, or rates change by 3 percent or more. It also reviews and updates all standard costs each December; this practice provides current standards that are appropriate for use in valuing year-end inventories on the company's financial statements.

Jody Elgar is in charge of standard costing at Taylor Industries. On November 30, she received a memo from the chief financial officer informing her that Taylor Industries was considering purchasing another company and that she and her staff were to postpone adjusting standard costs until late February; they were instead to concentrate on analyzing the proposed purchase.

In the third week of November, prices on more than 20 of Taylor Industries' direct materials had been reduced by 10 percent or more, and a new labor union contract had reduced several categories of labor rates. A revision of standard costs in December would have resulted in lower valuations of inventories, higher cost of goods sold because of inventory write-downs, and lower net income for the year. Elgar believed that the company was facing an operating loss and that the assignment to evaluate the proposed purchase was designed primarily to keep her staff from revising and lowering standard costs. She questioned the chief financial officer about the assignment and reiterated the need for updating the standard costs, but she was again told to ignore the update and concentrate on the proposed purchase. Elgar and her staff were relieved of the evaluation assignment in early February. The purchase never materialized.

Assess Jody Elgar's actions in this situation. Did she follow all ethical paths to solving the problem? What are the consequences of failing to adjust the standard costs?

Internet Case

LO1   **Resources for Developing Cost Standards**

C 7. Suppose you have recently taken a job at a company that manufactures parts for automobiles. You have been assigned the task of developing manufacturing cost standards. You want to gather as much background information as you can about these standards. Using a standard search engine, such as Google, search the Internet for websites that provide information about cost standards, manufacturing, and automobile manufacturers. Visit the sites that look most interesting, and list the five sites you think are most useful. Bring your list to class and compare your findings with those of your classmates.

Group Activity Case

LO2, LO3   **Standard Costs and Variance Analysis**

C 8. Domino's Pizza is a major purveyor of home-delivered pizzas. Although customers can pick up their orders at the shops where Domino's makes its pizzas, employees deliver most orders to customers' homes, and they use their own cars to do it.

Specify what standard costing for a Domino's pizza shop would entail. Where would you obtain the information for determining the cost standards? In what ways would the standards help in managing a pizza shop? If necessary to gain a better understanding of the operation, visit a pizzeria. (It does not have to be a Domino's.)

Your instructor will divide the class into groups to discuss the case. Summarize your group's discussion, and select one person from your group to report the group's findings to the class.

Business Communication Cases

LO3   Using Variance Analysis to Control Costs

C 9. Holding down operating costs is an ongoing challenge for managers. The lower the costs that a company incurs, the higher its profit will be. But two factors can make a target profit difficult to achieve. First, human error and unexpected machine breakdowns may cause dozens of operating inefficiencies, and each inefficiency will cause costs to rise. Second, a company may control its costs so strictly that it will use cheaper materials or labor, which may cause a decline in the quality of its product or service and in its sales. To control costs and still produce high-quality goods or services, managers must continually assess operating activities by analyzing both financial and nonfinancial data.

Write a one-page paper on how variance analysis helps managers control costs. Focus on both the financial and the nonfinancial data used in standard costing.

LO3, LO5, LO6   Preparing Performance Reports

C 10. Troy Corrente, the president of Forest Valley Spa, is concerned about the spa's operating performance during March. He budgeted his costs carefully so that he could reduce the annual membership fees. He now needs to evaluate those costs to make sure that the spa's profits are at the level he expected.

He has asked you, the spa's controller, to prepare a performance report on labor and overhead costs for March. He also wants you to analyze the report and suggest possible causes for any problems that you find. He wants to attend to any problems quickly, so he has asked you to submit your report as soon as possible. The following information for the month is available to you:

	Budgeted Costs	Actual Costs
Variable costs		
Operating labor	$10,880	$12,150
Utilities	2,880	3,360
Repairs and maintenance	5,760	7,140
Fixed overhead costs		
Depreciation, equipment	2,600	2,680
Rent	3,280	3,280
Other	1,704	1,860
Totals	$27,104	$30,470

Corrente's budget allows for eight employees to work 160 hours each per month. During March, nine employees worked an average of 150 hours each.

1. Answer the following questions:
   a. Why are you preparing this performance report?
   b. Who will use the report?
   c. What information do you need to develop the report? How will you obtain that information?
   d. When are the performance report and the analysis needed?
2. With the limited information available to you, compute the labor rate variance, the labor efficiency variance, and the variable and fixed overhead variances.
3. Prepare a performance report for the spa for March. Analyze the report and suggest causes for any problems that you find.

Short-Run Decision Analysis

Managers use both financial and nonfinancial quantitative information to analyze the effects of past and potential business actions on their organization's resources and profits. Although many short-term business problems are unique and cannot be solved by following strict rules, managers often take predictable actions when making decisions that will affect their organizations in the short run. In this chapter, we describe those actions. We also explain how managers use incremental analysis in making various types of short-term decisions.

LEARNING OBJECTIVES

LO1 Describe how managers make short-run decisions.

LO2 Define *incremental analysis,* and explain how it applies to short-run decision making.

LO3 Perform incremental analysis for outsourcing decisions.

LO4 Perform incremental analysis for special order decisions.

LO5 Perform incremental analysis for segment profitability decisions.

LO6 Perform incremental analysis for sales mix decisions involving constrained resources.

LO7 Perform incremental analysis for sell or process-further decisions.

- How do managers at Bank of America decide on new ways to increase business and protect customers' interests?

- How can incremental analysis help managers at Bank of America take advantage of the business opportunities that online banking offers?

Bank of America has customers in over 150 countries and more online customers than any other bank in the world. It has received numerous awards for online customer satisfaction and for its initiatives in preventing online fraud and identity theft. In 2006, it had more than 14.6 million online customers (34 percent of all online banking customers) and 7.2 million online bill payers (more than 58 percent of online bill payers in the United States).

Managers at Bank of America believe the trend to online commerce is good for business. As customers gain confidence in dealing with their finances online, the bank's managers plan to offer more products and services, such as portfolio management, online account statements and cancelled check images, and the ability to open a new account or apply for a loan over the Internet. In their quest to find safe and innovative ways to meet the needs of commercial, consumer, global corporate, and investment banking customers, managers at Bank of America make short-run decisions that affect the bank's profits, resources, and opportunities to increase online banking.[1]

Short-Run Decision Analysis and the Management Process

LO1 Describe how managers make short-run decisions.

Readers of financial reports want to know what happened to produce the results presented in these reports. The historical information in the reports answers that question. But for planning and control purposes, managers want to know why things happen and how these things could affect their organization. They use historical financial and nonfinancial quantitative information to analyze past and potential business alternatives and to determine how these alternatives could affect their organization's activities, resources, and profits.

Many of the decisions that managers make affect their organization's activities in the short run. Those decisions are the focus of this chapter. In making short-run decisions, managers need historical and estimated quantitative information that is both financial and nonfinancial in nature. Such information should be relevant, timely, and presented in a format that is easy to use in decision making.

Short-run decision analysis is the systematic examination of any decision whose effects will be felt over the course of the next year. The decision analysis must take into account the organization's strategic plan and tactical objectives, the related costs and revenues, as well as any relevant qualitative factors.

Although many business problems are unique and cannot be solved by following strict rules, managers frequently take five predictable actions when making short-run decisions. As shown in Figure 1, the first four actions are part of planning; the fifth takes place during evaluation.

Planning

When making short-run decisions, managers typically take the following four planning actions:

1. Discover a problem or need.

2. Identify all reasonable courses of action that can solve the problem or meet the need.

3. Prepare a thorough analysis of each possible solution, identifying its total costs, savings, other financial effects, and any qualitative factors.

4. Select the best course of action.

As a rule, the managers of companies like **Bank of America** make decisions that support the company's strategic plan. For example, the managers of a bank may have to make a decision about keeping or eliminating one of the bank's branch locations. Both quantitative and qualitative factors will influence the decision. The quantitative information includes the costs of operating the branch location and the fee revenues that the branch generates. Management may also want to know the number of customers serviced each year, the types of services offered, and the number and dollar amount of the branch's accounts.

The following qualitative factors will influence the managers' decision to keep or eliminate the branch:

▪ Competition (Do our competitors have a branch office located here?)

▪ Economic conditions (Is the community growing?)

■ **FIGURE 1**
The Management Process: To-Do's for Managers

To-Do's for Managers

- Plan
  - Discover a problem or need
  - Identify all reasonable courses of action that can solve the problem or meet the need
  - Prepare a thorough analysis of each possible solution, identifying its total costs, savings, other financial effects, and any qualitative effects (e.g., competition, economic conditions, social issues, product or service quality, timeliness)
  - Select the best course of action

- Perform
  - Make decisions that affect operations in the current operating period
  - Take advantage of opportunities that will improve organization's profitability and liquidity in the short run (e.g., accept a special order, examine the profitability of a segment, select the appropriate product mix given a resource constraint, contract with outside suppliers of goods and services, sell a product as is or process it further)

- Evaluate
  - Examine how each decision was carried out and how it affected the organization
  - Identify and prescribe corrective action

- Communicate
  - Prepare reports related to short-run decisions throughout the year

▶ Social issues (Will keeping this branch benefit the community we serve?)

▶ Product or service quality (Can we attract more business because of the quality of service at this branch?)

▶ Timeliness (Does the branch promote customer service?)

Managers must identify and assess the importance of all such qualitative and quantitative factors when they make short-run decisions.

Performing

Managers must adapt to changing environments and take advantage of opportunities that will improve their organization's profitability and liquidity in the short run. In the course of a year, managers may decide to accept a special order, examine the profitability of a segment, select the appropriate product mix given a resource constraint, contract with outside suppliers of goods and services, or sell a product as is or process it further. All of these decisions affect operations in the current operating period.

For example, a bank's management might eliminate a branch if the costs of the branch exceed the revenues that the branch generates. However, management may choose to keep the branch because the community expects the organization to provide this service.

Evaluating

When managers evaluate performance, they take the fifth predictable action associated with short-run decision analysis—that is, they review each decision to determine whether it produced the forecasted results. They examine how each decision was carried out and how it affected the organization. If results fell short, they identify and prescribe corrective action. This post-decision audit supplies feedback about the results of the short-run decision. If the solution is not completely satisfactory or if the problem remains, the management process begins again.

For example, if the bank decided to keep the branch location, the managers would evaluate the results of their decision in many ways. They would probably consider how successful the branch has been, how many people have benefited from the branch, and how well the branch fits in with the other kinds of services the bank offers. They would be interested in knowing how much operating income the branch has produced and in what other ways the branch has benefited the bank and the people that the bank serves. Depending on what they discover during their evaluation, the managers might consider ways to improve the branch, or they might decide to close the branch after all.

Communicating

Managers communicate with others regarding short-run decisions throughout the year. They prepare reports focusing on those decisions. They develop budgets that show the estimated costs and revenues related to alternative courses of action. They compile analyses of data that support their decisions. And they issue reports that measure the effect that their decisions had on the organization, including its operating income. When deciding whether to keep the branch location, the bank managers would develop budgets showing the costs and revenues that they expect the branch to generate. They would also

FOCUS ON BUSINESS PRACTICE

Have Accounting Scandals Affected CFOs' Workloads?

The documentation requirements that have resulted from recent accounting scandals are increasing the workload of chief financial officers (CFOs). Because of these requirements, it is taking CFOs more time to make and report decisions. The new regulations are designed to make corporations more accountable to their shareholders and the investing public. For example, the Sarbanes-Oxley Act requires that top corporate executives attest in writing to the accuracy of their company's earnings statements. CFOs must now confirm in writing with division heads and other executives that everything is in order—a more formal and time-consuming procedure than the previous one. In addition, CFOs are spending a significant amount of time thoroughly analyzing each rule and law to determine if their company is in compliance and, if not, how to bring the company into compliance. Although many CFOs have not computed how much adapting to all the new accounting standards is going to cost, they do know that their audit bills will be higher because of the increased scrutiny of corporate finances by regulators and investors and the detailed audits that outside auditors now perform.[2]

prepare written analyses of the expected costs and revenues and of the qualitative factors mentioned earlier. If the managers decided to keep the branch open, they would evaluate its success by comparing actual financial and nonfinancial results with the results predicted in the budget and the initial analyses. They would create reports showing how much operating income the branch has produced and how else the branch has benefited the bank and the people whom the bank serves.

S T O P • R E V I E W • A P P L Y

1-1. Give two examples of common short-run decisions.

1-2. Are qualitative factors important in short-run decision making?

Suggested answers to all Stop, Review, and Apply questions are available at http://college.hmco.com/accounting/needles/man_acc/8e/student_home.html.

Incremental Analysis for Short-Run Decisions

LO2   Define *incremental analysis,* and explain how it applies to short-run decision making.

Study Note

Incremental analysis is a technique used not only by businesses, but also by individuals to solve daily problems.

Once managers have determined that a problem or need is worthy of consideration and have identified alternative courses of action, they must evaluate the effect that each alternative will have on their organization. The method of comparing alternatives by focusing on the differences in their projected revenues and costs is called **incremental analysis**. If incremental analysis excludes revenues or costs that stay the same or that do not change between the alternatives, it is called *differential analysis.*

Irrelevant Costs and Revenues

A cost that changes between alternatives is known as a **differential cost** (also called an *incremental cost*). For example, suppose that Home State Bank managers are deciding which of two ATM machines—C or W—to buy. The ATMs have the same purchase price but different revenue and cost characteristics. The company currently owns ATM B, which it bought three years ago for $15,000 and which has accumulated depreciation of $9,000 and a book value of $6,000. ATM B is now obsolete as a result of advances in technology and cannot be sold or traded in.

The manager has prepared the following comparison of the annual revenue and operating cost estimates for the two new machines:

	ATM C	ATM W
Increase in revenue	$16,200	$19,800
Increase in annual operating costs		
Direct materials	4,800	4,800
Direct labor	2,200	4,100
Variable overhead	2,100	3,050
Fixed overhead (depreciation included)	5,000	5,000

EXHIBIT 1 ▶ | Incremental Analysis

Home State Bank
Incremental Analysis

	ATM C	ATM W	Difference in Favor of ATM W
Increase in revenue	$16,200	$19,800	$3,600
Increase in operating costs that differ between alternatives			
Direct labor	$ 2,200	$ 4,100	($1,900)
Variable overhead	2,100	3,050	(950)
Total relevant operating costs	$ 4,300	$ 7,150	($2,850)
Resulting change in operating income	$11,900	$12,650	$ 750

Study Note

Sunk costs cannot be recovered and are irrelevant in short-run decision making.

The first step in the incremental analysis is to eliminate any irrelevant revenues and costs. *Irrelevant revenues* are those that will not differ between the alternatives. *Irrelevant costs* include sunk costs and costs that will not differ between the alternatives. A **sunk cost** is a cost that was incurred because of a previous decision and cannot be recovered through the current decision. An example of a sunk cost is the book value of ATM B. A manager might be tempted to say that the ATM should not be junked because the company still has $6,000 invested in it. However, the manager would be incorrect because the book value of the old ATM represents money that was spent in the past and so does not affect the decision about whether to replace the old ATM with a new one. The old ATM would be of interest only if it could be sold or traded in, and if the amount received for it would be different, depending on which new ATM was chosen. In that case, the amount of the sale or trade-in value would be relevant to the decision because it would affect the future cash flows of the alternatives.

Another look at the financial data for ATMs C and W reveals two other irrelevant costs—the costs of direct materials and fixed overhead (depreciation included). These costs can also be eliminated from the analysis because they are the same under both alternatives.

Once the irrelevant revenues and costs have been identified, the incremental analysis can be prepared using only the differential revenues and costs that will change between the alternative ATMs, as shown in Exhibit 1. The analysis shows that ATM W would produce $750 more in operating income than ATM C. Because the costs of buying the two ATMs are the same, this report would favor the purchase of ATM W.

Opportunity Costs

Study Note

Opportunity costs arise when the choice of one course of action eliminates the possibility of another course of action.

Because incremental analysis focuses on only the quantitative differences among the alternatives, it simplifies management's evaluation of a decision and reduces the time needed to choose the best course of action. However, incremental analysis is only one input to the final decision. Management needs to consider other issues. For instance, the manufacturer of ATM C might have a reputation for better quality or service than the manufacturer of ATM W. **Opportunity costs** are the benefits that are forfeited or lost when one alternative is chosen over another.

Consider a plant nursery that has been in business for many years at the intersection of two highways. Suburbs have grown up around the nursery, and a bank has offered the nursery owner a high price for the land. The interest that could be earned from investing the proceeds of the land sale is an opportunity cost for the nursery owner. It is revenue that the nursery owner has chosen to forgo to continue operating the nursery in that location.

Opportunity costs often come into play when a company is operating at or near capacity and must choose which products or services to offer. For example, suppose that Debit Card Company, which currently services 20,000 cards, has the option of offering 15,000 premium debit cards, which is a higher-priced product, but it cannot do both. The amount of income from the 20,000 debit cards is an opportunity cost of the premium debit cards.

S T O P • R E V I E W • A P P L Y

2-1. What is incremental analysis? What types of decision analyses depend on the incremental approach?

2-2. What is an opportunity cost? When do opportunity costs arise?

Incremental Analysis for Outsourcing Decisions

LO3 Perform incremental analysis for outsourcing decisions.

Outsourcing is the use of suppliers outside the organization to perform services or produce goods that could be performed or produced internally. **Make-or-buy decisions**, which are decisions about whether to make a part internally or buy it from an external supplier, may lead to outsourcing. However, a company may decide to outsource entire operating activities, such as warehousing and distribution, that it has traditionally performed in-house.

To improve operating income and compete effectively in global markets, many companies are focusing their resources on their core competencies—that is, the activities that they perform best. One way to obtain the financial, physical, human, and technological resources needed to emphasize those competencies is to outsource expensive nonvalue-adding activities. Strong candidates for outsourcing include payroll processing, training, managing fleets of vehicles, sales and marketing, custodial services, and information management. Many such areas involve either relatively low skill levels (such as

To focus resources on their core competencies, many companies are outsourcing activities that they used to perform internally. Commonly outsourced activities include payroll processing, training, sales and marketing, and information management. In this photo, an employee at a call center in Bangalore, India, provides service support to international customers. India is the leader of emerging markets to which developed economies are outsourcing high-tech jobs.

payroll processing or custodial services) or highly specialized knowledge (such as information management) that could be better acquired from experts outside the company.

Outsourcing production or operating activities can reduce a company's investment in physical assets and human resources, which can improve cash flow. It can also help a company reduce its operating costs and improve operating income. Many companies, including **Bank of America** and **Amazon.com**, benefit from outsourcing. For example, because Amazon.com outsources the distribution of most of its products, it has been able to reduce its storage and distribution costs enough to offer product discounts of up to 40 percent off the list price. It is also able to provide additional value-adding services, such as online reviews by customers, personalized recommendations, and discussions and interviews on current products. Banks, too, are outsourcing to increase their online capabilities, especially in the areas of financial management software and analysis.

In manufacturing companies, a common decision facing managers is whether to make or to buy some or all of the parts used in product assembly. The goal is to select the more profitable choice by identifying the costs of each alternative and their effects on revenues and existing costs. Managers need the following information for this analysis:

Information About Making	*Information About Outsourcing*
Need for additional machinery	Purchase price of item
Variable costs of making the item	Rent or net cash flow to be generated from vacated space in the factory
Incremental fixed costs	Salvage value of unused machinery

To illustrate a manufacturer's outsourcing decision, let's suppose that for the past five years, Box Company has purchased packing cartons from an outside supplier at a cost of $1.25 per carton. The supplier has just informed Box Company that it is raising the price 20 percent, to $1.50 per carton, effective immediately. Box Company has idle machinery that could be adjusted to produce the cartons. Annual production and usage would be 20,000 cartons. The company estimates the cost of direct materials at $.84 per carton. Workers, who

EXHIBIT 2 ▶

Incremental Analysis: Outsourcing Decision

Box Company
Outsourcing Decision
Incremental Analysis

	Make	Outsource	Difference in Favor of Make
Direct materials			
(20,000 × $.84)	$16,800	—	($16,800)
Direct labor			
(20,000 × $.40)	8,000	—	(8,000)
Variable overhead			
(1,000 hours × $4)	4,000	—	(4,000)
To purchase completed cartons			
(20,000 × $1.50)	—	$30,000	30,000
Totals	$28,800	$30,000	$ 1,200

will be paid $8.00 per hour, can process 20 cartons per hour ($.40 per carton). The cost of variable overhead will be $4 per direct labor hour, and 1,000 direct labor hours will be required. Fixed overhead includes $4,000 of depreciation per year and $6,000 of other fixed costs. The company has space and machinery to produce the cartons; the machines are currently idle and will continue to be idle if the cartons are purchased. Should Box Company continue to outsource the cartons?

Exhibit 2 presents an incremental analysis of the two alternatives. All relevant costs are listed. Because the machinery has already been purchased and neither the machinery nor the required factory space has any other use, the depreciation costs and other fixed overhead costs are the same for both alternatives; therefore, they are not relevant to the decision. The cost of making the needed cartons is $28,800. The cost of buying 20,000 cartons at the increased purchase price will be $30,000. Since the company would save $1,200 by making the cartons, management will decide to make the cartons.

Study Note

When performing an incremental analysis for an outsourcing decision, do not incorporate irrelevant information, such as depreciation and other fixed costs. Include only costs that change between the alternatives.

S T O P • R E V I E W • A P P L Y

3-1. List at least two business activities that are likely to be outsourced. What makes them attractive for outsourcing?

3-2. What data are relevant to a manufacturer's make-or-buy decision?

Outsourcing Decision   Office Associates, Inc., is currently operating at less than capacity. The company thinks it could cut costs by outsourcing office cleaning to an independent cleaning service for $75 a week. Currently, a general office worker is employed for $10 an hour to do light cleaning and other general office duties. Cleaning the office usually takes one hour a day to perform and consumes $10 of supplies, $2 of variable overhead, and $18 of fixed overhead each week. Should Office Associates, Inc., continue to perform office cleanings, or should it begin to outsource them?

SOLUTION

Costs per Cleaning	Continue to Perform Cleanings	Outsource Cleanings	Difference in Favor of Continuing to Perform Cleanings
Employee labor	$50	—	($50)
Supplies	10	—	(10)
Variable overhead	2	—	(2)
Outside cleaning service	—	$75	75
Totals	$62	$75	$13

Office Associates should continue to perform office cleanings itself.

Incremental Analysis for Special Order Decisions

LO4   Perform incremental analysis for special order decisions.

Study Note

Special order decisions assume that excess capacity exists to accept the order and that the order, if accepted, will not have an impact on regular sales orders.

Managers are often faced with **special order decisions**, which are decisions about whether to accept or reject special orders at prices below the normal market prices. Special orders usually involve large numbers of similar products that are sold in bulk. Before a firm accepts a special product order, it must be sure that excess capacity exists to complete the order and that the order will not reduce unit sales from its full-priced regular product line.

The objective of a special order decision is to determine whether a special order should be accepted. A special order should be accepted only if it maximizes operating income. In many situations, sales commission expenses are excluded from a special order decision analysis because the customer approached the company directly. In addition, the fixed costs of existing facilities usually do not change if a company accepts a special order, and therefore these costs are usually irrelevant to the decision. If additional fixed costs must be incurred to fill the special order, they would be relevant to the decision. Examples of relevant fixed costs are the purchase of additional machinery, an increase in supervisory help, and an increase in insurance premiums required by a specific order.

One approach to a special order decision is to compare the price of the special order with the relevant costs of producing, packaging, and shipping the order. The relevant costs include the variable costs, variable selling costs, if any, and other costs directly associated with the special order (e.g., freight, insurance, and packaging and labeling the product). Another approach to this kind of decision is to prepare a special order bid price by calculating a minimum selling price for the special order. The bid price must cover the relevant costs and an estimated profit.

For example, suppose Home State Bank has been approved to provide and service four ATMs at a special event. The event sponsors want the fee reduced to $.50 per ATM transaction. At past special events, ATM use has averaged 2,000 transactions per machine. Home State Bank has located four idle ATMs and determined the following additional information:

ATM *Cost Data for Annual Use of One Machine* (400,000 *Transactions*)

Direct materials	$ .10
Direct labor	.05
Variable overhead	.20
Fixed overhead ($100,000 ÷ 400,000)	.25
Advertising ($60,000 ÷ 400,000)	.15
Other fixed selling and administrative expenses ($120,000 ÷ 400,000)	.30
Cost per transaction	$1.05
Regular fee per transaction	$1.25

Should Home State Bank accept the special event offer?

An incremental analysis of the decision in the contribution-margin reporting format appears in Exhibit 3. The report shows the contribution margin for Home State Bank operations both with and without the special order. Fixed costs are not included because the only costs affected by the order are direct materials, direct labor, and variable overhead. The net result of accepting the special order is a $1,200 increase in contribution margin (and, correspondingly, in operating income). The analysis reveals that Home State Bank should accept the special order. The $1,200 increase is verified by the following incremental analysis:

Special order sales (2,000 transactions × 4) × $.50		$4,000
Less variable costs		
Direct materials (8,000 transactions × $.10)	$ 800	
Direct labor (8,000 transactions × $.05)	400	
Variable overhead (8,000 transactions × $.20)	1,600	
Total variable costs		2,800
Special order contribution margin		$1,200

EXHIBIT 3 ▶

Incremental Analysis: Special Order Decision

Home State Bank
Special Order Decision
Incremental Analysis

	Without Order	With Order	Difference in Favor of Accepting Order
Sales	$2,400,000	$2,404,000	$4,000
Less variable costs			
Direct materials	$ 160,000	$ 160,800	($ 800)
Direct labor	80,000	80,400	(400)
Variable overhead	320,000	321,600	(1,600)
Total variable costs	$ 560,000	$ 562,800	($2,800)
Contribution margin	$1,840,000	$1,841,200	$1,200

Now let us assume that the event sponsor asks Home State Bank what its minimum special order price is. If the incremental costs for the special order are $2,800, the relevant cost per transaction is $.35 ($2,800 ÷ 8,000). The special order price should cover this cost and generate a profit. If Home State Bank would like to earn $800 from the special order, the special order price should be $.45 ($.35 cost per transaction plus $.10 profit per transaction [$800 ÷ 8,000 transactions]).

Of course, the decision that Home State Bank management makes must be consistent with the bank's strategic plan and tactical objectives, and it must take into account not only costs and revenues, but also relevant qualitative factors. Qualitative factors that might influence the decision are (1) the impact of the special order on regular customers, (2) the potential of the special order to lead into new sales areas, and (3) the customer's ability to maintain an ongoing relationship that includes good ordering and paying practices.

S T O P • R E V I E W • A P P L Y

4-1. What are two approaches to making a special order decision?

4-2. When should a special order be accepted?

Special Order Decision   Sample Company has received an order for Product EZ at a special selling price of $26 per unit (suggested retail price is $30). This order is over and above normal production, and budgeted production and sales targets for the year have already been exceeded. Capacity exists to satisfy the special order. No selling costs will be incurred in connection with this order. Unit costs to manufacture and sell Product EZ are as follows: direct materials, $7.00; direct labor, $10.00; variable overhead, $8.00; fixed manufacturing costs, $5.00; variable selling costs, $3.00; and fixed general and administrative costs, $9.00. Should Sample Company accept the order?

SOLUTION

Variable costs to produce Product EZ:

Direct materials	$ 7.00
Direct labor	10.00
Variable overhead	8.00
Total variable costs to produce	$25.00

Sample Company should accept the special order because the offered price exceeds the variable manufacturing costs.

Incremental Analysis for Segment Profitability Decisions

LO5   Perform incremental analysis for segment profitability decisions.

Another type of operating decision that management must make is whether to keep or drop unprofitable segments, such as product lines, services, sales territories, divisions, departments, stores, or outlets. Management must select the alternative that maximizes operating income. The objective of the decision analysis is to identify the segments that have a negative segment margin so that managers can drop them or take corrective action.

A **segment margin** is a segment's sales revenue minus its direct costs (direct variable costs and direct fixed costs traceable to the segment). Such costs are assumed to be **avoidable costs**. An avoidable cost could be eliminated if management were to drop the segment. If a segment has a positive segment margin—that is, the segment's revenue is greater than its direct costs—it is able to cover its own direct costs and contribute a portion of its revenue to cover common costs and add to operating income. In that case, management should keep the segment. If a segment has a negative segment margin—that is, the segment's revenue is less than its direct costs—management should eliminate the segment. However, certain common costs will be incurred regardless of the decision. Those are unavoidable costs, and the remaining segments must have sufficient contribution margin to cover their own direct costs and the common costs.

An analysis of segment profitability includes the preparation of a segmented income statement using variable costing to identify variable and fixed costs. The fixed costs that are traceable to the segments are called *direct fixed costs*. The remaining fixed costs are *common costs* and are not assigned to segments.

Suppose Home State Bank wants to determine if it should eliminate its Safe Deposit Division. Managers prepare a segmented income statement, separating variable and fixed costs to calculate the contribution margin. They separate the total fixed costs of $84,000 further by directly tracing $55,500 to Bank Operations and $16,500 to the Safe Deposit Division; the remaining $12,000 are common fixed costs. The following segmented income statement shows the segment margins for Bank Operations and the Safe Deposit Division and the operating income for the total company:

Home State Bank
Segmented Income Statement
For the Year Ended December 31, 20xx

	Bank Operations	Safe Deposit Division	Total Company
Sales	$135,000	$15,000	$150,000
Less variable costs	52,500	7,500	60,000
Contribution margin	$ 82,500	$ 7,500	$ 90,000
Less direct fixed costs	55,500	16,500	72,000
Segment margin	$ 27,000	($ 9,000)	$ 18,000
Less common fixed costs			12,000
Operating income			$ 6,000

The analysis of Situation I in Exhibit 4 demonstrates that dropping the Safe Deposit Division will increase operating income by $9,000. Unless the bank can increase the division's segment margin by increasing sales revenue or by reducing direct costs, management should drop the segment. The incremental approach to analyzing this decision isolates the segment and focuses on its segment margin, as shown in the last column of the exhibit.

The decision to drop a segment also requires a careful review of the other segments to see whether they will be affected. Let's extend the illustration by

EXHIBIT 4 ▶ | **Incremental Analysis: Segment Profitability Decision**

Home State Bank
Segment Profitability Decision
Incremental Analysis—Situation 1

	Keep Safe Deposit Division	Drop Safe Deposit Division	Difference in Favor of Dropping Safe Deposit Division
Sales	$150,000	$135,000	($15,000)
Less variable costs	60,000	52,500	7,500
Contribution margin	$ 90,000	$ 82,500	($ 7,500)
Less direct fixed costs	72,000	55,500	16,500
Segment margin	$ 18,000	$ 27,000	$ 9,000
Less common fixed costs	12,000	12,000	0
Operating income	$ 6,000	$ 15,000	$ 9,000

Home State Bank
Segment Profitability Decision
Incremental Analysis—Situation 2

	Keep Safe Deposit Division	Drop Safe Deposit Division	Difference in Opposition to Dropping Safe Deposit Division
Sales	$150,000	$108,000	($42,000)
Less variable costs	60,000	42,000	18,000
Contribution margin	$ 90,000	$ 66,000	($24,000)
Less direct fixed costs	72,000	55,500	16,500
Segment margin	$ 18,000	$ 10,500	($ 7,500)
Less common fixed costs	12,000	12,000	0
Operating income	$ 6,000	($ 1,500)	($ 7,500)

FOCUS ON BUSINESS PRACTICE
To Drop or Not to Drop a Segment?

When Steve Bennett arrived at **Intuit Corporation** in January 2000, he knew that the company should have been doing much better than was indicated by its $1 billion in annual revenues from such popular software products as Quicken, QuickBooks, and Turbo Tax. Building on the reliable demand for the company's tax and accounting software, Bennett has guided Intuit in making acquisitions and building one of the industry's leading online subscription services. At the same time, Bennett began examining parts of Intuit that either weren't producing an adequate return or did not fit well with Intuit's core competencies. Since Bennett's arrival, Intuit has sold its mortgage loan division and eliminated its online insurance business.[4]

assuming that Bank Operation's sales volume and variable costs will decrease 20 percent if management eliminates the Safe Deposit Division. The reduction in sales volume stems from the loss of customers who purchase products from both divisions. The analysis of Situation 2 in Exhibit 4 shows that dropping the division would reduce both the segment margin and the bank's operating income by $7,500. In this situation, Home State Bank would want to keep the Safe Deposit Division.

S T O P • R E V I E W • A P P L Y

5-1. How does a manager decide whether to keep or drop an unprofitable segment?

5-2. What is a segment margin?

Segment Profitability Decision   Sample Company is evaluating its two divisions, North Division and South Division.

Data for North Division include sales of $500,000, variable costs of $250,000, and fixed costs of $400,000, 50 percent of which are traceable to the division. South Division's data for the same period include sales of $600,000, variable costs of $350,000, and fixed costs of $450,000, 60 percent of which are traceable to the division.

Should either division be considered for elimination?

SOLUTION

	North Division	South Division	Total Company
Sales	$500,000	$600,000	$1,100,000
Less variable costs	250,000	350,000	600,000
Contribution margin	$250,000	$250,000	$ 500,000
Less direct fixed costs	200,000	270,000	470,000
Divisional income	$ 50,000	($ 20,000)	$ 30,000
Less common fixed costs			380,000
Operating income (loss)			($ 350,000)

The company should keep North Division because it is profitable. South Division does not seem to be profitable and should be considered for elimination. The home office and its very heavy overhead costs are causing the company's loss.

Incremental Analysis for Sales Mix Decisions

LO6   Perform incremental analysis for sales mix decisions involving constrained resources.

A company may not be able to provide the full variety of products or services that customers demand within a given time. Limits on resources like machine time or available labor may restrict the types or quantities of products or services that are available. Resource constraints can also be

FOCUS ON BUSINESS PRACTICE
Why Banks Prefer Ebanking

After performing segment analysis of online banking and face-to-face banking, bank managers worldwide are encouraging customers to do their banking over the Internet. Banks have found that linking global Internet access with customer relationship management (CRM), customer-friendly financial software, and online bill payment in a secure banking environment can reduce costs, increase service and product availability, and boost earnings.[5]

> **Study Note**
>
> When resources like direct materials, direct labor, or time are scarce, the goal is to maximize the contribution margin per unit of scarce resource.

associated with other activities, such as inspection and equipment setup. The question is, Which products or services contribute the most to profitability in relation to the amount of capital assets or other constrained resources needed to offer those items? To satisfy customers' demands and maximize operating income, management will choose to offer the most profitable product or service first. To identify such products or services, managers calculate the contribution margin per constrained resource (such as labor hours or machine hours) for each product or service.

The objective of a **sales mix decision** is to select the alternative that maximizes the contribution margin per constrained resource. The decision analysis, which uses incremental analysis to identify the relevant costs and revenues, consists of two steps. First, you calculate the contribution margin per unit for each product or service affected by the constrained resource. The contribution margin per unit equals the selling price per unit less the variable costs per unit. Second, you calculate the contribution margin per unit of the constrained resource. The contribution margin per unit of the constrained resource equals the contribution margin per unit divided by the quantity of the constrained resource required per unit.

Suppose Home State Bank offers three types of loans: commercial loans, auto loans, and home loans. The product line data are as follows:

	Commercial Loans	Auto Loans	Home Loans
Current loan application demand	20,000	30,000	18,000
Processing hours per loan application	2	1	2.5
Loan origination fee	$24.00	$18.00	$32.00
Variable processing costs	$12.50	$10.00	$18.75
Variable selling costs	$ 6.50	$ 5.00	$ 6.25

The current loan application capacity is 100,000 processing hours.

> **Question 1:** *Which loan type should be advertised and promoted first because it is the most profitable for the bank? Which should be second? Which last?*

Exhibit 5 shows the sales mix analysis. It indicates that the auto loans should be promoted first because they provide the highest contribution margin per processing hour. Home loans should be second, and commercial loans should be last.

> **Question 2:** *How many of each type of loan should the bank sell to maximize its contribution margin based on the current loan application activity of 100,000 processing hours? What is the total contribution margin for that combination?*

To begin the analysis, compare the current loan application activity with the activity required to meet the current loan demand. The company needs 115,000 processing hours to meet the current loan demand: 40,000 processing

EXHIBIT 5 ▶ | **Incremental Analysis: Sales Mix Decision Involving Constrained Resources**

Home State Bank
Sales Mix Decision: Ranking the Order of Loans
Incremental Analysis

	Commercial Loans	Auto Loans	Home Loans
Loan origination fee per loan	$24.00	$18.00	$32.00
Less variable costs			
Processing	$12.50	$10.00	$18.75
Selling	6.50	5.00	6.25
Total variable costs	$19.00	$15.00	$25.00
Contribution margin per loan (A)	$ 5.00	$ 3.00	$ 7.00
Processing hours per loan (B)	2	1	2.5
Contribution margin per processing hour (A ÷ B)	$ 2.50	$ 3.00	$ 2.80

Home State Bank
Sales Mix Decision: Number of Units to Make
Incremental Analysis

	Processing Hours
Total processing hours available	100,000
Less processing hours to produce auto loans	
(30,000 loans × 1 processing hour per loan)	30,000
Balance of processing hours available	70,000
Less processing hours to produce home loans	
(18,000 loans × 2.5 processing hours per loan)	45,000
Balance of processing hours available	25,000
Less processing hours to produce commercial loans	
(12,500 loans × 2 processing hours per loan)	25,000
Balance of processing hours available	0

hours for commercial loans (20,000 loans × 2 processing hours per loan), 30,000 processing hours for auto loans (30,000 loans × 1 processing hour per loan), and 45,000 processing hours for home loans (18,000 loans × 2.5 processing hours per loan). Because that amount exceeds the current capacity of 100,000 processing hours, management must determine the sales mix that maximizes the company's contribution margin, which will also maximize its operating income. The calculations in the second part of Exhibit 5 show that Home State Bank should sell 30,000 auto loans, 18,000 home loans, and 12,500 commercial loans. The total contribution margin is as follows:

Auto loans (30,000 loans × $3.00 per loan)	$ 90,000
Home loans (18,000 loans × $7.00 per loan)	126,000
Commercial loans (12,500 loans × $5.00 per loan)	62,500
Total contribution margin	$278,500

STOP • REVIEW • APPLY

6-1. What are the two steps in analyzing a sales mix decision?

6-2. How does a manager decide between alternatives in a sales mix decision?

Sales Mix Decision Surf, Inc., makes three kinds of surfboards, but it has a limited number of machine hours available to make them. Product line data are as follows:

	Fiberglass	Plastic	Graphite
Machine hours per unit	4	1	2
Selling price per unit	$1,500	$800	$1,300
Variable manufacturing cost per unit	500	200	800
Variable selling costs per unit	200	350	200

In what order should the surfboard product lines be produced?

SOLUTION

	Fiberglass	Plastic	Graphite
Selling price per unit	$1,500	$800	$1,300
Less variable costs			
Manufacturing	$ 500	$200	$ 800
Selling	200	350	200
Total unit variable costs	$ 700	$550	$1,000
Contribution margin per unit (A)	$ 800	$250	$ 300
Machine hours per unit (B)	4	1	2
Contribution margin per machine hour (A ÷ B)	$ 200	$250	$ 150

Surf, Inc., should produce plastic first, then fiberglass, and finally graphite surfboards.

Incremental Analysis for Sell or Process-Further Decisions

LO7 Perform incremental analysis for sell or process-further decisions.

Some companies offer products or services that can either be sold in a basic form or be processed further and sold as a more refined product or service to a different market. For example, a meatpacking company processes cattle into meat and meat-related products, such as bones and hides. The company may choose to sell sides of beef and pounds of bones and hides to other companies for further processing. Alternatively, it could choose to cut and package the meat for immediate sale in grocery stores, process bone into fertilizer for gardeners, or tan hides into refined leather for purses.

A **sell or process-further decision** is a decision about whether to sell a joint product at the split-off point or sell it after further processing. **Joint products** are two or more products made from a common material or

Study Note

Products are made by combining materials or by dividing materials, as in oil refining or ore extraction.

A sell or process-further decision is a decision about whether to sell a product as is or after further processing. A meatpacking company may decide to sell sides of beef to other companies for further processing, or it may decide, like the meatpacking company shown here, that it will itself process the beef into cooked meat for sale in grocery stores.

process that cannot be identified as separate products or services during some or all of the processing. Only at a specific point, called the **split-off point**, do joint products or services become separate and identifiable. At that point, a company may choose to sell the product or service as is or to process it into another form for sale to a different market.

The objective of a sell or process-further decision is to select the alternative that maximizes operating income. The decision analysis entails calculating the incremental revenue, which is the difference between the total revenue if the product or service is sold at the split-off point and the total revenue if the product or service is sold after further processing. You then compare the incremental revenue with the incremental costs of processing further. If the incremental revenue is greater than the incremental costs of processing further, a decision to process the product or service further would be justified. If the incremental costs are greater than the incremental revenue, you would probably choose to sell the product or service at the split-off point. Be sure to ignore *joint costs* (or common costs) in your analysis, because they are incurred *before* the split-off point and do not change if further processing occurs. Although accountants assign joint costs to products or services when valuing inventories and calculating cost of goods sold, joint costs are not relevant to a sell or process-further decision and are omitted from the decision analysis.

For example, as part of the company's strategic plan, Home State Bank's management is looking for new markets for banking services, and management is considering whether it would be profitable to bundle banking services. Home State Bank is considering adding two levels of service, Premier Checking and Personal Banker, beyond its current Basic Checking account services. The three levels have the following bundled features:

▶ Basic Checking: Online checking account, debit card, and online bill payment with a required minimum average balance of $500

▶ Premier Checking: Paper and online checking, a debit card, a credit card, and a small life insurance policy equal to the maximum credit limit on the credit card for customers who maintain a minimum average balance of $1,000

⌐ͻ Study Note

The common costs shared by two or more products before they are split off are called *joint costs*. Joint costs are irrelevant in a sell or process-further decision.

EXHIBIT 6 ▶

Incremental Analysis: Sell or Process-Further Decision

Home State Bank
Sell or Process-Further Decision
Incremental Analysis

	Premier Checking	Personal Banker
Incremental revenue per account if processed further:		
Process further	$50	$250
Split-off—Basic Checking	25	25
Incremental revenue	$25	$225
Less incremental costs	30	200
Operating income (loss) from processing further	($ 5)	$ 25

▶ Personal Banker: All of the features of Premier Checking plus a safe deposit box, a $5,000 personal line of credit at the prime interest rate, financial investment advice, and a toaster upon opening the account for customers who maintain a minimum average balance of $5,000

Assume that the bank can earn sales revenue of 5 percent on its checking account balances and that the total cost of offering basic checking services is currently $50,000. The bank's accountant provided these data for each level of service:

Product	Sales Revenue	Additional Costs
Basic Checking	$ 25	$ 0
Premier Checking	50	30
Personal Banker	250	200

The decision analysis in Exhibit 6 indicates that the bank should offer Personal Banking services in addition to Basic Checking accounts. Notice that the $50,000 joint costs of Basic Checking were ignored because they are sunk costs that will not influence the decision.

As we noted earlier, the decision analysis must take into account the organization's strategic plan and tactical objectives. In this example, the decision to process services further supports the bank's strategic plan to expand into new markets. In making the final decision, management must also consider other factors, such as the bank's ability to obtain favorable returns on its bank deposit investments.

STOP • REVIEW • APPLY

7-1. What is the role of joint costs in analyzing sell or process-further decisions?

7-2. What is the objective of a sell or process-further decision?

A Sell or Process-Further Decision In an attempt to provide superb customer service, Home Movie Rentals is considering expanding its product offerings from single movie or game rentals to complete movie or game evenings. Each evening would include a movie or game, candy, popcorn, and drinks. The accountant for Home Movie Rentals has compiled the following relevant information:

Product	Sales Revenue, No Additional Service	Sales Revenue if Processed Further	Additional Processing Costs
Movie	$2	$10	$5
Game	1	6	5

Determine which products Home Movie Rentals should offer.

SOLUTION

Incremental Revenue if Processed Further:	Movie	Game
Process further	$10	$6
Split-off	2	1
Incremental revenue	$ 8	$5
Less incremental costs	5	5
Operating income from further processing	$ 3	—

Home Movie Rentals should promote movie evenings first, then movies, and finally games or game evenings. There is no difference in profitability between the sale of games and the sale of game evenings.

BANK OF AMERICA

In this chapter's Decision Point, we commented on the dominance of **Bank of America** in online banking. We asked the following questions:

- How do managers at Bank of America decide on new ways to increase business and protect customers' interests?
- How can incremental analysis help managers at Bank of America take advantage of the business opportunities that online banking offers?

As managers at Bank of America make short-term decisions about which business alternatives to pursue that will increase business and give customers additional protection against fraud and identity theft, they will ask a number of questions—for example: When should bank products and services be outsourced? When should a special order for service be accepted? When is a bank segment profitable? What is the best sales mix when resource constraints exist? When should bank products be sold as is or processed further into different products?

To answer such questions and determine what could happen under alternative courses of action, the bank's managers need pertinent information that they can use in incremental analysis. On that basis, they can make sound, ethical decisions that will protect the bank's customers and increase both its traditional and online business.

CHAPTER REVIEW

REVIEW of Learning Objectives

LO1 Describe how managers make short-run decisions.

Both quantitative information and qualitative information are important in short-run decision analysis. Such information should be relevant, timely, and presented in a format that is easy to use in decision making. When managers plan, they discover a problem or need, identify alternative courses of action to solve the problem or meet the need, perform a complete analysis to determine the effects of each alternative on business operations, and choose the best alternative. As managers perform during the year, they contract with outside suppliers of goods and services, accept or reject special orders, examine the profitability of segments, select the appropriate product mix given a resource constraint, or sell a product as is or process it further. When managers evaluate actual performance, they review each decision to determine if the forecasted results were obtained, and if they were not, they take corrective action. In reports that managers prepare throughout the year, they communicate the information they used in making their decisions, the decisions they made, and the impact of those decisions on the organization.

LO2 Define *incremental analysis,* and explain how it applies to short-run decision making.

Incremental analysis helps managers compare alternative courses of action by focusing on the differences in projected revenues and costs. Any data that relate to future costs, revenues, or uses of resources and that will differ among alternative courses of action are considered relevant decision information. Examples of relevant information are projected sales or estimated costs, such as the costs of direct materials or direct labor, that differ for each alternative. The manager analyzes relevant information to determine which alternative contributes the most to profits or incurs the lowest costs. Only data that differ for each alternative are considered. Differential or incremental costs are costs that vary among alternatives and thus are relevant to the decision. Sunk costs are past costs that cannot be recovered; they are irrelevant to the decision process. Opportunity costs are revenue or income forgone as a result of choosing an alternative.

LO3 Perform incremental analysis for outsourcing decisions.

Outsourcing (including make-or-buy) decision analysis helps managers decide whether to use suppliers from outside the organization to perform services or provide goods that could be performed or produced internally. An incremental analysis of the expected costs and revenues for each alternative is used to identify the best alternative.

LO4 Perform incremental analysis for special order decisions.

A special order decision is a decision about whether to accept or reject a special order at a price below the normal market price. One approach is to compare the special order price with the relevant costs to see if a profit can be generated. Another approach is to prepare a special order bid price by calculating a minimum selling price for the special order. Generally, fixed costs are irrelevant to a special order decision because such costs are covered by regular sales activity and do not differ among alternatives.

LO5 Perform incremental analysis for segment profitability decisions.

Segment profitability decisions involve the review of segments of an organization, such as product lines, services, sales territories, divisions, or departments. Managers often must decide whether to add or drop a segment. A segment with a negative segment margin may be dropped. A segment margin is a segment's sales revenue minus its direct costs, which include variable costs and avoidable fixed costs. Avoidable costs are traceable to a specific segment. If the segment is eliminated, the avoidable costs will also be eliminated.

LO6 Perform incremental analysis for sales mix decisions involving constrained resources.

Sales mix decisions require the selection of the most profitable combination of sales items when a company makes more than one product or service using a common constrained resource. The product or service generating the highest contribution margin per constrained resource is offered and sold first.

LO7 Perform incremental analysis for sell or process-further decisions.

Sell or process-further decisions require managers to choose between selling a joint product at its split-off point or processing it into a more refined product. Managers compare the incremental revenues and costs of the two alternatives. Joint processing costs are irrelevant to the decision because they are identical for both alternatives. A product should be processed further only if the incremental revenues generated exceed the incremental costs incurred.

REVIEW of Concepts and Terminology

The following concepts and terms were introduced in this chapter:

Avoidable costs: Costs that can be eliminated by dropping a segment. **(LO5)**

Differential cost: A cost that changes among alternatives. Also called an *incremental cost*. **(LO2)**

Incremental analysis: A technique used in decision analysis that compares alternatives by focusing on the differences in their projected revenues and costs. Also sometimes called *differential analysis*. **(LO2)**

Joint products: Two or more products made from a common material or process that cannot be identified as separate products during some or all of the production process. **(LO7)**

Make-or-buy decisions: Decisions about whether to make a part internally or buy it from an external supplier. **(LO3)**

Opportunity costs: The benefits that are forfeited or lost when one alternative is chosen over another. **(LO2)**

Outsourcing: The use of suppliers outside the organization to perform services or produce goods that could be performed or produced internally. **(LO3)**

Sales mix decision: A decision to select the alternative that maximizes the contribution margin per constrained resource. **(LO6)**

Segment margin: A segment's sales revenue minus its direct costs (direct variable costs and direct fixed costs traceable to the segment). **(LO5)**

Sell or process-further decision: A decision about whether to sell a joint product at the split-off point or sell it after further processing. **(LO7)**

Short-run decision analysis: The systematic examination of any decision whose effects will have the greatest impact within the next year. **(LO1)**

Special order decisions: Decisions about whether to accept or reject special orders at prices below the normal market prices. **(LO4)**

Split-off point: A specific point in the production process at which two or more joint products become separate and identifiable. At that point, a company may choose to sell the product as is or process it into another form for sale to a different market. **(LO7)**

Sunk cost: A cost that was incurred because of a previous decision and that cannot be recovered through the current decision. **(LO2)**

REVIEW Problem

LO5 **Short-Run Decision Analysis**

Ten years ago, Dale Bandy formed Home Services, Inc., a company specializing in repair and maintenance services for homes and their surroundings. Home Services now has offices in six major cities across the country. During the past two years, the company's profitability has decreased, and Bandy wants to determine which service lines are not meeting the company's profit targets. Once the unprofitable service lines have been identified, he will either eliminate them or set higher prices. If higher prices are set, all variable and fixed operating, selling, and general administration costs will be covered by the price structure. Four service lines are under serious review. The following data from the most recent year-end closing were available for analysis:

	A	B	C	D	E	F	G
1			\multicolumn{5}{c}{**Home Services, Inc.**}	
2				**Segmented Income Statement**			
3				**For the Year Ended December 31, 20xx**			
4							
5					**Tile**		
6			**Auto**	**Boat**	**Floor**	**Tree**	**Total**
7			**Repair**	**Repair**	**Repair**	**Trimming**	**Impact**
8	Sales		$297,500	$114,300	$126,400	$97,600	$635,800
9	Less variable costs						
10		Direct labor	$119,000	$ 40,005	$ 44,240	$34,160	$237,405
11		Operating supplies	14,875	5,715	6,320	4,880	31,790
12		Small tools	11,900	4,572	5,056	7,808	29,336
13		Replacement parts	59,500	22,860	25,280	—	107,640
14		Truck costs	—	11,430	12,640	14,640	38,710
15		Selling costs	44,625	17,145	18,960	9,760	90,490
16		Other variable costs	5,950	2,286	2,528	1,952	12,716
17	Contribution margin		$ 41,650	$ 10,287	$ 11,376	$24,400	$ 87,713
18	Less direct fixed costs		35,800	16,300	24,100	5,200	81,400
19	Segment margin		$ 5,850	($ 6,013)	($ 12,724)	$19,200	$ 6,313
20	Less common fixed						
21		costs					32,100
22	Operating income						
23		(loss)					($ 25,787)
24							

Required

1. Analyze the performance of the four service lines. Should Dale Bandy eliminate any of them? Explain your answer.
2. Why might Bandy want to continue providing unprofitable service lines?
3. Even though some of the unprofitable services can be eliminated, the company still has an operating loss. Identify some possible causes for poor performance by the services. What actions do you recommend?

Answer to Review Problem

1. In deciding whether to eliminate any of the four service lines, Dale Bandy should concentrate on the service lines that have a negative segment margin. If the revenues from a service line are less than the sum of its variable and direct fixed costs, then other service lines must cover some of the losing line's costs while carrying the burden of the common fixed costs.

   By looking at the segmented income statement, Dale Bandy can see that the company will improve its operating income by $18,737 ($6,013 + $12,724) by eliminating the Boat Repair Service and the Tile Floor Repair

Service, both of which have a negative segment margin. Bandy's decision can also be supported by the analysis that follows.

		Keep Boat Repair and Tile Floor Repair	Drop Boat Repair and Tile Floor Repair	Difference in Favor of Dropping Boat Repair and Tile Floor Repair
	Home Services, Inc.			
	Segment Profitability Decision			
Sales		$635,800	$395,100	($240,700)
Less variable costs		548,087	329,050	219,037
Contribution margin		$ 87,713	$ 66,050	($ 21,663)
Less direct fixed costs		81,400	41,000	40,400
Segment margin		$ 6,313	$ 25,050	$ 18,737
Less common fixed costs		32,100	32,100	—
Operating income (loss)		($ 25,787)	($ 7,050)	$ 18,737

2. Bandy may want to continue offering the unprofitable service lines if their elimination would have a negative effect on the sale of the auto repair service or the tree trimming service. Bandy may also want to diversify into new markets by offering new services. If Bandy does decide to enter new markets, he should be prepared to suffer some initial losses.

3. The following are among the possible causes for poor performance by the four services:

   a. Service fees set too low
   b. Inadequate advertising
   c. High direct labor costs
   d. Other variable costs too high
   e. Poor management of fixed costs
   f. Excessive supervision costs

   To improve profitability, the company can eliminate nonvalue-adding costs, increase service fees, or increase the volume of services provided to customers.

CHAPTER ASSIGNMENTS

BUILDING Your Knowledge Foundation

Short Exercises

LO1 **Qualitative and Quantitative Information in Short-Run Decision Analysis**

SE 1. The owner of Mimi's, a French restaurant, is deciding whether to take chicken à l'orange off the menu. State whether each item of decision information that follows is qualitative or quantitative. If the information is quantitative, specify whether it is financial or nonfinancial.

1. The time needed to prepare the chicken
2. The daily number of customers who order the chicken
3. Whether competing French restaurants have this entrée on the menu
4. The labor cost of the chef who prepares the chicken
5. The fact that the president of a nearby company, who brings ten guests with him each week, always orders chicken à l'orange

LO2 **Using Incremental Analysis**

SE 2. Aries Corporation has assembled the following information related to the purchase of a new automated postage machine:

	Posen Machine	Valuet Machine
Increase in revenue	$43,200	$49,300
Increase in annual operating costs		
Direct materials	12,200	12,200
Direct labor	10,200	10,600
Variable overhead	24,500	26,900
Fixed overhead (including depreciation)	12,400	12,400

Using incremental analysis and only relevant information, compute the difference in favor of the Valuet machine.

LO3 **Outsourcing Decision**

SE 3. Marcus Company assembles products from a group of interconnecting parts. The company produces some of the parts and buys some from outside vendors. The vendor for Part X has just increased its price by 35 percent, to $10 per unit for the first 5,000 units and $9 per additional unit ordered each year. The company uses 7,500 units of Part X each year. Unit costs if the company makes the part are as follows:

Direct materials	$3.50
Direct labor	1.75
Variable overhead	4.25
Variable selling costs for the assembled product	3.75

Should Marcus continue to purchase Part X or begin making it?

LO3 **Outsourcing Decision**

SE 4. Dental Associates, Inc., is currently operating at less than capacity. The company thinks it could cut costs by outsourcing dental cleaning to an independent dental hygienist for $50 per cleaning. Currently, a dental hygienist is employed for $30 an hour. A dental cleaning usually takes one hour to perform and consumes $10 of dental supplies, $8 of variable overhead, and $16 of fixed overhead. Should Dental Associates, Inc., continue to perform dental cleanings, or should it begin to outsource them?

LO4 **Special Order Decision**

SE 5. Hadley Company has received a special order for Product R3P at a selling price of $20 per unit. This order is over and above normal production, and budgeted production and sales targets for the year have already been exceeded. Capacity exists to satisfy the special order. No selling costs will be incurred in connection with this order. Unit costs to manufacture and sell Product R3P are as follows: direct materials, $7.60; direct labor, $3.75; variable overhead, $9.25; fixed overhead, $4.85; variable selling costs, $2.75; and fixed general and administrative costs, $6.75. Should Hadley Company accept the order?

LO4 **Special Order Decision**

SE 6. Smith Accounting Services is considering a special order that it received from one of its corporate clients. The special order calls for Smith to prepare the individual tax returns of the corporation's four largest shareholders. The company has idle capacity that could be used to complete the special order. The following data have been gathered about the preparation of individual tax returns:

Materials cost per page	$1
Average hourly labor rate	$60
Standard hours per return	4
Standard pages per return	10
Variable overhead cost per page	$.50
Fixed overhead cost per page	$.50

Smith Accounting Services would be satisfied with a $40 gross profit per return. Compute the minimum bid price for the entire order.

LO5 **Segment Profitability Decision**

SE 7. Perez Company is evaluating its two divisions, West Division and East Division. Data for West Division include sales of $530,000, variable costs of $290,000, and fixed costs of $260,000, 50 percent of which are traceable to the division. East Division's efforts for the same period include sales of $610,000, variable costs of $340,000, and fixed costs of $290,000, 60 percent of which are traceable to the division. Should Perez Company consider eliminating either division? Is there any other problem that needs attention?

LO6 **Sales Mix Decision**

SE 8. Snow, Inc., makes three kinds of snowboards, but it has a limited number of machine hours available to make them. Product line data are as follows:

	Wood	Plastic	Graphite
Machine hours per unit	1.25	1.0	1.5
Selling price per unit	$100	$120	$200
Variable manufacturing cost per unit	45	50	100
Variable selling costs per unit	15	26	36

In what order should the snowboard product lines be produced?

LO7 **Sell or Process-Further Decision**

SE 9. Gomez Industries produces three products from a single operation. Product A sells for $3 per unit, Product B for $6 per unit, and Product C for $9 per unit. When B is processed further, there are additional unit costs of $3, and its new selling price is $10 per unit. Each product is allocated $2 of joint costs from the initial production operation. Should Product B be processed further, or should it be sold at the end of the initial operation?

LO7 **Sell or Process-Further Decision**

SE 10. In an attempt to provide superb customer service, Richard V. Meats is considering the expansion of its product offerings from whole hams and turkeys to complete ham and turkey dinners. Each dinner would include a carved ham or turkey, two side dishes, and six rolls or cornbread. The accountant for Richard V. Meats has compiled the relevant information that follows.

Product	Sales Revenue, No Additional Service	Sales Revenue if Processed Further	Additional Processing Costs
Ham	$30	$50	$15
Turkey	20	35	15

A cooked, uncarved ham costs Richard V. Meats $20 to produce. A cooked, uncarved turkey costs $15 to prepare. Use incremental analysis to determine which products Richard V. Meats should offer.

Exercises

LO2   Incremental Analysis

E 1. Max Wayco, the business manager for Essey Industries, must select a new computer system for his assistant. Rental of Model A, which is similar to the model now being used, is $2,200 per year. Model B is a deluxe system that rents for $2,900 per year and will require a new desk for the assistant. The annual desk rental charge is $750. The assistant's salary of $1,200 per month will not change. If Model B is rented, $280 in annual software training costs will be incurred. Model B has greater capacity and is expected to save $1,550 per year in part-time wages. Upkeep and operating costs will not differ between the two models.

1. Identify the relevant data in this problem.
2. Prepare an incremental analysis to aid the business manager in his decision.

LO2   Incremental Analysis

E 2. The managers of Lennox Company must decide which of two mill blade grinders—Y or Z—to buy. The grinders have the same purchase price but different revenue and cost characteristics. The company currently owns Grinder X, which it bought three years ago for $15,000 and which has accumulated depreciation of $9,000 and a book value of $6,000. Grinder X is now obsolete as a result of advances in technology and cannot be sold or traded in.

The accountant has collected the following annual revenue and operating cost estimates for the two new machines:

	Grinder Y	Grinder Z
Increase in revenue	$16,000	$20,000
Increase in annual operating costs		
Direct materials	4,800	4,800
Direct labor	3,000	4,100
Variable overhead	2,100	3,000
Fixed overhead (depreciation included)	5,000	5,000

1. Identify the relevant data in this problem.
2. Prepare an incremental analysis to aid the managers in their decision.
3. Should the company purchase Grinder Y or Grinder Z?

LO3   Outsourcing Decision

E 3. One component of a radio produced by Audio Systems, Inc., is currently being purchased for $225 per 100 parts. Management is studying the possibility of manufacturing that component. Annual production (usage) at Audio is 70,000 units; fixed costs (all of which remain unchanged whether the part is made or purchased) are $38,500; and variable costs are $.95 per unit for direct materials, $.55 per unit for direct labor, and $.60 per unit for variable overhead.

Using incremental analysis, decide whether Audio Systems, Inc., should manufacture the part or continue to purchase it from an outside vendor.

LO3 Outsourcing Decision

E 4. Sunny Hazel, the manager of Cyber Web Services, must decide whether to hire a new employee or to outsource some of the Web design work to Ky To, a freelance graphic designer. If she hires a new employee, she will pay $32 per design hour for the employee to work 600 hours and incur service overhead costs of $2 per design hour. If she outsources the work to Ky To, she will pay $36 per design hour for 600 hours of work. She can also redirect the use of a computer and server to generate $4,000 in additional revenue from Web page maintenance work.

Should Cyber Web Services hire a new designer or outsource the work to Ky To?

LO4 Special Order Decision

E 5. Antiquities, Ltd., produces antique-looking books. Management has just received a request for a special order for 1,000 books and must decide whether to accept it. Venus Company, the purchaser, is offering to pay $25.00 per book, which includes $3.00 per book for shipping costs.

The variable production costs per book include $9.20 for direct materials, $4.00 for direct labor, and $3.80 for variable overhead. The current year's production is 20,000 books, and maximum capacity is 25,000 books. Fixed costs, including overhead, advertising, and selling and administrative costs, total $70,000. The usual selling price is $25.00 per book. Shipping costs, which are additional, average $3.00 per book.

Determine whether Antiquities should accept the special order.

LO4 Special Order Decision

E 6. Jens Sporting Goods, Inc., manufactures a complete line of sporting equipment. Leiden Enterprises operates a large chain of discount stores. Leiden has approached Jens with a special order for 30,000 deluxe baseballs. Instead of being packaged separately, the balls are to be bulk packed in boxes containing 500 baseballs each. Leiden is willing to pay $2.45 per baseball. Jens knows that annual expected production is 400,000 baseballs. It also knows that the current year's production is 410,000 baseballs and that the maximum production capacity is 450,000 baseballs. The following additional information is available:

Standard unit cost data for 400,000 baseballs

Direct materials	$ .90
Direct labor	.60
Overhead:	
Variable	.50
Fixed ($100,000 ÷ 400,000)	.25
Packaging per unit	.30
Advertising ($60,000 ÷ 400,000)	.15
Other fixed selling and administrative	
expenses ($120,000 ÷ 400,000)	.30
Product unit cost	$ 3.00
Unit selling price	$ 4.00
Total estimated bulk packaging costs for	
special order (30,000 baseballs: 500 per box)	$2,500

1. Should Jens Sporting Goods, Inc., accept Leiden's offer?
2. What would be the minimum order price per baseball if Jens would like to earn a profit of $3,000 from the special order?

LO4 Special Order Decision

E 7. In September, a nonprofit organization, Toys for Homeless Children (THC), offers Virtually LLC $400 to prepare a custom web page to help the organization attract toy donations. The home page for the THC website will include special animated graphics of toys and stuffed animals. Virtually LLC estimates that it will take 12.5 design labor hours at $32 per design hour and 2 installation labor hours at $10 per installation hour to complete the job. Fixed costs are already covered by regular business. Should Virtually LLC accept THC's offer?

LO5 Elimination of Unprofitable Segment Decision

E 8. Guld's Glass, Inc., has three divisions: Commercial, Nonprofit, and Residential. The segmented income statement for last year revealed the following:

Guld's Glass, Inc.
Divisional Profit Summary and Decision Analysis

	Commercial Division	Nonprofit Division	Residential Division	Total Company
Sales	$290,000	$533,000	$837,000	$1,660,000
Less variable costs	147,000	435,000	472,000	1,054,000
Contribution margin	$143,000	$ 98,000	$365,000	$ 606,000
Less direct fixed costs	124,000	106,000	139,000	369,000
Segment margin	$ 19,000	($ 8,000)	$226,000	$ 237,000
Less common fixed costs				168,000
Operating income				$ 69,000

1. How will Guld's Glass, Inc., be affected if the Nonprofit Division is dropped?
2. If the Nonprofit Division is dropped, the sales of the Residential Division will decrease by 10 percent. How will Guld's Glass, Inc., be affected if the Nonprofit Division is dropped?

LO5 Elimination of Unprofitable Segment Decision

E 9. URL Services has two divisions: Basic Web Pages and Custom Web Pages. Ricky Vega, manager of Custom Web Pages, wants to find out why Custom Web Pages is not profitable and has prepared the reports that appear on the opposite page.

1. How will URL Services be affected if the Custom Web Pages Division is eliminated?
2. How will URL Services be affected if the Design segment of Custom Web Pages is eliminated?
3. What should Ricky Vega do? What additional information would be helpful to him in making the decision?

URL Services
Segmented Income Statement
For the Year Ended December 31

	Basic Web Pages (1,000 units)	Custom Web Pages (200 units)	Total Company
Service revenue	$200,000	$150,000	$350,000
Less variable costs			
Direct professional labor: design	$ 32,000	$ 80,000	$112,000
Direct professional labor: install	30,000	4,000	34,000
Direct professional labor: maintain	15,000	36,000	51,000
Total variable costs	$ 77,000	$120,000	$197,000
Contribution margin	$123,000	$ 30,000	$153,000
Less direct fixed costs			
Depreciation on computer equipment	$ 6,000	$ 12,000	$ 18,000
Depreciation on servers	10,000	20,000	30,000
Total direct fixed costs	$ 16,000	$ 32,000	$ 48,000
Segment margin	$107,000	($ 2,000)	$105,000
Less common fixed costs			
Building rent			$ 24,000
Supplies			1,000
Insurance			3,000
Telephone			1,500
Website rental			500
Total fixed costs			$ 30,000
Operating income			$ 75,000

Custom Web Pages Division
URL Services
Segment Profitability Decision
Incremental Analysis

	Design	Install	Maintain	Total
Service revenue	$60,000	$25,000	$65,000	$150,000
Less variable costs	80,000	4,000	36,000	120,000
Contribution margin	($20,000)	$21,000	$29,000	$ 30,000
Less direct fixed costs	6,000	13,000	13,000	32,000
Segment margin	($26,000)	$ 8,000	$16,000	($ 2,000)

LO6   Scarce Resource Usage

E 10. EZ, Inc., manufactures two products that require both machine processing and labor operations. Although there is unlimited demand for both products, EZ could devote all its capacities to a single product. Unit prices, cost data, and processing requirements follow.

	Product E	Product Z
Unit selling price	$80	$220
Unit variable costs	$40	$ 90
Machine hours per unit	.4	1.4
Labor hours per unit	2	6

Next year, the company will be limited to 160,000 machine hours and 120,000 labor hours. Fixed costs for the year are $1,000,000.

1. Compute the most profitable combination of products to be produced next year.
2. Prepare an income statement using the contribution margin format for the product volume computed in 1.

LO6 **Sales Mix Decision**

E 11. Grady Enterprises manufactures three computer games. They are called Rising Star, Ghost Master, and Road Warrior. The product line data are as follows:

	Rising Star	Ghost Master	Road Warrior
Current unit sales demand	20,000	30,000	18,000
Machine hours per unit	2	1	2.5
Selling price per unit	$24.00	$18.00	$32.00
Unit variable manufacturing costs	$12.50	$10.00	$18.75
Unit variable selling costs	$ 6.50	$ 5.00	$ 6.25

The current production capacity is 100,000 machine hours.

1. Which computer game should be manufactured first? Which should be manufactured second? Which last?
2. How many of each type of computer game should be manufactured and sold to maximize the company's contribution margin based on the current production activity of 100,000 machine hours? What is the total contribution margin for that combination?

LO6 **Sales Mix Decision**

E 12. Web Services, a small company owned by Simon Orozco, provides web page services to small businesses. His services include the preparation of basic pages and custom pages.

The following summary of information will be used to make several short-run decisions for Web Services:

	Basic Pages	Custom Pages
Service revenue per page	$200	$750
Variable costs per page	77	600
Contribution margin per page	$123	$150

Total annual fixed costs are $78,000.

One of Web Services' two graphic designers, Taylor Campbell, is planning to take maternity leave in July and August. As a result, there will be only one designer available to perform the work, and design labor hours will be a resource constraint. Orozco plans to help the other designer complete the projected 160 orders for basic pages and 30 orders for custom pages for those two months. However, he wants to know which type of page Web Services should advertise and market. Although custom pages have a higher contribution margin per service, each custom page requires 12.5 design hours, whereas basic pages require only 1 design hour per page. On which page type should his company focus? Explain your answer.

LO7   **Sell or Process-Further Decision**

E 13. H & L Beef Products, Inc., processes cattle. It can sell the meat as sides of beef or process it further into final cuts (steaks, roasts, and hamburger). As part of the company's strategic plan, management is looking for new markets for meat or meat by-products. The production process currently separates hides and bones for sale to other manufacturers. However, management is considering whether it would be profitable to process the hides into leather and the bones into fertilizer. The costs of the cattle and of transporting, hanging, storing, and cutting sides of beef are $125,000. The company's accountant provided these data:

Product	Sales Revenue if Sold at Split-off	Sales Revenue if Sold After Further Processing	Additional Processing Costs
Meat	$100,000	$200,000	$80,000
Bones	20,000	40,000	15,000
Hides	50,000	55,000	10,000

Should the products be processed further? Explain your answer.

LO7   **Sell or Process-Further Decision**

E 14. Six Star Pizza manufactures frozen pizzas and calzones and sells them for $4 each. It is currently considering a proposal to manufacture and sell fully prepared products. The following relevant information has been gathered by management:

Product	Sales Revenue, No Additional Processing	Sales Revenue if Processed Further	Additional Processing Costs
Pizza	$4	$ 8	$5
Calzone	$4	$10	$5

Use incremental analysis to determine which products Six Star should offer.

Problems

Outsourcing Decision

LO3

P 1. Stainless Refrigerator Company purchases ice makers and installs them in its products. The ice makers cost $138 per case, and each case contains 12 ice makers. The supplier recently gave advance notice that the price will rise by 50 percent immediately. Stainless Refrigerator Company has idle equipment that, with only a few minor changes, could be used to produce similar ice makers.

Cost estimates have been prepared under the assumption that the company could make the product itself. Direct materials would cost $100.80 per 12 ice makers. Direct labor required would be 10 minutes per ice maker at a labor rate of $18.00 per hour. Variable overhead would be $4.60 per ice maker. Fixed overhead, which would be incurred under either decision alternative, would be $32,420 a year for depreciation and $234,000 a year for other costs. Production and usage are estimated at 75,000 ice makers a year. (Assume that any idle equipment cannot be used for any other purpose.)

Required

1. Prepare an incremental analysis to determine whether the ice makers should be made within the company or purchased from the outside supplier at the higher price.
2. Compute the variable unit cost to (a) make one ice maker and (b) buy one ice maker.

LO4 **Special Order Decision**

P 2. On March 26, Sinker Industries received a special order request for 120 ten-foot aluminum fishing boats. Operating on a fiscal year ending May 31, the company already has orders that will allow it to produce at budget levels for the period. However, extra capacity exists to produce the 120 additional boats.

    The terms of the special order call for a selling price of $675 per boat, and the customer will pay all shipping costs. No sales personnel were involved in soliciting the order.

    The ten-foot fishing boat has the following cost estimates: direct materials, aluminum, two 4′ × 8′ sheets at $155 per sheet; direct labor, 14 hours at $15.00 per hour; variable overhead, $7.25 per direct labor hour; fixed overhead, $4.50 per direct labor hour; variable selling expenses, $46.50 per boat; and variable shipping expenses, $57.50 per boat.

Required

1. Prepare an analysis for management of Sinker Industries to use in deciding whether to accept or reject the special order. What decision should be made?
2. To make an $8,000 profit on this order, what would be the lowest possible price that Sinker Industries could charge per boat?

LO5 **Segment Profitability Decision**

P 3. Sports, Inc., is a nationwide distributor of sporting equipment. The corporate president, Wesley Coldwell, is dissatisfied with corporate operating results, particularly those of the Spring Branch, and has asked the controller for more information. The controller prepared the following segmented income statement (in thousands of dollars) for the Spring Branch:

Sports, Inc., Spring Branch
Segmented Income Statement
For the Year Ended December 31
(Amounts in Thousands)

	Football Line	Baseball Line	Basketball Line	Spring Branch
Sales	$3,500	$2,500	$2,059	$8,059
Less variable costs	2,900	2,395	1,800	7,095
Contribution margin	$ 600	$ 105	$ 259	$ 964
Less direct fixed costs	300	150	159	609
Segment margin	$ 300	($ 45)	$ 100	$ 355
Less common fixed costs				450
Operating income (loss)				($ 95)

Coldwell is considering adding a new product line, Kite Surfing. The controller estimates that adding this line to the Spring Branch will increase sales by $300,000, variable costs by $150,000, and direct fixed costs by $20,000. The new product line will have no effect on common fixed costs.

Required

1. How will operating income be affected if the Baseball line is dropped?
2. How will operating income be affected if the Baseball line is kept and a Kite Surfing line is added?
3. If the Baseball line is dropped and the Kite Surfing line is added, sales of the Football line will decrease by 10 percent and sales of the Basketball line will decrease by 5 percent. How will those changes affect operating income?
4. **Manager Insight:** What decision do you recommend? Explain.

LO6 **Sales Mix Decision**

P 4. Management at Generic Chemical Company is evaluating its product mix in an attempt to maximize profits. For the past two years, Generic has produced four products, and all have large markets in which to expand market share. Heinz Bexer, Generic's controller, has gathered data from current operations and wants you to analyze them for him. Sales and operating data are as follows:

	Product AZI	Product BY7	Product CX5	Product DW9
Variable production costs	$ 71,000	$ 91,000	$ 91,920	$ 97,440
Variable selling costs	$ 10,200	$ 5,400	$ 12,480	$ 30,160
Fixed production costs	$ 20,400	$ 21,600	$ 29,120	$ 18,480
Fixed administrative costs	$ 3,400	$ 5,400	$ 6,240	$ 10,080
Total sales	$122,000	$136,000	$156,400	$161,200
Units produced and sold	85,000	45,000	26,000	14,000
Machine hours used*	17,000	18,000	20,800	16,800

*Generic's scarce resource, machine hours, is being used to full capacity.

Required

1. Compute the machine hours needed to produce one unit of each product.
2. Determine the contribution margin per machine hour for each product.
3. Which product line(s) should be targeted for market share expansion?

LO6 **Sales Mix Decision**

P 5. Dr. Massy, who specializes in internal medicine, wants to analyze his sales mix to find out how the time of his physician assistant, Consuela Ortiz, can be used to generate the highest operating income.

Ortiz sees patients in Dr. Massy's office, consults with patients over the telephone, and conducts one daily weight-loss support group attended by up to 50 patients. Statistics for the three services are as follows:

	Office Visits	Phone Calls	Weight-Loss Support Group
Maximum number of patient billings per day	20	40	50
Hours per billing	.25	.10	1.0
Billing rate	$50	$25	$10
Variable costs	$25	$12	$ 5

Ortiz works seven hours a day.

Required

1. Determine the best sales mix. Rank the services offered in order of their profitability.
2. Based on the ranking in **1**, how much time should Ortiz spend on each service in a day? (**Hint:** Remember to consider the maximum number of patient billings per day.) What would be the daily total contribution margin generated by Ortiz?
3. Dr. Massy believes the ranking is incorrect. He knows that the daily 60-minute meeting of the weight-loss support group has 50 patients and should continue to be offered. If the new ranking for the services is (1) weight-loss support group, (2) phone calls, and (3) office visits, how much time should Ortiz spend on each service in a day? What would be the total contribution margin generated by Ortiz, assuming the weight-loss support group has the maximum number of patient billings?
4. Manager Insight: Which ranking would you recommend? What additional amount of total contribution margin would be generated if your recommendation is accepted?

Alternate Problems

LO7 **Sell or Process-Further Decision**

P 6. Bagels, Inc., produces and sells 20 types of bagels by the dozen. Bagels are priced at $6.00 per dozen (or $.50 each) and cost $.20 per unit to produce. The company is considering further processing the bagels into two products: bagels with cream cheese and bagel sandwiches. It would cost an additional $.50 per unit to produce bagels with cream cheese, and the new selling price would be $2.50 each. It would cost an additional $1.00 per sandwich to produce bagel sandwiches, and the new selling price would be $3.50 each.

Required

1. Identify the relevant per unit costs and revenues for the alternatives. Are there any sunk costs?
2. Based on the information in **1**, should Bagels, Inc., expand its product offerings?
3. Suppose that Bagels, Inc., did expand its product line to include bagels with cream cheese and bagel sandwiches. Based on customer feedback, the company determined that it could further process those two products into bagels with cream cheese and fruit and bagel sandwiches with cheese. The company's accountant compiled the following information:

Product (per unit)	Sales Revenue if Sold with No Further Processing	Sales Revenue if Processed Further	Additional Processing Costs
Bagels with cream cheese	$2.50	$3.50	Fruit: $1.00
Bagel sandwiches	$3.50	$4.50	Cheese: $ .50

Perform an incremental analysis to determine if Bagels, Inc., should process its products further. Explain your findings.

LO5 **Decision to Eliminate an Unprofitable Product**

P 7. Seven months ago, Naib Publishing Company published its first book (Book N). Since then, Naib has added four more books to its product list

(Books S, Q, X, and H). Management is considering proposals for three more new books, but editorial capacity limits the company to producing only seven books annually. Before deciding which of the proposed books to publish, management wants you to evaluate the performance of its existing book list. Recent revenue and cost data are as follows:

Naib Publishing Company
Product Profit and Loss Summary
For the Year Ended December 31

	Book N	Book S	Book Q	Book X	Book H	Company Totals
Sales	$813,800	$782,000	$634,200	$944,100	$707,000	$3,881,100
Less variable costs						
Materials and binding	$325,520	$312,800	$190,260	$283,230	$212,100	$1,323,910
Editorial services	71,380	88,200	73,420	57,205	80,700	370,905
Author royalties	130,208	125,120	101,472	151,056	113,120	620,976
Sales commissions	162,760	156,400	95,130	141,615	141,400	697,305
Other selling costs	50,682	44,740	21,708	18,334	60,700	196,164
Total variable costs	$740,550	$727,260	$481,990	$651,440	$608,020	$3,209,260
Contribution margin	$ 73,250	$ 54,740	$152,210	$292,660	$ 98,980	$ 671,840
Less total fixed costs	97,250	81,240	89,610	100,460	82,680	451,240
Operating income (loss)	($ 24,000)	($ 26,500)	$ 62,600	$192,200	$ 16,300	$ 220,600
Direct fixed costs included in total fixed costs above	$ 51,200	$ 65,100	$ 49,400	$ 69,100	$ 58,800	$ 293,600

Projected data for the proposed new books are Book P, sales, $450,000, contribution margin, $45,000; Book T, sales, $725,000, contribution margin, ($25,200); and Book R, sales, $913,200, contribution margin, $115,500. Projected direct fixed costs are: Book P, $5,000; Book T, $6,000; Book R, $40,000.

Required

1. Analyze the performance of the five books that the company is currently publishing.
2. Should Naib Publishing Company eliminate any of its present products? If so, which one(s)?
3. Identify the new books you would use to replace those eliminated. Justify your answer.

LO4   **Special Order Decision**

P 8. Keystone Resorts, Ltd., has approached Crystal Printers, Inc., with a special order to produce 300,000 two-page brochures. Most of Crystal's work consists of recurring short-run orders. Keystone Resorts is offering a one-time order, and Crystal has the capacity to handle the order over a two-month period.

The management of Keystone Resorts has stated that the company would be unwilling to pay more than $48 per 1,000 brochures. Crystal Printers' controller assembled the following cost data for this decision analysis. Direct materials (paper) would be $26.50 per 1,000 brochures. Direct labor costs would be $6.80 per 1,000 brochures. Direct materials (ink) would be

$4.40 per 1,000 brochures. Variable production overhead would be $6.20 per 1,000 brochures. Machine maintenance (fixed cost) is $1.00 per direct labor dollar. Other fixed production overhead amounts to $2.40 per direct labor dollar. Variable packing costs would be $4.30 per 1,000 brochures. Also, the share of general and administrative expenses (fixed costs) to be allocated would be $5.25 per direct labor dollar.

Required

1. Prepare an analysis for Crystal Printers management to use in deciding whether to accept or reject Keystone Resorts' offer. What decision should be made?
2. What is the lowest possible price Crystal Printers can charge per thousand and still make a $6,000 profit on the order?

ENHANCING Your Knowledge, Skills, and Critical Thinking

Conceptual Understanding Cases

LO1 ### Management Decision Process

C 1. Two weeks ago, your cousin Edna moved from New York City to Houston. She needs a car to drive to work and to run errands, but she has no experience in selecting a car and has asked for your help. Using the management process presented in this chapter, write her a letter explaining how she can approach making this decision.

How would your response change if the president of your company asked you to help make a decision about acquiring a fleet of cars for use by the sales personnel?

LO2 ### Identification of Sunk Costs and Opportunity Costs

C 2. Motorola, Inc., originated a $5 billion project, called Iridium, that launched 66 low-earth-orbit satellites for global communication using pagers and mobile phones. After its operations began, the Iridium Project had technical and marketing problems. Instead of the 600,000 subscribers it was expected to have, it had only 55,000. A basic problem with the system was that a subscriber had to buy a mobile phone that cost $3,000 and weighed more than 1 pound. Few potential users wanted to do this. As a result, Iridium had to file for bankruptcy. Motorola, which had an 18 percent ownership of Iridium, had invested $1.6 billion and had to decide if it was willing to invest more in an effort to save the project. Some investors wanted to see Motorola cut its losses and move on. Others were concerned about recouping the enormous expenditure that had already been made.[6]

What are sunk costs, and how do they differ from opportunity costs? How do these concepts apply to the decision by Motorola's management to continue or discontinue support for the Iridium Project?

LO2 ### Defining and Identifying Relevant Information

C 3. Bob's Burgers is in the fast-food restaurant business. One component of its marketing strategy is to increase sales by expanding in foreign markets. It uses both financial and nonfinancial quantitative and qualitative information when deciding whether to open restaurants abroad. Bob's decided to open a restaurant in Prague (Czech Republic) five years ago. The following information helped the managers in making that decision:

Financial Quantitative Information

Operating information

Estimated food, labor, and other operating costs (e.g., taxes, insurance, utilities, and supplies)

Estimated selling price for each food item

Capital investment information

Cost of land, building, equipment, and furniture

Financing options and amounts

Nonfinancial Quantitative Information

Estimated daily number of customers, hamburgers to be sold, employees to work

High-traffic time periods

Income of people living in the area

Ratio of population to number of restaurants in the market area

Traffic counts in front of similar restaurants in the area

Qualitative Information

Government regulations, taxes, duties, tariffs, political involvement in business operations

Property ownership restrictions

Site visibility

Accessibility of store location

Training process for local managers

Hiring process for employees

Local customs and practices

Bob's Burgers has hired you as a consultant and given you an income statement comparing the operating incomes of its five restaurants in Eastern Europe. You have noticed that the Prague location is operating at a loss (including unallocated fixed costs) and must decide whether to recommend closing that restaurant.

Review the information used in making the decision to open the restaurant. Identify the types of information that would also be relevant in deciding whether to close the restaurant. What period or periods of time should be reviewed in making your decision? What additional information would be relevant in making your decision?

LO5 **Decision to Add a New Department**

C 4. Management at Transco Company is considering a proposal to install a third production department in its factory building. With the company's existing production setup, direct materials are processed through the Mixing Department to produce Materials A and B in equal proportions. The Shaping Department then processes Material A to yield Product C. Material B is sold as is at $20.25 per pound. Product C has a selling price of $100.00 per pound. There is a proposal to add a Baking Department to process Material B into Product D. It is expected that any quantity of Product D can be sold for $30.00 per pound.

Costs per pound under this proposal appear on the next page.

1. If (a) sales and production levels are expected to remain constant in the foreseeable future and (b) there are no foreseeable alternative uses for the factory space, should Transco Company add a Baking Department and produce Product D, if 100,000 pounds of D can be sold? Show calculations of incremental revenues and costs to support your answer.

	Mixing Department (Materials A & B)	Shaping Department (Product C)	Baking Department (Product D)
Costs from Mixing Department	—	$52.80	$13.20
Direct materials	$20.00	—	—
Direct labor	6.00	9.00	3.50
Variable overhead	4.00	8.00	4.00
Fixed overhead			
Traceable (direct, avoidable)	2.25	2.25	1.80
Allocated (common, unavoidable)	.75	.75	.75
	$33.00	$72.80	$23.25

2. List at least two qualitative reasons why Transco Company may not want to install a Baking Department and produce Product D, even if this decision appears profitable.

3. List at least two qualitative reasons why Transco Company may want to install a Baking Department and produce Product D, even if it appears that this decision is unprofitable. (CMA adapted)

Interpreting Management Reports

LO4

Special Order Decision

C 5. Metallica Can Opener Company is a subsidiary of Maltz Appliances, Inc. The can opener that Metallica produces is in strong demand. Sales this year are expected to be 1,000,000 units. Full plant capacity is 1,150,000 units, but 1,000,000 units are considered normal capacity for the current year. The following unit price and cost breakdown is applicable:

	Per Unit
Sales price	$22.50
Less manufacturing costs	
Direct materials	$ 6.00
Direct labor	2.50
Overhead, variable	3.50
Overhead, fixed	1.50
Total manufacturing costs	$13.50
Gross margin	$ 9.00
Less selling and administrative expenses	
Selling, variable	$ 1.50
Selling, fixed	1.00
Administrative, fixed	1.25
Packaging, variable*	.75
Total selling and administrative expenses	$ 4.50
Operating income	$ 4.50

*Three types of packaging are available: deluxe, $.75 per unit; plain, $.50 per unit; and bulk pack, $.25 per unit.

During November, the company received three requests for special orders from large chain-store companies. Those orders are not part of the budgeted 1,000,000 units for this year, but company officials think that sufficient capacity exists for one order to be accepted. Orders received and their terms are as follows: Order 1—75,000 can openers @ $20.00 per unit, deluxe packaging; Order 2—90,000 can openers @ $18.00 per unit, plain packaging; Order 3—125,000 can openers @ $15.75 per unit, bulk packaging.

Because the orders were placed directly with company officials, no variable selling costs will be incurred.

1. Analyze the profitability of each of the three special orders.
2. Which special order should be accepted?

Decision Analysis Using Excel

LO7 **Sell or Process-Further Decision**

C 6. Marketeers, Inc., developed a promotional program for a large shopping center in Sunset Living, Arizona, a few years ago. Having invested $360,000 in developing the original promotion campaign, the firm is ready to present its client with an add-on contract offer that includes the original promotion areas of (1) a TV advertising campaign, (2) a series of brochures for mass mailing, and (3) a special rotating BIG SALE schedule for 10 of the 28 tenants in the shopping center. Presented below are the revenue terms from the original contract with the shopping center and the offer for the add-on contract, which extends the original contract terms.

	Original Contract Terms	Extended Contract Including Add-On Terms
TV advertising campaign	$520,000	$ 580,000
Brochure series	210,000	230,000
Rotating BIG SALE schedule	170,000	190,000
Totals	$900,000	$1,000,000

Marketeers, Inc., estimates that the following additional costs will be incurred by extending the contract:

	TV Campaign	Brochures	BIG SALE Schedule
Direct labor	$30,000	$ 9,000	$7,000
Variable overhead costs	22,000	14,000	6,000
Fixed overhead costs*	12,000	4,000	2,000

*80 percent are direct fixed costs applied to this contract.

1. Using an Excel spreadsheet, compute the costs that will be incurred for each part of the add-on portion of the contract.
2. Should Marketeers, Inc., offer the add-on contract, or should it ask for a final settlement check based on the original contract only? Defend your answer.
3. If management of the shopping center indicates that the terms of the add-on contract are negotiable, how should Marketeers, Inc., respond?

Ethical Dilemma Case

LO3 **Ethics of a Make-or-Buy Decision**

C 7. Tima Iski is the assistant controller for Tagwell Corporation, a leading producer of home appliances. Her friend Zack Marsh is the supervisor of the firm's

Cookware Department. Marsh has the authority to decide whether parts are purchased from outside vendors or manufactured in his department. Iski recently conducted an internal audit of the parts being manufactured in the Cookware Department, including a comparison of the prices currently charged by vendors for similar parts. She found more than a dozen parts that could be purchased for less than they cost the company to produce. When she approached Marsh about the situation, he replied that if those parts were purchased from outside vendors, two automated machines would be idled for several hours a week. Increased machine idle time would have a negative effect on his performance evaluation and could reduce his yearly bonus. He reminded Iski that he was in charge of the decision to make or purchase those parts and asked her not to pursue the matter any further.

What should Iski do in this situation? Discuss her options.

Internet Case

LO5   **Comparison of Segment Performance**

C 8. Public companies that operate in different businesses or segments are required to report operating results for those segments. This requirement makes it possible to evaluate the performance of comparable segments of different companies even though the rest of the companies' operations are not in comparable segments. Access the websites of **Time Warner** and **Walt Disney Company**. Both are diversified entertainment companies, but they operate in both similar and different segments. On their websites, find information about their major business segments and compare them. List the major business segments of each company. Which segments are comparable, and which are different?

Group Activity Case

LO2   **Identifying Relevant Decision Information**

C 9. Select two destinations for a two-week vacation, and gather information about them from brochures, magazines, travel agents, the Internet, and friends. Then list the relevant quantitative and qualitative information in order of its importance to your decision. Analyze the information, and select a destination.

Which factors were most important to your decision? Why? Which were least important? Why? How would the process of identifying relevant information differ if the president of your company asked you to prepare a budget for the next training meeting, to be held at a location of your choice?

Your instructor will divide the class into groups and ask each group to discuss this case. One student from each group will summarize his or her group's findings and debrief the entire class.

Business Communication Case

LO5   **Formulating a Segmented Income Statement**

C 10. Carmen Mendoza recently purchased the Mesa Grande Country Club in Tucson, Arizona. The club offers swimming, golf, and tennis as well as dining services for its members. Mendoza is unfamiliar with the actual operating activities of those areas. Because you are the controller for the country club's operations, Mendoza has asked you to prepare a memo that shows how each activity or service contributed to the profitability of the country club for the year ended December 31. The information you provide will assist Mendoza in her decision to keep or eliminate one or more areas.

1. In preparation for writing your memo, answer the following questions:
   a. What kinds of information about each area do you need?
   b. Why is such information relevant?
   c. Where would you find the information?
   d. When would you want to obtain the information?
2. Draft your memo. Omit actual numbers; show only headings and line items.
3. Assume that Carmen Mendoza wants to increase the membership of the country club and will invest a large sum of money to promote membership sales. How would you structure the memo differently to address such a decision?

Pricing Decisions, Including Target Costing and Transfer Pricing

In this chapter, we examine the various approaches that managers use to establish the prices of goods and services. There are many such approaches; however, each approach may very well produce a different price for the same product or service. The process of establishing a correct price is, in fact, more of an art than a science. It depends on a manager's ability to analyze the marketplace and anticipate customers' reactions to a product or service and its price.

LEARNING OBJECTIVES

LO1 Identify the objectives and rules used to establish prices of goods and services, and relate pricing issues to the management process.

LO2 Describe economic pricing concepts, including the auction-based pricing method used on the Internet.

LO3 Use cost-based pricing methods to develop prices.

LO4 Describe target costing, and use that concept to analyze pricing decisions and evaluate a new product opportunity.

LO5 Describe how transfer pricing is used for transferring goods and services and evaluating performance within a division or segment.

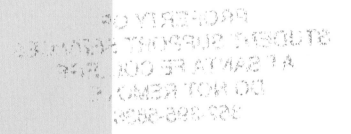

- Why do managers generally use several pricing approaches?
- Why did Palm's managers use target costing to establish a price for the Zire?

Palm invented and dominates the personal digital assistant (PDA) market. Its products range from simple two-button PDAs like the Zire to high-priced innovative models that combine the features of a cell phone and a digital organizer with wireless Internet access. Competition between Palm's products, BlackBerry, and other PDA and pocket PCs is very keen, and there is constant pressure to offer more technology-rich features to outdo competitors.

The Pricing Decision and the Manager

> **LO1** Identify the objectives and rules used to establish prices of goods and services, and relate pricing issues to the management process.

As we have noted, establishing a correct price depends on a manager's ability to analyze the marketplace and anticipate customers' reactions to a product or service and its price. Factors that managers consider when analyzing the marketplace include competitors' pricing strategies, the economic environment, and legal, political, and niche issues. In today's global marketplace, managers perfect the art of price setting through experience in dealing with customers and products within their company's industry.

The Objectives of a Pricing Policy

Setting appropriate prices is one of the most difficult decisions that managers must make on a day-to-day basis. Because such decisions affect the long-term survival of any profit-oriented enterprise, a company's long-term objectives should include a pricing policy. A pricing policy is one way in which companies differentiate themselves from their competitors. Compare, for example, the pricing policies of luxury brands like **Lexus** and **Nordstrom** with those of cost-driven companies like **Toyota** or **Wal-Mart**. Consider also how prices are set on **eBay** and **Priceline.com**. Although all these companies are successful, their pricing policies differ significantly because each company has different pricing objectives.

In addition, companies may use pricing policies to differentiate among their own brands. For example, companies like **Palm** (Treo versus Zire), **The Gap** (The Gap versus Old Navy), and **General Motors** (Cadillac versus Chevrolet) use price to differentiate their product brands and the market segments that each brand targets. Thus, for each product brand, the company has identified the market segment that it intends to serve and has developed pricing objectives to meet the needs of that market.

Possible objectives of a pricing policy include the following:

1. Identifying and adhering to both short-run and long-run pricing strategies
2. Maximizing profits
3. Maintaining or gaining market share
4. Setting socially responsible prices
5. Maintaining a minimum rate of return on investment
6. Being customer focused

Pricing strategies depend on many factors and conditions. The pricing strategies of companies that produce standard items or commodities for a competitive marketplace will differ from the pricing strategies of companies that make custom-designed items. In a competitive market, companies can reduce prices to win sales away from competing companies. They can also continuously add value-enhancing features and upgrades to their products and services to create the impression that customers are receiving more for their money. In contrast, a company that makes custom-designed items can be more conservative in its pricing strategy.

Maximizing profits has traditionally been the underlying objective of any pricing policy. One key indicator of profit potential is an increasing share of the market. Maintaining or gaining market share is closely related to pricing strategies. However, market share is important only if sales are profitable. To increase market share by reducing prices below cost can be economically disastrous unless such a move is accompanied by strategies that compensate for the lost revenues.

Maximizing profits remains a dominant factor in price setting. However, to enhance their standing with the public and thus ensure their long-term survival, companies today also consider whether their prices are socially responsible. The pricing policies of many companies now take into consideration a variety of social concerns, including environmental factors, the influence of an aging population, legal constraints, and ethical issues.

Other pricing policy objectives include maintaining a minimum return on investment and enhancing value to customers. Organizations view each product or service as an investment. They will not invest in making a product or providing a service unless it will provide a minimum return. To maintain a minimum return on investment, an organization, when setting prices, adds a markup percentage to each product's costs of production. This markup percentage is closely related to the objective of profit maximization. Taking customers' needs into consideration when setting prices or increasing a product's value to customers is important for at least three reasons. These reasons are as follows:

1. Sensitivity to customers is necessary to sustain sales growth.

2. Customers' acceptance is crucial to success in a competitive market.

3. Prices should reflect the enhanced value that the company adds to the product or service, which is another way of saying that prices are customer-driven.

Pricing and the Management Process

For an organization to stay in business, its selling price must (1) be competitive with the competition's price, (2) be acceptable to customers, (3) recover all costs incurred in bringing the product or service to market, and (4) return a profit. If a manager deviates from any of these four pricing rules, there must be a specific short-run objective that accounts for the change. Breaking those pricing rules for a long period will force a company into bankruptcy. Figure 1 illustrates the elements of pricing that managers need to consider at each step in the management process.

Planning When managers plan, they must consider how much to charge for each product or service and identify the maximum price that the market will accept and the minimum price that the company can sustain. Those prices form the foundation for budgets, as well as the foundation for projections of profitability.

Performing In the course of the year, managers implement the pricing strategies that they formulated during the planning stage. Products or services are sold either at the specified prices or on an auction market like **eBay** or **Priceline.com**.

■ **FIGURE 1**
The Management Process: To-Do's for Managers

To-Do's for Managers

- Plan
  - How much to charge for each product or service
  - Identify the maximum price the market will accept and the minimum price the company can sustain

- Perform
  - Sell products or services at the specified prices or on the auction market

- Evaluate
  - Analyze actual prices and profits versus targeted ones
  - Determine which pricing strategies were successful and which failed
  - Identify reasons for success or failure
  - Plan any necessary corrective action

- Communicate
  - Prepare reports to assess past pricing strategies and plan future strategies

Evaluating   When managers evaluate performance, they review sales to determine which pricing strategies were successful and which failed, identify the reasons for the success or failure, and take any necessary corrective action.

Communicating   When managers communicate about performance inside the organization, analyses of actual prices and profits versus targeted ones are prepared for use. Those analyses are used to assess past pricing strategies and plan future strategies.

External and Internal Pricing Factors

When making and evaluating pricing decisions, managers must consider many factors. As shown in Figure 2, some of those factors relate to the external market, and others relate to internal constraints. The external factors include demand for the product, customer needs, competition, and quantity and quality of competing products or services. The internal factors include constraints caused by costs, desired return on investment, quality and quantity of materials and labor, and allocation of scarce resources.

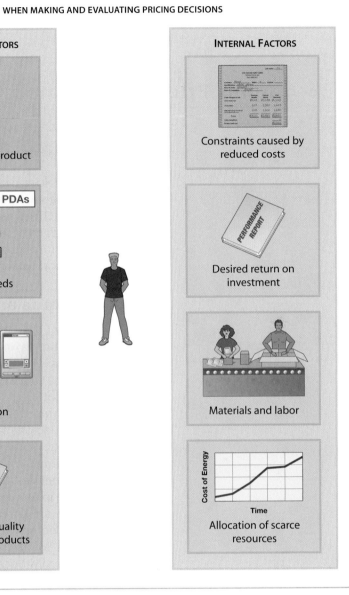

■ **FIGURE 2**
External and Internal Factors Affecting Pricing Decisions

WHEN MAKING AND EVALUATING PRICING DECISIONS

EXTERNAL FACTORS

Demand for the product

SALE ONE DAY ONLY · PDAs

Customer needs

Competition

CONSUMER REPORTS

Quantity and quality of competing products

INTERNAL FACTORS

Constraints caused by reduced costs

PERFORMANCE REPORT

Desired return on investment

Materials and labor

Cost of Energy / Time

Allocation of scarce resources

S T O P • R E V I E W • A P P L Y

1-1. Identify five possible pricing policy objectives. Discuss each one briefly.

1-2. If a manager's strategy is to price products so that total market share will increase, what considerations should go into selecting a price?

1-3. Do prices have a social effect? If so, in what way?

1-4. In setting a selling price, what four rules must an organization follow?

1-5. List four external factors to consider when establishing the price of a product or service.

1-6. Identify four internal factors that affect the price of a good or service.

Suggested answers to all Stop, Review, and Apply questions are available at http://college.hmco.com/accounting/needles/man_acc/8e/student_home.html.

Economic Pricing Concepts

LO2 Describe economic pricing concepts, including the auction-based pricing method used on the Internet.

The economic approach to pricing is based on microeconomic theory. Pricing plays a strong role in the concepts underlying microeconomic theory as it is practiced at individual firms. Every firm is in business to maximize profits. Although each product has its own set of revenues and costs, microeconomic theory states that profit will be greatest when the difference between total revenue and total cost is greatest.

Total Revenue and Total Cost Curves

It may seem that if a company could produce an infinite number of products, it would realize the maximum profit. But this is not the case, and microeconomic theory explains why. Figure 3A shows the economist's view of a breakeven chart. It contains two breakeven points, between which is a large space labeled "profit area." Notice that the total revenue line is curved rather than straight. The theory behind this is that as a product is marketed, because of competition and other factors, price reductions will be necessary if the firm is to sell additional units. Total revenue will continue to increase, but the rate of increase will diminish as more units are sold. Therefore, the slope of the total revenue line declines, and the line curves toward the right.

Costs react in an opposite way. Over the assumed relevant range, variable and fixed costs are fairly predictable, with fixed costs remaining constant and variable costs being the same per unit. The result is a straight line for total costs. However, following microeconomic theory, costs per unit will increase as more units are sold because fixed costs will change. As costs move into different relevant ranges, such fixed costs as supervision and depreciation increase, and competition causes marketing costs to rise. As the company pushes for more and more products from limited facilities, repair and maintenance costs also increase. And as the push from management increases, total costs per unit rise at an accelerating rate. The result is that the slope of the total cost line in Figure 3A increases, and the line begins curving upward. The total revenue line and the total cost line then cross again; beyond that point, the company suffers a loss on additional sales.

Profits are maximized at the point where the difference between total revenue and total cost is the greatest. In Figure 3A, this point is 6,000 units of sales. At that sales level, total revenue will be $195,000; total cost, $100,000; and profit, $95,000. In theory, if one additional unit is sold, profit per unit will drop because total cost is rising at a faster rate than total revenues. As you can see, if the company sells 11,000 units, total profits will be almost entirely depleted by the rising costs. Therefore, 6,000 sales units is the optimal operating level, and the price charged at that level is the optimal price.

■ **FIGURE 3**
Microeconomic Pricing Theory

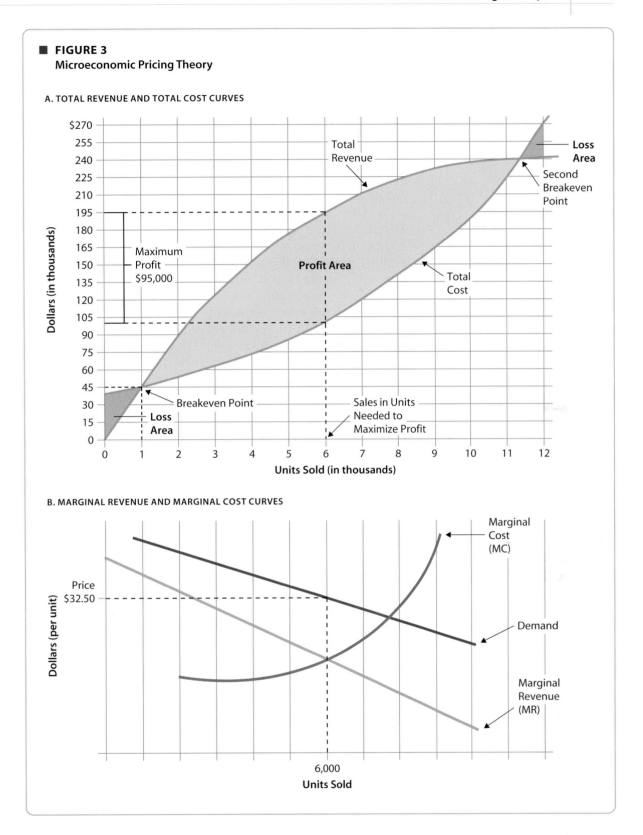

A. TOTAL REVENUE AND TOTAL COST CURVES

B. MARGINAL REVENUE AND MARGINAL COST CURVES

Marginal Revenue and Marginal Cost Curves

Economists use marginal revenue and marginal cost to help determine the optimal price for a good or service. **Marginal revenue** is the change in total revenue caused by a one-unit change in output. **Marginal cost** is the change in total cost caused by a one-unit change in output. Graphic curves for marginal revenue and marginal cost are created by measuring and plotting the rate of change in total revenue and total cost at various activity levels. If you computed marginal revenue and marginal cost for each unit sold in our example and plotted them on a graph, the lines would resemble those in Figure 3B. Notice that the marginal cost line crosses the marginal revenue line at 6,000 units. After that point, profit per unit will decrease as additional units are sold. Marginal cost will exceed marginal revenue for each unit sold over 6,000. Profit will be maximized when the marginal revenue and marginal cost lines intersect. By projecting this point onto the product's demand curve, you can locate the optimal price, which is $32.50 per unit.

If all the information used in microeconomic theory were certain, picking the optimal price would be fairly easy. But most information used in such an analysis relies on projected amounts for unit sales, product costs, and revenues. Nevertheless, developing such an analysis usually highlights cost patterns and the unanticipated influences of demand. For this reason, it is important that managers consider the microeconomic approach to pricing when setting product prices. However, the results of this type of analysis should not be the only data relied on.

Auction-Based Pricing

In recent years, as a result of Internet companies like eBay, **Yahoo**, and Price-line.com that host auction markets, auction-based pricing has skyrocketed in popularity. **Auction-based pricing** occurs in two ways: Either sellers post what they have to sell, ask for price bids, and accept a buyer's offer to purchase at a certain price, or buyers interested in buying something post what they want, ask for prices, and accept a seller's offer to sell at a certain price.

To illustrate the seller's auction-based price, suppose a corporation like **Intel** or **Sun Microsystems** has an excess of silicon wafers after a production run. The company posts a message on the Internet asking for the quantity of silicon wafers that prospective buyers are willing to buy and the price that they are willing to pay. After the offers are received, the company prepares a demand curve of all offers and selects the one that best fits the quantity of silicon wafers it has available for sale.

FOCUS ON BUSINESS PRACTICE
What's It Worth to Shop Online?

The Internet makes it possible to price efficiently at the level of marginal costs. For instance, **Priceline.com** is a bargain hunter's dream. At Priceline's website, travelers pick a destination and a price they are willing to pay for air or hotel reservations. The price must be guaranteed by credit card. An airline or hotel has one hour to accept or reject the bid. If the bid is accepted, the buyer is obligated to pay for the air or hotel reservation. The company claims that customers save 54 to 76 percent off the regular prices. The hotels and airlines are often willing to accept the low bid prices because the marginal cost of filling an additional seat on an airplane or an extra room in a hotel is very low. Even the low marginal revenue from the low bid prices is greater than the marginal cost.[1]

FOCUS ON BUSINESS PRACTICE

How Big a Problem Is Fraud on the Internet?

The Federal Bureau of Investigation and the National White Collar Crime Center formed the Internet Fraud Complaint Center in the spring of 2000. A breakdown of the center's complaints in 2001 showed that the following scams were most prevalent: auction fraud (42.8 percent), nondelivery of merchandise and payment (20.3 percent), the Nigerian letter fraud (15.5 percent), and credit/debit card fraud (9.4 percent).

eBay, the dominant player in Internet auction sites, battles fraud by using a customer rating system or "feedback forum" to rate the reputation of all eBay members. The ratings of both buyers and sellers are prominently displayed on the site. According to eBay, less than .001 percent of the millions of transactions it handles a year are fraudulent.[2]

To illustrate the buyer's auction-based price, consider an individual who wants to fly roundtrip to Europe on certain dates and posts his or her needs on one of the hosted auction markets. After receiving the offers to sell roundtrip tickets to Europe, the individual will accept the offer that best suits his or her needs.

Auction-based pricing will continue to grow in importance as a result of the escalating amount of business that is being conducted over the Internet by both organizations and individuals. Just about anything can be bought or sold via the Internet.

S T O P • R E V I E W • A P P L Y

2-1. In traditional economic theory, what role does total revenue play in maximizing profit?

2-2. Why is profit maximized at the point at which marginal revenue equals marginal cost?

2-3. What is auction-based pricing? Why is auction-based pricing popular?

Cost-Based Pricing Methods

LO3 Use cost-based pricing methods to develop prices.

Managers may use a variety of pricing methods. A good starting point for developing a price is to base it on the cost of producing a good or service. Two pricing methods based on cost are gross margin pricing and return on assets pricing. Remember that in a competitive environment, market prices and conditions also influence price; however, if prices do not cover a company's costs, the company will eventually fail.

To illustrate the two methods of cost-based pricing, we will consider the Energeez Company. This company buys parts from outside vendors and assembles them into portable solar panels. In the previous accounting period, the Energeez Company produced 14,750 solar panels. The total costs and unit costs incurred follow.

	Total Costs	Unit Costs
Variable production costs		
Direct materials and parts	$ 88,500	$ 6.00
Direct labor	66,375	4.50
Variable overhead	44,250	3.00
Total variable production costs	$199,125	$13.50
Fixed overhead	154,875	10.50
Total production costs	$354,000	$24.00
Selling, general, and administrative expenses		
Selling expenses	$ 73,750	$ 5.00
General expenses	36,875	2.50
Administrative expenses	22,125	1.50
Total selling, general, and administrative expenses	$132,750	$ 9.00
Total costs and expenses	$486,750	$33.00

No changes in unit costs are expected this period. The desired profit for the period is $110,625. The company uses assets totaling $921,875 in producing the solar panels and expects a 14 percent return on those assets.

Gross Margin Pricing

Study Note

The gross margin pricing method is also called the *income statement method.*

One cost-based approach emphasizes the use of income statement information to determine a selling price and is called the *gross margin pricing method.* Gross margin is the difference between sales and the total production costs of those sales. **Gross margin pricing** is a cost-based pricing approach in which the price is computed using a markup percentage based on a product's total production costs. The markup percentage is designed to include all costs other than those used in the computation of gross margin. Therefore, the gross margin markup percentage covers selling, general, and administrative expenses and the desired profit. Because an accounting system often provides management with unit production cost data, both variable and fixed, this method of determining selling price can be easily applied. The formulas are as follows:

$$\text{Markup Percentage} = \frac{\text{Desired Profit} + \text{Total Selling, General, and Administrative Expenses}}{\text{Total Production Costs}}$$

Gross Margin-Based Price = Total Production Costs per Unit + (Markup Percentage × Total Production Costs per Unit)

For the Energeez Company, the markup percentage and selling price are computed as follows:

$$\text{Markup Percentage} = \frac{\$110,625 + \$132,750}{\$354,000}$$

$$= 68.75\%$$

Gross Margin-Based Price = $24.00 + (68.75% × $24.00)

$$= \underline{\$40.50}$$

The numerator in the markup percentage formula is the sum of the desired profit ($110,625) and the total selling, general, and administrative expenses

($132,750). The denominator contains all production costs: variable costs of $199,125 and fixed production costs of $154,875. The gross margin markup is 68.75 percent of total production costs, or $16.50. Adding $16.50 to the total production costs per unit yields a selling price of $40.50.

Another way to express the gross margin–based price is to state the formula in terms of a company's desire to recover all of its costs and make a profit. This approach ignores the computation of the markup percentage, achieves the same gross margin–based price, and is stated as follows:

$$\text{Gross Margin–Based Price} = \frac{\text{Total Production Costs} + \text{Total Selling, General, and Administrative Expenses} + \text{Desired Profit}}{\text{Total Units Produced}}$$

Using this formula, the gross margin–based price for the Energeez Company is computed as follows:

$$\text{Gross Margin–Based Price} = \frac{\$88,500 + \$66,375 + \$44,250 + \$154,875 + \$73,750 + \$36,875 + \$22,125 + \$110,625}{14,750 \text{ Units}}$$

$$= \$597,375 \div 14,750$$

$$= \$40.50$$

Gross margin–based price can also be detailed on a per unit basis:

Gross Margin–Based Price = Direct Materials + Direct Labor
+ Variable Overhead + Fixed Overhead
+ Selling, General, and Administrative Expenses
+ Desired Profit per Unit

Applying this formula to the Energeez Company's data, the computations are as follows:

Gross Margin-Based Price = $6.00 + $4.50 + $3.00 + $10.50 + $5.00
+ $2.50 + $1.50 + ($110,625 ÷ 14,750)

$$= \$40.50$$

Study Note

Gross margin–based price per unit equals total production, selling, general, and administrative costs per unit plus a desired profit per unit.

Return on Assets Pricing

Return on assets pricing changes the objective of the price determination process. Earning a profit margin on total costs is replaced by earning a profit equal to a specified rate of return on the assets employed in the operation. Because this approach focuses on a desired minimum rate of return on assets, it is known as the *balance sheet approach to pricing*.

The following formula is used to calculate the return on assets–based price:

Study Note

The return on assets pricing method is also known as the *balance sheet method*.

Return on Assets–Based Price = Total Costs and Expenses per Unit
+ (Desired Rate of Return × Cost of
Assets Employed per Unit)

The formula can also be expressed as follows:

Study Note

Return on assets–based price per unit equals total production, selling, general, and administrative costs per unit plus a per-unit desired return on the assets employed.

Return on Assets–Based Price = [(Total Production Costs + Total Selling,
General, and Administrative Expenses)
÷ Units to Be Produced] + [Desired Rate of
Return × (Total Cost of Assets Employed ÷
Units to Be Produced)]

To compute the return on assets–based price, the total cost of the assets employed is divided by the projected number of units to be produced. The result is then multiplied by the rate of return to obtain the desired earnings per unit. Desired earnings per unit plus total costs and expenses per unit yields the unit selling price.

Recall that the Energeez Company has an asset base of $921,875. It plans to produce 14,750 units and would like to earn a 14 percent return on assets. If the company uses return on assets pricing, the selling price per unit would be calculated as follows:

$$\text{Return on Assets–Based Price} = \$24.00 + \$9.00$$
$$+ [14\% \times (\$921,875 \div 14,750)]$$
$$= \underline{\$41.75}$$

or as:

$$\text{Return on Assets–Based Price} = [(\$354,000 + \$132,750) \div 14,750]$$
$$+ [14\% \times (\$921,875 \div 14,750)]$$
$$= \$33.00 + \$8.75$$
$$= \underline{\$41.75}$$

Notice that the desired profit used in gross margin pricing is replaced by an overall company rate of return on assets. By dividing the cost of assets employed by projected units of output and multiplying the result by the desired minimum rate of return, a unit profit factor of $8.75 [14% × ($921,875 ÷ 14,750)] is obtained. Adding this profit factor to the total unit costs and expenses gives the selling price of $41.75.

Summary of Cost-Based Pricing Methods

Figure 4 summarizes the two cost-based pricing methods. If Energeez Company uses return on assets pricing and has a desired rate of return of 14 percent, it will need to set a higher selling price ($41.75) than it would under the gross margin method ($40.50). Companies select their pricing methods based on their degree of trust in a cost base. The cost bases from which they can choose are (1) total product costs per unit and (2) total costs and expenses per unit.

Often, total product costs per unit are readily available, which makes gross margin pricing a good way to compute selling prices. However, gross margin pricing depends on an accurate forecast of units because the fixed cost per unit portion of total production costs will vary if the actual number of units produced differs from the estimated number of units. Return on assets pricing is also a good pricing method if the assets used to manufacture a product can be identified and their cost determined. If this is not the case, the method yields inaccurate results.

Pricing Services

A service business's approach to pricing differs from that of a manufacturer. Although a service has no physical substance, it must still be priced and billed to the customer. Most service organizations use a form of **time and materials pricing** (also known as *parts and labor pricing*) to arrive at the price of a service. With this method, service companies, such as appliance repair shops, home-

Study Note

Time and materials pricing is also known as *parts and labor pricing*.

■ **FIGURE 4**
Cost-Based Pricing Methods : Energeez Company

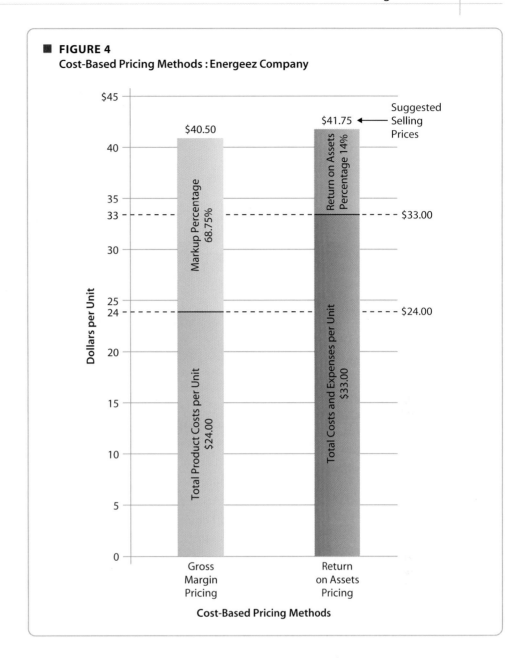

remodeling specialists, pool cleaners, and automobile repair shops, arrive at prices by using two computations: one for direct labor and one for materials and parts. Markup percentages are added to the costs of materials and labor to cover the cost of overhead and provide a profit factor. If the service does not require materials and parts, then only direct labor costs are used in developing the price. Professionals, such as attorneys, accountants, and consultants, apply a factor representing all overhead costs to the base labor costs to establish a price for their services.

To illustrate, suppose that Gil Marquis, the owner of an auto repair shop, has just completed work on Lucinda Lowe's Mercedes. The parts used to repair the vehicle cost $840. The company's 40 percent markup rate on parts covers parts-related overhead costs and profit. The repairs required four hours of labor by a certified Mercedes specialist, whose wages are $35 per hour. The company's overhead markup rate on labor is 80 percent. Marquis will compute Lucinda Lowe's bill as shown on the next page.

Auto repair shops like the one shown here commonly use time and materials pricing (also called *parts and labor pricing*). This method involves computing the costs of direct labor and materials and adding percentage markups to those costs to cover overhead and provide a profit factor.

Repair parts used	$840	
Overhead charges		
$840 × 40%	336	
Total parts charges		$1,176
Labor charges		
4 hours @ $35 per hour	$140	
Overhead charges		
$140 × 80%	112	
Total labor charges		252
Total billing		$1,428

Final Notes on Cost-Based Pricing Methods

In some areas of the economy, such as government contracts, cost-based pricing is widely used. Although a variety of cost-based methods may be used to mechanically compute a price, many factors external to the product or service still require a manager's attention. Once a cost-based price has been determined, the decision maker must consider such factors as competitors' prices, customers' expectations, and the cost of substitute products and services. Pricing is a risky part of operating a business, and care must be taken when establishing that all-important selling price.

S.T.O.P • R.E.V.I.E.W • A.P.P.L.Y

3-1. What is gross margin pricing? How is the markup percentage calculated under this method?

3-2. How does return on assets pricing differ from gross margin pricing?

3-3. In the pricing of services, what is time and materials pricing?

Pricing Based on Target Costing

LO4 Describe target costing, and use that concept to analyze pricing decisions and evaluate a new product opportunity.

⊂⊃ Study Note

Target costing is sometimes referred to as *target pricing*.

Target costing is designed to enhance a company's ability to compete, especially in new or emerging product markets. The Decision Point at the start of this chapter focused on **Palm**, which used target costing to price a new product, the Zire. This approach to pricing differs significantly from the cost-based methods we have just described. Instead of first determining the cost of a product or service and then adding a profit factor to arrive at a price, target costing reverses the procedure. **Target costing** is a pricing method that (1) identifies the price at which a product will be competitive in the marketplace, (2) defines the desired profit to be made on the product, and (3) computes the target cost for the product by subtracting the desired profit from the competitive market price. The formula is as follows:

$$\text{Target Price} - \text{Desired Profit} = \text{Target Cost}$$

The company's engineers and product designers then use the target cost as the maximum cost to be incurred for the materials and other resources needed to design and manufacture the product. It is their responsibility to create the product at or below its target cost.

Pricing based on target costing may not seem revolutionary, but a detailed look at its underlying principles reveals its strategic superiority. Target costing gives managers the ability to control or dictate the costs of a new product at the planning stage of the product's life cycle. In a competitive environment, the use of target costing enables managers to analyze a product's potential before they commit resources to its production.

Figure 5 compares the timing of a pricing decision that uses a traditional approach with one that uses target costing. The stages of the product life cycle, from the generation of the product idea to the final disposition of the product, are identified at the base of the figure. When traditional cost-based pricing practices are used, prices cannot be set until production has taken place and costs have been incurred and analyzed. At that point, a profit factor is added to the product's cost, and the product is ready to be offered to customers. In contrast, under target costing, the pricing decision takes place immediately after

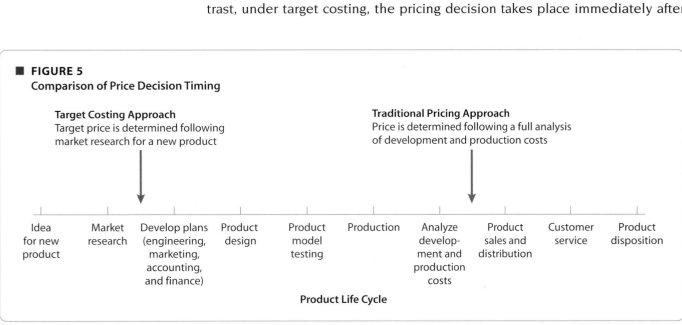

■ **FIGURE 5**
Comparison of Price Decision Timing

Target Costing Approach
Target price is determined following market research for a new product

Traditional Pricing Approach
Price is determined following a full analysis of development and production costs

| Idea for new product | Market research | Develop plans (engineering, marketing, accounting, and finance) | Product design | Product model testing | Production | Analyze development and production costs | Product sales and distribution | Customer service | Product disposition |

Product Life Cycle

the market research for a new product. The market research not only reveals the potential demand for the product, but also identifies the maximum price that a customer would be willing to pay for it. Once the price is determined, target costing enables the company's engineers to design the product with a fixed maximum target cost on which to base the product's features.

Differences Between Cost-Based Pricing and Target Costing

To illustrate how cost-based pricing differs from target costing, suppose that Cost First Company and Price First Company are about to enter the market with a new product called the Starbeam. Both companies have conducted market research and know that demand exists for the product. Cost First Company's strategy is to jump right into the planning phase, design the product, and get it into production as soon as possible. The product's prototype model will be tested during the production phase. The company assumes that flaws will be found, so changes in engineering orders will be necessary and the production process will have to be redesigned to fit the changes. Cost control will not be a part of this process. Only after the product has been produced successfully can a total unit cost be computed and a price determined.

Figure 6 shows the cost patterns associated with Cost First Company's new product. Once the company decides to produce a new product, new costs are incurred at each stage in the product's life cycle. The patterns of two kinds of cost are shown. **Committed costs** are the costs of design, development, engineering, testing, and production that are engineered into a product or service at the design stage of development. They should occur if all design specifications are followed during production. **Incurred costs** are the actual costs incurred in making the product. When cost-based pricing is used, it is very difficult to control costs from the planning phase through the production phase.

Study Note

Remember that when desired profit is defined as a percentage of target cost, target price is equal to 100 percent of target cost *plus* the percentage of target cost desired as profit.

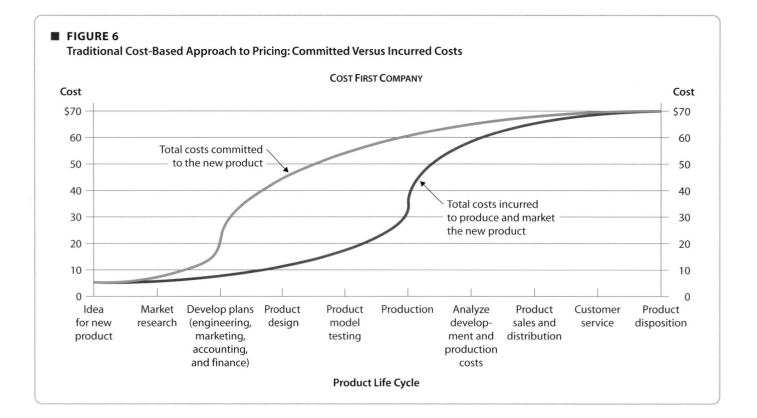

■ **FIGURE 6**
Traditional Cost-Based Approach to Pricing: Committed Versus Incurred Costs

COST FIRST COMPANY

Management has a hard time setting realistic targets because the product is being made for the first time. Because customers are expected to pay whatever amount cost-based pricing identifies, the focus is on sales, not on the design and manufacture of the product. Cost control efforts will focus on incurred costs after the product has been introduced to the marketplace. In this example, Cost First Company's new product will cost around $70, so to earn a profit of 20 percent of target cost, the company will need to price the product at around $84.

Now let's take a look at Price First Company's target costing approach. Market research indicated that the product would be successful if it were priced at or below $48. Using the target costing formula, the company conducted the following analysis:

$$\$48 - 20\% \text{ of Target Cost} = \text{Target Cost}$$
$$\$48 - .2X = X$$
$$\$48 = 1.2X$$
$$\underline{\underline{\$40 = X}}$$

The analysis showed that to be successful in the marketplace and profitable to the company, the product had to be produced for $40 or less. Engineers set about designing a product that would comply with that cost restriction. Production efforts were not started until the prototype model had met the requirements for both cost and quality. Figure 7 shows the patterns for the committed and incurred costs associated with Price First Company's new product. Because a $40 maximum cost was engineered into the design of the product, committed costs are set at that amount, much lower than the $70 committed costs for Cost First Company's product. Two Starbeams will now be marketed: one selling for $84 and the other for $48. If both are of equal quality, which do you think will dominate the market?

If a company's engineers determine that a product cannot be manufactured at or below its target cost, the company should examine the product's design

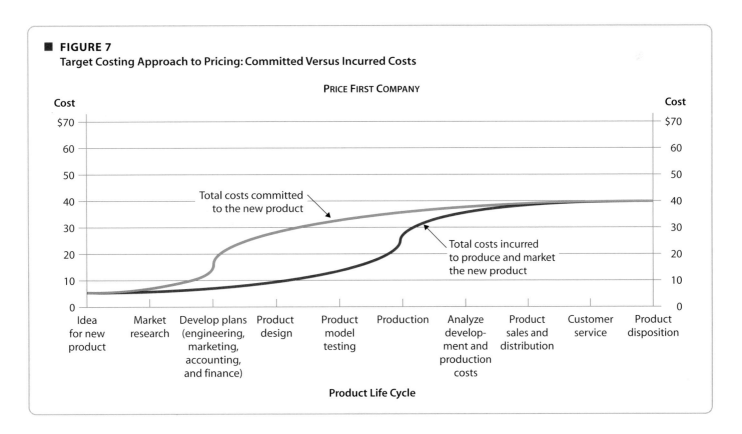

■ **FIGURE 7**
Target Costing Approach to Pricing: Committed Versus Incurred Costs

These shoppers at an Ikea store have a large selection of high-quality products to choose from. Target costing enables Ikea to offer its products at competitive prices and ensures that a product will earn a profit as soon as it is introduced. This method identifies the price at which a product will be competitive in the marketplace, defines the desired profit to be made on the product, and computes the target cost by subtracting the desired profit from the competitive market price.

and try to improve the approach to production. If the product still cannot be made at its target cost, the company must realize that it cannot compete in that particular market. It should either invest in new equipment and procedures or abandon its plans to make and market the product.

One of the primary benefits of using target costing is the ability to design and build a product to a specific cost goal. The increased emphasis on product design allows a company to engineer the target cost into the product before manufacturing begins. A new product is designed only if its projected costs are equal to or lower than its target cost. The company can thus focus on holding costs down while it plans and designs the product, before the costs are actually committed and incurred. Under the cost-based approach, concern about reducing costs begins only after the product has been produced. This often leads to random efforts to cut costs, which can reduce product quality and further erode the customer base. Under target costing, the product is expected to produce a profit as soon as it is marketed. Cost-cutting improvements in a product's design and production methods can still be made, but profitability is built into the selling price from the beginning. Companies like **Sony** and **Ikea** have used target costing successfully for years and have benefited from increased sales volume each time they have cut prices because of production improvements. These companies never sacrifice product quality.

Target Costing Analysis in an Activity-Based Management Environment

To see how target costing is implemented in a company that uses activity-based management, consider Zephyr Company's approach to new product decisions. A customer is seeking price quotations for two WiFi components: a special-purpose router and a wireless palm-sized computer. One German company and two Swedish companies are competing for the order. The current market-price ranges for the two products are as follows: router, $320–$380 per unit; computer, $750–$850 per unit.

One of Zepher's salespersons thinks that if the company could quote prices of $300 for the router and $725 for the computer, it would get the order and gain a significant share of the market for those products. Zephyr's usual

Study Note

Activity-based management (ABM) can be used successfully with target costing.

profit markup is 25 percent of total unit cost. The company's design engineers and accountants put together these specifications and costs for the new products:

Activity-based cost rates

Materials handling	$ 1.30	per dollar of direct materials and purchased parts cost
Production	$ 3.50	per machine hour
Product delivery	$24.00	per router
	$30.00	per computer

	Router	Computer
Projected unit demand	26,000	18,000
Per-unit data		
Direct materials cost	$25.00	$65.00
Purchased parts cost	$15.00	$45.00
Manufacturing labor		
Hours	2.6	4.8
Hourly labor rate	$12.00	$15.00
Assembly labor		
Hours	3.4	8.2
Hourly labor rate	$14.00	$16.00
Machine hours	12.8	28.4

The target cost for each product is computed as follows:

$$\text{Router} = \$300.00 \div 1.25 = \$240.00*$$
$$\text{Computer} = \$725.00 \div 1.25 = \$580.00$$

*Target Price − Desired Profit = Target Cost
$$\$300.00 - .25X = X$$
$$\$300.00 = 1.25X$$
$$X = \frac{\$300.00}{1.25} = \$240.00$$

The projected total unit cost of production and delivery is computed in the following way:

	Router	Computer
Direct materials cost	$ 25.00	$ 65.00
Purchased parts cost	15.00	45.00
Total cost of direct materials and parts	$ 40.00	$110.00
Manufacturing labor		
Router (2.6 hours × $12.00)	31.20	
Computer (4.8 hours × $15.00)		72.00
Assembly labor		
Router (3.4 hours × $14.00)	47.60	
Computer (8.2 hours × $16.00)		131.20
Activity-based costs		
Materials handling		
Router ($40.00 × $1.30)	52.00	
Computer ($110.00 × $1.30)		143.00
Production		
Router (12.8 machine hours × $3.50)	44.80	
Computer (28.4 machine hours × $3.50)		99.40
Product delivery		
Router	24.00	
Computer		30.00
Projected total unit cost	$239.60	$585.60

Using the target costing approach and the following data, we can determine whether Zephyr Company should produce the new products:

	Router	Computer
Target unit cost	$240.00	$580.00
Less projected unit cost	239.60	585.60
Difference	$ .40	($ 5.60)

The router can be produced below its target cost, so it should be produced. As currently designed, the computer cannot be produced at or below its target cost, so Zyphyr should either redesign it or drop plans to produce it.

S T O P • R E V I E W • A P P L Y

4-1. Describe pricing based on target costing, and state the formula used to compute a target cost.

4-2. Why is the target costing approach to pricing more useful in a competitive marketplace than cost-based pricing methods are?

Pricing Using Target Costing   Success Ltd. is considering a new product and must make a go or no-go decision when its planning team meets tomorrow. Market research shows that the unit selling price that would be agreeable to potential customers is $1,000, and the company's desired profit is 25 percent of target cost. The design engineer's preliminary estimate of the product's design, production, and distribution costs is $775 per unit. Using target costing, determine whether the company should market the new product.

SOLUTION

The company should market the new product. The target cost for the product is $800 ($1,000 ÷ 1.25). The engineer's projected cost is $775, or $25 below the amount needed to earn the desired profit.

Pricing for Internal Providers of Goods and Services

LO5   Describe how transfer pricing is used for transferring goods and services and evaluating performance within a division or segment.

So far in this chapter, we have focused on how a company sets prices for consumers outside the organization. We now turn our focus inside an organization and look at how it prices its products and services for internal transfers between divisions or segments.

As a business grows, its day-to-day operations often become too complex to be managed by a single person. To make operations more manageable, the business is usually organized into divisions or operating segments, and a separate manager is assigned to control the operations of each segment. Such a business is called a **decentralized organization**. Each division or segment often sells its goods and services both inside and outside the organization. For example, the beverage division of **Pepsico** sells its Pepsi drink products to

The average cost of a six-pack of Budweiser continues to rise. That's because **Anheuser-Busch Company**, the world's largest brewer, controls nearly half the U.S. beer market, and its competitors have traditionally followed its price lead. For many years, Anheuser-Busch has tracked the U.S. beer market by brand, market, package, and channel. The company knows that although beer consumption in the U.S. market appears recession-proof, there is little overall growth. Thus, Anheuser-Busch generally raises prices to keep pace with the consumer price index.[3]

internal customers like KFC and Taco Bell restaurants. It also sells to external customers like **Safeway** and Wal-Mart. And the **Anheuser-Busch Company's** beer segment produces and sells its products internally to Sea World amusement parks, as well as externally to unrelated entities like airlines and grocery stores.

Transfer Pricing

When divisions or segments within a company exchange goods or services and assume the role of customer or supplier for each other, they use transfer prices. A **transfer price** is the price at which goods and services are charged and exchanged between a company's divisions or segments. Transfer prices are an internal pricing mechanism that allows transactions between divisions or segments of a business to be measured and accounted for. Transfer prices affect the revenues and costs of the divisions involved. They do not affect the revenues and costs of the company as a whole. The transfer price just shifts part of the profits from the divisions or centers that externally charge for their goods or services to the divisions or centers that do not externally bill for their services and products. Transfer pricing enables a business to assess both the internal and the external profitability of its products or services. The three basic kinds of transfer prices are cost-plus transfer prices, market transfer prices, and negotiated transfer prices.

Cost-Plus Transfer Price

A **cost-plus transfer price** is based on either the full cost or the variable costs incurred by the producing division plus an agreed-on profit percentage. The weakness of the cost-plus pricing method is that cost recovery is guaranteed to the selling division. Guaranteed cost recovery prevents the company from detecting inefficient operating conditions and the incurrence of excessive costs, and it may even inappropriately reward inefficient divisions that incur excessive costs. This reduces overall company profitability and shareholder value.

Market Transfer Price

A **market transfer price** is based on the price that could be charged if a segment could buy from or sell to an external party. Some experts believe that the use of a market transfer price is preferable to the other methods. It forces the division that is "selling," or transferring, the product or service to another division to be competitive with market conditions, and it does not penalize the "buying," or receiving, division by charging it a higher price than it would have to pay if it bought from outside the firm.

However, using market prices may lead the selling division to ignore negotiation attempts from the buying division manager and to sell directly to outside customers. If this causes an internal shortage of materials and forces the buying division to purchase materials from the outside, overall company profits may decline even if the selling division makes a profit. Such use of market prices works against a company's overall operating objectives. Therefore, when market prices are used to develop transfer prices, they are usually used only as a basis for negotiation.

Negotiated Transfer Price A **negotiated transfer price** is arrived at through bargaining between the managers of the buying and selling divisions or segments. Such a transfer price may be based on an agreement to use a cost plus a profit percentage. The negotiated price will be between the negotiation floor (the selling division's variable cost) and the negotiation ceiling (the market price). This approach allows for cost recovery while still allowing the selling division to return a profit.

Study Note

A negotiated transfer price is often used for internal pricing.

Developing a Transfer Price

To illustrate the development of the three kinds of transfer prices, let's consider the Simple Box Company, a firm that makes cardboard boxes. As shown in Figure 8, this company has two divisions: the Pulp Division and the Cardboard Division. The Pulp Division produces pulp for the Cardboard Division. The Cardboard Division may also purchase pulp from outside suppliers. Exhibit 1 shows the development of a cost-plus transfer price for the Pulp Division. The Pulp Division's manager has created a one-year budget based on the expectation that the Cardboard Division will require 480,000 pounds of pulp. Unit costs appear in the last column of Exhibit 1. Notice that allocated corporate overhead is not included in the computation of the transfer price. Only the variable costs of $11.85 ($3.30 + $.70 + $1.60 + $2.40 + $1.90 + $1.95) and the fixed cost of $1.05 related to the Pulp Division are included. The profit markup of 10 percent adds $1.29, producing the final cost-plus transfer price of $14.19.

Management could now dictate that the $14.19 price be used. However, the Cardboard Division's manager could point out that it is possible to purchase pulp from an outside supplier for $13.00 per pound. Use of the $13.00 price would represent a market value approach and would be the ceiling price for

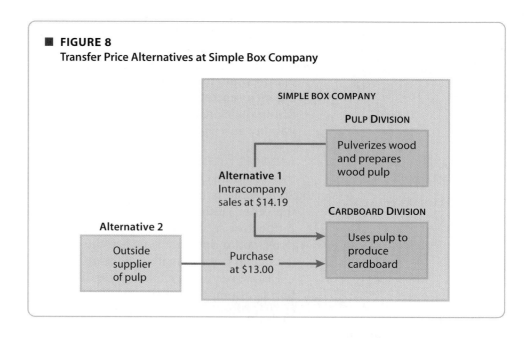

■ **FIGURE 8**
Transfer Price Alternatives at Simple Box Company

EXHIBIT 1 ▶   **Transfer Price Computation**

Simple Box Company
Pulp Division—Transfer Price Computation

Cost Categories	Budgeted Costs	Cost per Unit
Direct materials		
Wood	$1,584,000	$ 3.30
Scrap wood	336,000	.70
Direct labor		
Shaving/cleaning	768,000	1.60
Pulverizing	1,152,000	2.40
Blending	912,000	1.90
Overhead		
Variable	936,000	1.95
Fixed	504,000	1.05
Subtotals	$6,192,000	$12.90
Costs allocated from corporate office	144,000	
Target profit, 10% of division's costs	619,200	1.29
Total costs and profit	$6,955,200	
Cost-plus transfer price		$14.19

the negotiations. Usually, such situations are resolved by determining a negotiated transfer price. The best solution might be to agree on a negotiated transfer price between the variable costs of $11.85, the floor, and the outside market price of $13.00, the ceiling. The negotiation process will facilitate each manager's role in maximizing companywide profits and controlling his or her division's costs.

In this example, both managers brought their concerns to the attention of top management, and a settlement was reached. The negotiated transfer price allows for the sharing of the final product's companywide profits between the divisions when the boxes are sold on the outside market. Such an approach is often used to maintain harmony within an organization.

Additional issues may arise if the Cardboard Division chooses to purchase from outside suppliers. Because the Pulp Division has adequate capacity to fulfill the Cardboard Division's demands, it should sell to that division at any price that recovers its incremental costs. The incremental costs of intracompany sales include all variable costs of production and distribution plus any avoidable fixed costs that are directly traceable to intracompany sales. If the Cardboard Division can acquire products from outside suppliers at an annual cost that is less than the Pulp Division's incremental costs, then purchases should be made from the outside supplier because it will enhance the company's overall profits. Before making such a decision, a thorough analysis of the Pulp Division's operations should be conducted.

Study Note

The use of transfer pricing encourages accountability for seller-customer relationships.

Using Transfer Prices to Measure Performance

Because a transfer price contains an estimated amount of profit, a manager's ability to meet a targeted profit can be measured. Although transfer prices are

EXHIBIT 2 ▶ | Performance Report Using Transfer Prices

Simple Box Company
Pulp Division—Performance Report
For March 20xx

	Budget	Actual	Difference Under/(Over) Budget
Sales to Cardboard Division (42,000 lbs.)	$546,000	$546,000	$ 0
Costs Controllable by Manager			
Cost of goods sold			
Direct materials			
Wood	$138,600	$140,250	($1,650)
Scrap wood	29,400	29,750	(350)
Direct labor			
Shaving/cleaning	67,200	68,000	(800)
Pulverizing	100,800	102,000	(1,200)
Blending	79,800	80,750	(950)
Overhead			
Variable	81,900	82,875	(975)
Fixed	44,100	44,100	—
Total cost of goods sold	$541,800	$547,725	($5,925)
Gross margin from sales	$ 4,200	($ 1,725)	$5,925
Costs Uncontrollable by Manager			
Cost allocated from corporate office	12,600	12,600	—
Operating (loss)	($ 8,400)	($ 14,325)	$5,925

often called *artificial* or *created* prices, they and their related policies are closely connected with performance evaluation. When transfer prices are used, a division can be evaluated as a profit center, even if it does not sell to outsiders, because using transfer prices to value the division's output creates simulated revenues for the division. The operating income calculated in this way is not based on real sales to outsiders and is thus artificial. However, it is a valuable performance measure if the transfer prices are realistic and are determined using the methods described in this chapter.

Exhibit 2 shows a performance report for the Pulp Division of the Simple Box Company. The Pulp Division produced and transferred 42,000 pounds as budgeted at a negotiated transfer price of $13.00 per pound. The budgeted costs are based on the costs per unit in Exhibit 1. The performance report in Exhibit 2 shows that the Pulp Division's actual gross margin was ($1,725), whereas the budgeted gross margin was $4,200. The difference of $5,925 stems from cost overages in various materials, labor, and variable overhead accounts. Those differences will need to be investigated, as they would be for any division. The use of transfer prices to simulate revenues, however, allows further evaluation. For instance, the measures of operating income (loss) can be com-

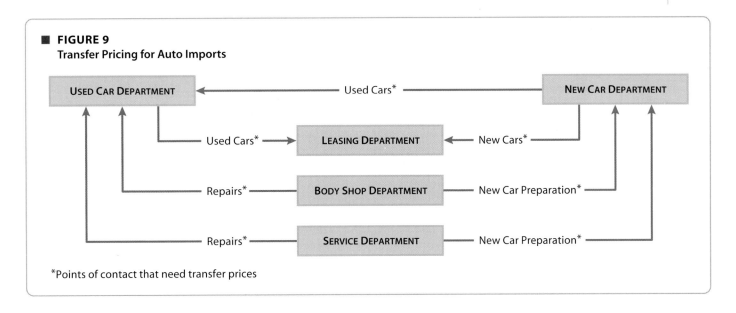

■ **FIGURE 9**
Transfer Pricing for Auto Imports

*Points of contact that need transfer prices

pared with the amount of capital the company has invested in the Pulp Division to determine whether the division is making an adequate return on the company's investment, and the impact on the division of uncontrollable costs from the corporate office can be assessed.

Transfer Pricing in Retail and Service Companies

The setting of transfer prices is an important issue for all types of businesses. For example, consider Auto Imports, an automobile dealership that sells and leases new and used cars and provides service through its Maintenance and Body Shop Departments. As shown in Figure 9, there is a need for transfer prices in at least seven points of contact among the five departments. For example, the Used Car Department receives trade-ins from the New Car Department. The Leasing Department obtains cars from both the New Car and the Used Car Departments. Auto Imports could use a cost-plus method to determine transfer prices, but because market prices are readily available for all points of contact, the company uses the market prices for transfer pricing. When market prices are used, each department may be evaluated on both its profitability and its competitiveness with outside suppliers.

STOP • REVIEW • APPLY

5-1. What is a transfer price? Why are transfer prices usually associated with decentralized companies?

5-2. Describe the cost-plus approach to setting transfer prices.

5-3. How are market prices used to develop a transfer price? Under what circumstances are market prices relevant to setting a transfer price?

5-4. "Most transfer prices are negotiated prices." Explain the meaning of this statement.

5-5. How can an organization use transfer pricing to evaluate a division's performance?

A LOOK BACK AT

PALM, INC.

In this chapter's Decision Point, we asked the following questions:

- **Why do managers generally use several pricing approaches?**
- **Why did Palm's managers use target costing to establish a price for the Zire?**

As you learned in this chapter, no one pricing method is superior because each business and market segment differs. Successful managers, like those at **Palm**, therefore generally use several pricing approaches.

Historically, in the PDA market, new models have been expensive, priced to recover the product's cost and earn a certain amount of profit. As models have aged and been replaced with newer technology, their prices have dropped. However, Palm's managers began using a different approach for their lowest-priced products. Rather than offering older technology at bargain prices, Palm decided to create a new product, the Zire, that was specifically targeted at the "under $100 market."[4] Palm's managers could not use a cost-based pricing strategy, since the price was set at less than $100 before the new product's cost was computed. Instead, they used target costing. They subtracted their desired profit from the proposed $99 price for the Zire to arrive at the maximum target cost. A team of engineering, accounting, and sales managers then analyzed each proposed product feature to verify that the product could be designed and manufactured at or below the target cost. The result is a lightweight, simple, and easy-to-use organizer.

CHAPTER REVIEW

REVIEW of Learning Objectives

LO1 Identify the objectives and rules used to establish prices of goods and services, and relate pricing issues to the management process.

A company's long-run objectives should include statements on pricing policy. Possible pricing policy objectives include (1) identifying and adhering to both short-run and long-run pricing strategies, (2) maximizing profits, (3) maintaining or gaining market share, (4) setting socially responsible prices, (5) maintaining a minimum rate of return on investment, and (6) being customer focused.

For a company to stay in business, a product's or service's selling price must (1) be competitive with the competition's price, (2) be acceptable to the customer, (3) recover all costs incurred in bringing the product or service to market, and (4) return a profit. If a manager deviates from any of these four pricing rules, there must be a specific short-run objective that accounts for the change. Breaking those pricing rules for a long period of time will force a company into bankruptcy.

Pricing issues are addressed at each step in the management process. When managers plan, they must determine how much to charge for each product or service and identify the maximum price that the market will accept and the minimum price that they can sustain. During the period, the products or services are sold at either an auction price or the specified prices. When managers evaluate performance, they analyze sales to determine which pricing strategies were successful and which failed. When managers communicate about performance inside the organization, analyses of actual versus targeted prices and profits are prepared for use.

LO2 Describe economic pricing concepts, including the auction-based pricing method used on the Internet.

The economic approach to pricing is based on microeconomic theory. Microeconomic theory states that profits will be maximized when the difference between total revenue and total cost is greatest. Total revenue then increases more slowly, because as a product is marketed, price reductions are necessary to sell more units. Total cost increases when larger quantities are produced because fixed costs change. To locate the point of maximum profit, marginal revenue and marginal cost must be computed and plotted. Profit is maximized at the point where the marginal revenue and marginal cost curves intersect. Auction-based pricing is growing in importance as a pricing mechanism as more businesses and individuals are conducting business over the Internet. Basically, the Internet allows sellers and buyers to solicit bids and transact exchanges in an open market environment. An auction-based price is set by a willing buyer and seller in a sales transaction.

LO3 Use cost-based pricing methods to develop prices.

Cost-based pricing methods include gross margin pricing and return on assets pricing. Under these two methods, a markup representing a percentage of production costs or a desired rate of return is added to the total costs. A pricing method often used by service businesses is time and materials pricing. Although managers may depend on one or two traditional approaches to pricing, they often also factor in their own experience.

LO4 Describe target costing, and use that concept to analyze pricing decisions and evaluate a new product opportunity.

Target costing enhances a company's ability to compete in the global marketplace. Instead of first determining the cost of a product and then adding a profit factor to arrive at its price, target costing reverses the procedure. Target costing (1) identifies the price at which a product will be competitive in the marketplace, (2) defines the desired profit to be made on the product, and

(3) computes the target cost for the product by subtracting the desired profit from the competitive market price. Target costing gives managers the ability to control or dictate the costs of a new product at the planning stage; under a traditional pricing system, managers cannot control costs until after the product has been manufactured. To identify a new product's target cost, the following formula is applied:

$$\text{Target Price} - \text{Desired Profit} = \text{Target Cost}$$

The target cost is then given to the engineers and product designers, who use it as a maximum cost to be incurred for materials and other resources needed to design and manufacture the product. It is their responsibility to create the product at or below its target cost. Sometimes, the cost requirements cannot be met. In such a case, the organization should try to adjust the product's design and the approach to production. If those attempts fail, the organization should either invest in new equipment and procedures or abandon its plans to market the product.

LO5 Describe how transfer pricing is used for transferring goods and services and evaluating performance within a division or segment.

A transfer price is the price at which goods and services are charged and exchanged between a company's divisions or segments. There are three primary approaches to developing transfer prices: (1) the price may be based on the cost of the item up to the point at which it is transferred to the next department or process; (2) the price may be based on market value if the item has an existing external market; or (3) the price may be negotiated by the managers of the buying and selling divisions. A cost-plus transfer price is the sum of costs incurred by the producing division plus an agreed-on profit percentage. A market-based transfer price is based on external market prices. In most cases, a negotiated transfer price is used, that is, a price is reached through bargaining between the managers of the selling and buying divisions. A division's performance may be evaluated by using transfer prices as the basis for determining revenues.

REVIEW of Concepts and Terminology

The following concepts and terms were introduced in this chapter:

Auction-based pricing: A pricing method used primarily on the Internet, where price is determined by willing buyers and sellers. **(LO2)**

Committed costs: The costs of design, development, engineering, testing, and production that are engineered into a product or service at the design stage of development and that should occur if all design specifications are followed during production. **(LO4)**

Cost-plus transfer price: A transfer price computed as the full cost or the sum of the variable costs incurred by the producing division plus an agreed-on profit percentage. **(LO5)**

Decentralized organization: An organization that has several divisions or operating segments; operating control of each segment's activities is the responsibility of the segment's manager. **(LO5)**

Gross margin pricing: A cost-based pricing approach in which the price is computed using a markup percentage based on a product's total production costs. **(LO3)**

Incurred costs: The actual costs to produce and market a product. **(LO4)**

Marginal cost: The change in total cost caused by a one-unit change in output. **(LO2)**

Marginal revenue: The change in total revenue caused by a one-unit change in output. **(LO2)**

Market transfer price: A transfer price based on the price that could be charged if a segment could buy from or sell to an external party. **(LO5)**

Negotiated transfer price: A transfer price that is arrived at through bargaining between the managers of the buying and selling divisions or segments. **(LO5)**

Return on assets pricing: A pricing method in which the objective is to earn a profit equal to a specific rate of return on the assets employed in the operation. Also called the *balance sheet approach to pricing*. **(LO3)**

Target costing: A pricing method that (1) identifies the price at which a product will be competitive in the marketplace, (2) defines the desired profit to be made on the product, and (3) computes the target cost for the product by subtracting the desired profit from the competitive market price. **(LO4)**

Time and materials pricing: An approach to pricing used by service businesses in which the total billing is composed of actual materials and parts costs and actual direct labor cost plus a percentage markup of each to cover overhead costs and a profit factor. Also called *parts and labor pricing*. **(LO3)**

Transfer price: The price at which goods and services are charged and exchanged between a company's divisions or segments. Also called *artificial* or *created prices*. **(LO5)**

REVIEW Problem

LO3   **Gross Margin Pricing**

The Enforcer Toy Company makes a complete line of toy vehicles, including a fire truck, a police cruiser, and an ambulance transport. The toys are produced on an assembly line, beginning with the Stamping Department and continuing through the Welding, Painting, and Detailing departments. The projected costs of each toy and the percentages for assigning unavoidable fixed and common costs are as follows:

Cost Categories	Total Projected Costs	Toy Fire Truck	Toy Police Cruiser	Toy Ambulance Transport
Direct materials				
Metal	$137,000	$62,500	$29,000	$45,500
Axles	5,250	2,500	1,000	1,750
Wheels	9,250	3,750	2,000	3,500
Paint	70,500	30,000	16,000	24,500
Direct labor				
Stamping	53,750	22,500	12,000	19,250
Welding	94,000	42,500	20,000	31,500
Painting	107,500	45,000	24,000	38,500
Detailing	44,250	17,500	11,000	15,750
Indirect labor	173,000	77,500	36,000	59,500
Operating supplies	30,000	12,500	7,000	10,500
Variable overhead	90,500	40,000	19,000	31,500
Fixed overhead	120,000	45%	25%	30%
Distribution expenses	105,000	40%	20%	40%
Variable marketing expenses	123,000	$55,000	$26,000	$42,000
Fixed marketing expenses	85,400	40%	25%	35%
General and administrative expenses	47,600	40%	25%	35%

Enforcer Toy's policy is to earn a minimum of 30 percent over total cost on each type of toy produced. Expected sales for the year are: fire truck, 50,000 units; police cruiser, 20,000 units; and ambulance transport, 35,000 units. Assume no change in inventory levels, and round all answers to two decimal places.

Required

1. Using the gross margin pricing method, compute the selling price for each kind of toy.
2. The competition is selling a similar fire truck for around $14. Should this influence Enforcer Toy's pricing decision? Give reasons for your answer.

Answer to Review Problem

Before the selling prices are computed, the cost analysis must be completed and restructured to supply the information that is required for the pricing computations.

Cost Categories	Total Projected Costs	Toy Fire Truck	Toy Police Cruiser	Toy Ambulance Transport
Total direct materials	$ 222,000	$ 98,750	$ 48,000	$ 75,250
Total direct labor	299,500	127,500	67,000	105,000
Indirect labor	173,000	77,500	36,000	59,500
Operating supplies	30,000	12,500	7,000	10,500
Variable overhead	90,500	40,000	19,000	31,500
Fixed overhead	120,000	54,000	30,000	36,000
Total production costs	$ 935,000	$410,250	$207,000	$317,750
Distribution expenses	$ 105,000	$ 42,000	$ 21,000	$ 42,000
Variable marketing expenses	123,000	55,000	26,000	42,000
Fixed marketing expenses	85,400	34,160	21,350	29,890
General and administrative expenses	47,600	19,040	11,900	16,660
Total selling, general, and administrative expenses	$ 361,000	$150,200	$ 80,250	$130,550
Total costs	$1,296,000	$560,450	$287,250	$448,300
Desired profit (30%)	$ 388,800	$168,135	$ 86,175	$134,490

1. Pricing using the gross margin approach

Markup percentage formula:

$$\text{Markup Percentage} = \frac{\text{Desired Profit} + \text{Total Selling, General, and Administrative Expenses}}{\text{Total Production Costs}}$$

Gross margin pricing formula:

$$\text{Gross Margin–Based Price} = \text{Total Production Costs per Unit} + (\text{Markup Percentage} \times \text{Total Production Costs per Unit})$$

Fire truck:

$$\text{Markup Percentage} = \frac{\$168,135 + \$150,200}{\$410,250} = 77.60\%$$

Gross Margin–Based Price = ($410,250 ÷ 50,000) + [77.6% × ($410,250 ÷ 50,000)] = $14.57

Police cruiser:

$$\text{Markup Percentage} = \frac{\$86,175 + \$80,250}{\$207,000} = 80.40\%$$

Gross Margin–Based Price = ($207,000 ÷ 20,000) + [80.4% × ($207,000 ÷ 20,000)] = $18.67

Ambulance transport:

$$\text{Markup Percentage} = \frac{\$134,490 + \$130,550}{\$317,750} = 83.41\%$$

Gross Margin–Based Price = ($317,750 ÷ 35,000) + [83.41% × ($317,750 ÷ 35,000)] = $16.65

2. Competition's influence on price: If the competition's toy fire truck is similar in quality and design, Enforcer Toy's management should consider reducing the price of its truck to the $14.00 range. At $14.57, Enforcer has a 30 percent profit built into its price. The fire truck's breakeven is at $11.21 ($14.57 ÷ 1.3). Therefore, the company could reduce its price below the competitor's price and still make a significant profit.

CHAPTER ASSIGNMENTS

BUILDING Your Basic Knowledge and Skills

Short Exercises

LO1 Rules for Establishing Prices

SE 1. Jason Kellam is planning to open a pizza restaurant next month in Flora, Alabama. He plans to sell his large pizzas for a base price of $18 plus $2 for each topping selected. When asked how he arrived at the base price, he said that his cousin developed that price for his pizza restaurant in New York City. What pricing rules has Jason Kellam not followed?

LO1 External Factors That Influence Prices

SE 2. Your client is about to introduce a very high-quality product that will remove an invasive form of pepper bush in the southern United States. The Marketing Department has established a price of $37 per gallon, and the company controller has projected total production, selling, and distribution costs of $26 per gallon. What other factors should your client consider before introducing the product into the marketplace?

LO2 Traditional Economic Pricing Concept

SE 3. You are to decide the total demand for a particular product. Assume that the product you are evaluating has the total cost and total revenue curves pictured in Figure 3A in this chapter. Also assume that the difference between total revenue and total cost is the same at the 4,000- and 9,000-unit levels. If you had to choose between those two levels of activity as goals for total sales over the life of the product, which would you prefer? Why?

LO3 Cost-Based Price Setting

SE 4. The Windwalker Company has collected the following data for one of its product lines: total production costs, $300,000; total selling, general, and administrative expenses, $112,600; desired profit, $67,400; and production costs per unit, $50. Using the gross margin pricing method, compute a suggested selling price for this product that would yield the desired profit.

LO3 Pricing a Service

SE 5. Evan Nathan runs a home repair business. Recently he gathered the following cost information about the repair of a client's pool deck: replacement wood, $650; deck screws and supplies, $112; and labor, 12 hours at $14 per hour. Nathan applies a 40 percent overhead rate to all direct costs of a job. Compute the total billing price for the repair of the pool deck.

LO4 **Committed Costs and Target Costing**

SE 6. Nanci Osborne is a design engineer for Dash Enterprises. In a discussion about a proposed new product, Osborne stated that the product's projected target cost was $6.50 below the committed costs identified by design estimates. Given this information, should the company proceed with the new product? Explain your answer, and include a definition of committed cost in your analysis.

LO4 **Pricing Using Target Costing**

SE 7. JTZ Furniture is considering a new product and must make a go or no-go decision before tomorrow's planning team meeting. Market research shows that the unit selling price agreeable to potential customers is $1,600, and the company's desired profit is 22 percent of target cost. The design engineer's preliminary estimate of the product's design, production, and distribution costs is $1,380 per unit. Using target costing, determine whether the company should market the new product.

LO5 **Decision to Use Transfer Prices**

SE 8. The production process at Premier Castings includes eight processes, each of which is currently treated as a cost center with a specific set of operations to perform on each casting produced. Following the fourth process's operations, the rough castings have an external market. The fourth process must also supply the fifth process with its direct materials. The management of Premier Castings wants to develop a new approach to measuring process performance. Is Premier a candidate for using transfer prices? Explain your answer.

LO5 **Cost-Based Versus Market-Based Transfer Prices**

SE 9. Refer to the information in SE 8. Should Premier Castings use economic-based, cost-based, market-based, or negotiated transfer prices?

LO5 **Developing a Negotiated Transfer Price**

SE 10. The Molding Process at Trophy Products has been treated as a cost center since the company was founded in 1968. Recently, management decided to change the performance evaluation approach and treat its processes as profit centers. Each process is expected to earn a 20 percent profit on its total production costs. One of Trophy's products is a plastic base for a display chest. The Molding Process supplies this base to the Cabinet Process, and it also sells the base to another company. Molding's total production cost for the base is $27.40. It sells the base to the other company for $38.00. What should the transfer price for the plastic base be?

Exercises

LO1 **Pricing Policy Objectives**

E 1. Old Denim, Ltd., is an international clothing company that retails medium-priced goods. Its retail outlets are located throughout the United States, France, Germany, and Great Britain. Management wants to maintain the company's image of providing the highest possible quality at the lowest possible prices. Selling prices are developed to draw customers away from competitors' stores. First-of-the-month sales are regularly held at all stores, and customers are accustomed to this practice. Company buyers are carefully trained to seek out quality goods at inexpensive prices. Sales are targeted to increase a minimum of 5 percent per year. All sales should yield a 15 percent return on assets. Sales personnel are expected to wear Old Denim clothing while working, and all personnel can purchase clothing at 10 percent above cost. All stores are required to be clean and well organized. Competitors' prices are checked daily. Identify the pricing policy objectives of Old Denim, Ltd.

LO1 **External and Internal Pricing Factors**

E 2. Towne's Tire Outlet features more than a dozen brands of tires in many sizes. Two of the brands are Gripper and Roadster, both imports. The tire size 205/70-VR15 is available in both brands. The following information about the two brands was obtained:

	Gripper	Roadster
Selling price:		
Single tire, installed	$125	$110
Set of four tires, installed	460	400
Cost per tire	90	60

As shown, selling prices include installation costs. Each Gripper or Roadster tire costs $20 to mount and balance.

1. Compute each brand's net unit selling price after installation for both a single tire and a set of four.
2. Was cost the main consideration in setting those prices?
3. What other factors could have influenced those prices?

LO2 **Traditional Economic Pricing Theory**

E 3. Texaza, a product design firm, has just completed a contract to develop a wireless phone keychain. The phone keychain needs to be recharged only once a week and can be used worldwide. Initial fixed costs for this product are $4,000. The designers estimate that the product will break even at the $5,000/100-unit mark. Total revenues will again equal total costs at the $25,000/900-unit point. Marginal cost is expected to equal marginal revenue when 550 units are sold.

1. Sketch total revenue and total cost curves for this product. Mark the vertical axis at each $5,000 increment and the horizontal axis at each 100-unit increment.
2. Based on your total revenue and total cost curves in 1, at what unit selling price will profits be maximized?

LO2 **ebusiness**

E 4. Visit the websites of **Priceline.com** and **eBay.com**. Write a brief comparison of each site's features. Which site do you prefer, and why?

LO3 **Price Determination**

E 5. Gillson Industries has just patented a new product called Gleam, an automobile wax for lasting protection against the elements. The company's controller has developed the following annual information for use in price determination meetings:

Variable production costs	$1,110,000
Fixed overhead	540,000
Selling expenses	225,000
General and administrative expenses	350,000
Desired profit	250,000
Cost of assets employed	1,000,000

Annual demand for the product is expected to be 250,000 cans. On average, the company now earns a 10 percent return on assets.

1. Compute the projected unit cost for one can of Gleam.
2. Using gross margin pricing, compute the markup percentage and selling price for one can.
3. Using return on assets pricing, compute the unit price for one can.

LO3   Pricing a Service

E 6. Texas has just passed a law making it mandatory to have every head of cattle inspected at least once a year for a variety of communicable diseases. Big Springs Enterprises is considering entering this inspection business. After extensive studies, Tex Autry, the owner of Big Springs Enterprises, has developed the following annual projections:

Direct service labor	$525,000
Variable service overhead costs	250,000
Fixed service overhead costs	225,000
Selling expenses	142,500
General and administrative expenses	157,500
Minimum desired profit	120,000
Cost of assets employed	750,000

Autry believes his company could inspect 250,000 head of cattle per year. On average, the company now earns a 16 percent return on assets.

1. Compute the projected cost of inspecting each head of cattle.
2. Determine the price to charge for inspecting each head of cattle. Use gross margin pricing.
3. Using return on assets pricing, compute the unit price to charge for this inspection service.

LO3   Cost-based Pricing

E 7. Hometown Bank is determining the price for its newest mini debit card. The card can be used at any retail outlet with a swipe reader and is small enough to attach to a key chain—no PIN number or signature is required. Sigrid Olmo has developed the following annual information for use in upcoming price determination meetings.

Variable processing costs	$50 million
Fixed processing costs	36 million
Selling expenses (fixed)	10 million
General and administrative expenses (fixed)	4 million
Desired profit	3 billion
Cost of assets employed	10 billion

Annual usage is expected to be 10 billion transactions. On average, the company now earns a 6 percent return on assets.

1. Compute the projected cost of one transaction.
2. Using gross margin pricing, compute the price to charge per transaction.
3. Using return on assets pricing, compute the price to charge per transaction.

LO3   Pricing Services

E 8. Gator Car Repair specializes in repairing rental cars. The company uses a 50 percent markup rate on parts to cover parts-related overhead costs and profit margin. It uses a 100 percent markup rate on labor to cover labor-related overhead costs and profit margin. Compute the bill for a recent job that used the following parts and labor:

Material and repair parts used	$600
Labor used	5 hours at $40 per hour

LO3 Time and Materials Pricing

E 9. Cruz's Home Remodeling Service specializes in refurbishing older homes. Last week Cruz was asked to bid on a remodeling job for the town's mayor. His list of materials and labor needed to complete the job is as follows:

Materials		Labor	
Lumber	$ 6,500	Carpenter	$2,000
Nails/bolts	160	Floor specialist	1,300
Paint	1,420	Painter	1,500
Glass	2,890	Supervisor	1,420
Doors	730	Helpers	1,680
Hardware	600	Total	$7,900
Supplies	400		
Total	$12,700		

The company uses an overhead markup percentage for materials (60 percent) and for labor (40 percent). Those markups cover all operating costs. In addition, Cruz expects to make at least a 25 percent profit on all jobs. Compute the price that Cruz should quote for the mayor's job.

LO4 Target Costing and Pricing

E 10. Environ Company has determined that its new fireplace screen would gain widespread customer acceptance if the company could price it at or under $90. Anticipated labor hours and costs for each unit of the new product are as follows:

Direct materials cost	$15
Direct labor cost	
Manufacturing labor	
Hours	1.2
Hourly labor rate	$12
Assembly labor	
Hours	1.5
Hourly labor rate	$10
Machine hours	2

The company currently uses the following three activity-based cost rates:

Materials handling	$1.30 per dollar of direct materials
Production	$3.00 per machine hour
Product delivery	$5.50 per unit

The company's minimum desired profit is 25 percent over total production and delivery cost. Compute the target cost for the new fireplace screen, and determine if the company should market it.

LO4 Target Costing

E 11. Assume the same facts as in **E 10** except that the company's minimum desired profit has been revised to 10 percent over production and delivery costs as a result of a recent economic downturn. Compute the revised target cost for the new fireplace screen, and determine if the company should market it.

LO4 Target Costing

E 12. Suppose that **Ikea**, the Swedish retailer, is developing a new chair targeted to sell for less than $100 and that it is considering the following two production alternatives. Rank the alternatives, assuming that the company's minimum desired profit is 30 percent over total production costs.

	Alternative A	Alternative B
Direct material costs	$35	$20
Direct labor cost	1 hour at $12 per hour	2 hours at $8 per hour
Overhead costs	200 percent of direct labor costs	$2 per dollar of direct materials

LO4 **Target Costing**

E 13. Management at Fox Valley Machine Tool Co. is considering the development of a new automated drill press called the AutoDrill. After conferring with the design engineers, the controller's staff assembled the following data about this product:

Target selling price	$7,500 per unit
Desired profit percentage	25% of total unit cost
Projected unit demand	4,500 Units
Activity-based cost rates	
Materials handling	5% of direct materials and purchased parts cost
Engineering	$300 per unit for AutoDrill
Production and assembly	$50 per machine hour
Delivery	$570 per unit for AutoDrill
Marketing	$400 per unit for AutoDrill
Per-unit data	
Direct materials cost	$1,620
Purchased parts cost	$840
Manufacturing labor	
Hours	6
Hourly labor rate	$14
Assembly labor	
Hours	10
Hourly labor rate	$15
Machine hours	30

1. Compute the product's target cost.
2. Compute the product's projected unit cost based on the design engineers' estimates.
3. Should management produce and market the AutoDrill? Defend your answer.

LO5 **Transfer Price Comparison**

E 14. Mary Janus is developing a transfer price for the housing section of an automatic pool-cleaning device. The housing for the device is made in Department A. It is then passed on to Department D, where final assembly occurs. Unit costs for the housing are as follows:

Cost Categories	Unit Costs
Direct materials	$5.20
Direct labor	2.30
Variable overhead	1.30
Fixed overhead	2.60
Profit markup, 20% of cost	?

An outside vendor can supply the housing for $13.00 per unit.

1. Develop a cost-plus transfer price for the housing.
2. What should the transfer price be? Support your answer.

LO5 **Transfer Pricing**

E 15. Patch Watch Company's Seconds Store offers refurbished or factory seconds time-keeping products to the public at substantially reduced prices. The factory controller is developing transfer price alternatives to present to management to determine the best price to use when transferring products from the factory to the store, using the following data:

Unit price if sold to outside retailers	$25
Variable product cost per unit	10
Fixed product cost per unit	5
Seconds store profit markup	40%

1. What is the market-based transfer price alternative?
2. What is the minimum transfer price alternative?
3. Compute the cost-plus transfer price alternative assuming cost includes variable costs only.

Problems

LO3 **Pricing Decision**

P 1. Ed Vetz & Company specializes in the assembly of home appliances. One division focuses most of its efforts on assembling a standard toaster oven. Projected costs of this product for 20xx are as follows:

Cost Description	Budgeted Costs
Toaster casings	$ 960,000
Electrical components	2,244,000
Direct labor	3,648,000
Variable indirect assembly costs	780,000
Fixed indirect assembly costs	1,740,000
Selling expenses	1,536,000
General operating expenses	840,000
Administrative expenses	816,000

The projected costs are based on an estimated demand of 600,000 toaster ovens per year. The company wants to make a $1,260,000 profit.

Competitors have just published their wholesale prices for the coming year. They range from $21.60 to $22.64 per oven. The Vetz toaster oven is known for its high quality and modern look. It competes with products at the top end of the price range. Even with its reputation, however, every $.20 increase above the top competitor's price causes a drop in demand of 60,000 units below the original estimate. Assume that all price changes are in $.20 increments.

Required

1. Prepare a schedule of total projected costs and unit costs.
2. Use gross margin pricing to compute the anticipated selling price.
3. Based on competitors' prices, what should the Vetz toaster sell for in 20xx (assume a constant unit cost)? Defend your answer. (Hint: Determine the total profit at various sales levels.)
4. Manager Insight: Would your pricing structure in **3** change if the company had only limited competition at its quality level? If so, in what direction? Explain why.

LO3 **Cost-Based Pricing**

P 2. Centered Publishing Company specializes in health awareness books. Because the field of health awareness is very competitive, Jay Rosenbek, the company's president, maintains a strict policy about selecting manuscripts to publish. Rosenbek wants to publish only books whose projected earnings are 20 percent above total projected costs. Three titles were accepted for publication during 20x8. The authors of those books are Tone, Tyme, and Klay. Projected costs for each book and allocation percentages for common costs are shown below.

Cost Categories	Tone Book	Tyme Book	Klay Book	Total Projected Costs
Direct labor	$146,250	$243,750	$97,500	$487,500
Royalty costs	36,000	60,000	24,000	120,000
Printing costs	74,580	124,300	49,720	248,600
Supplies	10,260	17,100	6,840	34,200
Variable production costs	42,600	71,000	28,400	142,000
Fixed production costs	35%	40%	25%	168,000
Distribution costs	30%	50%	20%	194,000
Marketing costs	$ 61,670	$ 90,060	$42,270	194,000
General and administrative costs	35%	40%	25%	52,400

Expected sales for 20x8 are as follows: Tone, 26,000 copies; Tyme, 32,000 copies; and Klay, 20,000 copies.

Required

1. Prepare a cost analysis that computes the desired profit for each of the three books and in total.
2. Use gross margin pricing to compute the selling price for each book. (Hint: Treat royalty costs as production costs.)
3. **Manager Insight:** If the competition's average selling price for a book similar to Klay's is $22, should this influence the pricing decision? Explain.

LO3   Time and Materials Pricing in a Service Business

P 3. Ace Maintenance, Inc., repairs heavy construction equipment and vehicles. Recently, the Shanti Construction Company had one of its giant earthmovers overhauled and its tires replaced. Repair work for a vehicle of that size usually takes from one week to ten days. The vehicle must be lifted up so that maintenance workers can gain access to the engine. Parts are normally so large that a crane must be used to put them into place.

The company uses the time and materials pricing system and data from the previous year to compute markup percentages for overhead related to parts and materials and overhead related to direct labor. It adds markups of 130 percent to the cost of materials and parts and 140 percent to the cost of direct labor to cover overhead and profit. The following materials, parts, and direct labor are needed to repair the giant earthmover:

Quantity		Unit Price	Hours		Hourly Rate
Materials and parts			Direct labor		
24	Spark plugs	$ 3.40	42	Mechanic	$18.20
20	Oil, quarts	2.90	54	Assistant mechanic	12.00
12	Hoses	11.60			
1	Water pump	764.00			
30	Coolant, quarts	6.50			
18	Clamps	5.90			
1	Distributor cap	128.40			
1	Carburetor	214.10			
4	Tires	820.00			

Required

Prepare a complete billing for this job. Include itemized amounts for each type of materials, parts, and direct labor. Follow the time and materials pricing approach, and show the total price for the job.

LO4 **Pricing Using Target Costing**

P 4. Young Joon Corp. is considering marketing two new graphing calculators, named Speed-Calc 4 and Speed-Calc 5. According to recent market research, the two products will surpass the current competition in both speed and quality and would be welcomed in the market. Customers would be willing to pay $98 for Speed-Calc 4 and $110 for Speed-Calc 5, based on their projected design capabilities. Both products have many uses, but the primary market interest comes from college students. Current production capacity exists for the manufacture and assembly of the two products. The company has a minimum desired profit of 25 percent above all costs for all of its products. Current activity-based cost rates are as follows:

Materials/parts handling	$1.20 per dollar of direct materials and purchased parts cost
Production	8.00 per machine hour
Marketing/delivery	4.40 per unit of Speed-Calc 4
	6.20 per unit of Speed-Calc 5

Design engineering and accounting estimates to produce the two new products are as follows:

	Speed-Calc 4	Speed-Calc 5
Projected unit demand	100,000	80,000
Per-unit data		
Direct materials cost	$5.50	$7.50
Computer chip cost	$10.60	$11.70
Production labor		
Hours	1.2	1.3
Hourly labor rate	$16.00	$16.00
Assembly labor		
Hours	0.6	0.5
Hourly labor rate	$12.00	$12.00
Machine hours	1	1.2

Required

1. Compute the target costs for each product.
2. Compute the projected total unit cost of production and delivery.
3. Using the target costing approach, decide whether the products should be produced.

LO5 **Developing Transfer Prices**

P 5. Cylinder Company has two divisions, Glass Division and Instrument Division. For several years, Glass Division has manufactured a special glass container, which it sells to Instrument Division at the prevailing market price of $20. Glass Division produces the glass containers only for Instrument Division and does not sell the product to outside customers. Annual production and sales volume is 20,000 containers. A unit cost analysis for Glass Division showed the following:

Cost Categories	Costs per Container
Direct materials	$ 3.50
Direct labor, 1 1/4 hours	2.30
Variable overhead	7.50
Avoidable fixed costs	
$30,000 ÷ 20,000	1.50
Corporate overhead, $18 per direct labor hour	4.50
Variable shipping costs	1.20
Unit cost	$20.50

Corporate overhead represents the allocated joint fixed costs of production—building depreciation, property taxes, insurance, and executives' salaries. A profit markup of 20 percent is used to determine transfer prices.

Required

1. What would be the appropriate transfer price for Glass Division to use in billing its transactions with Instrument Division?
2. If Glass Division decided to sell some containers to outside customers, would your answer to 1 change? Defend your response.
3. Manager Insight: What factors concerning transfer price should management consider when transferring products between divisions?

Alternate Problems

LO3 **Pricing Decision**

P 6. Sumac & Oak, Ltd., designs and assembles low-priced portable Internet devices. It estimates that there will be 235,000 requests for its most popular model. Budgeted costs for this product for the year are as follows:

Description	Budgeted Costs
Casing	$ 432,400
Battery chamber	545,200
Electronics	1,151,500
Direct labor	1,598,000
Variable indirect assembly costs	789,600
Fixed indirect assembly costs	338,400
Selling expenses	493,500
General operating expenses	183,300
Administrative expenses	126,900

The budget is based on the demand previously stated. The company wants to earn an annual operating income of $846,000.

Last week four competitors released their wholesale prices for the year. Their prices are as follows: Competitor A, $25.68; Competitor B, $24.58; Competitor C, $23.96; Competitor D, $25.30

Sumac & Oak portable devices are known for their high quality. However, every $1 price increase above the top competitor's price causes a 55,000-unit drop in demand from the original estimate. (Assume all price changes occur in $1 increments.)

Required

1. Prepare a schedule of total projected costs and unit costs.
2. Use gross margin pricing to compute the anticipated selling price.
3. Based on competitors' prices, what should Sumac & Oak's portable device sell for (assume a constant unit cost)? Defend your answer. (**Hint:** Determine the total operating income at various sales levels.)

4. **Manager Insight:** Would your pricing structure in **3** change if the company had only limited competition at this quality level? If so, in what direction? Explain why.

LO4 Pricing Using Target Costing

P 7. Clevenger Machine Tool Company designs and produces a line of high-quality machine tools and markets them throughout the world. Its main competition comes from French, British, and Korean companies. Five competitors have recently introduced two highly specialized machine tools, Y14 and Z33. The prices charged for Y14 range from $625 to $675 per tool, and the price range for Z33 is from $800 to $840 per tool. Clevenger is contemplating entering the market for these two products. Market research has indicated that if Clevenger can sell Y14 for $650 per tool and Z33 for $750 per tool, it will be successful in marketing the products worldwide. The company's profit markup is 25 percent over all costs to produce and deliver a product. Current activity-based cost rates are as follows:

Materials handling	$ 1.30 per dollar of direct materials and purchased parts cost
Production	$ 4.40 per machine hour
Product delivery	$34.00 per unit of Y14
	$40.00 per unit of Z33

Design engineering and accounting estimates for the production of the two new products are as follows:

	Product Y14	Product Z33
Projected unit demand	75,000	95,000
Per-unit data		
Direct materials cost	$50.00	$60.00
Purchased parts cost	$65.00	$70.00
Manufacturing labor		
Hours	6.2	7.4
Hourly labor rate	$14.00	$14.00
Assembly labor		
Hours	4.6	9.2
Hourly labor rate	$12.00	$12.00
Machine hours	14	16

Required

1. Compute the target cost for each product.
2. Compute the total projected unit cost of producing and delivering each product.
3. Using target costing, decide whether the products should be produced.

LO5 Developing Transfer Prices

P 8. Sims Corporation produces sound equipment for home use. Its Research and Development (R & D) Division is responsible for continually evaluating and updating critical electronic parts used in the corporation's products. Two years ago, R & D took on the added responsibility of producing all microchip circuit boards for the company's sound equipment. One of Sims's specialties is a sound dissemination board (SDB) that greatly enhances the quality of Sims's speakers.

Demand for the SDB has increased significantly in the past year. As a result, R & D has increased its production and assembly labor force. Three outside customers now want to purchase the SDB. To date, R & D has been producing SDBs for internal use only.

The R & D controller wants to create a transfer price for the SDBs that will apply to all intracompany transfers. Estimated demand over the next six months is 235,000 SDBs for internal use and 165,000 SDBs for external customers, for a total of 400,000 units. The following data show cost projections for the next six months:

Materials and parts	$2,600,000
Direct labor	1,920,000
Supplies	100,000
Indirect labor	580,000
Other variable overhead costs	200,000
Fixed overhead, SDBs	1,840,000
Other fixed overhead, corporate	560,000
Variable selling expenses, SDBs	1,480,000
Fixed selling expenses, corporate	520,000
General corporate operating expenses	880,000
Corporate administrative expenses	680,000

A profit markup of at least 20 percent must be added to total unit cost for internal transfer purposes. Outside customers are willing to pay $35 for each SDB. All categories of fixed costs are assumed to be unavoidable.

Required

1. Prepare a table that shows the total budgeted costs and the cost per unit for each component of the budget. Also show the profit markup and the cost-plus transfer price.
2. **Manager Insight:** Should R & D use the computed transfer price? Explain the factors that influenced your decision.

ENHANCING Your Knowledge, Skills, and Critical Thinking

Conceptual Understanding Cases

LO1, LO2 **Product Differentiation and Pricing**

C 1. Maytag Corporation can price its products higher than any other company in the home appliance industry and still maintain and even increase market share. How can it do this? Are its costs higher, resulting in higher prices than those of its competitors? No. Will customers shop around for products with lower price tags? No. Will competitors single out Maytag products in comparative ad campaigns and try to exploit the higher prices? No. Think about the Maytag repairman television commercials that you have seen over the past ten years. They feature a very lonely person who never gets a call to repair a Maytag product. The ads say nothing about price. They do not attack competitors' products. But the commercials do inspire customers to purchase Maytag products through what is known in the marketing field as product differentiation. Prepare a one-page memo to your teacher explaining how Maytag Corporation has differentiated its products from the competition. Is product cost a factor in Maytag's pricing strategy?

LO2 **Comparison of Pricing Policies**

C 2. E*TRADE and **Ameritrade** offer Internet stock-trading services at a very low price compared to traditional brokers. Both companies have been growing very rapidly in recent years. What internal and external factors influence the setting of prices? Why would the prices of online brokerage firms differ so greatly from the prices of traditional brokerage firms? Include in your answer a discussion of the role of marginal cost and marginal revenue as it may apply to such companies.

LO3, LO4 **Product Pricing in a Foreign Market**

C 3. Borner, Inc., is an international corporation that manufactures and sells home care products. Today, a meeting is being held at corporate headquarters in New York City. The purpose of the meeting is to discuss changing the price of the laundry detergent the company manufactures and sells in Brazil. During the meeting, a conflict develops between Carl Dickson, the corporate sales manager, and José Cabral, the Brazilian Division's sales manager.

Dickson insists that the selling price of the laundry detergent should be increased to the equivalent of U.S. $3. This increase is necessary because the Brazilian Division's costs are higher than those of other international divisions. The Brazilian Division is paying high interest rates on notes payable for the acquisition of a new manufacturing plant. In addition, a stronger, more expensive ingredient has been introduced into the laundry detergent, which has caused the product cost to increase by $.20.

Cabral believes that the laundry detergent's selling price should remain at $2.50 for several reasons. He argues that the market for laundry detergent in Brazil is highly competitive. Labor costs are low, and the costs of distribution are small because the target market is limited to the Rio de Janeiro metropolitan area. Inflation is extremely high in Brazil, and the Brazilian government continues to impose policies to control inflation. Because of these controls, Cabral insists, buyers will resist any price hikes.

1. What selling price do you believe Borner, Inc., should set for the laundry detergent? Explain your answer. Do you believe Borner should let the Brazilian Division set the selling price for laundry detergent in the future? When should corporate headquarters set prices?
2. Based on the information given above, should cost-based pricing or target costing be used to set the selling price for laundry detergent in Brazil? Explain your answer.

LO3 **Pricing Decisions**

C 4. The Fastener Company manufactures office equipment for retail stores. Carol Watson, the vice president of marketing, has proposed that Fastener introduce two new products: an electric stapler and an electric pencil sharpener. Watson has requested that the Profit Planning Department develop preliminary selling prices for the two new products for her review.

Profit Planning has followed the company's standard policy for developing potential selling prices. It has used all data available for each product. The data accumulated by Profit Planning are as follows:

	Electric Stapler	Electric Pencil Sharpener
Estimated annual demand in units	16,000	12,000
Estimated unit manufacturing costs	$14.00	$15.00
Estimated unit selling and administrative expenses	$3.00	Not available
Assets employed in manufacturing	$160,000	Not available

Fastener plans to use an average of $1,200,000 in assets to support operations in the current year. The condensed budgeted income statement that follows reflects the planned return on assets of 20 percent ($240,000 ÷ $1,200,000) for the entire company for all products.

Fastener Company
Budgeted Income Statement
For the Year Ended May 31
($000 omitted)

Revenue	$2,400
Cost of goods sold	1,440
Gross profit	$ 960
Selling and administrative expenses	720
Operating income	$ 240

1. Calculate a potential selling price for (a) the stapler, using return on assets pricing, and (b) the pencil sharpener, using gross margin pricing.
2. Could a selling price for the electric pencil sharpener be calculated using return on assets pricing? Explain your answer.
3. Which of the two pricing methods—return on assets pricing or gross margin pricing—is more appropriate for decision analysis? Explain your answer.
4. Discuss the additional steps Carol Watson is likely to take in setting an actual selling price for each of the two products after she receives their potential selling prices (as calculated in 1). (CMA adapted)

Interpreting Management Reports

LO5 **Transfer Pricing**

C 5. Cirrus Industries, Inc., has two major operating divisions, the Cabinet Division and the Electronics Division. The company's main product is a deluxe console television set. The TV cabinets are manufactured by the Cabinet Division, and the Electronics Division produces all electronic components and assembles the sets. The company has a decentralized organizational structure.

The Cabinet Division not only supplies cabinets to the Electronics Division, but also sells cabinets to other TV manufacturers. The following unit cost breakdown for a deluxe television cabinet was developed based on a typical sales order of 40 cabinets:

Direct materials	$ 32.00
Direct labor	15.00
Variable overhead	12.00
Fixed overhead	18.00
Variable selling expenses	9.00
Fixed selling expenses	6.00
Fixed general and administrative expenses	8.00
Total unit cost	$100.00

The Cabinet Division's usual profit margin is 20 percent, and the regular selling price of a deluxe cabinet is $120. The division's managers recently decided that $120 will also be the transfer price for all intracompany transactions.

Managers at the Electronics Division are unhappy with that decision. They claim that the Cabinet Division will show superior performance at the expense of the Electronics Division. Competition recently forced the company to lower its prices. Because of the newly established transfer price for the cabinet, the Electronics Division's portion of the profit margin on deluxe television sets was lowered to 18 percent. To counteract the new intracompany transfer price, the managers of the Electronics Division announced that effective immediately, all cabinets will be purchased from an outside supplier, in lots of 200 cabinets at a unit price of $110 per cabinet. The company president, Joe Springer, has called a meeting of both divisions to negotiate a fair intracompany transfer price. The following prices were listed as possible alternatives:

Current market price	$120 per cabinet
Current outside purchase price (This price is based on a large-quantity purchase discount. It will cause increased storage costs for the Electronics Division.)	$110 per cabinet
Total unit manufacturing costs plus a 20 percent profit margin: $77.00 + $15.40	$ 92.40 per cabinet
Total unit costs excluding variable selling expenses plus a 20 percent profit margin: $91.00 + $18.20	$109.20 per cabinet

1. What price should be established for intracompany transactions? Defend your answer by showing the shortcomings of each alternative.
2. If there were an outside market for all units produced by the Cabinet Division at the $120 price, would you change your answer to 1? Why?

Decision Analysis Using Excel

LO4 **Target Costing**

C 6. Every Electronics, Inc., produces circuit boards for electronic devices that are made by more than a dozen customers. Competition among the producers of circuit boards is keen, with over 30 companies bidding on every job request from those customers. The circuit boards can vary widely in their complexity, and their unit prices can range from $250 to more than $500.

Every's controller is concerned that the cost planning projection for a new complex circuit board, the CX35, is almost 6 percent above its target cost. The controller has asked the Engineering Design Department to review its design and projections and come up with alternatives that will reduce the proposed product's costs to equal to or below the target cost. The following information was used to develop the initial cost projections:

Target selling price	$590.00 per unit
Desired profit percentage	25% of total unit cost
Projected unit demand	13,600 units
Per-unit data	
Direct materials cost	$56.00
Purchased parts cost	$37.00
Manufacturing labor	
Hours	4.5
Hourly labor rate	$14.00
Assembly labor	
Hours	5.2
Hourly labor rate	$15.00
Machine hours	26
Activity-based cost rates	
Materials handling	10% of direct materials and purchased parts cost
Engineering	$13.50 per unit for CX35
Production	$8.20 per machine hour
Product delivery	$24.00 per unit for CX35
Marketing	$6.00 per unit for CX35

1. Compute the product's target cost.
2. Compute the product cost of the original estimate to verify that the controller's calculations were correct.
3. Rework the product cost calculations for each of the following alternatives recommended by the design engineers:

   a. Cut product quality, which will reduce direct materials cost by 20 percent and purchased parts cost by 15 percent.
   b. Increase the quality of direct materials, which will increase direct materials cost by 20 percent but will reduce machine hours by 10 percent, manufacturing labor hours by 16 percent, and assembly labor hours by 20 percent.

4. What decision should the management of Every Electronics, Inc., make about the new product? Defend your answer.

Ethical Dilemma Case

LO1, LO2   **Ethics in Pricing**

C 7. Barnes Company has been doing business with mainland China for the past three years. The company produces leather handbags that are in great demand in the cities of China. On a recent trip to Hong Kong, Kwan Cho, the purchasing agent for Shen Enterprises, approached Barnes salesperson Harriet Makay to arrange for a purchase of 2,500 handbags. Barnes's usual price is $75 per bag. Kwan Cho wanted to purchase the handbags at $65 per bag. After an hour of haggling, they agreed to a final price of $68 per item. When Makay returned to her hotel room after dinner, she found an envelope containing five new $100 bills and a note that said, "Thank you for agreeing to our order of 2,500 handbags at $68 per bag. My company's president wants you to have the enclosed gift for your fine service." Makay later learned that Kwan Cho was following her company's normal business practice. What should Harriet Makay do? Is the gift hers to keep? Be prepared to justify your opinion.

Internet Case

LO4   **Target Costing and the Internet**

C 8. Assume that you work for a company that wants to develop a product to compete with **Palm's** Zire. You have been assigned the task of using target costing to help in its development. Do a search for Zire product reviews and product specifications and get price quotes. Why would your company's management want to use target costing to help in its development of a competitive PDA? What retail price would you suggest be used as a basis for target costing? Assuming a desired profit of 25 percent of selling price, what is the resulting target cost? What actions should the company take now?

Group Activity Case

LO5   **Transfer Pricing**

C 9. One reason that companies use transfer prices is to allow cost centers to function and be evaluated as profit centers. Transfer prices are artificial prices charged to one department by another for internally manufactured parts and products that are used by the "purchasing" department. Transfer pricing policies and methods have generated much controversy in recent years. Use an Internet search engine like Google or Ask Jeeves to locate an article about transfer prices. Prepare a one-page summary of the article, and use it as the basis for a classroom presentation. Include in your summary the name and website of the publication, the article's title and author(s), a list of the issues being discussed, and a brief statement about the conclusions reached by the author(s).

Your instructor will divide the class into groups and ask each group to discuss this case. One student from each group will summarize his or her group's findings and debrief the entire class.

Business Communication Case

LO5   **Transfer Prices and Performance Evaluation**

C 10. "That Champions Division is robbing us blind!" This statement by the director of the Tournament Division was heard during the meeting of the board of directors at Golf-Brell Company. The company produces golf umbrellas in a two-step process. The Champions Division prepares the fabric tops and transfers them to the Tournament Division, which produces the ribs and handles, secures the tops, and packs all finished umbrellas for shipment.

Because of the directors' concern, the company controller gathered data for the past year, as shown in the following table:

	Champions Division	Tournament Division
Sales		
Regular	$700,000	$1,720,000
Deluxe	900,000	3,300,000
Direct materials		
Fabric tops (from Champions Division)	—	1,600,000
Cloth	360,000	—
Aluminum	—	660,000
Closing mechanisms	—	1,560,000
Direct labor	480,000	540,000
Variable overhead	90,000	240,000
Fixed divisional overhead—avoidable	150,000	210,000
Selling and general operating expenses	132,000	372,000
Company administrative expenses	84,000	108,000

During the year, 200,000 regular umbrellas and 150,000 deluxe umbrellas were completed and transferred or shipped by the two divisions. Transfer prices used by the Champions Division were as follows:

Regular $3.50
Deluxe   6.00

The regular umbrella wholesales for $8.60 and the deluxe model for $22.00. Company administrative costs are allocated to divisions by a predetermined formula. Management has indicated that the transfer price should include a 20 percent profit factor on total division costs.

1. Prepare a performance report on the Champions Division.
2. Prepare a performance report on the Tournament Division.
3. Compute each division's rate of return on controllable costs and on total division costs.
4. Do you agree with the statement made by the director of the Tournament Division? Explain your response.
5. What procedures would you recommend to the board of directors?

Capital Investment Analysis

When deciding when and how much to spend on expensive, long-term projects, such as the construction of a new building or the installation of a new production system, managers apply capital investment analysis to ensure that they use resources wisely and that their choices make the maximum contribution to future profits. This chapter explains the net present value method and other methods of capital investment analysis that managers use when making decisions about long-term capital investments.

LEARNING OBJECTIVES

LO1 Define *capital investment analysis,* and describe its relation to the management process.

LO2 State the purpose of the minimum rate of return, and identify the methods used to arrive at that rate.

LO3 Identify the types of projected costs and revenues used to evaluate alternatives for capital investment.

LO4 Apply the concept of the time value of money.

LO5 Analyze capital investment proposals using the net present value method.

LO6 Analyze capital investment proposals using the payback period method and the accounting rate-of-return method.

AIR PRODUCTS AND CHEMICALS INC.

- Why are capital investment decisions critical for a company like Air Products and Chemicals Inc.?

- How can managers evaluate capital investment alternatives and make wise allocations of limited resources?

- How can managers minimize the risks involved in capital investments?

Air Products and Chemicals Inc. is an industrial producer of gases that are piped directly into steel mills and other factories; it has many small gas plants located near its customers. What makes Air Products and Chemicals competitive is its use of a "lights-out" system, or, as the company describes it, "unattended operations with remote access." The system minimizes on-site labor by having regional operators remotely monitor several gas plants from a computer at their homes. If a problem occurs with a machine, an operator can repair it remotely or visit the plant.

Air Products and Chemicals is not alone in turning on-site labor's lights off. Using systems that link machines to the Internet so that managers can monitor operations at any time and from anywhere is common in industries that produce identical products in high volume, such as gears and dental-floss containers.[1] Automated systems of this kind are expensive, and managers must carefully weigh the risks involved in investing in them.

The Capital Investment Process

LO1 Define *capital investment analysis,* and describe its relation to the management process.

Among the most significant decisions that management must make are **capital investment decisions**, which are decisions about when and how much to spend on capital facilities and other long-term projects. Capital facilities and projects may include machinery, systems, or processes; new buildings or additions or renovations to existing buildings; entire new divisions or product lines; and distribution and software systems. For example, **Air Products and Chemicals Inc.** will make decisions about installing new equipment, replacing old equipment, expanding production by renovating or adding to a building, buying or building a new factory, or acquiring another company.

Capital facilities and projects are expensive. A new factory or production system may cost millions of dollars and require several years to complete. Managers must make capital investment decisions carefully so that they select the alternatives that will contribute the most to future profits.

Capital Investment Analysis

Study Note

Capital investment analysis is a decision process for the purchase of capital facilities, such as buildings and equipment.

Capital investment analysis, or *capital budgeting*, is the process of making decisions about capital investments. It consists of identifying the need for a capital investment, analyzing courses of action to meet that need, preparing reports for managers, choosing the best alternative, and allocating funds among competing needs. Every part of the organization participates in this process. Financial analysts supply a target cost of capital or desired rate of return and an estimate of how much money can be spent annually on capital facilities. Marketing specialists predict sales trends and new product demands, which help in determining which operations need expansion or new equipment. Managers at all levels help identify facility needs and often prepare preliminary cost estimates for the desired capital investment. They then work together to implement the project selected and to keep the results within revenue and cost estimates.

The capital investment process involves the evaluation of alternative proposals for large capital investments, including considerations for financing the projects. Capital investment analyses affect both short-term and long-term planning. Figure 1 illustrates the time span of the capital expenditure planning process. Most companies have a long-term plan—that is, a projection of operations for the next five or ten years. Large capital investments should be an integral part of that plan. Anticipated additions or changes to product lines, replacements of equipment, and acquisitions of other companies are examples of items to be included in long-term capital investment plans.

One element of budgeting is a capital investment budget. The capital investment budget fits into both the long-term planning process and the capital investment process. Long-term plans are not very specific; they are expressed in broad, goal-oriented terms. Each annual budget must help accomplish the organization's long-term goals. Look again at Figure 1. In 2009, the company plans to purchase a large, special-purpose machine. When the ten-year plan was developed, it included only a broad statement about a plan to purchase the machine. Nothing was specified about the cost of the machine or the anticipated operating details and costs. Those details are contained in

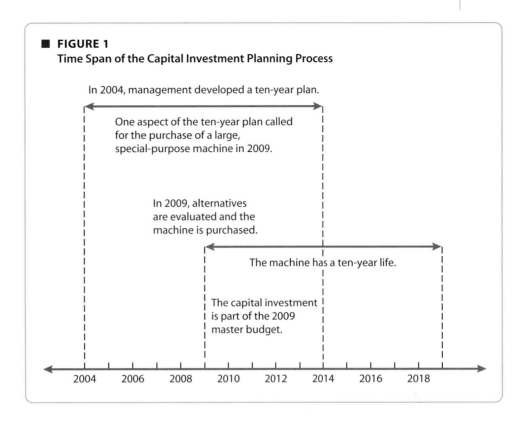

■ FIGURE 1
Time Span of the Capital Investment Planning Process

In 2004, management developed a ten-year plan.

One aspect of the ten-year plan called for the purchase of a large, special-purpose machine in 2009.

In 2009, alternatives are evaluated and the machine is purchased.

The machine has a ten-year life.

The capital investment is part of the 2009 master budget.

2004   2006   2008   2010   2012   2014   2016   2018

the annual master budget for 2009, and it is in 2009 that the capital investment analysis will occur. So although capital investment decisions that will affect the company for many years are discussed and estimates of future revenues and expenditures are made when the long-term plan is first developed, the capital investment analysis is performed in the period in which the expenditure will be made. This point is important to the understanding of capital investment analysis.

Capital Investment Analysis in the Management Process

Managers pay close attention to capital investments throughout the management process, as shown in Figure 2. However, the greatest portion of capital investment analysis takes place when they plan.

Planning   Each decision made about a capital investment is vitally important because it involves a large amount of money and commits a company to a course of action for years to come. For example, **Air Products and Chemicals**, **IBM**, and **Intel** must make capital investment decisions that fit into their strategic plans. A series of poor decisions about capital investments can cause a company to fail. To ensure high-quality capital investment decisions, managers follow six key steps when they plan.

Step 1: Identification of Capital Investment Needs   Identifying the need for a new capital investment is the starting point of capital investment analysis. Managers identify capital investment opportunities from past sales experience, changes in sources and quality of materials, employees' suggestions, production bottlenecks caused by obsolete equipment, new production or

Study Note

The six steps of capital investment analysis are performed for both long-term and short-term planning purposes.

■ **FIGURE 2**
Capital Investment Analysis in the Management Process

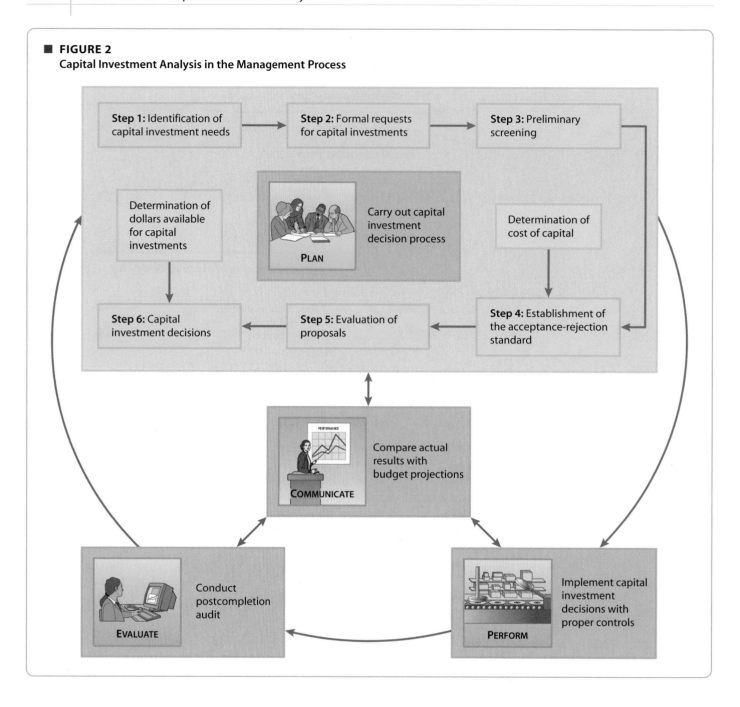

distribution methods, or customer complaints. In addition, capital investment needs are identified through proposals to:

1. Add new products to the product line.

2. Expand capacity in existing product lines.

3. Reduce production costs of existing products without altering operating levels.

4. Automate existing production processes.

Step 2: Formal Requests for Capital Investments To enhance control over capital investments, managers prepare formal requests for new capital investments. Each request includes a complete description of the investment under

A capital investment decision is one of the most significant decisions a manager can make. Such a decision often involves millions of dollars and commits a company to a course of action for many years. Shown here in 2005 is the CEO of Sanofi-Pasteur, a pharmaceutical company, announcing the start of construction of a new facility for the manufacture of flu vaccine. The facility was not expected to be ready for production until the 2009 flu season. Its estimated costs were $150.5 million.

review; the reasons a new investment is needed; the alternative means of satisfying the need; the timing, estimated costs, and related cost savings of each alternative; and the investment's engineering specifications, if necessary.

Step 3: Preliminary Screening Organizations that have several branches and a highly developed system for capital investment analysis require that all proposals go through preliminary screening. The purpose of preliminary screening is to ensure that the only proposals to receive serious review are those that both meet company strategic goals and produce the minimum rate of return set by management.

Step 4: Establishment of the Acceptance-Rejection Standard To attract and maintain funding for capital investments, an organization establishes an acceptance-rejection standard. Such a standard may be expressed as a minimum rate of return or a minimum cash-flow payback period. If the number of acceptable requests for capital investments exceeds the limited funds available for such investments, the proposals must next be ranked according to their rates of return. Acceptance-rejection standards are used to identify projects that are expected to yield inadequate or marginal returns. They also identify proposed projects for which high product demand and high financial returns are expected. Cost of capital information is often used to establish minimum rates of return on investments. The development of such rates is discussed later in this chapter.

Step 5: Evaluation of Proposals Proposals are evaluated by verifying decision variables and applying established proposal evaluation methods. The key decision variables are (1) expected life, (2) estimated cash flow, and (3) investment cost. Each variable in a proposal should be checked for accuracy. Three commonly used methods of evaluating proposed capital investments are the net present value method, the payback period method, and the accounting rate-of-return method. Using one or more evaluation methods and the minimum acceptance-rejection standard, management evaluates all proposals. In addition to this quantitative analysis, management will also consider qualitative factors, such as availability and training of employees, competition, anticipated future technological improvements, and the proposal's impact on other company operations.

Step 6: *Capital Investment Decisions* The proposals that meet the standards of the evaluation process are given to the appropriate manager for final review. When deciding which requests to implement, the manager must consider the funds available for capital investments. The acceptable proposals are ranked in order of net present value, payback period, or rate of return, and the highest-ranking proposals are funded first. Often there will not be enough money to fund all proposals. The final capital investment budget is then prepared by allocating funds to the selected proposals.

Performing During the year, capital investment decisions are implemented. This involves scheduling projects and overseeing their development, construction, or purchase. Managers must establish controls to make sure projects are completed on time, within budget, and at the desired level of quality.

Evaluating Each project undergoes a postcompletion audit to determine if it is meeting its goals and targets. Many projects can be modified in midprocess if changes are advisable. The postdecision audit may also identify weaknesses in the original planning process that can be corrected to avoid similar problems in the future.

The postcompletion audit is a difficult step in the management process. To isolate how a decision affects a company's overall operating results requires extensive analysis. The main problems are that (1) long-term projects must be evaluated by concentrating on cash flows over the project's life, (2) a particular decision may influence the operations of existing facilities, and (3) profitability resulting from a decision may be difficult to isolate and identify.

Communicating To communicate the results of capital investment decisions, managers prepare reports and distribute them within the organization. These reports include comparisons of budgeted expenditures and actual expenditures for each project. Once projects are in operation, the reports include comparisons of projected net cash flows or cost savings with actual results. Based on these comparisons, managers may decide to modify or curtail projects that are failing to meet expectations or to go forward with new projects. Such reports are critical to the postcompletion audit.

S T O P • R E V I E W • A P P L Y

1-1. What are capital investments? Give two examples.

1-2. Define *capital investment analysis.*

1-3. How is capital investment analysis part of both the long-term planning process and the annual budgeting process?

1-4. Arrange the following steps in the planning phase of the management process in their proper order:

a. Preliminary screening

b. Capital investment decisions, including determination of dollars available for capital investments

c. Establishment of acceptance-rejection standards, including determination of the cost of capital

d. Identification of capital investment needs

The Minimum Rate of Return on Investment

LO2 State the purpose of the minimum rate of return, and identify the methods used to arrive at that rate.

Most companies set a minimum rate of return, and any capital expenditure proposal that fails to produce that rate of return is automatically refused. The minimum rate of return is often referred to as a *hurdle rate* because it is the rate that must be exceeded, or hurdled. If none of the capital investment requests is expected to meet or exceed the minimum rate of return, or hurdle rate, all requests will be turned down.

Organizations set a minimum rate of return to guard their profitability. If the return from a capital investment falls below the minimum rate of return, the funds can be used more profitably in another part of the organization. Projects that produce poor returns will ultimately have a negative effect on an organization's profitability.

Choosing a minimum rate of return is not a simple task. Each measure that can be used to set a cutoff point has certain advantages. The most commonly used measures are (1) cost of capital, (2) corporate return on investment, (3) industry average return on investment, and (4) bank interest rates.

Cost of Capital

Of all the possible measures of minimum rates of return, cost of capital is the most widely used. The **cost of capital** is the weighted-average rate of return that a company must pay to its long-term creditors and shareholders for the use of their funds. The components of cost of capital are the cost of debt, the cost of preferred stock, the cost of common stock, and the cost of retained earnings. Sophisticated methods may be used to determine these costs. However, in this discussion, we use a simplified definition of each cost. The cost of debt is the after-tax interest on the debt (interest times one minus the tax rate). The after-tax amount is used because the interest is tax deductible. In contrast, the cost of preferred stock is the full dividend rate because dividends are not tax deductible. The cost of equity capital (common stock and retained earnings) is the return required by investors in the company.

The cost of capital is computed in four steps:

1. Identify the cost of each source of capital.

2. Compute the proportion (percentage) of the organization's total amount of debt and equity that each source of capital represents.

3. Multiply each source's cost by its proportion of the capital.

4. Total the weighted costs computed in Step **3**.

Study Note

Depending on the mixture of sources of capital, a company's cost of capital will vary.

Capital investments involve spending large amounts of money on a project in anticipation of profitable returns in the future. Cost is therefore always a consideration in a capital investment decision. However, it is not the only factor that should be considered. International trade and logistics can also be very important. A case in point is **Koss Corporation**, a maker of high-fidelity headphones for audio equipment that is located in Milwaukee, Wisconsin. Company managers moved much of the production to China, where costs were low. However, that caused a problem with making timely deliveries to customers.[2] The just-in-time inventory philosophy had to be abandoned, and inventories were tripled from $2 million to $6 million to avoid customer backorders and dissatisfaction. Now, finished products are stacked in the Milwaukee factory to ensure against dockworker strikes and missed deliveries. Looking beyond the numbers is thus an important consideration in capital investment decisions.

For example, suppose Wilson Company's financing structure is as follows:

Cost of Capital (Percentage)	Source of Capital	Amount	Proportion of Capital (Percentage)
6	Debt financing	$150,000	30
8	Preferred stock	50,000	10
12	Common stock	200,000	40
12	Retained earnings	100,000	20
	Totals	$500,000	100

The cost of capital of 9.8 percent would be computed as follows:

Source of Capital	Cost	×	Proportion of Capital	=	Weighted Cost
Debt financing	.06		.30		.018
Preferred stock	.08		.10		.008
Common stock	.12		.40		.048
Retained earnings	.12		.20		.024
Cost of capital					.098

Other Cutoff Measures

If cost of capital information is unavailable, management can use one of three less accurate but still useful amounts as the minimum rate of return. The first is the average total corporate return on investment. This measure is based on the notion that any capital investment that produces a lower return than the rate that the company has earned historically will negatively affect investors' perception of the firm's future market value. A second method is to use the industry's average cost of capital. Most sizable industry associations supply such information. As a last resort, a company might use the current bank-lending rate. But because most companies are financed by both debt and equity, the bank lending rate seldom reflects an accurate rate of return.

Ranking Capital Investment Proposals

The requests for capital investments that a company receives usually exceed the funds available for capital investments. Even after management evaluates and selects proposals under the minimum acceptance-rejection standard, there are often too many proposals to fund adequately. At that point, managers must rank the proposals according to their rates of return, or profitability, and begin a second selection process.

Suppose that Queens Enterprises has $4,500,000 to spend this year for capital improvements and that five acceptable proposals are competing for those funds. The company's current minimum rate of return is 18 percent, and it is considering the following proposals:

Project	Rate of Return (Percentage)	Capital Investment	Cumulative Investment
A	32	$1,460,000	$1,460,000
B	30	1,890,000	3,350,000
C	28	460,000	3,810,000
D	24	840,000	4,650,000
E	22	580,000	5,230,000
Total		$5,230,000	

The proposals are listed in the order of their rates of return. As you can see, Projects A, B, and C have the highest rates of return and together will cost a total of $3,810,000. That leaves $690,000 in capital funds for other projects. Project D should be examined first to see if it could be implemented for $150,000 less. If not, then Project E should be selected. The selection of Projects A, B, C, and E means that $110,000 in capital funds will be uncommitted for the year.

S T O P • R E V I E W • A P P L Y

2-1. Do all industries have the same cost of capital?

2-2. Identify two measures that companies use to determine a minimum rate of return for capital investment proposals.

Cost of Capital   Sample Industries is considering investing $20 million in a plant expansion. Management needs to know the average cost of capital to use in evaluating this capital investment decision. The company's capital structure consists of $2,000,000 of debt at 6 percent interest and $3,000,000 of stockholders' equity at 2 percent. What is Sample Industries' average cost of capital?

SOLUTION

The company's average cost of capital is 3.6 percent, which is computed as follows:

Source of Capital	Amount	Proportion of Capital		Cost of Capital		Weighted Cost
Debt	$2,000,000	40%	×	6%	=	0.024
Equity	3,000,000	60%	×	2%	=	0.012
Total	$5,000,000	100%				0.036

Measures Used in Capital Investment Analysis

> **LO3** Identify the types of projected costs and revenues used to evaluate alternatives for capital investment.

When evaluating a proposed capital investment, managers must predict how the new asset will perform and how it will benefit the company. Various measures are used to estimate the benefits to be derived from a capital investment.

Net Income and Net Cash Inflows

Each capital investment analysis must include a measure of the expected benefit from the investment project. The measure of expected benefit depends on the method of analyzing capital investment alternatives. One possible measure is net income, calculated in the usual way. Managers determine increases in net income resulting from the capital investment for each alternative.

A more widely used measure of expected benefit is projected cash flows. **Net cash inflows** are the balance of increases in projected cash receipts over increases in projected cash payments resulting from a capital investment. In some cases, equipment replacement decisions involve situations in which revenues are the same among alternatives. In such cases, **cost savings** measure the benefits, such as reduced costs, from proposed capital investments. Either net cash inflows or cost savings can be used as the basis for an evaluation, but the two measures should not be confused. If the analysis involves cash receipts, net cash inflows are used. If the analysis involves only cash outlays, cost savings are used. Managers must measure and evaluate all the investment alternatives consistently.

Equal Versus Unequal Cash Flows

Projected cash flows may be the same for each year of an asset's life, or they may vary from year to year. Unequal annual cash flows are common and must be analyzed for each year of an asset's life. Proposed projects with equal annual cash flows require less detailed analysis. Both a project with equal cash flows and one with unequal cash flows are illustrated and explained later in this chapter.

Carrying Value of Assets

Carrying value is the undepreciated portion of the original cost of a fixed asset—that is, the asset's cost less its accumulated depreciation. Carrying value is also referred to as *book value*. When a decision to replace an asset is

FOCUS ON BUSINESS PRACTICE

Counting Your Pennies the High-Tech Way

As noted in this chapter's Decision Point, "lights-out" machines are replacing human labor in factories. They are also replacing human labor in the counting of loose change. **Coinstar**, located in Bellevue, Washington, manufactures and sells high-tech coin counters. There are over 10,000 of these machines in supermarkets in the United States, Canada, and Great Britain. They are 99.99 percent accurate and can count 600 coins per minute. They are considered high-tech because each one is connected to a central data processing center that monitors and maintains it.[3]

being evaluated, the carrying value of the old asset is irrelevant because it is a past, or historical, cost and will not be altered by the decision. Net proceeds from the asset's sale or disposal are relevant, however, because the proceeds affect cash flows and may differ for each alternative.

Depreciation Expense and Income Taxes

The techniques of capital investment analysis discussed in this chapter compare the relative benefits of proposed capital investments by measuring the cash receipts and payments for a facility or project. Income taxes alter the amount and timing of cash flows of projects under consideration by for-profit companies. To assess the benefits of a capital project, a company must include the effects of taxes in its capital investment analyses. Depreciation expense is deductible when determining income taxes. (You may recall that the annual depreciation expense computation using the straight-line method is the asset's cost less its residual value, divided by the asset's useful life.) Thus, depreciation expense strongly influences the amount of income taxes that a company pays and can lead to significant tax savings.

Corporate income tax rates vary and can change yearly. To examine how taxes affect capital investment analysis, assume that a company has a tax rate of 30 percent on taxable income. It is considering a capital project that will make the following annual contribution to operating income:

Cash revenues	$400,000
Cash expenses	(200,000)
Depreciation	(100,000)
Operating income before income taxes	$100,000
Income taxes at 30%	(30,000)
Operating income	$ 70,000

The net cash inflows for this project can be determined in two ways:

1. Net cash inflows—receipts and disbursements

Revenues (cash inflows)	$400,000
Cash expenses (outflows)	(200,000)
Income taxes (outflows)	(30,000)
Net cash inflows	$170,000

2. Net cash inflows—income adjustment procedure

Income after income taxes	$ 70,000
Add back noncash expenses (depreciation)	100,000
Less noncash revenues	—
Net cash inflows	$170,000

In both computations, the net cash inflows are $170,000, and the total effect of income taxes is to lower the net cash inflows by $30,000.

Disposal or Residual Values

Proceeds from the sale of an old asset are current cash inflows and are relevant to evaluating a proposed capital investment. Projected disposal or residual values of replacement equipment are also relevant because they represent future cash inflows and usually differ among alternatives. Remember that the residual value, sometimes called the *disposal* or *salvage value*, of an asset will be received at the end of the asset's estimated life.

STOP • REVIEW • APPLY

3-1. Distinguish between cost savings and net cash inflows.

3-2. Why is it important to know whether a capital investment will produce equal or unequal cash flows?

3-3. "In capital investment analysis, the carrying value of an asset is irrelevant, whereas current and future residual values are relevant." Is this statement valid? Why or why not?

3-4. How does the relationship between depreciation and income taxes affect capital investment analysis? Why is depreciation of old equipment ignored in this type of analysis?

The Time Value of Money

LO4   Apply the concept of the time value of money.

An organization has many options for investing capital besides buying plant assets. Consequently, management expects a plant asset to yield a reasonable return during its useful life. A key question in capital investment analysis is how to measure the return on a plant asset. One way is to look at the cash flows that the asset will generate during its useful life. When an asset has a long useful life, management will usually analyze those cash flows in terms of the time value of money. The **time value of money** is the concept that cash flows of equal dollar amounts separated by an interval of time have different present values because of the effect of compound interest. The notions of interest, present value, future value, and present value of an ordinary annuity are all related to the time value of money.

Interest

Interest is the cost associated with the use of money for a specific period of time. Because interest is a cost associated with time and "time is money," interest is an important consideration in any business decision.

Simple interest is the interest cost for one or more periods when the amount on which the interest is computed stays the same from period to period. **Compound interest** is the interest cost for two or more periods when the amount on which interest is computed changes in each period to include all interest paid in previous periods. In other words, compound interest is interest earned on a principal sum that is increased at the end of each period by the interest for that period.

Example: Simple Interest   Jo Sanka accepts an 8 percent, $30,000 note due in 90 days. How much will she receive in total when the note comes due? The formula for calculating simple interest is as follows:

Study Note

Interest is a cost associated with the passage of time, whether or not there is a stated interest rate.

$$\text{Interest Expense} = \text{Principal} \times \text{Rate} \times \text{Time}$$
$$= \$30,000 \times 8/100 \times 90/360$$
$$= \$600$$

The total that Sanka will receive is computed as follows:

$$\text{Total} = \text{Principal} + \text{Interest}$$
$$= \$30,000 + \$600$$
$$= \$30,600$$

If the interest is paid and the note is renewed for an additional 90 days, the interest calculation will remain the same.

Example: Compound Interest

Andy Clayburn makes a deposit of $5,000 in a savings account that pays 6 percent interest. He expects to leave the principal and accumulated interest in the account for three years. What will be his account total at the end of three years? Assume that the interest is paid at the end of the year, that the interest is added to the principal at that time, and that this total in turn earns interest.

The amount at the end of three years is computed as follows:

(1) Year	(2) Principal Amount at Beginning of Year	(3) Annual Amount of Interest (col. 2 × .06)	(4) Accumulated Amount at End of Year (col. 2 + col. 3)
1	$5,000.00	$300.00	$5,300.00
2	5,300.00	318.00	5,618.00
3	5,618.00	337.08	5,955.08

At the end of three years, Clayburn will have $5,955.08 in his savings account. Note that the annual amount of interest increases each year by the interest rate times the interest of the previous year. For example, between year 1 and year 2, the interest increased by $18 ($318 − $300), which exactly equals 6 percent times $300.

Present Value

Suppose that you had the choice of receiving $100 today or one year from today. Intuitively, you would choose to receive the $100 today. Why? You know that if you have the $100 today, you can put it in a savings account to earn interest, so that you will have more than $100 a year from today. Therefore, we can say that an amount to be received in the future (future value) is not worth as much today as the same amount to be received today (present value) because of the cost associated with the passage of time.

Future value and present value are closely related. **Future value** is the amount that an investment will be worth at a future date if it is invested today at compound interest. **Present value** is the amount that must be invested today at a given rate of compound interest to produce a given future value.

For example, if Daschel Company needs $1,000 one year from now, how much should it invest today to achieve that goal if the interest rate is 5 percent? The following equation can be used to answer that question:

$$\text{Present Value} \times (1.0 + \text{Interest Rate}) = \text{Future Value}$$
$$\text{Present Value} \times 1.05 = \$1,000.00$$
$$\text{Present Value} = \$1,000.00 \div 1.05$$
$$\text{Present Value} = \$952.38$$

Thus, to achieve a future value of $1,000.00, a present value of $952.38 must be invested. Interest of 5 percent on $952.38 for one year equals $47.62, and the two amounts added together equal $1,000.00.

Present Value of a Single Sum Due in the Future

When more than one time period is involved, the calculation of present value is more complicated. For example, Reza Company wants to be sure of having $4,000 at the end of three years. How much must the company invest today in a 5 percent savings account to achieve that goal? By adapting the preceding equation, the present value of $4,000 at compound interest of 5 percent for three years in the future may be computed as follows:

Year	Amount at End of Year	Divide by		Present Value at Beginning of Year
3	$4,000.00	÷ 1.05	=	$3,809.52
2	3,809.52	÷ 1.05	=	3,628.11
1	3,628.11	÷ 1.05	=	3,455.34

Reza Company must invest a present value of $3,455.34 to achieve a future value of $4,000 in three years. This calculation is made easier by using the appropriate table from the appendix on future value and present value tables. In Table 3, we look down the 5 percent column until we reach period 3. There we find the factor .864. Multiplied by $1, this factor gives the present value of $1 to be received three years from now at 5 percent interest. Thus, we solve the problem as follows:

Future Value	×	Present Value Factor	=	Present Value
$4,000	×	.864	=	$3,456

Except for a rounding difference of $.66, this gives the same result as the previous calculation.

Present Value of an Ordinary Annuity

Study Note

The first payment of an ordinary annuity is always made at the end of the first year.

It is often necessary to compute the present value of a series of receipts or payments. When we calculate the present value of equal amounts equally spaced over a period of time, we are computing the present value of an ordinary annuity. An **ordinary annuity** is a series of equal payments or receipts that will begin one time period from the current date. For example, suppose that Fodor Company has sold a piece of property and is to receive $15,000 in three equal annual cash payments of $5,000, beginning one year from today. What is the present value of this sale, assuming a current interest rate of 5 percent?

This present value can be determined by calculating a separate present value for each of the three payments (using Table 3 in the appendix on future value and present value tables) and summing the results, as follows:

Future Cash Receipts (Annuity)				Present Value Factor at 5 Percent (from Table 3)		Present Value
Year 1	Year 2	Year 3				
$5,000			×	.952	=	$ 4,760
	$5,000		×	.907	=	4,535
		$5,000	×	.864	=	4,320
Total Present Value						$13,615

The present value of this sale is $13,615. Thus, there is an implied interest cost (given the 5 percent rate) of $1,385 associated with the payment plan that allows the purchaser to pay in three installments. We can calculate this present value more easily by using Table 4 in the appendix on future value and present value tables. We look down the 5 percent column until we reach period 3. There we find the factor 2.723. That factor, when multiplied by $1, gives the present value of a series of three $1 payments, spaced one year apart, at compound interest of 5 percent. Thus, we solve the problem as follows:

$$\text{Periodic Payment} \times \text{Present Value Factor} = \text{Present Value}$$
$$\$5,000 \times 2.723 = \$13,615$$

This result is the same as the one computed earlier. If Fodor Company is willing to accept a 5 percent rate of return, management will be equally satisfied to receive a single cash payment of $13,615 today or three equal annual cash payments of $5,000 spread over the next three years.

S T O P • R E V I E W • A P P L Y

4-1. Discuss the statement, "To treat all future income flows alike ignores the time value of money."

4-2. How are present value and future value different?

4-3. Which table in the appendix on future value and present value tables is used to determine the present value of a single sum to be received in the future? Which table is used to determine the present value of a series of payments (ordinary annuity) to be received in the future?

The Net Present Value Method

LO5 Analyze capital investment proposals using the net present value method.

The **net present value method** evaluates a capital investment by discounting its future cash flows to their present values and subtracting the amount of the initial investment from their sum. All proposed capital investments are evaluated in the same way, and the projects with the highest

FOCUS ON BUSINESS PRACTICE

How Would You Decide Whether to Buy Rare Dinosaur Bones?

Not-for-profit organizations can use the techniques of capital investment analysis just as for-profit ones do. For example, the officers of the Field Museum in Chicago applied these techniques when they decided to bid at auction on the most complete skeleton of a *Tyrannosaurus rex* ever found. The museum bought the bones for $8.2 million and spent another $9 million to restore and install the dinosaur, named Sue. The museum projected that Sue would attract 1 million new visitors, who would produce $5 million in admissions and spend several more million dollars on food, gifts, and the like. After deducting operating costs, museum officials used discounted present values to calculate a return on investment of 10.5 percent. Given that the museum's cost of capital was 8.5 percent, Sue's purchase was considered a financial success. Sue has been extremely popular with the public and more than met the museum's attendance goals in the first year after installation.[4]

net present value—the amount that exceeds the initial investment—are selected for implementation.

Advantages of the Net Present Value Method

A significant advantage of the net present value method is that it incorporates the time value of money into the analysis of proposed capital investments. Future cash inflows and outflows are discounted by the company's minimum rate of return to determine their present values. The minimum rate of return should at least equal the company's average cost of capital.

When dealing with the time value of money, use discounting to find the present value of an amount to be received in the future. To determine the present values of future amounts of money, use Tables 3 and 4 in the appendix on future value and present value tables. Remember that Table 3 deals with a single payment or amount, whereas Table 4 is used for a series of equal periodic amounts.

Tables 3 and 4 are used to discount each future cash inflow and cash outflow over the life of the asset to the present. If the net present value is positive (the total of the discounted net cash inflows exceeds the cash investment at the beginning), the rate of return on the investment will exceed the company's minimum rate of return, or hurdle rate, and the project can be accepted. Conversely, if the net present value is negative (the cash investment at the beginning exceeds the discounted net cash inflows), the return on the investment is less than the minimum rate of return and the project should be rejected. If the net present value is zero (if discounted cash inflows equal discounted cash outflows), the project meets the minimum rate of return and can be accepted.

The Net Present Value Method Illustrated

Suppose that Open Imaging Company is considering the purchase of a magnetic resonance imaging (MRI) machine that will improve efficiency in its Radiology Department. Management must decide between two models of the machine.

Model M costs $17,500 and will have an estimated residual value of $2,000 after five years. It is projected to produce cash inflows of $6,000, $5,500, $5,000, $4,500, and $4,000 during its five-year life.

Model N costs $21,000 and will have an estimated residual value of $2,000. It is projected to produce cash inflows of $6,000 per year for five years.

The company's minimum rate of return is 16 percent. Because Model M is expected to produce unequal cash inflows, Table 3 in the appendix on future

FOCUS ON BUSINESS PRACTICE
What Is Total Cost of Ownership, and Why Is It Important?

The concept of total cost of ownership (TCO) was developed to determine the total lifetime costs of owning an information technology (IT) asset, such as a computer system. TCO includes both the direct and indirect costs associated with the acquisition, deployment, operation, support, and retirement of the asset. Today, TCO is the industry standard for evaluating and comparing the costs associated with long-lived asset acquisitions. For example, if you buy a printer, TCO includes the direct costs of buying the printer, the annual supplies costs of ink and paper, and the indirect costs of maintaining it. Thus, the decision about which printer to buy is not based solely on the cost of the printer, but on all costs related to it over its useful lifetime.[5]

State lotteries use the net present value method to compute the lump-sum equivalent of the grand prize. In this photo, Mega Millions winners Margaret and James Jones hold a replica of their $77,744,832 check. Worth an annuity of $130 million, it was the second largest prize in Georgia's lottery history.

value and present value tables is used to determine the present value of each cash inflow from each year of the machine's life. The net present value of Model M is determined as follows:

Model M

Year	Net Cash Inflows	16% Factor	Present Value
1	$6,000	.862	$ 5,172.00
2	5,500	.743	4,086.50
3	5,000	.641	3,205.00
4	4,500	.552	2,484.00
5	4,000	.476	1,904.00
Residual value	2,000	.476	952.00
Total present value of cash inflows			$17,803.50
Less purchase price of Model M			17,500.00
Net present value			$ 303.50

All the factors for this analysis can be found in the column for 16 percent in Table 3. The factors are used to discount the individual cash flows, including the expected residual value, to the present. The amount of the investment in Model M is deducted from the total present value of the cash inflows to arrive at the net present value of $303.50. Since the entire investment of $17,500 in Model M is a cash outflow at the beginning—that is, at time zero—no discounting of the $17,500 purchase price is necessary. Because the net present value is positive, the proposed investment in Model M will achieve at least the minimum rate of return.

Because Model N is expected to produce equal cash receipts in each year of its useful life, Table 4 in the appendix on future value and present value tables is used to determine the combined present value of those future cash inflows. However, Table 3 is used to determine the present value of the machine's residual value because it represents a single payment, not an annuity. The net present value of Model N is calculated as follows:

Model N

Year	Net Cash Inflows	16% Factor	Present Value
1–5	$6,000	3.274	$19,644.00
Residual value	2,000	.476	952.00
Total present value of cash inflows			$20,596.00
Less purchase price of Model N			21,000.00
Net present value			($ 404.00)

Table 4 is used to determine the factor of 3.274 (found in the column for 16 percent and the row for five periods). Because the residual value is a single inflow in the fifth year, the factor of .476 must be taken from Table 3 (the column for 16 percent and the row for five periods). The result is a net present value of ($404). Because the net present value is negative, the proposed investment in Model N will not achieve the minimum rate of return and should be rejected.

The two analyses show that Model M should be chosen because it has a positive net present value and would exceed the company's minimum rate of return. Model N should be rejected because it does not achieve the minimum rate of return. Model M is the better choice because it is expected to produce cash inflows sooner and will thus produce a proportionately greater present value.

STOP • REVIEW • APPLY

5-1. Why is the net present value method superior to the other methods of capital investment analysis presented in this chapter?

5-2. What is the role of the average cost of capital when the net present value method is used to evaluate capital investment proposals?

Net Present Value Communications, Inc., is considering the purchase of a new piece of data transmission equipment. Estimated annual net cash inflows for the new equipment are $575,000. The equipment costs $2 million, has a five-year life, and will have no residual value at the end of the five years. The company's minimum rate of return is 12 percent. Compute the net present value of the equipment. Should the company purchase it?

SOLUTION

Net Present Value = Present Value of Future Net Cash Inflows − Cost of Equipment
= ($575,000 × 3.605*) − $2,000,000
= $2,072,875 − $2,000,000
= $72,875

The solution is positive, so the company should purchase the equipment. A positive answer means that the investment will yield more than the minimum 12 percent return required by the company.

─────
*From Table 4 in the appendix on future value and present value tables.

Other Methods of Capital Investment Analysis

LO6 Analyze capital investment proposals using the payback period method and the accounting rate-of-return method.

The net present value method is the best method for capital investment analysis. However, two other commonly used methods provide rough guides to evaluating capital investment proposals. These methods are the payback period method and the accounting rate-of-return method.

The Payback Period Method

 **Study Note**

The payback period method measures the estimated length of time necessary to recover in cash the cost of an investment.

Because cash is an essential measure of a business's health, many managers estimate the cash flow that the investment will generate. Their goal is to determine the minimum time it will take to recover the initial investment. If two investment alternatives are being studied, management should choose the investment that pays back its initial cost in the shorter time. That period of time is known as the payback period, and the method of evaluation is called the **payback period method**. Although the payback period method is simple to use, its use has declined because it does not consider the time value of money. The payback period is computed as follows:

$$\text{Payback Period} = \frac{\text{Cost of Investment}}{\text{Annual Net Cash Inflows}}$$

To apply the payback period method, suppose that Gordon Company is interested in purchasing a new bottling machine that costs $51,000 and has a residual value of $3,000. To evaluate this proposed capital investment, begin by determining the net cash inflows. First, find and eliminate the effects of all noncash revenue and expense items included in the analysis of net income. Assume that estimates for the proposal include revenue increases of $17,900 a year and operating cost increases of $11,696 a year (including depreciation and taxes). In this case, the only noncash expense or revenue is machine depreciation. To calculate this amount, you must know the asset's life and the depreciation method. Suppose the Gordon Company uses the straight-line method of depreciation, and the new bottling machine will have a ten-year service life. The annual depreciation is computed using this information and the facts given earlier, as follows:

$$\text{Annual Depreciation} = \frac{\text{Cost} - \text{Residual Value}}{10 \text{ (years)}}$$

$$= \frac{\$51,000 - \$3,000}{10}$$

$$= \$4,800 \text{ per year}$$

Study Note

In computing the payback period, depreciation is omitted because it is a noncash expense.

After removing the noncash annual depreciation amount from the operating costs, the payback period is computed as follows:

$$\text{Payback Period} = \frac{\text{Cost of Machine}}{\text{Cash Revenue} - \text{Cash Expenses}}$$

$$= \frac{\$51,000}{\$17,900 - (\$11,696 - \$4,800)}$$

$$= \frac{\$51,000}{\$11,004}$$

$$= 4.6 \text{ years}$$

If the company's desired payback period is five years or less, this proposal would be approved.

If a proposed capital investment has unequal annual net cash inflows, the payback period is determined by subtracting each annual amount (in chronological order) from the cost of the capital facility. When a zero balance is reached, the payback period has been determined. This will often occur in the middle of a year. The portion of the final year is computed by dividing the amount needed to reach zero (the unrecovered portion of the investment) by the entire year's estimated cash inflow. The Review Problem in this chapter illustrates that process.

The payback period method is widely used because it is easy to compute and understand. It is especially useful in areas in which technology changes rapidly, such as in Internet companies, and when risk is high, such as when investing in emerging countries. However, the disadvantages of this approach far outweigh its advantages. First, the payback period method does not measure profitability. Second, it ignores differences in the present values of cash flows from different periods; thus, it does not adjust cash flows for the time value of money. Finally, the payback period method emphasizes the time it takes to recover the investment rather than the long-term return on the investment. It ignores all future cash flows after the payback period is reached.

The Accounting Rate-of-Return Method

The **accounting rate-of-return method** is an imprecise but easy way to measure the estimated performance of a capital investment, since it uses financial statement information. This method does not use an investment's cash flows but considers the financial reporting effects of the investment instead. The accounting rate-of-return method measures expected performance using two variables: (1) estimated annual net income from the project and (2) average investment cost. The basic equation is as follows:

$$\frac{\text{Accounting Rate}}{\text{of Return}} = \frac{\text{Project's Average Annual Net Income}}{\text{Average Investment Cost}}$$

To compute the average annual net income, use the cost and revenue data prepared for evaluating the project. Average investment in a proposed capital facility is calculated as follows:

$$\frac{\text{Average Investment}}{\text{Cost}} = \left(\frac{\text{Total Investment} - \text{Residual Value}}{2}\right) + \text{Residual Value}$$

To see how this equation is used in evaluating a proposed capital investment, assume the same facts as before for the Gordon Company in its interest in purchasing a new bottling machine. Also assume that the company's management will consider only projects that promise to yield more than a 16 percent return. To determine if the company should invest in the machine, compute the accounting rate of return as follows:

$$\frac{\text{Accounting Rate}}{\text{of Return}} = \frac{\$17,900 - \$11,696}{\left(\dfrac{\$51,000 - \$3,000}{2}\right) + \$3,000}$$

$$= \frac{\$6,204}{\$27,000}$$

$$= 23\%$$

 Study Note

Payback period is expressed in time, net present value is expressed in money, and accounting rate of return is expressed as a percentage.

The projected rate of return is higher than the 16 percent minimum, so management should think seriously about making the investment.

The accounting rate-of-return method has been widely used because it is easy to understand and apply, but it does have several disadvantages. First, because net income is averaged over the life of the investment, it is not a reliable figure; actual net income may vary considerably from the estimates. Second, the method is unreliable if estimated annual net incomes differ from year to year. Third, it ignores cash flows. Fourth, it does not consider the time value of money; thus, future and present dollars are treated as equal.

S T O P • R E V I E W • A P P L Y

6-1. Why do the payback period method and the accounting rate-of-return method yield rough estimates?

6-2. Why is the payback period method widely used?

Payback Period Method   Communications, Inc., is considering the purchase of new data transmission equipment. Estimated annual net cash inflows from the new equipment are $575,000. The equipment costs $2 million and will have no residual value at the end of its five-year life. Compute the payback period for the equipment. Does this method yield a positive or negative response to the proposal to buy the equipment, assuming that the company has set a maximum payback period of four years?

SOLUTION

$$\text{Payback Period} = \text{Cost of Investment} \div \text{Annual Net Cash Inflows}$$
$$= \$2,000,000 \div \$575,000$$
$$= 3.5 \text{ years}$$

The piece of equipment should be purchased because its payback period is less than the company's maximum payback period.

Accounting Rate of Return   Sample Trucking is considering whether to purchase a delivery truck that will cost $26,000, last six years, and have an estimated residual value of $6,000. Average annual net income from the delivery truck is estimated at $4,000. Sample Trucking's owners want to earn an accounting rate of return of 20 percent. Compute the average investment cost and the accounting rate of return. Should the company make the investment?

SOLUTION

$$\frac{\text{Average}}{\text{Investment Cost}} = \left(\frac{\text{Total Investment} - \text{Residual Value}}{2}\right) + \frac{\text{Residual}}{\text{Value}}$$

$$\$16,000 = \left(\frac{\$26,000 - \$6,000}{2}\right) + \$6,000$$

$$\frac{\text{Accounting}}{\text{Rate of Return}} = \frac{\text{Project's Average Annual Net Income}}{\text{Average Investment Cost}}$$

$$= \frac{\$4,000}{\$16,000}$$

$$= 25\%$$

The project will exceed the desired return and should be undertaken.

AIR PRODUCTS AND CHEMICALS INC.

In this chapter's Decision Point, we asked the following questions:

- Why are capital investment decisions critical for a company like Air Products and Chemicals Inc.?
- How can managers evaluate capital investment alternatives and make wise allocations of limited resources?
- How can managers minimize the risks involved in capital investments?

Capital investments require making decisions about long-term projects that may have positive or negative consequences for a company for many years. It is therefore essential to take a systematic approach to evaluating such projects. Companies like Air Products and Chemicals have many equipment and factory needs, and installing completely automated systems is costly. Thus, when deciding whether to invest their company's capital in an expensive project like an automated plant, managers must focus on making the best decisions possible by using methods of capital investment analysis, such as the net present value method, the payback period method, or the accounting rate-of-return method. With these methods, they can make wise resource choices and minimize the risks involved in the decision. Air Products and Chemicals' management typically evaluates each proposed investment alternative to determine if it will generate an adequate return for the company before making far-reaching capital investment decisions.

CHAPTER REVIEW

REVIEW of Learning Objectives

LO1 Define *capital investment analysis,* and describe its relation to the management process.

Capital investment decisions focus on when and how much to spend on capital facilities and other long-term projects. Capital investment analysis, often referred to as *capital budgeting*, consists of identifying the need for a capital investment, analyzing courses of action to meet that need, preparing reports for management, choosing the best alternative, and dividing funds among competing resource needs.

Capital investment analysis spans all phases of the management process. When managers plan, they analyze capital investment alternatives by screening and evaluating them before making funding decisions. They implement their capital investment decisions as they perform their duties during the year. In the evaluation phase, they review the results of their decisions. They prepare reports to communicate the results of their capital investment decisions as the reports are needed. Based on such reports, they may decide to modify or curtail projects that are failing to meet expectations or to go forward with new projects.

LO2 State the purpose of the minimum rate of return, and identify the methods used to arrive at that rate.

The minimum rate of return, or hurdle rate, is used as a screening mechanism to eliminate from further consideration capital investment requests with anticipated inadequate returns. It saves executives' time by quickly identifying substandard requests. The most commonly used measures for determining minimum rates of return are (1) cost of capital, (2) corporate return on investment, (3) industry average return on investment, and (4) bank interest rates. The weighted-average cost of capital and the average return on investment are the most widely used measures.

LO3 Identify the types of projected costs and revenues used to evaluate alternatives for capital investment.

The accounting rate-of-return method requires measures of net income. Other methods of evaluating capital investments evaluate net cash inflows or cost savings. The analysis process must take into consideration whether each period's cash flows will be equal or unequal. Unless the after-income-tax effects on cash flows are being considered, carrying values and depreciation expense of assets awaiting replacement are irrelevant. Net proceeds from the sale of an old asset and estimated residual value of a new facility represent future cash flows and must be part of the estimated benefit of a project. Depreciation expense on replacement equipment is relevant to evaluations based on after-tax cash flows.

LO4 Apply the concept of the time value of money.

Cash flows of equal dollar amounts at different times have different values because of the effect of compound interest. This phenomenon is known as the time value of money. Of the evaluation methods discussed in this chapter, only the net present value method takes into account the time value of money.

LO5 Analyze capital investment proposals using the net present value method.

The net present value method incorporates the time value of money into the analysis of a proposed capital investment. A minimum required rate of return, usually the average cost of capital, is used to discount an investment's expected future cash flows to their present values. The present values are added together, and the amount of the initial investment is subtracted from their total. If the resulting amount, called the net present value, is positive, the rate of return on the investment will exceed the required rate of return, and the investment should be accepted. If the net present value is negative, the return on the investment will be less than the minimum rate of return, and the investment should be rejected.

LO6 Analyze capital investment proposals using the payback period method and the accounting rate-of-return method.

The payback period method of evaluating a capital investment focuses on the minimum length of time needed to get the amount of the initial investment back in cash. With the accounting rate-of-return method, managers evaluate two or more capital investment proposals and then select the alternative that yields the highest ratio of average annual net income to average cost of investment. Both methods are easy to use, but they are very rough measures that do not consider the time value of money. As a result, the net present value method is preferred.

REVIEW of Concepts and Terminology

The following concepts and terms were introduced in this chapter:

Accounting rate-of-return method: A method of evaluating capital investments designed to measure the estimated performance of a potential capital project. It is calculated by dividing the project's average annual net income by the average cost of the investment. **(LO6)**

Capital investment analysis: The process of making decisions about capital investments. It includes identifying the need for a capital investment, analyzing courses of action to meet that need, preparing reports for managers, choosing the best alternative, and dividing funds among competing needs. Also called *capital budgeting*. **(LO1)**

Capital investment decisions: Management decisions about when and how much to spend on capital facilities and other long-term projects. **(LO1)**

Carrying value: The undepreciated portion of the original cost of a plant asset. Also called *book value*. **(LO3)**

Compound interest: The interest cost for two or more periods when the amount on which interest is computed changes in each period to include all interest paid in previous periods. **(LO4)**

Cost of capital: The weighted-average rate of return that a company must pay to its long-term creditors and shareholders for the use of their funds. **(LO2)**

Cost savings: Benefits, such as reduced costs, from a proposed capital investment. **(LO3)**

Future value: The amount that an investment will be worth at a future date if it is invested today at compound interest. **(LO4)**

Interest: The cost associated with the use of money for a specific period of time. **(LO4)**

Net cash inflows: The balance of increases in projected cash receipts over increases in projected cash payments resulting from a proposed capital investment. **(LO3)**

Net present value method: A method of evaluating capital investments in which all future cash flows for each proposed project are discounted to their present values and the amount of the initial investment is subtracted from their sum. The projects with the highest positive net present value—the amount that exceeds the initial investment—are selected for implementation. **(LO5)**

Ordinary annuity: A series of equal payments or receipts that will begin one time period from the current date. **(LO4)**

Payback period method: A method of evaluating capital investments that bases the decision to invest in a capital project on the minimum length of time it will take to get back the amount of the initial investment in cash. **(LO6)**

Present value: The amount that must be invested today at a given rate of compound interest to produce a given future value. **(LO4)**

Simple interest: The interest cost for one or more periods when the amount on which the interest is computed stays the same from period to period. **(LO4)**

Time value of money: The concept that cash flows of equal amounts separated by an interval of time have different present values because of the effect of compound interest. **(LO4)**

REVIEW Problem

Capital Investment Analysis

The Rolla Construction Company specializes in developing large shopping centers. It is considering the purchase of a new earth-moving machine and has gathered the following information:

Purchase price $600,000
Residual value $100,000
Desired payback period   3 years
Minimum rate of return   15%

The cash flow estimates are as follows:

Year	Cash Inflows	Cash Outflows	Net Cash Inflows	Projected Net Income
1	$ 500,000	$260,000	$240,000	$115,000
2	450,000	240,000	210,000	85,000
3	400,000	220,000	180,000	55,000
4	350,000	200,000	150,000	25,000
Totals	$1,700,000	$920,000	$780,000	$280,000

Required

1. Analyze the company's investment in the new machine. In your analysis, use (a) the net present value method, (b) the accounting rate-of-return method, and (c) the payback period method.
2. Summarize your findings from **1**, and recommend a course of action.

Answer to Review Problem

1a. Net present value method (factors are from Table 3 in the appendix on future value and present value tables):

Year	Net Cash Inflows	Present Value Factor	Present Value
1	$240,000	.870	$208,800
2	210,000	.756	158,760
3	180,000	.658	118,440
4	150,000	.572	85,800
4	100,000 (residual value)	.572	57,200

Total present value $629,000
Less cost of original investment   600,000
Net present value $ 29,000

1b. Accounting rate-of-return method

$$\text{Accounting Rate of Return} = \frac{\text{Average Annual Net Income}}{\text{Average Investment Cost}}$$

$$= \frac{\$280,000 \div 4}{\left(\frac{\$600,000 - \$100,000}{2}\right) + \$100,000}$$

$$= \frac{\$70,000}{\$350,000}$$

$$= 20\%$$

1c. Payback period method

Total cash investment		$600,000
Less cash-flow recovery		
Year 1	$240,000	
Year 2	210,000	
Year 3 (5/6 of $180,000)	150,000	(600,000)
Unrecovered investment		0

Payback period: 2.833 (2⅚) years, or 2 years 10 months.

2. Rolla Construction Company: summary of decision analysis

	Decision Measures	
	Desired	**Calculated**
Net present value	—	$29,000
Accounting rate of return	15%	20%
Payback period	3 years	2.833 years

Based on the calculations in **1**, the proposed investment in the earth-moving machine meets all company criteria for such investments. Given these results, the company should invest in the machine.

CHAPTER ASSIGNMENTS

BUILDING Your Knowledge Foundation and Skills

Short Exercises

LO1

Manager's Role in Capital Investment Decisions

SE 1. Joe Pharr, the supervisor of the Logistics Department, has suggested to Nina Sadam, the plant manager, that a new machine costing $185,000 be purchased to improve material handling operations for the plant's newest product line. How should the plant manager proceed with this request?

LO2

Average Cost of Capital

SE 2. Orley Industries is considering a $1 million plant expansion. Management needs to know the average cost of capital to use in evaluating this capital investment decision. The company's capital structure consists of $2,000,000 of debt at 8 percent interest and $3,000,000 of stockholders' equity at 12 percent. What is Orley Industries' average cost of capital?

LO2

Ranking Capital Investment Proposals

SE 3. Zuni Corp. has the following capital investment requests pending from its three divisions: Request 1, $60,000, 11 percent projected return; Request 2, $110,000, 14 percent projected return; Request 3, $130,000, 16 percent projected return; Request 4, $160,000, 13 percent projected return; Request 5, $175,000, 12 percent projected return; and Request 6, $230,000, 15 percent projected return. Zuni's minimum rate of return is 13 percent, and $500,000 is available for capital investment this year. Which requests will be honored, and in what order?

LO3

Capital Investment Analysis and Revenue Measures

SE 4. Maize Corp. is analyzing a proposal to switch its factory over to a lights-out operation similar to what was discussed in the opening Decision

Point. To do so, it must acquire a fully automated machine. The machine will be able to produce an entire product line in a single operation. Projected annual net cash inflows from the machine are $180,000, and projected net income is $120,000. Why is the projected net income lower than the projected net cash inflows? Identify possible causes for the $60,000 difference.

LO4   Time Value of Money

SE 5. Heidi Layne recently inherited a trust fund from a distant relative. On January 2, the bank managing the trust fund notified Layne that she has the option of receiving a lump-sum check for $175,500 or leaving the money in the trust fund and receiving an annual year-end check for $20,000 for each of the next 20 years. Layne likes to earn at least an 8 percent return on her investments. What should she do?

LO5   Residual Value and Present Value

SE 6. Anna Joiner is developing a capital investment analysis for her supervisor. The proposed capital investment has an estimated residual value of $5,500 at the end of its five-year life. The company uses a 16 percent minimum rate of return. What is the present value of the residual value? Use Table 3 in the appendix on future value and present value tables.

LO5   Capital Investment Decision: Net Present Value Method

SE 7. Noway Jose Communications, Inc., is considering the purchase of a new piece of computerized data transmission equipment. Estimated annual net cash inflows for the new equipment are $590,000. The equipment costs $2 million, it has a five-year life, and it will have no residual value at the end of the five years. The company has a minimum rate of return of 12 percent. Compute the net present value of the piece of equipment. Should the company purchase it? Use Table 4 in the appendix on future and present value tables.

LO6   Capital Investment Decision: Payback Period Method

SE 8. Using the information about Noway Jose Communications, Inc., in **SE 7**, compute the payback period for the piece of equipment. Does this method yield a positive or a negative response to the proposal to buy the equipment, assuming that the company sets a maximum payback period of four years?

LO6   Capital Investment Decision: Payback Period Method

SE 9. East-West Cable, Inc., is considering the purchase of new data transmission equipment. Estimated annual cash revenues for the new equipment are $1 million, and operating costs (including depreciation of $400,000) are $825,000. The equipment costs $2 million, it has a five-year life, and it will have no residual value at the end of the five years. Compute the payback period for the piece of equipment. Does this method yield a positive or a negative response to the proposal to buy the equipment if the company has set a maximum payback period of four years?

LO6   Capital Investment Decision: Accounting Rate-of-Return Method

SE 10. Best Cleaners is considering whether to purchase a delivery truck that will cost $29,000, last six years, and have an estimated residual value of $5,000. Average annual net income from the delivery service is estimated to be $4,000. Best Cleaners' owners seek to earn an accounting rate of return of 20 percent. Compute the average investment cost and the accounting rate of return. Should the investment be made?

Exercises

LO1 Capital Investment Analysis

E 1. Genette Henderson was just promoted to supervisor of building maintenance for the Ford Valley Theater complex. The complex consists of 17 buildings. Allpoints Entertainment, Inc., Henderson's employer, uses a companywide system for evaluating capital investment requests from its 22 supervisors. Henderson has approached you, the corporate controller, for advice on preparing her first proposal. She would also like to become familiar with the entire decision-making process.

1. What advice would you give Henderson before she prepares her first capital investment proposal?
2. Explain the role of capital investment analysis in the management process, including the six key steps taken during planning.

LO2 Minimum Rate of Return

E 2. The controller of Olaf Corporation wants to establish a minimum rate of return and would like to use a weighted-average cost of capital. Current data about the corporation's financing structure are as follows: debt financing, 40 percent; preferred stock, 30 percent; common stock, 20 percent; and retained earnings, 10 percent. The cost of debt is $9\frac{1}{2}$ percent. The dividend rate on the preferred stock issue is $7\frac{1}{2}$ percent. The cost of common stock and retained earnings is 12 percent.

Compute the weighted-average cost of capital.

LO2 Ranking Capital Investment Proposals

E 3. Managers of the Emerald Bay Furniture Company have gathered all of the capital investment proposals for the year, and they are ready to make their final selections. The following proposals and related rate-of-return amounts were received during the period:

Project	Amount of Investment	Rate of Return (Percentage)
AB	$ 450,000	19
CD	500,000	28
EF	654,000	12
GH	800,000	32
IJ	320,000	23
KL	240,000	18
MN	180,000	16
OP	400,000	26
QR	560,000	14
ST	1,200,000	22
UV	1,600,000	20

Assume that the company's minimum rate of return is 15 percent, and that $5,000,000 is available for capital investments during the year.

1. List the acceptable capital investment proposals in order of profitability.
2. Which proposals should be selected for this year?

LO3 Income Taxes and Net Cash Flow

E 4. San Falesco Company has a tax rate of 25 percent on taxable income. It is considering a capital project that will make the following annual contribution to operating income:

Cash revenues	$500,000
Cash expenses	(300,000)
Depreciation	(150,000)
Operating income before income taxes	$ 50,000
Income taxes at 25%	(12,500)
Operating income	$ 37,500

1. Determine the net cash inflows for this project in two different ways. Are net cash flows the same under either approach?
2. What is the impact of income taxes on net cash flows?

LO4 **Using the Present Values Tables**

E 5. For each of the following situations, identify the correct factor to use from Table 3 or 4 in the appendix on future value and present value tables. Also, compute the appropriate present value.

1. Annual net cash inflows of $35,000 for five years, discounted at 16 percent
2. An amount of $25,000 to be received at the end of ten years, discounted at 12 percent
3. The amount of $28,000 to be received at the end of two years, and $15,000 to be received at the end of years 4, 5, and 6, discounted at 10 percent

LO4 **Using the Present Values Tables**

E 6. For each of the following situations, identify the correct factor to use from Table 3 or 4 in the appendix on future value and present value tables. Also, compute the appropriate present value.

1. Annual net cash inflows of $22,500 for a period of twelve years, discounted at 14 percent
2. The following five years of cash inflows, discounted at 10 percent:

Year 1	$35,000	Year 4	$40,000
Year 2	20,000	Year 5	50,000
Year 3	30,000		

3. The amount of $70,000 to be received at the beginning of year 7, discounted at 14 percent

LO5 **Present Value Computations**

E 7. Two machines—Machine M and Machine P—are being considered in a replacement decision. Both machines have about the same purchase price and an estimated ten-year life. The company uses a 12 percent minimum rate of return as its acceptance-rejection standard. Following are the estimated net cash inflows for each machine.

Year	Machine M	Machine P
1	$12,000	$17,500
2	12,000	17,500
3	14,000	17,500
4	19,000	17,500
5	20,000	17,500
6	22,000	17,500
7	23,000	17,500
8	24,000	17,500
9	25,000	17,500
10	20,000	17,500
Residual value	14,000	12,000

1. Compute the present value of future cash flows for each machine, using Tables 3 and 4 in the appendix on future value and present value tables.
2. Which machine should the company purchase, assuming that both involve the same capital investment?

LO5 **Capital Investment Decision: Net Present Value Method**

E 8. Qen and Associates wants to buy an automated coffee roaster/grinder/brewer. This piece of equipment would have a useful life of six years, would cost $219,500, and would increase annual net cash inflows by $57,000. Assume that there is no residual value at the end of six years. The company's minimum rate of return is 14 percent.

Using the net present value method, prepare an analysis to determine whether the company should purchase the machine. Use Tables 3 and 4 in the appendix on future value and present value tables.

LO5 **Capital Investment Decision: Net Present Value Method**

E 9. H and Y Service Station is planning to invest in automatic car wash equipment valued at $250,000. The owner estimates that the equipment will increase annual net cash inflows by $46,000. The equipment is expected to have a ten-year useful life with an estimated residual value of $50,000. The company requires a 14 percent minimum rate of return.

Using the net present value method, prepare an analysis to determine whether the company should purchase the equipment. How important is the estimate of residual value to this decision? Use Tables 3 and 4 in the appendix on future value and present value tables.

Capital Investment Decision: Net Present Value Method

LO5 **E 10.** Assume the same facts for H and Y Service Station as in **E 9**, except assume that the company requires a 20 percent minimum rate of return.

Using the net present value method, prepare an analysis to determine whether the company should purchase the equipment. Use Tables 3 and 4 in the appendix on future value and present value tables.

Capital Investment Decision: Payback Period Method

LO6 **E 11.** Perfection Sound, Inc., a manufacturer of stereo speakers, is thinking about adding a new plastic injection molding machine. This machine can produce speaker parts that the company now buys from outsiders. The machine has an estimated useful life of 14 years and will cost $425,000. The residual value of the new machine is $42,500. Gross cash revenue from the machine will be about $400,000 per year, and related cash expenses should total $310,050. Depreciation is estimated to be $30,350 annually. The payback period should be five years or less.

Use the payback period method to determine whether the company should invest in the new machine. Show your computations to support your answer.

Capital Investment Decision: Payback Period Method

LO6 **E 12.** Soaking Wet, Inc., a manufacturer of gears for lawn sprinklers, is thinking about adding a new fully automated machine. This machine can produce gears that the company now produces on its third shift. The machine has an estimated useful life of ten years and will cost $800,000. The residual value of the new machine is $80,000. Gross cash revenue from the machine will be about $520,000 per year, and related operating expenses, including depreciation, should total $500,000. Depreciation is estimated to be $80,000 annually. The payback period should be five years or less.

Use the payback period method to determine whether the company should invest in the new machine. Show your computations to support your answer.

LO6 Capital Investment Decision: Accounting Rate-of-Return Method

E 13. Assume the same facts as in **E 11** for Perfection Sound, Inc. Management has decided that only capital investments that yield at least a 20 percent return will be accepted.

Using the accounting rate-of-return method, decide whether the company should invest in the machine. Show all computations to support your decision.

LO6 Capital Investment Decision: Accounting Rate-of-Return Method

E 14. Assume the same facts as in **E 12** for Soaking Wet, Inc. Management has decided that only capital investments that yield at least a 5 percent return will be accepted.

Using the accounting rate-of-return method, decide whether the company should invest in the machine. Show all computations to support your decision.

LO6 Capital Investment Decision: Accounting Rate-of-Return Method

E 15. Boink Corporation manufactures metal hard hats for on-site construction workers. Recently, management has tried to raise productivity to meet the growing demand from the real estate industry. The company is now thinking about buying a new stamping machine. Management has decided that only capital investments that yield at least a 14 percent return will be accepted. The new machine would cost $325,000; revenue would increase by $98,400 per year; the residual value of the new machine would be $32,500; and operating cost increases (including depreciation) would be $74,600.

Using the accounting rate-of-return method, decide whether the company should invest in the machine. Show all computations to support your decision.

Problems

LO2, LO3 Minimum Rate of Return

P 1. Capital investment analysis is the main responsibility of Ginny Weiss, the special assistant to the controller of Nazzaro Manufacturing Company. During the previous 12-month period, the company's capital mix and the respective costs were as follows:

	Percentage of Total Financing	Cost of Capital (Percentage)
Debt financing	25	7
Preferred stock	15	9
Common stock	50	12
Retained earnings	10	12

Plans for the current year call for a 10 percent shift in total financing from common stock financing to debt financing. Also, the cost of debt financing is expected to increase to 8 percent, although the cost of the other types of financing will remain the same.

Weiss has already analyzed several proposed capital investments. Those projects and their projected rates of return are as follows: Project M, 9.5 percent; Equipment Item N, 8.5 percent; Product Line O, 15.0 percent;

Project P, 6.9 percent; Product Line Q, 10.5 percent; Equipment Item R, 11.9 percent; and Project S, 11.0 percent.

Required

1. Using the expected adjustments to cost and capital mix, compute the weighted-average cost of capital for the current year.
2. Identify the proposed capital investments that should be implemented based on the cost of capital calculated in 1.

LO4, LO5 **Net Present Value Method**

P 2. Sonja and Sons, Inc., owns and operates a group of apartment buildings. Management wants to sell one of its older four-family buildings and buy a new building. The old building, which was purchased 25 years ago for $100,000, has a 40-year estimated life. The current market value is $80,000, and if it is sold, the cash inflow will be $67,675. Annual net cash inflows from the old building are expected to average $16,000 for the remainder of its estimated useful life.

The new building will cost $300,000. It has an estimated useful life of 25 years. Net cash inflows are expected to be $50,000 annually.

Assume that (1) all cash flows occur at year end, (2) the company uses straight-line depreciation, (3) the buildings will have a residual value equal to 10 percent of their purchase price, and (4) the minimum rate of return is 14 percent. Use Tables 3 and 4 in the appendix on future value and present value tables.

Required

1. Compute the present value of future cash flows from the old building.
2. What will the net present value of cash flows be if the company purchases the new building?
3. Manager Insight: Should the company keep the old building or purchase the new one?

LO4, LO5 **Net Present Value Method**

P 3. The management of Better Plastics has recently been looking at a proposal to purchase a new plastic injection-style molding machine. With the new machine, the company would not have to buy small plastic parts to use in production. The estimated useful life of the machine is 15 years, and the purchase price, including all setup charges, is $400,000. The residual value is estimated to be $40,000. The net addition to the company's cash inflow as a result of the savings from making the parts is estimated to be $70,000 a year. Better Plastics' management has decided on a minimum rate of return of 14 percent. Use Tables 3 and 4 in the appendix on future value and present value tables.

Required

1. Using the net present value method to evaluate this capital investment, determine whether the company should purchase the machine. Support your answer.
2. Manager Insight: If the management of Better Plastics had decided on a minimum rate of return of 16 percent, should the machine be purchased? Show all computations to support your answer.

LO6 **Accounting Rate-of-Return and Payback Period Methods**

P 4. The Raab Company is expanding its production facilities to include a new product line, a sporty automotive tire rim. Tire rims can now be produced with little labor cost using new computerized machinery. The controller has advised management about two such machines. The details about each machine are as follows:

	XJS Machine	HZT Machine
Cost of machine	$500,000	$550,000
Residual value	50,000	55,000
Net income	34,965	40,670
Annual net cash inflows	91,215	90,170

The company's minimum rate of return is 12 percent. The maximum payback period is six years. (Where necessary, round calculations to the nearest dollar.)

Required

1. For each machine, compute the projected accounting rate of return.
2. Compute the payback period for each machine.
3. **Manager Insight:** Based on the information from **1** and **2**, which machine should be purchased? Why?

LO4, LO5, LO6   Capital Investment Decision: Comprehensive

P 5. The Arcadia Manufacturing Company, based in Arcadia, Florida, is one of the fastest-growing companies in its industry. According to Ms. Prinze, the company's production vice president, keeping up-to-date with technological changes is what makes the company successful.

Prinze feels that a machine introduced recently would fill an important need. The machine has an estimated useful life of four years, a purchase price of $250,000, and a residual value of $25,000. The company controller has estimated average annual net income of $11,250 and the following cash flows for the new machine:

	Cash Flow Estimates		
Year	Cash Inflows	Cash Outflows	Net Cash Inflows
1	$325,000	$250,000	$75,000
2	320,000	250,000	70,000
3	315,000	250,000	65,000
4	310,000	250,000	60,000

Prinze uses a 12 percent minimum rate of return and a three-year payback period for capital investment evaluation purposes.

Required

1. Analyze the data about the machine, and decide if the company should purchase it. Use the following evaluation approaches in your analysis: (a) the net present value method, (b) the accounting rate-of-return method, and (c) the payback period method. Use Tables 3 and 4 in the appendix on future value and present value tables.
2. Summarize the information generated in **1**, and make a recommendation to Prinze.

Alternate Problems

LO4, LO5   Comparison of Alternatives: Net Present Value Method

P 6. City Sights, Ltd., operates a tour and sightseeing business. Its trademark is the use of trolley buses. Each vehicle has its own identity and is specially made for the company. Gridlock, the oldest bus, was purchased 15 years ago and has 5 years of its estimated useful life remaining. The company paid $25,000 for Gridlock, and the bus could be sold today for $20,000. Gridlock is expected to generate average annual net cash inflows of $24,000 for the remainder of its estimated useful life.

Management wants to replace Gridlock with a modern-looking vehicle called Phantom. Phantom has a purchase price of $140,000 and an estimated useful life of 20 years. Net cash inflows for Phantom are projected to be $40,000 per year.

Assume that (1) all cash flows occur at year end, (2) each vehicle's residual value equals 10 percent of its purchase price, and (3) the minimum rate of return is 10 percent. Use Tables 3 and 4 in the appendix on future value and present value tables.

Required

1. Compute the present value of the future cash flows from Gridlock.
2. Compute the net present value of cash flows if Phantom were purchased.
3. **Manager Insight:** Should City Sights keep Gridlock or purchase Phantom?

LO4, LO5 **Net Present Value Method**

P 7. Mansion is a famous restaurant in the French Quarter of New Orleans. Bouillabaisse Sophie is Mansion's house specialty. Management is considering the purchase of a machine that would prepare all the ingredients, mix them automatically, and cook the dish to the restaurant's specifications. The machine will function for an estimated 12 years, and the purchase price, including installation, is $250,000. Estimated residual value is $25,000. This labor-saving device is expected to increase cash flows by an average of $42,000 per year during its estimated useful life. For capital investment decisions, the restaurant uses a 12 percent minimum rate of return. Use Tables 3 and 4 in the appendix on future value and present value tables.

Required

1. Using the net present value method, determine if the company should purchase the machine. Support your answer.
2. **Manager Insight:** If management had decided on a minimum rate of return of 14 percent, should the machine be purchased? Show all computations to support your answer.

LO4, LO5, LO6 **Capital Investment Decision: Comprehensive**

P 8. Pressed Corporation wants to buy a new stamping machine. The machine will provide the company with a new product line: pressed rubber food trays for kitchens. Two machines are being considered; the data for each machine are as follows:

	ETZ Machine	LKR Machine
Cost of machine	$350,000	$370,000
Net income	$39,204	$48,642
Annual net cash inflows	$64,404	$75,642
Residual value	$28,000	$40,000
Estimated useful life in years	10	10

The company's minimum rate of return is 16 percent, and the maximum allowable payback period is 5.0 years.

Required

1. Compute the net present value for each machine.
2. Compute the accounting rate of return for each machine.
3. Compute the payback period for each machine.
4. **Manager Insight:** From the information generated in **1**, **2**, and **3**, decide which machine should be purchased. Why?

ENHANCING Your Knowledge, Skills, and Critical Thinking

Conceptual Understanding Cases

LO1   **Factors in Capital Investment Decisions**

C 1. PPG Industries, founded in 1883, was the first commercially successful plate glass manufacturer in the United States. Today it is a global supplier of coatings, chemicals, and glass. Annually, its management approves capital spending for modernization and productivity improvements, expansion of existing businesses, and environmental control projects. Management will receive many proposals for projects to use this money, and it must set an appropriate acceptance-rejection standard. What factors should be considered in setting this standard? If more proposed projects meet the minimum standard than can be funded, what other factors should management consider, and what should management do?

LO2   **Weighted-Average Cost of Capital**

C 2. DaimlerChrysler is a multinational company that must evaluate many proposed capital investments. The company's investment policy is based on a weighted-average cost of capital. What is a weighted-average cost of capital? Briefly describe how DaimlerChrysler would go about calculating it.

LO1   **Evaluation of Proposed Capital Investments**

C 3. The board of directors of the Tanashi Corporation met to review a number of proposed capital investments that would improve the quality of company products. One production line manager requested the purchase of new computer-integrated machines to replace the older machines in one of the ten production departments at the Tokyo plant. Although the manager had presented quantitative information to support the purchase of the new machines, the board members asked the following important questions:

1. Why do we want to replace the old machines? Have they deteriorated? Are they obsolete?
2. Will the new machines require less cycle time?
3. Can we reduce inventory levels or save floor space by replacing the old machines?
4. How expensive is the software used with the new machines?
5. Will we be able to find highly skilled employees to maintain the new machines? Or can we find workers who are trainable? What would it cost to train workers? Would the training disrupt the staff by causing relocations?
6. Would the implementation of the machines be delayed because of the time required to recruit and train new workers?
7. How would the new machines affect the other parts of the manufacturing systems? Would the company lose some of the flexibility in its manufacturing systems if it introduced the new machines?

The board members believe that the qualitative information needed to answer their questions could lead to the rejection of the project, even though it would have been accepted based on the quantitative information.

1. Identify the questions that can be answered with quantitative information. Give an example of the quantitative information that could be used.
2. Identify the questions that can be answered with qualitative information. Explain why this information could negatively influence the capital investment decision even though the quantitative information suggests a positive outcome.

LO4, LO5 **Using Net Present Value**

C 4. The McCall Syndicate owns four resort hotels in Europe. Because the Paris operation (Hotel 1) has been booming over the past five years, management has decided to build an addition to the hotel. This addition will increase the hotel's capacity by 20 percent. A construction company has bid to build the addition at a cost of $30,000,000. The building will have an increased residual value of $3,000,000.

Da Van Dyke, the controller, has started an analysis of the net present value for the project. She has calculated the annual net cash inflows by subtracting the increase in cash operating expenses from the increase in cash inflows from room rentals. Her partially completed schedule follows.

Year	Net Cash Inflows
1–20 (each year)	$3,900,000

Capital investment projects must generate a 12 percent minimum rate of return to qualify for consideration.

Using net present value analysis, evaluate the proposal and make a recommendation to management. Explain how your recommendation would change if management were willing to accept a 10 percent minimum rate of return. Use Tables 3 and 4 in the appendix on future value and present value tables.

Interpreting Management Reports

LO5 **Capital Investment Analysis**

C 5. Automated teller machines (ATMs) have become common in the banking industry. San Angelo Federal Bank is planning to replace some old teller machines and has decided to use the York Machine. Nola Chavez, the controller, has prepared the analysis shown at the top of the opposite page. She has recommended the purchase of the machine based on the positive net present value shown in the analysis.

The York Machine has an estimated useful life of five years and an expected residual value of $35,000. Its purchase price is $385,000. Two existing ATMs, each having a carrying value of $25,000, can be sold to a neighboring bank for a total of $50,000. Annual operating cash inflows are expected to increase in the following manner:

Year 1	$79,900
Year 2	76,600
Year 3	79,900
Year 4	83,200
Year 5	86,500

The San Angelo Federal Bank uses straight-line depreciation. The minimum rate of return is 12 percent.

San Angelo Federal Bank
Capital Investment Analysis
Net Present Value Method

Year	Net Cash Inflows	Present Value Factor	Present Value
1	$ 85,000	.909	$ 77,265
2	80,000	.826	66,080
3	85,000	.751	63,835
4	90,000	.683	61,470
5	95,000	.621	58,995
5 (residual value)	35,000	.621	21,735
Total present value			$349,380
Initial investment	$385,000		
Less proceeds from the sale of existing teller machines	50,000		
Net capital investment			(335,000)
Net present value			$ 14,380

1. Analyze Chavez's work. What changes need to be made in her capital investment analysis?
2. What would be your recommendation to bank management about the purchase of the York Machine?

Decision Analysis Using Excel

LO5   Net Present Value of Cash Flows

C 6. CPC Corporation is an international plumbing equipment and supply company located in southern California. The manager of the Pipe Division is considering the purchase of a computerized copper pipe machine that costs $120,000.

The machine has a six-year life, and its expected residual value after six years of use will be 10 percent of its original cost. Cash revenue generated by the new machine is projected to be $50,000 in year 1 and will increase by $10,000 each year for the next five years. Variable cash operating costs will be materials and parts, 25 percent of revenue; machine labor, 5 percent of revenue; and overhead, 15 percent of revenue. First-year sales and marketing cash outflows are expected to be $10,500 and will decrease by 10 percent each year over the life of the new machine. Anticipated cash administrative expenses will be $2,500 per year. The company uses a 15 percent minimum rate of return for all capital investment analyses.

1. Prepare an Excel spreadsheet to compute the net present value of the anticipated cash flows for the life of the proposed new machine. Use the following format:

		Projected Cash Outflows							
Future Time Period	Projected Cash Revenue	Materials and Parts	Machine Labor	Overhead	Sales and Marketing	Administrative Expenses	Projected Net Cash Inflows	15% Factor	Present Value

Should the company invest in the new machine?

2. After careful analysis, the controller has determined that the variable rate for materials and parts can be reduced to 22 percent of revenue. Will this reduction in cash outflow change the decision about investing in the new machine? Explain your answer.

3. The marketing manager has determined that the initial estimate of sales and marketing cash expenses was too high and has reduced that estimate by $1,000. The 10 percent annual reductions are still expected to occur. Together with the change in **2**, will this reduction affect the initial investment decision? Explain your answer.

Ethical Dilemma Case

LO5 **Ethics, Capital Investment Decisions, and the New Globally Competitive Business Environment**

C 7. Marika Jonssen is the controller of Bramer Corporation, a globally competitive producer of standard and custom-designed window units for the housing industry. As part of the corporation's move to become automated, Jonssen was asked to prepare a capital investment analysis for a robot-guided aluminum extruding and stamping machine. This machine would automate the entire window-casing manufacturing line. She has just returned from an international seminar on the subject of qualitative inputs into the capital investment decision process and is eager to incorporate those new ideas into the analysis. In addition to the normal net present value analysis (which produced a significant negative result), Jonssen factored in figures for customer satisfaction, scrap reduction, reduced inventory needs, and reputation for quality. With the additional information included, the analysis produced a positive response to the decision question.

When the chief financial officer finished reviewing Jonssen's work, he threw the papers on the floor and said, "What kind of garbage is this! You know it's impossible to quantify such things as customer satisfaction and reputation for quality. How do you expect me to go to the board of directors and explain your work? I want you to redo the entire analysis and follow only the traditional approach to net present value. Get it back to me in two hours!"

What is Jonssen's dilemma? What ethical courses of action are available to her?

Internet Case

LO1, LO2 **Comparison of Capital Investment Disclosures by Two Large Companies**

C 8. Companies vary in the amount of information they disclose about their criteria for selecting capital investments. Access the websites of two companies—for example, **Coca-Cola** and **International Paper**. Find management's discussion and analysis (also called the *financial review*), which precedes the presentation of the financial statements. In that section, find the discussion of capital investments. Which company provides the more in-depth discussion? Does either disclose its criteria for making capital investment decisions? Also, look at the investing activities listed in the statement of cash flows for each company. What is the extent of capital expenditures for each company? Compare each company's capital investments with the amount of total assets on the balance sheet. Which company is more of a growth company? Explain your answer.

Group Activity Case

LO1 Capital Investment Analysis

C 9. Computers are essential in today's business world. Every business benefits from computers' capabilities, which include rapid data processing, timely report generation, automated accounting systems, and the use of specialized software packages for such areas as payroll, accounts receivable, accounts payable, and tax return preparation. Make a trip to a local computer retailer. Inquire about the various types of computers available, and identify one that would be useful to a local nursery selling landscape plants and gardening supplies and equipment. Find out the cost of this computer. Make notes of its model name, its special features and capabilities, and its cost. After gathering the data, identify the benefits that the nursery's controller would include in an analysis to justify the purchase of the computer. Describe the effect of each benefit on cash flow and profitability.

Your instructor will divide the class into groups, and ask each group to discuss this case. One student from each group will summarize his or her group's findings for the entire class.

Business Communication Case

LO3, LO4, LO5, LO6 Evaluating a Capital Investment Proposal

C 10. Smile Photo, Inc., is a nationally franchised company with over 50 outlets located in the southern states. Part of the franchise agreement promises a centralized photo developing process with overnight delivery to the outlets.

Because of the tremendous increase in demand for its photo processing, Emma DuBarry, the corporation's president, is considering the purchase of a new, deluxe photo processing machine by the end of this month. DuBarry wants you to formulate a memo showing your evaluation of this purchase. Your memo will be presented at the board of directors' meeting next week.

According to your research, the new machine will cost $320,000. It will function for an estimated five years and should have a $32,000 residual value. All capital investments are expected to produce a 20 percent minimum rate of return, and the investment should be recovered in three years or less. All fixed assets are depreciated using the straight-line method. The forecasted increases in operating results for the new machine are as follows:

	Cash Flow Estimates	
Year	Cash Inflows	Cash Outflows
1	$310,000	$210,000
2	325,000	220,000
3	340,000	230,000
4	300,000	210,000
5	260,000	180,000

1. In preparation for writing your memo, answer the following questions:
   a. What kinds of information do you need to prepare this memo?
   b. Why is the information relevant?
   c. Where would you find the information?
   d. When would you want to obtain the information?
2. Analyze the purchase of the machine and decide if the company should purchase it. Use (a) the net present value method, (b) the accounting rate-of-return method, and (c) the payback period method.

Quality Management and Measurement

Quality has many dimensions. Not only must a product or service be defect-free and dependable; it must also embody such intangibles as prestige and good taste. Managers must meet or exceed a variety of expectations about customer service and create innovative new products and services that anticipate the opportunities offered by an ever-changing marketplace. To compete successfully, managers need information that enables them to determine accurate product, service, and customer costs; to improve processes; and to provide timely feedback about their organization to all stakeholders. Such information can be produced only by an information system that captures both financial and nonfinancial information. In this chapter, we describe financial and nonfinancial measures of quality and how managers use these measures to evaluate operating performance.

LEARNING OBJECTIVES

LO1 Describe a management information system, and explain how it enhances management decision making.

LO2 Define *total quality management (TQM),* and identify financial and nonfinancial measures of quality.

LO3 Use measures of quality to evaluate operating performance.

LO4 Discuss the evolving concept of quality.

LO5 Recognize the awards and organizations that promote quality.

- How do Amazon.com's managers maintain the company's competitive edge?

- What measures of quality can Amazon.com use to evaluate operating performance?

Through its innovative approach to selling books and other merchandise online, Amazon.com has changed the rules of successful electronic retailing. To maintain a competitive advantage, Amazon.com's managers must have an information system that produces more than just financial data. They need an extensive information infrastructure that can capture all kinds of information in huge, secure databases. Amazon.com's databases presently contain over 1 trillion bytes of information that the company can privately mine and use in multiple applications.

Customers of online retailing firms have come to expect not only innovative features, but also a high standard of product reliability and service. Amazon.com can continue to challenge and experiment with the ever-evolving ecommerce business model only if its management information system remains on the cutting edge of database technology and produces pertinent information of the highest quality for its managers.[1]

The Role of Management Information Systems in Quality Management

LO1 Describe a management information system, and explain how it enhances management decision making.

Many traditional management information systems contain only financial data and do not produce the sort of information that is necessary in today's competitive business environment. To compete successfully, managers need information that enables them to determine accurate product, service, and customer costs; improve processes; and provide timely feedback to all stakeholders about their organization. Such information can be produced only by an information system that captures both financial and non-financial information. This kind of **management information system (MIS)** is a reporting system that identifies, monitors, and maintains continuous, detailed analyses of a company's activities and provides managers with timely measures of operating results. It is designed to support such management philosophies as just-in-time (JIT) operations, activity-based costing (ABC) and activity-based management (ABM), and total quality management (TQM).

The primary focus of an MIS is on the management of activities, not on costs. By focusing on activities, an MIS provides managers with improved knowledge of the processes for which they are responsible. Activity-related information that is needed to increase responsiveness to customers and reduce processing time is readily available. More accurate product and service costs lead to improved pricing decisions. Nonvalue-adding activities are highlighted, and managers can work to reduce or eliminate them. In addition to providing information about product profitability, an MIS can analyze the profitability of individual customers and look at all aspects of serving customers. Overall, the MIS identifies resource usage and cost for each activity and fosters managerial decisions that lead to continuous improvement throughout the organization.

Enterprise Resource Planning Systems

An MIS can be designed as a customized, informally linked series of systems for specific purposes, such as financial reporting, product costing, and business process measurement, or as a fully integrated database system known as an **enterprise resource planning (ERP) system**. An ERP system combines the management of all major business activities (e.g., purchasing, manufacturing, marketing, sales, logistics, and order fulfillment) with support activities (e.g., accounting and human resources) to form one easy-to-access, centralized data warehouse. An ERP system not only fosters communication within an organization; it can also communicate with other businesses' databases.

This chapter's Decision Point presents an example of an ERP system that has merged **Amazon.com's** operating, financial, and management systems. Because of its ability to access a variety of data types from multiple sources, both inside and outside the company, Amazon.com has developed a competitive advantage in achieving financial targets and quality results. Using improved knowledge of the activities and processes for which they are responsible, Amazon.com's managers have pinpointed resource usage and fostered managerial decisions that have led to continuous improvement throughout the organization.

> ⌐◯ Study Note
>
> The term *enterprise resource management (ERM)* can be used in place of *ERP*.

■ **FIGURE 1**
The Management Process: To-Do's for Managers

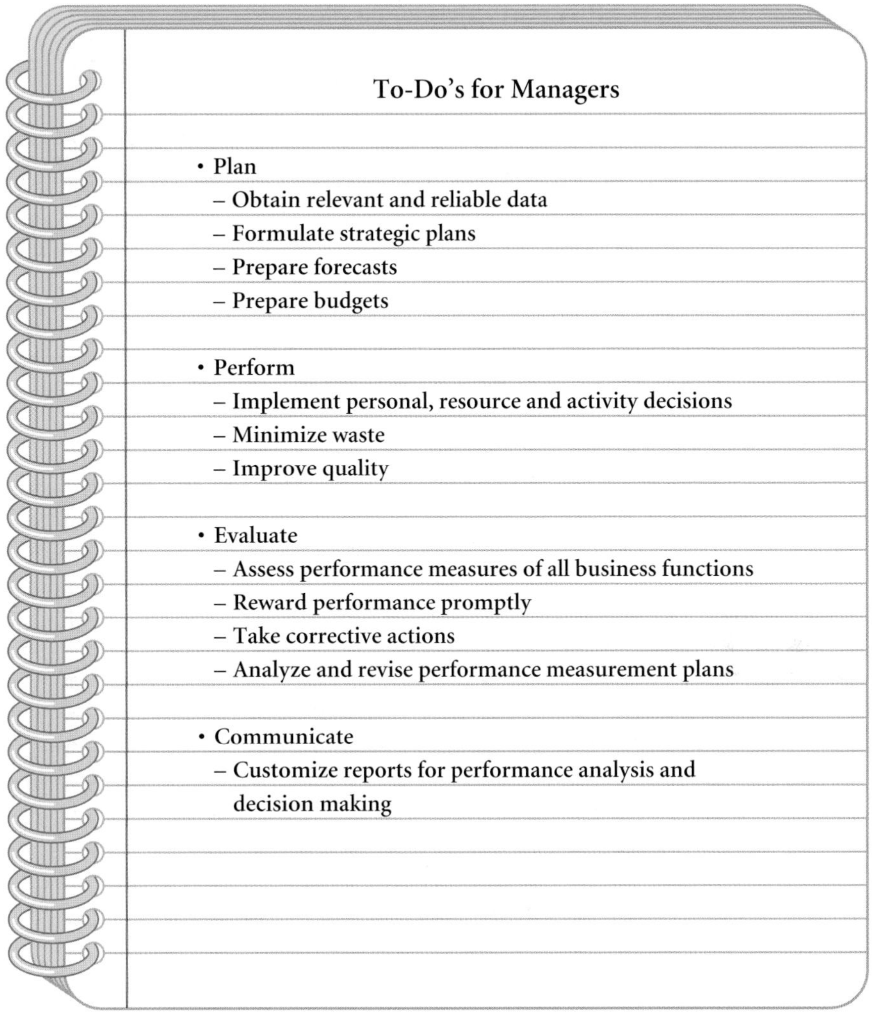

To-Do's for Managers

- Plan
  – Obtain relevant and reliable data
  – Formulate strategic plans
  – Prepare forecasts
  – Prepare budgets

- Perform
  – Implement personal, resource and activity decisions
  – Minimize waste
  – Improve quality

- Evaluate
  – Assess performance measures of all business functions
  – Reward performance promptly
  – Take corrective actions
  – Analyze and revise performance measurement plans

- Communicate
  – Customize reports for performance analysis and
    decision making

Managers' Use of MIS

Like the managers at Amazon.com, business managers today use their management information systems' detailed, real-time financial and nonfinancial information about customers, inventory, resources, and the supply chain to manage quality. Without the flexibility and power of database management information systems like ERP, managers would be at a disadvantage in today's rapidly changing and highly competitive business environment. Figure 1 illustrates how managers use a management information system.

Planning Managers use the MIS database to obtain relevant and reliable information for formulating strategic plans, making forecasts, and preparing budgets. For example, managers at Amazon.com use their MIS to develop forecasts and budgets for existing operations and to create plans for new value-adding products and services.

Performing Managers use the financial and nonfinancial information in the MIS database to implement decisions about personnel, resources, and activities that will minimize waste and improve the quality of their organization's products or services. At Amazon.com, managers use their supply-chain and value-chain software to manage operations in ways that ensure accurate order fulfillment and timely delivery.

Evaluating Managers identify and track financial and nonfinancial performance measures to evaluate all major business functions. By enabling the timely comparison of actual performance with expected performance, Amazon.com's MIS allows managers to reward good performance promptly, take speedy corrective actions, and analyze and revise performance measurement plans.

Communicating Managers can use an MIS to generate customized reports that evaluate performance and provide useful information for decision making. For example, managers at Amazon.com can consolidate customer profiles from their company's sophisticated database into a real-time report available on their desktops to continuously monitor the changing buying habits of their customers.

STOP • REVIEW • APPLY

1-1. What is a management information system?

1-2. Why is a management information system so important to managers?

1-3. How does an enterprise resource planning (ERP) system differ from other management information systems?

Suggested answers to all Stop, Review, and Apply questions are available at http://college.hmco.com/accounting/needles/man_acc/8e/student_home.html.

Financial and Nonfinancial Measures of Quality

LO2 Define *total quality management (TQM)*, and identify financial and nonfinancial measures of quality.

Over the past two decades, organizations have defined quality in terms of what their customers value. Organizations believe that customers want the highest-quality goods and services and that customers' willingness to pay for high quality will result in improved organizational profits. As a result, organizations strive to exceed customers' expectations and improve the quality of their products or services. Quality is not something that a company can simply add at some point in the production process or assume will happen automatically. Inspections can detect bad products, but they do not ensure quality. Managers need reliable measures of quality to help them meet the goal of producing high-quality, reasonably priced products or services. They need to create a total quality management environment.

Total quality management (TQM) is an organizational environment in which all business functions work together to build quality into the firm's products or services. The first step toward creating a TQM environment is to identify and manage the financial measures of quality, or the costs of quality. The second step is to analyze operating performance using nonfinancial measures and to require that all business processes and products or services be improved continuously.

Financial Measures of Quality

To the average person, *quality* means that one product or service is better than another—perhaps because of its design, its durability, or some other attribute. In a business setting, however, **quality** is the result of an operating environment in which a product or service meets or conforms to a customer's specifications the first time it is produced or delivered.

The **costs of quality** are the costs that are specifically associated with the achievement or nonachievement of product or service quality. Total costs of quality include (1) costs of good quality, incurred to ensure the successful development of a product or service, and (2) costs of poor quality, incurred to transform a faulty product or service into one that is acceptable to the customer.

The costs of quality can make up a significant portion of a product's or service's total cost. Therefore, controlling the costs of quality strongly affects profitability. Today's managers should be able to identify the activities associated with improving quality and should be aware of the cost of resources used to achieve high quality.

The costs of quality have two components: the **costs of conformance**, which are the costs incurred to produce a quality product or service, and the **costs of nonconformance**, which are the costs incurred to correct defects in a product or service. Costs of conformance are made up of prevention costs and appraisal costs.

- **Prevention costs** are the costs associated with the prevention of defects and failures in products and services.

- **Appraisal costs** are the costs of activities that measure, evaluate, or audit products, processes, or services to ensure their conformance to quality standards and performance requirements.

The costs of nonconformance include internal failure costs and external failure costs.

- **Internal failure costs** are the costs incurred when defects are discovered before a product or service is delivered to a customer.

- **External failure costs** are costs incurred after the delivery of a defective product or service.

Table 1 gives examples of each cost category. Note that there is an inverse relationship between the costs of conformance and the costs of nonconformance: If a company spends money on the costs of conformance, the costs of

Study Note

Costs of conformance include the costs of building quality into products and services by doing it right the first time.

Study Note

Internal failure costs are costs incurred to correct mistakes found by the company. External failure costs are costs incurred to correct mistakes discovered by customers.

TABLE 1. **Financial Measures of Quality**

Costs of Conformance to Customer Standards

Prevention Costs

Technical support for vendors	Quality-certified suppliers
Integrated system development	Quality circles
Quality improvement projects	Preventive maintenance
Quality training of employees	Statistical process control
Design review of products and processes	Process engineering

Appraisal Costs

Inspection of materials, processes, and machines	Maintenance of test equipment
End-of-process sampling and testing	Quality audits of products and processes
Vendor audits and sample testing	Field testing

Costs of Nonconformance to Customer Standards

Internal Failure Costs

Scrap and rework	Failure analysis
Reinspection and retesting of rework	Inventory control and scheduling
Quality-related downtime	Downgrading because of defects
Scrap disposal losses	

External Failure Costs

Lost sales	Returned goods and replacements
Restoration of reputation	Investigation of defects
Warranty claims and adjustments	Product recalls
Customer complaint processing	Product-liability settlements

Measures of Quality

Total costs of quality as a percentage of net sales

Ratio of costs of conformance to total costs of quality

Ratio of costs of nonconformance to total costs of quality

Costs of nonconformance as a percentage of net sales

nonconformance should be reduced. However, if little attention is paid to the costs of conformance, the costs of nonconformance may escalate.

An organization's overall goal is to avoid costs of nonconformance because both internal and external failures affect customers' satisfaction and the organization's profitability. High initial costs of conformance are justified when they minimize the total costs of quality over the life of a product or service. The cost-based measures of quality listed at the bottom of Table 1 are discussed later in the chapter.

Nonfinancial Measures of Quality

By measuring the costs of quality, a company learns how much it has spent in its efforts to improve product or service quality. But critics say that tracking historical data to monitor quality performance does little to enhance quality. What managers need is a measurement and evaluation system that signals poor quality early enough to allow problems to be corrected before a defective product or service reaches the customer. Implementing a policy of contin-

Before undergoing an operation, patients and their families want to evaluate the performance record of the hospital and the surgical team so that they can feel confident about the quality of care. Leading hospitals like the Cleveland Clinic enable them to make this assessment by publishing relevant facts and figures graphically on the Internet. Take a glance at the Cleveland Clinic's quality measures at www.clevelandclinic.org/quality/measures.

Study Note

Nonfinancial measures gauge quality and the value created throughout the supply and value chains.

uous improvement satisfies this need and is the second stage of total quality management.

Nonfinancial measures of performance, identified and reported to managers in a timely manner, are used to supplement cost-based measures. Although cost control is still an important consideration, a commitment to ongoing improvement encourages activities that enhance quality at every stage, from design to delivery. As explained earlier, those activities, or cost drivers, cause costs. By controlling the leading nonfinancial performance measures of activities, managers can ultimately maximize the resulting financial return from operations. Five categories of nonfinancial measures of quality are discussed in the following sections.

Product Design Problems with quality often are the result of poor design. Most automated production operations use **computer-aided design (CAD)**, a computer-based engineering system with a built-in program to detect product design flaws. Such computer programs automatically identify poorly designed parts or manufacturing processes, which means that engineers can correct these problems before production begins. Managers monitor the CAD reports on design flaws to ensure that products are properly designed and free

Product quality is a nonfinancial measure of performance. Poor product quality is often the result of poor design. This woman is using computer-aided design (CAD) to create a model of a new fuel cell scooter. CAD allows designs to be tested without expending the time and money required to build a working model.

of defects. Among the measures that they consider are the number and types of design defects detected, the average time between defect detection and correction, and the number of unresolved design defects at the time of product introduction.

Vendor Performance   Companies have recently changed the way they do business with suppliers of materials. Instead of dealing with dozens of suppliers in a quest for the lowest cost, companies now analyze their vendors to determine which ones are most reliable, furnish high-quality goods, have a record of timely deliveries, and charge competitive prices. Once a company has identified such vendors, they become an integral part of the production team's effort to ensure a continuing supply of high-quality materials. Vendors may even contribute to product design to ensure that the correct materials are being used.

Managers use measures of quality (such as defect-free materials as a percentage of total materials received) and measures of delivery (such as timely deliveries as a percentage of total deliveries) to identify reliable vendors and monitor their performance. The goal in doing so is to ensure that high-quality, reasonably priced materials are available when they are needed.

Production Performance   Management must always be concerned about the wasted time and money that can be traced to defective products, scrapped parts, machine maintenance, and downtime. To minimize such concerns, more and more companies have adopted **computer-integrated manufacturing (CIM) systems**, in which production and its support operations are coordinated by computers. Within a CIM system, computer-aided manufacturing (CAM) may be used to coordinate and control production activities, or a flexible manufacturing system (FMS) may be used to link together automated equipment into a computerized flexible production network.

In CIM systems, most direct labor hours are replaced by machine hours, and very little direct labor cost is incurred. In addition, a significant part of variable product cost is replaced by the cost of expensive machinery, a fixed cost. Today, the largest item on a company's balance sheet is often automated machinery and equipment. Each piece of equipment has a specific capacity, above which continuous operation is threatened. When managers evaluate such machines, their measures have two objectives:

1. To evaluate the performance of each piece of equipment in relation to its capacity

2. To evaluate the performance of maintenance personnel in following a prescribed maintenance program

Measures of production quality, parts scrapped, equipment utilization, machine downtime, and machine maintenance time help managers monitor production performance.

Delivery Cycle Time   Companies today are extremely interested in the amount of time they take to respond to customers. To evaluate their responsiveness to customers, companies examine their **delivery cycle time**, which is the time between the acceptance of an order and the final delivery of the product or service. When a customer places an order, it is important for a salesperson to be able to promise an accurate delivery date. A company's goal is to fill

> **Study Note**
>
> Delivery Cycle Time = Purchase-Order Lead Time + Production Cycle Time + Delivery Time.

its orders 100 percent of the time and to deliver its products 100 percent on time. To meet this goal, a company must establish and maintain consistency and reliability within its production process and be highly aware of its delivery cycle time.

Companies pay careful attention to delivery cycle time not only because on-time delivery is important to customers, but also because a decrease in delivery cycle time can lead to a significant increase in income from operations. Delivery cycle time consists of **purchase-order lead time** (the time it takes a company to process an order and organize so that production can begin), **production cycle time** (the time it takes to make a product) and **delivery time** (the time between the completion of a product and its receipt by the customer).

Managers should establish measures that emphasize the importance of minimizing the purchase-order lead time, production cycle time, and delivery time for each order. They should also track the average purchase-order lead time, production cycle time, and delivery time for all orders. Trends should be highlighted, and reports should be readily available. Other measures designed to monitor delivery cycle time include order backlogs, on-time delivery performance, percentage of orders filled, and waste time. Waste time is the production cycle time − (average process time + average setup time).

Customer Satisfaction The sale and shipment of a product does not mark the end of performance measurement. Customer follow-up helps in evaluating total customer satisfaction. Measures used to determine the degree of customer satisfaction include (1) the number and types of customer complaints, (2) the number and causes of warranty claims, and (3) the percentage of shipments returned by customers (or the percentage of shipments accepted by customers). Several companies have developed their own customer satisfaction indexes from these measures so that they can compare different product lines over different time periods.

Table 2 lists specific examples of the many nonfinancial measures used to monitor quality. These measures help a company continuously produce higher-quality products, improve production processes, and reduce throughput time and costs.

Measuring Service Quality

The quality of services rendered can be measured and analyzed. Many of the costs of conformance and nonconformance for a product apply to the development and delivery of a service. Flaws in service design lead to poor-quality services. Timely service delivery is as important as timely product shipments. Customer satisfaction in a service business can be measured by services accepted or rejected, the number of complaints, and the number of returning customers. Poor service development leads to internal and external failure costs.

Many of the costs-of-quality categories and several of the nonfinancial measures of quality can be applied directly to services and can be adopted by any type of service company. For example, the service departments of **Mercedes-Benz** dealers ask customers to complete a short three-question form when they pay their bills, **Chubb Insurance Company** sends a brief questionnaire to customers after every claim, and **PBS** provides phone, fax, and email addresses where viewers can record their comments about the system's programming.

TABLE 2.   Nonfinancial Measures of Quality

**Measures of
Product Design Quality**

Product design flaws	Number and types of design defects detected
	Average time between defect detection and correction
	Number of unresolved design defects at time of product introduction

**Measures of
Vendor Performance**

Vendor quality	Defect-free materials as a percentage of total materials received; prepared for each vendor
Vendor delivery	Timely deliveries of materials as a percentage of total deliveries; prepared for each vendor

**Measures of
Production Performance**

Production quality	Number of defective products per thousand produced
Parts scrapped	Number and type of materials spoiled during production
Equipment utilization rate	Productive machine time as a percentage of total time available for production
Machine downtime	Amount of time each machine is idle
Machine maintenance time	Amount of time each machine is idle for maintenance and upgrades

**Measures of
Delivery Cycle Time**

On-time deliveries	Shipments received by promised date as a percentage of total shipments
Orders filled	Orders filled as a percentage of total orders received
Average process time	Average time required to make a product available for shipment
Average setup time	Average amount of time elapsed between the acceptance of an order and the beginning of production
Purchase-order lead time	Time it takes a company to process an order and organize so that production can begin
Production cycle time	Time it takes to make a product
Delivery time	Time between a product's completion and its receipt by customer
Delivery cycle time	Time between the acceptance of an order and the final delivery of the product or service (purchase-order lead time + production cycle time + delivery time)
Waste time	Production cycle time − (average process time + average setup time)
Production backlog	Number and type of units waiting to begin processing

**Measures of
Customer Satisfaction**

Customer complaints	Number and types of customer complaints
Warranty claims	Number and causes of claims
Returned orders	Shipments returned as a percentage of total shipments

S T O P • R E V I E W • A P P L Y

2-1. What is total quality management?

2-2. Why are internal failure costs less likely than external failure costs to harm a business in the future?

2-3. What is the difference between delivery cycle time and delivery time?

2-4. How do the five categories of nonfinancial measures of quality apply to services as well as products?

Measures of Quality Internal reports on quality at the EMCAP Publishing Company generated the following information for the Trade Division for the first three months of the year:

Total sales	$60,000,000
Costs of quality:	
Prevention	$ 523,000
Appraisal	477,000
Internal failure	1,360,000
External failure	640,000

Compute the following:

a. Total costs of quality as a percentage of sales
b. Ratio of costs of conformance to total costs of quality
c. Ratio of costs of nonconformance to total costs of quality
d. Costs of nonconformance as a percentage of total sales

SOLUTION

Costs of Conformance	= Prevention Costs + Appraisal Costs
	= $523,000 + $477,000 = $1,000,000

Costs of Nonconformance	= Internal Failure Costs + External Failure Costs
	= $1,360,000 + $640,000 = $2,000,000

a. Total Costs of Quality
as a Percentage of Sales
= $3,000,000 ÷ $60,000,000 = 5%

b. Ratio of Costs of
Conformance to Total
Costs of Quality
= Costs of Conformance ÷ (Costs of Conformance + Costs of Nonconformance)
= $1,000,000 ÷ ($1,000,000 + $2,000,000)
= 0.33 to 1

c. Ratio of Costs of
Nonconformance to
Total Costs of Quality
= Costs of Nonconformance ÷ (Costs of Conformance + Costs of Nonconformance)
= $2,000,000 ÷ ($1,000,000 + $2,000,000)
= 0.67 to 1

d. Costs of Nonformance
as a Percentage of Total Sales = $2,000,000 ÷ $60,000,000 = 3.33%

Measuring Quality: An Illustration

LO3 Use measures of quality to evaluate operating performance.

Using many of the examples of the costs of quality identified in Table 1 and the nonfinancial measures of quality listed in Table 2, the following sections demonstrate how a company measures and evaluates its progress toward the goal of achieving total quality management.

Evaluating the Costs of Quality

As demonstrated in Part A of Exhibit 1, three companies, Able, Baker, and Cane, have taken different approaches to achieving product quality. All three companies are the same size, each having generated $15 million in sales last year.

▼ **EXHIBIT 1**

Measures of Quality—Data for Analysis

A. Costs of Quality

	Able Co.	Baker Co.	Cane Co.
Annual Sales	$15,000,000	$15,000,000	$15,000,000
Costs of Conformance to Customer Standards			
Prevention Costs			
Quality training of employees	$ 210,000	$ 73,500	$ 136,500
Process engineering	262,500	115,500	189,000
Design review of products	105,000	42,000	84,000
Preventive maintenance	157,500	84,000	115,500
Appraisal Costs			
End-of-process sampling and testing	$ 126,000	$ 63,000	$ 73,500
Inspection of materials	199,500	31,500	115,500
Quality audits of products	84,000	21,000	42,000
Vendor audits and sample testing	112,500	52,500	63,000
Costs of Nonconformance to Customer Standards			
Internal Failure Costs			
Scrap and rework	$ 21,000	$ 189,000	$ 126,000
Reinspection of rework	15,750	126,000	73,500
Quality-related downtime	42,000	231,000	178,500
Scrap disposal losses	26,250	84,000	52,500
External Failure Costs			
Warranty claims	$ 47,250	$ 94,500	$ 84,000
Returned goods and replacements	15,750	68,250	36,750
Investigation of defects	26,250	78,750	57,750
Customer complaint processing	120,750	178,500	126,000

We can evaluate each company's approach to quality enhancement by analyzing the costs of quality and by answering the following questions:

- Which company is most likely to succeed in the competitive marketplace?

- Which company has serious problems with its products' quality?

- What do you think will happen to the total costs of quality for each company over the next five years? Why?

Exhibit 2 summarizes and analyzes the three companies' costs of quality. It shows that each company spent between 10.22 and 10.48 percent of its sales dollars on costs of quality. The following discussion is based on that analysis:

Which company is most likely to succeed in the competitive marketplace? Able Co. spent the most money on costs of quality. What is more important, however, is that the company spent 80 percent of that money on costs of conformance, which will reap benefits in years to come. The company's focus

B. Nonfinancial Measures of Quality

	Able Co.	Baker Co.	Cane Co.
Vendor Performance			
Percentage of defect-free materials			
20x7	98.20%	94.40%	95.20%
20x8	98.40%	93.20%	95.30%
20x9	98.60%	93.10%	95.20%
Production Performance			
Production quality level (product defects per million)			
20x7	1,400	4,120	2,710
20x8	1,340	4,236	2,720
20x9	1,210	4,340	2,680
Delivery Cycle Time			
Percentage of on-time deliveries			
20x7	94.20%	76.20%	84.10%
20x8	94.60%	75.40%	84.00%
20x9	95.40%	73.10%	83.90%
Customer Satisfaction			
Percentage of returned orders			
20x7	1.30%	6.90%	4.20%
20x8	1.10%	7.20%	4.10%
20x9	0.80%	7.60%	4.00%
Number of customer complaints			
20x7	22	189	52
20x8	18	194	50
20x9	12	206	46

▼ **EXHIBIT 2**

Analysis of the Costs of Quality

	Able Co.	Baker Co.	Cane Co.
Annual Sales	$15,000,000	$15,000,000	$15,000,000
Costs of Conformance to Customer Standards			
Prevention Costs			
Quality training of employees	$ 210,000	$ 73,500	$ 136,500
Process engineering	262,500	115,500	189,000
Design review of products	105,000	42,000	84,000
Preventive maintenance	157,500	84,000	115,500
Subtotal	$ 735,000	$ 315,000	$ 525,000
Appraisal Costs			
End-of-process sampling and testing	$ 126,000	$ 63,000	$ 73,500
Inspection of materials	199,500	31,500	115,500
Quality audits of products	84,000	21,000	42,000
Vendor audits and sample testing	112,500	52,500	63,000
Subtotal	$ 522,000	$ 168,000	$ 294,000
Total Costs of Conformance	$ 1,257,000	$ 483,000	$ 819,000
Costs of Nonconformance to Customer Standards			
Internal Failure Costs			
Scrap and rework	$ 21,000	$ 189,000	$ 126,000
Reinspection of rework	15,750	126,000	73,500
Quality-related downtime	42,000	231,000	178,500
Scrap disposal losses	26,250	84,000	52,500
Subtotal	$ 105,000	$ 630,000	$ 430,500
External Failure Costs			
Warranty claims	$ 47,250	$ 94,500	$ 84,000
Returned goods and replacements	15,750	68,250	36,750
Investigation of defects	26,250	78,750	57,750
Customer complaint processing	120,750	178,500	126,000
Subtotal	$ 210,000	$ 420,000	$ 304,500
Total Costs of Nonconformance	$ 315,000	$ 1,050,000	$ 735,000
Total Costs of Quality	$ 1,572,000	$ 1,533,000	$ 1,554,000
Total costs of quality as a percentage of sales	10.48%	10.22%	10.36%
Ratio of costs of conformance to total costs of quality	.80 to 1	.32 to 1	.53 to 1
Ratio of costs of nonconformance to total costs of quality	.20 to 1	.68 to 1	.47 to 1
Costs of nonconformance as a percentage of sales	2.10%	7.00%	4.90%

on the costs of conformance means that only a small amount had to be spent on internal and external failure costs. The resulting high-quality products will lead to high customer satisfaction.

Which company has serious problems with its products' quality? Baker Co. spent the least on costs of quality, but that's not the reason it is in serious trouble. Over 68 percent of its costs of quality ($1,050,000 of a total of $1,533,000) was spent on internal and external failure costs. Scrap costs, reinspection costs, the cost of downtime, warranty costs, and customer complaint costs were all high. Baker's products are very low in quality, which will lead to hard times in the future.

What do you think will happen to the total costs of quality for each company over the next five years? Why? When money is spent on costs of conformance early in a product's life cycle, quality is integrated into the development and production processes. Once a high level of quality has been established, total costs of quality should be lower in future years. Able Co. seems to be in that position today.

Baker's costs of conformance will have to increase significantly if the company expects to stay in business. It is spending 7 percent of its sales revenue on internal and external failure costs. Because the marketplace is not accepting its products, its competitors have the upper hand, and the company is in a weak position.

Cane Co. is taking a middle road. This company is spending a little more than half (53 percent) of its cost-of-quality dollars on conformance, so product quality should be increasing. However, the company is still incurring high internal and external failure costs. Cane's managers must learn to prevent such costs if they expect the company to remain competitive.

Evaluating Nonfinancial Measures of Quality

From the information presented in Part B of Exhibit 1, we can evaluate each company's experience in its pursuit of total quality management. That part of the exhibit presents nonfinancial measures for each company for three years—20x7, 20x8, and 20x9. The trends shown there tend to support the findings in the analysis of the costs of quality in Exhibit 2.

Able Co. For Able Co., 98.2 percent of the materials received from suppliers in 20x7 were of high quality, and the quality has been increasing over the three years. The product defect rate, measured in number of defects per million, has been decreasing rapidly, proof that the costs of conformance are having a positive effect. The percentage of on-time deliveries has been increasing, and both the percentage of returned orders and the number of customer complaints have been decreasing, which means that customer acceptance and satisfaction have been increasing.

Baker Co. Baker Co.'s experience is not encouraging. The number of high-quality shipments of materials from vendors has been decreasing, the product defect rate has been increasing (it seems to be out of control), on-time deliveries were bad to begin with and have been getting worse, more goods have been returned each year, and customer complaints have been on the rise. All those signs reflect the company's high costs of nonconformance.

Cane Co. Cane Co. is making progress toward higher quality, but its progress is very slow. Most of the nonfinancial measures show a very slight positive trend. More money needs to be spent on the costs of conformance.

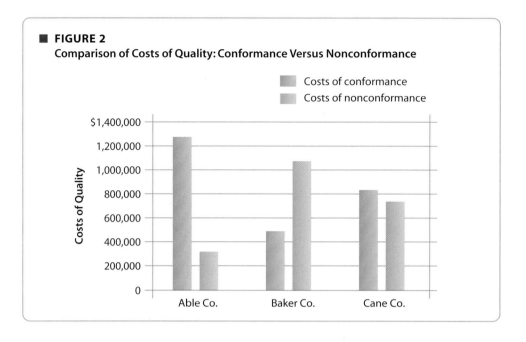

■ FIGURE 2
Comparison of Costs of Quality: Conformance Versus Nonconformance

A graphic analysis can be very useful when a manager is comparing the performance of several operating units. Mere columns of numbers do not always adequately depict differences in operating performance and may be difficult to interpret. In such cases, a chart or graph can help managers see what the data are saying. For example, the bar graph in Figure 2 illustrates the amounts that Able, Baker, and Cane are spending on costs of quality. It clearly shows that Able Co. is focusing on costs of conformance and has low costs of nonconformance. Baker Co., in contrast, is paying over $1,000,000 in costs of nonconformance because it has not tried to increase spending on prevention and appraisal. Cane Co. spends slightly more on costs of conformance than on costs of nonconformance, but, like Baker Co., it is spending too much on failure costs.

S T O P • R E V I E W • A P P L Y

3-1. Comment on the relationship between the costs of conformance and the costs of nonconformance.

3-2. Why is a graph or chart a useful communication tool?

The Evolving Concept of Quality

LO4 Discuss the evolving concept of quality.

Much of what organizations now know about quality can be traced to past manufacturing initiatives. Before the advent of TQM over 20 years ago, managers assumed that there was a trade-off between the costs and the benefits of improving quality. In economic terms, a **return on quality (ROQ)** results when the marginal revenues possible from a higher-quality good or service exceed the marginal costs of providing that higher quality. In other words, managers must weigh the high costs of consistent quality against the resulting higher revenues, and they must base the quality standards for a good or service on the expected return on quality.

In the 1980s, quality gave organizations a competitive edge in the global marketplace. W. Edwards Deming and other advocates of TQM stressed improved quality as a means of enhancing an organization's efficiency and profits. As a result, managers focused on increasing customer satisfaction and product or service quality, and organizations recognized the value of producing highly reliable products. Companies emphasized **kaizen**, or the gradual and ongoing improvement of products and processes while reducing costs. Quality control methods such as statistical analysis, computer-aided design, and Six Sigma eliminated defects in the design and manufacture of products. Today more than 90 percent of the Fortune 500 companies use a combination of those methods.

The story of **Motorola** and its Six Sigma quality standard illustrates how product quality quickly improved. In 1978, Motorola was losing market share as a result of aggressive competition from high-quality Japanese goods. In response, Motorola set the goal of Six Sigma quality, which meant that Motorola's customers would perceive the company's products and services as perfect. The company's goal was to hold defects to three standard deviations from the norm, or about 3.4 defects per million. Whatever the company measured had to improve 10 times by 1989, improve 100 times by 1991, and be Six Sigma quality by 1992. Motorola applied the Six Sigma quality standard to all aspects of its operations—not just to production. Even Motorola's Corporate Finance Department measures defects per unit, tracking its number of errors per monthly close and the time it takes to close the books each month.[3] Other companies, including **Amazon.com**, have embraced the Six Sigma method to reduce errors. At Amazon.com, employees are awarded "black belts" and "green belts" for quality innovation.[4]

As managers at Motorola and other companies achieved high levels of product reliability, they expanded their efforts to include the quality of their companies' nonmanufacturing processes. Two techniques, benchmarking and process mapping, allowed managers to understand and measure quality improvements.

▸ **Benchmarking** is the measurement of the gap between the quality of a company's process and the quality of a parallel process at the best-in-class company. For example, Motorola improved its order-processing system by studying order processing at **Lands' End**.

▸ **Process mapping** is a method of using a flow diagram to indicate process inputs, outputs, constraints, and flows to help managers identify unnecessary efforts and inefficiencies in a business process. Quality problems and their causes are visually tracked using control charts, histograms, cause-and-effect diagrams, and Pareto diagrams. As a result, customer satisfaction with

The Walt Disney character Minnie Mouse interacts with customers waiting in line at Disney's Magic Kingdom in Orlando, Florida. Disney theme parks use characters to keep waiting customers amused, thereby maximizing customers' satisfaction with the theme park experience.

a product or service and with the buying experience both before and after the sale is enhanced.

Service businesses also recognize the importance of quality and seek to maximize customers' satisfaction with their services. For example, **Disney** theme parks minimize customers' impatience as they wait in long lines by having Disney characters interact and play with the crowd. A potential customer problem becomes another opportunity to deliver Disney magic.

The Decision Point in this chapter pointed out how an ecommerce company like Amazon.com can manage the quality of a customer's shopping experience through customer-specific web pages and how it can also continuously experiment to improve that experience. The need to create fresh features and innovative uses for websites challenges managers to think of quality in new ways as their organizations adapt to Internet-based business models.

In summary, a manager's concept of quality must continuously evolve to fulfill customers' needs and expectations and to meet the demands of the changing business environment. Quality has many dimensions. Not only must a product or service be defect-free and dependable; it must also embody such intangibles as prestige and good taste. Managers must meet or exceed a variety of expectations about customer service and create innovative new products and services that anticipate the opportunities offered by an ever-changing marketplace. The concept of quality means more than having zero defects in a product or service; it means doing everything possible to have zero defections of customers.

S T O P • R E V I E W • A P P L Y

4-1. How has the focus on quality shifted over time for managers?

4-2. What is return on quality (ROQ)? How does ROQ affect managers' decisions about quality?

4-3. What is the Six Sigma quality standard?

4-4. What is process mapping, and how is it used to improve quality?

Recognition of Quality

| **LO5** | Recognize the awards and organizations that promote quality. |

Many awards and organizations have been established to recognize and promote the importance of quality. Two of the most prestigious awards are the Deming prizes and the Malcolm Baldrige Quality Award. In addition, the International Organization for Standardization works to promote quality standards worldwide.

In 1951, the Japanese Union of Scientists and Engineers established the Deming Application Prize to honor individuals or groups who have contributed to the development and dissemination of total quality control. Consideration for the prize was originally limited to Japanese companies, but interest in it was so great that the rules were revised to allow the participation of companies outside Japan. Today, the organization awards several **Deming prizes** to companies and individuals that achieve distinctive results by carrying out total quality control. Recent winners of Deming prizes include the following:

Hosei Brake Industry Co., Limited (Japan)

Krishna Maruti Limited, Seat Division (India)

Rane Engine Valves Limited (India)

Rane TRW Steering Systems Limited, Steering Gear Division (India)

GC Corporation (Japan)

Thai Acrylic Fibre Co., Limited (Thailand).[5]

In 1987, the U.S. Congress created the **Malcolm Baldrige Quality Award** to recognize U.S. organizations for their achievements in quality and business performance and to raise awareness of the importance of quality and performance excellence. Organizations are evaluated on the basis of the Baldrige performance excellence criteria, a set of standards that is divided into seven categories: leadership, strategic planning, customer and market focus, information and analysis, human resource focus, process management, and business results. Thousands of organizations throughout the world accept the Baldrige criteria as the standards for performance excellence and use them for training and self-assessment, whether they plan to compete for the award or not. Award winners are showcased annually on the Internet (www.quality.nist.gov) and are encouraged to share their best practices with others. The following were among the winners of the Baldrige Award in 2005:

Sunny Fresh Foods, Inc., Monticello, Minn. (manufacturing)

DynMcDermott Petroleum Operations, New Orleans, La. (service)

Park Place Lexus, Plano, Tex. (small business)

Richland College, Dallas, Tex. (education)

Jenks Public Schools, Jenks, Okla. (education)

Bronson Methodist Hospital, Kalamazoo, Mich. (health care)

The International Organization for Standardization (ISO) is a worldwide federation of national standards bodies from over 130 countries. It promotes standardization with a view to facilitating the international exchange of goods and services. For example, by developing a standard format for credit cards, standard film speed codes, and standard graphical symbols for use on equipment and diagrams, the ISO has saved time and money for both individuals and businesses worldwide.

To standardize quality management and quality assurance, the ISO has developed **ISO 9000**, a set of guidelines for businesses that covers the design, development, production, final inspection and testing, installation, and servicing of products, processes, and services. Because many organizations do business only with ISO-certified companies, these guidelines have been adopted worldwide. To become ISO certified, an organization must pass a rigorous third-party audit of its manufacturing and service processes. As a result, certified companies have detailed documentation of their operations. The ISO 14000 series provides a similar framework for environmental management.[6]

STOP • REVIEW • APPLY

5-1. Identify two awards for quality, and explain the purpose of each.

5-2. Why is ISO certification advantageous for a company?

A LOOK BACK AT

AMAZON.COM

This chapter's Decision Point posed the following questions:

● **How do Amazon.com's managers maintain the company's competitive edge?**

● **What measures of quality can Amazon.com use to evaluate operating performance?**

Doing business over the Internet has added a rich dimension to quality. At Amazon.com, the quality of a customer's experience is enhanced by the company's management information system. By maintaining customer profiles based on previous visits and purchases, Amazon.com can greet customers as they return to the site with a web page customized to their preferences. And by integrating its supply-chain software with its warehousing and data-mining applications, Amazon.com can ensure timely and efficient deliveries to its warehouses and its customers.

Amazon.com's managers also use their information system's highly developed infrastructure to meet the changing expectations of their diverse customer base. In assessing customer satisfaction and the responsiveness of the company's supply chain and value chain, these managers use both nonfinancial and financial measures. To maintain a competitive edge, they will continue to need detailed, real-time information, both financial and nonfinancial, about every aspect of the company's operations and the highly competitive environment of ecommerce.

CHAPTER REVIEW

REVIEW of Learning Objectives

LO1 Describe a management information system, and explain how it enhances management decision making.

In a management information system (MIS), the primary focus is on the management of activities, not on costs. By focusing on activities, an MIS provides managers with improved knowledge of the processes for which they are responsible. The MIS pinpoints resource usage for each activity and fosters managerial decisions that lead to continuous improvement throughout the organization.

As managers plan, they use the MIS database to obtain relevant and reliable information for formulating strategic plans, making forecasts, and preparing budgets. When managers perform their duties, they use the financial and non-financial information in the MIS database to implement decisions about personnel, resources, and activities that will minimize waste and improve the quality of their organization's products or services. When they evaluate performance, managers identify and track financial and nonfinancial performance measures to evaluate all major business functions. By enabling the timely comparison of actual to expected performance, the MIS allows managers to reward performance promptly, take speedy corrective actions, and analyze and revise performance measurement plans. And when they communicate, managers are able to generate customized reports that evaluate performance and provide useful real-time information for decision making.

LO2 Define *total quality management (TQM),* and identify financial and nonfinancial measures of quality.

Total quality management is an organizational environment in which all business functions work together to build quality into a firm's products or services. The costs of quality are measures of the costs that are specifically related to the achievement or nonachievement of product or service quality. The costs of quality have two components. One is the cost of conforming to a customer's product or service standards by preventing defects and failures and by appraising quality and performance. The other is the cost of nonconformance—the costs incurred when defects are discovered before a product is shipped and the costs incurred after a defective product or faulty service is delivered to the customer.

The objective of TQM is to reduce or eliminate the costs of nonconformance, the internal and external failure costs that are associated with customer dissatisfaction. To this end, managers can justify high initial costs of conformance if they minimize the total costs of quality over the product's or service's life cycle.

LO3 Use measures of quality to evaluate operating performance.

Nonfinancial measures of quality are related to product design, vendor performance, production performance, delivery cycle time, and customer satisfaction. Those measures, together with the costs of quality, help a firm meet its goal of continuously improving product or service quality and the production process.

LO4 Discuss the evolving concept of quality.

A manager's concept of quality must continuously evolve to fulfill customers' needs and expectations and to meet the demands of the changing business environment. Quality has many dimensions that extend beyond the mere creation and delivery of a product or service. Managers must satisfy customers today and create innovative products and services for tomorrow. The evolving concept of quality means more than having zero defects in a product or service; it means doing everything possible to have zero defections of customers.

LO5 Recognize the awards and organizations that promote quality.

The importance of quality has been acknowledged worldwide through the granting of numerous awards, certificates, and prizes for quality. Two of the most prestigious awards are the Deming prizes and the Malcolm Baldrige Quality Award. In addition, the International Organization for Standardization promotes quality management through the ISO 9000 standards.

REVIEW of Concepts and Terminology

The following concepts and terms were introduced in this chapter:

Appraisal costs: The costs of activities that measure, evaluate, or audit products, processes, or services to ensure their conformance to quality standards and performance requirements; a cost of conformance. **(LO2)**

Benchmarking: The measurement of the gap between the quality of a company's process and the quality of a parallel process at the best-in-class company. **(LO4)**

Computer-aided design (CAD): A computer-based engineering system with a built-in program to detect product design flaws. **(LO2)**

Computer-integrated manufacturing (CIM) systems: Systems in which manufacturing and its support operations are coordinated by computer. **(LO2)**

Costs of conformance: The costs incurred in producing a quality product or service. **(LO2)**

Costs of nonconformance: The costs incurred to correct defects in a product or service. **(LO2)**

Costs of quality: The costs that are specifically associated with the achievement or nonachievement of product or service quality. **(LO2)**

Delivery cycle time: The time between the acceptance of an order and the final delivery of the product or service. **(LO2)**

Delivery time: The time between the completion of a product and its receipt by the customer. **(LO2)**

Deming prizes: Prizes awarded by the Japanese Union of Scientists and Engineers to companies that achieve distinctive results by carrying out total quality control. **(LO5)**

Enterprise resource planning (ERP) system: An integrated information system that manages all major business functions of an organization through an easy-to-access, centralized data warehouse. **(LO1)**

External failure costs: The costs incurred after the delivery of a defective product or service; a cost of nonconformance. **(LO2)**

Internal failure costs: The costs incurred when defects are discovered before a product or service is delivered to a customer; a cost of nonconformance. **(LO2)**

ISO 9000: A set of quality management guidelines established by the International Organization for Standardization. **(LO5)**

Kaizen: The gradual and ongoing improvement of quality and cost reduction in a business. **(LO4)**

Malcolm Baldrige Quality Award: An award established by the U.S. Congress to recognize U.S. organizations for their achievements in quality and business performance and to raise awareness about the importance of quality and performance excellence. **(LO5)**

Management information system (MIS): A management reporting system that identifies, monitors, and maintains continuous, detailed analyses of a company's activities and provides managers with timely measures of operating results. **(LO1)**

Prevention costs: The costs associated with the prevention of defects and failures in products and services; a cost of conformance. **(LO2)**

Process mapping: A method of using a flow diagram to indicate process inputs, outputs, constraints, and flows to help managers identify unnecessary efforts and inefficiencies in a business process. **(LO4)**

Production cycle time: The time it takes to make a product. **(LO2)**

Purchase-order lead time: The time it takes a company to process an order and organize so that production can begin. **(LO2)**

Quality: The result of an operating environment in which a product or service meets or conforms to a customer's specifications the first time it is produced or delivered. **(LO2)**

Return on quality (ROQ): The earnings that result when the marginal revenues possible from a higher-quality good or service exceed the marginal costs of providing that higher quality. **(LO4)**

Total quality management (TQM): An organizational environment in which all business functions work together to build quality into the firm's products or services. **(LO2)**

REVIEW Problem

LO2, LO3   **Analysis of Nonfinancial Data**

Three months ago, the Cooper Motor Division of Cruz Products, Inc., installed a new manufacturing system in its Small Motors Department. A just-in-time approach is now followed for everything from ordering materials and parts to product shipment and delivery. The division's superintendent is very interested in the initial results of the venture. The following data have been collected for your analysis:

	A	B	C	D	E	F	G	H	I
1					Week				
2		1	2	3	4	5	6	7	8
3	Warranty claims	2	4	1	1	—	5	7	11
4	Average setup time								
5	(hours)	0.30	0.25	0.25	0.30	0.25	0.20	0.20	0.15
6	Purchase-order lead								
7	time (hours)	2.4	2.3	2.2	2.3	2.4	2.4	2.4	2.5
8	Production cycle time								
9	(hours)	2.7	2.6	2.5	2.6	2.6	2.6	2.6	2.7
10	Average process time								
11	(hours)	1.90	1.90	1.85	1.80	1.90	1.95	1.95	1.90
12	Customer complaints	12	12	10	8	9	7	6	4
13	Production backlog								
14	(units)	9,210	9,350	9,370	9,420	9,410	8,730	8,310	7,950
15	Machine downtime								
16	(hours)	86.5	83.1	76.5	80.1	90.4	100.6	120.2	124.9
17	Equipment utilization								
18	rate (%)	98.2	98.6	98.9	98.5	98.1	97.3	96.6	95.7
19	On-time deliveries (%)	93.2	94.1	96.5	95.4	92.1	90.5	88.4	89.3
20	Machine maintenance								
21	time (hours)	34.6	32.2	28.5	22.1	18.5	12.6	19.7	26.4
22									

Required

1. Analyze the nonfinancial measures of quality of the Cooper Motor Division for the eight-week period. Focus on the following areas of performance:
   a. Production performance
   b. Delivery cycle time
   c. Customer satisfaction

2. Summarize your findings in a report to the division's superintendent.

Answer to Review Problem

The data given were reorganized as shown on the next page, and one additional piece of information, average waste time, was calculated from the data.

1. Analysis of nonfinancial measures of performance:

				Weeks							Weekly
			1	2	3	4	5	6	7	8	Average
a.	**Production Performance**										
	Machine downtime (hours)		86.5	83.1	76.5	80.1	90.4	100.6	120.2	124.9	95.3
	Equipment utilization rate (%)		98.2	98.6	98.9	98.5	98.1	97.3	96.6	95.7	97.7
	Machine maintenance time (hours)		34.6	32.2	28.5	22.1	18.5	12.6	19.7	26.4	24.3
b.	**Delivery Cycle Time**										
	On-time deliveries (%)		93.2	94.1	96.5	95.4	92.1	90.5	88.4	89.3	92.4
	Average setup time (hours)		0.30	0.25	0.25	0.30	0.25	0.20	0.20	0.15	0.24
	Purchase-order lead time (hours)		2.4	2.3	2.2	2.3	2.4	2.4	2.4	2.5	2.4
	Production cycle time (hours)		2.7	2.6	2.5	2.6	2.6	2.6	2.6	2.7	2.6
	Average process time (hours)		1.90	1.90	1.85	1.80	1.90	1.95	1.95	1.90	1.89
	Production backlog (units)		9,210	9,350	9,370	9,420	9,410	8,730	8,310	7,950	8,969
	Average waste time (hours)		0.50	0.45	0.40	0.50	0.45	0.45	0.45	0.65	0.48
c.	**Customer Satisfaction**										
	Customer complaints		12	12	10	8	9	7	6	4	8.5
	Warranty claims		2	4	1	1	—	5	7	11	3.9

2. Memorandum to the division superintendent:
My analysis of the operating data for the Cooper Motor Division for the last eight weeks revealed the following:

- *Production Performance*: Machine downtime is increasing. Also, the equipment utilization rate is down. Machine maintenance time originally decreased, but it has increased in the past two weeks. Department managers should be aware of these potential problem areas.

- *Delivery Cycle Time*: We are having trouble maintaining the averages for delivery cycle time established eight weeks ago. On-time delivery percentages are slipping. Waste time is increasing, which is contrary to our goals. Backlogged orders are decreasing, which is a good sign from a JIT viewpoint but could spell problems in the future. On the positive side, setup time seems to be under control. Emphasis needs to be placed on reducing lead time, cycle time, and process time.

- *Customer Satisfaction*: Customer satisfaction seems to be improving, as the number of complaints is decreasing rapidly. However, warranty claims have risen significantly in the past three weeks, which may be a signal of quality problems.

Overall, we can see good signs from the new equipment, but we need to pay special attention to all potential problem areas.

CHAPTER ASSIGNMENTS

BUILDING Your Basic Knowledge and Skills

Short Exercises

LO1 **Traits of a Management Information System**

SE 1. What kinds of information does a management information system capture? How do managers use such information?

LO1 Continuous Improvement

SE 2. Maxine Lavon is the controller for Prater Industries. She has been asked to develop a plan for installing a management information system in her company. The president has already approved the concept and has given Lavon the go-ahead. What kind of information will Lavon need to give managers to help them with their decision making?

LO2 Costs of Quality in a Service Business

SE 3. McGriff-Elam Insurance Agency incurred the following activity costs related to service quality. Identify those that are costs of conformance (CC) and those that are costs of nonconformance (CN).

Policy processing improvements	$76,400
Customer complaints response	34,100
Policy writer training	12,300
Policy error losses	82,700
Policy proofing	39,500

LO2 Measures of Quality

SE 4. Internal reports on quality at the Lakeside Publishing Company generated the following information for the School Division for the first three months of the year:

Total sales	$50,000,000
Costs of quality:	
Prevention	$ 523,000
Appraisal	77,000
Internal failure	860,000
External failure	640,000

Compute the following:

a. Total costs of quality as a percentage of sales
b. Ratio of costs of conformance to total costs of quality
c. Ratio of costs of nonconformance to total costs of quality
d. Costs of nonconformance as a percentage of total sales

LO2 Nonfinancial Measures of Quality

SE 5. For a fast-food restaurant that specializes in deluxe cheeseburgers, identify two nonfinancial measures of good product quality and two nonfinancial measures of poor product quality.

LO2 Vendor Quality

SE 6. Cite some specific measures of vendor quality that Nick Michael could use when he installs a quality-certification program for the vendors that supply his company, Stamp It, Inc., with direct materials.

LO2, LO3 Measures of Delivery Cycle Time

SE 7. Quality Cosmetics, Inc., has developed a set of nonfinancial measures to evaluate on-time product delivery for one of its best-selling cosmetics. The following data have been generated for the past four weeks:

Week	Purchase-Order Lead Time	Production Cycle Time	Delivery Time
1	2.4 days	3.5 days	4.0 days
2	2.3 days	3.5 days	3.5 days
3	2.4 days	3.3 days	3.4 days
4	2.5 days	3.2 days	3.3 days

Compute total delivery cycle time for each week. Evaluate the delivery performance. Is there an area that needs management's attention?

LO4 Return on Quality

SE 8. For many years June Pirolo has used return on quality (ROQ) to evaluate quality. What assumptions about quality did she make?

LO4 Quality and Cycle Time

SE 9. Motorola's Finance Department has adapted the concept of delivery cycle time to include the measurement of cycle times for processing customer credit memos, invoices, and orders. Why would such performance measures contribute to Motorola's quest for Six Sigma quality?

LO5 Quality Award Recipients

SE 10. What types of organizations are represented by recent recipients of the Malcolm Baldrige Award? Consult the website at www.quality.nist.gov.

Exercises

LO1 Adapting to Changing Information Needs

E 1. "What's all the fuss about managers' needing to focus on activities instead of costs?" demanded Sam Edwards, the controller of Tyme Flies. "The bottom line is all that matters, and our company's current management information system is just fine for figuring that out. I know that our system is ten years old, but if it isn't broken, why should we fix it?"

How would you respond to Sam Edwards?

LO2 Costs of Conformance in a Service Business

E 2. Home Health Care, LLP, incurred the following service-related activity costs for the month. Prepare an analysis of the costs of conformance by identifying the prevention costs and appraisal costs, and compute the percentage of sales represented by prevention costs, appraisal costs, and total costs of conformance.

Total sales	$22,000
Quality training of employees	500
Vendor audits	400
Quality-certified vendors	100
Preventive maintenance	300
Quality sampling of services	200
Field testing of new services	250
Quality circles	50
Quality improvement projects	150
Technical service support	75
Inspection of services rendered	175

LO2 Costs of Nonconformance in a Service Business

E 3. Home Health Care, LLP, incurred the following service-related activity costs for the month. Prepare an analysis of the costs of nonconformance by identifying the internal failure costs and external failure costs, and compute the percentage of sales represented by internal failure costs, external failure costs, and total costs of nonconformance.

Total sales	$22,000
Reinspection of rework	50
Investigation of service defects	300
Lawsuits	0

Quality-related downtime	$ 75
Failure analysis	50
Customer complaint processing	500
Retesting of service scheduling	25
Restoration of reputation	0
Lost sales	100
Replacement services	1,000

LO2   Measures of Quality in a Service Business

E 4. Rehab Health Care, LLC, incurred the following service-related activity costs for the month:

Total sales	$42,000
Customer complaint processing	1,200
Employee training	400
Reinspection and retesting	500
Design review of service procedures	300
Technical support	200
Investigation of service defects	800
Sample testing of vendors	100
Inspection of supplies	150
Quality audits	250
Quality-related downtime	300

Prepare an analysis of the costs of quality for Rehab Health Care, LLC. Categorize the costs as (a) costs of conformance, with subsets of prevention costs and appraisal costs, or (b) costs of nonconformance, with subsets of internal failure costs and external failure costs. Compute the percentage of sales represented by prevention costs, appraisal costs, total costs of conformance, internal failure costs, external failure costs, total costs of nonconformance, and total costs of quality. Also compute the ratio of costs of conformance to total costs of quality and the ratio of costs of nonconformance to total costs of quality.

LO2, LO3   Costs of Quality

E 5. Hauschlager Corp. produces and supplies automotive manufacturers with the mechanisms used to adjust the positions of front seating units. Several competitors have recently entered the market, and management is concerned that the quality of the company's current products may be surpassed by the quality of the new competitors' products. The controller was asked to conduct an analysis of the efforts in January to improve product quality. His analysis generated the following costs of quality:

Training of employees	$22,400
Customer service	13,600
Reinspection of rework	28,000
Quality audits	31,300
Design review	27,500
Warranty claims	67,100
Sample testing of materials	27,400
Returned goods	98,700
Preventive maintenance	26,500
Quality engineering	18,700
Setup for testing new products	42,100
Scrap and rework	76,500
Losses caused by vendor scrap	65,800
Product simulation	28,400

1. Prepare a detailed analysis of the costs of quality.
2. Comment on the company's current efforts to improve product quality.

LO2, LO3 **Measuring Costs of Quality**

E 6. A corporation has two departments that produce two separate product lines. The company has been implementing total quality management over the past year. Revenue and costs of quality for that year are presented below.

	Dept. C	Dept. D	Totals
Annual sales	$9,200,000	$11,000,000	$20,200,000
Costs of quality			
Prevention costs	$ 186,000	$ 124,500	$ 310,500
Appraisal costs	136,000	68,000	204,000
Internal failure costs	94,000	197,500	291,500
External failure costs	44,000	160,000	204,000
Totals	$ 460,000	$ 550,000	$ 1,010,000

Which department is taking a more serious approach to implementing TQM? Base your answer on the following computations:

a. Total costs of quality as a percentage of sales
b. Ratio of costs of conformance to total costs of quality
c. Ratio of costs of nonconformance to total costs of quality
d. Costs of nonconformance as a percentage of sales

LO2 **Measures of Product Design Quality**

E 7. Being first to market with its newest product, the pocket e-book, was the goal of management at Read It, Inc. Comment on how the company's measures of product design quality, which follow, compare with the industry benchmarks.

Measures of Product Design Quality	Read It, Inc.	Industry Benchmark
Number of design defects detected	50	50
Unresolved design defects at time of product introduction	10	5
Average time between defect detection and correction (hours)	4	8
Time to market (time from design idea to market) (days)	60	100

LO2 **Measures of Vendor Performance**

E 8. Hal Justin, the manager of a hotel that caters to traveling businesspeople, is reviewing the nonfinancial measures of quality for the hotel's dry cleaning service. Six months ago, he contracted with a local dry cleaning company to provide the service to hotel guests. The cleaner promised a four-hour turnaround on all dry cleaning orders. Comment on the following measures for the past six months.

	January	February	March	April	May	June
Percentage of complaints	1%	2%	1%	2%	2%	1%
Percentage of on-time deliveries	100%	75%	100%	80%	85%	100%
Number of orders	300	400	400	500	600	600

LO2 **Measures of Production Performance**

E 9. Analyze the following nonfinancial measures of quality for Holiday Express, Inc., a supplier of mistletoe, for a recent four-week period. Focus specifically on measures of production performance.

Measures of Quality	Week 1	Week 2	Week 3	Week 4
Percentage of defective products per million produced	1.0%	0.8%	0.6%	0.5%
Equipment utilization rate	90%	91%	89%	90%
Machine downtime (hours)	12	10	13	12
Machine maintenance time (hours)	8	8	8	8
Machine setup time (hours)	4	2	5	4

LO2 **Measures of Delivery Cycle Time**

E 10. Compute the missing numbers for **a**, **b**, **c**, and **d** for the delivery cycle time for Companies M, N, Q, and P.

Company	Purchase-Order Lead Time	Production Cycle Time	Delivery Time	Total Delivery Cycle Time
M	a	2	1	4
N	2	4	b	9
Q	10	c	15	30
P	2	7	1	d

LO2 **Analysis of Waste Time**

E 11. Calculate the missing numbers for **a**, **b**, **c**, and **d** to analyze the waste time for the following orders. Comment on your findings.

Name of Order	Production Cycle Time	Average Process Time	Average Setup Time	Waste Time
Howe	6	a	1	1
Smith	b	9	4	2
Gomez	9	5	c	3
Patel	8	3	1	d

LO2, LO3 **Nonfinancial Measures of Quality and TQM**

E 12. "A satisfied customer is the most important goal of this company!" was the opening remark of the corporate president, Alice Nunes, at the monthly executive committee meeting of Santiago Company. The company manufactures tube products for customers in 16 western states. It has four divisions, each producing a different type of tubing material. Nunes, a proponent of total quality management, was reacting to the latest measures of quality from the four divisions. The data for the four divisions follow.

	Brass Division	Plastics Division	Aluminum Division	Copper Division	Company Averages
Vendor on-time delivery	97.20%	91.40%	98.10%	88.20%	93.73%*
Production quality rates (defective parts per million)	1,440	2,720	1,370	4,470	2,500
On-time shipments	89.20%	78.40%	91.80%	75.60%	83.75%
Returned orders	1.10%	4.60%	0.80%	6.90%	3.35%
Number of customer complaints	24	56	10	62	38
Number of warranty claims	7	12	4	14	9.3*

*Rounded.

Why was Nunes upset? Which division or divisions do not appear to have satisfied customers? What criteria did you use to make your decision?

LO4 Nonfinancial Data Analysis

E 13. Takada Company makes racing bicycles. Its Lightning model is considered the top of the line in the industry. Three months ago, to improve quality and reduce production time, Takada Company purchased and installed a computer-integrated manufacturing system for the Lightning model. Management is interested in cutting time in all phases of the delivery cycle. The controller's office gathered these data for the past four-week period:

	Week			
	1	2	3	4
Average process time (hours)	24.6	24.4	23.8	23.2
Average setup time (hours)	1.4	1.3	1.2	1.1
Customer complaints	7	6	8	9
Delivery time (hours)	34.8	35.2	36.4	38.2
On-time deliveries (%)	98.1	97.7	97.2	96.3
Production backlog (units)	8,230	8,340	8,320	8,430
Production cycle time (hours)	28.5	27.9	27.2	26.4
Purchase-order lead time (hours)	38.5	36.2	35.5	34.1
Warranty claims	2	3	3	2

Analyze the performance of the Lightning model for the four-week period, focusing specifically on product delivery cycle time and on customer satisfaction.

LO4 **Innovation and Quality**

E 14. Ecommerce has changed the way goods and services are obtained. How do companies like **Amazon.com** continue to anticipate customer needs? To answer this question, visit Amazon.com's website.

LO5 **Quality Awards**

E 15. How do the Malcolm Baldrige Quality Award and the ISO 9000 standards differ? Consult their websites at www.quality.nist.gov and www.iso.org.

Problems

LO2 **Costs and Nonfinancial Measures of Quality**

P 1. Minturn Enterprises, Inc., operates as three autonomous companies, each with a chief executive officer who oversees its operations. At a recent corporate meeting, the company CEOs agreed to adopt total quality management and to track, record, and analyze their costs and nonfinancial measures of quality. All three companies are operating in highly competitive markets. Sales and quality-related data for September follow.

	Carbondale Company	Wolcott Company	Silverthorne Company
Annual sales	$11,600,000	$13,300,000	$10,800,000
Costs of quality			
Vendor audits	$ 69,000	$ 184,800	$ 130,800
Quality audits	58,900	115,550	141,700
Failure analysis	188,500	92,400	16,350
Design review of products	80,500	176,700	218,000
Scrap and rework	207,000	160,800	21,200
Quality-certified suppliers	49,200	105,600	231,600
Preventive maintenance	92,000	158,400	163,500
Warranty adjustments	149,550	105,600	49,050
Product recalls	201,250	198,000	80,050
Quality training of employees	149,500	237,600	272,500
End-of-process sampling and testing	34,500	145,200	202,700
Reinspection of rework	126,500	66,000	27,250
Returned goods	212,750	72,600	16,350
Customer complaint processing	109,250	162,450	38,150
Total costs of quality			
Nonfinancial measures of quality	$ 1,728,400	$ 1,981,700	$ 1,609,200
Number of warranty claims	61	36	12
Customer complaints	107	52	18
Defective parts per million	4,610	2,190	1,012
Returned orders	9.20%	4.10%	0.90%

Required

1. Prepare an analysis of the costs of quality for the three companies. Categorize the costs as (a) costs of conformance, with subsets of prevention costs

and appraisal costs, or (b) costs of nonconformance, with subsets of internal failure costs and external failure costs. Compute the total costs in each category for each company.

2. For each company, compute the percentage of sales represented by prevention costs, appraisal costs, total costs of conformance, internal failure costs, external failure costs, total costs of nonconformance, and total costs of quality.

3. Interpret the cost-of-quality data for each company. Is its product of high or low quality? Why? Is each company headed in the right direction to be competitive?

4. **Manager Insight:** Evaluate the nonfinancial measures of quality in terms of customer satisfaction. Are the results consistent with your analysis in **3**? Explain your answer.

LO2, LO3 **Analysis of Nonfinancial Data**

P 2. Enterprises, Inc., manufactures several lines of small machinery. Before the company installed automated equipment, the total delivery cycle time for its Coin machine models averaged about three weeks. Last year, management decided to purchase a new computer-integrated manufacturing system for the Coin line. The following is a summary of operating data for the past eight weeks for the Coin line:

				Week				
	1	2	3	4	5	6	7	8
Average process time (hours)	7.20	7.20	7.10	7.40	7.60	7.20	6.80	6.60
Average setup time (hours)	2.20	2.20	2.10	1.90	1.90	1.80	2.00	1.90
Customer complaints	5	6	4	7	6	8	9	9
Delivery time (hours)	36.20	37.40	37.20	36.40	35.90	35.80	34.80	34.20
Equipment utilization rate (%)	98.10	98.20	98.40	98.10	97.80	97.60	97.80	97.80
Machine downtime (hours)	82.30	84.20	85.90	84.30	83.40	82.20	82.80	80.40
Machine maintenance time (hours)	50.40	52.80	49.50	46.40	47.20	45.80	44.80	42.90
On-time deliveries (%)	92.40	92.50	93.20	94.20	94.40	94.10	95.80	94.60
Production backlog (units)	15,230	15,440	15,200	16,100	14,890	13,560	13,980	13,440
Production cycle time (hours)	12.20	12.60	11.90	11.80	12.20	11.60	11.20	10.60
Purchase-order lead time (hours)	26.20	26.80	26.50	25.90	25.70	25.30	24.80	24.20
Warranty claims	2	2	3	2	3	4	3	3

Required

1. Analyze the performance of the Coin machine line for the eight-week period. Focus on performance in the following areas:

   a. Production performance
   b. Delivery cycle time
   c. Customer satisfaction

   Carry your answers to two decimal places.

2. Summarize your findings in a report to the company's president, Wilhem Devore.

LO2   **Costs of Quality**

P 3. Karen Setten, regional manager of Heavenly Pies, is evaluating the performance of four pie kitchens in her region. In accordance with the company's costs-of-quality standards of performance, the four locations provided these data for the past six months:

	Aspen	Basalt	Frisco	Dillon
Sales	$1,800,000	$1,500,000	$1,400,000	$1,200,000
Prevention costs	$ 32,000	$ 48,000	$ 16,000	$ 20,000
Appraisal costs	42,000	32,000	18,000	25,000
Internal failure costs	24,000	21,000	42,000	30,000
External failure costs	33,000	16,000	45,000	25,000
Total costs of quality	$ 131,000	$ 117,000	$ 121,000	$ 100,000

Required

1. For each location, compute the percentages of sales represented by prevention costs, appraisal costs, total costs of conformance, internal failure costs, external failure costs, total costs of nonconformance, and total costs of quality. Carry your answers to two decimal places.
2. For each location, calculate the ratio of costs of conformance to costs of quality and the ratio of costs of nonconformance to costs of quality.
3. **Manager Insight:** Interpret the cost of quality data for each location. Rank the locations in terms of quality.

LO2   **Costs of Quality**

P 4. Creed Napier, the regional manager of E-Taxes, Inc., is evaluating the performance of four ecommerce tax preparation sites in her region. The following data for the past six months were presented to her by each site in accordance with the company's costs-of-quality standards of performance:

	Small Business Portal	Big Business Portal	Self-Employed Portal	Partnership Portal
Sales	$5,000,000	$10,000,000	$8,000,000	$6,000,000
Prevention costs	$ 62,000	$ 58,000	$ 16,000	$ 20,000
Appraisal costs	32,000	42,000	28,000	15,000
Internal failure costs	54,000	31,000	32,000	40,000
External failure costs	23,000	26,000	55,000	35,000
Total costs of quality	$ 171,000	$ 157,000	$ 131,000	$ 110,000

Required

1. For each site, compute the percentages of sales represented by prevention costs, appraisal costs, total costs of conformance, internal failure costs, external failure costs, total costs of nonconformance, and total costs of quality.
2. For each site, calculate the ratio of costs of conformance to costs of quality and the ratio of costs of nonconformance to costs of quality.
3. **Manager Insight:** Interpret the cost-of-quality data for each site. Rank the sites in terms of quality.

LO2, LO3 Interpreting Measures of Quality

P 5. Watts Corporation supplies electronic circuitry to major appliance manufacturers in all parts of the world. Producing a high-quality product in each of the company's four divisions is the mission of management. Each division is required to record and report its efforts to achieve quality in all of its primary product lines. The following information was submitted to the chief financial officer for the most recent three-month period:

	Glenwood Division		Lakes Division		Springs Division		Gilman Division	
	Amount	% of Revenue	Amount	% of Revenue	Amount	% of Revenue	Amount	% of Revenue
Costs of Quality								
Costs of Conformance								
Prevention costs:								
Quality training of employees	$ 4,400		$ 15,600		$ 23,600		$ 8,900	
Process engineering	3,100		19,700		45,900		9,400	
Preventive maintenance	5,800		14,400		13,800		11,100	
Total prevention costs	$ 13,300	0.95%	$ 49,700	3.11%	$ 83,300	5.55%	$ 29,400	1.73%
Appraisal costs:								
End-of-process sampling and testing	$ 3,500		$ 19,500		$ 21,400		$ 6,900	
Quality audits of products	6,100		11,900		17,600		8,700	
Vendor audits	4,100		10,100		9,800		7,300	
Total appraisal costs	$ 13,700	0.98%	$ 41,500	2.59%	$ 48,800	3.25%	$ 22,900	1.35%
Total costs of conformance	$ 27,000	1.93%	$ 91,200	5.70%	$132,100	8.80%	$ 52,300	3.08%
Costs of Nonconformance								
Internal failure costs:								
Quality-related downtime	$ 26,800		$ 8,300		$ 6,500		$ 22,600	
Scrap and rework	17,500		9,100		7,800		16,200	
Scrap disposal losses	31,200		7,200		3,600		19,900	
Total internal failure costs	$ 75,500	5.39%	$ 24,600	1.54%	$ 17,900	1.19%	$ 58,700	3.45%
External failure costs:								
Warranty claims	$ 22,600		$ 4,400		$ 2,500		$ 17,100	
Customer complaint processing	31,600		8,100		6,400		22,300	
Returned goods	29,900		5,600		3,100		19,800	
Total external failure costs	$ 84,100	6.01%	$ 18,100	1.13%	$ 12,000	.80%	$ 59,200	3.48%
Total costs of nonconformance	$159,600	11.40%	$ 42,700	2.67%	$ 29,900	1.99%	$117,900	6.93%
Total costs of quality	$186,600	13.33%	$133,900	8.37%	$162,000	10.79%	$170,200	10.01%

Ratios of Nonfinancial Measures:	Glenwood Division	Lakes Division	Springs Division	Gilman Division
Number of sales to number of warranty claims	168 to 1	372 to 1	996 to 1	225 to 1
Number of products produced to number of products reworked	1,420 to 1	3,257 to 1	6,430 to 1	2,140 to 1
Change in throughput time (positive amount means time reduction)	(−4.615%)	2.163%	5.600%	(−1.241%)
Total number of deliveries to number of late deliveries	86 to 1	168 to 1	290 to 1	128 to 1

Required

1. Rank the divisions in order of their apparent product quality.
2. What three measures were most important in your rankings in **1**? Why?
3. Which division is most successful in its bid to improve quality? What measures illustrate its high-quality rating?
4. **Manager Insight:** Consider the two divisions producing the lowest-quality products. What actions would you recommend to the management of each division? Where should their quality dollars be spent?

Alternate Problems

LO2 Costs and Nonfinancial Measures of Quality

P 6. The Janelle Company operates as three autonomous divisions. Each division has a general manager in charge of product development, production, and distribution. Management recently adopted total quality management, and the divisions now track, record, and analyze their costs and nonfinancial measures of quality. All three divisions are operating in highly competitive marketplaces. Sales and quality-related data for April are summarized on the next page.

Required

1. Prepare an analysis of the costs of quality for the three divisions. Categorize the costs as (a) costs of conformance, with subsets of prevention costs and appraisal costs, or (b) costs of nonconformance, with subsets of internal failure costs and external failure costs. Compute the total costs for each category for each division.
2. For each division, compute the percentage of sales represented by prevention costs, appraisal costs, total costs of conformance, internal failure costs, external failure costs, total costs of nonconformance, and total costs of quality.
3. Interpret the cost-of-quality data for each division. Is each division's product of high or low quality? Explain your answers. Are the divisions headed in the right direction to be competitive?

	East Division	Central Division	West Division
Annual sales	$8,500,000	$9,500,000	$13,000,000
Costs of quality			
Field testing	$ 51,600	$ 112,800	$ 183,950
Quality audits	17,200	79,100	109,650
Failure analysis	103,100	14,700	92,700
Quality training of employees	60,200	188,000	167,700
Scrap and rework	151,000	18,800	154,800
Quality-certified suppliers	34,400	94,000	108,200
Preventive maintenance	65,800	148,000	141,900
Warranty claims	107,500	42,300	106,050
Customer complaint processing	151,500	108,100	154,800
Process engineering	94,600	235,000	232,200
End-of-process sampling and testing	24,700	178,600	141,900
Scrap disposal losses	77,400	23,500	64,500
Returned goods	152,500	16,200	45,150
Product recalls	64,500	32,900	64,500
Total costs of quality	$1,156,000	$1,292,000	$1,768,000
Nonfinancial measures of quality			
Defective parts per million	3,410	1,104	1,940
Returned orders	7.40%	1.10%	3.20%
Customer complaints	62	12	30
Number of warranty claims	74	16	52

4. **Manager Insight:** Evaluate the nonfinancial measures of quality in terms of customer satisfaction. Are the results consistent with your analysis in **3**? Explain your answers.

LO2, LO3 **Analysis of Nonfinancial Data**

P 7. Park Electronics Company is known for its high-quality products and on-time deliveries. Six months ago, it installed a computer-integrated manufacturing system in its Sensitive Components Department. The new equipment produces the entire component, so the finished product is ready to be shipped when needed. During the past eight-week period, the controller's staff gathered the data that appear at the top of the next page.

Required

1. Analyze the performance of the Sensitive Components Department for the eight-week period. Focus on performance in the following areas: (a) production performance, (b) delivery cycle time, and (c) customer satisfaction. Carry your answers to two decimal places.

	Week							
	1	**2**	**3**	**4**	**5**	**6**	**7**	**8**
Average process time (hours)	10.90	11.10	10.60	10.80	11.20	11.80	12.20	13.60
Average setup time (hours)	2.50	2.60	2.60	2.80	2.70	2.40	2.20	2.20
Customer complaints	11	10	23	15	9	7	5	6
Delivery time (hours)	26.20	26.40	26.10	25.90	26.20	26.60	27.10	26.40
Equipment utilization rate (%)	96.20	96.10	96.30	97.20	97.40	96.20	96.40	95.30
Machine downtime (hours)	106.40	108.10	120.20	110.40	112.80	102.20	124.60	136.20
Machine maintenance time (hours)	64.80	66.70	72.60	74.20	76.80	66.60	80.40	88.20
On-time deliveries (%)	97.20	97.50	97.60	98.20	98.40	96.40	94.80	92.60
Production backlog (units)	10,246	10,288	10,450	10,680	10,880	11,280	11,350	12,100
Production cycle time (hours)	16.50	16.40	16.30	16.10	16.30	17.60	19.80	21.80
Purchase-order lead time (hours)	15.20	15.10	14.90	14.60	14.60	13.20	12.40	12.60
Warranty claims	4	8	2	1	6	4	2	3

2. Summarize your findings in a report to the department's superintendent, André Park.

ENHANCING Your Knowledge, Skills, and Critical Thinking

Conceptual Understanding Cases

LO4 **Comparison of Ecommerce Quality**

C 1. Airlines, real estate agencies, retailers, and most other businesses have developed an Internet presence to sell their goods and services. Select two automobile companies, and evaluate their websites to determine the quality of their ecommerce efforts. What features does each site offer its customers? What features are missing? Do the sites offer both pre- and post-sale assistance? In your opinion, how have these websites affected the way cars are sold?

LO2, LO3 **Evaluating Performance Measures**

C 2. Ahern Company and Siedle Company compete in the same industry. Each company is located in a large midwestern city, and each employs between 300 and 350 people. Both companies have adopted a total quality management approach, and both want to improve their ability to compete in the marketplace. They have installed common performance measures to help track their quest for quality and a competitive advantage.

During the most recent three-month period, Ahern Company and Siedle Company generated the data that follow.

Performance Measures	Ahern Company		Siedle Company	
	Financial	Nonfinancial	Financial	Nonfinancial
Production performance				
Equipment utilization rate		89.4%		92.1%
Machine downtime (in machine hours)		720		490
Delivery cycle time				
On-time deliveries		92.1%		96.5%
Purchase-order lead time (hours)		17		18
Production cycle time (hours)		14		16
Waste time (hours)		3		2
Customer satisfaction				
Customer complaints		28		24
Scrap and rework costs	$14,390		$13,680	
Field service costs	9,240		7,700	

1. For each measure, indicate which company has the better performance.
2. Which company is more successful in achieving a total quality environment and an improved competitive position? Explain your answer.

LO4   **Quality Measures and Techniques**

C 3. **Motorola's** Total Customer Satisfaction (TCS) Teams are cross-functional teams that use customer-focused methods to solve quality and process problems. One TCS Team success story involved an international supplier with quality and delivery problems. These problems required additional order expediting and rework and were causing customer dissatisfaction. The TCS Team's report to management disclosed the following:

- By evaluating and revising the product's design with input from the international supplier, the team created a more robust finished product.
- The team's adoption of process capability studies, together with continuous monitoring, resulted in improved quality for the international supplier.
- When sourcing was moved to a local supplier, the number of times the inventory turned over annually improved. It went from 26 to 52 times a year.
- Over the three-year life of the product, the team's changes resulted in $831,438 in cost savings.[7]

1. From the TCS Team's report, identify the key issues involved in solving the international supplier's quality and process problems.
2. How could the team have applied the process-based techniques of benchmarking and process mapping to improve quality?

Interpreting Management Reports

LO2, LO3   **Reports on Quality Data**

C 4. Jim Macklin is chief executive officer of Red Cliff Machinery, Inc. The company adopted a JIT operating environment five years ago. Since then, each segment of the company has been converted, and a complete computer-integrated manufacturing system operates in all parts of the company's five plants. Processing of Red Cliff Machinery's products now averages less than four days once the materials have been put into production.

Macklin is worried about customer satisfaction and has asked you, as the controller, for some advice and help. He has also asked the Marketing Department to perform a quick survey of customers to determine weak areas in customer relations. Here is a summary of four customers' replies:

Customer A Customer for five years; waits an average of six weeks for delivery; located 1,200 miles from plant; returns an average of 3 percent of products; receives 90 percent on-time deliveries; never hears from salesperson after placing order; likes quality or would go with competitor.

Customer B Customer for seven years; waits an average of five weeks for delivery; orders usually sit in backlog for at least three weeks; located 50 miles from plant; returns about 5 percent of products; receives 95 percent on-time deliveries; has great rapport with salesperson; salesperson is why this customer is loyal.

Customer C Customer for twelve years; waits an average of seven weeks for delivery; located 1,500 miles from plant; returns about 4 percent of products; receives 92 percent on-time deliveries; salesperson is available but of little help in getting faster delivery; customer is thinking about dealing with another source for its product needs.

Customer D Customer for fifteen years; very pleased with company's product; waits almost five weeks for delivery; located 120 miles from plant; returns only 2 percent of goods received; rapport with salesperson is very good; follow-up service of salesperson is excellent; would like delivery cycle time reduced to equal that of competitors; usually deals with three-week backlog.

1. Identify the areas of concern, and give at least three examples of reports that will help managers improve the company's response to customer needs.

2. Assume that you are asked to write a report that will provide information about customer satisfaction. In preparation for writing the report, answer the following questions:

   a. What kinds of information do you need to prepare this report?
   b. Why is this information relevant?
   c. Where would you find this information (i.e., what sources would you use)?
   d. When would you want to obtain this information?

Decision Analysis Using Excel

LO2, LO3   **Interpreting Measures of Quality**

C 5. Travis Corporation has five divisions, each manufacturing a product line that competes in the global marketplace. The company is planning to compete for the Malcolm Baldrige Award, so management requires that each division record and report its efforts to achieve quality in its product line. The information on the following page was submitted to the company's controller for the most recent six-month period.

1. Prepare an analysis of the costs of quality for each division. Categorize the costs as costs of conformance or costs of nonconformance. Carry your answers to two decimal places.

2. For each division, compute the percentage of total revenue for each of the four cost-of-quality categories and the ratios for the nonfinancial data.

3. Rank the divisions in order of their apparent product quality.

4. What three measures were most important in your rankings in **3**? Why?

			Division A	Division B	Division C	Division D	Division E
Total Revenue			$886,000	$1,040,000	$956,000	$1,225,000	$1,540,000
Costs of Quality							
	Customer complaint processing		$ 10,400	$ 12,600	$ 12,300	$ 10,100	$ 15,600
	Scrap and rework		26,800	13,500	38,700	11,900	34,800
	Quality audits of products		13,600	28,400	6,300	25,600	11,700
	Returned goods		18,700	11,400	38,400	11,300	36,000
	Warranty claims		21,100	6,400	36,200	6,500	42,600
	Quality training of employees		8,900	12,600	4,600	11,400	4,200
	Preventive maintenance		11,300	18,700	8,300	13,600	6,300
	Failure analysis		34,800	9,800	46,900	10,200	56,900
	Inspection of materials		12,500	18,700	7,800	17,500	5,600
Nonfinancial Measures of Quality							
	Number of warranty claims versus		22	12	46	12	62
	number of sales		6,500	8,900	7,200	9,800	9,600
	Number of products reworked versus		150	140	870	70	900
	number of products manufactured		325,000	456,000	365,000	450,000	315,600
	Throughput time in hours versus		6.20	8.50	6.80	9.20	11.60

5. Which division has been most successful in its bid to improve quality? What measures illustrate its high quality rating?

6. Consider the two divisions producing the lowest-quality products. What actions would you recommend to the management of each division? Where should their quality dollars be spent?

Ethical Dilemma Case

LO1 **MIS and Ethics**

C 6. Three months ago, Maxwell Enterprises hired a consultant, Stacy Slone, to assist in the design and installation of a new management information system for the company. Mike Carns, one of Maxwell's systems design engineers, was assigned to work with Slone on the project. During the three-month period, Slone and Carns met six times and developed a tentative design and installation plan for the MIS. Before the plan was to be unveiled to top management, Carns asked his supervisor, Todd Bowman, to look it over and comment on the design.

Included in the plan was the consolidation of three engineering functions into one. Both of the supervisors of the other two functions had seniority over Bowman, so he believed that the design would lead to his losing his management position. He communicated this to Carns and ended his comments with the following statement: "If you don't redesign the system to accommodate all three of the existing engineering functions, I will give you an unsatisfactory performance evaluation for this year!"

How should Carns respond to Bowman's assertion? Should he handle the problem alone, keeping it inside the company, or communicate the comment to Slone? Outline Carns's options, and be prepared to discuss them in class.

Internet Case

LO5 **ISO Standards**

C 7. Visit ISO's electronic information service at www.iso.org to learn more about ISO 9000 and ISO 14000 standards. Click on "Press Releases," "ISO

Focus," and "ISO Café" to learn more about these worldwide standards. Share your findings in a brief email message to your instructor.

Group Activity Case

LO2, LO3 **Just-in-Time Production and Quality**

C 8. Many large multinational companies have installed automated just-in-time production processes to improve product quality and compete for new domestic and foreign business. Locate an article about a company that has installed a JIT system to help it improve product quality. Conduct your search using an Internet search engine like Google, the company annual reports in your campus library, the business section of your local newspaper, or *The Wall Street Journal*.

Choose a source that describes the changes the company made within its plant to increase product quality and compete as a world-class manufacturer. Prepare a one-page description of those changes. Include in your report the name of the company, its geographic location, the name of the chief executive officer and/or president, and the dollar amount of the company's total sales for the most recent year, if stated.

Your instructor will divide the class into groups to discuss the case. Each group will prepare a summary of its findings and select a member of the group to present the summary to the rest of the class.

Business Communication Case

LO2 **Total Quality Management and Employee Attitudes**

C 9. For the total quality management philosophy to work, everyone in an organization must buy into the concept. Lane Lordon has been with Boyer Industries for 25 years and is managing one of its JIT work areas. He has just been told that he needs to attend four two-hour training sessions on his company's new "Quality or Else" approach to operations. His response to the training program was, "Who needs it? I know this operation better than anyone else in the organization. My work area outproduces all other work areas in this division. Give the training to the new people, especially those new M.B.A.s in middle management who are still wet behind the ears."

You are Lordon's supervisor. Write a memo to him explaining why every employee of Boyer Industries needs to go through a special training program to learn about TQM.

Allocation of Internal Service Costs and Joint Product Costs

All organizations have departments or centers that provide services internally to support the activities of their business. How an organization assigns the cost of these internal service providers affects its prices, product costs, and the decisions its managers make. This chapter explains the various methods managers use to allocate internal service costs.

LEARNING OBJECTIVES

LO1 Discuss the allocation of internal service costs and explain its impact on decision making.

LO2 Describe the two kinds of responsibility centers used in allocating service costs.

LO3 Use the direct method to assign service costs.

LO4 Use the step method to assign service costs.

LO5 Describe the two-step method, the simultaneous equation method, the ability to pay method, and the physical measures method of assigning service costs.

LO6 Explain how service cost allocation relates to overhead rates.

LO7 Apply allocation methods to the costs associated with joint products.

- How should Publix apportion internal service costs among its stores and support departments?

- How should Publix apportion the costs of its other service departments, such as human resources and the dairy, deli, and bakery facilities, among the many departments that use these services?

Publix Super Markets, Inc., is the largest employee-owned grocery chain in the United States. To support the operations of its grocery stores, Publix has many internal service providers, including eight regional distribution centers; dairy, deli, and bakery facilities; as well as service departments, such as human resources. The services that they provide benefit all the Publix stores and contribute to their profitability. Because these services benefit multiple stores and departments within the Publix organization, the stores and departments share the costs of the services.

As Publix ventures into new business activities, such as walk-in medical clinics and cooking school classes, its managers will have to decide on the best method of assigning the costs of internal services to the new activities in a fair and effective way.

Internal Service Providers

> **LO1** Discuss the allocation of internal service costs and explain its impact on decision making.

Publix.

To support their business activities, all organizations have departments or centers that provide services within the organization. For example, **Publix's** eight distribution centers fill store inventory needs daily. Because most of Publix's stores stock over 50,000 items, many of them perishable, this can be a logistical challenge. Goods from vendors arrive by truck or rail on one side of the distribution center, are inspected for quality as they are received, and are entered into the company's inventory system. The distribution center may further process some bulk goods, such as vegetables and fruits, by repackaging them into bar-coded, customer-sized portions. At the other side of the distribution center, all goods are sorted by store and loaded onto company trucks for delivery. Delivery schedules fluctuate with seasonal demand and store needs. Some trucks deliver to only one store, and others deliver to multiple stores. Some trucks deliver produce; others, dairy or bakery goods; and still others, all types of goods.[1]

Internal services like those provided by Publix's distribution centers are commonly provided in all kinds of businesses to achieve organizational goals. For example, **Eli Lilly**, a pharmaceutical company, **Dollar Stores**, a retail business, and **Schlumberger**, an oilfield and information services company, all have internal service departments. In an earlier chapter, we identified the departments that provide such services as the primary processes or support services in an organization's value chain. To ensure its long-term profitability, an organization must include the costs of these internal services in the full cost of its products or services. The **full cost** includes not only the costs of direct materials and direct labor, but also the costs of all production and nonproduction activities in the organization's value chain that are required to satisfy customers.

For example, during a visit to the emergency room at his local hospital, Tony Chewinowski received a tetanus shot. The bill for the tetanus shot was much higher than he had expected. He questioned a patient services representative, who explained that the charges were based on the full cost of a tetanus shot. The amount billed to a patient includes both traceable and assigned costs. *Traceable costs* are direct costs that can be traced to the administration of the shot, such as the costs of the syringe and the tetanus vaccine. *Assigned costs* are other essential but not necessarily traceable indirect costs that must be assigned to the shot; they include the costs of patient accounting and of maintaining the examining room, medical records, and the skilled support staff.

Allocation of Common Service Costs

Indirect costs may not have a clear cause-and-effect relationship to the tetanus shot Tony Chewinowski received because they come from the many services the hospital renders to its patients. Such mutually beneficial indirect costs are called **common costs** because they support many different service activities that are billed to patients. To determine the full cost of the services they offer, hospitals and other service providers must devise a fair way to assign common costs to the users of those services. The process of assigning common costs to specific cost objects (in this case, the users) using an allocation base is called **cost allocation**. Cost allocation does not change an organization's total costs.

Study Note

Managers allocate common costs to determine the full cost of providing a product or service. By comparing the full cost of a product or service with the revenue it generates, managers can determine its profitability.

Study Note

An organization's total cost remains the same before and after cost allocation. Cost allocation merely shifts internal service costs to the consuming centers.

They remain the same before and after allocation. The allocation process merely shifts costs from the internal service providers or support services, which do not charge any of their services to users outside the organization, to the responsibility centers that benefit from those services and bill their services or products to external users. By moving all costs to the centers that produce revenue, a business is able to calculate the full cost of its products or services and set prices accordingly. It can then assess the profitability of a product or service or a specific customer.

Managers and Service Cost Allocation

How an organization assigns the costs of internal services strongly affects its prices, its other costs, its profitability, and the decisions its managers make. We will use **Publix Supermarkets** to illustrate how the allocation of internal service costs affects managers and the decisions they make (see Figure 1).

Planning Managers of each of Publix's regional distribution centers identify the activities within their centers. Typical activity centers are receiving, shipping, repackaging, distribution, truck maintenance, fuel, utilities, and logistics administration. Because distribution centers do not charge external customers for these services, the activity centers generate only costs and no revenues. A supervisor oversees each activity center and reports to the manager of the distribution center. Together, representatives from the distribution center and the stores that it serves select an allocation base to measure the stores' use of each activity center and a method for assigning the costs of the activity centers to the user stores.

Performing Managers of Publix's activity centers control the costs of their respective areas of responsibility. The costs of the activity centers are assigned to stores using the agreed-upon allocation bases and method. Stores add the assigned costs to their store overhead costs to compute a store overhead rate. The overhead rate is applied to products and services to determine the total cost and unit cost of a product or service.

Evaluating Store managers evaluate customer profitability and product or service performance. Store and distribution center managers also review the

■ **FIGURE 1**
The Management Process: To-Do's for Managers

To-Do's for Managers

- Plan
  - Identify activities within each center
  - Select allocation base
  - Select allocation method

- Perform
  - Control costs of revenue and service centers
  - Assign costs using allocation base and method
  - Compute and apply overhead rate
  - Determine unit cost of products and services

- Evaluate
  - Customer profitability
  - Product and service performance

- Communicate
  - Cost-allocation and performance reports
  - Appropriateness of allocation base and method

appropriateness of the cost-allocation bases and the method used and revise them as needed.

Communicating Cost-allocation reports are prepared by and for managers to monitor costs, allocation bases, and the cost-allocation method. Managers who understand how internal service costs are assigned and how these costs affect overhead rates and product or service costs can make more informed decisions about their areas of responsibility. By improving their understanding of full cost, managers become informed consumers of internal services and able evaluators of the effectiveness of those services.

STOP • REVIEW • APPLY

1-1. Why is cost allocation necessary?

1-2. What is a common cost?

1-3. How does the way in which an organization assigns internal costs affect the organization?

Suggested answers to all Stop, Review, and Apply questions are available at http://college.hmco.com/accounting/needles/man_acc/8e/student_home.html.

Responsibility Centers and the Allocation of Service Costs

LO2 Describe the two kinds of responsibility centers used in allocating service costs.

The process of cost allocation begins with a company's responsibility centers. As you will recall, a **responsibility center** is an organizational unit whose manager is responsible for managing a portion of the company's resources. The activity of a responsibility center dictates the extent of its manager's responsibility. Costs are incurred and controlled at the center level. All center costs, such as direct materials, direct labor, and overhead, can be logically traced to the center's activities. For example, all the costs incurred by one of **Publix's** regional distribution center's repackaging activities can be logically traced to that cost center, and the costs incurred to maintain that regional center's trucks can be tracked specifically to the truck maintenance center.

Responsibility centers are classified into two categories for the allocation of service costs: revenue centers and service centers.

Revenue Centers

A **revenue center** is a responsibility center that is directly responsible for producing products or services that are sold to external buyers. Such centers are also known as *producing centers* or *operating centers*. Revenue centers not only incur their own traceable costs but are also assigned the costs of other responsibility centers that they benefit from. Notice that the term *revenue center* has a broader meaning in the context of internal service cost allocation than it has in the classification of responsibility centers for reporting purposes.

Service Centers

A **service center** is a responsibility center that provides benefits to other responsibility centers. Service centers are also known as *support centers* because they indirectly support the activities of the revenue centers and other service centers. They are sometimes also referred to as *discretionary cost centers*. The traceable costs of a service center are collected and controlled by that center and then assigned to other centers using an allocation base, or *cost driver*.

A **cost driver** is an activity that causes another center's use of a service center. For example, a hospital may assign the costs of the Housekeeping Services Department to other departments based on the square footage that the departments occupy. A consulting firm may assign the cost of the Human Resources Department to other departments based on the number of persons the departments employ. A Publix regional distribution center may assign the costs of logistics administration to the supermarkets it serves based on the number of items shipped, the dollar amount shipped, or some other measurable cost driver. Table 1 gives additional examples of service centers that are mentioned in this chapter and the typical cost drivers that cause their use.

 *Study Note*

Revenue centers charge external customers for goods and services sold. Internal service centers charge internal customers for goods and services provided by assigning costs to them.

 *Study Note*

The buyers of the services that support centers provide are other internal users—that is, other service and revenue centers of the business that use the services provided by support centers.

TABLE 1. Examples of Service Centers and Related Cost Drivers

Service Centers	Possible Cost Drivers
Patient Accounting	Number of transactions, number of patient bills
Exam Room	Square feet, patient visits, patient room time
Medical Records	Patient visits, patient-days, number of entries
Patient Care	Patient-days, number of beds, patient visits
Truck Maintenance	Number of work orders, minutes spent, number of deliveries
Fuel	Number of gallons pumped, number of miles driven
Utilities	Kilowatt hours, square feet, number of stores
Repackaging	Pounds processed, number of packages, process time
Distribution	Number of sorted and repacked items, weight of sorted and repacked items, dollar amount of sorted and repacked items
Receiving Dock	Number of truckloads, shipment weight, shipment cost
Shipping Dock	Number of truckloads, number of items in shipment, shipment weight

Once managers have determined which responsibility centers are service centers and which are revenue centers, they must select a method of cost allocation, decide the order in which service costs will be assigned, and choose cost drivers. The two most common methods of assigning internal service costs are the direct method and the step method. Allocation may also be based on full recognition of service users, ability to pay, or number of users.

STOP • REVIEW • APPLY

2-1. What is the difference between a revenue center and a service center? Give an example of each.

2-2. Why are cost drivers important in cost allocation?

2-3. List the decisions that managers must make before cost allocation can occur.

The Direct Method of Service Cost Allocation

LO3 Use the direct method to assign service costs.

Study Note

Under the direct method, costs of service centers are assigned only to revenue centers.

The simplest of the commonly used activity-based cost-allocation methods is the **direct method**, which assigns the costs of service centers only to revenue centers. The direct method ignores the fact that service centers provide service and support to other service centers as well as to revenue centers. This method is easy and straightforward. However, because it assigns service center costs only to revenue centers, the allocations may not reflect the revenue centers' actual use of services.

TABLE 2. Cost Driver Information at City Hospital

Cost Drivers	Service Centers			Revenue Centers			Total
	House-keeping	Human Resources	Marketing	Emergency Room	Radiology	Laboratory	
Percentage of square feet	5	10	15	15	25	30	100
Number of employees	10	20	30	90	210	240	600
Sales dollars	0	0	0	600	800	900	2,300

To illustrate, suppose that City Hospital has three service centers—Housekeeping, Human Resources, and Marketing—and three revenue centers—Emergency Room, Radiology, and Laboratory. The costs of the service centers are assigned to other centers using the following cost drivers: Housekeeping, percentage of square feet occupied by the center; Human Resources, number of employees in the center; and Marketing, sales dollars generated by the center. During the accounting period, Housekeeping had total costs of $100, Human Resources had total costs of $120, and Marketing had total costs of $150. Allison Batson, City Hospital's management accountant, has measured each cost driver for each center. Her findings are presented in Table 2.

Once Batson has identified and measured the relevant cost drivers, she follows the three steps of the direct method to assign the costs of the service centers to the revenue centers.

Step 1: Calculate Allocation Fractions

Under the direct method, an allocation fraction is a revenue center's specific cost driver amount divided by the sum of all the revenue centers' cost driver amounts. With this method, only the cost driver amounts for the revenue centers are used in determining the allocation fractions. For example, to assign the costs of Housekeeping, Allison Batson calculates the following allocation fractions:

$$\text{Emergency Room:} \quad 15/(15 + 25 + 30) = 15/70$$
$$\text{Radiology:} \quad 25/(15 + 25 + 30) = 25/70$$
$$\text{Laboratory:} \quad 30/(15 + 25 + 30) = 30/70$$

The allocation fractions for the costs of Human Resources are

$$\text{Emergency Room:} \quad 90/(90 + 210 + 240) = 90/540$$
$$\text{Radiology:} \quad 210/(90 + 210 + 240) = 210/540$$
$$\text{Laboratory:} \quad 240/(90 + 210 + 240) = 240/540$$

FOCUS ON BUSINESS PRACTICE

Virtual Environments Bring IT Departments Home

Historically, chief information officers (CIOs) have outsourced many of their information technology (IT) tasks to external distribution centers. Doing so has enabled them to improve performance by making use of the latest IT features and to cut costs by consolidating services. Now, however, some CIOs have shifted their focus to making better use of their own existing resources by linking company desktops, servers, and storage resources to create secure, subsecond-response infrastructures. These virtual environments allow IT resources to be available wherever and whenever they are needed and have transformed IT departments into agile internal service providers.[2]

The direct method of allocating the costs of service centers, such as human resource departments, assigns those costs only to revenue centers like the hospital laboratory shown here. It is the simplest of the commonly used activity-based methods of cost allocation. A drawback of the direct method is that its allocation of costs may not reflect a revenue center's actual use of services.

The allocation fractions for the costs of Marketing are

Emergency Room: 600/(600 + 800 + 900) = 600/2,300
Radiology: 800/(600 + 800 + 900) = 800/2,300
Laboratory: 900/(600 + 800 + 900) = 900/2,300

Step 2: Determine the Dollar Amount to Assign to Each Revenue Center

This is done by multiplying each service center's total costs by the corresponding revenue center allocation fraction calculated in Step 1. For example, Housekeeping's $100 of costs are assigned as follows:

Emergency Room: (15/70)($100) = $21
Radiology: (25/70)($100) = $36
Laboratory: (30/70)($100) = $43

Human Resources' $120 of costs are assigned as follows:

Emergency Room: (90/540)($120) = $20
Radiology: (210/540)($120) = $47
Laboratory: (240/540)($120) = $53

Marketing's $150 of costs are assigned as follows:

Emergency Room: (600/2,300)($150) = $39
Radiology: (800/2,300)($150) = $52
Laboratory: (900/2,300)($150) = $59

Step 3: Total the Costs for Each Revenue Center

Add the assigned service costs to the other costs incurred in the revenue centers. At City Hospital, before the assignment of service costs, Emergency Room had costs of $400, Radiology had costs of $500, and Laboratory had costs of $600. Batson calculates the totals for each revenue center as follows:

TABLE 3. Direct Method of Assigning Service Costs

	House-keeping	Human Resources	Marketing	Allocation Fraction: Emergency Room	Emergency Room	Allocation Fraction: Radiology	Radiology	Allocation Fraction: Laboratory	Laboratory	Total
Total center costs	$100	$120	$150		$400		$500		$600	$1,870
Assign Housekeeping costs	$100			15/70	21	25/70	36	30/70	43	
Assign Human Resources costs		$120		90/540	20	210/540	47	240/540	53	
Assign Marketing costs			$150	600/2,300	39	800/2,300	52	900/2,300	59	
Total revenue center costs after allocation					$480		$635		$755	$1,870

Emergency Room: $400 + $21 (assigned from Housekeeping) + $20 (assigned from Human Resources) + $39 (assigned from Marketing) = $480

Radiology: $500 + $36 + $47 + $52 = $635

Laboratory: $600 + $43 + $53 + $59 = $755

The total revenue center costs after allocation are the same as the total center costs before allocation. No dollars are lost or gained in the allocation process. The calculations of the assigned service costs for each revenue center using the direct method are summarized in Table 3.

S T O P • R E V I E W • A P P L Y

3-1. How does a business decide on a method of service cost allocation?

3-2. How are service center costs assigned under the direct method?

Applying the Direct Method A large supermarket chain has a centralized facility that prepares soup for the kitchens in its many retail stores. The $20,000 cost of preparing the soup is assigned on the basis of containers of soup used. Based on the following data for five stores, assign soup costs using the direct method: Store A, 200 containers; Store B, 400 containers; Store C, 150 containers; Store D, 120 containers; and Store E, 130 containers.

SOLUTION

	Store A	Store B	Store C	Store D	Store E	Total
Cost Assigned	$4,000	$8,000	$3,000	$2,400	$2,600	$20,000
Cost Driver used	200 / 1,000	400 / 2,000	150 / 2,000	120 / 1,000	130 / 1,000	1,000

Store A: (200 / 1,000) ($20,000) = $4,000
Store B: (400 / 1,000) ($20,000) = $8,000
Store C: (150 / 1,000) ($20,000) = $3,000
Store D: (120 / 1,000) ($20,000) = $2,400
Store E: (130 / 1,000) ($20,000) = $2,600

The Step Method of Service Cost Allocation

LO4 Use the step method to assign service costs.

Another commonly used activity-based cost-allocation method is the step method. The **step method** assigns service center costs to both service and revenue centers based on descending order of use. Thus, the costs of the service center that is used most by other centers are assigned first, and so on, until the costs of the service center that is used least by other service centers are assigned last. Once the costs of a service center have been assigned, that center cannot receive any assigned costs from any other service center. It is, in effect, closed to the process.

The step method requires a sequence of allocation steps. In fact, it is also known as the *step-down method* because the process resembles stair steps. The step method recognizes the fact that service centers provide service and support to other service centers as well as to revenue centers. However, although the step method attempts to recognize some interdepartmental use, other methods must be used to recognize the full reciprocal usage of services.

To illustrate, we will use the facts about City Hospital given in Table 2 and assume that the hospital's managers have ranked the service centers in the order of services provided and used. Housekeeping provides the most service to other centers and makes the least use of the other service centers. Human Resources ranks next, and Marketing provides the smallest amount of service.

Using the information about costs, cost drivers, and use that she has already gathered, Allison Batson follows the three steps of the step method to assign the costs of the service centers to both service centers and revenue centers.

Step 1: Calculate the Allocation Fraction

Under the step method, a center's allocation fraction is its specific cost driver amount divided by the sum of all the consuming service and revenue centers' driver amounts. Only the cost driver amounts for the consuming centers are used in determining an allocation fraction.

For example, to assign the costs of Housekeeping, Allison Batson calculates the following allocation fractions:

$$
\begin{aligned}
\text{Human Resources:} \quad & 10/(10 + 15 + 15 + 25 + 30) = 10/95 \\
\text{Marketing:} \quad & 15/(10 + 15 + 15 + 25 + 30) = 15/95 \\
\text{Emergency Room:} \quad & 15/(10 + 15 + 15 + 25 + 30) = 15/95 \\
\text{Radiology:} \quad & 25/(10 + 15 + 15 + 25 + 30) = 25/95 \\
\text{Laboratory:} \quad & 30/(10 + 15 + 15 + 25 + 30) = 30/95
\end{aligned}
$$

FOCUS ON BUSINESS PRACTICE
How Are the Data for Cost Allocation Gathered?

Companies like **MRO** sell software that tracks resources critical to a business's performance. Managers use these real-time business systems to facilitate the provision of timely services and the appropriate allocation of costs for both internal service providers and outsourced business contracts. These software systems enable managers to set realistic internal and external customer expectations, establish trust, and charge a reasonable amount for the work actually done.

To assign the costs of Human Resources, the allocation fractions are

Marketing:	30/(30 + 90 + 210 + 240) = 30/570
Emergency Room:	90/(30 + 90 + 210 + 240) = 90/570
Radiology:	210/(30 + 90 + 210 + 240) = 210/570
Laboratory:	240/(30 + 90 + 210 + 240) = 240/570

To assign the costs of Marketing, the allocation fractions are

Emergency Room:	600/(600 + 800 + 900) = 600/2,300
Radiology:	800/(600 + 800 + 900) = 800/2,300
Laboratory:	900/(600 + 800 + 900) = 900/2,300

Step 2: Determine the Dollar Amount to Assign to Each Service Center and Each Revenue Center

Step 2 of the step method is accomplished by multiplying each service center's total costs by the corresponding service or revenue center allocation fraction calculated in Step 1. When assigning the costs of a service center under the step method, it is important to include both that service center's own costs and any costs that have been assigned to it. It is also important to recall that once a service center's costs have been assigned, that center cannot receive any more assigned costs. For example, Housekeeping's costs of $100 are assigned as follows:

Human Resources:	(10/95)($100) = $10 (rounded down)
Marketing:	(15/95)($100) = $16
Emergency Room:	(15/95)($100) = $16
Radiology:	(25/95)($100) = $26
Laboratory:	(30/95)($100) = $32

Human Resources' costs of $130 (center costs of $120 plus $10 of assigned costs) are assigned as follows:

Marketing:	(30/570)($130) = $ 7
Emergency Room:	(90/570)($130) = $20 (rounded down)
Radiology:	(210/570)($130) = $48
Laboratory:	(240/570)($130) = $55

Marketing's costs of $173 (center costs of $150 plus assigned costs of $16 from Housekeeping and $7 from Human Resources) are assigned as follows:

Emergency Room:	(600/2,300)($173) = $45
Radiology:	(800/2,300)($173) = $60
Laboratory:	(900/2,300)($173) = $68

Step 3: Total the Costs for Each Revenue Center

Add the assigned service costs to the other costs incurred in the revenue centers. Allison Batson calculates the totals for each revenue center as follows:

Emergency Room:	$400 + $16 (assigned from Housekeeping) + $20 (assigned from Human Resources) + $45 (assigned from Marketing) = $481
Radiology:	$500 + $26 + $48 + $60 + $634
Laboratory:	$600 + $32 + $55 + $68 + $755

TABLE 4.   Step Method of Assigning Service Costs

	House-keeping	Allocation Fraction: Human Resources	Human Resources	Allocation Fraction: Marketing	Marketing	Allocation Fraction: Emergency Room	Emergency Room	Allocation Fraction: Radiology	Radiology	Allocation Fraction: Laboratory	Laboratory	Total
Total center costs	$100		$120		$150		$400		$500		$600	$1,870
Assign Housekeeping costs	$100	10/95	10*	15/95	16	15/95	16	25/95	26	30/95	32	
Assign Human Resources costs			$130	30/570	7	90/570	20*	210/570	48	240/570	55	
Assign Marketing costs					$173	600/2,300	45	800/2,300	60	900/2,300	68	
Total revenue center costs after allocation							$481		$634		$755	$1,870

*Rounded down.

Note that the total revenue center costs after allocation are the same as the total center costs before allocation. No dollars are lost or gained in the allocation process. (Sometimes assigned amounts are rounded up or down to ensure that the two total figures are equal.) The calculations of the assigned service costs for each revenue center using the step method are summarized in Table 4.

In our example, the total amount of service costs assigned to a given revenue center under the direct method differs little from the amount assigned under the step method. In actual practice, however, the total costs assigned to a revenue center may differ significantly from method to method. Such differences will be due largely to the order of allocation, the number of service centers involved, and the cost drivers used.

STOP • REVIEW • APPLY

4-1. What is the primary difference between the direct method and the step method of assigning service costs?

4-2. Are total costs the same before and after allocation regardless of the allocation method used?

4-3. Under the step method, what is the basis for allocating service center costs, and which responsibility centers receive assigned costs?

4-4. Under the step method, in what order are the costs of service departments assigned to revenue centers?

Applying the Step Method   A large supermarket chain has a centralized produce facility that prepares fruit and vegetables for the produce departments in its many retail stores. The chain has no other service centers. The $30,000 cost of prepackaging the produce is assigned on the basis of pounds packaged. Based on the following data for five stores, assign the $30,000 cost of packaging using the step method: Store A, 10,000 pounds; Store B, 20,000 pounds; Store C, 15,000 pounds; Store D, 12,000 pounds; and Store E, 13,000 pounds.

SOLUTION

	Store A	Store B	Store C	Store D	Store E	Total
Cost Assigned	$4,286	$8,571	$6,429	$5,143	$5,571	$30,000
Cost Driver used	10,000 / 70,000	20,000 / 70,000	15,000 / 70,000	12,000 /70,000	13,000 / 70,000	70,000

Store A:	(10 / 70) ($30,000) = $4,286
Store B:	(20 / 70) ($30,000) = $8,571
Store C:	(15 / 70) ($30,000) = $6,429
Store D:	(12 / 70) ($30,000) = $5,143
Store E:	(13 / 70) ($30,000) = $5,571

Other Methods of Service Cost Allocation

LO5 Describe the two-step method, the simultaneous equation method, the ability to pay method, and the physical measures method of assigning service costs.

Organizations may use a variety of other approaches to service cost allocation, depending on their business goals and cost considerations. In addition, some businesses do not assign service costs at all, but instead charge departments for the goods and services they use. For example, if the Product Design Department uses the services of the company's Legal Department, the Legal Department will send the Product Design Department a bill. Under this approach, the Legal Department must bill enough services to pay for its costs of operation. Although such an approach has benefits, it also has problems. For instance, departments may refuse to use the services of the internal Legal Department and hire outside law firms instead. Under such circumstances, the Legal Department may not have enough internal clients to support its costs and may be forced either to send extremely high bills to internal users or to ask for a subsidy from the parent organization.

Some organizations believe that their method of assigning internal service costs must fully recognize the reciprocal use of services among service centers, whereas other organizations prefer to base their allocation of service costs on ability to pay or number of users.

 Study Note

A manager's selection of a method of service cost allocation may change the utilization of internal services, depending on how the using centers perceive its fairness in measuring use.

Full Recognition of Service Users Method

A business that is interested in fully recognizing the reciprocal use of services among service centers can use either the two-step method or the simultaneous equation method of service cost allocation. Under the **two-step method**, the step method is performed twice—first to apportion all service costs among the service centers, with no service center being closed to accepting costs, and second to assign all service center costs to the revenue centers. Under the **simultaneous equation method**, a cost formula is set up for each service and revenue center that expresses the center's full use of all other centers' services. All the formulas are then solved simultaneously to determine the full cost of each revenue department. The simultaneous equation method is also known as the *reciprocal method*.

FOCUS ON BUSINESS PRACTICE

Hollywood Accounting

The costs of making movies extend far beyond the costs of film and actors. In fact, such traceable costs are minor when all of a movie's costs are totaled. In *Movie Money: Understanding Hollywood's (Creative) Accounting Practices,* Steven Sills explains that studio practices have evolved to allow studios to recover all or most of their investment before a film shows a profit. For example, studios deduct between 15 and 50 percent of the film's revenue for distribution expenses, which has no relation to the actual cash outlays for the film's distribution. In other words, distribution costs are allocated using the ability to pay method, and actual expenses are not traced back to individual films.[3]

Ability to Pay Method

In some organizations, it may not be important or desirable to measure the use of internal services precisely and assign their costs accordingly. Instead, management may decide to use the **ability to pay method**. Under this method, the revenue centers with the greatest ability to pay absorb most of the service center costs. If service costs are assigned using a readily accessible cost driver such as sales dollars, the revenue centers with the highest dollar sales will be assigned more of the service center costs than their less successful counterparts. Unfortunately, the selection of a cost driver such as sales dollars can affect managers' behavior.

For example, assume that in year 1, three revenue centers all have the same sales and cost structures. If sales dollars are used as a cost driver, each revenue center will be assigned the same amount of service center costs regardless of actual service use. Now assume that in year 2, one revenue center increases its sales, one center's sales remain the same, and one center's sales decline. Under such circumstances, an allocation based on sales dollars will fall most heavily on the revenue center that increased its sales, and the manager of that center may feel penalized instead of rewarded.

The movie industry frequently uses the ability to pay method to allocate studio costs. The higher the box-office gross, the greater the allocation of studio costs to the movie. Shown here is a scene being filmed for *Pirates of the Caribbean,* which was a major box-office draw.

Physical Measures Method

The easiest method of service cost allocation, the **physical measures method**, is based on the number of centers instead of on an activity of the centers. A service center's costs are divided by the number of centers that use its services and are assigned in equal portions. For example, if a service center has total costs of $100 and four revenue centers use its services, each revenue center would be assigned one-quarter of the costs, or $25, regardless of the amount of service usage. Consider the behavioral implications of this very simple allocation process: If centers will pay the same amount for a service regardless of their actual use of that service, they may be tempted to use the service more than necessary.

S T O P • R E V I E W • A P P L Y

5-1. What are two of the reasons that total service costs assigned to a revenue center vary depending on the method used?

5-2. How does the two-step method of cost allocation differ from the step method?

5-3. If an organization is interested in fully recognizing the reciprocal use of services among service centers, which method or methods of cost allocation should it use?

Applying the Physical Measures Method A large supermarket chain has a centralized kitchen that prepares salads and ready-to-eat foods for its many retail stores. Use the physical measures method to assign the $100,000 cost of food preparation for five stores (Stores A–E).

SOLUTION

	Store A	Store B	Store C	Store D	Store E	Total
Cost Assigned	$20,000	$20,000	$20,000	$20,000	$20,000	$100,000
Cost Driver used	1 / 5	1 / 5	1 / 5	1 / 5	1 / 5	5 / 5

Application of Overhead Rates

LO6 Explain how service cost allocation relates to overhead rates.

Once service center costs have been assigned to revenue centers, they are combined with each revenue center's overhead (that is, the center's traceable indirect costs). Either a single departmental overhead rate or several activity-based overhead rates are then computed for each revenue center. The resulting rate or rates are used to apply indirect costs to products and services. The allocation of costs from service centers to revenue centers to products or services is illustrated in Figure 2.

> **Study Note**
>
> Traditional overhead rates are based on both the traceable costs of a department and the allocated costs from the department's use of internal services.

Departmental Overhead Rates

A **departmental overhead rate** is a single rate that is based on all of a department's overhead costs and that is used to determine the full cost of a product

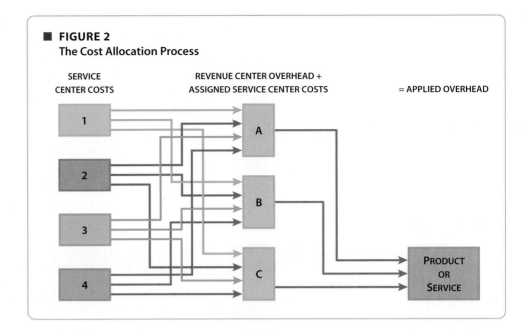

■ **FIGURE 2**
The Cost Allocation Process

or service. It is computed by dividing departmental overhead costs (traceable indirect costs plus assigned service center costs) by an activity-based cost driver, such as direct labor hours or machine hours:

$$\frac{\text{Revenue Center Overhead} + \text{Assigned Service Costs}}{\text{Cost Driver}} = \text{Overhead Rate}$$

For example, if Allison Batson, the management accountant at City Hospital, wants to compute a single departmental overhead rate for Radiology, she will add the center's traceable indirect costs to its assigned service center costs and divide that total by Radiology's activity-based cost driver: total machine minutes. The result will be Radiology's overhead rate per machine minute. Using the same method, she will compute a separate departmental overhead rate for each revenue center and apply that rate to determine the full cost of that center's products and services.

Activity-Based Costing Rates

Using several activity-based overhead rates instead of a single departmental overhead rate improves a revenue center manager's ability to manage and control different types of overhead costs. Under activity-based costing (ABC), a revenue center has multiple overhead rates based on the activities of that center. Those rates are used to assign the costs of their respective activities to a product or service to determine its full cost.

For example, under ABC, Allison Batson would compute a number of activity-based costing rates for each revenue center. She would add the costs of an activity, including the assigned service center costs, and divide the total by an activity-based cost driver that reflects the use of that activity by the product or service the revenue center produces. She would compute a separate activity-based costing rate for each activity in a revenue center and apply those rates to determine the full cost of the revenue center's product or service.

The True Cost of a Product or Service

One of the fundamental questions that managers try to answer is, "How much does a product or service cost?" In previous chapters, we considered product or service costs that included only direct materials, direct labor, and overhead. This chapter showed that the costs of services provided by other departments must also be included in product or service costs, even if managers must use judgment in assigning service costs.

Managers realize that the long-term performance and profitability of their organization depends on their ability to manage and control the full cost of products and services, not just the easily traceable costs that are under their direct control. Savvy managers recognize the limitations of cost-allocation policies—for example, that arbitrary cost-allocation methods can lead to poor product pricing or the rejection of potentially lucrative business opportunities. But they also recognize the benefits, including improved information for decision making and full knowledge of all the costs of products and services.

S T O P • R E V I E W • A P P L Y

6-1. What is the difference between service center costs and overhead costs if both are indirect costs?

6-2. Why might a manager use ABC instead of a single departmental rate?

6-3. How do activity-based rates differ from a single departmental overhead rate?

Allocation of Joint Product Costs

LO7 Apply allocation methods to the costs associated with joint products.

Products can be made by combining materials or by splitting materials apart. If two or more products are extracted, distilled, or refined from a common material, the products are called **joint products.** For example, raw milk is processed into the joint products of milk, cream, and butter. Some joint products are called **byproducts** because their sales value is minor relative to the value of the other joint products that were simultaneously produced. For example, a byproduct from processing pineapples into crushed, sliced, or cubed canned pineapple is the pineapple skins and cores, which can be used for animal feed.

The processing costs and material costs that joint products share are called **joint costs**. Joint costs are incurred before the separation of joint products. Costs incurred after the separation of joint products are called **separable costs**. The point at which joint products first become separate, identifiable products is known as the **split-off point**. Costs incurred up to the split-off point must be allocated to the joint products for financial purposes like inventory valuation. The three allocation methods used for joint costs are the physical measures method, the relative sales value method, and the net realizable value method.

Allocation Methods for Joint Costs

To illustrate the three methods of allocating joint costs, suppose that **Publix's** Meat Department processes 2,000 pounds of beef into steaks, hamburger, and soup bones. As Figure 3 shows, the cost of 2,000 pounds of beef is $1,000. Joint processing costs of $200 result in 500 pounds of steak, 750 pounds of hamburger, and 750 pounds of soup bones. At split-off, the steak can be sold at

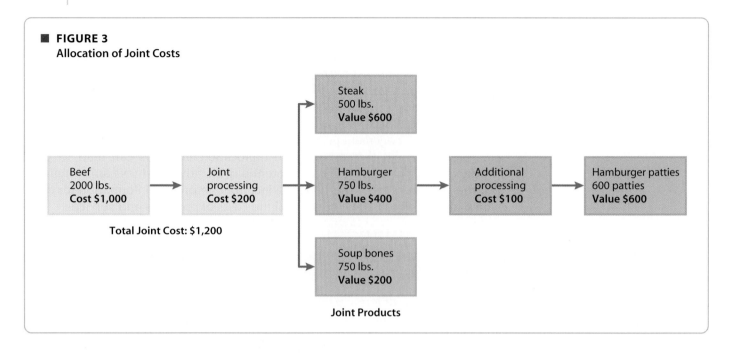

■ **FIGURE 3**
Allocation of Joint Costs

Total Joint Cost: $1,200

Joint Products

wholesale for $600, the hamburger for $400, and the soup bones for $200. Hamburger meat can be processed further at a cost of $100 into 600 hamburger patties that can be sold for $1 per patty to customers.

The Physical Units Method   The **physical units method** allocates joint costs to products based on their relative physical quantities, such as weight, volume, or units. In the beef example, the joint products' total weight of 2,000 pounds (500 + 750 + 750) is used as the denominator to allocate the $1,200 joint cost. The first part of Table 5 shows the physical units method of allocation. The advantages of this method are its objectivity and its ease of use. Its primary drawback is that it ignores the revenue value of the products. For example, if weight were used to allocate the joint cost of processing beef into steak, hamburger, and bones, much of the cost would be allocated to the heaviest part—bones—which could cause managers using this method for decision making to reach an incorrect conclusion.

The Relative Sales Value Method   The **relative sales value method** allocates joint costs to products based on their relative market value at the split-off point. In the beef example, the denominator for allocating the $1,200 joint cost is the total relative sales value at the split-off point, or $1,200 (steak $600 + hamburger $400 + soup bones $200). The second part of Table 5 shows the relative sales value method of allocation. The advantage of this method is its fairness in allocating costs to the products that are most likely to be able to absorb them. In this respect, it is similar to the ability to pay method used for internal service cost allocation. The primary drawback of the relative sales value method is the frequent inability to determine market value at split-off because of fluctuating market prices or because the product cannot be sold at split-off without further processing.

The Net Realizable Value Method   The **net realizable value method** allocates joint costs to products based on their eventual sales value less any separable costs necessary to make them salable. In the beef example, the relative sales value and the net realizable value are the same for steak and soup bones, since there are no separable costs. If hamburger is processed fur-

TABLE 5.   Joint Cost-Allocation Methods

Physical Units Method:

Joint Products	Weight at Split-off	Proportion	Joint Cost
Steaks	500	500/2,000	$ 300
Hamburger	750	750/2,000	450
Soup bones	750	750/2,000	450
Total	2,000 lbs.		$1,200

Relative Sales Value Method:

Joint Products	Sales Value at Split-off	Proportion	Joint Cost
Steak	$ 600	600/1,200	$ 600
Hamburger	400	400/1,200	400
Soup bones	200	200/1,200	200
Total	$1,200		$1,200

Net Realizable Value Method:

Joint Products	Net Realizable Value	Proportion	Joint Cost
Steak	$ 600	600/1,300	$ 554*
Hamburger ($600 − $100)	500	500/1,300	461*
Soup bones	200	200/1,300	185*
Total	$1,300		$1,200

*Rounded.

ther into hamburger patties, its net realizable value is $500 ($600 − separable costs of $100). Thus, the denominator used for joint cost allocation is $1,300 (the sum of steak $600 + hamburger patties $500 + soup bones $200). The last part of Table 5 shows the net realizable value method of allocation. An advantage of this method is the comparability of profits among products for allocation and decision-making purposes.

Sell or Process-Further Decisions and Joint Costs

Our analysis of a short-run management decision in an earlier chapter focused on how to determine which costs are relevant when deciding whether to sell a product or process it further into another product. You may recall that joint costs were ignored in the analysis and only the separable costs were used, since they were the only costs that changed between the alternatives.

Byproducts

The difference between byproducts and joint products is their relative market value. Joint products are the primary products produced. Byproducts are produced simultaneously with joint products but have minimal market value. Sometimes, byproducts become joint products as a result of changing market preferences for products. For example, broken cookies were a byproduct of cookies until products like cookies-and-cream ice cream were introduced. Similarly, sawdust was a byproduct until it was compressed and sold as particleboard or fireplace logs. Generally, for accounting purposes, joint costs are not allocated to byproducts.

S T O P • R E V I E W • A P P L Y

7-1. What types of products are produced at the split-off point?

7-2. Of the three methods of assigning joint costs, which one is preferred?

A LOOK BACK AT

PUBLIX SUPER MARKETS, INC.

The Decision Point at the beginning of this chapter focused on **Publix Super Markets, Inc.,** the largest employee-owned grocery chain in the United States. It posed these questions.

- **How should Publix apportion internal service costs among its stores and support departments?**

- **How should Publix apportion the costs of its other service departments, such as human resources and the dairy, deli, and bakery facilities, among the many departments that use these services?**

The services provided by Publix's distribution and communication centers—as well as by its other service departments, such as human resources or the dairy, deli, and bakery facilities—benefit multiple stores and departments within the organization. Their costs are therefore apportioned among all users. Publix management knows that how it assigns the costs of internal services can strongly affect the company's prices, costs, and profitability and the decisions its managers make. There are several methods of assigning internal service costs, and Publix managers realize that they must understand the pros and cons of each and select the one that best suits their situation for current or new business activities. They want to be sure that the method chosen not only assigns costs effectively, but also seems fair to the managers of the affected stores and departments and motivates them to perform their best.

CHAPTER REVIEW

REVIEW of Learning Objectives

LO1 Discuss the allocation of internal service costs and explain its impact on decision making.

All organizations have departments or centers that provide services internally to support the activities of the business. The costs of such services must be included in the full cost of a business's products and services to ensure the business's long-term survival. The full cost encompasses both the directly traceable product and service costs and the indirect internal service costs.

How an organization assigns the costs of internal services strongly affects its prices, its other costs, its profitability, and the decisions its managers make. Managers plan the cost-allocation methods and allocation bases that they will use to assign service costs. As they perform their duties, they control the costs for individual centers or departments, assign service center costs to revenue centers, and compute overhead rates. Managers evaluate customer profitability, analyze the performance of products and services, review the allocation methods and bases used, and make the needed adjustments. Finally, they prepare and use reports on cost allocation to monitor costs and the allocation bases and methods.

LO2 Describe the two kinds of responsibility centers used in allocating service costs.

Responsibility centers are classified into two categories for the allocation of service costs: revenue centers and service centers. Revenue centers are directly responsible for producing the products or services sold to external buyers. They not only incur their own traceable costs, but are also assigned the costs of other responsibility centers from which they benefit.

Service centers provide benefits to other responsibility centers. Service centers are also called *support centers* because they indirectly support the activities of the revenue centers and other service centers. The traceable costs of a service center are first collected and controlled by that center and then assigned to other centers based on a logical measure or cost driver.

LO3 Use the direct method to assign service costs.

The simplest of the commonly used activity-based cost-allocation methods is the direct method, which assigns the costs of service centers only to revenue centers. However, because the direct method ignores the fact that service centers provide service and support to other service centers as well as to revenue centers, the distribution of costs may not reflect the actual use of services.

LO4 Use the step method to assign service costs.

The step method assigns service center costs to both service and revenue centers based on descending order of use. The costs of the service center that is used most by other centers are assigned first. The costs of the service center that is used least by other service centers are assigned last. Managers must decide on the order of allocation. Once the costs of a service center have been assigned, that center cannot receive any assigned costs from any other service center. Although the step method attempts to recognize some interdepartmental use, other methods must be used to recognize the full reciprocal usage of services.

LO5 Describe the two-step method, the simultaneous equation method, the ability to pay method, and the physical measures method of assigning service costs.

A business that is interested in fully recognizing the reciprocal use of services among service centers can use either the two-step method or the simultaneous equation method of service cost allocation. Organizations that do not need precise measurements of the internal use of services may decide to allocate service center costs based on a revenue center's ability to pay. Under this system, if sales dollars are used as a cost driver, a revenue center's actual use of service centers is irrelevant. The easiest method of service cost allocation, physical measures, is based on the number of centers instead of on an activity of the centers. A service center's costs are divided by the number of centers that use its services and assigned in equal portions.

LO6 Explain how service cost allocation relates to overhead rates.

When a revenue center applies overhead costs to the product or service it produces, either a single departmental overhead rate or several activity-based costing (ABC) rates are used. These rates include the overhead costs of the revenue center and any assigned service center costs. Revenue center managers may use several activity-based rates instead of a single departmental overhead rate to improve their ability to manage and control different types of overhead costs.

LO7 Apply allocation methods to the costs associated with joint products.

Joint products and byproducts are produced simultaneously from a common source. Joint products are the primary products produced. Some joint products are called byproducts because their sales value is minor relative to the value of the other simultaneously produced joint products. Joint costs are the common costs incurred before the separation of joint products. The split-off point is the point in the production process at which products first become separate, identifiable products or byproducts. Costs incurred after the split-off point that can be traced to the individual products are called *separable costs.*

Three methods are commonly used to allocate joint costs to products. The physical units method assigns joint costs to products based on a physical quantity, such as weight, volume, or units. The relative sales value method assigns joint costs to products based on their sales value at the split-off point of production. The net realizable value method assigns joint costs to products based on the eventual sales value of each product less any separable costs needed to make it salable.

REVIEW of Concepts and Terminology

The following concepts and terms were introduced in this chapter:

Ability to pay method: A method of service cost allocation in which the revenue centers with the highest dollar sales will be expected to absorb most of the service center costs. **(LO5)**

Byproducts: Products with minor sales value that are produced simultaneously with joint products from a common source. **(LO7)**

Common costs: Mutually beneficial indirect costs that may not have a clear cause-and-effect relationship to a specific product or service because they come from a service center that benefits and supports many products and services. **(LO1)**

Cost allocation: The process of assigning collected indirect costs, known as common costs, to specific cost objects using an allocation base. **(LO1)**

Cost driver: An activity that causes another center's use of a service center. **(LO2)**

Departmental overhead rate: A single rate that is based on all of a department's overhead costs and that is used to determine the full cost of a product or service; departmental overhead costs (traceable indirect costs plus assigned service center costs) divided by an activity-based cost driver, such as direct labor hours or machine hours. **(LO6)**

Direct method: An activity-based cost-allocation method that assigns the costs of service centers only to revenue centers. **(LO3)**

Full cost: A cost that includes not only the costs of direct materials and direct labor, but also the costs of all production and nonproduction activities in an organization's value chain that are required to satisfy customers. **(LO1)**

Joint costs: Costs incurred before the separation of products made from a common source. **(LO7)**

Joint products: Two or more major products that are produced from a common source. **(LO7)**

Net realizable value method: A cost-allocation method that assigns joint costs to products based on the eventual sales value of the products less any separable costs needed to make them salable. **(LO7)**

Physical measures method: A cost-allocation method based on the number of centers instead of on an activity of the centers. A service center's costs are divided by the number of centers that use its services and are assigned in equal portions. **(LO5)**

Physical units method: A cost-allocation method that assigns joint costs to products based on their relative physical quantities. **(LO7)**

Relative sales value method: A cost-allocation method that assigns joint costs to products based on their sales value at the split-off point of production. **(LO7)**

Responsibility center: An organizational unit whose manager is responsible for managing a portion of the company's resources. **(LO2)**

Revenue center: A responsibility center that is directly responsible for producing products or services that are sold to external buyers. Also known as a *producing center* or an *operating center*. **(LO2)**

Separable costs: Costs incurred after split-off that are traceable to the individual products. **(LO7)**

Service center: A responsibility center that provides benefits to other responsibility centers. Also known as a *support center* or a *discretionary cost center*. **(LO2)**

Simultaneous equation method: An activity-based cost-allocation method in which a cost formula is set up for each service and revenue center and that expresses the center's full use of all other centers' services. All the formulas are solved simultaneously to determine the full cost of each revenue department. Also known as the *reciprocal method*. **(LO5)**

Split-off point: The point in the production process at which products first become separate, identifiable products or byproducts. **(LO7)**

Step method: An activity-based cost-allocation method that assigns service center costs to both service and revenue centers based on descending order of use. Also called the *step-down method*. **(LO4)**

Two-step method: An activity-based method of service cost allocation in which the step method is performed twice—first to apportion all service costs among the service centers, with no service center's being closed to accepting costs, and second to assign all service center costs to the revenue centers. **(LO5)**

REVIEW Problem

LO3, LO4, LO6   **Cost Allocation and Overhead Rates**

The Live Oak Clinic is a rural health facility with three revenue centers and four service centers. The three revenue centers are Clinic, Radiology, and Laboratory. In order of utilization, the service centers are Administration, Housekeeping, Medical Records, and Patient Accounting. The allocation of Administration's costs is based on percentage of time spent. The allocation of Housekeeping's costs is based on the number of square feet. The allocation of Medical Records' costs is based on the number of entries. The allocation of Patient Accounting's costs is based on the percentage of patient visits. The following data have been collected:

	A / B	C Administration	D House-keeping	E Medical Records	F Patient Accounting	G Clinic	H Radiology	I Laboratory	J Total
4	Percentage of time spent	10	10	10	10	30	20	10	100
5	Number of square feet	1,000	500	1,500	1,000	5,000	3,000	2,000	14,000
6	Number of entries				500	2,000	500	1,500	4,500
7	Percentage of patient visits					50	10	40	100

Traceable indirect costs for all departments total $2,200. They are as follows:

Administration	$250	Clinic	$800
Housekeeping	50	Radiology	500
Medical Records	80	Laboratory	400
Patient Accounting	120		

Required

1. The clinic's administrators want to determine the overhead costs for the three revenue centers—Clinic, Radiology, and Laboratory. Prepare the cost allocations using (a) the direct method and (b) the step method.
2. Prepare departmental overhead rates for the three revenue centers using these activity-based cost drivers: Clinic, 1,000 patient visits; Radiology, 250 x-rays; and Laboratory, 5,000 lab tests. Use both the direct method and the step method. Carry your answers to two decimal places.

Answer to Review Problem

1a. Service cost allocations computed using the direct method:

	Admini-stration	House-keeping	Medical Records	Patient Account-ing	Allocation Fraction: Clinic	Clinic	Allocation Fraction: Radiology	Radio-logy	Allocation Fraction: Laboratory	Labo-ratory	Total
Method: Direct											
Total center costs	$250	$50	$80	$120		$ 800		$500		$400	$2,200
Assign costs:											
Administration	$250				30/60	125	20/60	83	10/60	42	
Housekeeping		$50			5,000/10,000	25	3,000/10,000	15	2,000/10,000	10	
Medical											
Records			$80		2,000/4,000	40	500/4,000	10	1,500/4,000	30	
Patient											
Accounting				$120	50/100	60	10/100	12	40/100	48	
Total revenue											
center costs											
after allocation						$1,050		$620		$530	$2,200

1b. Service cost allocations computed using the step method:

	Admini-stration	Allocation Fraction: House-keeping	House-keeping	Allocation Fraction: Medical Records	Medical Records	Allocation Fraction: Patient Accounting	Patient Account-ing	Allocation Fraction: Clinic	Clinic	Allocation Fraction: Radiology	Radio-logy	Allocation Fraction: Laboratory	Labo-ratory	Total
Method: Step														
Total center														
costs	$250		$50		$ 80		$120		$ 800		$500		$400	$2,200
Assign costs:														
Administration	$250	10/90	28	10/90	28	10/90	28	30/90	83	20/90	55*	10/90	28	
Housekeeping			$78	1,500/12,500	9	1,000/12,500	6	5,000/12,500	31	3,000/12,500	19	2,000/12,500	13*	
Medical														
Records					$117	500/4,500	13	2,000/4,500	52	500/4,500	13	1,500/4,500	39	
Patient														
Accounting							$167	50/100	83*	10/100	17	40/100	67	
Total revenue														
center costs														
after allocation									$1,049		$604		$546	$2,200

* Rounded

2. Departmental overhead rates computed:
Direct Method

Clinic:	$1,050/1,000	= $1.05 per patient visit
Radiology:	$620/250	= $2.48 per x-ray
Laboratory:	$530/5,000	= $.11 per lab test

Step Method

Clinic:	$1,049/1,000	= $1.05 per patient visit
Radiology:	$604/250	= $2.42 per x-ray
Laboratory:	$547/5,000	= $.11 per lab test

Notice that in the computation of departmental overhead rates, rounding can affect the outcome.

CHAPTER ASSIGNMENTS

BUILDING Your Basic Knowledge and Skills

Short Exercises

LO1 Classifying Costs

SE 1. Identify the following as either directly traceable costs or common costs for a store in a restaurant chain:

a. Food prepared in the store
b. Company newsletter and website
c. Centralized purchasing
d. Wait staff
e. Depreciation of restaurant equipment

LO2 Categorizing Responsibility Centers

SE 2. Suppose you are the manager of a resort and spa. List some of the responsibility centers you would manage, and categorize each as either a revenue center or a service center.

LO3 Applying the Direct Method

SE 3. A large supermarket chain has a centralized bakery facility that prepares frosting for the bakeries in its many retail stores. The $30,000 cost of preparing the frosting is assigned on the basis of containers of frosting used. Based on the following data for five store bakeries, assign frosting costs using the direct method: Store A, 200 containers; Store B, 400 containers; Store C, 150 containers; Store D, 120 containers; and Store E, 130 containers.

LO3 Applying the Direct Method

SE 4. A large supermarket chain has a centralized bakery facility that prepares bread dough for the bakeries in its many retail stores. The $21,000 cost of preparing the dough is assigned on the basis of pounds baked. Based on the following data for five store bakeries, assign the cost of the bread dough using the direct method: Store A, 10,000 pounds; Store B, 20,000 pounds; Store C, 15,000 pounds; Store D, 12,000 pounds; and Store E, 13,000 pounds.

LO3 **Applying the Direct Method**

SE 5. A large supermarket chain has a centralized bakery facility that makes cupcakes for three service centers and two stores (revenue centers). The $50,000 cost of preparing the cupcakes is assigned on the basis of cupcake pans used. Based on the following data, assign the cost of the cupcakes using the direct method: Center A, 50,000 pans; Center B, 20,000 pans; Center C, 30,000 pans; Store D, 60,000 pans; and Store E, 40,000 pans.

LO4 **Applying the Step Method**

SE 6. A large supermarket chain has a centralized bakery facility that prepares frosting for three service centers and two stores (revenue centers). The $40,000 cost of preparing the frosting is assigned on the basis of containers of frosting used. Based on the following data, assign the cost of the frosting using the step method: Center A, 200 containers; Center B, 400 containers; Center C, 150 containers; Store D, 120 containers; and Store E, 130 containers. Assume an allocation order of A, B, and C. (**Hint:** Refer to the exercise in the Stop, Review, and Apply section of LO4.)

LO4 **Applying the Step Method**

SE 7. A large supermarket chain has a centralized bakery facility that prepares bread dough for the bakeries in its many retail stores.. The chain has no other service centers. The $28,000 cost of preparing the dough is assigned on the basis of pounds baked. Based on the following data for five store bakeries, assign the cost of the bread dough using the step method: Store A, 10,000 pounds; Store B, 20,000 pounds; Store C, 15,000 pounds; Store D, 12,000 pounds; and Store E, 13,000 pounds. (**Hint:** Refer to the exercise in the Stop, Review, and Apply section of LO4.)

LO4 **Applying the Step Method**

SE 8. A large supermarket chain has a centralized bakery facility that makes cupcakes for three service centers and two stores (revenue centers). The $40,000 cost of preparing the cupcakes is assigned on the basis of cupcake pans used. Based on the following data, assign the cost of the cupcakes using the step method: Center A, 50,000 pans; Center B, 20,000 pans; Center C, 30,000 pans; Store D, 60,000 pans; and Store E, 40,000 pans. Assume an allocation order of A, B, and C. (**Hint:** Refer to the exercise in the Stop, Review, and Apply section of LO 4.)

LO5 **Applying the Physical Measures Method**

SE 9. A large supermarket chain has a centralized delicatessen distribution center that prepares ready-to-eat food for its many retail stores. The company uses the physical measures method to allocate the $50,000 cost of preparing the food. Using that method, assign the $50,000 of food preparation costs to five stores (Stores A–E). (**Hint:** Refer to the exercise in the Stop, Review, and Apply section of LO5.)

LO5 **Applying the Physical Measures Method**

SE 10. A large supermarket chain has a centralized delicatessen distribution center that prepares meat for its many retail stores. The $100,000 cost of preparing the meat is assigned on the basis of store revenues. Based on the following data, allocate the $100,000 of meat preparation costs among these five stores: Store A, $10,000,000 sales; Store B, $20,000,000 sales; Store C, $30,000,000 sales; Store D, $25,000,000 sales; and Store E, $15,000,000 sales.

Exercises

LO1 **Identifying Direct and Common Costs**

E 1. Rugged Outfitters, an outdoor clothing retailer, sells its products in stores and online. Identify the following service costs as either directly traceable store costs or common costs that benefit multiple internal users:

a. Payroll processing
b. Information services
c. Sales staff
d. Store administration
e. Distribution center shipping and receiving
f. Inventory
g. In-store customer service department
h. Central accounting services
i. Utilities
j. Strategic Planning Department

LO1 **Classifying Costs**

E 2. Tasty Juice is a citrus growers' cooperative. Should each of the following costs be internally assigned to producing centers or directly charged to external parties?

a. Housekeeping
b. Grounds maintenance
c. Citrus pulp
d. Juice concentrate
e. Equipment depreciation
f. Purchasing
g. Engineering
h. Employee benefits
i. Safety
j. Quality testing and control

LO2 **Categorizing Responsibility Centers**

E 3. Classify each of the following responsibility centers at Regents Circle Hospital as either a revenue center or a service center:

a. Radiology
b. Housekeeping
c. Maintenance
d. Laundry
e. Prescriptions
f. Physical Therapy
g. Nursing Services
h. Laboratory
i. Hazardous Waste Disposal
j. Shipping and Receiving

LO2 **Identifying Cost Drivers**

E 4. Happy Trails Ranch charges a weekly fee for meals, lodging, and activities for each of its package vacations. Packages include a Western Getaway and a Wilderness Getaway. Each of the packages uses the same five service centers. For each of these service centers, identify at least one cost driver:

a. Horse Barn   d. Reservations
b. Cookouts   e. White Water Rafting
c. Lodging

LO3 **Applying the Direct Method**

E 5. Climax Mines uses the direct method for assigning service center costs to Revenue Centers M and N. The costs, cost drivers, and statistics are as follows:

	Costs	Cost Drivers
Mine Administration	$500,000	Number of employees
Equipment Maintenance	$50,000	Number of square feet

Center	Number of Employees	Number of Square Feet
Mine Administration	10	1,800
Equipment Maintenance	24	3,200
Mine M	58	6,000
Mine N	62	8,000

Using the direct method, assign service center costs to Mine M and Mine N. Carry your answers to three decimal places.

LO3 **Applying the Direct Method**

E 6. Recent operational data for Broomfield Occupational Therapy Services are as follows:

	Service Center A	Service Center B	Revenue Center C	Revenue Center D
Costs incurred	$40,000	$30,000	$80,000	$70,000
Percentage of square feet occupied	30	10	40	20
Number of procedures	200	600	1,800	2,400
Number of patient visits			900	1,800

Center A's costs are assigned on the basis of square feet occupied, and Center B's costs are assigned on the basis of the number of procedures performed. The number of patient visits is the basis for applying overhead. Assign all service center costs using the direct method, and determine the total cost of the revenue centers after allocation.

LO3 **Applying the Direct Method**

E 7. Ouray Peaks, an ecotourism business, has two service centers, Human Resources and Financial Resources. They provide services to each other as well as to two revenue centers, Mountain Adventures and River Adventures. Data for the summer season follow:

	Human Resources	Financial Resources	Mountain Adventures	River Adventures
Number of employees	2	3	15	20
Number of transactions	1,000	500	2,500	7,000
Trips sold	—	—	2,000	6,000

Human Resources had total costs of $40,000, and Financial Resources had total costs of $50,000. Human Resources' costs are assigned based on the number of employees, and Financial Resources' costs are assigned based on the number of transactions. Overhead costs are applied on the basis of trips sold. Assign service center costs using the direct method.

LO4   Applying the Step Method

E 8. Climax Mines has decided to use the step method for assigning service center costs to Revenue Centers M and N. The costs, cost drivers, and statistics are as shown in **E 5**. Assign service center costs to Mine M and Mine N using the step method. Assign the costs of Mine Administration first and Equipment Maintenance second.

LO4   Applying the Step Method

E 9. These data summarize the recent operations of Blue River Physical Therapy Services:

	Service Center W	Service Center X	Revenue Center Y	Revenue Center Z
Costs incurred	$40,000	$50,000	$80,000	$70,000
Percentage of square feet occupied	30	10	40	20
Number of procedures	200	600	1,800	2,400
Patient visits			900	1,800

Center W's costs are assigned on the basis of square feet occupied, and Center X's costs are assigned on the basis of the number of procedures performed. The number of patient visits is the basis for applying overhead. Assign the costs of Service Center W and then Service Center X using the step method, and determine the total cost of the revenue centers after allocation.

LO4   Applying the Step Method

E 10. Ouray Peaks, an ecotourism business, has two service centers—Human Resources and Financial Resources—that provide services to each other as well as to two revenue centers, Mountain Adventures and River Adventures. Data for the summer season are presented in **E 7**. Human Resources had total costs of $40,000; Financial Resources had total costs of $50,000. Human Resources' costs are assigned based on the number of employees; Financial Resources' costs are assigned based on the number of transactions. Overhead costs are applied on the basis of trips sold. Assign service center costs of Human Resources first and Financial Resources second using the step method.

LO5   Using Other Allocation Methods

E 11. Climax Mines assigns service center costs to Revenue Centers M and N. The costs, cost drivers, and statistics are as follows:

	Costs	Cost Drivers
Mine Administration	$500,000	Number of mines
Equipment Maintenance	$50,000	Revenue dollars

Center	Number of Mines	Revenue Dollars
Mine M	1	$3,600,000
Mine N	1	$8,400,000

Assign service center costs to Mine M and Mine N using the physical measures method for Mine Administration and the ability to pay method for Equipment Maintenance.

LO5   Using Other Allocation Methods

E 12. Pecos Flats, an ecotourism business, has two service centers, Human Resources and Financial Resources. They provide services to each other as well as to two revenue centers, Desert Adventures and Sea Adventures. Data for the revenue centers' summer season are as follows:

	Desert Adventures	Sea Adventures
Center revenue	$200,000	$300,000
Number of revenue centers	1	1
Trips sold	2,000	6,000

Human Resources had total costs of $250,000, and Financial Resources had total costs of $120,000. Human Resources' costs are assigned based on the number of revenue centers, and Financial Resources' costs are assigned based on center revenue. Overhead costs are applied on the basis of trips sold. Assign service center costs to the revenue centers.

LO6 Computing Overhead Rates Using the Direct Method

E 13. Using the information in **E 6** about the operations of Broomfield Occupational Therapy Services and assuming that the costs incurred in the revenue centers are for overhead, determine the overhead rate per patient visit for each revenue center. Revenue Center C had 900 patient visits, and Revenue Center D had 1,800 patient visits.

LO6 Computing Overhead Rates Using the Step Method

E 14. Using the information in **E 9** about the operations of Blue River Physical Therapy Services and assuming that the costs incurred in the revenue centers are for overhead, determine the overhead rate per patient visit for each revenue center. Revenue Center Y had 900 patient visits, and Revenue Center Z had 1,800 patient visits.

LO7 Joint Costing Methods

E 15. St. Simons Silicon, LLC, produces two joint products: Chip A and Chip B. Joint production costs for the month were $40,000. During the month, further processing was necessary to convert the products into salable form. Separable costs were $25,000 for Chip A and $35,000 for Chip B. Total output for the month was 1,800 units of Chip A and 600 units of Chip B. Chip A sells for $60, and Chip B sells for $120. The company currently uses the physical units method for allocating joint costs but is considering adopting the net realizable value method. Prepare a report that shows the allocation of joint costs using both the physical units method and the net realizable value method. Compare the results, and comment on your findings.

Problems

LO1, LO2 Classifying Costs

P 1. Some of State University's responsibility centers are President, Provost, Central Receiving, Housing, Food Service, Bookstore, Physical Plant, Power Plant, College of Arts and Sciences, College of Business, Foundation, Online Registration, College Website, and Health Center.

Required

1. Classify each responsibility center as either a revenue center or a service center.
2. Identify at least one cost driver for each service center.

LO3, LO4   **Applying the Direct and Step Methods**

P 2. Columbine Incubator for Emerging Technologies nurtures fledgling businesses by providing tenants with a variety of services. Support services in descending order of use are Secretarial Services, Computer and Network Services, Fund Raising, Management Consulting, and Wet Lab Space. The service center costs are assigned to the centers and the tenant companies using the cost drivers that are listed below.

Service Center	Cost	Cost Driver
Secretarial Services	$25,000	Number of phone calls
Computer and Network Services	45,000	Number of computer connections
Fund Raising	15,000	Dollars raised
Management Consulting	35,000	Number of tenants
Wet Lab Space	65,000	Percentage of reserved time

Support Centers and Tenants	Number of Phone Calls	Number of Computer Connections	Dollars Raised	Number of Tenants	Percentage of Reserved Time
Secretarial Services	—	5	—	—	—
Computer and Network Services	25	15	—	—	—
Fund Raising	35	6	—	—	—
Management Consulting	15	5	—	—	—
Wet Lab Space	5	4	—	—	—
Tenant: Clean Air	55	10	100,000	1	0
Tenant: NuBones	45	35	600,000	1	40
Tenant: Genetic Fish	20	15	300,000	1	60

Required

1. Use the direct method of allocation to determine the three tenants' support costs.
2. Use the step method of allocation to determine the three tenants' support costs. Assign the service centers' costs in descending order of use. (For example, assign the costs of Secretarial Services first and Computer and Network Services second.)
3. Manager Insight: Did each tenant's total service costs differ depending on the allocation method? Did the total center costs of Columbine Incubator for Emerging Technologies change?

LO3, LO4, LO6   **Using Allocation Methods and Computing Overhead Rates**

P 3. The following data summarize a small publishing firm's indirect costs:

	Printing Services	Editing Services	Proofing Services	Trade Publishing	Custom Publishing
Indirect costs	$140,000	$120,000	$40,000	$80,000	$70,000
Number of pages		5,000	10,000	40,000	20,000
Number of inquiries			1,000	2,600	2,400
Number of errors				900	1,800

Printing Services' costs are assigned on the basis of number of pages printed, Editing Services' costs are assigned based on the number of editor inquiries, and Proofing Services' costs are assigned based on the number of errors corrected. The number of books produced is the basis for applying overhead for the Trade Publishing and Custom Publishing revenue centers. Each of the revenue centers produced 200 books.

Required

1. Use the direct method of cost allocation to determine the two revenue centers' overhead costs.
2. Use the step method of cost allocation to determine the two revenue centers' overhead costs. Assign the service costs of Printing Services first, Editing Services second, and Proofing Services third.
3. Compute departmental overhead rates for Trade Publishing and Custom Publishing under the direct method of cost allocation.
4. Compute departmental overhead rates for Trade Publishing and Custom Publishing under the step method of cost allocation.

LO3, LO4, LO6   **Using Allocation Methods and Computing Overhead Rates**

P 4. The Dentist Group is an upscale dental clinic with four service centers and three revenue centers. In order of utilization, the service centers are Administration, Housekeeping, Anesthesia, and Patient Accounting. The three revenue centers are General Dentistry, Oral Surgery, and Orthodontics. Administration's costs are assigned based on the percentage of time spent. Housekeeping's costs are assigned based on the number of square feet. Anesthesia's costs are assigned based on the minutes of surgery. Patient Accounting's costs are assigned based on the percentage of patient visits.

The following statistics have been collected:

Center	Percentage of Time Spent	Number of Square Feet	Number of Minutes of Surgery	Percentage of Patient Visits	Number of Patient Visits
Administration	15	1,000	—	—	—
Housekeeping	5	500	—	—	—
Anesthesia	10	1,000	—	—	—
Patient Accounting	10	500	—	—	—
General Dentistry	30	3,500	500	50	500
Oral Surgery	10	2,500	5,000	10	100
Orthodontics	20	2,000	1,500	40	400
Total	100	11,000	7,000	100	1,000

Managers report these traceable indirect costs for their departments:

Administration	$ 2,500
Housekeeping	500
Anesthesia	1,800
Patient Accounting	1,200
General Dentistry	8,000
Oral Surgery	5,000
Orthodontics	4,000
Total	$23,000

Required

1. Use the direct method of cost allocation to determine the three revenue centers' overhead costs.
2. Use the step method of cost allocation to determine the three revenue centers' overhead costs.
3. Compute departmental overhead rates for General Dentistry, Oral Surgery, and Orthodontics, assuming that the direct method of cost allocation is used and that the activity base is number of patient visits.
4. Compute departmental overhead rates for General Dentistry, Oral Surgery, and Orthodontics, assuming that the step method of cost allocation is used and that the activity base is number of patient visits.
5. Did each revenue center's departmental overhead rates vary depending on the allocation method used? Did the total center costs change?

LO3, LO4, LO5 **Using Allocation Methods**

P 5. Wild Bluebonnets, an ecotourism business, has two service centers, Human Resources and Financial Resources. They provide services to each other as well as to two revenue centers, Solo Adventures and Team Adventures. Data for the company's summer season are as follows:

	Human Resources	Financial Resources	Solo Adventures	Team Adventures
Number of employees	2	3	15	20
Number of transactions	1,000	500	2,500	7,000
Trips sold	—	—	3,000	6,000

Human Resources had total costs of $250,000, and Financial Resources had total costs of $100,000. Human Resources' costs are assigned based on the number of employees, and Financial Resources' costs are assigned based on the number of transactions.

Required

1. Assign service center costs using the direct method. Compute the costs of the revenue centers after allocation.
2. Assign service center costs using the step method. Assign the costs of Human Resources first and Financial Resources second. Compute the costs of the revenue centers after allocation.
3. Wild Bluebonnets is considering other allocation bases for assigning service center costs. Using the physical measures method and the ability to pay method, assign service center costs if Human Resources costs are assigned on the basis of number of revenue centers and Financial Resources' costs are assigned on the basis of center revenue:

	Solo Adventures	Team Adventures
Center revenue	$200,000	$300,000
Number of revenue centers	1	1

Compute the costs of the revenue centers after allocation.

Alternate Problems

LO3, LO4, LO6 **Applying the Direct and Step Methods and Computing Overhead Rates**

P 6. A small metropolitan airport has three service centers: Maintenance, Air Traffic Control, and Ground Crew. They provide services to one another as well as to two revenue centers: Commercial Planes and Private Planes. During the fall season, the service and revenue centers generated the following data:

	Maintenance	Air Traffic Control	Ground Crew	Commercial Planes	Private Planes
Number of work orders	—	10	30	470	200
Number of controller minutes	—	—	—	2,500	6,500
Number of passenger seats	—	—	—	80	20
Number of flights	—	—	—	1,000	6,000

Maintenance had total costs of $150,000, which are assigned on the basis of the number of work orders. Air Traffic Control had total costs of $200,000, which are assigned on the basis of the number of controller minutes. Ground Crew had total costs of $80,000, which are assigned on the basis of the number of passenger seats. Commercial Planes had indirect costs of $100,000, and Private Planes had indirect costs of $50,000. Overhead rates for Commercial Planes and Private Planes are computed on the basis of number of flights.

Required

1. Use the direct method of cost allocation to determine the two revenue centers' overhead costs.
2. Use the step method of cost allocation to determine the two revenue centers' overhead costs. Allocate in the order presented: Maintenance, Air Traffic Control, Ground Crew, Commercial Planes, and Private Planes.
3. Prepare departmental overhead rates for Commercial Planes and Private Planes under the direct method of cost allocation.
4. Prepare departmental overhead rates for Commercial Planes and Private Planes under the step method of cost allocation.

LO3, LO4, LO6 **Using Allocation Methods and Computing Overhead Rates**

P 7. Oakhaven Financial Planners has four service centers and three revenue centers. In order of use, the service centers are Administration, Information Services, Customer Service, and Client Accounting. The three revenue centers are Insurance, Investments, and Financial Plans.

Administration's costs are assigned based on percentage of time spent. Information Services' costs are assigned based on the percentage of computer and Internet access time. Customer Service's costs are assigned based on percentage of clients. Client Accounting's costs are assigned based on the percentage of client transactions. Statistics for the service and revenue centers appear at the top of the facing page.

Managers report these indirect costs for their departments:

Administration	$ 2,500
Information Services	1,800
Customer Service	5,000
Client Accounting	1,000
Insurance	2,600
Investments	8,000
Financial Plans	2,400
Total	$23,300

Center	Percentage of Time Spent	Percentage of Access Time	Percentage of Clients	Percentage of Client Transactions	Labor Hours
Administration	5	15	—	—	—
Information Services	6	5	—	—	—
Customer Service	25	25	—	—	—
Client Accounting	4	12	—	—	—
Insurance	25	13	20	25	830
Investments	15	20	60	70	500
Financial Plans	20	10	20	5	664
Total	100	100	100	100	1,994

Required

1. Use the direct method of cost allocation to determine the three revenue centers' overhead costs.
2. Use the step method of cost allocation to determine the three revenue centers' overhead costs.
3. Prepare departmental overhead rates for Insurance, Investments, and Financial Plans, assuming that the direct method of cost allocation is used and that the activity base is labor hours.
4. Prepare departmental overhead rates for Insurance, Investment, and Financial Plans, assuming that the step method of cost allocation is used and that the activity base is labor hours.
5. **Manager Insight:** Did the departmental overhead rates computed using the direct method and the step method of cost allocation differ? Why?

LO7 **Joint Costing Methods**

P 8. Corn Palace Processors purchases field corn and processes it into cornmeal, corncobs, and cornhusks. Cornmeal can be processed further into corn chips. Corncobs can be processed further into animal feed. Cornhusks can be processed further into tamales. In a recent month, $500 was spent on field corn.

Data regarding the products at separation and their sales values and weights, separable costs, and resulting products after further processing with their sales values are as follows:

	At Separation	Sales Value	Separable Costs After Processing	Sales Value
Cornmeal 400 lbs.	$300	$500	Corn chips	$ 950
Corncobs 500 lbs.	250	150	Animal feed	250
Cornhusks 100 lbs.	50	750	Tamales	1,100

Required

1. Use the physical units method of joint cost allocation to determine the joint costs allocated to cornmeal, corncobs, and cornhusks.
2. Use the relative sales value method of joint cost allocation to determine the joint costs allocated to cornmeal, corncobs, and cornhusks.
3. Use the net realizable method of joint cost allocation to determine the joint costs allocated to each product.
4. What is the net income if all products are sold at the split-off point?
5. What is the net income if all products are sold after further processing?
6. **Manager Insight:** Which products should be sold at split-off, and which should be processed further? Why?

ENHANCING Your Knowledge, Skills, and Critical Thinking

Conceptual Understanding Cases

LO1, LO5 **Evaluating Service Centers**

C 1. A local municipality operates a Transportation Center that provides services and maintains municipal vehicles. Some departments use Transportation Center trucks on a daily basis to maintain streets. Other departments own their own vehicles, such as garbage trucks and school buses, and use the Transportation Center only for repairs and general maintenance. Still other departments occasionally reserve vehicles for out-of-town trips. Assume that you are a manager of one of the departments that uses the Transportation Center. What reasons do you have for being interested in how the Transportation Center assigns its costs to users? How would you evaluate the effectiveness and efficiency of the Transportation Center's services? Briefly state your responses. Be prepared to defend your positions in a class discussion.

LO5 **Evaluating Cost-Allocation Methods**

C 2. Flyaway Airlines is facing a common airline decision: whether to maintain its own online reservation center or outsource reservation management to an ecommerce company like **Expedia.com** or **Travelocity.com**. Travelocity.com would charge Flyaway a small percentage of the ticket price per online reservation in exchange for hosting all the airline's Internet information needs. Flyaway would assign the resulting reservation service fees to scheduled flights and then to passenger seats to determine the cost per passenger seat. If Flyaway maintains its own online reservation center, the total cost of the center would be divided by the number of scheduled flights and assigned to passenger seats on the flight to determine the cost per seat.

You have been called in as a consultant to give Flyaway managers some idea of the possible effects of the two cost-allocation alternatives and to advise them on their outsourcing decision. Describe the two types of activity-based allocation methods proposed. What are the implications of using such methods? What other factors should be considered?

LO1, LO5 **Cost-Plus Contracts**

C 3. Governments around the world inoculate their military troops against various diseases. Suppose an international drug company is planning to negotiate a cost-plus contract to sell a vaccine to government-sponsored military forces worldwide. The cost-plus contract price is more than double the price the company previously offered. Knowing that cost-plus contracts allow for the recovery of a product's cost plus a fixed amount or percentage of costs, speculate on the reasons for the price increase in the vaccine.

Interpreting Management Reports

LO1, LO2 **Management Information Systems**

C 4. **Blue Cross and Blue Shield of Florida, Inc.**, developed a management information system (MIS) that provides timely and accurate reports on products, customers, and business segments, as well as information on internal services. The system includes a four-step ROSA (Resource, Operational, Support, and Administrative) cost-allocation process. First, the costs of resources are assigned. Resource costs include the costs of services and supplies, such as telephone, printing, and postage. Second, the costs of operational centers are assigned. Operational centers, such as claims and customer service, serve specific external users. Third, the costs of support centers are assigned. Support centers primarily support internal users and include medical affairs and claims management. Finally, the costs of administrative centers are assigned. Administrative centers benefit the whole organization or have no specific user group; they include human resources and employee communications.

Accounting personnel and the managers of the centers work together to develop appropriate cost drivers. Each manager is responsible for supplying accurate cost data for cost-allocation purposes.[4]

1. Compare the definition of the four ROSA cost types with this chapter's definition of a service center. Do all types of ROSA costs qualify as service center costs?
2. In what ways does the MIS at Blue Cross and Blue Shield of Florida benefit the centers' managers?
3. What benefits or opportunities do reports containing ROSA cost-allocation information provide the organization's managers?

Decision Analysis Using Excel

Cost-Allocation Analysis

LO3, LO4   **C 5.** Using the data in this chapter's Review Problem for the direct and step methods of service cost allocation, construct two spreadsheets. Build the spreadsheets so that they can be used as templates for any problem in direct or step cost allocation presented in this chapter. The following tables provide row and column headings to begin building the templates:

		House-keeping	Admini-stration	Medical Records	Patient Account-ing	Allocation Fraction: Clinic	Clinic	Allocation Fraction: Radiology	Radio-logy	Allocation Fraction: Laboratory	Labo-ratory	Total
Total center costs		$50	$250	$80	$120		$800		$500		$400	$2,200
Assign costs:												
Housekeeping												
Administration												
Medical												
Records												
Patient												
Accounting												
Total revenue												
center costs												
after allocation												
Overhead rate for												
clinic:												
$/1,000 = $												
Overhead rate for												
radiology:												
$/250 = $												
Overhead rate for												
laboratory:												
$/5,000 = $												

Spreadsheet Template for Direct Method of Service Cost Allocation

			House-keeping	Allocation Fraction: Admini-stration	Admini-stration	Allocation Fraction: Medical Records	Medical Records	Allocation Fraction: Patient Accounting	Patient Account-ing	Allocation Fraction: Clinic	Clinic	Allocation Fraction: Radiology	Radio-logy	Allocation Fraction: Laboratory	Labo-ratory	Total
		Spreadsheet Template for Step Method of Service Cost Allocation														
6	Total center costs		$50			$250		$80		$120		$800		$500		$400	$2,200
7	Assign costs:																
8	Housekeeping																
9	Administration																
10	Medical																
11	Records																
12	Patient																
13	Accounting																
14	Total revenue																
15	center costs																
16	after allocation																

1. Assume that the order of allocation in the Review Problem is Housekeeping, Administration, Medical Records, and Patient Accounting. This change in allocation order may affect the total cost in each revenue center. Use the spreadsheet template for the direct method to assign service center costs.
2. Assume that the order of allocation is the same as in requirement 1. Use the spreadsheet template for the step method to assign service center costs.

Ethical Dilemma Case

LO1, LO2, LO6 **Ethics and Cost Allocation**

C 6. Harold Gyllstrom is a professor of psychiatry at the Medical College of Whiting, which is part of the state university system. Gyllstrom is preparing a National Science Foundation grant application to do brain research. The application requires him to submit a proposed budget that discloses the full cost of the project, and it states that the full cost cannot exceed a certain amount.

So far, Gyllstrom has listed the direct costs of the research: laboratory supplies, scanner time, and pay for research workers and subjects. He is now considering what support costs to include in the budget. Specifically, which overhead rates should he include—the rates of the department, the rates of the university, and/or the rates for research that the university has negotiated? He is approaching the grant's spending limits. What would you advise?

Internet Case

LO1 **Virtual Distribution Centers**

C 7. Distribution centers similar to those discussed in this chapter's Decision Point exist not only in bricks-and-mortar companies, but in cyberspace as well. Like **Publix's** distribution centers and those of **Fresh Direct**, Internet distribution centers attempt to move their product (i.e., content) to individual users as quickly as possible. Internet companies like **Akamai** and **SAVVIS Inc.** minimize download time by bringing their content to the edges of cyberspace and finding the best delivery routes.[5]

Conduct an Internet search for the latest developments in content distribution. Use key terms like *content distribution, streaming media, geographic targeting, content targeting,* and *Internet infrastructure technologies,* and consult the websites akamai.com and savvis.net. Report your findings in a brief email to your instructor or in a short oral report to your class.

Group Activity Case

LO1, LO2 **Responsibility Center Concepts**

C 8. Select a local business that you understand, and try to identify its service and revenue centers. For each service center, list possible cost drivers and the departments or centers that would use its services. State the order of cost allocation—that is, which service center's costs should be allocated first, second, and so on. Prepare an email-style memo to the president of the business stating the business's name, location, and activities; the centers you have identified; possible service center cost drivers; the users of the service centers; and the allocation order.

Your instructor will divide the class into groups of four to six students to complete the assignment. Each group member will take the perspective of a different revenue or service center. The group should become familiar with the background of the business it has chosen and interview the business's manager or accountant. The group should then prepare a summary report to be presented to the class that identifies the most appropriate service center cost drivers, the responsibility centers to which each service center's costs should be assigned, the allocation order of the service center costs, and the preferred cost-allocation method.

Business Communication Case

LO1, LO2 **Applying Service Organization Concepts**

C 9. Arrange to interview the manager or controller of a local health care provider, such as a hospital, clinic, home health agency, assisted living facility, or skilled nursing home. During the interview, ask the following questions:

1. What different revenue centers does your business have? What are some types of revenue that they generate?
2. What different service centers does your business have? What are some of the services they provide?
3. Does your business assign service center costs to other responsibility centers? What method of cost allocation is used? If some service center costs are not assigned, why not? What are some of the cost drivers used to assign service center costs?
4. Who is responsible for controlling service center costs? What measures are used to evaluate service center performance?

Prepare a summary of the manager's or controller's responses, and be prepared to share your findings in class.

Financial Performance Measurement

The ultimate purpose of financial reporting is to enable managers, creditors, investors, and other interested parties to evaluate a company's financial performance. In earlier chapters, we discussed the various measures used in assessing a company's financial performance; here, we provide a comprehensive summary of those measures. Because these measures play a key role in executive compensation, there is always the risk that they will be manipulated. Users of financial statements therefore need to be familiar with the analytical tools and techniques used in performance measurement and the assumptions that underlie them.

LEARNING OBJECTIVES

LO1 Describe the objectives, standards of comparison, sources of information, and compensation issues in measuring financial performance.

LO2 Apply horizontal analysis, trend analysis, vertical analysis, and ratio analysis to financial statements.

LO3 Apply ratio analysis to financial statements in a comprehensive evaluation of a company's financial performance.

STARBUCKS CORPORATION

- What standards should be used to evaluate Starbucks' performance?

- What analytical tools are available to measure performance?

- How successful has the company been in creating value for shareholders?

Formed in 1985, Starbucks is today a well-known specialty retailer. The company purchases and roasts whole coffee beans and sells them, along with a variety of freshly brewed coffees and other beverages and food items, in its retail shops. It also produces and sells bottled coffee drinks and a line of premium ice creams.

Like many other companies, Starbucks uses financial performance measures, primarily earnings per share, in determining compensation for top management. Earnings per share and some of the measures that drive earnings per share appear in the company's Financial Highlights below.[1] By linking compensation to financial performance, Starbucks provides its executives with incentive to improve the company's performance. Compensation and financial performance are thus linked to increasing shareholders' value.

STARBUCKS' FINANCIAL HIGHLIGHTS
(In thousands, except profit margin and earnings per share)

	2005	2004	2003
Net revenues	$6,369,300	$5,294,247	$4,075,522
Net earnings	494,467	388,973	265,355
Profit margin	7.8%	7.3%	6.5%
Earnings per share—basic	0.63	0.49	0.34

Foundations of Financial Performance Measurement

LO1 Describe the objectives, standards of comparison, sources of information, and compensation issues in measuring financial performance.

Financial performance measurement, also called *financial statement analysis*, uses all the techniques available to show how important items in a company's financial statements relate to the company's financial objectives. Persons with a strong interest in measuring a company's financial performance fall into two groups:

1. A company's top managers, who set and strive to achieve financial performance objectives; middle-level managers of business processes; and lower-level employees who own stock in the company

2. Creditors and investors, as well as customers who have cooperative agreements with the company

Financial Performance Evaluation and the Management Process

As shown in Figure 1, financial performance evaluation plays a key role in all phases of the management process.

Planning During the planning phase of the management process, managers set the financial performance objectives that will enable them to achieve the company's goals. All the strategic and operating plans that management formulates to achieve a company's goals must eventually be stated in terms of financial objectives. A primary objective is to increase the wealth of the company's stockholders, but this objective must be divided into categories. A complete financial plan should have financial objectives and related performance objectives in all the following categories:

Financial Objective	*Performance Objective*
Liquidity	The company must be able to pay bills when due and meet unexpected needs for cash.
Profitability	It must earn a satisfactory net income.
Long-term solvency	It must be able to survive for many years.
Cash flow adequacy	It must generate sufficient cash through operating, investing, and financing activities.
Market strength	It must be able to increase stockholders' wealth.

Performing During the performing phase, management's main responsibility is to carry out the plans for achieving the financial performance objectives. For example, **Starbucks'** management will need to focus on increasing revenues and improving profitability by expanding the business, investing in technology, managing assets, and controlling costs.

Evaluating Management must constantly monitor key financial performance measures, determine the cause of any deviations in the measures, and propose corrective actions. Annual measures provide data for long-term trend analysis. For Starbucks, a key performance measure is growth in revenues and earnings per share, but other measures related to asset management and cost control will be important as well.

■ **FIGURE 1**
The Management Process: To-Do's for Managers

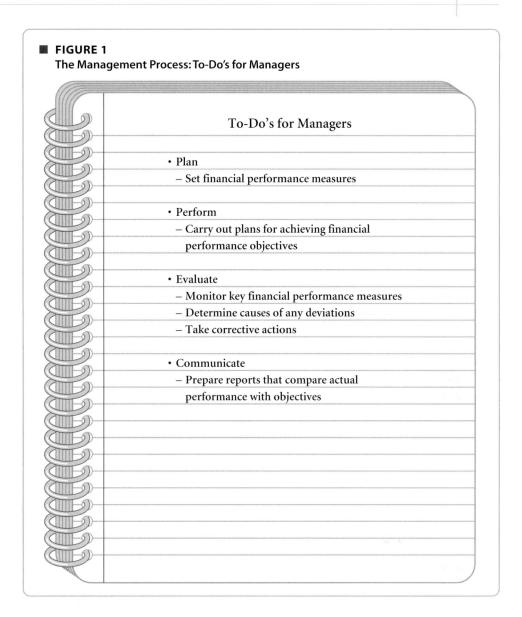

To-Do's for Managers

- Plan
  - Set financial performance measures

- Perform
  - Carry out plans for achieving financial
    performance objectives

- Evaluate
  - Monitor key financial performance measures
  - Determine causes of any deviations
  - Take corrective actions

- Communicate
  - Prepare reports that compare actual
    performance with objectives

Communicating Management develops monthly, quarterly, and annual reports that compare actual performance with planned performance in achieving the key business objectives of liquidity, profitability, long-term solvency, cash flow adequacy, and market strength. Reports at Starbucks will focus on financial performance measures that relate to the company's specific long-term strategies, such as cash flow and return on assets.

Financial Performance Measurement: Creditors' and Investors' Objectives

Creditors and investors use financial performance evaluation to judge a company's past performance and present position. They also use it to assess a company's future potential and the risk connected with acting on that potential. An investor focuses on a company's potential earnings ability because that ability will affect the market price of the company's stock and the amount of dividends the company will pay. A creditor focuses on the company's potential debt-paying ability.

Past performance is often a good indicator of future performance. To evaluate a company's past performance, creditors and investors look at trends in past sales, expenses, net income, cash flow, and return on investment. To evaluate its current position, they look at its assets, liabilities, cash position, debt in relation to equity, and levels of inventories and receivables. Knowing a company's past performance and current position can be important in judging its future potential and the related risk.

The risk involved in making an investment or loan depends on how easy it is to predict future profitability or liquidity. If an investor can predict with confidence that a company's earnings per share will be between $2.50 and $2.60 in the next year, the investment is less risky than if the earnings per share are expected to fall between $2.00 and $3.00. For example, the potential of an investment in an established electric utility company is relatively easy to predict on the basis of the company's past performance and current position. In contrast, the potential of an investment in a new Internet firm that has not yet established a record of earnings is very hard to predict. Investing in the Internet firm is therefore riskier than investing in the electric utility company.

In return for taking a greater risk, investors often look for a higher expected return (an increase in market price plus dividends). Creditors who take a greater risk by advancing funds to a company like the new Internet firm mentioned above may demand a higher interest rate and more assurance of repayment (a secured loan, for instance). The higher interest rate reimburses them for assuming the higher risk.

Standards of Comparison

When analyzing financial statements, decision makers must judge whether the relationships they find in the statements are favorable or unfavorable. Three standards of comparison that they commonly use are rule-of-thumb measures, a company's past performance, and industry norms.

Rule-of-Thumb Measures
Many financial analysts, investors, and lenders apply general standards, or rule-of-thumb measures, to key financial ratios. For example, most analysts today agree that a current ratio (current assets divided by current liabilities) of 2:1 is acceptable.

In its *Industry Norms and Key Business Ratios*, the credit-rating firm of Dun & Bradstreet offers such rules of thumb as the following:

> *Current debt to tangible net worth*: A business is usually in trouble when this relationship exceeds 80 percent.
>
> *Inventory to net working capital*: Ordinarily, this relationship should not exceed 80 percent.

Although rule-of-thumb measures may suggest areas that need further investigation, there is no proof that the levels they specify apply to all companies. A company with a current ratio higher than 2:1 may have a poor credit policy (causing accounts receivable to be too large), too much inventory, or poor cash management. Another company may have a ratio lower than 2:1 but still have excellent management in all three of those areas. Thus, rule-of-thumb measures must be used with caution.

Past Performance
Comparing financial measures or ratios of the same company over time is an improvement over using rule-of-thumb measures. Such a comparison gives the analyst some basis for judging whether the measure or ratio is getting better or worse. Thus, it may be helpful in showing future trends. However, trends reverse at times, so such projections must be made with care.

Study Note

Rules of thumb evolve and change as the business environment changes. Not long ago, an acceptable current ratio was higher than today's 2:1.

FOCUS ON BUSINESS PRACTICE
Take the Numbers with a Grain of Salt.

Traditionally, pro forma statements presented financial statements as they would appear after the occurrence of certain agreed-upon transactions, such as mergers or acquisitions. However, in recent years, companies have increasingly used pro forma statements as a way of presenting a better picture of their operations than would be the case in reports prepared under GAAP. According to a survey by the National Investor Relations Institute, 57 percent of companies across a range of industries use pro forma reporting.[2] In one quarter, Amazon.com reported a

"pro forma operating" loss of $49 million and a "pro forma net" loss of $76 million; under GAAP, its net loss was $234 million. Pro forma statements, which are unaudited, have come to mean whatever a company's management wants them to mean. As a result, the SEC has issued new rules that prohibit companies from giving more prominence to non-GAAP measures and from using terms that are similar to GAAP measures. Although this helps, analysts should rely exclusively on financial statements that are prepared using GAAP and that are audited by an independent CPA.[3]

Another problem with trend analysis is that past performance may not be enough to meet a company's present needs. For example, even though a company improves its return on investment from 3 percent in one year to 4 percent the next year, the 4 percent return may not be adequate for the company's current needs. In addition, using a company's past performance as a standard of comparison is not helpful in judging its performance relative to that of other companies.

Industry Norms   Using industry norms as a standard of comparison overcomes some of the limitations of comparing a company's measures or ratios over time. Industry norms show how a company compares with other companies in the same industry. For example, if companies in a particular industry have an average rate of return on investment of 8 percent, a 3 or 4 percent rate of return is probably not adequate. Industry norms can also be used to judge trends. Suppose that because of a downturn in the economy, a company's profit margin dropped from 12 percent to 10 percent, while the average drop in profit margin of other companies in the same industry was from 12 to 4 percent. By this standard, the company would have done relatively well. Sometimes, instead of industry averages, data for the industry leader or a specific competitor are used for analysis.

Using industry norms as standards has three limitations:

1. Companies in the same industry may not be strictly comparable. Consider two companies in the oil industry. One purchases oil products and markets them through service stations. The other, an international company, discovers, produces, refines, and markets its own oil products. Because of the disparity in their operations, these two companies cannot be directly compared.

2. Many large companies have multiple segments and operate in more than one industry. Some of these **diversified companies**, or *conglomerates*, operate in many unrelated industries. The individual segments of a diversified company generally have different rates of profitability and different degrees of risk. In analyzing a diversified company's consolidated financial statements, it is often impossible to use industry norms as a standard because there simply are no comparable companies.

The FASB provides a partial solution to this problem. It requires diversified companies to report profit or loss, certain revenue and expense items, and assets for each of their segments. Segment information may be

Study Note

Each segment of a diversified company represents an investment that the home office or parent company evaluates and reviews frequently.

EXHIBIT 1 ▶

Selected Segment Information for Goodyear Tire & Rubber Company			
(In millions)	**2005**	**2004**	**2003**
Sales			
North American Tire	$ 9,091	$ 8,569	$ 7,279
European Union Tire	4,676	4,476	3,922
Eastern Europe, Africa, and Middle East Tire	1,437	1,279	1,073
Latin American Tire	1,466	1,245	1,041
Asia Tire	1,423	1,312	582
Total Tires	**18,093**	**16,881**	**13,897**
Engineered Products	1,630	1,472	1,205
Total Segment Sales	**19,723**	**18,353**	**15,102**
Income			
North American Tire	$ 167	$ 74	($ 103)
European Union Tire	317	253	130
Eastern Europe, Africa, and Middle East Tire	198	194	147
Latin American Tire	295	251	149
Asia Tire	84	60	49
Total Tires	**1,061**	**832**	**372**
Engineered Products	103	114	47
Total Segment Income	**1,164**	**946**	**419**
Assets*			
North American Tire	$ 5,438	$ 5,504	$ 5,494
European Union Tire	3,690	4,056	4,207
Eastern Europe, Africa, and Middle East Tire	1,227	1,315	1,103
Latin American Tire	900	846	710
Asia Tire	1,126	1,154	669
Total Tires	**12,381**	**12,875**	**12,183**
Engineered Products	799	764	681
Total Segment Assets	**13,180**	**13,639**	**12,864**

*2003 assets estimated.
Source: Goodyear Tire & Rubber Company, *Annual Report*, 2005.

reported for operations in different industries or different geographical areas, or for major customers.[4] Exhibit 1 shows how **Goodyear Tire & Rubber Company** reports data on sales, income, and assets for its engineered products segment. These data allow the analyst to compute important profitability performance measures, such as profit margin, asset turnover, and return on assets, for each segment and to compare them with the appropriate industry norms.

3. Another limitation of industry norms is that even when companies in the same industry have similar operations, they may use different acceptable accounting procedures. For example, they may use different methods of valuing inventories and different methods of depreciating assets.

Despite these limitations, if little information about a company's past performance is available, industry norms probably offer the best available standards for judging current performance—as long as they are used with care.

Sources of Information

The major sources of information about public corporations are reports published by the corporations themselves, reports filed with the SEC, business periodicals, and credit and investment advisory services.

Reports Published by the Corporation A public corporation's annual report is an important source of financial information. From a financial analyst's perspective, the main parts of an annual report are management's analysis of the past year's operations; the financial statements; the notes to the financial statements, which include a summary of significant accounting policies; the auditors' report; and financial highlights for a five- or ten-year period.

Most public corporations also publish **interim financial statements** each quarter and sometimes each month. These reports, which present limited information in the form of condensed financial statements, are not subject to a full audit by an independent auditor. The financial community watches interim statements closely for early signs of change in a company's earnings trend.

Reports Filed with the SEC Public corporations in the United States must file annual reports, quarterly reports, and current reports with the Securities and Exchange Commission (SEC). If they have more than $10 million in assets and more than 500 shareholders, they must file these reports electronically at www.sec.gov/edgar.shtml, where anyone can access them free of charge.

The SEC requires companies to file their annual reports on a standard form, called Form 10-K. Form 10-K contains more information than a company's annual report and is therefore a valuable source of information.

Companies file their quarterly reports with the SEC on Form 10-Q. This report presents important facts about interim financial performance.

The current report, filed on Form 8-K, must be submitted to the SEC within a few days of the date of certain significant events, such as the sale or purchase of a division or a change in auditors. The current report is often the first indicator of significant changes that will affect a company's financial performance in the future.

Business Periodicals and Credit and Investment Advisory Services Financial analysts must keep up with current events in the financial world. A leading source of financial news is *The Wall Street Journal*. It is the most complete financial newspaper in the United States and is published every business day. Useful periodicals that are published every week or every two weeks include *Forbes*, *Barron's*, *Fortune*, and the *Financial Times*.

Credit and investment advisory services also provide useful information. The publications of Moody's Investors Service and Standard & Poor's provide details about a company's financial history. Data on industry norms, average ratios, and credit ratings are available from agencies like Dun & Bradstreet. Dun & Bradstreet's *Industry Norms and Key Business Ratios* offers an annual analysis of 14 ratios for each of 125 industry groups, classified as retailing, wholesaling, manufacturing, and construction. *Annual Statement Studies*, published by Risk Management Association (formerly Robert Morris Associates), presents many facts and ratios for 223 different industries. The publications of a number of other agencies are also available for a yearly fee.

An example of specialized financial reporting readily available to the public is Mergent's *Handbook of Dividend Achievers*. It profiles companies that have increased their dividends consistently over the past ten years. A listing from that publication—for **PepsiCo Inc.**—is shown in Exhibit 2. As you can see, a wealth of information about the company, including the market action of its stock, its business operations, recent developments and prospects, and earnings and dividend data, is summarized on one page. We use the kind of data contained in Mergent's summaries in many of the analyses and ratios that we present later in this chapter.

Executive Compensation

As we noted earlier in the text, one intent of the Sarbanes-Oxley Act of 2002 was to strengthen the corporate governance of public corporations. Under this act, a public corporation's board of directors must establish a **compensation committee** made up of independent directors to determine how the company's top executives will be compensated. The company must disclose the components of compensation and the criteria it uses to remunerate top executives in documents that it files with the SEC. The components of **Starbucks'** compensation of executive officers are typical of those used by many companies:

- Annual base salary
- Incentive bonuses
- Stock option awards[5]

Incentive bonuses are based on performance measures that the compensation committee identifies as important to the company's long-term success. Many companies tie incentive bonuses to such measures as growth in revenues and return on assets, or return on equity. Starbucks bases 80 percent of its incentive bonus on an "earnings per share target approved by the compensation committee" and 20 percent on the executive's "specific individual performance." The Financial Highlights at the beginning of the chapter show the growth in the Starbucks' earnings per share.

Stock option awards are usually based on how well the company is achieving its long-term strategic goals. In 2005, a very good year for Starbucks, the company's CEO received a base salary of $1,190,000, an incentive bonus of an equal amount, and a stock option award of 200,000 shares of common stock.[6]

From one vantage point, earnings per share is a "bottom-line" number that encompasses all the other performance measures. However, using a single performance measure as the basis for determining compensation has the potential of leading to practices that are not in the best interests of the company or its stockholders. For instance, management could boost earnings per share by reducing the number of shares outstanding (the denominator in the earnings per share equation) while not improving earnings. It could accomplish this by using cash to repurchase shares of the company's stock (treasury stock), rather than investing the cash in more profitable operations. An understanding of the performance measures used in determining executive compensation and the factors that underlie them is critical in evaluating their fairness. ●

S T O P ● R E V I E W ● A P P L Y

1-1. How are the objectives of investors and creditors in using financial performance evaluation similar? How do they differ?

EXHIBIT 2 ▶ | **Listing from Mergent's Handbook of Dividend Achievers**

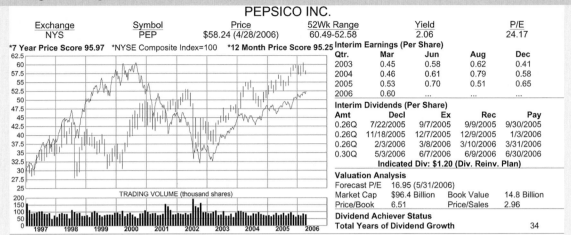

PEPSICO INC.

Exchange	Symbol	Price	52Wk Range	Yield	P/E
NYS	PEP	$58.24 (4/28/2006)	60.49-52.58	2.06	24.17

*7 Year Price Score 95.97   ***NYSE Composite Index=100**   ***12 Month Price Score 95.25**

Interim Earnings (Per Share)

Qtr.	Mar	Jun	Aug	Dec
2003	0.45	0.58	0.62	0.41
2004	0.46	0.61	0.79	0.58
2005	0.53	0.70	0.51	0.65
2006	0.60	...	...	...

Interim Dividends (Per Share)

Amt	Decl	Ex	Rec	Pay
0.26Q	7/22/2005	9/7/2005	9/9/2005	9/30/2005
0.26Q	11/18/2005	12/7/2005	12/9/2005	1/3/2006
0.26Q	2/3/2006	3/8/2006	3/10/2006	3/31/2006
0.30Q	5/3/2006	6/7/2006	6/9/2006	6/30/2006

Indicated Div: $1.20 (Div. Reinv. Plan)

Valuation Analysis
Forecast P/E   16.95 (5/31/2006)
Market Cap $96.4 Billion   Book Value   14.8 Billion
Price/Book   6.51   Price/Sales   2.96

Dividend Achiever Status
Total Years of Dividend Growth   34

Business Summary: Food (MIC: 4.1 SIC: 2086 NAIC: 312111)

PepsiCo is a global snack and beverage company. Co. manufactures, markets and sells a variety of salty, convenient, sweet and grain-based snacks, carbonated and non-carbonated beverages and foods. Co.'s Frito-Lay North America division's brands include Lay's potato chips, Fritos corn chips, Quaker Chewy granola bars and Rold Gold pretzels. PepsiCo Beverages North America brands include Pepsi, Mountain Dew, Sierra Mist, Mug, SoBe, Gatorade, Tropicana Pure Premium and Propel. PepsiCo International brands include Sabritas in Mexico, Walkers in the UK, and Smith's in Australia. Quaker Foods North America's products include Quaker oatmeal and Cap'n Crunch and Life ready-to-eat cereals.

Recent Developments: For the twelve weeks ended Mar 25 2006, net income increased 11.7% to $1.02 billion compared with $912.0 million in the corresponding year-earlier period. Revenues were $7.21 billion, up 9.4% from $6.59 billion the year before. Operating income was $1.35 billion versus $1.25 billion in the prior-year quarter, an increase of 8.1%. Direct operating expenses rose 10.8% to $3.18 billion from $2.87 billion in the comparable period the year before. Indirect operating expenses increased 8.5% to $2.68 billion from $2.47 billion in the equivalent prior-year period.

Prospects: Co. continues to see strong revenue momentum across all its businesses, which is being driven by product innovation and strong marketplace execution. For instance, Co.'s net revenue in its Pepsico Beverages North America division is reflecting volume growth, a positive mix effect from the strong performance of its non-carbonated beverage portfolio, increased pricing, and the timing of concentrate shipments to bottlers. In addition, Co. is benefiting from solid profit performance despite continued pressure from inflation in some of its key input costs. Looking ahead to full-year 2006, Co. expects earnings of at least $2.93 per share.

Financial Data

(US$ in Thousands)	3 Mos	12/31/2005	12/25/2004	12/27/2003	12/28/2002	12/29/2001	12/30/2000	12/25/1999
Earnings Per Share	2.41	2.39	2.44	2.05	1.85	1.47	1.48	1.37
Cash Flow Per Share	3.16	3.45	2.99	2.53	2.65	2.39	2.66	2.07
Tang Book Value Per Share	5.50	5.20	4.84	3.82	4.93	2.17	1.91	1.47
Dividends Per Share	1.040	1.010	0.850	0.630	0.595	0.575	0.555	0.535
Dividend Payout %	43.15	42.26	34.84	30.73	32.16	39.12	37.50	39.05
Income Statement								
Total Revenue	7,205,000	32,562,000	29,261,000	26,971,000	25,112,000	26,935,000	20,438,000	20,367,000
EBITDA	1,718,000	7,732,000	6,848,000	6,269,000	6,077,000	5,189,000	4,209,000	4,843,000
Depn & Amortn	286,000	1,253,000	1,209,000	1,165,000	1,067,000	1,008,000	854,000	942,000
Income Before Taxes	1,415,000	6,382,000	5,546,000	4,992,000	4,868,000	4,029,000	3,210,000	3,656,000
Income Taxes	396,000	2,304,000	1,372,000	1,424,000	1,555,000	1,367,000	1,027,000	1,606,000
Net Income	1,019,000	4,078,000	4,212,000	3,568,000	3,313,000	2,662,000	2,183,000	2,050,000
Average Shares	1,695,000	1,706,000	1,729,000	1,739,000	1,789,000	1,807,000	1,475,000	1,496,000
Balance Sheet								
Current Assets	9,502,000	10,454,000	8,639,000	6,930,000	6,413,000	5,853,000	4,604,000	4,173,000
Total Assets	30,994,000	31,727,000	27,987,000	25,327,000	23,474,000	21,695,000	18,339,000	17,551,000
Current Liabilities	8,160,000	9,406,000	6,752,000	6,415,000	6,052,000	4,998,000	3,935,000	3,788,000
Long-Term Obligations	2,288,000	2,313,000	2,397,000	1,702,000	2,187,000	2,651,000	2,346,000	2,812,000
Total Liabilities	16,253,000	17,476,000	14,464,000	13,453,000	14,183,000	13,021,000	11,090,000	10,670,000
Stockholders' Equity	14,812,000	14,320,000	13,572,000	11,896,000	9,298,000	8,648,000	7,249,000	6,881,000
Shares Outstanding	1,656,000	1,656,000	1,679,000	1,705,000	1,722,000	1,756,000	1,446,000	1,455,000
Statistical Record								
Return on Assets %	13.74	13.44	15.84	14.66	14.71	13.34	11.97	10.22
Return on Equity %	28.49	28.77	33.17	33.76	37.02	33.58	30.40	30.95
EBITDA Margin %	23.84	23.75	23.40	23.24	24.20	19.26	20.59	23.78
Net Margin %	14.14	12.52	14.39	13.23	13.19	9.88	10.68	10.07
Asset Turnover	1.09	1.07	1.10	1.11	1.11	1.35	1.12	1.02
Current Ratio	1.16	1.11	1.28	1.08	1.06	1.17	1.17	1.10
Debt to Equity	0.15	0.16	0.18	0.14	0.24	0.31	0.32	0.41
Price Range	60.49-52.29	59.90-51.57	55.55-45.39	48.71-37.30	53.12-35.50	50.28-41.26	49.75-30.50	41.81-30.50
P/E Ratio	25.10-21.70	25.06-21.58	22.77-18.60	23.76-18.20	28.71-19.19	34.20-28.07	33.61-20.61	30.52-22.26
Average Yield %	1.83	1.82	1.66	1.43	1.29	1.25	1.36	1.46

Address: 700 Anderson Hill Road, Purchase, NY 10577-1444
Telephone: 914-253-2000
Web Site: www.pepsico.com

Officers: Steven S. Reinemund - Chmn., C.E.O. Indra K. Nooyi - Pres., C.F.O. **Transfer Agents:** The Bank of New York

Investor Contact: 914-253-3035
No of Institutions: 1209
Shares: 1,093,426,688 **% Held:** 66.17

Source: Listing from *Handbook of Dividend Achievers*, 2005. Reprinted by permission of Mergent.

1-2. What role does risk play in making loans and investments?

1-3. What standards of comparison are commonly used to evaluate financial statements, and what are their relative merits?

1-4. Why would a financial analyst compare the ratios of Steelco, a steel company, with the ratios of other companies in the steel industry? What factors might invalidate such a comparison?

1-5. Where can investors find information about public corporations in which they are thinking of investing?

1-6. What is the role of a corporation's compensation committee, and what are three common components of executive compensation?

Suggested answers to all Stop, Review, and Apply questions are available at http://college.hmco.com/accounting/needles/man_acc/8e/student_home.html.

Tools and Techniques of Financial Analysis

LO2 Apply horizontal analysis, trend analysis, vertical analysis, and ratio analysis to financial statements.

To gain insight into a company's financial performance, one must look beyond the individual numbers to the relationship between the numbers and their change from one period to another. The tools of financial analysis—horizontal analysis, trend analysis, vertical analysis, and ratio analysis—are intended to show these relationships and changes. To illustrate how these tools are used, we devote the rest of this chapter to a comprehensive financial analysis of **Starbucks Corporation**.

Horizontal Analysis

Comparative financial statements provide financial information for the current year and the previous year. To gain insight into year-to-year changes, analysts use **horizontal analysis**, in which changes from the previous year to the current year are computed in both dollar amounts and percentages. The percentage change relates the size of the change to the size of the dollar amounts involved.

Exhibits 3 and 4 present **Starbuck Corporation's** comparative balance sheets and income statements and show both the dollar and percentage changes. The percentage change is computed as follows:

$$\text{Percentage Change} = 100 \times \left(\frac{\text{Amount of Change}}{\text{Base Year Amount}}\right)$$

The **base year** is always the first year to be considered in any set of data. For example, when comparing data for 2004 and 2005, 2004 is the base year. As the balance sheets in Exhibit 3 show, between 2004 and 2005, Starbucks' total current assets decreased by $141,561 thousand, from $1,350,895 thousand to $1,209,334 thousand, or by 10.5 percent. This is computed as follows:

$$\text{Percentage Change} = 100 \times \left(\frac{\$141,561 \text{ thousand}}{\$1,350,895 \text{ thousand}}\right) = 10.5\%$$

Study Note

It is important to ascertain the base amount used when a percentage describes an item. For example, inventory may be 50 percent of *total current assets* but only 10 percent of *total assets*.

▼ **EXHIBIT 3**

Comparative Balance Sheets with Horizontal Analysis

Starbucks Corporation
Consolidated Balance Sheets
October 2, 2005 and October 3, 2004

(Dollar amounts in thousands)	2005	2004	Increase (Decrease) Amount	Percentage
	Assets			
Current assets:				
Cash and cash equivalents	$ 173,809	$ 145,053	$ 28,756	19.8
Short-term investments	133,227	507,956	(374,729)	(73.8)
Accounts receivable, net of allowances of $3,079 and $2,231, respectively	190,762	140,226	50,536	36.0
Inventories	546,299	422,663	123,636	29.3
Prepaid expenses and other current assets	94,429	71,347	23,082	32.4
Deferred income taxes, net	70,808	63,650	7,158	11.2
Total current assets	$1,209,334	$1,350,895	$(141,561)	(10.5)
Long-term investments	261,936	302,919	(40,983)	(13.5)
Property, plant, and equipment, net	1,842,019	1,551,416	290,603	18.7
Other assets	72,893	85,561	(12,668)	(14.8)
Other intangible assets	35,409	26,800	8,609	32.1
Goodwill	92,474	68,950	23,524	34.1
Total assets	$3,514,065	$3,386,541	$127,524	3.8
	Liabilities and Shareholders' Equity			
Current liabilities:				
Accounts payable	$ 220,975	$ 199,346	$ 21,629	10.8
Accrued compensation and related costs	232,354	208,927	23,427	11.2
Accrued occupancy costs	44,496	29,231	15,265	52.2
Accrued taxes	78,293	62,959	15,334	24.4
Short-term borrowings	277,000	—	277,000	N/A
Other accrued expenses	198,082	123,684	74,398	60.2
Deferred revenue	175,048	121,377	53,671	44.2
Current portion of long-term debt	748	735	13	1.8
Total current liabilities	$1,226,996	$ 746,259	$480,737	64.4
Deferred income taxes, net	—	21,770	(21,770)	(100.0)
Long-term debt	2,870	3,618	(748)	(20.7)
Other long-term liabilities	193,565	144,683	48,882	33.8
Shareholders' equity	2,090,634	2,470,211	(379,577)	(15.4)
Total liabilities and shareholders' equity	$3,514,065	$3,386,541	$127,524	3.8

Source: Data from Starbucks Corporation, 10K, 2005.

▼ **EXHIBIT 4**

Comparative Income Statements with Horizontal Analysis

Starbucks Corporation
Consolidated Income Statements
For the Years Ended October 2, 2005, and October 3, 2004

(Dollar amounts in thousands, except per share amounts)	2005	2004	Increase (Decrease) Amount	Percentage
Net revenues	$6,369,300	$5,294,247	$1,075,053	20.3
Cost of sales, including occupancy costs	2,605,212	2,191,440	413,772	18.9
Gross margin	$3,764,088	$3,102,807	$ 661,281	21.3
Operating expenses				
Store operating expenses	$2,165,911	$1,790,168	$ 375,743	21.0
Other operating expenses	197,024	171,648	25,376	14.8
Depreciation and amortization expenses	340,169	289,182	50,987	17.6
General and administrative expenses	357,114	304,293	52,821	17.4
Total operating expenses	$3,060,218	$2,555,291	$ 504,927	19.8
Operating income	$ 703,870	$ 547,516	$ 156,354	28.6
Other income, net	92,574	73,211	19,363	26.4
Earnings before income taxes	$ 796,444	$ 620,727	$ 175,717	28.3
Income taxes	301,977	231,754	70,223	30.3
Net earnings	$ 494,467	$ 388,973	$ 105,494	27.1
Net earnings per common share—basic	$ 0.63	$ 0.49	$ 0.14	28.6
Net earnings per common share—diluted	$ 0.61	$ 0.47	$ 0.14	29.8
Shares used in calculation of net earnings per common share—basic	789,570	794,347	(4,777)	(0.6)
Shares used in calculation of net earnings per common share—diluted	815,417	822,930	(7,513)	(0.9)

Source: Data from Starbucks Corporation, 10K, 2005.

When examining such changes, it is important to consider the dollar amount of the change as well as the percentage change in each component. For example, the percentage increase in prepaid expenses and other current assets (32.4 percent) is slightly greater than the increase in inventories (29.3 percent). However, the dollar increase in inventories is more than five times the dollar increase in prepaid expenses and other current assets ($123,636 thousand versus $23,082 thousand). Thus, even though the percentage changes differ by only 3.1 percent, inventories require much more investment.

Starbucks' balance sheets for this period, illustrated in Exhibit 3, also show an increase in total assets of $127,524 thousand, or 3.8 percent. This reflects an increase of property, plant, and equipment, net, of $290,603 thousand, or 18.7 percent, while short-term investments decreased by $374,729 thousand, or 73.8 percent. Starbucks is redeploying its assets for growth. In addition, shareholders' equity decreased by $379,577 thousand, or 15.4 percent. Starbucks' equity declined despite an increase in retained earnings because the company repurchased its common stock during the period.

Starbucks' income statements in Exhibit 4 show that net revenues increased by $1,075,053 thousand, or 20.3 percent, while gross margin increased by $661,281 thousand, or 21.3 percent. This indicates that cost of sales did not grow faster than net revenues. In fact, cost of sales increased only 18.9 percent compared with the 20.3 percent increase in net revenues.

Starbucks' total operating expenses increased by $504,927 thousand, or 19.8 percent, also not as fast as the 20.3 percent increase in net revenues. As a result, operating income increased by $156,354 thousand, or 28.6 percent, and net income increased by $105,494 thousand, or 27.1 percent. The primary reason for the increases in operating income and net income is that total cost of sales and operating expenses increased at a slower rate (18.9 and 19.8 percent, respectively) than net revenues (20.3 percent).

Trend Analysis

Trend analysis is a variation of horizontal analysis. With this tool, the analyst calculates percentage changes for several successive years instead of for just two years. Because of its long-term view, trend analysis can highlight basic changes in the nature of a business.

Many companies present a summary of key data for five or more years in their annual reports. Exhibit 5 shows a trend analysis of **Starbucks'** five-year summary of net revenues and operating income.

Trend analysis uses an **index number** to show changes in related items over time. For an index number, the base year is set at 100 percent. Other years are measured in relation to that amount. For example, the 2005 index for Starbucks' net revenues is figured as follows (dollar amounts are in thousands):

$$\text{Index} = 100 \times \left(\frac{\text{Index Year Amount}}{\text{Base Year Amount}} \right)$$

$$= 100 \times \left(\frac{\$6,369,300}{\$2,648,980} \right) = 240.4\%$$

The trend analysis in Exhibit 5 shows that Starbucks' net revenues increased over the five-year period, as did operating income. Overall, revenue grew 240.4 percent, while operating income grew 278.8 percent. The percentage changes reveal that Starbucks' management has the ability to control its costs while growing the revenue, resulting in faster growth in operating income. Figure 2 illustrates these trends.

Study Note

To reflect the general five-year economic cycle of the U.S. economy, trend analysis usually covers a five-year period. Cycles of other lengths exist and are tracked by the National Bureau of Economic Research. Trend analysis needs to be of sufficient length to show a company's performance in both up and down markets.

EXHIBIT 5 ▶

Trend Analysis

Starbucks Corporation
Net Revenues and Operating Income
Trend Analysis

	2005	2004	2003	2002	2001
Dollar values (In thousands)					
Net revenues	$6,369,300	$5,294,247	$4,075,522	$3,288,908	$2,648,980
Operating income*	703,870	547,516	383,947	282,893	252,479
Trend analysis (In percentages)					
Net revenues	240.4	199.9	153.9	124.2	100.0
Operating income*	278.8	216.9	152.1	112.0	100.0

*Excludes income from equity investees.
Source: Data from Starbucks Corporation, 10K, 2005.

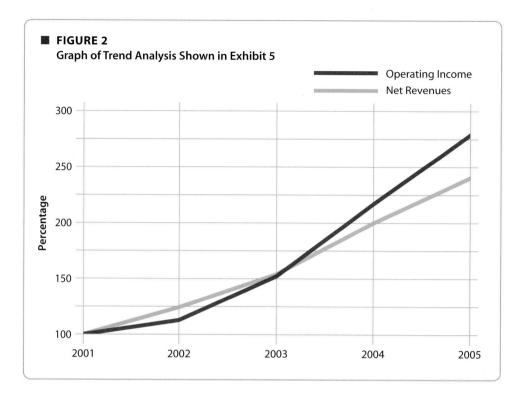

■ **FIGURE 2**
Graph of Trend Analysis Shown in Exhibit 5

Vertical Analysis

Vertical analysis shows how the different components of a financial statement relate to a total figure in the statement. The analyst sets the total figure at 100 percent and computes each component's percentage of that total. (On the balance sheet, the figure would be total assets or total liabilities and stockholders' equity, and on the income statement, it would be net revenues or net sales.) The resulting financial statement, which is expressed entirely in percentages, is called a **common-size statement**. Common-size balance sheets and common-size income statements for **Starbucks Corporation** are shown in pie-chart form in Figures 3 and 4 and in financial statement form in Exhibits 6 and 7.

Vertical analysis and common-size statements are useful in comparing the importance of specific components in the operation of a business and in identifying important changes in the components from one year to the next. The main conclusions to be drawn from our analysis of Starbucks are that the company's assets consist largely of current assets and property, plant, and equipment; that the company finances assets primarily through equity and current liabilities; and that it has few long-term liabilities.

Looking at the pie charts in Figure 3 and the common-size balance sheets in Exhibit 6, you can see that the composition of Starbucks' assets shifted from property, plant, and equipment to current assets. You can also see that the relationship of liabilities and equity shifted slightly from stockholders' equity to current liabilities.

The common-size income statements in Exhibit 7, illustrated in Figure 4, show that Starbucks reduced its operating expenses from 2004 to 2005 by 0.3 percent of revenues (48.3% − 48.0%). In other words, operating expenses did not grow as fast as revenues.

Common-size statements are often used to make comparisons between companies. They allow an analyst to compare the operating and financing characteristics of two companies of different size in the same industry. For example, the analyst might want to compare Starbucks with other specialty

■ **FIGURE 3**
Common-Size Balance Sheets Presented Graphically

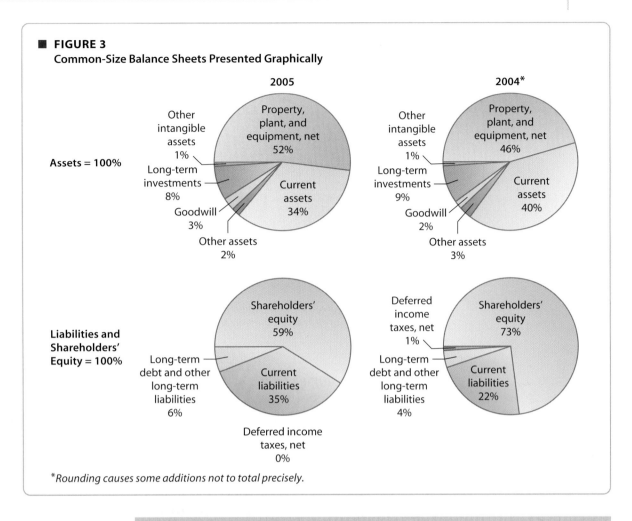

Rounding causes some additions not to total precisely.

EXHIBIT 6 ▶ **Common-Size Balance Sheets**

Starbucks Corporation
Common-Size Balance Sheets
October 2, 2005, and October 3, 2004

	2005	2004
Assets		
Current assets	34.4%	39.9%
Property, plant, and equipment, net	52.4	45.8
Long-term investments	7.5	8.9
Other assets	2.1	2.5
Goodwill	2.6	2.0
Other intangible assets	1.0	0.8
Total assets	100.0%	100.0%
Liabilities and Shareholders' Equity		
Current liabilities	34.9%	22.0%
Deferred income taxes, net	—	0.6
Long-term debt and other long-term liabilities	5.6	4.4
Shareholders' equity	59.5	72.9
Total liabilities and shareholders' equity	100.0%	100.0%

Source: Data from Starbucks Corporation, 10K, 2005.

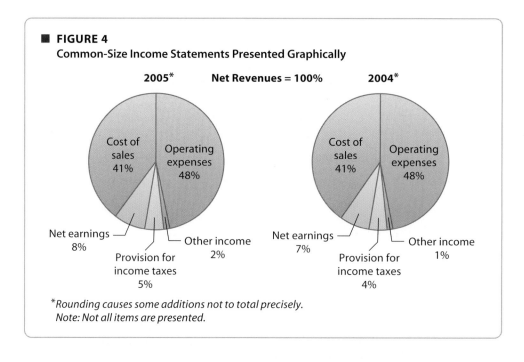

■ **FIGURE 4**
Common-Size Income Statements Presented Graphically

2005*   **Net Revenues = 100%**   2004*

2005: Cost of sales 41%, Operating expenses 48%, Net earnings 8%, Provision for income taxes 5%, Other income 2%

2004: Cost of sales 41%, Operating expenses 48%, Net earnings 7%, Provision for income taxes 4%, Other income 1%

*Rounding causes some additions not to total precisely.
Note: Not all items are presented.

retailers in terms of percentage of total assets financed by debt or in terms of operating expenses as a percentage of net revenues. Common-size statements would show those and other relationships. These statements can also be used to compare the characteristics of companies that report in different currencies.

EXHIBIT 7 ▶

Common-Size Income Statements

Starbucks Corporation
Common-Size Income Statements
For the Years Ended October 2, 2005, and October 3, 2004

	2005	2004
Net revenues	100.0%	100.0%
Cost of sales, including occupancy costs	40.9	41.4
Gross margin	59.1%	58.6%
Operating expenses		
Store operating expenses	34.0%	33.8%
Other operating expenses	3.1	3.2
Depreciation and amortization expenses	5.3	5.5
General and administrative expenses	5.6	5.7
Total operating expenses	48.0%	48.3%
Operating income	11.1%	10.3%
Other income, net	1.5	1.4
Earnings before income taxes	12.5%	11.7%
Income taxes	4.7	4.4
Net earnings	7.8%	7.3%

Note: Amounts do not precisely total 100 percent in all cases due to rounding.
Source: Data from Starbucks Corporation, 10K, 2005.

Ratio Analysis

Ratio analysis is an evaluation technique that identifies key relationships between the components of the financial statements. Ratios are useful tools for evaluating a company's financial position and operations and may reveal areas that need further investigation. To interpret ratios correctly, the analyst must have a general understanding of the company and its environment, financial data for several years or for several companies, and an understanding of the data underlying the numerator and denominator.

Ratios can be expressed in several ways. For example, a ratio of net income of $100,000 to sales of $1,000,000 can be stated as follows:

1. Net income is 1/10, or 10 percent, of sales.

2. The ratio of sales to net income is 10 to 1 (10:1), or sales are 10 times net income.

3. For every dollar of sales, the company has an average net income of 10 cents.

S T O P • R E V I E W • A P P L Y

2-1. Why would an investor want to see both horizontal and trend analyses of a company's financial statements?

2-2. What does this sentence mean: "Based on a 1990 index equaling 100, net income increased from 240 in 2000 to 260 in 2001"?

2-3. What is the difference between horizontal and vertical analysis?

2-4. What is the purpose of ratio analysis?

Comprehensive Illustration of Ratio Analysis

LO3 Apply ratio analysis to financial statements in a comprehensive evaluation of a company's financial performance.

In this section, to illustrate how analysts use ratio analysis in evaluating a company's financial performance, we perform a comprehensive ratio analysis of **Starbucks'** performance in 2004 and 2005. The following excerpt from the discussion and analysis section of Starbucks' 2005 annual report provides the context for our evaluation of the company's liquidity, profitability, long-term solvency, cash flow adequacy, and market strength:

> During the fiscal year ended October 2, 2005, all areas of Starbucks business, from U.S. and International Company-operated retail operations to the Company's specialty businesses, delivered strong financial performance. Starbucks believes the Company's ability to achieve the balance between growing the core business and building the foundation for future growth is the key to increasing long-term shareholder value. Starbucks fiscal 2005 performance reflects the Company's continuing commitment to achieving this balance.

Evaluating Liquidity

As you know, liquidity is a company's ability to pay bills when they are due and to meet unexpected needs for cash. Because debts are paid out of working capital, all liquidity ratios involve working capital or some part of it. (Cash flow ratios are also closely related to liquidity.)

Exhibit 8 presents **Starbucks'** liquidity ratios in 2004 and 2005. The **current ratio** and the **quick ratio** are measures of short-term debt-paying ability. The principal difference between the two ratios is that the numerator of the current ratio includes inventories and prepaid expenses. Inventories take longer to convert to cash than the current assets included in the numerator of the quick ratio. Starbucks' quick ratio was 1.1 times in 2004 and decreased to 0.4 times in 2005, primarily because of the more than $374 million decrease in short-term investments (marketable securities). Its current ratio was 1.8 times in 2004 and 1.0 in 2005. From 2004 to 2005, its current assets decreased $141,561 thousand due to the decline in short-term investments. At the same time, current liabilities increased, primarily because of new, short-term borrowing of $277,000 thousand.

Starbucks' management of receivables and inventories worsened from 2004 to 2005. The **receivable turnover**, which measures the relative size of accounts receivable and the effectiveness of credit policies, fell from 41.6 times in 2004 to 38.5 times in 2005. The related ratio of **days' sales uncollected** increased by almost one day, from 8.8 days in 2004 to 9.5 days in 2005. The number of days is quite low because the majority of Starbucks' revenues are from cash sales. The **inventory turnover**, which measures the relative size of inventories, decreased from 5.7 times in 2004 to 5.4 times in 2005. This resulted in almost a four-day increase in **days' inventory on hand**, from 64.0 days in 2004 to 67.6 days in 2005.

Starbucks' **operating cycle**, or the time it takes to sell products and collect for them, increased from 72.8 days in 2004 (8.8 days + 64.0 days, or the days' sales uncollected plus the days' inventory on hand) to 77.1 days in 2005 (9.5 days + 67.6 days). Related to the operating cycle is the number of days a company takes to pay its accounts payable. Starbucks' **payables turnover** increased from 12.3 times in 2004 to 13.0 times in 2005. This resulted in **days' payable** of 29.7 days in 2004 and 28.1 days in 2005. If the days' payable is subtracted from the operating cycle, Starbucks' financing period—the number of days of financing required—was 43.1 days in 2004 and 49.0 days in 2005 (see Figure 5). Overall, Starbucks' liquidity declined.

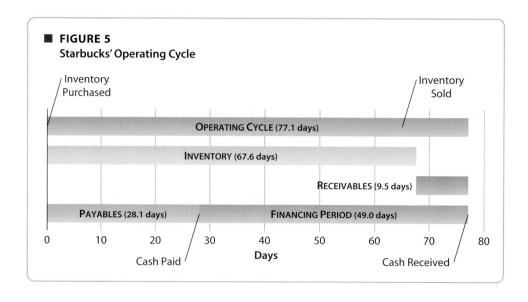

■ **FIGURE 5**
Starbucks' Operating Cycle

▼ **EXHIBIT 8**

Liquidity Ratios of Starbucks Corporation

(Dollar amounts in thousands)	2005	2004

Current ratio: Measure of short-term debt-paying ability

$$\frac{\text{Current Assets}}{\text{Current Liabilities}} \qquad \frac{\$1,209,334}{\$1,226,996} = 1.0 \text{ times} \qquad \frac{\$1,350,895}{\$746,259} = 1.8 \text{ times}$$

Quick ratio: Measure of short-term debt-paying ability

$$\frac{\text{Cash} + \text{Short-Term Investments} + \text{Receivables}}{\text{Current Liabilities}} \qquad \frac{\$173,809 + \$133,227 + \$190,762}{\$1,226,996} \qquad \frac{\$145,053 + \$507,956 + \$140,226}{\$746,259}$$

$$= \frac{\$497,798}{\$1,226,996} = 0.4 \text{ times} \qquad = \frac{\$793,235}{\$746,259} = 1.1 \text{ times}$$

Receivable turnover: Measure of relative size of accounts receivable and effectiveness of credit policies

$$\frac{\text{Net Revenue}}{\text{Average Accounts Receivable}} \qquad \frac{\$6,369,300}{(\$190,762 + \$140,226) \div 2} \qquad \frac{\$5,294,247}{(\$140,226 + \$114,448^*) \div 2}$$

$$= \frac{\$6,369,300}{\$165,494} = 38.5 \text{ times} \qquad = \frac{\$5,294,247}{\$127,337} = 41.6 \text{ times}$$

Days' sales uncollected: Measure of average days taken to collect receivables

$$\frac{\text{Days in Year}}{\text{Receivable Turnover}} \qquad \frac{365 \text{ days}}{38.5 \text{ times}} = 9.5 \text{ days} \qquad \frac{365 \text{ days}}{41.6 \text{ times}} = 8.8 \text{ days}$$

Inventory turnover: Measure of relative size of inventory

$$\frac{\text{Costs of Sales}}{\text{Average Inventory}} \qquad \frac{\$2,605,212}{(\$546,299 + \$422,663) \div 2} \qquad \frac{\$2,191,440}{(\$422,663 + \$342,944^*) \div 2}$$

$$= \frac{\$2,605,212}{\$484,481} = 5.4 \text{ times} \qquad = \frac{\$2,191,440}{\$382,804} = 5.7 \text{ times}$$

Days' inventory on hand: Measure of average days taken to sell inventory

$$\frac{\text{Days in Year}}{\text{Inventory Turnover}} \qquad \frac{365 \text{ days}}{5.4 \text{ times}} = 67.6 \text{ days} \qquad \frac{365 \text{ days}}{5.7 \text{ times}} = 64.0 \text{ days}$$

Payables turnover: Measure of relative size of accounts payable

$$\frac{\text{Costs of Sales} +/- \text{Change in Inventory}}{\text{Average Accounts Payable}} \qquad \frac{\$2,605,212 + \$123,636}{(\$220,975 + \$199,346) \div 2} \qquad \frac{\$2,191,440 + \$79,719^*}{(\$199,346 + \$168,984^*) \div 2}$$

$$= \frac{\$2,728,848}{\$210,161} = 13.0 \text{ times} \qquad = \frac{\$2,271,159}{\$184,165} = 12.3 \text{ times}$$

Days' payable: Measure of average days taken to pay accounts payable

$$\frac{\text{Days in Year}}{\text{Payables Turnover}} \qquad \frac{365 \text{ days}}{13.0 \text{ times}} = 28.1 \text{ days} \qquad \frac{365 \text{ days}}{12.3 \text{ times}} = 29.7 \text{ days}$$

*Figures for 2003 are from the balance sheet in Starbucks' 10K of 2004.
Source: Data from Starbucks Corporation, 10K, 2005; 10K, 2004.

Evaluating Profitability

Investors and creditors are interested in evaluating not only a company's liquidity, but also its profitability—that is, its ability to earn a satisfactory income. Profitability is closely linked to liquidity because earnings ultimately produce the cash flow needed for liquidity. Exhibit 9 shows **Starbucks'** profitability ratios in 2004 and 2005.

Profit margin measures how well a company manages its costs per dollar of sales. Starbucks' profit margin increased from 7.3 to 7.8 percent between 2004 and 2005. Its **asset turnover**, which measures how efficiently assets are used to produce sales (or net revenues), increased from 1.7 to 1.8 times. The result is an increase in the company's earning power, or **return on assets**, from 12.6 percent in 2004 to 14.3 percent in 2005. These computations show the relationships (the small difference in the two sets of return on assets figures results from the rounding of the ratios):

$\overbrace{}$*Study Note*

In accounting literature, *profit* is expressed in different ways—for example, as income before income taxes, income after income taxes, or operating income. To draw appropriate conclusions from profitability ratios, analysts must be aware of the content of net income data.

Profit Margin		*Asset Turnover*		*Return on Assets*
$\dfrac{\text{Net Income}}{\text{Net Sales}}$	$\times$	$\dfrac{\text{Net Sales}}{\text{Average Total Assets}}$	$=$	$\dfrac{\text{Net Income}}{\text{Average Total Assets}}$
2004 7.3%	$\times$	1.7	$=$	12.4%
2005 7.8%	$\times$	1.8	$=$	14.0%

In addition to using EVA (economic value added) to determine executive compensation, Target uses it to guide capital investment decisions. The company uses a benchmark of 9 percent for the estimated after-tax cost of capital invested in retail operations and a benchmark of 5 percent for capital invested in credit card operations. Target believes that a focus on EVA fosters its objective of increasing average annual earnings per share by 15 percent or more over time.

▼ **EXHIBIT 9**

Profitability Ratios of Starbucks Corporation

(Dollar amounts in thousands)	2005	2004

Profit margin: Measure of net income produced by each dollar of sales

$$\frac{\text{Net Income}}{\text{Net Sales}} \qquad \frac{\$494,467}{\$6,369,300} = 7.8\% \qquad \frac{\$388,973}{\$5,294,247} = 7.3\%$$

Asset turnover: Measure of how efficiently assets are used to produce sales

$$\frac{\text{Net Sales}}{\text{Average Total Assets}} \qquad \frac{\$6,369,300}{(\$3,514,065 + \$3,386,541) \div 2} \qquad \frac{\$5,294,247}{(\$3,386,541 + \$2,776,112^*) \div 2}$$

$$= \frac{\$6,369,300}{\$3,450,303} = 1.8 \text{ times} \qquad = \frac{\$5,294,247}{\$3,081,327} = 1.7 \text{ times}$$

Return on assets: Measure of overall earning power or profitability

$$\frac{\text{Net Income}}{\text{Average Total Assets}} \qquad \frac{\$494,467}{\$3,450,303} = 14.3\% \qquad \frac{\$388,973}{\$3,081,327} = 12.6\%$$

Return on equity: Measure of the profitability of stockholders' investments

$$\frac{\text{Net Income}}{\text{Average Stockholders' Equity}} \qquad \frac{\$494,467}{(\$2,090,634 + \$2,470,211) \div 2} \qquad \frac{\$388,973}{(\$2,470,211 + \$2,068,689^*) \div 2}$$

$$= \frac{\$494,467}{\$2,280,423} = 21.7\% \qquad = \frac{\$388,973}{\$2,269,450} = 17.1\%$$

*Figures for 2003 are from the five-year selected financial data in Starbucks' 10K of 2004.
Source: Data from Starbucks Corporation, 10K, 2005; 10K, 2004.

 Study Note

The analysis of both asset turnover and return on assets is improved if only productive assets are used in the calculations. For example, when investments in unfinished new plant construction or in plants that are now obsolete or nonoperating are removed from the asset base, the result is a better picture of the productivity of assets.

Starbucks' **return on equity** also improved, from 17.1 percent in 2004 to 21.7 percent in 2005 due to stock repurchases during 2005.

Although we have used net income in computing profitability ratios for Starbucks, net income is not always a good indicator of a company's sustainable earnings. For instance, if a company has discontinued operations, income from continuing operations may be a better measure of sustainable earnings. For a company that has one-time items on its income statement—such as restructurings, gains, or losses—income from operations before these items may be a better measure. Some analysts like to use earnings before interest and taxes, or EBIT, for the earnings measure because it excludes the effects of the company's borrowings and the tax rates from the analysis. Whatever figure one uses for earnings, it is important to try to determine the effects of various components on future operations.

Evaluating Long-Term Solvency

Long-term solvency has to do with a company's ability to survive for many years. The aim of evaluating long-term solvency is to detect early signs that a company is headed for financial difficulty. Increasing amounts of debt in a company's capital structure mean that the company is becoming more heavily leveraged. This condition has a negative effect on long-term solvency because it represents increasing legal obligations to pay interest periodically and the principal at maturity. Failure to make those payments can result in bankruptcy.

Declining profitability and liquidity ratios are key indicators of possible failure. Two other ratios that analysts consider when assessing long-term solvency are debt to equity and interest coverage, which are shown in Exhibit 10.

▼ **EXHIBIT 10**

Long-term Solvency Ratios of Starbucks Corporation		
(Dollar amounts in thousands)	2005	2004

Debt to equity ratio: Measure of capital structure and leverage

$$\frac{\text{Total Liabilities}}{\text{Stockholders' Equity}} \qquad \frac{\$1,423,431}{\$2,090,634} = .7 \text{ times} \qquad \frac{\$916,330}{\$2,470,211} = .4 \text{ times}$$

Interest coverage ratio: Measure of creditors' protection from default on interest payments

$$\frac{\text{Income Before Income Taxes} +}{\text{Interest Expense}} \qquad \text{[Starbucks does not report interest expense]}$$

Source: Data from Starbucks Corporation, *Annual Report*, 2005.

 Study Note

Liquidity is a firm's ability to meet its current obligations; solvency is its ability to meet maturing obligations as they come due without losing the ability to continue operations.

 Study Note

Because of innovative financing plans and other means of acquiring assets, lease payments and similar types of fixed obligations should be considered when evaluating long-term solvency.

The **debt to equity ratio** measures capital structure and leverage by showing the amount of a company's assets provided by creditors in relation to the amount provided by stockholders. **Starbucks'** debt to equity ratio was at .4 times in 2004 and .7 times in 2005. Recall from Exhibit 3 that the company increased most of its liabilites from 2004 to 2005, while equity decreased. Although moving toward higher financial risk in absolute terms, Starbucks' long-term solvency is still strong.

If debt is risky, why have any? The answer is that the level of debt is a matter of balance. Despite its riskiness, debt is a flexible means of financing certain business operations. The interest paid on debt is tax-deductible, whereas dividends on stock are not. Because debt usually carries a fixed interest charge, the cost of financing can be limited, and leverage can be used to advantage. If a company can earn a return on assets greater than the cost of interest, it makes an overall profit. In addition, being a debtor in periods of inflation has advantages because the debt, which is a fixed dollar amount, can be repaid with cheaper dollars. However, the company runs the risk of not earning a return on assets equal to the cost of financing the assets, thereby incurring a loss.

The **interest coverage ratio** measures the degree of protection creditors have from default on interest payments. The amount of interest that Starbucks expensed is quite small. In such cases, the resulting interest coverage ratio is not meaningful. However, given Starbucks' improving profitability, its interest-paying ability is very strong.

Evaluating the Adequacy of Cash Flows

Because cash flows are needed to pay debts when they are due, cash flow measures are closely related to liquidity and long-term solvency. Exhibit 11 presents **Starbucks'** cash flow adequacy ratios in 2004 and 2005.

Cash flow yield shows the cash-generating ability of a company's operations; it is measured by dividing cash flows from operating activities by net income. Starbucks' net cash flows from operating activities increased from $858,537 thousand in 2004 to $923,608 thousand in 2005. Its cash flow yield actually decreased from 2.2 to 1.9 times, revealing that net income increased faster than net cash provided by operating activities. The primary reasons for this result are the increase in inventories consuming cash of $121,618 in 2005 compared with $77,662 in 2004 and the increase in accounts receivables of $49,311 in 2005 (representing revenue recorded but cash not yet received) compared with $24,977 in 2004.

▼ **EXHIBIT 11**

Cash Flow Adequacy Ratios of Starbucks Corporation		
(Dollar amounts in thousands)	**2005**	**2004**

Cash flow yield: Measure of the ability to generate operating cash flows in relation to net income

Net Cash Flows from Operating Activities / Net Income

$$\frac{\$923,608^*}{\$494,467} = 1.9 \text{ times}$$ $$\frac{\$858,537^*}{\$388,973} = 2.2 \text{ times}$$

Cash flows to sales: Measure of the ability of sales to generate operating cash flows

Net Cash Flows from Operating Activities / Net Sales

$$\frac{\$923,608}{\$6,369,300} = 14.5\%$$ $$\frac{\$858,537}{\$5,294,247} = 16.2\%$$

Cash flows to assets: Measure of the ability of assets to generate operating cash flows

Net Cash Flows from Operating Activities / Average Total Assets

$$\frac{\$923,608}{(\$3,514,065 + \$3,386,541) \div 2}$$ $$\frac{\$858,537}{(\$3,386,541 + \$2,776,112^\dagger) \div 2}$$

$$= \frac{\$923,608}{\$3,450,303} = 26.8\%$$ $$= \frac{\$858,537}{\$3,081,327} = 27.9\%$$

Free cash flow: Measure of cash remaining after providing for commitments

Net Cash Flows from Operating Activities − Dividends − Net Capital Expenditures

$923,608 − $0 − $643,989* $858,537* − $0 − $412,537*

= $279,619   = $446,000

*These figures are from the statement of cash flows in Starbucks' 10K of 2005.
†The 2003 figure is from the five-year selected financial data in Starbucks' 10K of 2004.
Source: Data from Starbucks Corporation, 10K, 2005; 10K, 2004.

 Study Note

When the computation for free cash flow uses "net capital expenditures" in place of "purchases of plant assets minus sales of plant assets," it means that the company's sales of plant assets were too small or immaterial to be broken out.

Starbucks' ratios for cash flows to sales and cash flows to assets also declined. While the company's net sales and average total assets increased, the cash flows provided by its operations did not increase as fast. **Cash flows to sales**, or the cash-generating ability of sales, decreased from 16.2 to 14.5 percent. **Cash flows to assets**, or the ability of assets to generate operating cash flows, decreased from 27.9 to 26.8 percent.

Starbucks' **free cash flow**, the cash remaining after providing for commitments, also decreased. While the company's net capital expenditures increased by over $231 million, the net cash provided by its operating activities increased by only $65 million. Another factor in Starbucks' free cash flows is that the company pays no dividends. Management's comment with regard to cash flows in the future is as follows:

The Company manages its cash, cash equivalents and liquid investments in order to internally fund operating needs. The $421 million decline in total cash and cash equivalents and liquid investments from October 3, 2004 to October 2, 2005, was nearly all due to the sale of securities to fund common stock repurchases. The Company intends to use its available cash resources, including any borrowings under its revolving credit facility described below, to invest in its core businesses and other new business opportunities related to its core businesses. The Company may use its available cash resources to make proportionate capital contributions to its equity method and cost method investees, as well as purchase larger ownership interests in selected equity method investees, particularly in

▼ **EXHIBIT 12**

Market Strength Ratios of Starbucks Corporation

	2005	2004

Price/earnings (P/E) ratio: Measure of investors' confidence in a company

$$\frac{\text{Market Price per Share}}{\text{Earnings per Share}} \qquad \frac{\$24.72^*}{\$0.63} = 39.2 \text{ times} \qquad \frac{\$22.62^*}{\$0.49} = 46.2 \text{ times}$$

Dividends yield: Measure of a stock's current return to an investor

$$\frac{\text{Dividends per Share}}{\text{Market Price per Share}} \qquad \text{Starbucks does not pay a dividend.}$$

*Market price is the average for the fourth quarter reported in Starbucks' annual report.
Source: Data from Starbucks Corporation, 10K, 2005.

international markets. Depending on market conditions, Starbucks may repurchase shares of its common stock under its authorized share repurchase program. Management believes that strong cash flow generated from operations, existing cash and investments, as well as borrowing capacity under the revolving credit facility, should be sufficient to finance capital requirements for its core businesses.[8]

Evaluating Market Strength

Market price is the price at which a company's stock is bought and sold. It indicates how investors view the potential return and risk connected with owning the stock. Market price by itself is not very informative, however, because companies have different numbers of shares outstanding, different earnings, and different dividend policies. Thus, market price must be related to earnings by considering the price/earnings (P/E) ratio and the dividends yield. Those ratios for **Starbucks** appear in Exhibit 12. We computed them by using the average market prices of Starbucks' stock during the fourth quarter of 2004 and 2005.

The **price/earnings (P/E) ratio**, which measures investors' confidence in a company, is the ratio of the market price per share to earnings per share. The P/E ratio is useful in comparing the earnings of different companies and the value of a company's shares in relation to values in the overall market. With a higher P/E ratio, the investor obtains less underlying earnings per dollar invested. Starbucks' P/E ratio decreased from 46.2 times in 2004 to 39.2 times in 2005, which signals that investors expect less growth in the future.

The **dividends yield** measures a stock's current return to an investor in the form of dividends. Because Starbucks pays no dividends, its stockholders must expect their return to come from increases in the stock's market value.

S T O P • R E V I E W • A P P L Y

3-1. Company A and Company B both have net incomes of $1,000,000. Is it possible to conclude from this information that these companies are equally successful? Why or why not?

3-2. Circo Company has a return on assets of 12 percent and a debt to equity ratio of .5. Would you expect return on equity to be more or less than 12 percent?

3-3. Consider the following statement: "Supermarket executives are beginning to look back with some nostalgia on the days when the standard profit margin was 1 percent of sales. Last year the industry overall margin came to a thin .72 percent." How could a supermarket earn a satisfactory return on assets with such a small profit margin?

3-4. What amount is common to all cash flow adequacy ratios? To what other groups of ratios are the cash flow adequacy ratios most closely related?

3-5. Which ratios are most relevant to determining the financing period?

3-6. Company J's stock and Company Q's stock have the same market price. How might you determine whether investors are equally confident about the future of these companies?

Effects of Transactions on Ratios Sasah's, a retail firm, engaged in the transactions listed below. Opposite each transaction is a ratio and space to mark the transaction's effect on the ratio.

Transaction	Ratio	Increase	Decrease	None
a. Accrued salaries.	Current ratio			
b. Purchased inventory.	Quick ratio			
c. Increased allowance for uncollectible accounts.	Receivable turnover			
d. Purchased inventory on credit.	Payables turnover			
e. Sold treasury stock.	Profit margin			
f. Borrowed cash by issuing bond payable.	Asset turnover			
g. Paid wages expense.	Return on assets			
h. Repaid bond payable.	Debt to equity			
i. Accrued interest expense.	Interest coverage			
k. Sold merchandise on account.	Return on equity			
l. Recorded depreciation expense.	Cash flow yield			
m. Sold equipment.	Free cash flow			

Show that you understand the effect of business activities on performance measures by placing an X in the appropriate column to show whether the transaction increased, decreased, or had no effect on the ratio.

SOLUTION

Transaction	Ratio	Increase	Decrease	None
a. Accrued salaries.	Current ratio		X	
b. Purchased inventory.	Quick ratio		X	
c. Increased allowance for uncollectible accounts.	Receivable turnover	X		
d. Purchased inventory on credit.	Payables turnover		X	
e. Sold treasury stock.	Profit margin			X
f. Borrowed cash by issuing bond payable.	Asset turnover		X	
g. Paid wages expense.	Return on assets		X	
h. Repaid bond payable.	Debt to equity	X		
i. Accrued interest expense.	Interest coverage		X	
k. Sold merchandise on account.	Return on equity	X		
l. Recorded depreciation expense	Cash flow yield	X		
m. Sold equipment.	Free cash flow	X		

A LOOK BACK AT

STARBUCKS CORPORATION

To assess a company's financial performance, managers, stockholders, creditors, and other interested parties use measures that are linked to creating shareholder value. The Financial Highlights at the beginning of the chapter show steady increases in Starbucks' revenues, earnings, profit margin, and earnings per share—all good signs, but for a comprehensive view of the company's performance, users of its financial statements must consider the following questions:

- **What standards should be used to evaluate Starbucks' performance?**
- **What analytical tools are available to measure performance?**
- **How successful has the company been in creating value for shareholders?**

Starbucks' performance should be compared with the performance of other companies in the same industry—the specialty retail business. In addition, Starbucks' performance in the current year should be compared with its performance in past years. To make this comparison, users of Starbucks' financial statements employ such techniques as horizontal or trend analysis, vertical analysis, and ratio analysis.

Our comprehensive ratio analysis of Starbucks clearly shows that the company's financial condition improved from 2004 to 2005, as measured by its liquidity, profitability, long-term solvency, and cash flow adequacy ratios. This performance resulted in an increase in earnings per share from $.49 to $.63 and an increase in shareholders' value, as represented by an increase in the market price per share from $22.60 to $24.70.

CHAPTER REVIEW

REVIEW of Learning Objectives

LO1 Describe the objectives, standards of comparison, sources of information, and compensation issues in measuring financial performance.

A primary objective in management's use of financial performance measurement is to increase the wealth of the company's stockholders. Creditors and investors use financial performance measurement to judge a company's past performance and current position, as well as its future potential and the risk associated with it. Creditors use the information gained from their analyses to make reliable loans that will be repaid with interest. Investors use the information to make investments that will provide a return that is worth the risk.

Three standards of comparison commonly used in evaluating financial performance are rule-of-thumb measures, a company's past performance, and industry norms. Rule-of-thumb measures are weak because of a lack of evidence that they can be widely applied. A company's past performance can offer a guideline for measuring improvement, but it is not helpful in judging performance relative to the performance of other companies. Although the use of industry norms overcomes this last problem, its disadvantage is that firms are not always comparable, even in the same industry.

The main sources of information about public corporations are reports that the corporations publish themselves, such as annual reports and interim financial statements; reports filed with the SEC; business periodicals; and credit and investment advisory services.

In public corporations, a committee made up of independent directors appointed by the board of directors determines the compensation of top executives. Although earnings per share can be regarded as a "bottom-line" number that encompasses all the other performance measures, using it as the sole basis for determining executive compensation may lead to management practices that are not in the best interests of the company or its stockholders.

LO2 Apply horizontal analysis, trend analysis, vertical analysis, and ratio analysis to financial statements.

Horizontal analysis involves the computation of changes in both dollar amounts and percentages from year to year.

Trend analysis is an extension of horizontal analysis in that it calculates percentage changes for several years. The analyst computes the changes by setting a base year equal to 100 and calculating the results for subsequent years as percentages of the base year.

Vertical analysis uses percentages to show the relationship of the component parts of a financial statement to a total figure in the statement. The resulting financial statements, which are expressed entirely in percentages, are called common-size statements.

Ratio analysis is a technique of financial performance evaluation that identifies key relationships between the components of the financial statements. To interpret ratios correctly, the analyst must have a general understanding of the company and its environment, financial data for several years or for several companies, and an understanding of the data underlying the numerators and denominators.

LO3 Apply ratio analysis to financial statements in a comprehensive evaluation of a company's financial performance.

A comprehensive ratio analysis includes the evaluation of a company's liquidity, profitability, long-term solvency, cash flow adequacy, and market strength. The ratios for measuring these characteristics are illustrated in Exhibits 8 through 12.

REVIEW of Concepts and Terminology

The following concepts and terms were introduced in this chapter:

Asset turnover: A measure of how efficiently assets are used to produce sales; Net Sales ÷ Average Total Assets. **(LO3)**

Base year: In financial analysis, the first year to be considered in any set of data. **(LO2)**

Cash flows to assets: A measure of the ability of assets to generate operating cash flows; Net Cash Flows from Operating Activities ÷ Average Total Assets. **(LO3)**

Cash flows to sales: A measure of the ability of sales to generate operating cash flows; Net Cash Flows from Operating Activities ÷ Net Sales. **(LO3)**

Cash flow yield: A measure of a company's ability to generate operating cash flows in relation to net income; Net Cash Flows from Operating Activities ÷ Net Income. **(LO3)**

Common-size statement: A financial statement in which the components are expressed as percentages of a total figure in the statement. **(LO2)**

Compensation committee: A committee of independent directors appointed by a public corporation's board of directors to determine how top executives will be compensated. **(LO1)**

Current ratio: A measure of short-term debt-paying ability; Current Assets ÷ Current Liabilities. **(LO3)**

Days' inventory on hand: A measure that shows the average number of days taken to sell inventory; Days in Year ÷ Inventory Turnover. **(LO3)**

Days' payable: A measure that shows the average number of days taken to pay accounts payable; Days in Year ÷ Payables Turnover. **(LO3)**

Days' sales uncollected: A measure that shows the number of days, on average, that a company must wait to receive payment for credit sales; Days in Year ÷ Receivable Turnover. **(LO3)**

Debt to equity ratio: A measure that shows the relationship of debt financing to equity financing, or the extent to which a company is leveraged; Total Liabilities ÷ Stockholders' Equity. **(LO3)**

Diversified companies: Companies that operate in more than one industry. Also called *conglomerates*. **(LO1)**

Dividends yield: A measure of a stock's current return to an investor; Dividends per Share ÷ Market Price per Share. **(LO3)**

Financial performance measurement: An evaluation method that uses all the techniques available to show how important items in financial statements relate to a company's financial objectives. Also called *financial statement analysis*. **(LO1)**

Free cash flow: A measure of cash remaining after providing for commitments; Net Cash Flows from Operating Activities − Dividends − (Purchases of Plant Assets − Sales of Plant Assets). **(LO3)**

Horizontal analysis: A technique for analyzing financial statements in which changes from the previous year to the current year are computed in both dollar amounts and percentages. **(LO2)**

Index number: In trend analysis, a number that shows changes in related items over time and that is calculated by setting the base year equal to 100 percent. **(LO2)**

Interest coverage ratio: A measure of the degree of protection creditors have from default on interest payments; (Income Before Income Taxes + Interest Expense) ÷ Interest Expense. **(LO3)**

Interim financial statements: Financial statements issued for a period of less than one year, usually a quarter or a month. **(LO1)**

Inventory turnover: A measure of the relative size of inventory; Cost of Goods Sold ÷ Average Inventory. **(LO3)**

Operating cycle: The time it takes to sell products and collect for them; days' inventory on hand plus days' sales uncollected. **(LO3)**

Payables turnover: A measure of the relative size of accounts payable; (Cost of Goods Sold +/− Change in Inventory) ÷ Average Accounts Payable. **(LO3)**

Price/earnings (P/E) ratio: A measure of investors' confidence in a company and a means of comparing stock values; Market Price per Share ÷ Earnings per Share. **(LO3)**

Profit margin: A measure that shows the percentage of each revenue dollar that contributes to net income; Net Income ÷ Net Sales. **(LO3)**

Quick ratio: A measure of short-term debt-paying ability; (Cash + Marketable Securities + Receivables) ÷ Current Liabilities. **(LO3)**

Ratio analysis: A technique of financial performance evaluation that identifies key relationships between components of the financial statements. **(LO2)**

Receivable turnover: A measure of the relative size of accounts receivable and the effectiveness of credit policies; Net Sales ÷ Average Accounts Receivable. **(LO3)**

Return on assets: A measure of overall earning power, or profitability, that shows the amount earned on each dollar of assets invested; Net Income ÷ Average Total Assets. **(LO3)**

Return on equity: A measure of how much income was earned on each dollar invested by stockholders; Net Income ÷ Average Stockholders' Equity. **(LO3)**

Trend analysis: A variation of horizontal analysis in which percentage changes are calculated for several successive years instead of for two years. **(LO2)**

Vertical analysis: A technique for analyzing financial statements that uses percentages to show how the different components of a statement relate to a total figure in the statement. **(LO2)**

REVIEW Problem

LO3 **Comparative Analysis of Two Companies**

Maggie Washington is considering investing in a fast-food restaurant chain because she believes the trend toward eating out more often will continue. She has narrowed her choice to Quik Burger or Big Steak. The balance sheets of Quik Burger and Big Steak appear below. Their income statements are presented on the next page.

	A	B	C
1	**Balance Sheets**		
2	**December 31, 20xx**		
3	**(In thousands)**		
4			
5		**Quik Burger**	**Big Steak**
6	**Assets**		
7	Cash	$ 2,000	$ 4,500
8	Accounts receivable (net)	2,000	6,500
9	Inventory	2,000	5,000
10	Property, plant, and equipment (net)	20,000	35,000
11	Other assets	4,000	5,000
12	Total assets	$30,000	$56,000
13			
14	**Liabilities and Stockholders' Equity**		
15	Accounts payable	$ 2,500	$ 3,000
16	Notes payable	1,500	4,000
17	Bonds payable	10,000	30,000
18	Common stock, $1 par value	1,000	3,000
19	Additional paid-in capital	9,000	9,000
20	Retained earnings	6,000	7,000
21	Total liabilities and stockholders' equity	$30,000	$56,000

	A	B	C
1	**Income Statements**		
2	**For the Year Ended December 31, 20xx**		
3	(In thousands, except per share amounts)		
4			
5		**Quik Burger**	**Big Steak**
6	Net sales	$53,000	$86,000
7	Costs and expenses		
8	Cost of goods sold	$37,000	$61,000
9	Selling expenses	7,000	10,000
10	Administrative expenses	4,000	5,000
11	Total costs and expenses	$48,000	$76,000
12	Income from operations	$ 5,000	$10,000
13	Interest expense	1,400	3,200
14	Income before income taxes	$ 3,600	$ 6,800
15	Income taxes	1,800	3,400
16	Net income	$ 1,800	$ 3,400
17	Earnings per share	$ 1.80	$ 1.13

Quik Burger's statement of cash flows shows that it had net cash flows from operations of $2,200,000. Big Steak's statement of cash flows show that its net cash flows from operations were $3,000,000. Net capital expenditures were $2,100,000 for Quik Burger and $1,800,000 for Big Steak. Quik Burger paid dividends of $500,000, and Big Steak paid dividends of $600,000. The market prices of the stocks of Quik Burger and Big Steak were $30 and $20, respectively. Financial information pertaining to prior years is not readily available to Maggie Washington. Assume that all notes payable of these two companies are current liabilities and that all their bonds payable are long-term liabilities.

Required

Perform a comprehensive ratio analysis of both Quik Burger and Big Steak following the steps outlined below. Show dollar amounts in thousands, use end-of-year balances for averages, assume no change in inventory, and round all ratios and percentages to one decimal place.

1. Prepare an analysis of liquidity.
2. Prepare an analysis of profitability.
3. Prepare an analysis of long-term solvency.
4. Prepare an analysis of cash flow adequacy.
5. Prepare an analysis of market strength.
6. In each analysis, indicate the company that apparently had the more favorable ratio. (Consider differences of .1 or less to be neutral.)
7. In what ways would having access to prior years' information aid this analysis?

Answer to Review Problem

	A	B	C	D	E	F	G	H	I	J	K	L
1		**Ratio Name**			**Quik Burger**				**Big Steak**			**6. Company with More Favorable Ratio**
2												
3	1.	**Liquidity analysis**										
4												
5	a.	Current ratio		$2,000 + $2,000 + $2,000				$4,500 + $6,500 + $5,000				
6					$2,500 + $1,500				$3,000 + $4,000			
7												
8				$6,000				$16,000				
9				$4,000	=	1.5 times		$7,000	=	2.3 times		Big Steak
10												
11	b.	Quick ratio			$2,000 + $2,000				$4,500 + $6,500			
12					$2,500 + $1,500				$3,000 + $4,000			
13												
14				$4,000				$11,000				
15				$4,000	=	1.0 times		$7,000	=	1.6 times		Big Steak
16												
17	c.	Receivable turnover		$53,000				$86,000				
18				$2,000	=	26.5 times		$6,500	=	13.2 times		Quik Burger
19												
20	d.	Days' sales uncollected		365				365				
21				26.5	=	13.8 days		13.2	=	27.7 days		Quik Burger
22												
23	e.	Inventory turnover		$37,000				$61,000				
24				$2,000	=	18.5 times		$5,000	=	12.2 times		Quik Burger
25												
26	f.	Days' inventory on hand		365				365				
27				18.5	=	19.7 days		12.2	=	29.9 days		Quik Burger
28												
29	g.	Payables turnover		$37,000				$61,000				
30				$2,500	=	14.8 times		$3,000	=	20.3 times		Big Steak
31												
32	h.	Days' payable		365				365				
33				14.8	=	24.7 days		20.3	=	18.0 days		Big Steak
34												
35		* This analysis indicates the company with the apparently more favorable ratio. Class discussion may focus on conditions under which different conclusions may be drawn.										

(Continued)

	A	B	C	D	E	F	G	H	I	J	K	L
1		Ratio Name			Quik Burger				Big Steak			6. Company with More Favorable Ratio
2												
3	2.	**Profitability analysis**										
4												
5	a.	Profit margin		$1,800	=	3.4%		$3,400	=	4.0%		Big Steak
6				$53,000				$86,000				
7												
8	b.	Asset turnover		$53,000	=	1.8 times		$86,000	=	1.5 times		Quik Burger
9				$30,000				$56,000				
10												
11	c.	Return on assets		$1,800	=	6.0%		$3,400	=	6.1%		Neutral
12				$30,000				$56,000				
13												
14	d.	Return on equity			$1,800				$3,400			
15				$1,000 + $9,000 + $6,000				$3,000 + $9,000 + $7,000				
16												
17				$1,800	=	11.3%		$3,400	=	17.9%		Big Steak
18				$16,000				$19,000				

	A	B	C	D	E	F	G	H	I	J	K	L
1		Ratio Name			Quik Burger				Big Steak			6. Company with More Favorable Ratio
2												
3	3.	**Long-term solvency analysis**										
4												
5	a.	Debt to equity ratio		$2,500 + $1,500 + $10,000				$3,000 + $4,000 + $30,000				
6				$1,000 + $9,000 + $6,000				$3,000 + $9,000 + $7,000				
7												
8				$14,000	=	.9 times		$37,000	=	1.9 times		Quik Burger
9				$16,000				$19,000				
10												
11	b.	Interest coverage ratio			$3,600 + $1,400				$6,800 + $3,200			
12				$1,400				$3,200				
13												
14				$5,000	=	3.6 times		$10,000	=	3.1 times		Quik Burger
15				$1,400				$3,200				

	A	B	C	D	E	F	G	H	I	J	K	L
1		Ratio Name			Quik Burger				Big Steak			6. Company with More Favorable Ratio
2												
3	4.	**Cash flow adequacy analysis**										
4												
5	a.	Cash flow yield		$2,200	=	1.2 times		$3,000	=	.9 times		Quik Burger
6				$1,800				$3,400				
7												

(*Continued*)

	Ratio Name		Quik Burger				Big Steak				6. Company with More Favorable Ratio
8											
9											
10	b. Cash flows to sales		$2,200	=	4.2%		$3,000	=	3.5%		Quik Burger
11			$53,000				$86,000				
12											
13	c. Cash flows to assets		$2,200	=	7.3%		$3,000	=	5.4%		Quik Burger
14			$30,000				$56,000				
15											
16	d. Free cash flow		$2,200 - $500 - $2,100				$3,000 - $600 - $1,800				Big Steak
17			= ($400)				= $600				

	Ratio Name		Quik Burger				Big Steak				6. Company with More Favorable Ratio
1											
2											
3	5. Market strength analysis										
4											
5	a. Price/earnings ratio		$30	= 16.7 times			$20	= 17.7 times			Big Steak
6			$1.80				$1.13				
7											
8	b. Dividends yield		$500,000/1,000,000	=	1.7%		$600,000/3,000,000	=	1.0%		Quik Burger
9			$30				$20				

7. Prior years' information would be helpful in two ways. First, turnover, return, and cash flows to assets ratios could be based on average amounts. Second, a trend analysis could be performed for each company.

CHAPTER ASSIGNMENTS

BUILDING Your Basic Knowledge and Skills

Short Exercises

LO1 **Objectives and Standards of Financial Performance Evaluation**

SE 1. Indicate whether each of the following items is (a) an objective or (b) a standard of comparison of financial statement analysis:

1. Industry norms
2. Assessment of a company's past performance
3. The company's past performance
4. Assessment of future potential and related risk
5. Rule-of-thumb measures

LO1 **Sources of Information**

SE 2. For each piece of information in the list that follows, indicate whether the best source would be (a) reports published by the company, (b) SEC reports, (c) business periodicals, or (d) credit and investment advisory services.

1. Current market value of a company's stock
2. Management's analysis of the past year's operations
3. Objective assessment of a company's financial performance
4. Most complete body of financial disclosures
5. Current events affecting the company

LO2   Trend Analysis

SE 3. Using 20x7 as the base year, prepare a trend analysis for the following data, and tell whether the results suggest a favorable or unfavorable trend. (Round your answers to one decimal place.)

	20x9	20x8	20x7
Net sales	$316,000	$272,000	$224,000
Accounts receivable (net)	86,000	64,000	42,000

LO2   Horizontal Analysis

SE 4. The comparative income statements and balance sheets of Obras, Inc., appear on the opposite page. Compute the amount and percentage changes for the income statements, and comment on the changes from 20x8 to 20x9. (Round the percentage changes to one decimal place.)

LO2   Vertical Analysis

SE 5. Express the comparative balance sheets of Obras, Inc., as common-size statements, and comment on the changes from 20x8 to 20x9. (Round computations to one decimal place.)

LO3   Liquidity Analysis

SE 6. Using the information for Obras, Inc., in **SE 4** and **SE 5**, compute the current ratio, quick ratio, receivable turnover, days' sales uncollected, inventory turnover, days' inventory on hand, payables turnover, and days' payable for 20x8 and 20x9. Inventories were $8,000 in 20x7, $10,000 in 20x8, and $14,000 in 20x9. Accounts receivable were $12,000 in 20x7, $16,000 in 20x8, and $20,000 in 20x9. Accounts payable were $18,000 in 20x7, $20,000 in 20x8, and $24,000 in 20x9. The company had no marketable securities or prepaid assets. Comment on the results. (Round computations to one decimal place.)

LO3   Profitability Analysis

SE 7. Using the information for Obras, Inc., in **SE 4** and **SE 5**, compute the profit margin, asset turnover, return on assets, and return on equity for 20x8 and 20x9. In 2007, total assets were $200,000 and total stockholders' equity was $60,000. Comment on the results. (Round computations to one decimal place.)

LO3   Long-term Solvency Analysis

SE 8. Using the information for Obras, Inc., in **SE 4** and **SE 5**, compute the debt to equity ratio and the interest coverage ratio for 20x8 and 20x9. Comment on the results. (Round computations to one decimal place.)

Obras, Inc.
Comparative Income Statements
For the Years Ended December 31, 20x9 and 20x8

	20x9	20x8
Net sales	$360,000	$290,000
Cost of goods sold	224,000	176,000
Gross margin	$136,000	$114,000
Operating expenses	80,000	60,000
Operating income	$ 56,000	$ 54,000
Interest expense	14,000	10,000
Income before income taxes	$ 42,000	$ 44,000
Income taxes expense	14,000	16,000
Net income	$ 28,000	$ 28,000
Earnings per share	$ 2.80	$ 2.80

Obras, Inc.
Comparative Balance Sheets
December 31, 20x9 and 20x8

	20x9	20x8
Assets		
Current assets	$ 48,000	$ 40,000
Property, plant, and equipment (net)	260,000	200,000
Total assets	$308,000	$240,000
Liabilities and Stockholders' Equity		
Current liabilities	$ 36,000	$ 44,000
Long-term liabilities	180,000	120,000
Stockholders' equity	92,000	76,000
Total liabilities and stockholders' equity	$308,000	$240,000

LO3 **Cash Flow Adequacy Analysis**

SE 9. Using the information for Obras, Inc., in **SE 4**, **SE 5**, and **SE 7**, compute the cash flow yield, cash flows to sales, cash flows to assets, and free cash flow for 20x8 and 20x9. Net cash flows from operating activities were $42,000 in 20x8 and $32,000 in 20x9. Net capital expenditures were $60,000 in 20x8 and $80,000 in 20x9. Cash dividends were $12,000 in both years. Comment on the results. (Round computations to one decimal place.)

LO3 **Market Strength Analysis**

SE 10. Using the information for Obras, Inc., in **SE 4**, **SE 5**, and **SE 9**, compute the price/earnings (P/E) ratio and dividends yield for 20x8 and 20x9. The company had 10,000 shares of common stock outstanding in both years. The price of Obras' common stock was $60 in 20x8 and $40 in 20x9. Comment on the results. (Round computations to one decimal place.)

Exercises

LO1, LO2 **Discussion Questions**

E 1. Develop brief answers to each of the following questions:

1. Why is it essential that management compensation, including bonuses, be linked to financial goals and strategies that achieve shareholder value?
2. How are past performance and industry norms useful in evaluating a company's performance? What are their limitations?
3. In a five-year trend analysis, why do the dollar values remain the same for their respective years while the percentages usually change when a new five-year period is chosen?

LO3 **Discussion Questions**

E 2. Develop brief answers to each of the following questions:

1. Why does a decrease in receivable turnover create the need for cash from operating activities?
2. Why would ratios that include one balance sheet account and one income statement account, such as receivable turnover or return on assets, be questionable if they came from quarterly or other interim financial reports?
3. Can you suggest a limitation of free cash flow in comparing one company to another?

LO1 **Issues in Financial Performance Evaluation: Objectives, Standards, Sources of Information, and Executive Compensation**

E 3. Identify each of the following as (a) an objective of financial statement analysis, (b) a standard for financial statement analysis, (c) a source of information for financial statement analysis, or (d) an executive compensation issue:

1. Average ratios of other companies in the same industry
2. Assessment of the future potential of an investment
3. Interim financial statements
4. Past ratios of the company
5. SEC Form 10-K
6. Assessment of risk
7. A company's annual report
8. Linking performance to shareholder value

LO2 **Trend Analysis**

E 4. Using 20x5 as the base year, prepare a trend analysis of the following data, and tell whether the situation shown by the trends is favorable or unfavorable. (Round your answers to one decimal place.)

	20x9	20x8	20x7	20x6	20x5
Net sales	$51,040	$47,960	$48,400	$45,760	$44,000
Cost of goods sold	34,440	30,800	31,080	29,400	28,000
General and administrative expenses	10,560	10,368	10,176	9,792	9,600
Operating income	6,040	6,792	7,144	6,568	6,400

LO2 **Horizontal Analysis**

E 5. Compute the amount and percentage changes for the following balance sheets, and comment on the changes from 20x8 to 20x9. (Round the percentage changes to one decimal place.)

Davis Company
Comparative Balance Sheets
December 31, 20x9 and 20x8

	20x9	20x8
Assets		
Current assets	$ 18,600	$ 12,800
Property, plant, and equipment (net)	109,464	97,200
Total assets	$128,064	$110,000
Liabilities and Stockholders' Equity		
Current liabilities	$ 11,200	$ 3,200
Long-term liabilities	35,000	40,000
Stockholders' equity	81,864	66,800
Total liabilities and stockholders' equity	$128,064	$110,000

LO2 Vertical Analysis

E 6. Express the partial comparative income statements that follow as common-size statements, and comment on the changes from 20x7 to 20x8. (Round computations to one decimal place.)

Davis Company
Partial Comparative Income Statements
For the Years Ended December 31, 20x8 and 20x7

	20x8	20x7
Net sales	$212,000	$184,000
Cost of goods sold	127,200	119,600
Gross margin	$ 84,800	$ 64,400
Selling expenses	$ 53,000	$ 36,800
General expenses	25,440	18,400
Total operating expenses	$ 78,440	$ 55,200
Operating income	$ 6,360	$ 9,200

LO3 Liquidity Analysis

E 7. Partial comparative balance sheet and income statement information for Allen Company is as follows:

	20x9	20x8
Cash	$ 13,600	$ 10,400
Marketable securities	7,200	17,200
Accounts receivable (net)	44,800	35,600
Inventory	54,400	49,600
Total current assets	$120,000	$112,800
Accounts payable	$ 40,000	$ 28,200
Net sales	$322,560	$220,720
Cost of goods sold	217,600	203,360
Gross margin	$104,960	$ 17,360

In 20x7, the year-end balances for Accounts Receivable and Inventory were $32,400 and $51,200, respectively. Accounts Payable was $30,600 in 20x7 and is the only current liability. Compute the current ratio, quick ratio, receivable turnover, days' sales uncollected, inventory turnover, days' inventory on hand, payables turnover, and days' payable for each year. (Round computations to one decimal place.) Comment on the change in the company's liquidity position, including its operating cycle and required days of financing from 20x8 to 20x9.

LO3   Turnover Analysis

E 8. Diamond Tuxedo Rental has been in business for four years. Because the company has recently had a cash flow problem, management wonders whether there is a problem with receivables or inventories. Here are selected figures from the company's financial statements (in thousands):

	20x9	20x8	20x7	20x6
Net sales	$144.0	$112.0	$96.0	$80.0
Cost of goods sold	90.0	72.0	60.0	48.0
Accounts receivable (net)	24.0	20.0	16.0	12.0
Merchandise inventory	28.0	22.0	16.0	10.0
Accounts payable	13.0	10.0	8.0	5.0

Compute the receivable turnover, inventory turnover, and payables turnover for each of the four years, and comment on the results relative to the cash flow problem that the firm has been experiencing. Merchandise inventory was $11,000, accounts receivable were $11,000, and accounts payable were $4,000 in 20x5. (Round computations to one decimal place.)

LO3   Profitability Analysis

E 9. Barr Company had total assets of $320,000 in 20x7, $340,000 in 20x8, and $380,000 in 20x9. Its debt to equity ratio was .67 times in all three years. In 20x8, Barr had net income of $38,556 on revenues of $612,000. In 20x9, it had net income of $49,476 on revenues of $798,000. Compute the profit margin, asset turnover, return on assets, and return on equity for 20x8 and 20x9. Comment on the apparent cause of the increase or decrease in profitability. (Round the percentages and other ratios to one decimal place.)

LO3   Long-term Solvency and Market Strength Ratios

E 10. An investor is considering investing in the long-term bonds and common stock of Companies M and N. Both firms operate in the same industry. Both also pay a dividend per share of $8 and have a yield of 10 percent on their long-term bonds. Other data for the two firms are as follows:

	Company M	Company N
Total assets	$4,800,000	$2,160,000
Total liabilities	2,160,000	1,188,000
Income before income taxes	576,000	259,200
Interest expense	194,400	106,920
Earnings per share	6.40	10.00
Market price of common stock	80	95

Compute the debt to equity, interest coverage, and price/earnings (P/E) ratios, as well as the dividends yield, and comment on the results. (Round computations to one decimal place.)

LO3 **Cash Flow Adequacy Analysis**

E 11. Using the data below from the financial statements of Braugh, Inc., compute the company's cash flow yield, cash flows to sales, cash flows to assets, and free cash flow. (Round computations to one decimal place.)

Net sales	$3,200,000
Net income	352,000
Net cash flows from operating activities	456,000
Total assets, beginning of year	2,890,000
Total assets, end of year	3,120,000
Cash dividends	120,000
Net capital expenditures	298,000

Problems

LO2 **Horizontal and Vertical Analysis**

P 1. Sanborn Corporation's condensed comparative income statements for 20x8 and 20x7 appear below. The corporation's condensed comparative balance sheets for 20x8 and 20x7 appear on the next page.

Sanborn Corporation
Comparative Income Statements
For the Years Ended December 31, 20x8 and 20x7

	20x8	20x7
Net sales	$3,276,800	$3,146,400
Cost of goods sold	2,088,800	2,008,400
Gross margin	$1,188,000	$1,138,000
Operating expenses		
Selling expenses	$ 476,800	$ 518,000
Administrative expenses	447,200	423,200
Total operating expenses	$ 924,000	$ 941,200
Income from operations	$ 264,000	$ 196,800
Interest expense	65,600	39,200
Income before income taxes	$ 198,400	$ 157,600
Income taxes expense	62,400	56,800
Net income	$ 136,000	$ 100,800
Earnings per share	$ 3.40	$ 2.52

Required

1. Prepare schedules showing the amount and percentage changes from 20x7 to 20x8 for the comparative income statements and the balance sheets.
2. Prepare common-size income statements and balance sheets for 20x7 and 20x8.

Sanborn Corporation
Comparative Balance Sheets
December 31, 20x8 and 20x7

	20x8	20x7
Assets		
Cash	$ 81,200	$ 40,800
Accounts receivable (net)	235,600	229,200
Inventory	574,800	594,800
Property, plant, and equipment (net)	750,000	720,000
Total assets	$1,641,600	$1,584,800
Liabilities and Stockholders' Equity		
Accounts payable	$ 267,600	$ 477,200
Notes payable	200,000	400,000
Bonds payable	400,000	—
Common stock, $10 par value	400,000	400,000
Retained earnings	374,000	307,600
Total liabilities and stockholders' equity	$1,641,600	$1,584,800

3. **Manager Insight:** Comment on the results in requirements **1** and **2** by identifying favorable and unfavorable changes in the components and composition of the statements.

LO3 **Effects of Transactions on Ratios**

P 2. Koz Corporation engaged in the transactions listed in the first column of the following table. Opposite each transaction is a ratio and space to indicate the effect of each transaction on the ratio.

		Effect		
Transaction	**Ratio**	**Increase**	**Decrease**	**None**
a. Sold merchandise on account.	Current ratio			
b. Sold merchandise on account.	Inventory turnover			
c. Collected on accounts receivable.	Quick ratio			
d. Wrote off an uncollectible account.	Receivable turnover			
e. Paid on accounts payable.	Current ratio			
f. Declared cash dividend.	Return on equity			
g. Incurred advertising expense.	Profit margin			
h. Issued stock dividend.	Debt to equity ratio			
i. Issued bonds payable.	Asset turnover			
j. Accrued interest expense.	Current ratio			
k. Paid previously declared cash dividend.	Dividends yield			
l. Purchased treasury stock.	Return on assets			
m. Recorded depreciation expense.	Cash flow yield			

Required

Manager Insight: Show that you understand the effect of business activities on performance measures by placing an X in the appropriate column to show whether the transaction increased, decreased, or had no effect on the indicated ratio.

LO3 **Comprehensive Ratio Analysis**

P 3. Data for Sanborn Corporation in 20x8 and 20x7 follow. These data should be used in conjunction with the data in **P 1**.

	20x8	20x7
Net cash flows from operating activities	($196,000)	$144,000
Net capital expenditures	$40,000	$65,000
Dividends paid	$44,000	$34,400
Number of common shares	40,000,000	40,000,000
Market price per share	$18	$30

Selected balances at the end of 20x6 were accounts receivable (net), $206,800; inventory, $547,200; total assets, $1,465,600; accounts payable, $386,600; and stockholders' equity, $641,200. All Sanborn's notes payable were current liabilities; all its bonds payable were long-term liabilities.

Required

Perform a comprehensive ratio analysis following the steps outlined below. Round all answers to one decimal place.

1. Prepare a liquidity analysis by calculating for each year the (a) current ratio, (b) quick ratio, (c) receivable turnover, (d) days' sales uncollected, (e) inventory turnover, (f) days' inventory on hand, (g) payables turnover, and (h) days' payable.
2. Prepare a profitability analysis by calculating for each year the (a) profit margin, (b) asset turnover, (c) return on assets, and (d) return on equity.
3. Prepare a long-term solvency analysis by calculating for each year the (a) debt to equity ratio and (b) interest coverage ratio.
4. Prepare a cash flow adequacy analysis by calculating for each year the (a) cash flow yield, (b) cash flows to sales, (c) cash flows to assets, and (d) free cash flow.
5. Prepare a market strength analysis by calculating for each year the (a) price/earnings (P/E) ratio and (b) dividends yield.
6. **Manager Insight:** After making the calculations, indicate whether each ratio improved or deteriorated from 20x7 to 20x8 (use F for favorable and U for unfavorable and consider changes of .1 or less to be neutral).

LO3 **Comprehensive Ratio Analysis of Two Companies**

P 4. Ginger Adair is considering an investment in the common stock of a chain of retail department stores. She has narrowed her choice to two retail companies, Lewis Corporation and Ramsey Corporation, whose income statements and balance sheets are presented on the next page.

During the year, Lewis Corporation paid a total of $100,000 in dividends. The market price per share of its stock is currently $60. In comparison, Ramsey Corporation paid a total of $228,000 in dividends, and the current market price of its stock is $76 per share. Lewis Corporation had net cash flows from operations of $543,000 and net capital expenditures of $1,250,000. Ramsey Corporation had net cash flows from operations of $985,000 and net capital expenditures of $2,100,000. Information for prior years is not readily available. Assume that all notes payable are current liabilities and all bonds payable are long-term liabilities and that there is no change in inventory.

Income Statements

	Lewis	Ramsey
Net sales	$25,120,000	$50,420,000
Costs and expenses		
Cost of goods sold	$12,284,000	$29,668,000
Selling expenses	9,645,200	14,216,400
Administrative expenses	1,972,000	4,868,000
Total costs and expenses	$23,901,200	$48,752,400
Income from operations	$ 1,218,800	$ 1,667,600
Interest expense	388,000	456,000
Income before income taxes	$ 830,800	$ 1,211,600
Income taxes expense	400,000	600,000
Net income	$ 430,800	$ 611,600
Earnings per share	$ 4.31	$ 10.19

Balance Sheets

	Lewis	Ramsey
Assets		
Cash	$ 160,000	$ 384,800
Marketable securities (at cost)	406,800	169,200
Accounts receivable (net)	1,105,600	1,970,800
Inventory	1,259,600	2,506,800
Prepaid expenses	108,800	228,000
Property, plant, and equipment (net)	5,827,200	13,104,000
Intangibles and other assets	1,106,400	289,600
Total assets	$9,974,400	$18,653,200
Liabilities and Stockholders' Equity		
Accounts payable	$ 688,000	$ 1,145,200
Notes payable	300,000	800,000
Income taxes payable	100,400	146,800
Bonds payable	4,000,000	4,000,000
Common stock, $20 par value	2,000,000	1,200,000
Additional paid-in capital	1,219,600	7,137,200
Retained earnings	1,666,400	4,224,000
Total liabilities and stockholders' equity	$9,974,400	$18,653,200

Required

Conduct a comprehensive ratio analysis for each company, using the available information. Compare the results. Round percentages and ratios to one decimal place, and consider changes of .1 or less to be indeterminate.

1. Prepare a liquidity analysis by calculating for each company the (a) current ratio, (b) quick ratio, (c) receivable turnover, (d) days' sales uncollected,

(e) inventory turnover, (f) days' inventory on hand, (g) payables turnover, and (h) days' payable.

2. Prepare a profitability analysis by calculating for each company the (a) profit margin, (b) asset turnover, (c) return on assets, and (d) return on equity.

3. Prepare a long-term solvency analysis by calculating for each company the (a) debt to equity ratio and (b) interest coverage ratio.

4. Prepare a cash flow adequacy analysis by calculating for each company the (a) cash flow yield, (b) cash flows to sales, (c) cash flows to assets, and (d) free cash flow.

5. Prepare an analysis of market strength by calculating for each company the (a) price/earnings (P/E) ratio and (b) dividends yield.

6. Manager Insight: Compare the two companies by inserting the ratio calculations from 1 through 5 in a table with the following column headings: Ratio, Name, Lewis, Ramsey, and Company with More Favorable Ratio. Indicate in the last column which company had the more favorable ratio in each case.

7. Manager Insight: How could the analysis be improved if information about these companies' prior years were available?

Alternate Problems

LO3 **Effects of Transactions on Ratios**

P 5. Benson Corporation, a clothing retailer, engaged in the transactions listed in the first column of the table below. Opposite each transaction is a ratio and space to mark the effect of each transaction on the ratio.

		Effect		
Transaction	Ratio	Increase	Decrease	None
a. Issued common stock for cash.	Asset turnover			
b. Declared cash dividend.	Current ratio			
c. Sold treasury stock.	Return on equity			
d. Borrowed cash by issuing note payable.	Debt to equity ratio			
e. Paid salaries expense.	Inventory turnover			
f. Purchased merchandise for cash.	Current ratio			
g. Sold equipment for cash.	Receivable turnover			
h. Sold merchandise on account.	Quick ratio			
i. Paid current portion of long-term debt.	Return on assets			
j. Gave sales discount.	Profit margin			
k. Purchased marketable securities for cash.	Quick ratio			
l. Declared 5% stock dividend.	Current ratio			
m. Purchased a building.	Free cash flow			

Required

Manager Insight: Show that you understand the effect of business activities on performance measures by placing an X in the appropriate column to show whether the transaction increased, decreased, or had no effect on the indicated ratio.

LO3 **Comprehensive Ratio Analysis**

P 6. The condensed comparative income statements and balance sheets of Basie Corporation appear on the next page. All figures are given in thousands of dollars, except earnings per share.

Basie Corporation
Comparative Income Statements
For the Years Ended December 31, 20x8 and 20x7

	20x8	20x7
Net sales	$800,400	$742,600
Cost of goods sold	454,100	396,200
Gross margin	$346,300	$346,400
Operating expenses		
Selling expenses	$130,100	$104,600
Administrative expenses	140,300	115,500
Total operating expenses	$270,400	$220,100
Income from operations	$ 75,900	$126,300
Interest expense	25,000	20,000
Income before income taxes	$ 50,900	$106,300
Income taxes expense	14,000	35,000
Net income	$ 36,900	$ 71,300
Earnings per share	$ 1.23	$ 2.38

Basie Corporation
Comparative Balance Sheets
December 31, 20x8 and 20x7

	20x8	20x7
Assets		
Cash	$ 31,100	$ 27,200
Accounts receivable (net)	72,500	42,700
Inventory	122,600	107,800
Property, plant, and equipment (net)	577,700	507,500
Total assets	$803,900	$685,200
Liabilities and Stockholders' Equity		
Accounts payable	$104,700	$ 72,300
Notes payable	50,000	50,000
Bonds payable	200,000	110,000
Common stock, $10 par value	300,000	300,000
Retained earnings	149,200	152,900
Total liabilities and stockholders' equity	$803,900	$685,200

Additional data for Basie Corporation in 20x8 and 20x7 follow.

	20x8	20x7
Net cash flows from operating activities	$64,000	$99,000
Net capital expenditures	$119,000	$38,000
Dividends paid	$31,400	$35,000
Number of common shares	30,000	30,000
Market price per share	$40	$60

Balances of selected accounts at the end of 20x6 were accounts receivable (net), $52,700; inventory, $99,400; accounts payable, $64,800; total assets, $647,800; and stockholder's equity, $376,600. All of the bonds payable were long-term liabilities.

Required

Perform the following analyses. Round percentages and ratios to one decimal place.

1. Prepare a liquidity analysis by calculating for each year the (a) current ratio, (b) quick ratio, (c) receivable turnover, (d) days' sales uncollected, (e) inventory turnover, (f) days' inventory on hand, (g) payables turnover, and (h) days' payable.
2. Prepare a profitability analysis by calculating for each year the (a) profit margin, (b) asset turnover, (c) return on assets, and (d) return on equity.
3. Prepare a long-term solvency analysis by calculating for each year the (a) debt to equity ratio and (b) interest coverage ratio.
4. Prepare a cash flow adequacy analysis by calculating for each year the (a) cash flow yield, (b) cash flows to sales, (c) cash flows to assets, and (d) free cash flow.
5. Prepare an analysis of market strength by calculating for each year the (a) price/earnings (P/E) ratio and (b) dividends yield.
6. **Manager Insight:** After making the calculations, indicate whether each ratio improved or deteriorated from 20x7 to 20x8 (use F for favorable and U for unfavorable and consider changes of .1 or less to be neutral).

ENHANCING Your Knowledge, Skills, and Critical Thinking

Conceptual Understanding Cases

LO1, LO3   **Standards for Financial Performance Evaluation**

C 1. In a dramatic move, **Standard & Poor's Ratings Group**, the large financial company that evaluates the riskiness of companies' debt, downgraded its rating of **General Motors** and **Ford Motor Co**. debt to "junk" bond status because of concerns about the companies' profitability and cash flows. Despite aggressive cost cutting, both companies still face substantial future liabilities for health-care and pension obligations. They are losing money or barely breaking even on auto operations that concentrate on slow-selling SUVs. High gas prices and competition force them to sell the cars at a discount. The companies are counting on SUVs to make a comeback.[9] What standards do you think Standard & Poor's would use to evaluate Ford's progress? What performance measures would Standard & Poor's most likely use in making its evaluation?

LO1   **Using Segment Information**

C 2. Refer to Exhibit 1, which shows the segment information of **Goodyear Tire & Rubber Company**. In what business segments does Goodyear operate? What is the relative size of its business segments in terms of sales and income in the most recent year shown? Which segment is most profitable in terms of return on assets? In which region of the world is the tires segment largest, and which tire segment is most profitable in terms of return on assets?

LO1   **Using Investors' Services**

C 3. Refer to Exhibit 2, which contains the **PepsiCo Inc**. listing from Mergent's *Handbook of Dividend Achievers*. Assume that an investor has asked you to assess

PepsiCo's recent history and prospects. Write a memorandum to the investor that addresses the following points:

1. PepsiCo's earnings history. What has been the general relationship between PepsiCo's return on assets and its return on equity over the last seven years? What does this tell you about the way the company is financed? What figures back up your conclusion?
2. The trend of PepsiCo's stock price and price/earnings (P/E) ratio for the seven years shown.
3. PepsiCo's prospects, including developments likely to affect the company's future.

Interpreting Financial Reports

LO2 **Trend Analysis**

C 4. **H. J. Heinz Company** is a global company engaged in several lines of business, including food service, infant foods, condiments, pet foods, and weight-control food products. Below is a five-year summary of operations and other related data for Heinz.[10] (Amounts are expressed in thousands.)

H. J. Heinz Company and Subsidiaries
Five-Year Summary of Operations and Other Related Data

	2006	2005	2004	2003	2002
Summary of operations					
Sales	$8,643,438	$8,103,456	$7,625,831	$7,566,800	$7,040,934
Cost of products sold	5,550,364	5,069,926	4,733,314	4,825,462	4,441,194
Interest expense	316,296	232,088	211,382	222,729	230,027
Provision for income taxes	250,700	299,511	352,117	283,541	363,465
Net income (before special items)	442,761	688,004	715,451	478,303	593,042
Other related data					
Dividends paid: common	408,137	398,854	379,910	521,592	562,547
Total assets	9,737,767	10,577,718	9,877,189	9,224,751	10,278,354
Total debt	4,411,982	4,695,253	4,974,430	4,930,929	5,345,613
Shareholders' equity	2,048,823	2,602,573	1,894,189	1,199,157	1,718,616

Prepare a trend analysis for Heinz with 2002 as the base year and discuss the results. Identify important trends and state whether the trends are favorable or unfavorable. Discuss significant relationships among the trends.

Decision Analysis Using Excel

LO2, LO3 **Effect of a One-Time Item on a Loan Decision**

C 5. Apple a Day, Inc., and Unforgettable Edibles, Inc. are food catering businesses that operate in the same metropolitan area. Their customers include Fortune 500 companies, regional firms, and individuals. The two firms reported similar profit margins for the current year, and both base bonuses for managers on the achievement of a target profit margin and return on equity. Each firm has submitted a loan request to you, a loan officer for City National Bank. They have provided you with the following information:

	Apple a Day	Unforgettable Edibles
Net sales	$625,348	$717,900
Cost of goods sold	225,125	287,080
Gross margin	$400,223	$430,820
Operating expenses	281,300	371,565
Operating income	$118,923	$ 59,255
Gain on sale of real estate	—	81,923
Interest expense	(9,333)	(15,338)
Income before income taxes	$109,590	$125,840
Income taxes expense	25,990	29,525
Net income	$ 83,600	$ 96,315
Average stockholders' equity	$312,700	$390,560

1. Perform a vertical analysis and prepare a common-size income statement for each firm. Compute profit margin and return on equity.
2. Discuss these results, the bonus plan for management, and loan considerations. Identify the company that is the better loan risk.

Annual Report Case: CVS Corporation

LO3 **Comprehensive Ratio Analysis**

C 6. Access the website for **CVS Corporation** and locate the company's 2005 annual report. Conduct a comprehensive ratio analysis that compares the company's performance in 2005 and 2004. If you have computed ratios for CVS in previous chapters, you may prepare a table that summarizes the ratios and show calculations only for the ratios not previously calculated. If this is the first ratio analysis you have done for CVS, show all your computations. In either case, after each group of ratios, comment on the performance of CVS. Round your calculations to one decimal place. Prepare and comment on the following categories of ratios:

Liquidity analysis: current ratio, quick ratio, receivable turnover, days' sales uncollected, inventory turnover, days' inventory on hand, payables turnover, and days' payable. (Accounts Receivable, Inventories, and Accounts Payable were [in millions] $1,349.6, $4,016.5, and $1,666.4, respectively, in 2003.)

Profitability analysis: profit margin, asset turnover, return on assets, and return on equity. (Total assets and total shareholders' equity were [in millions] $10,543.1 and $6,021.8, respectively, in 2003.)

Long-term solvency analysis: debt to equity ratio and interest coverage ratio.

Cash flow adequacy analysis: cash flow yield, cash flows to sales, cash flows to assets, and free cash flow.

Market strength analysis: price/earnings (P/E) ratio and dividends yield.

Comparison Case: CVS Versus Southwest

LO3 **Comparison of Key Financial Performance Measures**

C 7. Access the websites for **CVS Corporation** and **Southwest Airlines Co.** and locate each company's 2005 annual report. Prepare a table for the following key financial performance measures for the two most recent years for both companies. Use your computations in **C6** or perform those analyses if you have not done so. Total assets for Southwest in 2003 were $9,878 million.

Profitability:	profit margin
	asset turnover
	return on assets
Long-term solvency:	debt to equity ratio
Cash flow adequacy:	cash flow yield
	free cash flow

Evaluate and comment on the relative performance of the two companies with respect to each of the above categories.

Ethical Dilemma Case

LO1 Executive Compensation

C 8. Executive compensation is often based on meeting certain targets for revenue growth, earnings, earnings per share, return on assets, or other performance measures. But what if performance is not living up to expectations? Some companies are simply changing the targets. For instance, **Sun Microsystems'** proxy as quoted in *The Wall Street Journal* states that "due to economic challenges experienced during the last fiscal year, our earnings per share and revenues are significantly below plan. As such, the Bonus Plan was amended to reduce the target bonus to 50% of the original plan and base the target bonus solely on the third and fourth quarters."[11] Sun Microsystems was not alone. Other companies, such as **AT&T Wireless**, **Estee Lauder**, and **UST**, also lowered targets for executive bonuses. Do you think it is acceptable to change the bonus targets for executives during the year if the year turns out to be not as successful as planned? What if an unexpected negative event like 9/11 happens? What are three standards of comparison? Which of these might justify changing the bonus targets during the year?

Internet Case

LO1 Using Investors' Services

C 9. Go to the website for **Moody's Investors Service**. Click on "ratings," which will show revisions of debt ratings issued by Moody's in the past few days. Choose a rating that has been upgraded or downgraded and read the short press announcement related to it. What reasons does Moody's give for the change in rating? What is Moody's assessment of the future of the company or institution? What financial performance measures are mentioned in the article? Summarize your findings and be prepared to share them in class.

Group Activity Case

LO3 Analyzing the Airline Industry

C 10. Divide into groups. Assume your group is analyzing the fate of the larger airlines, such as **United** and **American**. You have the following information:

a. Between 1999 and now, the long-term debt, including lease obligations, of the largest airlines more than doubled.
b. The price of fuel has increased by one-third.
c. Passenger loads are only now getting back to pre-9/11 levels.
d. Severe price competition from discount airlines exists.

Identify the ratios that you consider most important to consider in assessing the future of the large airlines and discuss the effect of each of the above factors on the ratios. Be prepared to present all or part of your findings in class.

Business Communication Case

LO3 **Comparison of International Companies' Operating Cycles**

C 11. Ratio analysis enables one to compare the performance of companies whose financial statements are presented in different currencies. Selected data from 2005 for two large pharmaceutical companies—one American, **Pfizer, Inc.**, and one Swiss, **Roche**—are presented below (in millions).[12]

	Pfizer, Inc. (U.S.)	Roche (Swiss)
Net sales	$51,298	SF35,511
Cost of goods sold	8,525	9,304
Accounts receivable	9,765	7,698
Inventories	6,039	5,041
Accounts payable	2,226	2,373

For each company, calculate the receivable turnover, days' sales uncollected, inventory turnover, days' inventory on hand, payables turnover, and days' payable. Then determine the operating cycle and days of financing required for each company. (Accounts receivable in 2004 were $9,367 for Pfizer and SF7,014 for Roche. Inventories in 2004 were $6,660 for Pfizer and SF4,614 for Roche. Accounts payable in 2004 were $2,672 for Pfizer and SF1,844 for Roche.) Prepare a memo containing your analysis of the operating cycles of these companies.

Future Value and Present Value Tables

Table 1 provides the multipliers necessary to compute the future value of a *single* cash deposit made at the *beginning* of year 1. Three factors must be known before the future value can be computed: (1) the time period in years, (2) the stated annual rate of interest to be earned, and (3) the dollar amount invested or deposited.

Example—Table 1. Determine the future value of $5,000 deposited now that will earn 9 percent interest compounded annually for five years.

TABLE 1. Future Value of $1 After a Given Number of Time Periods

Periods	1%	2%	3%	4%	5%	6%	7%	8%	9%	10%	12%	14%	15%
1	1.010	1.020	1.030	1.040	1.050	1.060	1.070	1.080	1.090	1.100	1.120	1.140	1.150
2	1.020	1.040	1.061	1.082	1.103	1.124	1.145	1.166	1.188	1.210	1.254	1.300	1.323
3	1.030	1.061	1.093	1.125	1.158	1.191	1.225	1.260	1.295	1.331	1.405	1.482	1.521
4	1.041	1.082	1.126	1.170	1.216	1.262	1.311	1.360	1.412	1.464	1.574	1.689	1.749
5	1.051	1.104	1.159	1.217	1.276	1.338	1.403	1.469	1.539	1.611	1.762	1.925	2.011
6	1.062	1.126	1.194	1.265	1.340	1.419	1.501	1.587	1.677	1.772	1.974	2.195	2.313
7	1.072	1.149	1.230	1.316	1.407	1.504	1.606	1.714	1.828	1.949	2.211	2.502	2.660
8	1.083	1.172	1.267	1.369	1.477	1.594	1.718	1.851	1.993	2.144	2.476	2.853	3.059
9	1.094	1.195	1.305	1.423	1.551	1.689	1.838	1.999	2.172	2.358	2.773	3.252	3.518
10	1.105	1.219	1.344	1.480	1.629	1.791	1.967	2.159	2.367	2.594	3.106	3.707	4.046
11	1.116	1.243	1.384	1.539	1.710	1.898	2.105	2.332	2.580	2.853	3.479	4.226	4.652
12	1.127	1.268	1.426	1.601	1.796	2.012	2.252	2.518	2.813	3.138	3.896	4.818	5.350
13	1.138	1.294	1.469	1.665	1.886	2.133	2.410	2.720	3.066	3.452	4.363	5.492	6.153
14	1.149	1.319	1.513	1.732	1.980	2.261	2.579	2.937	3.342	3.798	4.887	6.261	7.076
15	1.161	1.346	1.558	1.801	2.079	2.397	2.759	3.172	3.642	4.177	5.474	7.138	8.137
16	1.173	1.373	1.605	1.873	2.183	2.540	2.952	3.426	3.970	4.595	6.130	8.137	9.358
17	1.184	1.400	1.653	1.948	2.292	2.693	3.159	3.700	4.328	5.054	6.866	9.276	10.760
18	1.196	1.428	1.702	2.026	2.407	2.854	3.380	3.996	4.717	5.560	7.690	10.580	12.380
19	1.208	1.457	1.754	2.107	2.527	3.026	3.617	4.316	5.142	6.116	8.613	12.060	14.230
20	1.220	1.486	1.806	2.191	2.653	3.207	3.870	4.661	5.604	6.728	9.646	13.740	16.370
21	1.232	1.516	1.860	2.279	2.786	3.400	4.141	5.034	6.109	7.400	10.800	15.670	18.820
22	1.245	1.546	1.916	2.370	2.925	3.604	4.430	5.437	6.659	8.140	12.100	17.860	21.640
23	1.257	1.577	1.974	2.465	3.072	3.820	4.741	5.871	7.258	8.954	13.550	20.360	24.890
24	1.270	1.608	2.033	2.563	3.225	4.049	5.072	6.341	7.911	9.850	15.180	23.210	28.630
25	1.282	1.641	2.094	2.666	3.386	4.292	5.427	6.848	8.623	10.830	17.000	26.460	32.920
26	1.295	1.673	2.157	2.772	3.556	4.549	5.807	7.396	9.399	11.920	19.040	30.170	37.860
27	1.308	1.707	2.221	2.883	3.733	4.822	6.214	7.988	10.250	13.110	21.320	34.390	43.540
28	1.321	1.741	2.288	2.999	3.920	5.112	6.649	8.627	11.170	14.420	23.880	39.200	50.070
29	1.335	1.776	2.357	3.119	4.116	5.418	7.114	9.317	12.170	15.860	26.750	44.690	57.580
30	1.348	1.811	2.427	3.243	4.322	5.743	7.612	10.060	13.270	17.450	29.960	50.950	66.210
40	1.489	2.208	3.262	4.801	7.040	10.290	14.970	21.720	31.410	45.260	93.050	188.900	267.900
50	1.645	2.692	4.384	7.107	11.470	18.420	29.460	46.900	74.360	117.400	289.000	700.200	1,084.000

From Table 1, the necessary multiplier for five years at 9 percent is 1.539, and the answer is $5,000 × 1.539 = $7,695.

Where r is the interest rate and n is the number of periods, the factor values for Table 1 are

$$FV\ Factor = (1 + r)^n$$

Situations requiring the use of Table 2 are similar to those requiring Table 1 except that Table 2 is used to compute the future value of a *series* of *equal* annual deposits at the end of each period.

Example—Table 2.   What will be the future value at the end of 30 years if $1,000 is deposited each year on January 1, beginning in year 1, assuming 12 percent interest compounded annually? The required multiplier from Table 2 is 241.3, and the answer is $1,000 × 241.3 = $241,300.

The factor values for Table 2 are

$$FVa\ Factor = \frac{(1 + r)^n - 1}{r}$$

TABLE 2.   Future Value of $1 Paid in Each Period for a Given Number of Time Periods

Periods	1%	2%	3%	4%	5%	6%	7%	8%	9%	10%	12%	14%	15%
1	1.000	1.000	1.000	1.000	1.000	1.000	1.000	1.000	1.000	1.000	1.000	1.000	1.000
2	2.010	2.020	2.030	2.040	2.050	2.060	2.070	2.080	2.090	2.100	2.120	2.140	2.150
3	3.030	3.060	3.091	3.122	3.153	3.184	3.215	3.246	3.278	3.310	3.374	3.440	3.473
4	4.060	4.122	4.184	4.246	4.310	4.375	4.440	4.506	4.573	4.641	4.779	4.921	4.993
5	5.101	5.204	5.309	5.416	5.526	5.637	5.751	5.867	5.985	6.105	6.353	6.610	6.742
6	6.152	6.308	6.468	6.633	6.802	6.975	7.153	7.336	7.523	7.716	8.115	8.536	8.754
7	7.214	7.434	7.662	7.898	8.142	8.394	8.654	8.923	9.200	9.487	10.090	10.730	11.070
8	8.286	8.583	8.892	9.214	9.549	9.897	10.260	10.640	11.030	11.440	12.300	13.230	13.730
9	9.369	9.755	10.160	10.580	11.030	11.490	11.980	12.490	13.020	13.580	14.780	16.090	16.790
10	10.460	10.950	11.460	12.010	12.580	13.180	13.820	14.490	15.190	15.940	17.550	19.340	20.300
11	11.570	12.170	12.810	13.490	14.210	14.970	15.780	16.650	17.560	18.530	20.650	23.040	24.350
12	12.680	13.410	14.190	15.030	15.920	16.870	17.890	18.980	20.140	21.380	24.130	27.270	29.000
13	13.810	14.680	15.620	16.630	17.710	18.880	20.140	21.500	22.950	24.520	28.030	32.090	34.350
14	14.950	15.970	17.090	18.290	19.600	21.020	22.550	24.210	26.020	27.980	32.390	37.580	40.500
15	16.100	17.290	18.600	20.020	21.580	23.280	25.130	27.150	29.360	31.770	37.280	43.840	47.580
16	17.260	18.640	20.160	21.820	23.660	25.670	27.890	30.320	33.000	35.950	42.750	50.980	55.720
17	18.430	20.010	21.760	23.700	25.840	28.210	30.840	33.750	36.970	40.540	48.880	59.120	65.080
18	19.610	21.410	23.410	25.650	28.130	30.910	34.000	37.450	41.300	45.600	55.750	68.390	75.840
19	20.810	22.840	25.120	27.670	30.540	33.760	37.380	41.450	46.020	51.160	63.440	78.970	88.210
20	22.020	24.300	26.870	29.780	33.070	36.790	41.000	45.760	51.160	57.280	72.050	91.020	102.400
21	23.240	25.780	28.680	31.970	35.720	39.990	44.870	50.420	56.760	64.000	81.700	104.800	118.800
22	24.470	27.300	30.540	34.250	38.510	43.390	49.010	55.460	62.870	71.400	92.500	120.400	137.600
23	25.720	28.850	32.450	36.620	41.430	47.000	53.440	60.890	69.530	79.540	104.600	138.300	159.300
24	26.970	30.420	34.430	39.080	44.500	50.820	58.180	66.760	76.790	88.500	118.200	158.700	184.200
25	28.240	32.030	36.460	41.650	47.730	54.860	63.250	73.110	84.700	98.350	133.300	181.900	212.800
26	29.530	33.670	38.550	44.310	51.110	59.160	68.680	79.950	93.320	109.200	150.300	208.300	245.700
27	30.820	35.340	40.710	47.080	54.670	63.710	74.480	87.350	102.700	121.100	169.400	238.500	283.600
28	32.130	37.050	42.930	49.970	58.400	68.530	80.700	95.340	113.000	134.200	190.700	272.900	327.100
29	33.450	38.790	45.220	52.970	62.320	73.640	87.350	104.000	124.100	148.600	214.600	312.100	377.200
30	34.780	40.570	47.580	56.080	66.440	79.060	94.460	113.300	136.300	164.500	241.300	356.800	434.700
40	48.890	60.400	75.400	95.030	120.800	154.800	199.600	259.100	337.900	442.600	767.100	1,342.000	1,779.000
50	64.460	84.580	112.800	152.700	209.300	290.300	406.500	573.800	815.100	1,164.000	2,400.000	4,995.000	7,218.000

TABLE 3. Present Value of $1 to Be Received at the End of a Given Number of Time Periods

Periods	1%	2%	3%	4%	5%	6%	7%	8%	9%	10%	12%
1	0.990	0.980	0.971	0.962	0.952	0.943	0.935	0.926	0.917	0.909	0.893
2	0.980	0.961	0.943	0.925	0.907	0.890	0.873	0.857	0.842	0.826	0.797
3	0.971	0.942	0.915	0.889	0.864	0.840	0.816	0.794	0.772	0.751	0.712
4	0.961	0.924	0.888	0.855	0.823	0.792	0.763	0.735	0.708	0.683	0.636
5	0.951	0.906	0.883	0.822	0.784	0.747	0.713	0.681	0.650	0.621	0.567
6	0.942	0.888	0.837	0.790	0.746	0.705	0.666	0.630	0.596	0.564	0.507
7	0.933	0.871	0.813	0.760	0.711	0.665	0.623	0.583	0.547	0.513	0.452
8	0.923	0.853	0.789	0.731	0.677	0.627	0.582	0.540	0.502	0.467	0.404
9	0.914	0.837	0.766	0.703	0.645	0.592	0.544	0.500	0.460	0.424	0.361
10	0.905	0.820	0.744	0.676	0.614	0.558	0.508	0.463	0.422	0.386	0.322
11	0.896	0.804	0.722	0.650	0.585	0.527	0.475	0.429	0.388	0.350	0.287
12	0.887	0.788	0.701	0.625	0.557	0.497	0.444	0.397	0.356	0.319	0.257
13	0.879	0.773	0.681	0.601	0.530	0.469	0.415	0.368	0.326	0.290	0.229
14	0.870	0.758	0.661	0.577	0.505	0.442	0.388	0.340	0.299	0.263	0.205
15	0.861	0.743	0.642	0.555	0.481	0.417	0.362	0.315	0.275	0.239	0.183
16	0.853	0.728	0.623	0.534	0.458	0.394	0.339	0.292	0.252	0.218	0.163
17	0.844	0.714	0.605	0.513	0.436	0.371	0.317	0.270	0.231	0.198	0.146
18	0.836	0.700	0.587	0.494	0.416	0.350	0.296	0.250	0.212	0.180	0.130
19	0.828	0.686	0.570	0.475	0.396	0.331	0.277	0.232	0.194	0.164	0.116
20	0.820	0.673	0.554	0.456	0.377	0.312	0.258	0.215	0.178	0.149	0.104
21	0.811	0.660	0.538	0.439	0.359	0.294	0.242	0.199	0.164	0.135	0.093
22	0.803	0.647	0.522	0.422	0.342	0.278	0.226	0.184	0.150	0.123	0.083
23	0.795	0.634	0.507	0.406	0.326	0.262	0.211	0.170	0.138	0.112	0.074
24	0.788	0.622	0.492	0.390	0.310	0.247	0.197	0.158	0.126	0.102	0.066
25	0.780	0.610	0.478	0.375	0.295	0.233	0.184	0.146	0.116	0.092	0.059
26	0.772	0.598	0.464	0.361	0.281	0.220	0.172	0.135	0.106	0.084	0.053
27	0.764	0.586	0.450	0.347	0.268	0.207	0.161	0.125	0.098	0.076	0.047
28	0.757	0.574	0.437	0.333	0.255	0.196	0.150	0.116	0.090	0.069	0.042
29	0.749	0.563	0.424	0.321	0.243	0.185	0.141	0.107	0.082	0.063	0.037
30	0.742	0.552	0.412	0.308	0.231	0.174	0.131	0.099	0.075	0.057	0.033
40	0.672	0.453	0.307	0.208	0.142	0.097	0.067	0.046	0.032	0.022	0.011
50	0.608	0.372	0.228	0.141	0.087	0.054	0.034	0.021	0.013	0.009	0.003

Table 3 is used to compute the value today of a single amount of cash to be received sometime in the future. To use Table 3, you must first know (1) the time period in years until funds will be received, (2) the stated annual rate of interest, and (3) the dollar amount to be received at the end of the time period.

Example—Table 3. What is the present value of $30,000 to be received 25 years from now, assuming a 14 percent interest rate? From Table 3, the required multiplier is .038, and the answer is $30,000 × .038 = $1,140.

14%	15%	16%	18%	20%	25%	30%	35%	40%	45%	50%	Periods
0.877	0.870	0.862	0.847	0.833	0.800	0.769	0.741	0.714	0.690	0.667	1
0.769	0.756	0.743	0.718	0.694	0.640	0.592	0.549	0.510	0.476	0.444	2
0.675	0.658	0.641	0.609	0.579	0.512	0.455	0.406	0.364	0.328	0.296	3
0.592	0.572	0.552	0.516	0.482	0.410	0.350	0.301	0.260	0.226	0.198	4
0.519	0.497	0.476	0.437	0.402	0.328	0.269	0.223	0.186	0.156	0.132	5
0.456	0.432	0.410	0.370	0.335	0.262	0.207	0.165	0.133	0.108	0.088	6
0.400	0.376	0.354	0.314	0.279	0.210	0.159	0.122	0.095	0.074	0.059	7
0.351	0.327	0.305	0.266	0.233	0.168	0.123	0.091	0.068	0.051	0.039	8
0.308	0.284	0.263	0.225	0.194	0.134	0.094	0.067	0.048	0.035	0.026	9
0.270	0.247	0.227	0.191	0.162	0.107	0.073	0.050	0.035	0.024	0.017	10
0.237	0.215	0.195	0.162	0.135	0.086	0.056	0.037	0.025	0.017	0.012	11
0.208	0.187	0.168	0.137	0.112	0.069	0.043	0.027	0.018	0.012	0.008	12
0.182	0.163	0.145	0.116	0.093	0.055	0.033	0.020	0.013	0.008	0.005	13
0.160	0.141	0.125	0.099	0.078	0.044	0.025	0.015	0.009	0.006	0.003	14
0.140	0.123	0.108	0.084	0.065	0.035	0.020	0.011	0.006	0.004	0.002	15
0.123	0.107	0.093	0.071	0.054	0.028	0.015	0.008	0.005	0.003	0.002	16
0.108	0.093	0.080	0.060	0.045	0.023	0.012	0.006	0.003	0.002	0.001	17
0.095	0.081	0.069	0.051	0.038	0.018	0.009	0.005	0.002	0.001	0.001	18
0.083	0.070	0.060	0.043	0.031	0.014	0.007	0.003	0.002	0.001		19
0.073	0.061	0.051	0.037	0.026	0.012	0.005	0.002	0.001	0.001		20
0.064	0.053	0.044	0.031	0.022	0.009	0.004	0.002	0.001			21
0.056	0.046	0.038	0.026	0.018	0.007	0.003	0.001	0.001			22
0.049	0.040	0.033	0.022	0.015	0.006	0.002	0.001				23
0.043	0.035	0.028	0.019	0.013	0.005	0.002	0.001				24
0.038	0.030	0.024	0.016	0.010	0.004	0.001	0.001				25
0.033	0.026	0.021	0.014	0.009	0.003	0.001					26
0.029	0.023	0.018	0.011	0.007	0.002	0.001					27
0.026	0.020	0.016	0.010	0.006	0.002	0.001					28
0.022	0.017	0.014	0.008	0.005	0.002						29
0.020	0.015	0.012	0.007	0.004	0.001						30
0.005	0.004	0.003	0.001	0.001							40
0.001	0.001	0.001									50

The factor values for Table 3 are

$$PV \text{ Factor} = (1 + r)^{-n}$$

Table 3 is the reciprocal of Table 1.

TABLE 4. Present Value of $1 Received Each Period for a Given Number of Time Periods

Periods	1%	2%	3%	4%	5%	6%	7%	8%	9%	10%	12%
1	0.990	0.980	0.971	0.962	0.952	0.943	0.935	0.926	0.917	0.909	0.893
2	1.970	1.942	1.913	1.886	1.859	1.833	1.808	1.783	1.759	1.736	1.690
3	2.941	2.884	2.829	2.775	2.723	2.673	2.624	2.577	2.531	2.487	2.402
4	3.902	3.808	3.717	3.630	3.546	3.465	3.387	3.312	3.240	3.170	3.037
5	4.853	4.713	4.580	4.452	4.329	4.212	4.100	3.993	3.890	3.791	3.605
6	5.795	5.601	5.417	5.242	5.076	4.917	4.767	4.623	4.486	4.355	4.111
7	6.728	6.472	6.230	6.002	5.786	5.582	5.389	5.206	5.033	4.868	4.564
8	7.652	7.325	7.020	6.733	6.463	6.210	5.971	5.747	5.535	5.335	4.968
9	8.566	8.162	7.786	7.435	7.108	6.802	6.515	6.247	5.995	5.759	5.328
10	9.471	8.983	8.530	8.111	7.722	7.360	7.024	6.710	6.418	6.145	5.650
11	10.368	9.787	9.253	8.760	8.306	7.887	7.499	7.139	6.805	6.495	5.938
12	11.255	10.575	9.954	9.385	8.863	8.384	7.943	7.536	7.161	6.814	6.194
13	12.134	11.348	10.635	9.986	9.394	8.853	8.358	7.904	7.487	7.103	6.424
14	13.004	12.106	11.296	10.563	9.899	9.295	8.745	8.244	7.786	7.367	6.628
15	13.865	12.849	11.938	11.118	10.380	9.712	9.108	8.559	8.061	7.606	6.811
16	14.718	13.578	12.561	11.652	10.838	10.106	9.447	8.851	8.313	7.824	6.974
17	15.562	14.292	13.166	12.166	11.274	10.477	9.763	9.122	8.544	8.022	7.120
18	16.398	14.992	13.754	12.659	11.690	10.828	10.059	9.372	8.756	8.201	7.250
19	17.226	15.678	14.324	13.134	12.085	11.158	10.336	9.604	8.950	8.365	7.366
20	18.046	16.351	14.878	13.590	12.462	11.470	10.594	9.818	9.129	8.514	7.469
21	18.857	17.011	15.415	14.029	12.821	11.764	10.836	10.017	9.292	8.649	7.562
22	19.660	17.658	15.937	14.451	13.163	12.042	11.061	10.201	9.442	8.772	7.645
23	20.456	18.292	16.444	14.857	13.489	12.303	11.272	10.371	9.580	8.883	7.718
24	21.243	18.914	16.936	15.247	13.799	12.550	11.469	10.529	9.707	8.985	7.784
25	22.023	19.523	17.413	15.622	14.094	12.783	11.654	10.675	9.823	9.077	7.843
26	22.795	20.121	17.877	15.983	14.375	13.003	11.826	10.810	9.929	9.161	7.896
27	23.560	20.707	18.327	16.330	14.643	13.211	11.987	10.935	10.027	9.237	7.943
28	24.316	21.281	18.764	16.663	14.898	13.406	12.137	11.051	10.116	9.307	7.984
29	25.066	21.844	19.189	16.984	15.141	13.591	12.278	11.158	10.198	9.370	8.022
30	25.808	22.396	19.600	17.292	15.373	13.765	12.409	11.258	10.274	9.427	8.055
40	32.835	27.355	23.115	19.793	17.159	15.046	13.332	11.925	10.757	9.779	8.244
50	39.196	31.424	25.730	21.482	18.256	15.762	13.801	12.234	10.962	9.915	8.305

Table 4 is used to compute the present value of a *series* of *equal* annual cash flows.

Example—Table 4. Arthur Howard won a contest on January 1, 20x7, in which the prize was $30,000, payable in 15 annual installments of $2,000 each December 31, beginning in 20x7. Assuming a 9 percent interest rate, what is the present value of Howard's prize on January 1, 20x7? From Table 4, the required multiplier is 8.061, and the answer is $2,000 × 8.061 = $16,122.

The factor values for Table 4 are

$$\text{PVa Factor} = 1 - \frac{(1 + r)^{-n}}{r}$$

Table 4 is the columnar sum of Table 3. Table 4 applies to *ordinary annuities*, in which the first cash flow occurs one time period beyond the date for which the present value is computed.

14%	15%	16%	18%	20%	25%	30%	35%	40%	45%	50%	Periods
0.877	0.870	0.862	0.847	0.833	0.800	0.769	0.741	0.714	0.690	0.667	1
1.647	1.626	1.605	1.566	1.528	1.440	1.361	1.289	1.224	1.165	1.111	2
2.322	2.283	2.246	2.174	2.106	1.952	1.816	1.696	1.589	1.493	1.407	3
2.914	2.855	2.798	2.690	2.589	2.362	2.166	1.997	1.849	1.720	1.605	4
3.433	3.352	3.274	3.127	2.991	2.689	2.436	2.220	2.035	1.876	1.737	5
3.889	3.784	3.685	3.498	3.326	2.951	2.643	2.385	2.168	1.983	1.824	6
4.288	4.160	4.039	3.812	3.605	3.161	2.802	2.508	2.263	2.057	1.883	7
4.639	4.487	4.344	4.078	3.837	3.329	2.925	2.598	2.331	2.109	1.922	8
4.946	4.772	4.607	4.303	4.031	3.463	3.019	2.665	2.379	2.144	1.948	9
5.216	5.019	4.833	4.494	4.192	3.571	3.092	2.715	2.414	2.168	1.965	10
5.453	5.234	5.029	4.656	4.327	3.656	3.147	2.752	2.438	2.185	1.977	11
5.660	5.421	5.197	4.793	4.439	3.725	3.190	2.779	2.456	2.197	1.985	12
5.842	5.583	5.342	4.910	4.533	3.780	3.223	2.799	2.469	2.204	1.990	13
6.002	5.724	5.468	5.008	4.611	3.824	3.249	2.814	2.478	2.210	1.993	14
6.142	5.847	5.575	5.092	4.675	3.859	3.268	2.825	2.484	2.214	1.995	15
6.265	5.954	5.669	5.162	4.730	3.887	3.283	2.834	2.489	2.216	1.997	16
6.373	6.047	5.749	5.222	4.775	3.910	3.295	2.840	2.492	2.218	1.998	17
6.467	6.128	5.818	5.273	4.812	3.928	3.304	2.844	2.494	2.219	1.999	18
6.550	6.198	5.877	5.316	4.844	3.942	3.311	2.848	2.496	2.220	1.999	19
6.623	6.259	5.929	5.353	4.870	3.954	3.316	2.850	2.497	2.221	1.999	20
6.687	6.312	5.973	5.384	4.891	3.963	3.320	2.852	2.498	2.221	2.000	21
6.743	6.359	6.011	5.410	4.909	3.970	3.323	2.853	2.498	2.222	2.000	22
6.792	6.399	6.044	5.432	4.925	3.976	3.325	2.854	2.499	2.222	2.000	23
6.835	6.434	6.073	5.451	4.973	3.981	3.327	2.855	2.499	2.222	2.000	24
6.873	6.464	6.097	5.467	4.948	3.985	3.329	2.856	2.499	2.222	2.000	25
6.906	6.491	6.118	5.480	4.956	3.988	3.330	2.856	2.500	2.222	2.000	26
6.935	6.514	6.136	5.492	4.964	3.990	3.331	2.856	2.500	2.222	2.000	27
6.961	6.534	6.152	5.502	4.970	3.992	3.331	2.857	2.500	2.222	2.000	28
6.983	6.551	6.166	5.510	4.975	3.994	3.332	2.857	2.500	2.222	2.000	29
7.003	6.566	6.177	5.517	4.979	3.995	3.332	2.857	2.500	2.222	2.000	30
7.105	6.642	6.234	5.548	4.997	3.999	3.333	2.857	2.500	2.222	2.000	40
7.133	6.661	6.246	5.554	4.999	4.000	3.333	2.857	2.500	2.222	2.000	50

An *annuity due* is a series of equal cash flows for N time periods, but the first payment occurs immediately. The present value of the first payment equals the face value of the cash flow; Table 4 then is used to measure the present value of N − 1 remaining cash flows.

Example—Table 4. Determine the present value on January 1, 20x7, of 20 lease payments; each payment of $10,000 is due on January 1, beginning in 20x7. Assume an interest rate of 8 percent.

Present Value = Immediate Payment + Present Value of
19 Subsequent Payments at 8%

= $10,000 + ($10,000 × 9.604) = $106,040

Chapter 1

1. "Wal-Mart CEO Pleased with Sales," *Fort Meyers News-Press*, January 5, 2006.
2. *Statement No. 1A* (New York: Institute of Management Accountants, 1982).
3. Kathleen Day, "Wal-Mart Rattles Bankers," *Gainesville Sun*, February 19, 2006.
4. Andrew Ross Sorkin, "Albertsons Nears Deal, Yet Again, to Sell Itself," *New York Times*, January 23, 2006.
5. "A Profile for Leadership," *Pink* magazine, December/January 2006, p. 104.
6. Andra Gumbus and Susan D. Johnson, "The Balanced Scorecard at Futura Industries," *Strategic Finance*, July 2003.
7. American Institute of Certified Public Accountants, "Summary of Sarbanes-Oxley Act of 2002," www.aicpa.org/info/sarbanes_oxley_summary.htm; Securities and Exchange Commission, "Final Rule: Certification of Disclosure in Companies' Quarterly and Annual Reports," August 28, 2002, www.sec.gov/rules/final/33-8124.htm.
8. "Combating Corporate Fraud," Accounting Web, January 13, 2006, www.accountingweb.com/cgi-bin/item.cgi?id=101663.

Chapter 2

1. Southwest Airlines, "Fact Sheet," www.southwest.com.
2. Melanie Trottman, "Vaunted Southwest Slips in On-Time Performance," *The Wall Street Journal*, September 25, 2002.
3. Robert Frank and Sarah Ellison, "Meltdown in Chocolate-town," *The Wall Street Journal*, September 19, 2002.
4. United Parcel Service, "About UPS," www.ups.com.
5. "A Global Look at Women on Boards," *Pink* magazine, June–July 2005, pp. 96–97, or www.globalwomen.com.

Chapter 3

1. Information from www.coldstonecreamerycom and Alycia de Mesa, "Cold Stone Creamery—the Scoop," www.brandchannel.com, June 21, 2004.
2. Robert L. Simison, "Toyota Finds Way to Make Custom Car in 5 Days," *The Wall Street Journal*, August 6, 1999.
3. Cheryl Dahle, "Sneak Previews Make Good Project Reviews," *Fast Company*, July–August 1999.
4. P. Kelly Mooney, "The Experienced Customer," *Fast Company*, Fall 1999, pp. 25–29. Reprinted by permission of Gruner & Jahr USA Publishing.

Chapter 4

1. Don Clark, "Intel, Shaking Off Downturn, to Unveil New Chip Technology," *The Wall Street Journal*, August 13, 2002.
2. "Fraud Examiners Rate the Scams," *Journal of Accountancy*, June 2002.
3. Intel Corporation, "Corporate Overview," www.intel.com.

Chapter 5

1. Dan Morse, "Tennessee Producer Tries New Tactic in Sofas: Speed," *The Wall Street Journal*, November 19, 2002.
2. Mylene Mangalindan, "Oracle Puts Priority on Customer Service," *The Wall Street Journal*, January 21, 2003.

3. Lance Thompson, "Examining Methods of VBM," *Strategic Finance*, December 2002.
4. Robert Kaplan and Steven Anderson, "Time Driven Activity-Based Costing," *Harvard Business Review*, November 2004.
5. "Just In Time, Toyota Production System & Lean Manufacturing," http://www.strategosinc.com/just_in_time.htm.
6. Dan Morse, "Tennessee Producer Tries New Tactic in Sofas: Speed," *The Wall Street Journal*, November 19, 2002.
7. Gina Imperato, "Time for Zero Time," *Net Company*, Fall 1999.
8. Sally Beatty, "Levi's Strive to Keep a Hip Image," *The Wall Street Journal*, January 23, 2003.

Chapter 6

1. Kraft Foods, "Profile," www.kraft.com.
2. http://investor.google.com/conduct.html.
3. Kraft Foods, "Inside Kraft: A Company Overview," http://164.109.16.145/investors/overview.html.

Chapter 7

1. Johnson & Johnson, "Our Company," www.jnj.com.
2. "A Global Look at Women on Boards," *Pink* magazine, June–July 2005, pp. 96–97.
3. Richard Barrett, "From Fast Close to Fast Forward," *Strategic Finance*, January 2003.
4. Omar Aguilar, "How Strategic Performance Management Is Helping Companies Create Business Value," *Strategic Finance*, January 2003.
5. Jeremy Hope and Robin Frase, "Who Needs Budgets?" *Harvard Business Review*, February 2003.
6. Minnesota Mining and Manufacturing Company, "About 3M," www.3m.com.

Chapter 8

1. PEAKS Resorts, www.peakscard.com.
2. Mark Beasley, Al Chen, Karen Nunez, and Lorraine Wright, "Working Hand in Hand: Balanced Scorecards and Enterprise Risk Management," *Strategic Finance*, March 2006.
3. Marc J. Epstein and Jean-François Manzoni, "The Balanced Scorecard and Tableau de Bord: Translating Strategy into Action," *Management Accounting*, August 1997.
4. Kerry A. McDonald, "Meyners Does a Reality Check," *Journal of Accountancy*, February 2006.
5. V. G. Narayanan and Ananth Raman, "Aligning Incentives in Supply Chains," *Harvard Business Review*, November 2004.

Chapter 9

1. Erin White, "How Stodgy Turned Stylish," *The Wall Street Journal*, May 3, 2002.
2. Katy McLaughlin, "Factory Tours," *The Wall Street Journal*, October 29, 2002.
3. David E. Keys and Anton Van Der Merwe, "Gaining Effective Organizational Control with RCA," *Strategic Finance*, May 2002.
4. Gabriel Kahn, "Still Going for Gold," *The Wall Street Journal*, January 28, 2003.
5. www.coach.com/corporate/governance/integrityProgram.asp.

Chapter 10

1. Betty Riess, "Bank of America Expands Online Security Feature to the Northeast," Bank of America Newsroom Press Release, January 4, 2006, http://www.bankofamerica.com/newsroom/press.
2. Jonathan Eig, "One CFO Finds His Orderly World Upset After Enron," *Wall Street Journal*, November 14, 2002.
3. Stephanie Miles, "What's a Check?" *Wall Street Journal*, October 21, 2002.
4. Michael Liedtke, "Keeping the Books," *Gainesville Sun*, August 22, 2002.
5. Alan Fuhrman, "Your E-Banking Future," *Strategic Finance*, April 2002.
6. "The Ball and Chain," *Wireless Week*, June 21, 1999; "Iridium to be Reborn Relatively Debt-Free?" *Newbytes News Network*, August 19, 1999, www.iridium.com.

Chapter 11

1. Kathy Williams, "Tom D'Angelo, Priceline.com's Mr. Inside," *Strategic Finance*, July 2002.
2. Nick Wingfield, "Are You Satisfied?" *The Wall Street Journal*, September 16, 2002.
3. Christopher Lawton, "Anheuser-Busch Rolls Out the Price Jump," *The Wall Street Journal*, October 23, 2002.
4. Walter S. Mossberg, "An Affordable Palm Even Paper Lovers Might Use," *The Wall Street Journal*, October 16, 2002; Palm, Inc., "About Palm, Inc.," www.palm.com.

Chapter 12

1. Timothy Aeppel, "Workers Not Included," *The Wall Street Journal*, November 19, 2002.
2. Paulette Thomas, "Case Study: Electronics Firm Ends Practice Just in Time," *The Wall Street Journal*, October 29, 2002.
3. Kristina Shevory, "Heads or Tails?" *Seattle Times*, September 5, 2002.
4. From a speech by Jim Croft, Vice President of Finance and Administration of the Field Museum, Chicago, November 14, 2000.
5. From *Business Driven Information Technology: Answers to 100 Critical Questions for Every Manager*, edited by David R. Laube and Raymond F. Zammuto. Copyright © 2003.

Chapter 13

1. Nick Wingfield, "Amazon Takes Page from Wal-Mart to Prosper on Web," *The Wall Street Journal*, November 22, 2002.

2. Ross L. Fink, "Quality Improvement Technology Using the Taguchi Method," CPA *Journal Online*, December 1993, http://www.nysscpa.org/cpajournal.
3. Julia Winn, "Quality Is Doing It Right the First Time," *Insight*, October 1993.
4. Nick Wingfield, "Amazon Takes Page from Wal-Mart to Prosper on Web," *The Wall Street Journal*, November 22, 2002.
5. www.juse.or.jp.
6. International Organization for Standardization, "ISO 9000/ISO 14000," www.iso.ch.
7. Motorola Internet and Networking Group, "Why Motorola?" www.motorola.com/MIMS/ISG/ING/quality.

Chapter 14

1. Publix Asset Management Company, "About Publix," www.publix.com.
2. Michael Singer, "Internal Service Providers," www.internetnews.com, April 21, 2004.
3. Steven Sills, ". . . Hide Profits," *New York Times Magazine*, November 3, 2002.
4. Kenneth L. Thurston, Dennis M. Kelemen, and John B. MacArthur, "Cost for Pricing at Blue Cross and Blue Shield of Florida," *Management Accounting Quarterly*, Spring 2000.
5. Sarah L. Roberts-Witt, "Future Distribution," *Business 2.0*, June 13, 2000.

Chapter 15

1. Starbucks Corporation, *Annual Report*, 2005.
2. David Henry, "The Numbers Game," *BusinessWeek*, May 14, 2001.
3. Jonathan Weil, "'Pro forma' in Earnings reports? . . . As If," *The Wall Street Journal*, April 24, 2003.
4. *Statement of Financial Accounting Standards No.131*, "Segment Disclosures" (Norwalk, Conn.: Financial Accounting Standards Board, 1997).
5. Starbucks Corporation, *Annual Report*, 2005.
6. Ibid.
7. Target Corporation, *Proxy Statement*, May 18, 2005.
8. Starbucks Corporation, *Annual Report*, 2005.
9. Lee Hawkins Jr., "S&P Cuts Rating on GM and Ford to Junk Status," *The Wall Street Journal*, May 6, 2005.
10. H.J. Heinz Company, *Annual Report*, 2005.
11. Jesse Drucker, "Performance Bonus Out of Reach? Move the Target," *The Wall Street Journal*, April 29, 2003.
12. Pfizer, Inc., *Annual Report*, 2005; Roche Group, *Annual Report*, 2005.

Instructor Supplements

Course Management Systems

The Eduspace® (powered by Blackboard™) online learning tool pairs the widely recognized resources of Blackboard with quality, text-specific content from Houghton Mifflin. Using auto-graded homework, students can complete end-of-chapter assignments (short exercises, exercises, and problems) and receive immediate feedback on their work. Assignments are automatically graded and entered into a gradebook. Within the "Learn on Your Own" section, students can choose from a variety of resources aimed at helping them review, apply, and practice. Demonstration Videos, HMAccounting Tutor tutorials, audio (MP3) files of chapter summaries and quizzes, and links to SMARTHINKING online tutoring and the Online Study Center provide a wealth of review options. Algorithmic practice exercises let students work through exercises with different numbers every time. A **multimedia ebook** is available for quick access to text content and links to relevant tutorials and videos.

For instructors who use other course management systems (CMS), such as Blackboard and Web-CT, to manage their online courses, much of the text-specific content included in Eduspace is available in course cartridge form.

HMTesting with Algorithms

HMTesting—now powered by D*iploma*®—contains the computerized version of the printed test bank and is available on CD-ROM. With HMTesting, instructors can create, customize, and deliver multiple types of tests; import questions from the test bank; add their own questions; or edit existing questions, all within D*iploma's* powerful electronic platform. Online Testing and Gradebook functions allow instructors to administer tests via their local area network or the Internet, set up classes, record grades from tests or assignments, analyze grades, and compile class and individual statistics. HMTesting can be used on both PCs and Macintosh computers.

Online Teaching Center

The Online Teaching Center website provides instructors with password-protected course materials such as completely revised PowerPoint slides; Classroom Response System content; sample syllabi; Accounting Instructor's Report with teaching strategies for introductory accounting; and Electronic Solutions, which are fully functioning Excel spreadsheets for all exercises, problems, and cases.

PowerPoint Slides

Completely revised, the Premium Slides include video, photographs, line art, and additional Stop, Review, and Apply questions. Basic Slides provide a teaching outline of the text chapter. PowerPoint Slides are included on the Online Teaching Center website and within the Course Management Systems.

Instructor's Solutions Manual

This resource contains answers to all text exercises, problems, and cases. Also available as **Solutions Transparency Masters.**

Electronic Solutions

Contains all solutions from the Instructor's Solutions Manual in fully formatted Excel, with a new interface that makes it easy to find the solution you need. The electronic format allows instructors to manipulate the numbers in the classroom or distribute solutions via e-mail or the web. The solutions are available at the Online Teaching Center website and within Course Management Systems.

Printed Test Bank

The Test Bank provides more than 2,000 true/false, multiple-choice, short essay, and critical-thinking questions, as well as exercises and problems, all of which test students' ability to recall, comprehend, apply, and analyze information. Also included are two Achievement Tests per chapter.

Course Manual

Available on the Online Teaching Center website and through Course Management Systems, the Course Manual is filled with advice and teaching tips. It contains a planning matrix and time/difficulty chart, instructional materials, and quizzes.